The Army of Francis Joseph

The Army of Francis Joseph

Gunther E. Rothenberg

Purdue University Press
West Lafayette, Indiana

First paperback edition, 1998
Published in the United States by Purdue University Press
Cover design by David Black

Copyright © 1976 by Purdue Research Foundation
Library of Congress Catalog Number 75-16051
International Standard Book Number 1-55753-145-5
Printed in the United States of America

For my wife, Joy

Contents

	Introduction	ix
	A Note on Ranks and Names	xiii
1	The Evolution of the Army: Origins to Archduke Charles	1
2	The Austrian Army in the Age of Metternich: 1815–1847	9
3	Guardians of an Empire: The Army 1848–1849	22
4	The Emperor's Personal Command: 1849–1859	38
5	The End of an Age: 1860–1866	56
6	Dualism and Reorganization: 1867–1874	74
7	The Army and the Balkans: 1874–1881	90
8	The Era of Beck and Albrecht: 1881–1895	105
9	Foreign Equilibrium and Internal Crisis: 1895–1905	123
10	The Conrad Era from His Appointment to the Annexation Crisis: 1906–1909	139
11	Conrad, Moltke, Aehrenthal, and the Balkan Crises: 1909–1913	157
12	Austria-Hungary's Last War: 1914–1915	172
13	War on Many Fronts and the Death of Emperor Francis Joseph: 1915–1916	187
14	Emperor Charles and the Dissolution of the Habsburg Army: 1916–1918	201
15	Epilogue	219
	Notes	223
	Index	273

Introduction

The army was one of the most important, if not the most important, single institution in the multinational empire of the Habsburgs. Since the days of Ferdinand I, the dynasty had survived through the military power it could command, and the rise and decline in the fortunes of the Habsburgs were mirrored with a high degree of accuracy in the state of its military establishment. Not only did the army preserve the empire from external enemies and provide it with considerable weight in the affairs of Europe, but it was also an important pillar of the dynasty as a reliable instrument against foes within the empire. Although the Habsburgs had been moving towards a centralized state structure since the early eighteenth century, this goal, intermittently and at times half-heartedly pursued, was never wholly achieved, and particularistic national elements survived in considerable strength and gained renewed vigor in the nineteenth century. But in 1848 and 1849, the army proved capable of holding together the Habsburg Monarchy by force of arms, and when later in the century the rising tide of nationalism seemed likely to disrupt the empire, the army, above all loyal to the dynasty, became one of the strongest centripetal forces. Indeed, after 1867 it remained as one of the few institutions functioning in both parts of the monarchy where, by and large, it escaped, even at the price of isolation from civilian society, the conflicts of language and nationality, politics, religions, and economics raging in Austria-Hungary.

In the *kaiserlich und königliche Armee,* as it was designated after 1889, there remained a common language, common ideals, and a common loyalty, and it was in the army alone that the concept of a great empire headed by an emperor was at least partially translated into reality. At the moment of great peril Grillparzer had pronounced to the army that *"In deinem Lager ist Österreich,"* and this tradition the army preserved. Although it did not entirely escape the corroding effects of nationalism, it remained an effective fighting force under the stress of war. Contrary to often-expressed opinion, the balance sheet of the Austro-Hungarian forces during the long years of World War I speaks in its favor. "This loosely knit conglomeration of races," wrote B. H. Liddell Hart, "withstood the shock and strain of war for four years in a way that surprised and dismayed her opponents."[1] In fact, so strong proved its cohesion that at the very end the Habsburg standard was flown not by the imperial authorities in Vienna, but by a military commander in a remote part of the Balkans.

Despite its paramount importance, however, the Austrian army never became separate from or achieved superior standing to the political authorities. The Habsburg Empire never became a *Militärstaat* in the Prussian sense; in fact, "the 'military monarchy' of the Habsburgs was the least militarized state in Europe."[2] Again, despite its importance and partially self-imposed isolation, it also remained true of the Habsburg army that a military establishment is an extension of society and reflects in sharp focus the political system, the social structure, and the economic and technological vigor of a state. "The qualities of its courts of law and its armies," wrote Goethe, "give the most minute insight into the essence of an empire," and much the same was said by Engels who drew attention to the close reflection of the dominant political and economic characteristics of the nineteenth-century states in their military establishment. The theme of this work then is to reconstruct in some detail the major facts about the old Austrian and later Austro-Hungarian army and the trends in the body politic that molded its major and distinctive facets. The book sets out to describe one of the oldest armies of Europe during the last century of its existence, and if the narrative is not always simple or clear-cut, this is because the army and its various components often were sprawling, contradictory, and confusing.

This army which, as Schiller put it, Wallenstein called forth from the void, is gone. Its bugles no longer sound across the plains of Podolia and Hungary; its signal horns no longer shrill across the valleys of the Alps and the Carpathians, and the fife and drum of its bands is no longer heard in the squares of the many small garrison towns scattered from the Adriatic coast to Galicia. But in many capitals, in Vienna, Prague, Budapest, and Zagreb, and in many smaller towns in central and eastern Europe, in Goricia, Czernowitz, Ostrava, Tarnopol, Karlovać, and in many others, there still stand the barracks painted in the characteristic faded Habsburg yellow where soldiers still live. And there are still old men, though fewer of them each day, to whom the memory of the old army remains dear. And to people of many nationalities the memory of the imperial standard floating over public buildings, barracks, and forts is a poignant reminder of a lost and perhaps better world where, by and large, values were more secure and life more humane.

But it is not the object of this book to provide an exercise in nostalgia; the author will attempt to fill a gap in historical knowledge of military institutions and fighting men. Historians have not dealt kindly with this army, and so far no full-length analytical study of its history during the period from 1815 to 1918 has appeared. There exists, to be sure, a very considerable literature dealing with leaders, battles, and campaigns, though much of it, written by former officers, tends to be highly biased. Such material introduces us to the heroes in the service and the villains on the outside; the army is sacrosanct and its leaders wise, while the politicians and the public are generally shortsighted and blamed for the army's shortcomings. Again, this is not the object of these pages. While the author does not deny the merits of the Habsburg army, he is not unaware of its shortcomings and he hopes to deal fairly with both sides of the ledger.

Given the scope of the theme, this study makes no claim to have said the last word about the army of Francis Joseph. But it will try to fill at least partially the

Introduction xi

gaps existing in our knowledge of the institutions, organization, administration, doctrine, and armament of the *k.u.k. Armee*. Campaigns, battles, and leaders will receive some consideration, but the main emphasis will be placed on an analysis of the overall developments in the military establishment, its role in foreign and internal policy, and above all on its struggle against the disintegration of the empire under the stress of growing national divisions.

Briefly stated, the main thesis is that in an age of nationalism the army could not save a multinational state by itself. Tradition and circumstances cast it into the role of a loyal servant to the dynasty, a role which proved inadequate to deal with the problems of the age. Although the army fought well and preserved its integrity and cohesion, its very character made it obsolete and isolated. Tied to a historical and dynastic past, it thought too much about its tradition and heritage and too little about the future.

Many individuals and institutions helped in the preparation of this study. I am grateful for financial assistance from the American Council of Learned Societies, the American Philosophical Society, and the Research Allocations Committee of the University of New Mexico. Seminal work basic to this study was made possible by a fellowship from the Guggenheim Foundation. At the same time I would like to express my appreciation to the scholars, archivists, librarians, and staff of the Kriegsarchiv, Wien, for giving me unrestricted access to their rich holdings and for facilitating my work with advice and help. Above all I want to thank archivists Dr. Kurt Peball and Dr. Walter Wagner and librarian A. Moser. I am most grateful for the suggestions and support provided by Dr. Johann C. Allmayer-Beck, director of the Kriegsgeschichtliches Museum in Vienna. I would also like to express my gratitude for encouragement and help to the doyens of Austrian military history, General Rudolf Kiszling and Dr. Oskar Regele. In this country I have profited greatly from the suggestions of Professors George Barany, Thomas M. Barker, Gordon A. Craig, Robert A. Kann, Béla K. Király, Arthur J. May, Peter Paret, R. John Rath, and Theodore Ropp.

Grateful acknowledgments are also made to the publishers of the *Journal of Modern History,* the *Austrian History Yearbook,* and the *Slavic Review* for permission to utilize materials from my previous writings. Last, but by no means least, to my wife Joy go thanks for supporting and encouraging me during the process of writing.

Albuquerque, New Mexico GER
West Lafayette, Indiana

A Note on Ranks and Names

The highest rank in the Habsburg armies was *Feldmarschall*, followed either by *Feldzeugmeister* for officers of the artillery, infantry, or engineers, or *General der Kavallerie* for mounted troops. In 1908 the designation *General der Infanterie* was introduced, and in September 1915 the rank of *Generaloberst*, between *Feldzeumeister* and *Feldmarschall*, was established. The lower commissioned and the enlisted ranks generally followed the pattern of other European armies.

Officers are introduced with the rank they held at the time mentioned, and the first textual reference includes their full name. In the interest of brevity, however, the noble title usually has been rendered in abbreviated form; for example, Feldmarschall Leutnant Josef Count Radetzky will be used instead of Feldmarschall Leutnant Josef Count Radetzky von Radetz.

The rendition of geographical and personal names is one of the difficulties in dealing with a multinational empire with fourteen different languages. The author decided to adopt a rough-and-ready solution; German was the official army language and therefore the German version has been used, except where any location has a name in common English usage such as Vienna or Prague or Milan.

The spelling of personal names also has been simplified. In general, as far as possible, the version actually used by the individual has been employed, except that the author has not followed the Hungarian custom of putting the surname first. When a person is so familiar to English readers that there exists an English version of this name—Francis Joseph, Charles, or Francis Ferdinand—this version has been used.

1

The Evolution of the Army: Origins to Archduke Charles

Although the birthdate of the Habsburg army usually is regarded as 1649, when the regiments which Albrecht von Wallenstein raised for the emperor in 1627 were retained in permanent service, this is not strictly accurate.[1] The origins of the military establishment of what became the "Austrian Monarchy" reach back a century before Wallenstein when the Turkish danger as well as dynastic ambitions led to the development of military institutions separate both from the indigenous hosts and from the Spanish imperial establishment.

Overall, the evolution of the army to 1815 can be divided into three major stages. In the seminal stage, from 1522 to about 1625, the crown managed to establish certain basic institutions; during the second stage, to 1743, it raised a standing army which placed the Danubian monarchy into the ranks of the great powers; after an interval of abrupt decline, the third stage, from 1744 to 1815, brought a series of reforms which fashioned a military instrument that withstood the impact of the Prussian and French wars. Throughout this long process, the evolution of a strong Habsburg military establishment was hampered by opposition from the party of the estates in each of the various lands, while in Hungary resistance to military policies of the dynasty, as well as to administrative and fiscal ones, persisted to the very end of the monarchy.

Ferdinand I, younger brother of Emperor Charles V, came to to rule Austria in 1522. When soon thereafter he added to his dominions Bohemia and Hungary, where his claim to rule was disputed and the Turks were in occupation of most of the country, he possessed no troops of his own. There existed in these lands, as in most of Europe, considerable relics of two obsolescent medieval military institutions—the old militia or *Landesaufgebot,* and the feudal levy or *Lehensaufgebot*—while in Hungary, as far as it was under Habsburg control, there remained the mounted noble *insurrectio,* a feudal host, augmented by armed peasants, the *banderial* or *portal* militia.[2] While useful auxiliaries, these bodies had political and tactical limitations. Mobilization depended on the Austrian and Bohemian estates and the Hungarian diet, and not on the ruler. From the purely military point of view, these levies were too cumbersome to cope with swift Turkish raids, and against major bodies their lack of professional expertise could lead to disaster.

Of course, Ferdinand's imperial brother commanded professional troops superior to the Turks, but neither the Habsburgs nor the Ottomans were able to employ their first-line troops against each other for protracted periods. Charles needed his veteran regiments to fight France and the rising tide of Lutheranism in the Holy Roman Empire; the Ottomans faced trouble in the East. On occasion, to be sure, the main Ottoman host appeared in Hungary and threatened the empire. Both times, in 1529 and in 1532, the advance of the Turks brought a temporary suspension of the political and religious divisions in the empire and produced forces strong enough to deflect the immediate threat. But even after the sultan and his army had retired, the Ottomans continued hostilities along the extensive frontier in an unbroken series of raids, incursions, and ambuscades. Ferdinand's immediate strategic problem then was to provide for the defense of his southeastern frontiers.[3]

He solved the problem through fortifications and military colonies. In Hungary a crude but effective chain of forts, little more than earthworks surmounted by palisades, was built and garrisoned by small groups of mercenaries. To the south, covering the Croatian uplands, Ferdinand established a network of fortified villages, watchtowers, and blockhouses, and settled Christian Balkan refugees in this region. In return for military service, he granted these colonists substantial privileges: land, freedom of worship, and above all, immunity from the usual manorial obligations. In time, the Habsburgs appointed officers to fill the major command positions and fashioned the colonies into a substantial military institution, the *Militärgrenze*. Eventually this was to become an permanent component of the Habsburg military system, furnishing cheap and reliable manpower for the dynasty; immediately, these defenses contained minor incursions and, as the fruitless Turkish campaign of 1566 demonstrated, they could compel the Ottomans to expend their brief campaigning season in sieges. Hungary-Croatia became a less promising target, and the main Ottoman expansionist drive was channelled in other directions for nearly a century.[4]

But neither Ferdinand nor his successors ever became quite reconciled to an exclusive Danubian destiny. After Charles V resigned in 1556 and passed the imperial dignity to Ferdinand, the Austrian Habsburgs continued to seek supremacy in Germany; for this, they needed more sophisticated forces than those employed against the Turks. To provide the necessary administrative base for the creation of such an army, Ferdinand established in 1556 a mixed military-civilian body, the *Hofkriegsrat,* in Vienna, to supervise the military affairs of his entire realm. And while in the immediate future this office would not be of great importance, it eventually became the highest command agency directing the military affairs of the entire Habsburg Empire until 1848.[5]

Ferdinand I had created two important and lasting military institutions, but thereafter opposition from the estates impeded further progress. Both the *Militärgrenze* and the *Hofkriegsrat,* direct instruments of the crown, were resented by the estates and the weakening of the Turkish threat removed restraints. Opposition, frequently justified by recourse to religious argumentation, was building toward a confrontation; the weakness of the Habsburgs, who after the death of Ferdinand in 1564 divided into three lines in Vienna, Graz, and Innsbruck, provided the opportunity. Each line maintained a separate court and a separate military establishment and generally was too weak to oppose local estate particularism. In 1578 Charles of Styria was obliged to grant to his predominantly Lutheran estates religious concessions as well as control over the Military Border in Croatia and a separate Inner-Austrian *Hofkriegsrat*.[6] Some years later, another such office was established in the Tyrol and the military affairs of the Habsburgs were divided among three competing agencies in Vienna, Graz, and Innsbruck. Moreover, this caused damage to their military potential, though after 1590 the Habsburg rulers commenced to retake power, repeal their religious concessions, and reestablish a measure of administrative unity. Although, except in Bohemia, this effort did not encounter active resistance, it alienated the nobility. Many went into exile; those who remained were reluctant to vote money for troops which might be used against them. The outbreak of a Turkish war in 1593 forced a reluctant accommodation by both sides, but for the next thirty years the Austrian Habsburgs repeatedly had to be propped up by aid from the Spanish line.[7]

The weakness of the Habsburgs was demonstrated both during the small-scale war against Venice, from 1615 to 1617, and during the opening phases of the Thirty Years' War. In both conflicts Ferdinand II, now heading a reunited Austrian Habsburg line, was forced to fall back on contingents furnished by Spain and by his Catholic allies in Germany.

To improve his position, in 1625 Ferdinand entrusted Wallenstein, a Bohemian noble, with raising an army. For the next nine years, Wallenstein, with a force largely maintained with his own resources, fought with considerable success, but in the end reliance on this ambitious and most probably treacherous commander proved dangerous and his assassination was encouraged, if not ordered, by the emperor. The Wallenstein affair left a deep scar on the Habsburg minds and memories, and from that time on there was hardly an Austrian ruler or statesman who was not in some degree suspicious of outstanding soldiers.[8]

Even as the Thirty Years' War revealed the Habsburgs without an adequate or loyal military establishment, they accomplished an important breakthrough in principle during this period. In 1627 Ferdinand issued the Revised Land Ordinance, depriving the Bohemian estates of their military rights, and stipulating that it was the sovereign's exclusive prerogative to raise troops.[9] This was a decisive step clarifying the division of authority between the crown, the estates, and the military. Still, into the time of Maria Theresa, the estates retained the right to vote military funds and thus the opportunity to obstruct, but the precedent was set. Moreover, the experiences of the Thirty Years' War demonstrated that well-organized and trained forces, professional troops that could deploy, maneuver, attack, and defend, had become a *sine qua non* for the security of a government. After Wallenstein's fall, the crown had retained most of his regiments under arms and at the end of the war, in 1649, Emperor Ferdinand III decided to keep nine regiments of foot, ten of horse, and a small body of artillery in his service. These, together with the frontier troops, constituted the standing army, rising in strength from about twenty-five thousand in 1649, to sixty-five thousand in 1664, and to nearly a hundred thousand by the end of the century.[10]

Maintenance of a standing army, feared by the estates as an instrument that could break the traditional checks on the crown, required a fairly efficient bureaucracy, and this was provided by the *Hofkriegsrat*. Although its machinery was cumbersome, frequently inefficient, and always slow, and although there was a schism between the soldiers and the civilians, the agency somehow managed to discharge its many diverse functions. It served as the central administrative agency, a military chancery, as well as a staff for the emperor, directing and coordinating the field armies. In addition, the *Hofkriegsrat* conducted relations with the Ottoman Empire and administered the Military Border, a function complicated by the continued existence of the Inner-Austrian agency, which retained a voice in the affairs of the border until 1743.[11]

But the defects of this agency could be overcome by outstanding leadership, and for some fifty years the military fortunes of the Habsburgs were in the hands of two outstanding soldier-administrators, Count Raimondo Montecuccoli and Prince Eugene of Savoy. The first, a well-educated military theorist, an able commander and administrator, repulsed a new Turkish offensive in the battle of St. Gotthard in 1664. As president of the *Hofkriegsrat* from 1668 to 1681, he laid the foundations for the exploits of the army under his eventual successor, the great Eugene of Savoy, one of the most brilliant soldiers of the age.[12] Under Eugene's command Habsburg armies drove the Turks from Hungary, participated with great success in the War of the Spanish Succession, and between 1716 and 1718 won another series of victories in the Balkans. His seventeen major victories raised Austria to the rank of a great European power. Appointed president of the *Hofkriegsrat* in 1703, he sternly enforced the chain of command, created the Quartermaster-General Staff, and promoted technical and scientific military education. He failed, however, to abolish the noxious practice of promotion by purchase or to root out corruption in the military establishment. Moreover, his influence declined after 1718, though he remained in office until 1736.[13]

Neither Montecuccoli nor Eugene could solve the financial problems of the army, which were common, to be sure, in most military establishments during an age of luxurious courts and wide-spread corruption. Funds for the army came from the estates, the imperial diet, and cameral revenues, but generally they were insufficient to meet requirements. While the court lived in high style, the army often went hungry. During the critical year 1683, Leopold I found it difficult to pay his troops, and Vienna was saved with papal donations.[14] As many other monarchs were doing, Leopold I often resorted to Jewish court-financiers, especially Samuel Oppenheimer, who was named *Kriegsfaktor* in 1676. He too was unable to close the gap and, after expending his personal fortunes, was forced into bankruptcy. In 1697 Leopold created the *Deputation,* an agency to apportion available funds between civilian and military requirements, but this did not improve matters much. Towards the end of the War of the Spanish Succession, at the time of Charles IV, civilian expenditures still outstripped military and, while British subsidies helped, Eugene complained that beggars were less destitute than his army in the field.[15]

The financial picture was complicated by Hungary's continuing refusal to subordinate itself to the overall control of the dynasty in military and fiscal matters. Montecuccoli already had found the Magyars "a proud, fickle, and obdurate people" who would have to be controlled with an iron rod, and little changed in the next century.[16] An attempt to introduce Habsburg controls in the country provoked a revolt which ended in 1711 with the reconfirmation of Hungary's special position. And Charles VI, above all concerned to obtain the agreement of the various diets and estates for the succession of his daughter Maria Theresa, the Pragmatic Sanction, was willing to purchase this by relaxing the central administration. In 1715 the Hungarian Diet accepted a standing army, at least in principle. In 1722 it conceded its command to the king, but retained control over recruitment and supply, and specifically reaffirmed the tax exemption of the nobility as justified by its service in the *insurrectio*.[17] And Emperor Charles, grateful to the Hungarians for recognizing the Pragmatic Sanction in 1722, never seriously tried to enforce his rights in Hungary or solve the question, which would be raised again and again in the future, whether in accepting the Pragmatic Sanction the diet also had accepted an unitary Habsburg army or merely agreed to a joint defense.

During the last years of the emperor's reign, the condition of the army deteriorated, despite Eugene's warnings that political agreements were no substitute for a strong military force. The War of the Polish Succession, 1733 to 1735, and the disasters of the Austro-Turkish War of 1737 to 1739 revealed just how far the decline had gone. When Charles died in October 1740, he left a ruined treasury and a disorganized and indisciplined army to Maria Theresa.[18] "Who would believe," she complained, "that no sort of rule was in force among my troops? Each unit had a different order of marching, a different drill, etc. The same words of command were differently interpreted in each unit, and it is really no wonder that ten years before my accession the Emperor was defeated every time, and the subsequent state of the army beggars description."[19] To save her possessions, the queen initiated a series of military reforms, continued after 1756 by her son, co-ruler, and successor, Joseph II. Organization, administration, recruitment, training, equipment, and fighting methods were overhauled and recast on the Prussian model.[20] To obtain better officers, the queen hoped to attract the Austrian nobility to follow military careers, but a commission deliberating this question in 1749 concluded that this would "require improvements in the status of this estate that is clearly beyond the capacity of the public finances."[21] To attract officers, she opened her new military academy, founded in 1752, to the sons of the small nobility and even the bourgeoisie, and encouraged the transfer of able officers from foreign armies into her own. Finally, to improve the social position of the officers, she decreed that all officers were to be admitted to her court in uniform and that commoners were to be enobled after thirty years of meritorious service.

Most importantly, Maria Theresa consolidated army finances. In 1747 the queen adopted a program by which the estates of Austria and Bohemia no longer set their own military contributions, but instead accepted fixed ten-year obligations to support a standing army of one hundred ten thousand men. Although all these reforms were resented, the queen persisted in carrying them through and as a result, by the outbreak of the Seven Years' War in 1756, the Austrian army had again become an effective fighting instrument, quite different from the collection of disparate units before 1740.

But even Maria Theresa failed to change matters in Hungary, which, despite protestations of loyalty and devotion, provided little support during the Prussian wars. In fact, the queen did not even try. Realizing that coercion would be counterproductive, she wrote that "in the Kingdom of Hungary I did think it better not to introduce any change . . . special considerations apply in the case of the Hungarians who are extremely sensitive on such points."[22] She did, however, disregard Hungarian aspirations to control the Military Border. Impressed by the showing of the frontier troops, she greatly expanded the system and decreed that in the future the *Grenzer* were to be trained and employed as troops of the line.[23] The queen was correct. Hungary was touchy about all attempts to expand Vienna's authority and when after her death Joseph II tried to introduce a greater measure of centralization, there was a noble revolt which contributed to the reverses sustained during the Turkish War from 1788 to 1791.[24] Even so, the professional standing army of the Habsburgs, the *kaiserlich-königliche Armee,* as it now was styled, had become a solid body of unquestionable loyalty to the dynasty, and within a year after the Turkish War it began the struggle against the armies of the French Revolution and Napoleon.

For twenty-three long years, from 1792 to 1815, the Austrian army was almost constantly at war. Repeatedly defeated by superior forces and superior generalship, it always found internal strength to rise and fight again, and in the end served as the major instrument in the overthrow of Napoleon.[25] The army's recuperative powers were remarkable, especially because the army made few concessions to the new style of revolutionary warfare. To be sure, prodded by Archduke Charles, the brother of the reigning Emperor Francis I, who for several years between 1801 and 1809 combined most military authority in his hands, the army made certain adjustments in its strategy and tactics, but in its most basic characteristics, in the overall command structure, recruitment, and dynastic orientation, it made but few changes and remained a typical eighteenth-century dynastic organization.

The reasons for this posture are clear. The conservatism of the rulers and their dislike of radical innovations, combined with the very nature of the empire with its diverse political institutions and peoples, all discouraged basic changes. Emperor Francis, like all Habsburg monarchs, deeply apprehensive about the concentration of military power in any one hand, never backed his brother decisively and, except for a brief period, preserved the command dualism between the *Hofkriegsrat* and the field commanders. For that matter, Charles was no revolutionary; basically, he retained the thought pattern of limited dynastic war and did not accept the new concepts of national war. He considered war the "greatest evil a state or nation can experience," and though not deficient in personal courage, lacked the will to seek victory at any price. He was cautious rather than daring, and perceiving the army as the ultimate guarantor of the dynasty, he never was prepared to risk its total defeat in order to achieve total victory. He remained, a recent writer concluded, "a conservative contending against soundly entrenched reactionaries."[26]

And on the most fundamental issue, whether the army should be transformed into a broadly based popular force or remain a dynastic instrument, Charles, as well as most senior generals, agreed with the arch-conservatives. Although his army regulations issued in 1807 humanized discipline and appealed to the common soldier's sense of honor, Charles was quite content to retain the selective conscription system introduced between 1770 and 1777 by Joseph II, and rejected all suggestions for an army based on universal service. He feared that such an army, engaging the people's passions, would tend to escalate the level of warfare and also that discharged soldiers might provide expert leadership for popular revolts. Only after Napoleon deposed the Spanish Bourbons in 1808, and then largely on the insistence of Count Stadion, the foreign minister, did he agree to the formation of a militia, the *Landwehr.* It was, he wrote, the only way to "remedy after fifteen years of fighting and fifteen years of misfortunes the paucity of our resources."[27] From the outset the *Landwehr* was limited to the Austrian and Bohemian lands. Concern about the loyalty of the Poles precluded establishing the *Landwehr* in Galicia, and it also was never introduced in Hungary, partly because Charles and Stadion feared that it might become the opening wedge for a national Hungarian army, a demand already voiced during the feudal revolt of 1790. For that matter, the diet, too, was not eager to arm the lower classes, but promised to call out the *insurrectio* and provide additional recruits for the regular forces.[28]

Charles had accepted the *Landwehr* only as a last resort and favored a peace policy towards Napoleon. But, as in 1805, he was pushed aside by the war party, and in 1809 Austria once again went to war. In the hard-fought battle of Aspern, the first major victory against Napoleon on land, Charles prevailed largely because of the stubborn bravery of his troops. Cautious to a fault, however, he failed to follow up his success and in the end was defeated at Wagram. Discredited and accused of entertaining devious schemes, he then was abruptly dismissed, while the emperor signed the Treaty of Schönbrunn which deprived Austria of much territory, including most of the Military Border in Croatia, imposed a crippling indemnity, and restricted her army to one hundred fifty thousand men.

After 1809 the *Hofkriegsrat* regained its former position as the main control agency of the army, though much influence also was wielded by Klemens Prince Metternich, a firm believer in civilian supremacy, who now emerged as the crown's chief minister. Charles never again obtained command, but many of his innovations were retained, and his army regulations remained in force until superseded in 1873. By that time much had been forgotten and Charles, once suspected by the emperor, had become the very symbol of the dynastic soldier. Meanwhile, the unenviable responsiblity for rebuilding military strength fell to the much-maligned *Hofkriegsrat*. Despite the chaotic financial conditions and the shortage of every kind of military equipment, it managed not only to keep the army together, but also conducted covert preparations for a huge expansion. In 1813, when Metternich offered Austria's armed mediation, he was able to back up his position with two large mobilized armies, and when Austria eventually entered the coalition against Napoleon, the size of her forces, three hundred thousand combat troops, entitled her to name the supreme allied commander.

Although there were suggestions that Charles should be recalled to fill the position, Metternich insisted on Feldmarschall Karl Prince Schwarzenberg, a soldier-diplomat. Though chosen primarily because he accepted the principle of military subordination to political direction, and also because his background enabled him to harmonize the conflicting claims of three sovereigns and their ambitious generals, Schwarzenberg proved to be a most able coalition commander. Together with his chief of staff, Feldmarschall Leutnant Josef Count Radetzky, the prince not only imposed a measure of strategic cooperation on his reluctant allies, but also commanded the Austrian army in a way that won him the approbation of his political superiors in Vienna. Aware that Austria had only limited war aims and could not afford to hazard her last great army, Schwarzenberg was careful in his operations, though when the occasion demanded, his command team revealed an almost Napoleonic talent for the exploitation of time and space. The showing of the army restored Austria's great power position and earned Radetzky a lasting reputation.

At the same time, the army's performance confirmed the emperor's and

Metternich's faith in the traditional system of command and the dynastic army, while the spectacle of the Prussian generals feuding with their monarch reinforced their distrust of politically motivated forces. The experiences of 1813 and 1814 did much to set the pattern for the future evolution of the Habsburg army in which, perhaps too often, military effectiveness would be subordinated to dynastic concerns.

2

The Austrian Army in the Age of Metternich: 1815-1847

The fall of Napoleon ushered in a period of relative stability in Europe based primarily on the new balance of power established by the treaties of 1815 and the rigorous suppression of all domestic disorders. Preservation of this state of affairs fell in large part to Austria which had emerged from the French wars with enlarged prestige and power. Its ruling circles and, above all, its chancellor and chief minister, Klemens Prince Metternich, were determined to defend this new order both by diplomacy and armed force. "Austria not only had carried the main burden in the struggle against the subversive influences of liberalism and Napoleonic ambitions," Feldmarschall Leutnant Karl Friedrich Baron Langenau wrote in 1836, but, he continued, "even today the legitimate part of Europe can look with full confidence only towards the Austrian army."[1]

To perform this role as guardian of the international and domestic tranquility, the Austrian empire, now numbering some thirty million inhabitants, maintained an impressive military establishment with a mobilization strength, on paper at least, of nearly four hundred thousand men. Behind this imposing facade, however, there existed severe shortcomings in finances, administration, leadership, and training. In large part these shortcomings could be traced to the political conservatism of Austria's rulers which was matched by an equal hostility to military innovations.[2] Realizing that radical innovations in the military sphere were closely linked to changes in government and society, they chose to retain a military establishment resembling that of the pre-revolutionary period.

Of course, many of the defects also could be traced to the impoverished condition of the state. The strain of the French wars had left the empire financially exhausted, burdened with a heavy public debt and a mass of depreciated paper money. Financial recovery, moreover, was impeded by complicated and sometimes contradictory economic regulations and an inefficient system of taxation. Under these circumstances there was considerable pressure to reduce military expenditures. As early as the summer of 1814, Radetzky, then still chief of staff to Prince Schwarzenberg, commander in chief of the allied armies, had protested to the Emperor Francis that the Austrian army did not receive financial support on the same level as the Russian and Prussian forces. Later that year, following his appointment as president of the *Hofkriegsrat,* Schwarzenberg himself had voiced his misgivings about the proposed peace establishment to the emperor.[3]

Within the imperial administration, Metternich, assisted by Karl Josef Count Clam-Martinitz, adjutant general to the emperor, consistently fought to maintain a strong, if traditional, army. But after 1826, when Anton Count Kolowrat had gained decisive influence over internal and fiscal matters, the budget of the military was continually reduced. Emperor Francis laid down a rule that ordinary army expenditures were not to exceed forty million florins a year, and though that sum was eventually raised to forty-four million, it was inadequate in an inflationary period. In 1817 the army still received half of the total revenues; by 1830 it received only twenty-three percent, and by 1848 its share had sunk to twenty percent.[4]

At the same time, the army continued to suffer from an obsolescent and cumbersome command and control system. At the highest level, subject, of course, to the supreme authority of the emperor, was the venerable *Hofkriegsrat,* one of the four boards making up the *Staatsrat.* The *Hofkriegsrat* in turn was subdivided into various sections dealing with different aspects of the military establishment, and while in theory all sections were subordinate to the president of the council, there was considerable and continuous friction between the various sections. Decision making took a very long time and usually was arrived at only after much circulation of papers, quibbling, argument, and counterargument. Moreover, there was friction between the military and civilian elements within the *Hofkriegsrat.* While the presidents always were soldiers, though often men of limited vision, the majority of the section chiefs were civilian bureaucrats with soldiers merely acting as expert advisors.[5] And finally the *Hofkriegsrat* could be, and sometimes was, overridden by the *Staatsrat.* The military commanders generally resented this civilian supremacy and tried, though without much success, to achieve a greater degree of independence. "The army," grumbled Radetzky, looking back in 1848, "has no reason to be greatly attached to the system. This system, if one wishes to call it despotic, was a civilian and not a military despotism, and one in which the army was neglected."[6]

The most neglected part of the army, without a doubt, was the operational staff, the so-called Quartermaster-General Staff (*General-Quartiermeister Stab*) which occupied a very modest position within the military hierarchy. A permanent part of the army only since 1801, the staff had gained some prestige under Radetzky during the final campaigns against Napoleon. In 1811, using his new-found influence, the general had submitted a memorandum, "Concerning an improvement of the Quartermaster-General Staff establishment," which had drawn some favorable attention.[7] After 1815, however, while the general staff grew in power and prestige in other countries, especially in Prussia, in Austria the staff remained but a section of the *Hofkriegsrat* and in the army table of organization, the *Militär-Schematismus,* the staff officer corps appeared between the Pioneers and the Sappers.[8]

Even conservative military men were dissatisfied by this arrangement and during this period there were periodic attempts to raise the competence and the authority of the Quartermaster-General Staff. In 1830, for example, General der Kavallerie Johann Prince Frimont, newly appointed president of the *Hofkriegsrat,* submitted a reform proposal,[9] and after the death of Emperor Francis in 1835

Clam-Martinitz tried to enlist the cooperation of the then acting chief of staff, Feldmarschall Leutnant Leonhard von Rothkirch und Panthen, for a reform scheme.[10] At the same time, Archduke Charles, still the revered hero of the French wars, suggested the revival of the position of generalissimo in charge of all the armed forces, a post he had held between 1806 and 1809. But his proposal was promptly rebuffed by the new Emperor Ferdinand, who declared that such an arrangement contravened the fundamental principle that the "leading institutions of the monarchy, and especially the military command, should rest in the hands of permanent and continuing agencies and not be vested in any single person."[11] Reflecting the traditional supremacy of the civilian over the military authorities maintained since the days of Wallenstein, the emperor's decision was endorsed by Metternich who well appreciated the need for military power, but who on an earlier occasion also had asserted that "we need a commander who makes war and not a politician."[12] Therefore the antiquated and often exasperatingly slow command structure was retained.

The army itself also reflected the conservatism of the government in its essentially eighteenth-century character. The officer corps, especially in its upper ranks, retained an international composition. To be sure, the majority was of German descent, both from the Habsburg provinces and from the Germanies, but there also were officers of Spanish, French, Walloon, Danish, Irish, and English derivation. In 1843 one Austrian writer complained that "the Hungarian hussar regiments especially have virtually become English colonies," and that foreigners gained more rapid promotion than natives. At the same time, the number of bourgeois officers declined. At the end of the Napoleonic wars, bourgeoisie constituted nineteen percent of the generalcy, but by 1848, out of 253 generals on active duty, only 20 did not possess a patent of nobility.[13] As for the lower grades, the aristocratic element remained strong, though the bulk of the regimental officers came from quite humble origins and often received their patents of nobility by long service, promotion, or acts of outstanding bravery. Entry into the officer corps was possible in a number of ways: by direct appointment, through the military academies in Wiener-Neustadt and Vienna, or through the military schools maintained in the provinces by individual corps and regiments. In the latter, a considerable number of the cadets came from military families, including those of non-commissioned status.[14]

The long period of peace and reduction in the army establishment led to a stagnation in promotions. In many cases young officers who had become captains at the time of Wagram had to wait twenty or more years for their majority and it was not at all unusual for ensigns to remain in rank for eight to ten years.[15] At the same time, the continued existence of the system of regimental colonel proprietors, often well-connected absentee owners, tended to retard and limit promotions. Until the system was finally abolished in 1868, the proprietor held considerable influence over promotions. Seniority of rank existed only within each regiment and the proprietor had the right to issue direct commissions, a prerogative often abused to appoint relatives and friends, or to permit the purchase of commissions.[16] Although officially outlawed since 1803, the practice continued under different designations. An officer's billet was considered his property, and its sale was not considered to be an affair of the government. Such an arrangement, now styled a "convention," was regarded as a private transaction and the main reason that the regimental commander had to be informed was so that the officer quitting the service could not later demand a pension. Expenses of such a transaction could run rather high; in some cavalry regiments a lieutenantcy sold for as much as two thousand florins.

The price tended to limit the practice which, for the majority of officers, was out of the question. In fact, the financial position of the lower grades often was precarious. Radetzky had called the material status of Austrian officers "totally inadequate" as early as 1814, but there was little improvement in pay and allowances.[17] In 1838, to be sure, the average pay of subalterns was raised thirty percent, but in a period of rapidly rising prices and over-emphasis on smart turnout and extravagant uniforms, these additional expenses constituted a very heavy burden on junior officers without private incomes.[18] In the 1830s one Austrian officer bitterly complained that many subalterns were envious of "salesclerks and lackeys who at least had a full stomach."[19]

This, of course, was an exaggeration, but the peculiar institution of "regimental agents," civilians holding semi-official appointments to transact the private and semi-official affairs of officers, was symptomatic of the financial squeeze. These agents not only executed purchase orders, but provided security bonds, obtained marriage permits, extended loans to officers at a high rate of interest, bought and sold property, and performed many other similar services. In 1846, for instance, three such agents were listed in Vienna. A certain Franz Dempscher serviced fifty-seven regiments; Dr. Alois Spitzer took care of thirty-six, while Herr Heinrich Meyer had to content himself with only eight.[20]

Professionally, the officer corps tended to reflect, albeit with some significant exceptions, the prevailing resistance to any kind of progress. At the highest levels there was a marked inclination to cling to the methods developed during the Napoleonic wars and to shun innovations. In part, this was due to the prevailing conservatism in government, but it was also due to the fact that army commanders too often were selected both because of their good connections and because of their seniority, which often rendered them physically unfit and mentally out of date. On the middle and lower levels, too, the corps as a whole was not studious but rather contemptuous of learning; the grizzled and grim-faced regimental officers, especially, often regarded roughness and even brutality as the marks of a good soldier. They were unimaginative and very devoted to routine, and the typical officer came to look no further than the orders issued by his immediate superior or the appropriate military regulation.[21] There was considerable fear of responsibility at every level of the military hierarchy, compounded by frequent reports, returns, and memoranda. But on the other hand, the corps was courageous, honest, trustworthy, faithful to its role as an instrument of the state, and, above all, utterly devoted to a personal concept of loyalty to the sovereign.[22]

Moreover, the spark of professional learning was kept alive, especially in the technical services and the artillery. And there were officers like Radetzky who kept urging the establishment of an advanced military college, a *Kriegsschule,* a suggestion which was not implemented, however, until 1852.[23] Meanwhile, some professional learning was maintained by officers detached to the *Kriegsarchiv.* In a memorandum to the *Hofkriegsrat* in 1810, concerning the role of the Quartermaster-General Staff, Radetzky had argued that the "proper development of military historical writing and research requires the establishment of a special bureau,"[24] and though the full implementation of this proposal was delayed, a historical research nucleus was actually established in 1808, and from 1811 on a modicum of intellectual activity was maintained in the army by the *Österreichische militärische Zeitschrift,* edited by officers of the archival staff. But the journal had only limited circulation and apparently was not read with great interest. As one hostile critic wrote in 1846, Austrian officers tended to look outside the country for military learning,[25] and in 1837 a memorandum reminded officers to read the *Zeitschrift* carefully and not merely to scan it.[26]

As for the enlisted ranks, the army discontinued without much delay the last remnants of the people's army, the *Landwehr,* introduced during the Napoleonic wars. Although the *Landwehr* had acquitted itself rather well in 1809, it was progressively dismantled and completely shelved in 1831.[27] To be sure, the abolition of the *Landwehr* did not go unchallenged. In a collection of military essays published in 1820, one anonymous author advocated the idea of a people's army, and in 1828 Radetzky submitted a memorandum advocating the retention of such a force as the most "valuable foundation of strength."[28] But such ideas found no hearing in the decision-making circles which believed that only a strongly aristocratic officer corps, bound by personal ties to the dynasty, and a politically inert rank and file of long-service troops, strictly supervised and under iron discipline, could be relied upon to carry out the mission assigned to the army. In 1827, for instance, during a discussion of the new conscription and recruitment regulations, Emperor Francis remarked that he intended as soon as possible to dissolve even the last remnants of the *Landwehr* in order to be rid of an institution which he had only accepted under the pressure of circumstances.[29] Moreover, Radetzky also changed his mind. Like so many men of his generation and class, he believed that the ghost of the French Revolution had been inadequately banished, and the events of July 1830 in Paris and the Polish revolt the same year led him to change his opinion regarding the value of the *Landwehr.* He now believed that only the German areas of the monarchy would furnish reliable militia forces. There were, he wrote, "several provinces which never should become martial lands since their loyalty was suspect." As a result, the main burden would fall on the German Austrian duchies alone and this would be altogether too heavy a responsibility.[30]

Therefore, enlisted personnel for the Austrian army continued to be procured by the system of selective conscription dating back to the Josephinian reforms. Although in theory based on universal liability to serve, it provided numerous exemptions so that in practice the rank and file were drawn from the lowest classes only. Moreover, the system was not uniform in all the lands of the empire. The service law of 1827 provided that except for Hungary, the Tyrol, and Lombardy-Venetia, the term of service was fourteen years. In Hungary enlistment was for life. In the Tyrol the service obligation was for fourteen years, with an additional six years in the reserve, while in the Lombard-Venetian kingdom only eight years in all were required. In 1840 the duration of service was reduced to ten years in Hungary and in 1845, after considerable discussion, the term of service was set at an uniform eight years throughout the empire.[31]

Conscripts were obtained by drawing lots, though some communities met their quotas by turning their undesirable elements over to the army. In Hungary, especially, misfits and criminals were thought fit for military service. This reflected the common popular attitude towards the army. To be conscripted into the ranks was regarded as a disaster and indeed the life of the common soldier was harsh and had few compensations. Rations and pay were at a wretched level, lower than that of any other continental power except Russia, and soldiers often were forced to eke out a living by performing odd jobs during their off-duty hours.[32] Enlisted men were still regarded either as potential criminals to be punished severely or as children whose every action should be watched. Corporal punishments, caning, flogging, running the gauntlet, tying up, and other punishments were common, though there were some efforts to mitigate the worst excesses.[33] In 1835 Clam-Martinitz, one of the more perceptive officers, suggested that since the "army constituted the major unifying force in the monarchy," its rank and file should be well treated and flogging should be abolished.[34] This proposal proved unacceptable to the authorities, but in 1838 a *Hofkriegsrat* circular limited the amount of time a company commander could keep a man confined under close arrest and also restricted the punishments which could be inflicted by officers and non-commissioned officers without formal court martial proceedings. Even these limited reforms caused considerable lamentations among the old style officers who claimed that this would undermine all discipline.[35]

Understandably, the conditions of the unfortunate enlisted men resulted in a high incidence of desertion. When units shifted stations, and this was frequent, desertions were a common occurence, and the mountainous regions, especially Carniola and Carinthia, which lay on the route between Hungary and Italy, provided shelter for many bands of deserters who constituted an intermittent threat to the security of the civilian population.[36]

There existed, however, two exceptions to the general system of recruitment—the Tyrol and the Military Border. Although in 1815 Emperor Francis had ended the special privileged position of the Tyroleans and had introduced conscription, only one regiment, the Tyrolean *Jäger,* were recruited there, and the land provided proportionally fewer recruits than other parts of the monarchy. On the other hand, the emperor allowed the Tyroleans to maintain the old militia obligations going back to the *Libell* of 1511, which stipulated that in case of necessity the country would raise twenty thousand *Schützen* (marksmen enrolled and trained on a volunteer basis on publicly supported ranges), and if it became necessary the entire male population could be called out to serve in volunteer companies. Until 1848 these obligations remained mainly on paper, but when during that year Italian freecorps under Garibaldi threatened the frontiers, some sixteen thousand Tyrolean *Landesschützen* were called into service.[37]

In the meanwhile, during the period 1815 to 1847, with the army perennially short of funds, the ever-ready and cheaply maintained regiments of the Military Border assumed greater importance. From 1822 on the Military Border comprised of four major *Generalkommandos*: the Croatian, the Slavonian-Syrmian, the Banat, and the Transylvanian, subdivided into eighteen regiments and one independent battalion. Normally each regiment raised four battalions, grouped into three levies according to age. The first two battalions were on active service, and in rotation furnished troops for frontier guard and other duties. When necessary, the third and fourth battalions could be mobilized, and in case of dire necessity every man who could carry a musket was called out to form the fifth battalion or *Landesaufgebot*. In addition the Croatian command had the so-called *Seressaner*, a number of special units, about one thousand men in all, who dressed in national costume and were used for special police and scout duties. In all, the total strength of the Military Border, when fully mobilized, numbered over one hundred thousand men and the first and second battalions formed not only a cheap defense against the Turks but could be used for a variety of tasks. In 1820, for instance, the Ogulin Regiment furnished three companies to guard the Congress of Laibach, and in 1820 and 1821, and again in 1831, some twelve battalions went to reinforce the army in Italy.[38] On the Military Border the principle of universal military service was carried out to the fullest, and no other part of Europe made a comparable military effort in terms of its total population.

Financial problems, the conservatism of the highest command echelons, the character of the officer corps, and the composition of the rank and file also affected organization, equipment, and training of the army. In general, organization and equipment were similar to those of other European forces of the day, except that Austria boasted no special corps of guards, such as those of the French, British, Russian, and Prussian forces. Security of the emperor and his court was in the hands of special aristocratic semi-military bodies, such as the *Trabanten Leibgarde,* the Hungarian Noble Guard, the *Arcièren Leibgarde,* and others, assisted by a company-strength detachment of the army, the *Hofburgwache* (renamed in 1884 the *k.u.k. Leibgarde Infantrie Kompanie*).[39] Of course, there were some distinctions within the army. The cavalry was the most prestigious branch of the service, while the artillery and the engineering branches were regarded as middle class. The infantry regiments of the line, though they constituted the backbone of the army, rated low on the scale, and finally service in the *Grenz Infantrie* was, except for native sons, the last resort of a young man who sought financial solvency in exchange for no social prestige at all. Significantly, the *Grenzer* regiments had only honorary colonel proprietors and no purchase of commissions.

In early 1848 the army was divided into three hundred fifteen thousand men in the infantry, forty-nine thousand in the cavalry, twenty-six thousand in the artillery, five thousand four hundred in the technical troops, and a wagon train of four thousand.[40] These troops were distributed in twelve generalcies (*General-Militärkommanden*): Agram, Brünn, Graz, Hermannstadt, Lemberg, Buda, Peterwardein, Prague, Temesvár, Verona, Vienna, and Zara. Generally speaking, these commands functioned as administrative organizations only. Normally no higher tactical formations than regiments existed except in Italy where the *Generalkommando* in Verona was kept on a near-war footing and disposed of two corps, and on the Croatian sector of the Military Border where brigades of two regiments each were formed in the 1820s. Italy was considered the most important strategic area of the monarchy, but the Habsburg army also had commitments in Germany where the military constitution of the federation provided that in case of war Austria would provide the largest contingent, 158,040 men, and where during peacetime small Austrian contingents were stationed in the federal fortresses of southern Germany.[41]

A constant source of weakness was that due to the financial position of the state the establishment of many units was constantly understrength. As a further means of economy, the traditional expedient of sending men on unpaid furloughs after their initial training and recalling them only for maneuvers and emergencies was utilized. With a nominal establishment of four hundred thousand, actual army strength was close to two hundred fifty thousand men.[42] Administratively and tactically, the basic unit in most branches was the regiment. The infantry was composed of fifty-eight line regiments, eighteen *Grenzer* regiments, and one regiment of Tyrolean *Jäger*. In addition, there existed twenty independent Grenadier, twelve *Feld-Jäger*, and one amphibious *Grenzer* battalions. The cavalry consisted of fourteen heavy and twenty-three light regiments, eight Cuirasseer, six Dragoon, seven *Chevauxlegers,* twelve Hussar, and four Uhlan, while the artillery was divided into garrison and field artillery as well as an ordnance office, the *Feldzeugamt*. The main strength of this arm was in the five field regiments, one each stationed in Prague, Vienna, Olmütz, Budweis, and Pest. In addition there existed two special artillery formations, the Rocket Corps (*Feuerwerker Corps*) and the *Bombardeur Corps,* with the latter serving primarily as an instructional and experimental unit. Technical troops were formed into units of battalion strength. Finally, there existed a number of garrison units, fortress and town commands, remount farms, a small medical corps, educational institutions, and other auxiliary services.[43]

Strategy, tactics, armament, and equipment largely dated from the Napoleonic period. The artillery was still equipped entirely with smoothbore bronze barrelled muzzleloaders, standardized in the field regiments at 6- and 12-pounder cannon and 7- and 12-pounder howitzers. In addition there were rocket batteries using improved Congreve rockets. Due to the financial situation, there were no major changes in the artillery materiel during this period.[44] The cavalry branch, splendidly mounted, differed in training, equipment, and employment. The heavy regiments—Cuirasseers and Dragoons—were trained for the mounted charge during the battle, while the Hussars and Uhlans were to provide reconnaissance and security. The *Chevauxlegers* held an intermediate position. All regiments, except for the Uhlans who carried lances, relied primarily on the saber, though the Dragoons and *Chevauxlegers* carried carbines. In addition, all horsemen were equipped with clumsy horse pistols.

Infantry arms, however, were slowly changing. During the earlier part of the period all units were equipped with smoothbore flintlock muskets, but starting in 1835 first-line units were gradually equipped with weapons converted to a percussion pill-lock model Console, and special percussion rifles were issued to selected sharpshooters and to the *Jäger* formations. In 1842 the pill-lock was further improved by Feldmarschall Leutnant Vincenz Baron Augustin.[45] The engineers were the technically most advanced branch and their field bridging equipment, developed by Major Karl Birago and introduced in 1847, was highly mobile and engineer officers and men displayed a very high state of training and technical proficiency.[46]

The same, however, could not be said of the rest of the army where training tended to be defective. Economy played a considerable role here. The practice of sending men on extended leaves was highly detrimental, and there were other defects, too. Marksmanship was neglected and ammunition for training purposes was limited to twenty rounds annually for the line infantry and sixty rounds for the *Jäger*.[47] Of course, this deficiency applied to most European armies of the day. A single round cost almost as much as a soldier's daily ration and only Great Britain was wealthy enough to be able to afford adequate target practice for its infantry.

But there were other shortcomings. Mechanical drill, the manual of arms, and parade ground exercises were stressed to the detriment of realistic field training.

Maneuvers were rarely held, as they were expensive and usually consisted of grand exhibitions designed to achieve a spectacular effect to impress visiting dignitaries.[48] Adherence to an obsolescent tactical doctrine further inhibited realistic combat training. Although Austria had pioneered in the use of light troops in the seventeenth and eighteenth centuries, the official doctrine now stressed close formations, élan, and the use of the bayonet. And while the French were discovering the value of skirmishers in Algeria, the Austrian infantry manual of 1844 relegated skirmishers to an unimportant role and warned against any weakening of the main assault column.[49] Even the *Jäger* units were more and more given to ceremonial drill, tight formations, and neglect of their true function.[50] On the whole, the Austrian army was not well prepared for actual operations, despite the warnings of the aged Archduke Charles who wrote in 1841 that it "is not the number of soldiers which counts, but their efficiency and mobility."[51]

There were two exceptions to the general unpreparedness of the army. On the Military Border, especially in the Croatian sector facing turbulent Bosnia, the *Grenzer* were almost constantly engaged in small wars which on several occasions, in 1819, 1831, 1834, and again in 1845–1846, escalated into regimental-size battles.[52] The more important exception, and indeed it might be called the all-important exception, was the army stationed in Lombardy-Venetia. According to Metternich and the Austrian government, any new threat to the European order would come from "revolution," supported once again by France. With the other great continental powers—Russia and Prussia—Austria maintained cordial relations based on monarchical solidarity. Troops were disposed to forestall a Polish rising and not for use against each other. The armies of the three monarchies looked west, and on occasion their concentrations were designed for mutual support. In 1821, for instance, when Austria was engaged in Italy, Russia assembled an army of one hundred fifty thousand in Wolhynia to provide backing if needed. Of course, Austria also had interests and a certain amount of support in the lesser states of the German Federation, though here the political climate was volatile. In 1832 Metternich was prepared to act against radical trends in southwestern Germany and a small contingent, a mixed brigade, was readied for action.[53] But the cornerstone of Austrian military policy in Germany, and especially for the defense of the Rhine against France, was cooperation with Prussia, and specific military conventions covering such contingency were signed in 1832 and 1840.[54]

The bulk of the Austrian army was stationed in Italy and the security of the peninsula was considered her particular mission. As Metternich phrased it in his instructions to Wenzl Graf Kaunitz-Rietberg, the monarchy's ambassador at the Holy See, "Austria's military power in Italy provides the best guarantee for internal tranquility and peace abroad."[55] Not only was Italy the traditional invasion route to Inner Austria and thus a vital strategic area, but in Italy and specifically in her Italian possession the Habsburgs defended their traditional dynastic claims as well as the inviolability of the international settlements made in 1815.

The army was employed in 1821 to support the legitimate rulers in Naples and Piedmont; it intervened in Central Italy in 1831, and was committed to action in Parma and Modena in 1847. Even so, the army in Italy did not escape the general reduction in troop strength. From a maximum of 104,500 men in 1831, it was reduced to 75,000 in 1833, and finally to 49,297 in 1846, of whom, moreover, only 34,000 were available for field operations.[56] The remainder were scattered in a number of garrisons and small fortified places, most importantly guarding the four fortresses of the Quadrilateral—Verona, Legnano, Mantua, and Pesciera. These four great fortresses had been provided with up-to-date works and together formed a secure base and regroupment area for the army. But these were the only modern and fully armed fortresses in the empire. Except for the large fortified encampment around Linz, the fortress Komorn in Hungary, and the hastily constructed Franzensfeste in Tyrol, none of which was either fully armed or completed, the fortifications of the monarchy had become obsolete.[57]

But more important than numbers and fortifications were the unique spirit and the high state of preparedness of the army in Italy. In large part this was due to Radetzky. After 1817 the general, in disfavor because of his advocacy of advanced ideas, had been relegated to minor commands in Hungary and Bohemia, but when Austria reacted to the revolutions of 1830 by stepping up her military efforts, his talents could no longer remain unused. He was appointed chief of staff to General Frimont in Verona and later that year was elevated to commanding general in Italy.[58]

Radetzky found his army in indifferent shape. To be sure, it was adequately housed and fed, but its combat readiness left much to be desired. During his long career since entering the service in 1787, Radetzky had developed some very forward-looking ideas. For him the army was a corporate body in which all ranks, from the commander in chief to the lowest private, were linked by their military oath. Therefore, he carefully cultivated the morale of his men, abolished most of the brutal and degrading punishments, and introduced a new system of field training in which exercises were held in progressive stages, culminating in vast and well-planned corps maneuvers.[59] To be sure, there was some criticism that the maneuvers placed excessive demands on the troops, but generally his methods were widely acclaimed.[60] "Of all our forces," wrote Archduke Charles, "those in Italy are best prepared for war."[61]

But even Radetzky could not deal with the fundamental malaise of the army: the problem of nationalism. Under his leadership the heterogeneous elements that made up the army—Germans, Czechs, Italians, Magyars, Rumanians, Croats, Ruthenes, and others—were welded into a loyal and cohesive body, but elsewhere nationalist ideas penetrated, albeit slowly, into the military establishment. Metternich had hoped to keep the army separate and uncontaminated from the nationalist currents and the long terms of service were in part designed to break the rank and file from all attachments to their civilian lives. But the problem could not be dealt with exclusively within the army. Especially in Hungary, there was continual agitation for a national army, a goal supported by wide elements in the nation. These demands stemmed in part out of the old particularistic aspirations of the nobility, but were reinforced by the Hungarian Jacobins of the 1790s. At first the Magyar nobility aspired to reestablish the old "insurrection" as the base for a national army, but the last time this feudal levy had taken the field in 1809 had been a fiasco. Thereafter, nationalist Hungarian agitation centered on the proposition that the regiments recruited in Hungary should wear national insignia, use the Hungarian language, be officered exclusively by Hungarians, and be stationed exclusively within the kingdom. Such demands were voiced during the diets of 1832 to 1836 and emerged in even greater force in 1840.[62]

And while Hungarian aspirations were the most vocal, similar sentiments appeared among other contingents of the army. At the lowest level there was animosity between the rank and file of different nationalities. In the Bohemian regiments there was friction between Germans and Czechs, while in 1838 and 1839 German and Hungarian troops in Vienna clashed so frequently that the garrison commander had to assign different districts of the town to each regiment for their off-duty hours. More serious was a conspiracy involving Polish officers and men discovered in 1840 and the agitation of Italian nationalists, especially by followers of Mazzini's "Young Italy," among units recruited on the peninsula.[63] In fact, the *Hofkriegsrat* was concerned enough about "Young Italy's" activities that in 1833 it ordered that all soldiers belonging to that society were to be considered guilty of high treason and should be court martialled.[64] By the 1840s even the traditionally South Slav *Grenzer* were affected by nationalist stirrings, though after due investigation the *Hofkriegsrat* concluded that, especially in case of trouble with Hungary, they would not hesitate to perform their duty.[65]

To counteract nationalist influences, Vienna adopted a policy of distributing troops outside their ethnic areas, and in addition troops were transferred frequently to avoid their becoming too friendly with the local inhabitants. One regiment, for instance, Infantry Regiment Hoch-und Deutschmeister Nr. 4, was stationed in Milan in 1815, moved to St. Pölten the next year, switched to Bergamo in 1820, to Naples in 1822, to Capua in 1825, to Linz in 1830, to Görz in 1831, to Verona in 1833, to Kaisers-Ebersdorf in 1836, to Vienna in 1840, and finally to Tarnów and Lemberg in 1846.[66] Overall, late in 1847, out of thirty-five so-called "German" infantry regiments, a designation embracing all non-Hungarian and non-*Grenzer* units, six were in Italy and four in Hungary, while out of the fifteen Hungarian regiments, six were garrisoned in Italy, four were stationed in Austria, and only five remained in Hungary. At the same time, out of eight Italian regiments only four were in Italy and the remainder distributed in Austria and Hungary. Finally, during this period, out of the twenty-five non-Hungarian cavalry regiments thirteen were located in Hungary, while the twelve Hungarian Hussar regiments were evenly divided between their homeland and stations abroad.[67]

In general this policy was effective and, in the absence of an effective police or gendarmerie force able to deal with large-scale disorders, troops could be, and were, used to deal with such events. The earliest regulations regarding the use of troops "against rioters and unlawful assemblies and tumults," dated back to 1671 when Leopold I ordered the army to give assistance when so requested by the civil authorities. Repeatedly renewed during the eighteenth century, these instructions were amplified in 1783 when it was decreed that if troops were employed they should under no circumstances use blanks or fire into the air. In 1844 instructions concerning the use of arms against civilians were made more specific. If the local civilian authorities decided that no other means sufficed to disperse an unlawful assembly, the troops were to act sternly, yet with humane considerations. The instructions left it to the discretion of the commanding officer whether the soldiers were to use saber, bayonet, or firearms. If, however, firearms were to be used, the order to fire was to be given by an officer and a decision was to be made whether to employ individually aimed fire or volleys.[68]

Troops were used extensively to supplement the inadequate police resources in the empire and for this purpose considerable garrisons, some ten thousand each in Vienna and Milan, for instance, were maintained in the major cities.[69] In 1844 soldiers put down a textile workers' strike in Prague; in 1845 an Italian regiment suppressed riots in Agram;[70] and in the following year troops, assisted by loyal local peasants, rapidly squelched nationalist disorders in Galicia and occupied the Free City of Cracow.[71]

By 1847, however, the internal situation began to deteriorate in Italy where the inauguration of Pope Pius IX, considered a liberal and a nationalist, further increased tension. In the face of mounting unrest the Austrian authorities in Italy were divided. Viceroy Archduke Rainer favored a conciliatory policy, while Radetzky demanded a strong, uncompromising stand.[72] By January 1847, the general had already advised his corps commanders to prepare to reinforce Ferrara, one of the central Italian papal "legations" where Austria had garrison rights. Following disorders during the summer, Austrian troops occupied the town and surrounding area.[73] And when in the late fall of that year the Habsburg rulers of Modena and Parma asked for assistance, Radetzky dispatched small bodies of troops there.[74] At the same time, a civil war between the liberal and conservative cantons broke out in Switzerland which forced Radetzky to establish a cordon along the frontier between Lombardy and the Tessin.[75] His forces were becoming dangerously stretched out and he now strongly urged the immediate reinforcement of his army.[76]

But in Vienna, Metternich was growing uneasy. The prince had lost much of his former energy and had turned profoundly pessimistic. Moreover, always suspicious of the military, he felt that Radetzky had overstepped his authority in Ferrara and he was concerned with the continuing rift between the civil and military authorities in Italy. Therefore he dispatched a soldier-diplomat, General der Kavallerie Karl Ludwig Count Ficquelmont, to Milan to act as his special representative.[77] By October 1847, Metternich, who briefly had considered military intervention in Switzerland, was having second thoughts; he wrote to Fiquelmont that nothing more than a military demonstration should be undertaken.[78]

Although Metternich was restraining the military, he realized the urgent need to raise military expenditures and to augment the army, especially since he did support the decision to send troops to Modena and Parma.[79] But since all such major decisions had to be coordinated between the *Staatsrat*, the *Hofkriegsrat*, and the various military commands, it took time to implement such resolutions. To be sure, the military budget for 1847 was raised to 62.96 million florins, but it actually took longer to strengthen the army at the danger points. Thus on December 3, 1847, the emperor sanctioned the dispatch of seven *Grenzer* battalions to reinforce Radetzky in northern Italy, but despite the general's plea for prompt action, execution of the order was delayed until the end of February 1848.[80]

As 1847 was drawing to a close, Metternich no longer had much confidence in the future of his system. He need not have worried about the army, however. With all its shortcomings, many of which it shared with other contemporary forces, the Austrian army reflected a strong sense of mission and purpose. "In this union of heterogeneous provinces inclined to dissolution," Clam-Martinitz once wrote, "the army constituted the only symbol of unity and strength." It was, he continued, "not a part of the nation as in other states, but a nation unto itself which keeps together the various parts."[81] This was a proud boast, but soon it was to be proved true. The Austrian army not only enabled Metternich to play his role as the "coachman of Europe" for thirty years, it also managed to preserve much of his system. When the great wave of revolutions rolled over the empire in 1848, crumbling the government and sweeping Metternich out of office, the army by and large remained steadfast, the corporate guardian of the state which saved the empire and the dynasty.

To be sure, the army paid a price. By constituting itself as a "nation within itself," in Clam-Martinitz's phrase, it became increasingly more isolated from the population, and when in later years the popular will gained more power in Austria, it found itself cut off from the support of the people. But this still was in the future. For the moment the white-coated sentries still manned the citadels of the empire, visible evidence of the warning, as Radetzky put it in his famous message to the Milanese on January 15, 1848, not to make light of the power of the Austrian double eagle: "the saber is still firm in my hand . . . the strength of its talons still remains."[82]

3

Guardians of an Empire: The Army 1848-1849

The February Revolution in France set off revolts across half of Europe. Victory in Paris induced liberal hopes elsewhere that the crowned heads and their governments would hasten to come to terms. Such expectations appeared justified when the second wave of upheavals in March ousted established regimes with surprising ease and substituted in their stead liberal, or at least liberal-tinged, ministries. But such an assessment was unrealistic. The February and March developments demonstrated the power of the street against regimes which temporarily lost their nerve, and success remained more apparent than real as long as the ultimate instrument of power, the army, remained secure in the hands of the old establishment. This held true in the Austrian Empire where in March 1848 the Metternichean system collapsed with incredible swiftness and where, for a time at least, there was an almost complete disintegration of the traditional centers of authority. But the military authorities retained their grip, and ultimately they provided the rallying force for a complete counterrevolution.

Upon receiving news of the events in Paris, Metternich at once moved to contain the revolution which he perceived as a French threat to the international order. On March 4, 1848, he called on Prussia to implement the Military Convention of 1840 and on March 20, a week after the chancellor had left office, a punctation providing for a common defense against French aggression was signed in Vienna.[1] But Metternich had misjudged the situation. The real threat to the empire came from within and not from without. While the Austrian revolutions were inspired by events in France, they gained critical momentum from Hungary where for several months the diet had been sitting in Pressburg, only forty miles from Vienna, considering constitutional reforms. On March 3, the leader of the radicals, Louis Kossuth, made a fiery speech on liberty; copies of his address heightened existing unrest in Vienna. On March 13, a clash between demonstrating students and working men and the military escalated into full-scale rioting in the city and the suburbs. The commandant of Vienna, Feldmarschall Leutnant Archduke Albrecht, the son of the famous Archduke Charles, had been expecting trouble. But although the garrison had been alerted, live ammunition issued, and detachments deployed at strategic points in the Inner City, the force, some fourteen thousand men of all arms, was not adequate to contain a major uprising in a city of over four hundred thousand. Although by evening the military had restored control in the Inner City, unrest, looting, and violence continued in the outlying districts.

Fearing further proletarian disorders, the mayor of Vienna demanded that the preservation of public safety should be entrusted to the civic guard, the *k.k. privilegierte Bürgerwehr*, a well-equipped though inexperienced force of some fifteen thousand. In addition he suggested that this force be expanded into a national guard and that the students be armed and enrolled in an academic legion. But at the same time, the middle class was not prepared to act as a mere auxiliary to the military. The city authorities also demanded that army units be withdrawn from the streets. At court, meanwhile, there was a debate and after some discussion it was decided to appease the liberals. At the same time, these events enabled a court faction, led by the Archduchess Sophie, to pressure Emperor Ferdinand into jettisoning Metternich and to the amazement of Europe the chancellor resigned that very night. The next day the jubilant students formed their academic legion, arms were issued, and the emperor placed the security of his capital into the hands of the new national guard. Except for some guards at court, troops were withdrawn to their barracks outside the glacis of the Inner City, while Albrecht, compromised by his actions in the eyes of the radicals, and accused by some officers of not having shown enough resolution, was replaced by the amenable and popular Feldmarschall Leutnant Count Auersperg.[2]

Archduchess Sophie and her cabal had engineered the overthrow of Metternich in the hope of obtaining a revitalized conservative government, but the result was the constitution of a provisional government of bureaucrats, headed by Count Kolowrat on March 17. And when Kolowrat vanished from the scene after a few days, he was succeeded by Count Ficquelmont, the soldier-diplomat, who had been Metternich's special envoy to Radetzky and who, for a few days in March, had served as president of the *Hofkriegsrat*. But Ficquelmont too was unable to maintain himself and when he was driven from office in May, responsibility fell into the hands of Franz Freiherr von Pillersdorf, an elderly civil servant with an undeserved reputation for liberalism. None of these men was able to govern, and continued unrest in Vienna was met by dropping some unpopular figures from the ministry and by making new concessions to liberal and radical demands.

Only the army was an exception to the prevailing drift. At first the new ministry did not control the military whose direction remained in the hands of the *Hofkriegsrat*. On April 2, however, acting on the advice of Kolowrat, it was decided to end this venerable institution and to transfer its functions to a new War Ministry. The same day the emperor appointed Feldmarschall Leutnant Peter Zanini, one of the few non-noble general officers, as war minister over the head of several more senior generals. The appointment of Zanini was regarded by public opinion as a further concession to liberalism, and the aristocratic generalcy tended to be sceptical, if not actually hostile, towards the new minister.[3] And when in addition Zanini received confusing instructions regarding the powers of his office and was faced with obstruction from the conservative officials, he resigned in frustration before the end of the month. His successor, Feldzeugmeister Count Theodor Baillet de Latour, a stout-hearted and energetic conservative, took office on April 30.[4] The new minister faced a difficult task. Not only would be have to deal with the administrative problems presented by the transfer of powers to the new War

Ministry, but he was also confronted with the more urgent task of maintaining the integrity and the unity of the army in the face of mounting separatist pressure from Hungary and also the provision of all possible support to Radetzky, who was leading his army in suppressing a national war of liberation in northern Italy.[5]

In Hungary the fall of Metternich induced the diet to enact a series of measures on March 15 creating a unitary national Hungarian state. The diet was replaced by a parliament and there was to be a separate Hungarian army, budget, and foreign policy. On April 3, the emperor assented to the formation of a Hungarian ministry in Budapest, headed by Count Louis Batthyány and including Kossuth as minister of finance, and on April 7, the monarch promised that in future he would exercise his rights in "all civil, church, and military affairs," only through the medium of the responsible ministers.[6] The entire new constitutional system of Hungary was confirmed by the emperor on April 11.

From the outset, however, the implementation of these far-reaching concessions, especially in the military sphere, was subject to widely different interpretations in Vienna and Budapest. Although the conservative military held that the new order was only provisional and that the Diet of 1715 had established a unitary army once and for all, the more liberal Zanini had instructed imperial troops stationed in Hungary to swear loyalty to the new Hungarian ministry and to take their orders from the Hungarian minister of defense. But even this did not settle the status of the Military Borders. The Hungarians demanded their formal incorporation into the kingdom and the civilian ministers in Vienna were, at first, prepared to give in on this point. But even Zanini had balked. Control over the Military Border, he claimed, was one of the rights reserved to the monarch and therefore the War Ministry, as the legal successor to the *Hofkriegsrat,* remained in exclusive command.[7] To be sure, he received little guidance on this issue from the emperor and his ministers. When Zanini asked for further clarification of his competence in Hungary, he merely was told to find the "most effective and least controversial methods of conducting military affairs in that kingdom."[8] Undoubtedly, such instructions added to the problems which led to his resignation.

Latour, his successor, fared little better at first. The day that he took office he issued an army order which stressed the continued unity of the military establishment, "the bulwark of the constitutional throne against all foreign and domestic enemies." A week later, however, an imperial letter informed him that on all matters concerning the entire army, including the Military Borders and especially in the employment of Hungarian troops outside their country, he was to consult and act in agreement with the Hungarian War Ministry, temporarily headed by Major General Franz Ottinger.[9] At the same time, the ministry hoped that the permanent minister designate, Colonel Lázár Mészáros, a hussar officer on duty in Italy, would be cooperative, and orders were issued to speed his return.[10]

Confusing and contradictory policies were common during these months and the emperor was playing a double game. On the one hand he made concessions to Hungary's demand for military autonomy, and on the other he listened to the suggestions of loyalist Croatian conservatives who urged a firm stand against Hungary. On March 23, without consulting Budapest, he appointed Colonel Joseph Jelačić, an old *Grenzer* who combined absolute devotion to the dynasty with fervent Croat patriotism, as Ban of Croatia and within two weeks promoted him to feldmarschall leutnant and commanding officer in Croatia and its Military Border districts.¹¹ Determined to assert Croatia's special position against centralizing efforts from Budapest, Jelačić ordered all Croatian officials to accept no further directives from the Hungarian ministry and in May, claiming that the country was in danger, he mobilized his *Grenzer* regiments.¹²

In Hungary, however, these actions, coupled with unrest and even open defiance by the other Slav communities within the kingdom, were regarded as open threats against the new order. With Mészáros reluctant to act, Kossuth, although at the time he was merely minister of finance, took the first steps toward creating a national Hungarian army. During the last week in April he called for volunteers and placed orders for the manufacture of one hundred thousand muskets. At the same time, since manufacturing capacity was limited to about five hundred a week, he ordered the conversion of scythes into pikes to arm the popular levy.¹³ Both sides were arming and conditions for a confrontation between Vienna and Budapest were emerging.

Meanwhile the imperial and royal army already was engaged in an open war to maintain Habsburg rule in northern Italy where Lombardy-Venetia had been in turmoil for some time. In January 1848 there were riots and assaults on the military in Milan and in several other cities, accompanied by reports that Sardinia was arming for intervention.¹⁴ Aware of the coming storm, Radetzky warned the Italians on January 15 that "His Majesty, the Emperor, is fully determined to maintain the Lombard-Venetian Kingdom against all internal and external attacks," and, added the feldmarschall, he fully intended to carry out his orders as long as his hand could still wield the sword.¹⁵ But actually, Radetzky's brave words were masking weakness. He had received only minor reinforcements and his army numbered only seventy-three thousand of whom about twenty thousand were Italians of dubious reliability.¹⁶ As he bitterly complained, "I asked for troops and had to argue over every battalion; I requested rations and instead received instructions which only an ancient historian could decipher."¹⁷ Still, he made the best dispositions he could. The army was divided into two corps; I Corps, with Feldmarschall Leutnant Johann Wenzel Count Wratislaw commanding some forty thousand men, was stationed in Lombardy with ten thousand men in garrison at Milan. Feldmarschall Leutnant Constantin Baron D'Aspre's II Corps, with thirty-three thousand men, was located in Venetia with headquarters at Pavia. Radetzky would have preferred to concentrate his forces, but was obliged to accede to the wishes of the civil authorities, especially the Viceroy Archduke Rainer, who asked for a military presence in as many localities as possible.¹⁸

News about the revolution in Vienna reached Venice on March 17 and Milan the following day. In Milan the population, rather well provided with arms, rose at once and though the garrison maintained itself, it soon became evident that the city could not be held for long. Intelligence received indicated that the entire countryside was in revolt, that the Sardinians were ready to intervene, and that in Venice a weak commander actually was seeking terms from the insurgents. Under these circumstances, Radetzky decided to fall back on the Quadrilateral and call in his outlying garrisons. He evacuated Milan during the night of March 22. The same day the Habsburg flag was hauled down in Venice and the restoration of the republic proclaimed.¹⁹

The evacuation of Milan and the regroupment of the army were carried out in good order. Attempts by local insurgents to impede the march were brushed aside.[20] Still, it was a retreat and if Charles Albert of Sardinia had advanced while the fighting still raged in the city he might have cut off Radetzky's main body. But the king was not a bold leader. He hesitated until March 25 to cross the frontier with forty thousand men, a well-equipped, but indifferently led, army. But the Sardinians, reinforced by contingents from other Italian states, were regarded as liberators and everywhere received the active support of the population. Caught up in the wave of national enthusiasm, most of the Italian troops in the Habsburg service went over to the national cause; indeed, as one report noted, "it was astonishing that out of a draft of 380 men of the 26th Infantry (Ferdinand d'Este), 125 remained true to their duty and oath." Numerous fortified places and several important arms depots were lost at this point.[21] Popular uprisings even threatened the vital but weakly garrisoned Quadrilateral. Verona was saved when D'Aspre evacuated Padua and threw most of his corps into the fortress. Meanwhile in Mantua the resolute General Carl Ritter von Gorzkowski prevented a coup by the citizenry until reinforcements arrived.[22]

While the army stabilized its positions, the Vienna government lost heart. There was talk of writing off Lombardy and using Radetzky's troops to save Venetia. Some even mentioned negotiating peace in Italy and using the army to save Hungary and the German and Czech areas from revolution. But Radetzky refused to go along. He never had liked Viennese interference in his command and on April 2 he wrote to the ministry that "we cannot, and must not, let Italy go."[23] Although weakened by defections, he still commanded some fifty thousand concentrated in the Quadrilateral with detachments covering the Tyrol and his communications with Austria. While the Sardinians hesitated to push beyond Milan, the War Ministry in Vienna was supporting Radetzky's policy. Special priority was given to his demands for reinforcements and enough troops were scraped up to form a reserve corps to protect his rear and to blockade Venice.[24] And when the Sardinians finally advanced, they were defeated on May 6 at Santa Lucia, just west of Verona. With this victory, won against a numerically superior enemy, Radetzky turned the tide in Italy and regained the initiative.[25]

The Italian war was popular in Vienna, even among the liberals, but even so dissatisfaction with the constitution handed down in April led to a second upheaval on May 15, which compelled the feeble government to concede elections for a constituent assembly on a democratic franchise. This was followed on May 26 by another and even more radical uprising. Frightened by these developments, the imperial family left on May 17 for the security of loyal Innsbruck.

At the same time, the trend towards radicalism thoroughly disquieted the military leadership, who now began to assume a more active political role. Despite the virtual disintegration of the traditional centers of authority, the army retained its cohesion and, except for the defection of some Italian and later most Magyar troops, the rank and file never wavered in its obedience. Indeed, during March and April over one hundred thousand reservists and men on furlough returned to their units and new recruits were raised without trouble.[26]

The officers were even more resolved to fight the revolution. As early as April, officers in most garrisons communicated with each other, formed committees to fight subversion, and prepared to defy the constitutional arrangements if these threatened the authority of the emperor. The army, they reasoned, had to save the emperor, and "to save him, can under no circumstances, be considered a breach of the military oath."[27] In Vienna, Latour ably seconded their efforts. Latour outwardly played the role of a constitutional minister and in May rejected a proposal by General der Kavallerie Wilhelm Baron Hammerstein, commanding in Galicia, to transfer his twenty thousand troops reinforced by loyal peasant levies to the revolutionary capital. But at the same time, he quietly encouraged Jelačić in his continued defiance of the Hungarian ministry and was also filtering aid to the Serbs of southern Hungary who at the end of May had taken up arms against Budapest.[28] Following the May upheavals in Vienna, when a frightened government prepared to make additional concessions to the revolution, Latour indicated that while he would not actively oppose them, he nonetheless felt that his place was in Innsbruck with the emperor.[29] But Latour did not leave Vienna. He remained, perhaps none too reluctantly, at his post which remained the nerve center of the military administration.

Latour was quietly supporting the military counterrevolution, but it seems clear that he was not prepared to act without clear instructions from the emperor. No such scruples, however, troubled Feldmarschall Leutnant Alfred Prince Windischgrätz, commanding in Bohemia. A man with curiously changeable moods, a well-connected member of the high aristocracy, and a determined champion of absolutism, Windischgrätz "believed firmly that Providence had designed him to be the savior of the Habsburg Empire."[30] In March he fleetingly had attempted to play the role of military dictator in Vienna, but had resigned within a week. Since then he had watched the continued concessions to liberalism and the revolution with growing concern and he had maintained close contact with that court faction headed by Archduchess Sophie and Empress Marie Anna which now was scheming a counterrevolution during which Emperor Ferdinand was to lay down the crown and be succeeded by his young nephew, the Archduke Francis.

On May 20, Windischgrätz returned to Prague after an extended leave and from there, on May 29, he wrote to Joseph Count Lobkowitz, the emperor's adjutant general, that should the revolutionaries attempt to extract any additional concessions from the monarch, or should his security appear endangered, then the emperor, guarded by as many troops as could be found, should be conducted to the safety of Olmütz in Moravia. "After that," Windischgrätz asserted, "I shall seize Vienna, His Majesty will abdicate in favor of his nephew Archduke Francis, and we will then proceed to take Pest."[31] Here, as early as May, the complete program for a military counterrevolution was proclaimed. But the time was not yet. Immediately, Windischgrätz was preparing to deal a blow to the revolution in Bohemia.

Until June, Bohemia had been spared violence on the scale that had shaken Vienna, but its capital, Prague, was far from tranquil. Although the imperial government had conceded autonomy for Bohemia in principle, there was a considerable amount of political, social, and ethnic unrest. Windischgrätz's return to Prague did nothing to ease tensions because the general, having repressed the textile workers strike in 1844, was highly unpopular. Anticipating trouble, Windischgrätz took precautions. Strong patrols in fighting order were on the streets and cannon were emplaced at strategic points. Plans were laid to reinforce the garrison and to isolate the city from outside support in case of a rising.[32] Trouble materialized soon after a Pan Slav Congress convened in Prague on June 2. Although most of the delegates, representing above all the Slavs of the empire, were friendly to the dynasty, congress rhetoric inflamed passions and on June 12 a clash between soldiers and demonstrators escalated into a full-scale insurrection.

For six days there was intense fighting in Prague. The students, as usual, were in the forefront and had obtained weapons. At first the Vienna government wavered and sent a delegation to attempt mediation, while on June 14 Windischgrätz unaccountably offered to resign. But mediation failed and the general withdrew his offer within hours. Then, regaining the initiative, he concentrated his forces against the ill-sited barricades, bombarded strongpoints, and forced the city into submission.[33] On the face of it, the revolt in Prague was no different from others which had forced Vienna into abject concessions. The difference lay in Windischgrätz who "in dealing with the insurgents . . . could count on his popularity with his officers and on the loyalty of his troops."[34] He demonstrated that as long as troops remained available, urban insurrections could be overcome. "The street fighting in Prague," an English historian concluded, "was the first serious battle against the revolution; and in this battle the revolution was defeated."[35] Perhaps this statement underrated the importance of the battle of Santa Lucia, but certainly the events in Prague were a psychological turning point. Windischgrätz had demonstrated that as long as the troops remained loyal, urban insurrections could be mastered. Moreover, his stand showed that the power which the government had not been willing to employ in March now was becoming free of restraints. In short, victory in Prague allowed Windischgrätz to enact the role as the military savior of the dynasty.

Even while the military were moving to launch their counterrevolution, the vacillating emperor made one more attempt at appeasement. In response to Hungarian pressure, he confirmed on June 8 the authority on the Budapest War Ministry over all troops stationed in the lands of the crown of St. Stephen, including those of the Military Border, and on June 10 he signed a decree deposing Jelačić. But Jelačić ignored this action. The Hungarian government, however, choosing to take the decrees at face value, now ordered military execution against the Serbs in southern Hungary who had declared their independence and proclaimed the establishment of an autonomous Vojvodina. Hungarian attempts to restore control over this region failed, and by July a bitter war was raging in southern Hungary.[36]

At the same time Radetzky had moved out of the Quadrilateral in June and had taken the offensive. Although the Sardinians fought bravely, their leaders were quite unequal to the old feldmarschall and on July 25 they were decisively defeated at Custozza. On August 9 Charles Albert concluded an armistice which obliged him to evacuate all Austrian territory.[37] His Italian allies now left the war, Austrian troops returned to Milan and occupied the central Italian duchies, and only Venice, shielded by her lagoons, still held out against a desultory siege.

Victory in Italy not only vindicated Radetzky's strategy but also permitted a decisive confrontation with Hungary. Throughout the summer Count Batthyány, the moderate Hungarian premier, had tried to avoid open conflict with the imperial government, and together with Mészáros had resisted the radical demands for the creation of an independent Hungarian army. Instead he had relied on the imperial units stationed in the country that had been ordered by Zanini to take their instructions from the new Hungarian ministry. But with fierce fighting in progress in southern Hungary and with Jelačić continuing his defiance in Croatia, it was easy for Kossuth to sway parliament; on July 11 that body voted credits for a two hundred thousand strong national army, the *Honvéd*. This army, Magyar regiments with the Magyar language of command and Magyar officers, was to be formed around a core of regular imperial units, twenty battalions of infantry, ten regiments of hussars, and two *Székler* regiments of the Transylvanian Military Border. In addition to these Magyar units, eight companies of the two Italian infantry regiments stationed in Hungary and elements of the Fifth Bohemian Artillery Regiment took service with the new force. Even so, by September 1848, the Budapest government disposed only of some fifty thousand well-trained soldiers, while *Honvéd*, national guards, and local militia bodies were not considered able to hold their own against regulars.[38]

In Vienna, where the court had returned in August to attend the opening of the constituent assembly, the *Reichstag*, opinion was divided. For the moment the majority of the new and democratic-leaning Doblhoff government disliked the idea of open conflict within the empire, and as a further concession on August 20 obtained an imperial decree ordering the recall of all non-Hungarian units from Hungary.[39] But this was the last concession. Continued workers' riots in Vienna on August 22 raised the specter of social revolution, and at this point the terms of the problem changed. In the city the national guard became polarized between bourgeois and radical units, while the ministry, perceiving a connection between Austrian radicalism and Hungarian demands, changed its stand and decided that the extensive concessions made to Budapest should be modified. On August 29 the government decided to reintroduce centralization in the fiscal and military affairs of the empire. Hungary was told to halt formation of its national army and control over the Military Borders was returned to Vienna.[40] Hungarian protests were dismissed and on September 4, as further indication of the new course, the emperor formally reinstated Jelačić in all his offices.[41] The issue of war or peace with Hungary would soon be removed from the political arena.

Throughout the late summer Jelačić was under heavy pressure from military and conservative groups, as well as from the Serbs actually fighting in southern Hungary, to invade that country with the army of forty-five thousand men which he had raised in Croatia. Although Jelačić would have preferred to receive a direct imperial command, he finally decided to act; on September 11 his advance guard crossed the frontier.[42] But the hope that the campaign was going to be easy was soon dispelled. In Budadapest the Batthyány ministry resigned and the fiery Kossuth took over defense of the country. Jelačić confidently expected that the regular components of the *Honvéd* would rally to his side, but he was bitterly disappointed. At first there was considerable confusion indeed in the *Honvéd* ranks. The regulars, officers as well as men, were reluctant to engage their old comrades and under their commander, General Adam Teleky, they fell back towards the capital with little fighting.[43] But on September 29 the Croatian army encountered the main Hungarian body, now commanded by General Moga, at Pákozd-Velence, covering the approaches to Budapest. "The hope that regular troops would not fight against us," Jelačić reported, "has unfortunately not been realized." Only some Bohemian and Italian units reconsidered their allegiance; the remaining regulars fought against the Habsburg flag. "I shudder," continued the Ban, "at the thought of training my cannon on hussars. If this happens a chasm will open, perhaps forever, within the ranks of the army."[44] But it did happen. There was some heavy fighting, though the battle itself was indecisive. Jelačić, however, lost his nerve and under the cover of a three-day armistice he retreated northwards to Austria.[45]

Jelačić was able to extract himself from the consequences of defeat by proclaiming that he deliberately had diverted his forces in order to deal with the latest and by far most radical revolt yet in Vienna. The immediate spark for this outbreak had been provided by Latour's decision to send reinforcements to Jelačić. On October 6 the Richter Grenadier Battalion, ordered to entrain for Hungary, mutinied. Although this was due not so much to the radicalism of the soldiers as to their reluctance to fight Hungarian troops still considered by them as comrades-in-arms, the mutiny found immediate support among the radical units of the national guard. Fighting spread and within hours Latour was besieged in his ministry and brutally murdered by an aroused mob. The city fell into the hands of the radicals and at dawn the next day the emperor and the court fled the capital for the second time and took refuge at Olmütz.[46]

These events set the stage for the scenario outlined by Windischgrätz which did not come as a surprise to informed observers. Since March the generals had been unhappy with developments in Vienna, disliked the concessions made to Hungary, and distrusted the concept of ministerial responsibility and the constituent assembly. Relations between them and civilians were not improved when the *Reichstag* refused a vote of thanks to Radetzky's army and shouted Latour down during the debate.[47] Deeply annoyed, Radetzky wrote to Latour on September 30 that though the army was not necessarily tied to the old regime and was willing to abide a constitutional government, it could not tolerate a state of affairs in which the press was free to attack the officer corps and where control was in the "hands of mere boys and despicable agitators." The troops under his command, Radetzky continued, were loyal to the emperor and his constitution, but would resist any further encroachment on the imperial powers and react violently against any threat to the personal security of the monarch.[48] And at the same time, Lord Ponsonby, the well-connected British ambassador, reported to London that, "I think that the Austrian Empire is rising and that the ancient power it once had may be nearly restored ere long to its military."[49]

Actual execution of the military counterrevolution was carried out by Windischgrätz who for seveal weeks now had been concentrating forces for just this contingency and had taken steps to secure their rail transportation to Vienna.[50] When the October Revolution occurred, the Vienna garrison, depleted to eight thousand men, had evacuated the city and had taken up positions in the outer suburbs, and there had been reinforced on October 12 by Jelačić.[51] The advance elements of the Bohemian army arrived before the capital on October 16 and by the third week of that month a formidable force, fifty-nine battalions, sixty-seven squadrons, and two hundred guns, were concentrated under the personal command of Windischgrätz.[52] After several demands to surrender were refused, a general assault was ordered on October 28. Fierce fighting with severe casualties continued for two days, but after a Hungarian relief column was repulsed at Schwechat on October 30, resistance collapsed and the city capitulated.[53]

It had, in any case, been an uneven contest, for the radicals in Vienna never mustered more than fifty thousand ill-trained men, and the Hungarian relief corps, hesitant to cross the Austrian frontier, had appeared with inadequate strength and too late.⁵⁴ Vienna now was placed under martial law and garrisoned in strength, though the situation was somewhat eased by the consideration shown by Windischgrätz who, though stern and even brutal during the actual fighting, showed himself to be moderate in victory, and there were relatively few reprisals.⁵⁵ On November 3 actual control of the city was transferred to Feldzeugmeister Ludwig Baron Welden.⁵⁶

But moderation in reprisals did not mean that Windischgrätz had given up his program. Quite the contrary. Elevated on October 16 to the rank of feldmarschall and appointed commander-in-chief of all imperial forces, except the army of Italy, his headquarters at the imperial palace in Schönbrunn became the hub of political affairs.⁵⁷ From Italy Radetzky hailed the prince's victory as the base for a reconstruction of the empire, while from St. Petersburg Tsar Nicholas I sent his congratulations and expressed the hope that in the near future the army would also deal with the revolutionaries in other parts of the monarchy.⁵⁸ The next step was the formation of a strong ministry, amenable to the wishes of the army, and a forceful man to head such a government was at hand in the person of Feldmarschall Leutnant Felix Prince Schwarzenberg, Windischgrätz's brother-in-law.

Schwarzenberg, then forty-eight years old, had made a dual career as a soldier and diplomat. Recently he had distinguished himself with the army in Italy and had arrived in Vienna just before the October rising to provide closer liaison between Windischgrätz and Radetzky. He was appointed prime minister in November. A staunch protagonist of centralization, he was determined to reduce Hungary by peaceful means if possible, but if necessary, as he wrote to Radetzky, "an appeal will have to be made to the brave and loyal army and its leaders."⁵⁹ In the meantime, Schwarzenberg cooperated with the military in the final move, a change at the very head of the empire which on December 2, 1848, replaced Ferdinand with his young nephew who took the name of Francis Joseph. To be sure, Schwarzenberg soon revealed that he was his own man and in many ways stronger than Windischgrätz, but for the moment, and in the historical tradition, it was the military triumvirate of Windischgrätz, Jelačić, and Radetzky—the famous WJR—which effected the change on the throne.

The circumstances of Francis Joseph's elevation to the imperial dignity, his upbringing and education, all were of considerable significance for the future of the army. Throughout his long reign Francis Joseph would remember his debt to the military, cherish his position as supreme warlord, and regard the army as his chief support and main concern.⁶⁰ It also was natural that the army occupied the most important place in his first official pronouncements. In his accession manifesto Francis Joseph predicted that the disorders in Hungary soon would be terminated, and in his first order of the day he confirmed Windischgrätz as commander-in-chief and called on the "misguided" troops in Hungary to return to their proper allegiance.⁶¹

Thus the way was cleared for the final point in the military program—the reduction of Hungary. There is evidence that Windischgrätz did not aim at an exclusive military solution. Instead, he believed that a determined show of force, coupled with the occupation of Budapest, would be sufficient to overthrow the radicals and return the conservative Magyar high nobility, with whom he had retained rapport and which was traditionally amenable to Habsburg rule, to power.⁶² To accomplish this he concentrated two corps, backed by a small reserve of some forty-five thousand men, northwest of Pressburg, with other elements to operate out of Inner-Austria and Slovakia. In addition, some sixteen thousand men were deployed in Transylvania, while the imperial forces in southern Hungary, augmented by Serb volunteers, numbered thirty thousand. In all, the imperial army poised for intervention in Hungary numbered some one hundred thirty thousand men. To oppose them the Hungarians mustered about one hundred twenty thousand of whom about half had adequate training. The Magyars, however, had the advantage of being well acquainted with Austrian tactics, and their cavalry arm was superior to the imperial horse.[63]

A glaring weakness in the Hungarian forces was the quality and the reliability of the officer corps. Many of the newly appointed officers, though devoted to the cause, had no technical qualifications whatsoever, while the regulars were still wavering in their allegiance. The resignation of Emperor-King Ferdinand, who had taken an oath to the Hungarian constitution, and the accession of Francis Joseph, who had not become the duly crowned king of Hungary, created deep inner conflicts. For the moment, however, many of them, patriots rather than revolutionaries, decided to continue to serve the national authority, the Committee of National Defense, headed by Kossuth, established in October.[64]

This was the situation when on December 16 imperial forces crossed the Leitha, their shakoes marked with a white linen band to distinguish them from their adversaries, most of whom still wore the old imperial uniforms. Windischgrätz planned to advance on a broad front towards Budapest, while his supporting forces delivered concentric attacks from the east and the south.[65] At first all went well. Although Hungarian forces in the east and south achieved local successes, the main drive against the capital could not be stopped. Defense of the approaches to Budapest was in the hands of General Arthur Görgey, a former regular officer. Although he had orders to stand fast, Görgey did not intend to sacrifice his thirty thousand men and retreated eastwards. The Hungarian government was forced to abandon Budapest which Windischgrätz entered on January 5, 1849.[66] Exulted by this easy victory, Windischgrätz issued a proclamation calling on the country to submit, and on January 12 he called on all regular troops in the Hungarian service to return to their duty. At this point many of the officers wanted to return, but found themselves ordered to appear first before a commission of investigation which, in all too many cases, punished rather than rehabilitated. And when this became known, most regular officers decided that they had little to gain by submission.[67]

In any case, regardless of the decisions made by the officers, Kossuth had no intention of giving in and was preparing to wage war to the bitter end. Although Görgey perhaps was the most able Magyar general, he was now (temporarily, as it turned out) relieved from command, and Count Henry Dembinszki, a Polish émigré officer, was appointed to lead the insurgent forces. Dembinszki promptly attempted to retake Budapest, but on February 26 and 27 he was repulsed with heavy losses at Kapolna. Elated, Windischgrätz now informed Vienna that the campaign was as good as over.[68]

The prince did not understand the nature of a war of national liberation. Though their capital was occupied and their main field army defeated, the Hungarians were far from ready to submit and still retained the nucleus around which to raise new forces. At Debreczen, 150 miles east of Budapest, the Kossuth government was rapidly reorganizing a new army. In this crisis, Görgey settled his differences with Kossuth and in early April he resumed command of the revitalized Hungarian military.

Meanwhile Windischgrätz, despite repeated urgings from Vienna, remained almost inactive and failed to follow up his success.[69] During the critical weeks he failed to press beyond Budapest, apparently expecting that the occupation of the capital would be the signal for the Hungarian conservatives to rush to his support. But, in his favor, there also were compelling military reasons. He now stood at the end of an exposed supply line, threatened by the fortress of Komorn which was staunchly holding out against a siege conducted by Welden.[70] Under these circumstances, the prince was unable to provide the reinforcements asked for by his corps commanders, and on April 6 Görgey defeated an Austrian corps at Gyöngyös.[71] The same week imperial forces sustained defeats in Transylvania and southern Hungary, while Komorn continued to hold out against all efforts. "The Hungarian army," proclaimed Görgey, "marching from success to success is now approaching the capital."[72] Windischgrätz tried to minimize these developments, but the picture was all too clear and on April 14 he was recalled for "consultation."[73] In reality, of course, he had been summarily relieved.

Windischgrätz's relief was due to military as well as political considerations. Throughout the spring his conduct of operations was harshly criticized by his subordinate commanders, especially Welden, who in two memoranda, dated April 11 and 21, charged Windischgrätz with grave errors in his dispositions and suggested that the situation could be restored, provided "suitable men were appointed to command."[74]

Of course, this blatantly self-serving appeal would have been lost if the Hungarians had been less successful and if there had not been a deep rift between the prince and his brother-in-law, Schwarzenberg, over basic political issues. Essentially Windischgrätz wanted to restore the pre-March monarchy; Schwarzenberg was determined to create a unitary, centralized Austrian state. On March 4, 1849, Schwarzenberg, strongly supported by Minister of the Interior Alexander Bach, brushed aside a constitutional proposal by the *Reichstag* now sitting at Kremsier, and issued a constitution designed to end once and for all the troublesome historic rights of the various Habsburg lands. But to implement this proposal, Hungary had to be totally conquered and any possible military or political opposition had to be eliminated. Even the most conservative Magyar magnate could not have accepted this scheme, and therefore the war in Hungary had to be prosecuted until all defiance had been broken.[75]

This plan was not acceptable to Windischgrätz who so informed Baron Hübner, Schwarzenberg's special envoy, in mid-March. Here then was a military-civilian confrontation which Windischgrätz might have won if he had still enjoyed the confidence of his officers. But this he no longer had. Returning to Vienna, Hübner reported that because of Windischgrätz's mistakes the situation in Hungary was rapidly becoming catastrophic, and Schwarzenberg now decided to press for the prince's immediate removal.[76] To be sure, Francis Joseph was reluctant to dismiss the man who had saved his dynasty in October, but his military and political advisors prevailed and he signed the orders recalling Windischgrätz and appointed Welden as his predecessor. Determined to assert his own prerogatives, the emperor did not give Welden the plenary powers entrusted to his predecessor.[77] Moreover, on April 30 an imperial circular informed Feldmarschall Leutnant Franz Baron Cordon, Latour's successor in the War Ministry, that Francis Joseph himself had taken over supreme direction of all armies and established a military chancery for this purpose.[78]

Welden had been eager for command and was determined to prove that he could produce a quick decision. By April 14, he had already issued orders to all corps commanders to take the offensive.[79] But this was beyond the capability of the demoralized imperial forces. On April 19 Görgey defeated the Austrians at Nagy-Sarlö and relieved Komorn, and on April 23 the Austrians were forced to evacuate Pest. Görgey, however, was deflected when Buda, staunchly defended by General Hentzi, a native Magyar on whose defection the Hungarians had counted, held out for over a month. The defense of Buda probably saved Austria from a projected Hungarian invasion, which Kossuth had hoped would have provoked revolutions throughout Europe. But even so, Welden had clearly failed to make good on his boasts; on May 24 he was removed from command and resumed the military governor's post in Vienna.[80]

He was replaced by the energetic and capable, but also absolutely ruthless, Feldmarschall Leutnant Johann Baron Haynau, who had gained an unenviable reputation during the suppression of a revolt in Brescia. For the moment, however, Haynau too was unable to do much because his forces now numbered only sixty thousand against a Hungarian army of eighty thousand, buoyed up by their recent victories.[81]

While the fortunes of war were changing on the Hungarian plain, there had been momentous developments in Italy. Encouraged by the Magyar victories and pressured by the war party in Turin, Charles Albert broke the truce and on March 16, 1849, he once again crossed into Lombardy at the head of a reorganized and re-equipped army. This time, however, Radetzky was waiting and ready. On March 12 he informed his troops that hostilities were imminent; on the fifteenth he issued movement orders, and on the nineteenth, in a campaign which would not have disgraced Napoleon, the eighty-three year old leader invaded Sardinia, defeated the Italians at Mortara on the twenty-first, and two days later smashed the main force at Novara. The Sardinian army ceased to be an effective fighting force, and Charles Albert resigned in favor of his son Victor Emanuel who signed an armistice the next day. It was a brilliant campaign, but even so Radetzky did not escape criticism. Schwarzenberg, always suspicious of military interference in civilian affairs, complained that the fieldmarshal should have marched on Turin and had overstepped his authority by concluding the armistice.[82]

Radetzky, in fact, had taken both military and political factors into account when he permitted the House of Savoy to escape the consequences of defeat. By penetrating into Sardinia, Radetzky feared that he might unleash popular resistance and that Sardinia would be pushed into a radical revolution which might topple the dynasty.[83] Then too, Venice, protected by her lagoons, still was not subdued. But with his main front quiet, Radetzky was able to send in more troops and, under command of the energetic Gorzkowski, the siege was pushed and the republic capitulated in August.[84]

Meanwhile, radical revolution had overtaken Hungary where, encouraged by the successes of early April, parliament formally deposed the Habsburg dynasty and elected Kossuth as a temporary dictator. At this point, though the Habsburg Monarchy had successfully defended itself against the revolution in Bohemia, Austria, and Italy, it decided to call in outside aid. It was not so much that the Habsburgs feared defeat; that was unlikely, especially now, since the army of Italy was available to reinforce the Hungarian theatre. But continued Magyar resistance was seen as damaging to the imperial prestige and threatened to cause a resurgence of revolutionary spirits in Bohemia and elsewhere.[85] Therefore, on May 1, 1849, Francis Joseph officially asked Tsar Nicholas I to intervene, "to prevent," as he put it, "the Hungarian insurrection developing into a European calamity."[86]

The Austrian court and cabinet had been in touch with St. Petersburg from the very outset of the revolution, and help from Russia was always a possibility within the framework of the Münchengrätz agreement of 1833. The specific decision to ask for military intervention, however, came as a result of the deteriorating position in Hungary. As early as January, Windischgrätz had suggested calling for Russian assistance, and in April Welden too urged accepting aid from the tsar.[87] Although Schwarzenberg did not want to do this until the existence of the monarchy was at stake, he swallowed his pride and in April agreed to this step.[88] For his part, Nicholas was ready to heed a call from Vienna. By March 1848 he had already placed his army on a partial war footing and began to build up forces in Poland and Galicia. Moreover, in the summer, when there were disorders in Moldavia-Wallachia, a Russian corps had entered these principalities, and during the winter Russian units had entered Transylvania and supported the hard-pressed Austrians there.[89] Now, following a meeting between the two monarchs on May 21 in Warsaw, plans for major joint Russo-Austrian operations were prepared.[90]

The Austrians under Haynau, now reinforced to one hundred twenty thousand, massed in the west, with a second field army under Jelačić operating from the south. Meanwhile the Russians under Fieldmarshal Prince Ivan Paskievich, about one hundred fifty thousand strong, assembled in Galicia. On May 31 Schwarzenberg urged Paskievich to move with all possible speed, and a week later the Russians pushed through the Dukla Pass into Hungary.[91] The Hungarians were outnumbered hopelessly. On June 11 Haynau defeated Görgey at Zsigard and Komorn, reoccupied Budapest, and forcing a passage over the Theiss, defeated the main Hungarian body on August 9 near Temesvár. Encircled by the Austrian and Russian armies, Görgey capitulated on August 13 at Világos to Paskievich. Kossuth, accompanied by a small body of followers, fled the country; the remaining Magyar forces surrendered, and only isolated fortresses still held out. The last, Komorn, surrendered in early October.[92]

Hungary was subdued, but victory had been bought at the price of seriously strained relations with Russia. Friction between the allies had occurred as soon as the tsar's army had crossed the Carpathians. Both sides were critical of the other's performance and accused each other of avoiding battle.[93] Moreover, the Russians made no secret of their feelings before the Hungarians. As Görgey reported, they "openly honored Hungarian prisoners in the presence of Austrian officers," and Haynau complained to Schwarzenberg that "from the moment that they first appeared in Hungary, Russian officers and generals have shown open sympathy for the rebels."[94] Moreover, Haynau suspected that the tsar had designs on the country and, as he wrote to Radetzky, intended to offer the Hungarian crown to a Russian prince.[95] Relations were not improved when Paskievich, who had not fought a major action, accepted Görgey's surrender and the tsar's express command allowed the defeated general to retire unpunished to Carinthia.

The bulk of the Hungarian army, however was not so lucky. The war had been fought with exasperation and bitterness, and the vanquished were treated severely. It would, of course, have been wise to give lenient treatment, and Austrian commanders generally were not given to bloody reprisals. Both Radetzky and Windischgrätz had been moderate in victory, but Haynau, a man of morbid and sanguinary character, was different, and took harsh punitive measures which aroused opposition even within the army.[96] At the same time, however, Vienna also issued detailed instructions concerning the disposition of the prisoners.[97] Officers, especially those who formerly held commissions in the *k.k. Armee,* were singled out for punishment. In all, 490 former officers were courtmartialled, and of these, 231 were condemned to death, though in the great majority of cases these sentences were commuted to long prison terms. But there was no commutation for the major leaders. At Arad on October 6, thirteen Hungarian officers were executed, an event which aroused bitter resentment in Hungary and in Europe.[98] Officers who had not previously held imperial commissions were sentenced to serve as privates in the ranks of the regular army and finally 114 civilians, including Count Batthyány, were put to death and 1,765 were imprisoned.[99]

The savagery of retributions can also be explained by the fears which the Russian army aroused. Vienna regarded all national aspirations with equal distrust, and though the Slavs of Hungary had rallied to the dynasty, their ultimate ambitions were suspect. Fears of Pan-Slavism were strengthened when Orthodox *Grenzer* participated in field masses celebrated by Russian regiments.[100] Despite their proven loyalty, the Slavs in the Hungarian kingdom were denied their aspirations. Their ambitions for an independent Vojvodina in southern Hungary were denied and Vienna refused Croatian demands that the local *Grenzer* regiments be administered by national authorities.[101]

After November 1, 1849, largely in response to Haynau's excesses, but also as part of the now-prevailing centralist drive, investigation of subversive activities during the revolutions was taken over by the Central Military Investigating Commission in Vienna. A total of 4,628 cases were brought before the commission. Of twenty-four generals only one, Feldmarschall Leutnant Johann Baron Hrabowsky, formerly commanding officer in Hungary and Slavonia, was condemned to death, though the sentence was commuted to life imprisonment. Three other generals were stripped of their rank, two were rehabilitated, and none were pensioned off with prejudice. The cases of three others had not been decided when proceedings were suspended in December of 1850, and one officer had died during the investigation.[102] In fact, once the first few cases had been judged, punishments tended to become quite moderate. Seventy-one field grade officers were brought before the commission, but only four were cashiered, eight were pensioned off, and the rest reinstated. Most of the accused, of course, had been of Hungarian nationality and though many of them were returned to the army Hungarians were regarded with suspicion for many years.[103]

And this was the greatest liability the army inherited from the revolution. On the whole, it had weathered the storm better than the civilian institutions of the state, and while many generals had been indecisive and timid, others, especially the aged Radetzky, had reaped new glory. At the same time, the army had shown itself flexible in response to new demands, and despite the upheavals had managed to increase in strength. In October 1849, the *k.k. Armee* numbered six hundred forty-eight thousand men with one thousand two hundred mobile guns.[104]

On the other hand, old problems remained. The empire had been saved by the military and they naturally expected to retain their preeminent position in the state. But the old conflict between soldiers and civilians had not abated. The new prime minister, though once a soldier, had revealed already that he was not prepared to abdicate policy-making to the generals. Above all, nationalism, repressed but not eliminated, was still unresolved, and was sure to become an ever more serious question. Hungary would never forgive or forget; South Slavs were bitterly disappointed, and Italian nationalism would not recede. The Habsburg army had been victorious, but it had not resolved its basic problems.

4

The Emperor's Personal Command: 1849-1859

Grapeshot and bayonet had preserved the Habsburg dynasty and its empire, but a strong military establishment still was needed to preserve Austria's great power position. In Italy internal and external conditions required that a large army be kept on a near-war footing; Prussian aspirations in Germany needed watching, and because of fears about renewed revolutionary violence, a state of siege was maintained in Hungary, Italy, and Galicia, as well as in some of the major cities such as Vienna and Prague. Under these circumstances, the army played a major role during this decade. Troop strength, at least on paper, was increased even beyond the October 1849 level, and soldiers occupied positions of great power in the imperial administration. Liberal critics as well as conservative bureaucrats feared the monarchy was turning into a military state. In November 1849, after dining with the imperial family at Schönbrunn, Carl Friedrich Baron Kübeck entered in his diary: "Apotheosis of the army!"[1] And yet during this decade the army deteriorated as a fighting force.

Much of the blame for this must fall on the Emperor Francis Joseph. Attempting to achieve in military affairs the absolutist position he acquired for a time in the political realm, he was not content to remain supreme commander in title only, but tried to exercise actual control over the military establishment. The results, however, were far from salutary because his talents were ill-suited for this role. To be sure, Francis Joseph had received a military education, but one largely confined to indoctrination in the values of a regimental officer. Loyalty, unquestioning obedience, and strict observance of regulations ranked foremost in his mind, and he never understood the developments in the military art which changed the nature of war during his long reign. Regarding the army primarily as the guarantor of the dynasty, he perceived but dimly that the forces unleashed by the industrial revolution provided the means to mobilize, equip, and deploy immense armies, requiring control and direction by complex professional staffs and the support of the socio-economic potential of the entire nation. To be sure, in a multinational empire such support would have been almost impossible to achieve in any case, but Francis Joseph also remained unreceptive and suspicious of intellect and learning required for the professional direction of war. "The quality of my army," he remarked, "does not depend on learned officers, but on brave and chivalrous men."[2] Accustomed to flattery and deference, he rarely listened to contrary opinions, and chose his military advisors from the conservative high aristocracy who shared his outlook.

The most important of these men and the emperor's chief military advisor from 1849 to 1859 was his first adjutant general, Feldmarschall Leutnant (later General der Kavallerie) Karl Ludwig Count Grünne. Although the count's actual military experience was quite limited, he held the confidence of the emperor's mother, the Archduchess Sophie, and he had served as Francis Joseph's head chamberlain and military mentor. Shortly after Francis Joseph's accession to the throne, Grünne was appointed to his new office in which he continued to have daily contact and great influence with the emperor.[3]

Grünne's conception of the army essentially was pre-industrial; he distrusted scientific and technological developments likely to upset the status quo and he shared the emperor's distaste for military learning. At the same time, he was extremely ambitious and encouraged the emperor to assume personal command and to introduce a centralized command structure in which the first adjutant general became paramount while the War Ministry disappeared and the Quartermaster-General Staff was completely emasculated. The count has been harshly judged and made the main scapegoat for the shortcomings of the Habsburg military establishment during this decade.[4] However, though his influence was great, it is only fair to say that a very similar process was going on at the same time in Prussia where the Royal Military Chancery, representing the reactionaries, was engaged in bitter conflict with the more progressive War Ministry. Of course, in Prussia the progressives eventually won, while in Austria the reactionaries prevailed. This different outcome was in large measure due to Francis Joseph who in the final analysis acted as his own counsel in military affairs and who threw his power to the side of the reactionaries.

The process of making the emperor the actual head of the military establishment took several years. The imperial constitution of March 1849 designated him supreme commander of all armed forces, but this was merely a formality. Except for Joseph II, no Habsburg ruler had ever exercised actual command, but Francis Joseph was determined to do just that. In January 1849 he had informed Archdukes Johann and Ludwig that he regarded the army as the most important institution in the state and was resolved to gain firm control over it.[5] Then, on April 30, he informed War Minister Major General Franz Baron Cordon that he was taking over command. From now on, the emperor declared, he personally would pass on all senior promotions, major troop movements, and changes in regulations. To transact these matters the emperor announced the creation of a new position, a personal chief of staff, the *General Quartiermeister bei meiner Person,* and the expansion of the imperial military chancery into a *Militärzentralkanzlei* headed by the first adjutant general.[6] In September Francis Joseph appointed Feldmarschall Leutnant Heinrich Baron Hess, an able but pliant staff officer, as quartermaster-general of the army as well as his personal chief of staff. Hess previously had been chief of staff to Radetzky and had been proposed for his new position by the field marshal to counterbalance Grünne's growing influence. Above all, however, he was appointed because the emperor considered him a useful tool. Hess, Francis Joseph wrote to the Archduchess Sophie, was "clever, industrious and wholly of the opinion that I should control the army."[7]

The emperor, Radetzky, Hess, and Grünne jointly elaborated plans for army reorganization in October 1849. The new organization provided for a supreme command, the *Allerhöchstes Armee Oberkommando,* consisting of the emperor, with his personal chief of staff in charge of operations, and the adjutant general in charge of personnel. Below this level the military establishment consisted of four armies with headquarters in Vienna, Verona, Buda, and Lemberg. In addition, there remained the Military Border districts in Croatia and the Banat, their special status and institutions reconfirmed by edict in 1850.[8] But this was only the beginning. During the next seven years there was an endless reshuffling of the agencies of the high command, contributing little to efficiency, with much of it designed to enhance Grünne's position. At first Hess and Grünne collaborated on most of these changes, but after 1853 they became estranged and Major General Karl Baron Schlitter, Grünne's adjutant, assumed ever-growing influence in the military structure.[9]

In itself, centralization might well have improved the effectiveness of the army, but Grünne had little administrative talent and believed that a high social position qualified its possessor for high command. Increasingly the senior positions in the army, the number of which nearly doubled in the course of the constant reorganizations, were given to members of the great noble families who were usually lacking in strategic, tactical, or administrative talents.

Although centralization had now become formal policy, the four army commanders, especially Haynau in Buda and Radetzky in Verona, both holding extensive political as well as civil power, resented Grünne and interference from Vienna. Therefore Grünne supported Prime Minister Felix Prince Schwarzenberg in his dispute with Haynau over occupation policy in Hungary and helped to engineer the general's dismissal in the summer of 1850. But Radetzky's fame was far too great to allow similar action. In 1853, however, egged on by Grünne, the emperor, who also had grown weary of Radetzky and his "senile regime," sent Johann Bernhard Count Rechberg to Verona, ostensibly to relieve the field marshal of the pressure of civil administrative matters. Radetzky resented Rechberg, and his relationship with the *Militärzentralkanzlei* did not improve. Even so, Radetzky could not be induced to retire until 1857 when he reached the age of ninety.[10]

If Grünne encountered difficulties with Radetzky, he found it easier to eliminate, albeit temporarily, the War Ministry which Francis Joseph always regarded as an unwelcome reminder of his role as a nominally constitutional monarch. Influenced by Grünne, he decided to exclude this ministry from any participation in the shaping of policy and to relegate it to purely routine administration. In the summer of 1849, this led to the resignation of Cordon, who was replaced by Feldmarschall Leutnant Franz Count Gyulai, a well-connected Hungarian aristocrat and a Grünne favorite.[11] But even Gyulai, who was not consulted during the deliberations on further reorganization of the army, could not maintain himself in office and he resigned after little more than a year.[12] The last war minister during the period, Feldmarschall Leutnant Anton Baron Csorich, an unassuming man, carried on the ever-diminishing volume of ministerial business until 1853, when the ministry's remaining functions were transferred to the *Armee Oberkommando.*[13]

After May 1853 the supreme command agencies of the Habsburg army consisted of the emperor, who transmitted his orders through the *Militärkanzlei*, and the *Armee Oberkommando*, headed by Archduke Wilhelm, which now was organized into four sections—adjutancy, operations, administration, and military educational institutes.[14] This command structure enabled the emperor to intervene directly in all aspects of the military establishment and, though modified repeatedly, it continued in its essentials until 1859. In this fashion, Francis Joseph completed in military affairs the transition from a nominally constitutional monarch to a theoretically absolute ruler, a process which in the political sphere had already been accomplished by the Sylvester Patent of December 1851 and the abolition of the prime minister's office following the death of Schwarzenberg in April 1852.[15]

At the same time Grünne gradually encroached on the competence of the Quartermaster-General Staff. In a period when the growing size of armies, the increasing reliance on railroads, and the rapid changes in armament made military learning and professional staff work imperative, there continued after 1848 in Austria a "tendency in high places not merely to disregard learning but to distrust it."[16] Originally Hess had occupied a coequal place with Grünne, but by 1853 the Quartermaster-General Staff had been reduced to operating under the control of the first adjutant general and was deprived of funds, prestige, and personnel. Hess was unable to keep his own against Grünne and the only professional advance he could made was permission to provide, beginning in April 1852, a formal staff course, the foundation of the later *Kriegsschule*.[17] During the first years of its existence, however, the course as well as the school conformed to the prevailing anti-intellectual trends, emphasizing rote learning and horsemanship, and it was not until the 1870s that Austrian staff training approached the level of serious professionalism practiced in Prussia.[18]

Hess, moreover, was unable to prevent the adjutant general from interfering with the actual functions of the staff. During the campaigns of 1848 and 1849, adjutants had interfered frequently with the work of staff officers; this became much worse after 1856 when, ostensibly to ease the burdens of the shorthanded staff, Grünne formed a new body, the *Adjutanten Corps*, to supervise administrative procedures at all higher headquarters.[19] Recruited from noble and well-connected families, army, corps, and divisional adjutants outranked their opposite numbers on the staff. They reported directly to Grünne and all orders, including operational orders, had to be processed by them; thus, the prestige of the staff suffered while the operational machinery became exceedingly cumbersome.[20]

Constant reshufflings and rivalries at the very top of the military hierarchy did not make for efficiency, and even large financial outlays did little to improve the army's effectiveness. As in the pre-March period, there existed after 1849 sharp disputes between the soldiers and the budget-minded civilian finance ministers, but this time the soldiers won out. Before 1848 military expenditures had hovered around 50 million florins annually, though they had doubled during the revolution. From 1849 on, however, there was no year in which Austria spent less than 100 million on her army. During the 1854 crisis, the outlay rose to 198,219,783 florins, over 42 percent of the total budget, and reached 211,002,721 florins the next year. Thereafter the army budget was reduced, though in 1858, the low year for the decade, it still stood at 110,980,087 florins.[21] While some of it was accounted for by inflation, the complaints of the finance ministers were not unjustified. Much of the money was wasted in gross extravagances—splendid uniforms and accoutrements—sanctioned by the *Armee Oberkommando,* and too little on weapons and equipment. The supply system was shot through with corruption, and contractors made fortunes at the expense of the troops. At the same time, these expenditures unbalanced budgets, caused delays in railroad construction, and some important lines, above all those in northern Italy, fell into the hands of foreign capitalists.[22]

Unbalanced budgets covered by increased circulation of paper money, together with a steady rise in prices, created severe hardships for junior officers whose pay had remained at the 1818 levels. Lieutenants still received about one florin a day and promotion, except for those favored by Grünne, was glacially slow. But the first adjutant general cared little for the plight of his junior officers and on one occasion he informed a group of subalterns pleading for a pay raise that he "could always find enough lieutenants at twenty-four florins a month."[23] In fact, there was no shortage of officers. Ranks continued to be filled from the military academies, the cadet schools, and by direct entry. Military careers, however, became less and less desirable for the sons of the Austrian lower nobility and the educated middle classes. By 1859, 52 percent of the officer corps was recruited from outside the country, mainly from the Germanies; there also was a considerable English contingent. And these officers not only had very little understanding of their men, but also little internal camaraderie. A Prussian observer noted that the Habsburg officer corps was not tightly knit socially, and that everyone tended to go his own way after duty hours. Overall, reflecting the attitudes prevailing at the highest levels, the corps became more rigid and dominated by men who valued physical courage and connections over intelligence and professional education.[24]

Such defects did not disturb the emperor who looked with pride on this large army and in 1854 wrote to his mother that Austria was the only state "where two hundred thousand recruits could be levied without difficulty each year."[25] This, however, was a gross exaggeration. Austria did not effectively tap her manpower potential and the rank and file continued to be enlisted by the selective system of conscription dating back to the Josephinian era. In July 1852 a new recruitment law decreed all male subjects liable to service and extended conscription to the previously exempt provinces—Hungary, Tyrol, Lombardy, and Venetia.[26] The law also set the length of service at a uniform eight years with colors and two in the reserves, but in practice the propertied classes remained exempt and the reserve system non-functioning. Military commanders considered long-service soldiers more immune to subversive influences, and in practice few of the annual recruits, their number never exceeding eighty thousand, were kept on duty. Instead, after a short period of training, they usually were furloughed for indefinite periods and inadequately prepared when called up in an emergency.[27] Within the ranks conditions remained harsh. Corporal punishment was both frequent and severe; living conditions were poor, and the mortality rate for soldiers high. In 1857, for instance, the mortality rate in the army stood at 19.2 per 1,000 whereas the average for the civilian population of military age was only 10 per 1,000.[28]

During this decade there was little change in training, armament, tactics, or strategic doctrine. The most important and salutary innovation was the permanent creation of higher formations. Below the four armies there now existed brigades, divisions, and corps. The basic unit was the brigade, usually consisting of six infantry battalions, including a light battalion, either *Jäger* or *Grenzer*, a field battery of eight 4-pounders, and some auxiliary services. Three or four brigades formed a division and several divisions were grouped into a corps of twenty-five thousand to thirty thousand men including a cavalry brigade, an artillery reserve, and some technical troops.[29] Outside the overall structure of corps and divisions, although usually furnishing some battalions for their use, stood the regiments of the Military Border in Croatia-Slavonia and the Banat of Temesvár which still maintained their ancient roles as frontier guards against Turkey and as enforcers of the military sanitary cordon.[30] Of the fourteen corps, six usually were stationed in Italy, still regarded as the most vital strategic area.[31]

In all, at its peak strength in 1854, the army's paper mobilization strength passed a half million.[32] This number, which some Austrian diplomats tended to cite with overconfidence, was composed of sixty-two line infantry regiments, twelve *Grenzer* regiments, the outsize (twelve battalions) Tyrolean *Jäger* regiment, and twenty-five *Feldjäger* battalions. The cavalry consisted of forty regiments, while the artillery was organized in twelve field regiments and one regiment of garrison artillery. Technical troops still comprised a very small portion of the whole, less than twenty-five thousand at war strength. On the other hand, there existed a considerable body of internal security troops, nineteen gendarmerie regiments and twenty-three detachments of military police.[33]

Within the three main fighting branches, there were few major tactical or technological changes. The infantry continued to underestimate the effect of fire, and neglected marksmanship in favor of close order and the bayonet. And while the campaigns of 1848 and 1849 had proven their value, the number of light infantry troops was not substantially increased because, though the *Jäger* battalions were doubled, the Transylvanian *Grenzer* regiments, shown to be unreliable, were dissolved in 1851.[34] Infantry arms were somewhat improved. Beginning in 1855 the worn-out converted Augustin muskets were withdrawn and replaced by the Lorenz muzzle-loading percussion rifle, a weapon effective against individual targets up to four hundred paces and double that distance against formations. Foreign experts rated the Lorenz rifle a sturdy and accurate weapon, though in service its effectiveness was much reduced by the prevailing tactical doctrines and training, and by the slow delivery of the new arm which as late as 1859 had not been issued to all regiments.[35]

The cavalry arm, in view of the difficulty of raising and training mounts, always was kept close to war strength, some sixty-six thousand men in peace and seventy thousand in war time.[36] Because lancers had proven useful during the Hungarian campaign, the *Chevauxlegers* regiments were converted to *Uhlans* so that the branch now comprised twelve Hussar, twelve *Uhlan*, eight Cuirasseer, and eight Dragoon regiments. All regiments were equipped with pistol and carbine, but still relied primarily on shock tactics with lance and saber. Their training was directed towards producing battle cavalry and neglected reconaissance duties.[37] Except for the light brigades attached to individual corps, the bulk of mounted troops was concentrated in Galicia and Hungary where for a short time in 1854 and 1855 there existed a separate cavalry corps.[38]

The artillery, finally, saw perhaps the greatest change. At long last, it shed the remnants of its old medieval guild characteristics and became the coequal of the other two fighting branches. Based on the experience of the recent campaigns, in

1850 Feldmarschall Leutnant Vincenz Baron Augustin prepared a plan to expand and reorganize the artillery service. Above all he wanted to separate the heavy (or garrison) and the light (or field) artillery and provide the latter with organic transportation and permanent tactical formations. Batteries were to remain the basic tactical units, but for concentrating fire, as well as for administrative reasons, Augustin proposed the creation of fifteen field artillery regiments, each made up of eight gun and one rocket batteries.[39] This scheme was only partially put into effect. The *Bombardeur Corps,* suspected after 1848 of a tendency to sympathize with radical student elements in Vienna, was disbanded in 1851 and replaced by the Artillery Academy in Olmütz.[40] The Rocket Regiment remained as an administrative unit, though its batteries were divided among the field regiments. Only twelve field regiments were activated, while of the five projected garrison regiments, there was but one. Even so, the size of Austria's artillery branch nearly doubled between 1849 and 1851.[41]

But size was not all-important. Financial difficulties prevented the field artillery from receiving its full quota of draft animals and it also prevented radical improvements in materiel. While other armies were introducing breech-loading artillery, the Austrian service retained its obsolescent smoothbore muzzle-loaders. In 1856 the Artillery Committee, a permanent board set up in 1854 to evaluate technical developments, reviewed the lessons of the Crimean War. While conceding that rifled guns had greater range, better penetration, and were more accurate, the committee considered that muzzle-loaders were far less expensive. In conclusion, the committee found that "muzzle-loaders are superior to breechloaders in simplicity of construction and compare favorably in their efficiency for active service,"[42] and it recommended retention of the existing bronze-barrelled muzzle-loading gun types.

Even so, largely because the high quality of its personnel, the Austrian artillery maintained its well-deserved reputation. Its officers, while conservative and economy-minded, were serious professionals, while its non-commissioned officers were rated by one sapient critic as "superior to those in all other armies."[43]

The *k.k. Armee* did not lack willingness to fight or courage in battle. Its greatest weakness during this period lay in its unimaginative senior commanders who, after two years of fighting, were only too glad to return to ceremonial parades, barrack square drill, audit boards, inventories and inspections, and doing everything by the numbers to the music of the regimental bands. Many of the old generals heartily disliked the large-scale maneuvers pioneered by Radetzky and deprecated military learning. They knew how to move their formations about on the parade ground, but had little appreciation of the need for cooperation between the fighting branches. After observing the maneuvers of 1854, the Prussian military attaché noted that training and equipment of the army were obsolescent and that joint exercises revealed poor coordination and an astonishingly low level of leadership.[44]

One reason for this state of affairs could, of course, be found in the personal attitude of the emperor and his chief advisor. There were, however, even more basic reasons. During this period the government aimed at the creation of a unitary authoritarian state, and, unwilling to make any concessions to either liberalism or nationalism, it relied on the proven loyalty of the army to maintain internal security. And since any great changes in the employment and the nature of the army would not only affect military life, but also impinge on a multitude of other state concerns, the ruler and his advisors refrained from such a course. Recruitment and organization, strategy and tactics, all were affected by this concern much to the detriment of the combat effectiveness of the army.[45]

Indeed, the army was heavily committed to the maintenance of internal security. The state of siege prevailed in many cities and provinces, lasting in Vienna, Graz, and Prague until September 1853, in Hungary and Lombardy-Venetia until May 1854, and in Transylvania until the end of that year.[46] Vienna, of course, was especially critical and though the city was outwardly calm, extraordinary precautions were taken by Welden and his successor, Feldmarschall Leutnant Johann Freiherr Kempen von Fichtenstamm, who also acted as minister of police and commander of the gendarmerie. During the first year after the capital's occupation, strong patrols in fighting order moved about at frequent intervals while reinforcements were kept at the ready and cannon menaced the city from a number of emplacements. Perhaps these measures were excessive, but the military were unpopular in Vienna and there were occasional clashes between troops and civilians. The high command suspected that some soldiers, especially the "Children of Vienna" of the Hoch-und Deutschmeister Infantry Regiment Nr. 4, were in sympathy with the populace.[47] And the emperor regarded his subjects with ill-concealed distrust and suspicion. "The situation here," he wrote to his mother in 1853, "is steadily getting worse, though the people are afraid to attempt an armed collision. . . . Last Sunday there was a great church parade on the glacis to impress the Viennese that troops and guns are still at hand."[48]

Apprehensions about a second revolution also induced the government to take more permanent measures to secure the city. For some years the question of razing the old city walls and extending the city into the suburbs had been under discussion. Nothing, however, had been done by October 1848 when the walls served as cover for the insurgents. Therefore, in November of that year, a military-civilian commission was convened to consider the matter. Although some civilian officials favored retaining the walls around the Inner City to protect the wealthier and presumably more well-disposed citizens from the suburban workers, the military felt that the best method to command the capital was to place fortified barracks at strategic points from which artillery could dominate the suburbs. Consequently, early in 1850, construction of the fortified Franz Josef barracks was begun at the eastern outskirts of the city, while on the heights to the southeast near the *Südbahnhof* there arose a new arsenal.[49] The arsenal, strongly fortified, served a dual purpose. The authorities remembered how easily the old *Zeughaus* had been stormed by the insurgents and the new installation not only concentrated the manufacture of war materiel and provided safe storage, but was also an excellent fire base. Construction started in 1850 and was completed in 1856. Competent foreign observers praised the installation for its excellence. "The new arsenal in Vienna," reported Major Delafield of the United States Army, "is an establishment for the manufacture of every description of small arms, every caliber of artillery. . . . No arsenal in Europe will compare with it in extent; none in which there is more unity of design. It is doubtless perfect in all respects."[50]

These installations were linked together with an optical telegraph and in 1853 and again in 1857 special instructions for action in case of an uprising were issued to the Vienna garrison.⁵¹ In 1859, on the eve of the war with Sardinia, preparations were made by Archduke Wilhelm to reinforce the capital by troops from garrisons as far as Cracow and Laibach, and it was estimated that some fifteen thousand additional men could be brought to the city in one to three days.⁵²

Similar though less elaborate measures were taken in the other big cities of the monarchy while for the maintenance of public order and security the authorities relied on the newly formed gendarmerie. First established in 1850 with a strength of thirteen regiments, the force soon was expanded to sixteen and finally nineteen regiments.⁵³ Headed by a general officer, the force was given very extensive powers and privileges, including better pay and quarters than their equivalent ranks in the regular army. Gendarmes could arrest civilians as well as soldiers and even officers were not immune from their action; within a short time, the new corps was heartily disliked. "It was an open question," one soldier wrote, "whether the military of all grades or the civilians hated the gendarmes more."⁵⁴ Even the emperor, always jealous of his power, became perturbed by the activities of the gendarmerie which, for a time, was becoming more and more a political police and less a military force.⁵⁵

Even so, the new organization survived and became a valuable addition to the military establishment. Distributed in small units across the monarchy, it not only provided police and security functions for the rural areas, but it also gave the authorities an alternative instrument for use in dispersing demonstrations, riots, and strikes. To be sure, the gendarmerie, though well disciplined and honest, remained disliked and during the 1850s it was not always able to carry out its assigned mission. Endemic banditry, sometimes motivated by nationalism, which the gendarmes were not able to eradicate continued, especially in Hungary.⁵⁶ In war time the gendarmerie passed completely under military control and, with one regiment attached to each corps, acted as a field security police.

During this decade the *k.k. Armee* was committed heavily to the maintenance of internal security while Schwarzenberg and his successor Alexander Bach were determined to press reforms designed to transform the empire into a unitary centralized state. But this course aroused considerable opposition. Only in the German-speaking areas did the government find support for its designs, and even here the financial crisis tended to erode the government's position. In the non-German areas the government had to rely on force, or the threat of force, and so, though between 1849 and 1859 there was a decline in overt political activity among the nationalities, separate aspirations and desires persisted. This situation was, of course, highly detrimental to the army. It forced it to deploy much of its strength to meet the threat of new upheavals and also undermined the internal cohesion of the military establishment. "No one can predict," one observer wrote in 1855, "to what degree and how long this army will stay together and under what circumstances, and how many regiments might desert it."⁵⁷ Apprehension about the effect of nationalist aspirations on the troops inhibited not only the introduction of new tactics, but also forced the high command to station troops outside their ethnic areas and to retain the pre-revolutionary system of frequent garrison changes which, given the poor railroad system, made mobilization slow and cumbersome.⁵⁸

The nationality problem was particularly acute in Hungary and Italy. In Hungary, temporarily deprived of its ancient prerogatives, tension continued even after Haynau's removal, and though the new gendarmerie became increasingly effective, large numbers of troops had to remain on guard in the country.[59] Though most regular Hungarian regiments had been reconstituted since Világos, Magyar officers and men were regarded with suspicion for many years, and the presence of former *Honvéd* officers, sentenced to serve in the ranks, provided a particularly volatile element.[60] If the government showed too little consideration for the Magyars, it might have done well to cultivate ties with the nationalities formerly subject to the Crown of St. Stephen. But Serbs, Croats, Slovaks, and Rumanians were governed just as autocratically. Though the Serbs had rendered conspicuous service in the defense of the dynasty, their national ambitions were suppressed, and the military authorities purported to detect "dangerous tendencies hiding behind an outward mask of loyalty." As for the Croatians, their dream of a greater Croatia was denied and consequently even the proverbially loyal *Grenzer* regiments began to show signs of disaffection.[61]

Italy, of course, was another danger spot. In spite of their defeat in 1849, the Italians remained unreconciled to Austrian domination. In Sardinia the patient and discerning Count Camillo Cavour worked to gain effective foreign support for another round against Austria, a hope coming closer to realization when in December 1851 Louis Napoleon became Emperor Napoleon III of the French. Meanwhile the Lombard-Venetian kingdom was far from pacification. Perhaps, as one senior Austrian officer wrote, the Italians were treated far too leniently and the Hungarians were treated too harshly.[62] But lenient or not, the bulk of the population above peasant level resented Austrian rule and simmered with discontent, and only the presence of one hundred thirty thousand men prevented the outbreak of a major insurrection.[63] Even so, in February 1853 there occurred a number of terrorist attacks against the military, culminating on February 26 in an abortive attempt to overpower the main guard in Milan. In all, ten officers and men were killed and fifty-five wounded. There was some evidence that these attacks were aided by Mazzinian elements based on Swiss and Sardinian soil.[64] Radetzky took stern countermeasures. He confirmed seventy-nine executions, had hundreds imprisoned, and demanded from Vienna authority to pursue infiltrators in hot pursuit across the frontier.[65]

With the army so heavily committed to internal security missions, it might have been wise to modify the empire's foreign policy. But neither Schwarzenberg nor his successor in the post of foreign minister, Karl Count Buol-Schauenstein, who had served in the army and attained the rank of general, were able to formulate a mutually supporting internal, economic, foreign, and military policy. At the cabinet level, during the ministerial conferences, the army usually was represented by Grünne, occasionally seconded by Hess. But neither Grünne nor Hess had the vision or the strength to press for an overall coordinated policy; their view of the army and its role was limited and they usually confined themselves to matters of a strictly military character. And despite his role as an absolute monarch conducting his own policy, Francis Joseph too lacked the wisdom to direct an integrated policy. Therefore Austria simultaneously pursued a program of internal centralization, a poorly planned economic policy, and an ambitious foreign policy aiming to make the monarchy supreme in Central Europe. Such a design, of course, required a strong military posture, but though the soldiers did occasionally warn that the grand schemes were beyond the capabilities of the army, they were not consistent and on occasion appeared bellicose and aggressive. The result of all this was a policy which alienated both Prussia and Russia and in 1859, with her internal problems unresolved and her army unprepared, Austria faced a rearmed Sardinia backed by a French expeditionary force.

The first major foreign policy development after 1849 was a move to assert Habsburg supremacy in Germany. Here Prussia, convinced that the empire's preoccupation in Italy and Hungary made it important to act, tried to capitalize on national aspirations. In May 1849 delegates from the various German states convened at Erfurt to revise the constitution of the *Bund* and to create a restricted union under Prussian leadership. But Schwarzenberg was unwilling to tolerate this. He succeeded in getting Hannover and Saxony to withdraw from the proposed union and to delay completion of Prussia's design by shrewd diplomatic moves. At the same time, as early as the winter of 1849, Vienna did not exclude the possibility of armed conflict and formulated tentative war plans.[66] And when in the spring of 1850 Prussia persisted in her plans, more concrete measures were taken. The army in Bohemia and Moravia was reinforced, the main fortresses in Bohemia—Königgrätz, Josephstadt, and Theresienstadt—were armed and provisioned. Hess made a tour of the country, and possible march routes to Silesia were surveyed.[67] War seemed very near and Schwarzenberg instructed Hess to seek close cooperation with the allied Saxon army.[68] This time, however, and much to the relief of senior Austrian commanders appalled at the idea of having to fight their old comrades-in-arms, Prussia appeared to back down; in April Schwarzenberg called on all German states to send delegates to Frankfurt to reestablish the old confederation.[69]

By early fall, however, the situation had deteriorated, and a constitutional crisis in Hesse brought about a military confrontation. In September 1850 the sovereign of Hesse was driven from his grand duchy by an insurrection. While Austria belligerently supported the prince and pressed the reconstituted federal diet for intervention, Prussia sent troops into the grand duchy to secure her military communications with the Rhineland. Capitalizing on the rail transportation experience gained in 1848, the Quartermaster-General Staff responded by quickly shifting some seventy-five thousand men, eight thousand horses, and eighteen hundred vehicles and guns from the Vienna-Budapest region to Bohemia. Moreover, Schwarzenberg negotiated military assistance treaties, signed on October 12, with Bavaria and Württemberg. The war plan called for five Austrian corps from Bohemia, joined by the Saxon army, to advance on Berlin while an Austrian corps under Feldmarschall Leutnant Ignaz von Legeditsch and south German contingents were to exert pressure against the Prussian flank.[70] Both sides now advanced troops into Hesse and when in November Prussian and Bavarian advance guards actually exchanged fire, hostilities appeared imminent. At this point Austrian mobilized strength stood at two hundred fifty thousand in Bohemia, Moravia, and Germany, with eighty-two thousand still remaining on guard in Italy, and another ninety thousand remaining in Hungary and the Military Border, while Austria's German allies mobilized some ninety thousand men. To command this imposing array, the aged Radetzky arrived in Vienna from Verona.[71]

Although outnumbered by the Austrian and allied armies, the war faction in Berlin was willing to accept the gamble, believing that the *k.k. Armee* had not yet recuperated from the effects of the revolution.[72] In the end, however, Frederick

IV, the Prussian king, recoiled from war. Essentially a conservative, he did not wish to challenge the ancient position of the Habsburgs and he also feared the intervention of Russia on the Austrian side. Some Austrian military leaders, especially Hess, were indeed thinking back to the Seven Years' War and planned for a concentric Austrian-Russian-Allied offensive against Prussia,[73] but Schwarzenberg was willing to settle for a diplomatic triumph. Taking advantage of Frederick IV's conciliatory attitude, he called for a conference; on November 29, 1850, Prussia signed the Punctation of Olmütz, accepting the reestablishment of the old confederation and withdrawing her troops from Hesse.

Clearly the confrontation had ended in a victory for Austria, though from a long-range point of view the advantage was not as clear cut. Austria's determined stand and Prussia's retreat gave a rather mistaken picture of the real war potential of the two powers. To be sure, at the moment Austria clearly was the stronger of the two, both in actual troop strength and in combat experience, but in the long run the Habsburg Monarchy, though it had the resources, lacked the national cohesion and will to sustain a really first-rate army. In Prussia, however, the "Humiliation of Olmütz" set off reforms in the army which in a short time dramatically reversed the mobilization potential of the two states.

Then too, Austria had enjoyed Prussia's military support since 1813, and this was now lost. To be sure, when in 1851 and 1852 the rise of Louis Napoleon once again raised the specter of French aggression, another Prussian-Austrian military convention was signed on January 8, 1852, followed in May by a formal alliance which even guaranteed Austria's Italian possession. Hess was optimistic and even began to formulate plans for joint Austro-Prussian operations against France.[74] But these agreements were temporary expedients, covering up but not ending the struggle for domination in Germany.

This, however, became increasingly difficult because of an estrangement with Russia. Although the monarchy had sought and obtained the tsar's support in 1849 and 1850, and though Nicholas I also joined in the anti-Napoleonic alignment of 1852, there existed basic geopolitical conflicts between the two empires. The main issue was rivalry in the Balkans. As early as the days of Joseph II, Russian ambitions in this area had aroused serious misgivings; during the Napoleonic Wars, Archduke Charles repeatedly warned about the potential danger from the East. This clash of interests continued after the Congress of Vienna, and in an 1828 memorandum Radetzky called Russia the one power presenting a major military threat to the Habsburg Empire.[75]

This situation did not improve after 1850. Schwarzenberg was determined not to allow the tsar to become the final arbiter in Germany, and he was equally resolved to prevent Russian control over the Balkans even at the risk of conflict.[76] After his death, however, opinion in Vienna became divided. The rapidly advancing decay of the Ottoman power inspired Count Buol with the ambition to recover the heritage of Prince Eugene of Savoy and if possible to divide the Turkish possessions in Europe in agreement with Russia. This design was supported by a number of senior generals, above all Radetzky, who for many years had looked with misgivings on the rise of the Serbian state and regarded it as a potential base for a South Slav insurrection which not only might compromise the allegiance of the *Grenzer* but also constitute a menace to all South Slav areas of the monarchy.[77] Therefore the generals advocated the occupation and annexation of Serbia, Bosnia, and Albania. On the other hand, Alexander Bach and Karl Baron Bruck, the finance minister, advocated cooperation with England and France and opposition to any Russian advance. Finally, having returned from exile, Prince Metternich argued for the maintenance of the Ottoman Empire as a conservative bulwark to exclude western liberalism as well as Russian influence from this sensitive area, and he persuaded the emperor to support his policy.[78] "Austria desires to maintain the integrity of Turkey and to prevent her submission to Great Britain," read the instructions issued in 1852 to the Austrian ambassador in St. Petersburg, "at the same time, however, Austria is not willing to allow Russian domination of the Ottoman Empire."[79] The decision that neither Russia nor the West should be permitted to control large parts of the Balkan produced a policy which, in conjunction with the stand taken against Prussia, alienated Russia as well as the western powers and left the monarchy diplomatically and militarily isolated.

The latent Austro-Russian conflict came into the open in February 1853 during the Montenegrin-Turkish hostilities, when the monarchy mobilized an observation corps of fifty thousand *Grenzer* and sent an ultimatum to the Porte halting a Turkish advance on Cetinje.[80] The intent here was not so much to aid the Montenegrins as to forestall any Russian intervention and to warn Belgrade that Austria would not tolerate any escalation of the conflict into a great South Slav war of national liberation. Indeed, throughout this spring and summer, the military were disturbed by rumors of Russian and Serb propaganda on the Military Border, and the mobilization of the *Grenzer* revealed some instances of disaffection.[81]

The situation became even more acute when in July 1853 Russian troops entered Moldavia and Wallachia to enforce the tsar's claims to a protectorate over the Orthodox Christians within the sultan's dominions. Within a year this step led to the outbreak of the Crimean War. Austria felt that she could not suffer Russian troops at the mouth of the Danube, and during the fall of 1853 she mobilized an army of observation, one hundred thirty thousand strong, in Slavonia, Hungary, and Transylvania. Austria, however, refrained from open threats and did not concentrate any large bodies in Galicia, the natural offensive base against Russia. In the late fall and winter of 1853, however, events began to assume larger proportions. The sultan declared war on the tsar in October while England and France were moving towards intervention. By March 1854 Buol, supported by the "liberal press and the stock exchange," was willing to risk a military confrontation with Russia, apparently believing that even if this led to hostilities, these could be limited to the principalities.[82] This time he was opposed by Hess who argued that even a limited war would require two hundred thousand men and an alliance with Prussia.[83] On the other hand, the generals also disliked a Russian presence at the mouth of the Danube, though their preference, especially that of Radetzky and Jelačić, was for a policy of expansion in the western Balkans.[84]

In April 1854, after prolonged negotiations, Prussia finally signed the desired military convention with Austria, promising her support if Russia refused to evacuate the principalities.[85] This agreement negotiated by Hess was a very limited commitment only, but it encouraged the emperor to follow a more forward policy. To effectively threaten Russia required a full-scale shift in the deployment of the Austrian field army. At this point IX, X, XI, and XIII Corps were concentrated in Transylvania, and a provisional corps, the Serb-Banat Corps, was stationed on the lower Danube. Only two corps, II at Cracow and IV at Lemberg, were deployed in Galicia.[86] Even before the convention with Prussia was signed, the emperor ordered further military measures. The Third Army, commanded by Archduke Albrecht, mobilized in Hungary, and on May 15 the Fourth Army, commanded by General der Kavallerie Franz Count Schlik, mobilized in Galicia.[87] Reservists were recalled and Hess was appointed in overall command of the field armies.

Meanwhile Buol continued to pressure Russia for the immediate evacuation of the principalities and, threatened by the Austrian concentrations in Galicia and Hungary, the tsar complied. In mid-August 1854, Russian troops evacuated the principalities and with this the *casus foederis* was eliminated for Prussia. Buol, however, continued in his challenge to Russia, but now, with the notable exception of Archduke Albrecht, he was opposed by most senior officers.[88] From Verona, Radetzky strongly remonstrated that the mobilization of two armies in the east denuded Italy of troops and he actually succeeded in having VI Corps, slated for transfer to Galicia, halted and turned around in Treviso.[89] Hess was also skeptical about the prospects of war against Russia, but complying with an imperial order, he prepared, late in the summer of 1854, a war plan calling for an offensive thrust northeast from Galicia with the main weight of the attack to be delivered between the Vistula and the Bug.[90]

Francis Joseph had indeed become most bellicose. In October 1854 he wrote that Austria's future lay in the Orient and that Russia had to be restrained even at the cost of war.[91] On October 22, 1854, he decreed full mobilization of his army to be completed in time to begin offensive operations in the coming spring. The order of battle deployed a total of eleven corps against Russia, leaving three corps in Italy and one in Hungary. In all, Hess wanted to deploy 327,380 combat and some 100,000 support troops.[92] Even so, he continued to warn against such a war. At best, he pointed out in a memorandum of October 26, such a conflict was a risky enterprise. Russia could field eight hundred thousand men and to oppose this force with equal strength it would be necessary to strip the empire of troops which might have disastrous consequences. Victory, moreover, would not necessarily improve the position of the monarchy. It might result in the reestablishment of Poland and he concluded that "we shall then face France in the east as well as in the west." He repeated his arguments during the ministerial councils of November 15 and 17, adding that war would bankrupt the state.[93]

Hess actually overestimated Russian's war potential. Instead of eight hundred thousand men the tsar could at best produce three hundred fifty thousand, and it might be argued that the war from which the generals recoiled in 1854 had to be fought under even less favorable circumstances sixty years later. Still, neither Francis Joseph nor Buol were really prepared to go over the brink. Mobilization was suspended at the end of November, though the Third and Fourth Armies remained poised in Galicia and the occupation troops remained in the principalities.[94] But though Austria formally joined the western allies in December, it did not participate in the fighting. Prussia declared her neutrality and, much to the monarchy's discomfort, Sardinia actively entered the war and sent an expeditionary force to the Crimea. In the end, after the fall of Sebastopol, internal difficulties, allied victories, and continued Austrian pressure brought Russia to the peace table, though the results did not profit the Habsburg Empire.

Both in the short and in the long run, the army paid dearly for the policies pursued by Francis Joseph and Buol. Mobilization had exposed dire deficiencies especially in the medical and supply services, and there were fearful losses from disease.[95] Then, too, the huge armament against Russia had been expensive. The entire military budget for 1854 was used up during the first three months of that year. A forced loan had to be floated and Austrian currency depreciated even further.[96] In all, the affair cost 610 million florins and the financial crisis caused a cut in the army's budget for 1857 from 209 to 104 million florins.[97] The ill effects of the financial crisis delayed any further efforts towards the modernization of the Austrian military establishment and had long-range effects well into the latter part of the century.[98] Finally, the crisis had brought about an open rift between civilian and military policy makers, and from now to 1859 there was even less cooperation than before.[99]

The rift was to have serious consequences when Austria's diplomatic and military isolation tempted Napoleon III to revive his dreams of French influence in Italy. In 1858 he agreed with Cavour to expel Austria from northern Italy. To provoke war, Cavour exploited the continued national discontent; to this, Austria could find no other response than to flounder into war with Sardinia. But this time Austria had to go it alone because Francis Joseph was unwilling to obtain Prussian support by recognizing her dominant role in northern Germany.

Historians have differed in their assessment of direct responsibility for Austria's blunder into war, unprepared and without allies.[100] In balance, however, Buol must carry the largest share of the blame because his insistence on a tough policy towards Sardinia made war inevitable, while at the same time he refused to admit that the situation was serious enough to warrant full-scale military preparations.[101] When on January 1, 1859, Napoleon III publicly announced that relations between France and Austria were no longer as happy as he would have desired, the military at once pressed the council of ministers for reinforcements in Italy and indeed received the emperor's permission to send III Corps. Buol, however, denied that Cavour really wanted war or that Napoleon was serious about supporting Sardinia. In any case, he argued, Prussia would restrain France from any offensive action. While troops were assembling on both sides of the frontier, Archduke Albrecht was dispatched to Berlin to secure this support, and on April 6 Buol informed the emperor that he was certain of Prussian aid. Albrecht, however, received a cool reception and no assurances. Meanwhile, Buol pressed for the dispatch of an ultimatum to Turin demanding a halt in Sardinia's military preparations and the cessation of all propaganda in Lombardy-Venetia. Although Grünne and Hess had urged that mobilization should precede any ultimatum, no such full-scale measures were ordered. It might have been expensive and Buol's assurances were taken at face value by Francis Joseph. On April 19 the emperor openly sided with Buol and on April 23 a three-day ultimatum was dispatched. When this was promptly rejected by Turin, the foreign minister cavalierly washed his hands of the matter and, in answer to a question by Grünne as to whether France was to be considered hostile and what allies the army could expect, he replied that while negotiations were still in progress the problem now had moved from the diplomatic into the military sphere.[102] Under these circumstances little was left but to order the army in Italy to take the offensive, an action for which it was ill-prepared. If Buol really had counted on active Prussian support or expected that the French would not fight, it was a miscalculation of staggering proportions. When this became clear, he resigned and later claimed that he had not wanted war but had been driven into it by the exaggerated claims of the soldiers.[103]

Buol was wrong. The record clearly shows that both Grünne and Hess repeatedly warned that the army was not prepared to undertake a campaign, although it is doubtful that they realized the extent of the damage done to the army since 1849. The army went to war unprepared. Logistic and supply services were inefficient and corrupt and the troops lacked engineering stores, rations, and clothing. Infantry weapons were adequate, but the artillery much inferior to that of the French. Above all, command was in the hands of a man who failed to recognize the need for seizing the initiative.

The field army was entrusted to Count Gyulai, who had never held an active major command and who had so little confidence in his own ability that he asked to be relieved on the eve of the campaign.[104] Though the Austrian army had not been fully mobilized, the reinforced Second Army, with 107,000 men and 364 guns, should have been adequate to defeat the Sardinians, with about 60,000 men and 322 guns, from debouching out of the alpine passes. This was the plan drawn up by Colonel Franz Baron Kuhn, Gyulai's able chief of staff. Gyulai, however, was leery of endangering his army and barely on speaking terms with the colonel. So the fleeting opportunity to deal with the enemy forces separately was not exploited.

Even after the ultimatum expired on April 26, four precious days were lost before the army, five corps and one cavalry division, moved across the Ticino. Feldzeugmeister Gyulai and his staff, all splendidly mounted, "had taken up positions along the side of the bridge and had III Corps pass in review as it crossed into enemy territory. The troops were in high spirits."[105] The same, however, was not true of their leader. Although encountering little resistance because the Sardinians fell back to avoid battle, Gyulai remained apprehensive about the state of his army. On May 3, he telegraphed Vienna, complaining about the lack of gun teams for his artillery reserve and the poor condition of the train.[106] He did not dare to remedy his shortages by local requisitioning for fear of arousing popular resistance, and lack of coordination between the Quartermaster-General Staff and the Adjutant Corps led to the issuance of conflicting orders. Troops were marched and countermarched aimlessly and morale ruined even before the first serious encounter.[107]

By the end of May the French had arrived in strength, but Gyulai had also received another corps so that the armies were approximately equal in strength. But Gyulai clearly lost the initiative and was beginning to panic. On May 28 he reported that he expected a general offensive against his lines with diversionary thrusts into Venetia.[108] Even now all could still have been remedied by a great tactical success. Yet, in their battle dispositions and in their moral resolution the Austrian commanders, with some exceptions, also failed to come up to expectations. After the indecisive battle of Magenta on June 4, during which the only partially committed army fought with courage and determination, Gyulai lost his nerve. He hastily evacuated Milan and retreated to the cover of the Quadrilateral.

Gyulai, to be sure, had not been equal to his task, but considerable blame also attached to Grünne, who from far-off Vienna repeatedly interfered with the conduct of operations.[109] And when, after Magenta, Gyulai was relieved and the emperor appeared in the field to take supreme command in person with Hess acting as his chief of staff, this was hardly an unmixed blessing. Hess, who had been Radetzky's chief of staff in 1848 and 1849, was not given any real authority. He was saddled with an assistant, Feldmarschall Leutnant Wilhelm Baron Ramming, with whom he found it difficult to cooperate, and he was never permitted to run the war in his own way. Grünne had accompanied the emperor from Vienna and, acting as the emperor's personal representative, insisted that all orders had to be cleared through his office. As a result, orders and counterorders were issued in a bewildering succession. Hess favored standing on the defensive in the Quadrilateral while Ramming, supported by Grünne, wanted to cross the Mincio to attack the French. Francis Joseph overruled Hess and in June the army, having meanwhile received substantial reinforcements, moved out of the Quadrilateral. This time, however, morale was low and officers and men were weary and dispirited.[110]

On June 24 the Austrians met the French at Solferino, an encounter battle pure and simple. In bitter and bloody fighting, the Austrians sustained heavy casualties. The rifled French guns far outranged the Austrian artillery and inflicted heavy losses on the tight formations. No final decision, however, had been reached when Francis Joseph, appalled at the casualties, decided to break off the battle and to retire behind the Mincio. As almost always, the Austrian rear guards covered the retreat with skill and courage.

By this time, both sides were uneasy about continuing the war. Napoleon was disturbed about Prussia's mobilization of six corps, and he too was shaken by the sights of battle. Moreover, he had no wish to engage in a protracted war with Austria still holding the Quadrilateral and able to call on extensive reserves. For his part, Francis Joseph was unwilling to pay Prussia's price for active intervention—supreme command over all forces of the German Federation—and he also was concerned about internal repercussions, especially in Hungary.[111] On July 11, to the disappointment of the Sardinians, the preliminary peace of Villafranca in which Austria ceded Lombardy to France was signed.

The debacle of 1859 was in part due to the poor generalship and the confused Austrian staff and command system. But internal factors also played an important role. Mobilization and deployment of Austria's army had been delayed because of the fear of internal revolts, and throughout the war Austrian strategy was inhibited by internal considerations. During the summer of 1859, some units had to be diverted to Hungary and Croatia to guard against uprisings, while Cavour as well as Napoleon III played on these fears.[112] In Turin the exiled Louis Kossuth was encouraged to plan another great insurrection in Hungary and this time he hoped to obtain support on the discontented Military Border. At the same time Napoleon had plans for a landing on the Dalmatian coast, also supported by the *Grenzer*, and followed by a national rising in Hungary.[113] Perhaps these plans were farfetched, but the threat contributed to Francis Joseph's decision to end an unpopular war.

Although the conduct of the campaign revealed a very low level of Austrian military competence, it did not reflect adversely on the valor of the troops who fought and died there. As critical an observer as Friedrich Engels admitted that the *k.k. Armee* fought in Lombardy with a heroism that surprised its enemies.[114] Even so, appeals to nationalist sentiments showed their effects on the battlefield. At Solferino, for instance, two Hungarian regiments, the 19th and the 34th Infantry, deserted almost en masse and an eminent British historian estimated that some fifteen thousand men, about 6 percent of the troops involved, deserted during the war.[115] The predominantly Hungarian corps of Eduard Count Clam-Gallas had to be withdrawn from combat and even some of the *Grenzer* units showed poor morale.[116] "Suppressed nations and classes," commented one liberal Austrian officer, "do not make very enthusiastic soldiers."[117]

The prestige of the army had been raised high by Radetzky, but now it stood at the end of a decade of professional and moral decline. Its doctrine, methods of command, and equipment were out of date and its leadership incompetent and overly cautious. The debacle in Italy was not, as comforting legend would have it, due to the sudden and unexpected failure on the part of the field commanders; it was the result of ten years of misadministration for which the emperor must bear a large share of the responsibility. Beyond that, the poor state of the army reflected that of a state and a society increasingly out of step with the times. The question remained as to whether these shortcomings could be remedied.

5

The End of an Age: 1860-1866

On the field of Solferino, Francis Joseph lost confidence in his generalship. Thereafter, although he was personally brave, he no longer assumed actual command in battle, though on occasion he did not hesitate to interfere from afar with the conduct of operations. Above all, he jealously guarded his prerogatives as supreme war lord and he remained intensely involved in all questions concerning the military establishment, though his interests focused on matters of regimental detail. As Bardolff put it rather tactfully, the emperor had great enthusiasm for the "purely soldierly matters: discipline, élan, and aggressiveness."[1] Indeed, Francis Joseph first and foremost considered himself a soldier and, much to the distress of the liberal middle classes, he continued to wear uniform on almost every occasion.[2]

But even the emperor's enthusiastic support could not hide the fact that the army had given a very inept performance in Italy. Military discomfiture led to a crisis in the empire and to certain changes in the military establishment. In the empire the neo-absolutist course was first modified and eventually abandoned in favor of a constitutional accommodation with the two strongest nationalities—the Germans and the Magyars. In turn, the emergence of constitutional government, though without much effect on internal military administration, brought about new patterns of army control. But these changes were made reluctantly and neither the problem of military-civilian coordination in the shaping of policy nor the vexing nationality problems were resolved. In fact, the new political dispensations tended to render these conflicts even more acute.

The nationality problem acted both as the incentive and as the brake on military reform. Shortly after the close of the Italian campaign, a Swiss observer, Colonel Wilhelm Rüstow, remarked that the multinational Habsburg army achieved and maintained its cohesion by appealing to the soldier's pride in his calling and by fostering his corporate loyalty. But these two factors, Rüstow continued, were extremely vulnerable to the stresses imposed by defeat.[3] The lessons of the Italian campaign revealed the necessity for a new departure in military affairs, but the problem of divisive nationalism, of which the leading soldiers were only too well aware, created a dilemma. Any fundamental solution depended on a complete reorganization of the political structure of the monarchy. The generals, however, were conservative men whose dynastic allegiance and preoccupation with tradition conflicted with drastic changes.[4]

Even within these limits, flexibility and minor concessions might have remedied much, but the traditionalists considered all innovations dangerous. Archduke Albrecht, who had returned to active duty and gained a good reputation as a corps commander under Radetzky, and Feldzeugmeister Ludwig von Benedek, the newly promoted popular hero of Solferino, were convinced that the army was the only reliable barrier between the throne and renewed revolution. They believed that it had to be protected at all costs from the pernicious influences of liberalism and nationalism and that this could only be done by holding fast to the traditional values, the "old army spirit." As Albrecht told his confidant, Feldmarschall Leutnant Count Franz Folliot de Crenneville-Poutet, a conservative high aristocrat who had replaced Grünne as adjutant general, "let us hope that our supreme war lord stands firm against the war minister's innovation craze. If he gives in, then he no longer can count on the old Austrian army."[5] Crenneville, Benedek, and most other leading soldiers fully shared the archduke's sentiments. Loyalty to the dynasty was the prime article of their faith; they considered civilians, especially the professional and business classes, suspect and even dangerous. Benedek described them in a confidential circular to his officers. There were, he wrote "international revolutionaries, lawyers and doctors without practices, ambitious and money-hungry journalists, dissatisfied professors and schoolteachers," who, together with "debt-ridden nobles and cowardly magnates," plotted against the monarchy.[6] And, as he proclaimed during an imperial review at Verona in 1862, it was against the external and the internal enemies that the army existed "to serve, fight, and if necessary die with honor for their emperor and supreme warlord."[7] In this fashion the army leadership isolated itself from criticism and from the pressures for change.

At the same time, defeat produced a crisis of confidence in the leading soldiers who displayed what an Austrian historian recently described as "the desire to avoid responsibility, coupled with a remarkable lack of energy and drive."[8] This lack of will and confidence, already demonstrated by Gyulai in 1859, was repeated in 1860 when Feldzeugmeister August Count Degenfeld-Schonburg tried to avoid taking office as war minister, in 1864 when Feldmarschall Leutnant Alfred Baron Henikstein declared that he lacked the qualifications for a chief of staff, and culminated during this period in Benedek's famous doubts regarding his competence to command the army against Prussia. Together, these incidents indicated a deep spiritual malaise affecting the highest echelons of the army.

This malaise must be seen against the background of a number of constitutional experiments. In October 1860 an imperial edict, the October Diploma, constituted an enlarged crown council for the entire monarchy with deputies chosen from the resurrected provincial diets. But, encountering opposition both from the German and the Hungarian liberals, the diploma was replaced early in 1861 with the so-called February Patent which established a bicameral *Reichsrat* with, among other powers, control over the military budget. This constitutional concession, with its strong centralist orientation in which the various provincial diets were reduced to mere electoral colleges for the lower chamber of the *Reichsrat*, pleased the German Liberals, but was opposed and largely boycotted by Magyars, Slavs, and Italians. Even so, it functioned as a parliament for four years until continued opposition led to the recall of the patent in September 1865. There followed another brief interlude of absolutist government during which negotiations ultimately leading to the Compromise of 1867 were begun.

The fact that the *Reichsrat* functioned at all was due to the support of the German Liberals who regarded the concessions made in 1861 merely as a first step towards a complete parliamentary regime and were especially pleased with the *Reichsrat*'s control of the military budget. Moreover, with most of the other nationalities in opposition to the monarchy, the German Liberals, having no desire to dissolve the empire, were willing to retain the army's capability to carry out its internal security functions.[9] Even so, the military remained unreconciled to parliamentary budget control, which they regarded as the futile, even ill-intentioned, meddling of men who knew nothing about the business of fighting. Moreover, despite their feeling that the army should be preserved, the economy-minded ministers as well as the parliamentarians regarded the military establishment as the most suitable place to cut expenses.[10] The military budget stood at 179 million florins in 1860 and 1861, was reduced to 139 million in 1862, and to 118 million in the following years. It rose to 155 million during the conflict with Denmark in 1864, but the next year it was drastically cut to 96 million, though the military actually overspent their allocation by some eleven percent.[11]

Military men charged that the civilians willfully and needlessly starved the army, a change repeated in the years before the World War.[12] To be sure, the Austrian military budget did not keep up with expenditures made by the other European powers, but in large part this was the result of the economic crisis which dated back to the French and Napoleonic wars and had been intensified by the mistaken policies of the fifties. At the mercy of economic forces not fully understood, each year a bewildered *Reichsrat* found itself asked to allocate huge sums for the upkeep of a military establishment whose leaders were openly contemptuous of civilian values. The civilians naturally resented this and charged the military with financial irresponsibility and with concealing certain sources of revenue, such as the land holdings on the Military Border and the sale of surplus armament to America.[13] Revelations in 1859 of wide-spread corruption in the military supply system, followed by the suicide of Feldmarschall Leutnant August Baron Eynatten, chief of procurement, did not improve the army's case.[14] Moreover, the procurement system did not improve much during the following years. In 1866 one observer considered it among the chief weaknesses of the army, "a den of bribery and corruption."[15]

If relations between the army and a German-dominated and on the whole loyal *Reichsrat* left much to be desired, the military position concerning the other nationalities was even worse. There was continued apprehension about possible insurrections and even during external emergencies about a quarter of the troops had to be earmarked for internal security duties.[16] At that, there were fears about the reliability of the rank and file. In Hungary, where Francis Joseph was eager to conciliate popular sentiment, the inflexible Albrecht was replaced as commanding officer and governor general by Benedek, a Magyar by birth and at the moment a popular figure. But this did not halt agitation among the troops, and in July 1860 the emperor advised Benedek to take "stern measures to preserve the morale of the troops and to show foreign powers that there is no lack of will and determination."[17] By this time, however, elements of the army, especially the *Grenzer* in

Croatia-Slavonia, had become politically unreliable. When called upon to exercise their new constitutional rights in August 1861, the delegates from the *Grenzer* regiments furnished the decisive margin of votes against Croatian participation in the *Reichsrat*.[18] Other *Grenzer*, mainly of Serb origin, deserted to the Serbian army then being formed across the Danube.[19]

Military commitments also remained high in Italy. During 1860 when Cavour and Garibaldi set about to complete unification of the country, there was some talk about reviving the Holy Alliance and some speculation about Austrian intervention to halt the conquest of central Italy. In the end nothing was done, but the formation of the Kingdom of Italy and the repercussions of the Polish Revolt of 1863 stimulated irredentist activities in Venetia, Istria, and Dalmatia, and this required increased guard, patrol, and intelligence activities. And in 1864, with Austria involved against Denmark, there were a number of insurrectionary projects in Venetia and an attempted coup against Friaul. Martial law had to be imposed and troops were alerted in Carinthia, Carniola, and the Tyrol.[20]

The inflexibility of the leading soldiers, the difficulties with the *Reichsrat*, and the continuing threat of nationalism all contributed to limit the scope of military reform. Grünne, already under attack in the summer of 1859, was forced to resign and was replaced by Crenneville, a much more experienced officer. Though the powers of the adjutant general were somewhat reduced, Crenneville still held a pivotal position and his conservative aristocratic views and his friendship with Archduke Albrecht placed him in the traditionalist camp.[21] But while the traditionalists could prevent a basic reorientation of the military establishment, the confusion and discord at the higher command levels, as well as the corruption of the supply services displayed in Italy, demanded some retribution. While the memory of the humiliation was still fresh, one hundred and thirty-five generals were relieved from duty. Even Hess, who hardly could be blamed for the debacle, was first promoted and then pensioned off, but many highly placed and well-connected officers of proven incompetence retained their positions.[22] For instance, Count Clam-Gallas, whose performance at Magenta had been poor, remained to do the same at Königgrätz.

But with Grünne gone, there was a limited amount of reform in the command structure and in the establishment in general. At the very top, the *Armee Oberkommando* was discontinued in the fall of 1860 and the War Ministry was resurrected. Because of parliamentary control over army finances, it was deemed inadvisable to appoint a member of the imperial house as war minister and instead of Archduke Wilhelm, the outgoing head of the *Armee Oberkommando* who would have liked the post, Feldzeugmeister Degenfeld was chosen. The general, realizing the continued opposition to reform in high places, was reluctant to accept the appointment and did so only after a personal appeal by the emperor.[23] Despite this unpromising debut, he and his successor after 1864, Feldmarschall Leutnant Karl Ritter von Franck, succeeded in making much-needed improvements in the artillery and the cavalry, but were less successful with the infantry.

Unfortunately, there was also little progress in staff work, which continued to be held in low esteem. The emperor evidently did not consider the position of chief of the Quartermaster-General Staff worth a full-time appointment. On January 31, 1860, Benedek was appointed to replace Hess, but in April 1861 he was made governor general in Hungary, and even though he relinquished this post within six months to assume command of the Second Army in Verona, he still remained chief of staff. And despite his repeated requests to be relieved of this dual responsibility, it was not until November 1864 that he was finally replaced by Henikstein.[24] In the meantime most of the actual staff work had to be delegated to deputies lacking in authority, first to Ramming and after 1862 to Feldmarschall Leutnant Ladislaus Baron Nagy.[25]

In any case, Benedek was not a very happy choice as chief of staff. To be sure, he had received good training. Appointed to the staff corps in 1833, he had served under Radetzky and risen to become his chief of staff from 1849 to 1853. But at heart Benedek always remained a combat officer, courageous and energetic, popular with his troops, though on uneasy terms with many of his fellow officers. He rejected the scientific approach to operations and believed that victories were achieved by dash and enthusiasm. He disliked or even despised intellectual soldiers and once boasted, "I conduct the business of war according to simple rules and I am not impressed by complicated calculations."[26]

Holding such views, he opposed the Prussian concept of a general staff, a body of officers selected for their intellect and outstanding professional competence to serve as the collective brain of the army. Although there was much talk about the need for such an organization in the Austrian army, the concept met with a great deal of resistance because the creation of a real general staff would constitute a considerable shift in the power structure of the army and lessen the authority of the commanding generals.[27] Despite his position as chief of staff, Benedek favored the continued existence of the *Adjutanten Corps* and opposed Degenfeld's proposal to merge the adjutants and the staff corps into one general staff.[28] He was, however, given to rapid changes of mind and in October 1862 he relented and permitted the establishment of a general staff structure. But with Benedek as its head, actual changes were limited to the cartographic and historical sections. While in other countries, notably Prussia, considerable planning was undertaken for troop movements by rail and the control of such movements by telegraph, Austrian officers argued that the telegraph would never replace well-mounted staff officers.[29] Therefore the creation of a railway section within the staff was delayed until 1865. Moreover, the level of work remained low and on one occasion, so it is told, a staff officer sent to make a topographical survey went to a fashionable resort instead and compiled his report from a travel guide book.[30]

And Henikstein, Benedek's handpicked successor, chosen largely because he had been the general's highly compatible chief of staff in Verona, was hardly more suitable. In fact, even Benedek had some misgivings and in his letter to Crenneville recommending Henikstein, he pointed out that "at this time it is impossible to judge whether he indeed has the gifts of a great chief of staff or the genius for strategy."[31] Henikstein, for that matter, was none too sure of himself. "I am not the man for this important position," he explained, "I lack the ability, the knowledge, and therefore the necessary self-confidence."[32] Nonetheless, he was appointed. His effectiveness was further reduced by his lack of control over the staff officers at corps levels and by attacks on the competence of the general staff, both from within and without the army, which were so bitter that even the usually non-assertive Henikstein was moved to issue an official complaint against the critics.[33]

Clearly the new *k.k.* general staff did not enjoy the prestige and the power of its

Prussian counterpart, and as Craig so rightly pointed out, "this persistent refusal to take the staff problem seriously was unfortunate even in peacetime. As war approached, it menaced the very security of the state."[34] And after 1859 the Habsburg Monarchy found itself in an increasingly dangerous situation, lacking allies and facing two potential enemies—Prussia and Italy. Under these circumstances, close cooperation between the foreign minister and the chief of staff would have appeared imperative. But although Johann Bernhard Count Rechberg, foreign minister from 1859 to 1864, and after him Alexander Count Mensdorff-Pouilly, another soldier-diplomat who had reached general rank, were more compatible with the soldiers than Buol, there is nothing in the records to indicate joint deliberations concerning a national security policy. Usually only the war minister participated in the ministerial conferences and there he limited himself to defending the military budget.

At the same time the condition and the composition of the *k.k. Armee* changed but little in the six years between Solferino and Königgrätz. In 1860 the army again was divided into ten administrative area commands, the *Generalate*. In addition there remained two Military Border districts, the Croatian-Slavonian and the Banat, directly administered by a special section of the War Ministry. Actual strength of the army fluctuated. In theory the recruitment law of 1852 provided a conscript force of eight annual intakes—or ten if required—since men could be recalled during their two years in the reserves. Therefore, with cadres and the *Grenzer,* the peace establishment should have been around six hundred thousand and its mobilized strength should have exceed eight hundred fifty thousand, a number which Austrian diplomats were fond of quoting. In reality, however, numbers were much lower. Because of the economic squeeze most men served only a short term with the colors. In the cavalry, to be sure, men were retained for the full eight years, but gunners and engineers trained for only three years, while foot soldiers were furloughed after eighteen months of training.[35] In 1865 the peace establishment of the army stood at 374,371, while the war establishment was projected at 729,915.[36] In actuality, this figure was not reached and in 1866 only 528,000 men could be raised.[37]

The law of 1852 largely abolished the differences in military obligations between the various lands and the composition of the rank and file reflected the heterogeneity of the Habsburg Monarchy. In 1865 the army had 128,286 Germans, 96,300 Czechs and Slovaks, 52,700 Italians, 22,700 Slovenes, 20,700 Rumanians, 19,000 Serbs, 50,100 Ruthenes, 37,700 Poles, 32,500 Magyars, 27,600 Croats, and 5,100 men of other nationalities on its muster rolls.[38] Because of the generally low level of education and because the law still permitted the purchase of exemptions, only fewer than 10 percent of the enlisted men were able to read and write.[39] Combined with the short term of service, this made the procurement and retention of capable non-commissioned officers difficult,[40] and the average Austrian sergeant was not as well qualified as his equal in the Prussian army.[41]

Despite these difficulties, Austrian officers angrily rejected proposals made by a Prussian writer that the empire should adopt a system of truly universal conscription with a short period of training followed by a long reserve liability.[42] In reply, one Austrian officer maintained that the system had proved unworkable in Prussia and that a long-service army was much more ready for war than an army which first had to mobilize its reserves. Moreover, so the writer argued, the "purchase of substitutes by the wealthier classes actually was a benevolent institution, suitable to the social conditions of the empire." The rich paid for their exemptions a sum of four to five million florins annually and this went into the army funds to provide benefits for the rank and file.[43]

Thus, in substance, little changed in the enlisted ranks. Defeat, however, left some impression on the officer corps. Many of the high aristocracy, so favored by Grünne, had failed, and after 1859 the high aristocrats began to gradually withdraw from the army. Their positions were filled by men from the lesser nobility, or even from more humble backgrounds, who had made their way through the military schools. Whereas in 1848 and 1849 fewer than 3 percent of the generalcy came from these classes, by 1866 almost 20 percent of the generals in the Austrian field armies were of middle-class origin, thus reestablishing, at least in the field, the proportions prevailing at the end of the French wars.[44] Even so, the high nobility gave ground slowly. The highest ranks remained their preserve and among the feldmarschall leutnants on active duty in 1865, there were eleven archdukes, three princes, sixteen counts, thirty barons, thirteen lesser nobles, and only two without a noble title.[45]

Overall, the courage and devotion of the regimental officers could not be questioned, but many had stagnated too long in the service and were unwilling or unable to change with the times. Personal bravery, dash, and élan were preferred to careful study or rational planning, views which reflected the attitudes of Albrecht, Benedek, and Crenneville, the most important officers in the army.[46] In order to improve the technical and intellectual competence of the corps, the War Ministry revived in 1860 the *Österreichische Militärische Zeitschrift*, defunct since 1848.[47] But despite this official sponsorship, its circulation was poor. In 1863 out of 216 general officers, only 98 were subscribers, and out of 464 staff officers serving with the infantry, only 81 had taken subscriptions.[48] In addition, beginning in 1865, the War Ministry issued a number of technical journals for engineers and gunners, but these also had only a very limited circulation.[49] Attempts to start private military journals with broader appeal were regarded with displeasure in high places. Crenneville remarked that one could not be strict enough in watching this sort of activity. "Except for purely technical studies," he wrote, "soldiers should not be allowed to publish; otherwise, both discipline and *esprit de corps* will be endangered."[50] In fact, reading matter of all kinds was suspect and Benedek and Albrecht banned all non-German literature from officer messes within their commands.[51]

Finally, and this too remained a familiar complaint, the material conditions of the officers, especially in the junior ranks without a private income, remained precarious. In 1860, when permission was given for officers to resign with a two-year pay gratuity, more than eight hundred availed themselves of the opportunity. It became increasingly difficult to attract and retain good officers and, without the continued influx of candidates from military families and from the smaller German states, the problem might have become critical.[52]

In the 1860s too there was a fleeting opportunity for impecunious officers to escape the rigid conventions and the circumscribed life of the small garrisons. Late in 1861 Francis Joseph had given permission to his brother Maximilian, then contemplating acceptance of the Mexican crown, to recruit volunteers in Austria. When the project became an actuality in 1864, Maximilian, in return for renouncing all dynastic claims, was allowed to recruit six thousand volunteers from the Habsburg Empire.[53] Moreover, in 1866 when the French were about to depart from Mexico and Maximilian was in desperate straits, he was allowed to recruit an additional four thousand men.[54] Several hundred *k.k.* officers served in Mexico, usually in higher grades and with higher pay than they had enjoyed at home. But the dream evaporated, and in the end the bulk of the Austrian volunteers were evacuated together with the French early in 1866.[55]

Meanwhile, the army at home continued to make slow and half-hearted changes. Based on the 1859 experience, the operational structure again was modified. Divisions, considered too unwieldy, were abolished and replaced by four beefed-up battalion brigades. Four to six infantry brigades, a light cavalry brigade, a field artillery regiment, and some auxiliary troops constituted an army corps. As always, infantry constituted the most numerous branch of service: eighty line regiments, the Tyrolean *Jäger* Regiment, and thirty-two independent *Jäger* battalions.[56] In addition there still existed fourteen *Grenzer* regiments, now classified as line infantry though their combat value was disputed.[57] The mounted arm, divided between heavy and light cavalry, consisted of eleven *Cuirasseer*, two Dragoon, fourteen Hussar, and thirteen *Uhlan* regiments, while the artillery was organized in twelve field and one coast defense regiments. Technical troops still were very limited in number, only 2.5 percent of the total establishment, and did not form units larger than battalions.[58]

The lessons of the war brought about a certain amount of change in the three combat arms. Heavy cavalry had not been very useful in Italy, and there was pressure for reducing this expensive branch. In 1862 the number of squadrons in each regiment was reduced and, though on paper the cavalry still numbered 39,188 men, only some 28,000 troopers were actually present for duty by 1864.[59] In addition, though cavalry doctrine still placed the main emphasis on the well-executed charge, Major General Leopold Baron Edelsheim-Gyulai argued that new developments in rifled arms required a faster and more maneuverable light cavalry, trained for reconaissance and dismounted firefights. His ideas found but limited acceptance, though the *Cuirasseers* discarded their heavy breastplates, and new regulations promulgated in 1863 and 1864 stressed individual training and rapid evolutions.[60] But the dismounted firefight remained anathema to the traditionalists and only on the eve of war, in May 1866, were short rifles issued to the light cavalry.[61]

Of course, the artillery displayed more interest in the new advances in firepower. In 1859 its guns had been outranged by the rifled French pieces, and therefore considerable efforts were made to procure new materiel. Although experiments with rifled breech-loading cannons had been conducted since the 1830s, the problems of making the pieces gas tight and not too heavy had not been solved. In 1863, therefore, the Austrians introduced a modification of the French system, bronze muzzle-loading guns with large grooved rifling and studded shot. By 1866 all of the field regiments were equipped with 4- and 8-pounder guns of remarkable accuracy and a range of nearly four thousand yards.[62] In general, Austrian artillery doctrine centralized guns on the battlefield, and if necessary the artillery was to be sacrificed to save the troops, a concept which stood up to the test at Königgrätz.[63]

In the end, of course, infantry tactics were most important and here the changes had unfortunate results. The new infantry regulations of 1862 were based on a misunderstanding of the French fighting methods in Italy. There the French, only partially equipped with rifles and outranged by the Austrian weapons, had relied on fast moving columns to pass through the zone of fire to attack with the bayonet. What the Austrians failed to realize was that this had been an expedient, facilitated in part by the curved trajectory of the Lorenz rifle which created a gap in the zone covered by fire. Mistaking the bayonet attack as the crucial factor, the Austrians now adopted the so-called *Stosstaktik,* which further reduced the importance of fire and open order.[64]

The new doctrine assigned open-order fighting to special units such as the *Jäger*. Line infantry retained a skirmish line, but the distance between it and the *soutiens,* assault columns, formed in divisions of two companies, was reduced, and the regulations stated that the primary function of infantry was "to deliver the mass assault with the bayonet." In fact, the bayonet was considered the supreme weapon and the regulations declared that it was "not only useful in driving the enemy out of his position, but also appealing to the honor of brave men when called to stand on the defensive."[65] Offensive tactics, close-order fighting, and neglect of musketry had always been characteristic of the *k.k.* infantry, but now these methods were reaffirmed as official doctrine at a time when improvements in weaponry tended to make them most costly. At least one writer suggested that the continued reliance on obsolete close formations was due to the need to keep the troops under strict supervision.[66]

The first test of the new weapons and doctrine came during the Danish War of 1864. In this conflict Austria, trying to uphold her influence in German affairs, joined Prussia in intervening in the tangled affairs of Schleswig-Holstein. In December 1863, Holstein had been occupied by Saxon and Hanoverian troops acting on behalf of the German Confederation, and the Austro-Prussian political-strategic goal was limited to forcing the Danes out of Schleswig and compelling them to renounce their claims to the duchies.

In keeping with this limited aim, Austria and Prussia only fielded one corps each. The Austrian VI Corps, one cavalry and four infantry brigades, twenty-three thousand men in all, was commanded by Feldmarschall Leutnant Ludwig von Gablenz, the son of a Saxon general.[67] The Prussian contribution was larger, a reinforced corps of some thirty-seven thousand, and therefore command of the allied forces was entrusted to the Prussian Feldmarschal Friedrich von Wrangel. The Danes mustered a field army of thirty-six thousand, with another thirty thousand in reserves and fortresses. Moreover, the Danes could count on two major defensive works: the Danewerk blocking the way into Schleswig and the field fortifications at Düppel covering the shortest route from the mainland to the Danish islands. In addition, the superior Danish navy could threaten the flanks of the Austro-Prussian advance. Strategically, the Danes hoped to avoid fighting a decisive battle and by protracting the conflict obtain foreign and above all British intervention.[68] In contrast, allied strategies aimed to destroy the Danish field army as soon as possible, within the shortest time and within the boundaries of Schleswig.[69]

The allies entered Schleswig on February 1, 1864, and on February 3 Austrian troops demonstrating against the Danewerk won encounters with Danish screening forces.[70] The enemy evacuated the line and retired north, pursued by Austrian

The End of an Age 65

units which fought a major engagement with the Danish rearguard at Oeversee on February 6.[71] The Danes evacuated most of the mainland except for a garrison at Frederica in northern Jutland, under siege by the Austrians, and strong forces in the lines at Düppel. After Prussian troops stormed these fortifications on April 18, the Danish high command ordered the evacuation of Frederica and agreed to an armistice beginning May 12, 1865.[72]

Throughout their advance, and especially during the siege of Frederica, the Austrian command had been much concerned with the threat of popular resistance. The existence of a strong Danish navy and rumored Danish attempts at promoting a small war preoccupied Gablenz, and he took great care to prevent escalating hostilities into national resistance. Even in those few instances in which civilians did aid the Danish forces, he limited reprisals to internment and he kept his troops under strict control.[73] At the same time, mindful of his instructions to limit the war and to end it as soon as possible, he opposed Prussian proposals for a landing on the island of Fünen.[74] Therefore, when hostilities reopened at the end of June, Gablenz limited himself to a demonstration against Fünen, while the Prussians successfully invaded Alsen. There was no foreign intervention and the operation ended the war. In the Peace of Vienna, October 30, 1864, Denmark was forced to renounce her claims on Schleswig-Holstein in favor of Austria and Prussia.

Austrian troops had distinguished themselves during the fighting and Gablenz had carried out his instructions. Before departing from Vienna, Francis Joseph had told the general to maintain good relations with the Prussian ally, to keep strict discipline, and, above all, to "resurrect the spirit of Radetzky so that my troops, whose morale has suffered through the misfortunes of 1859, may find new heart."[75] Austrian morale certainly soared. The domestic and foreign press and many military men acclaimed the Austrian army and commented favorably on its dash and gallantry.[76] But a few observers were less impressed. One Prussian officer noted that the Austrian *Stosstaktik* resulted in prohibitive casualties.[77] Even some Austrian officers realized that emphasis placed on the all-out attack caused unacceptable losses and Feldzeugmeister Franz Ritter von Hauslab proposed more intensive use of artillery to prepare for infantry assaults.[78] Such dissenting opinions, however, were largely discounted in Vienna. Instead, as the future Austrian chief of staff, Lieutenant Colonel Friedrich Beck, noted, the Danish campaign was used to prove the contention that everything could be achieved with the bayonet and that the army now was prepared to face all comers.[79]

Faith in the bayonet prevented the timely rearmament of the infantry. Although it has been claimed, and widely accepted, that the "supreme warlord, general staff, War Ministry, veterans of 1864, and ordnance experts all favored introduction of the breechloader," and that only the penny-pinching parliamentarians prevented this vital measure, this is, to say the least, a distortion.[80] In reality, the emperor and the dominant figures in the military establishment were opposed to this innovation.

The Prussian needle gun was known in Austria since 1849, and for a decade there was no parliamentary obstacle to the introduction of a new weapon. In the fall of 1851, a commission headed by Feldzeugmeister Augustin conducted extensive trials with twenty needle guns. The commission rendered a negative verdict.

"Although the needle gun," Augustin reported, "permits rapid fire as long as there is no stoppage, this does not constitute any real advantage, because rapid fire will merely exhaust the ammunition supply."[81] The Danish campaign revealed that this supposition was not true, but still there was no change in attitude. Some officers commented favorably on Prussian use of the needle gun, but others, sent to Prussia in 1863 for further study of the new weapon, discounted its effectiveness. In addition, there were indications that the emperor did not favor breechloaders and regarded the bayonet as the more honorable weapon.[82]

Adoption of a breechloader did in fact present a problem for the Austrian army because the average educational level of the rank and file was low and the practice of furloughing men after a short initial training period left many of them unskilled even in the handling of the simpler Lorenz rifle. And, finally, the ordnance experts opposed the needle gun because they wanted to retain their monopoly in the production of military arms. Although the Vienna arsenal had been hard pressed to produce enough weapons for the army in 1859, production had been stepped up and by 1862 new machinery was able to manufacture a thousand Lorenz rifles a day. Retooling would have been expensive and complicated. To be sure, by this time private firms, especially the Josef Werndl factory in Steyr, were ready to supply breechloaders, but the military were not prepared to give up their monopoly. Instead they alleged that "private firms have neither the expertise nor the capability to meet the requirements of the army."[83]

For these reasons the army did not press the adoption of the new weapon, although when war appeared imminent in the spring of 1866, it did hold troop trials with a number of models from different sources.[84] As for parliament, the question of rearming the infantry had been discussed in 1865 when the Belcredi ministry had been formed, but the civilians had been reluctant and the army had not been insistent.[85] Between April and June 1866, however, parliament appropriated over 130 million florins for extraordinary military expenditures and it would appear that it was not the civilians but the military who were responsible for failing to reequip the infantry.[86] Frantic last-minute attempts were made to produce breechloaders or to purchase then abroad, but now it was too late and five thousand Remington rifles ordered in Belgium did not arrive until after the conclusion of the war with Prussia.[87]

Even so, and despite occasional misgivings, the Habsburg Monarchy entered into the conflict with confidence. War came as a result of the determination by both sides to force a solution to the question of supremacy in Germany. On the whole, Austrian army leaders were not eager for the conflict, though they believed that their army, because of its greater combat experience, was superior to the Prussian.[88] Moreover, Austria had stepped up her intelligence effort and by the spring of 1866 the k.k. general staff was reasonably well informed about Prussian preparations.[89] At that most foreign experts believed that despite the needle gun, military odds favored Austria. If the Prussians "refuse to be beaten in the first great battle by the superior leadership, organization, tactics, and morale of the Austrians," Friedrich Engels expostulated, "then they certainly are of different mettle from that of which a peace army of fifty years' standing may be expected to be."[90]

Therefore, when there was contention regarding the final disposition of the duchies, Austria, confident in her strength, remained adamant. For his part, Bismarck now saw a clear road to war. In January 1866, Prussia accused Austria of intrigues in Holstein and in February a crown council in Berlin discussed the possibility of conflict. The next month Austria began to place her regiments in Bohemia and Venetia on a war footing, mobilized the *Grenzer* regiments, and began to arm her fortresses. Clearly, Austria was preparing for a two-front war. On April 8 Prussia signed a short-term military alliance with Italy which substantiated Austrian fears and at the same time placed the monarchy in a difficult position. Because of the size of the empire and the distribution of her army, Austria needed seven to eight weeks for full mobilization while Prussia required only three. If there were to be an open race towards war, Austria would have to bear the onus of starting it. The Austrians were willing to hold back if Bismarck would promise that Prussia would not mobilize, but he was not willing to do this without reservations. Italy, moreover, made extensive preparations and on April 21 Vienna decided to mobilize the Southern Army. It soon became obvious, however, that no such separate mobilization could be carried out and in April 27 the Northern Army in Bohemia was also placed on a war footing.[91]

Mobilization raised the problem of command. Clearly the Bohemian theater was the most decisive and here the two outstanding contenders for command were Archduke Albrecht and Benedek. Despite the latter's protestations that he had no first-hand knowledge of the region, hardly a valid excuse, the emperor selected Benedek to lead the Northern Army. The appointment has been criticized as an attempt to avoid compromising the dynasty in the event of defeat, but this does not appear to have been the reason. Benedek was immensely popular both in the army and with the public at large and his appointment was thought to give heart to Austria's wavering allies and dismay the Prussians. His reputation was considered by the liberal press almost as a guarantee of success and having an Hungarian as the senior commander was likely to ensure the uncertain loyalty of the Magyar regiments. To deny Benedek the senior command would have raised charges of aristocratic bias. On the other hand, Albrecht was disliked by vast segments of the population and his military talents were not widely recognized outside the army. To argue that the emperor wanted at all costs to spare the dynasty the onus of defeat also has little foundation in history. Members of the imperial house had led armies and had been defeated, and, in fact, Albrecht fully expected to lead the Bohemian army.[92]

As it turned out, the emperor's decision to give the command to Benedek was a grave mistake. Even in his best days, Benedek never had revealed any great strategic gifts; his main strength had been combativeness and drive. But now, by all accounts, he was no longer his old self. He had aged and lost most of his self-confidence and had accepted the position with resignation. Appointed in early March, he stayed in his beloved Verona for nearly two months, displaying little interest in the forces assembling in Bohemia. On May 12 he finally arrived in Vienna and after further delay established his headquarters at Olmütz on May 26.[93] To make matters worse, he was accompanied by two chiefs of staff—Generalmajor Gideon Ritter von Krismanić, recommended by Albrecht and in actual charge of staff work for the Northern Army, and his personal friend and chief of the general staff, Henikstein. Krismanić was, to be sure, an able technician, but his strategic concepts were hopelessly old-fashioned and primarily concerned with establishing defensive positions and secure lines of communication. As one perceptive Austrian officer, Generalmajor Karl Moering, wrote to a friend in 1866, "My overlearned but lazy friend Krismanić and my unlearned friend Henikstein, who is as fit for his place as I am for composing an opera, appear to have bungled."[94] He hardly was the man to encourage Benedek to energetic action and his position was further compromised by Henikstein, his senior, who had been formally gazetted as chief of staff to the Northern Army, while still retaining his position as chief of the general staff. And Henikstein was pessimistic about the outcome of the campaign from the outset and as early as March 1866 had recommended the fortification of Vienna in case a retreat became necessary.[95] Naturally, his views permeated the headquarters, while his absence from Vienna left no one there to coordinate the Northern and Southern Armies.

Meanwhile the opposing forces were mustering for war. Although the Habsburg Empire had nearly twice the population of Prussia, 35 to 18 million, it only could raise an army of five hundred twenty eight thousand while Prussia mobilized three hundred fifty-five thousand and still had reserves at its disposal. Moreover, when Austrian fortress, base, service, and internal security troops were subtracted, this only left a fighting force of one hundred seventy-five thousand in the north and about seventy-five thousand in the south. To be sure, in the north, the Austrians could count on reinforcements from the Saxon Army and on some diversionary efforts by her south German allies on the Main, so that in Bohemia, the decisive theater of operations, Austria could count on a slight numerical superiority.[96]

Austrian war plans against Prussia dated back to the schemes developed during the 1850s which assumed a forward concentration in Bohemia followed by a joint Austrian-Saxon offensive against Berlin. But these offensive plans had envisaged neither a two-front war nor the accelerated Prussian mobilization capacity. Under the new conditions, concentration in Bohemia was ruled out by Austria's slow mobilization, the limited rail system, and by the fact that to join the Saxons would have required the troops to march six days beyond the railhead. Moreover, political reasons induced Austria to assume a defensive posture. It was therefore decided to assembly the army around Olmütz in Moravia and to move up into the strategic Bohemia fortress triangle—Josefstadt, Theresienstadt, Königgrätz—only after the buildup was completed. The Saxons, thirty-two thousand strong, were to fall back into Bohemia.[97]

The decision illustrated the *k.k.* general staff's preoccupation with the eighteenth-century maxims of secure operational bases, good positions, and safe lines of communications and, of course, it surrendered the initiative to Prussia.[98] It left Austria's north German allies, Hanover and Electoral Hesse, to their fate and induced the south German states to remain on the defensive. When on June 14 Prussia declared the German Federation ended and invaded Hanover and Hesse, the Austrians rendered no assistance, while the Saxons, also facing attack, withdrew into Bohemia to await the arrival of the Northern Army. Prussia and Italy declared war against Austria on June 18, but still Benedek's forces remained in their assembly areas at Olmütz.

Although it is true that the army was in poor shape with some regiments understrength, some containing a high percentage of raw recruits, and others still deficient in equipment and clothing, Benedek bears the major responsibility for the delay. His original intention was to await Prussian attack in the fortified positions around Olmütz, a strategy reinforced by the fact that mobilization went even more slowly than expected, and by his reluctance, shared by both Krismanić and Henikstein, to have the flank of the army moving north exposed to a Prussian thrust from Bohemia. But Benedek's inactivity aroused apprehension in Vienna and though Francis Joseph had resolved not to intervene in the conduct of the war, he dispatched Lieutenant Colonel Friedrich Beck, a member of his personal staff, to Olmütz. Beck, who had been involved in the preliminary planning of the campaign, tried to persuade Benedek to move forward to link up with Austria's German allies, but the general, supported by his staff, claimed that his army was not ready.[99]

And so the army remained at Olmütz while Benedek busied himself issuing a great number of orders, instructions, and circulars, stressing strict adherence to regulations, dress, and ceremonials, and more importantly emphasizing the importance of the *Stosstaktik*.[100] The best way to beat the Prussians, the general maintained, was to move rapidly to the attack and overrun the Prussians in closed order with cold steel.[101] Insistence on the *Stosstaktik* was curious because Benedek must have been aware of the Prussian fire potential, explained in great detail in an article by Moltke published in the *Österreichische Militärische Zeitschrift* in 1865.[102]

On June 15, with the Prussians invading Saxony, Beck returned to Olmütz. Now Benedek was finally willing to advance. On June 18 the army moved north in three parallel columns, with I Corps shielding its right flank against attack. Though the strain of such a marching arrangement was considerable, the North Army reached its goal quickly and in good order. Between June 26 and 29 it massed at Josefstadt with detached corps watching the mountain passes into Saxony and Silesia. Thus deployed, Benedek awaited the Prussians.

While indecision clouded the campaign in the north, victory had been achieved in Italy. Archduke Albrecht, ably assisted by his chief of staff, Generalmajor Franz Freiherr von John, had taken the offensive. Aided by an excellent intelligence system, he fell on the enemy before he had time to fully concentrate, and on June 28 at Custozza, Albrecht's troops, though greatly inferior in numbers, inflicted a shattering defeat on the main Italian army. Superior strategy and energetic leadership were victorious against any army not yet fully matured and not in possession of superior weaponry. Even so, the shock tactics were expensive and Austrian losses proportionately higher than those of the Italians. Especially significant was the large number of missing, 2666, largely from Italian and Magyar regiments.[103] Then too, the battle had been fought and won in defense of a province which Vienna, anxious to obtain Napoleon's benevolent neutrality, had already ceded to France by the secret treaty of June 12. Perhaps the troops fighting here would have turned the balance in the north. But on the other hand, there was no guarantee that Italy would have been content with Venetia and to give up the province without a fight might well have destroyed the morale of the army. As it was, victory at Custozza showed that despite her defeat in Bohemia, Austria still remained a major military power.[104]

Meanwhile, between June 26 and July 1, the Prussians invaded Bohemia in three major thrusts. Benedek, torn by conflicting counsel and doubts, did not make use of the opportunity offered by his interior lines. He should have fallen with all his strength on one of the separate Prussian armies, though in view of the Austrian inferiority in infantry, weapons, and tactics, this might have constituted a gamble. Still it was his best and perhaps his only chance. But he did not act and the Austrian covering forces were pushed back everywhere except at Trautenau on June 27, where they defended themselves with great determination and inflicted a sharp setback on the Prussians.[105] Even here, however, Austrian losses were so severe that they prevented exploitation of the victory.

The reports coming from the frontier battles finally convinced Benedek of the destructive firepower of the needle gun. He realized that this could be partially compensated for by the greater range of the Austrian artillery and the Lorenz rifle, provided, of course, that tactics were changed radically. On June 28 he issued an order to this effect. "The not negligible losses suffered by the infantry," Benedek wrote, "have convinced me that infantry should go into action, and especially into the bayonet charge, only after the enemy has been shaken by artillery fire."[106] Even now, however, he could not give up his preoccupation with the tactical offense and concluded that "I do not wish to inhibit the offensive spirit." To change basic tactics in the middle of a campaign was a desperate measure indeed and it was only partially implemented.

Troop morale, in any case, already was shaky while something like despair seized the North Army's headquarters. And when on June 29, I Corps, badly handled by Clam-Gallas, suffered defeat at Gitschin, Benedek decided to withdraw from Bohemia and to make a stand at Olmütz. The retreat began the next day in the direction of Königgrätz. During the march Benedek met Beck who had been sent up from Vienna and the general now informed the emperor's personal representative that only a speedy peace could save the army. Krismanić and Henikstein concurred and together with Beck they drew up a telegram to the emperor. "Beg Your Majesty most urgently to make peace. Catastrophe unavoidable for the army." The telegram was dispatched shortly before noon on June 30 and within hours Francis Joseph replied. "Impossible to make peace," the reply ran. "If unavoidable, I authorize an orderly retreat. Has a battle taken place?" The final query, added by Crenneville, though with the emperor's knowledge and consent, was interpreted by Benedek as an order not to retreat before fighting a major battle. Therefore, he halted at Königgrätz and with the Elbe in his rear drew up his army for battle.[107]

He deployed his army, still over two hundred sixty thousand strong, in a triangle with a base of six miles. About a fourth of the army was placed in reserve. Benedek hoped first to fight the Prussians on the defensive and then, at the crucial moment, to deliver a counterstroke to break their center.[108] But Benedek, disregarding the warnings of his chief intelligence officer, expected to fight the First Prussian Army only. When during the battle on July 3, the Second Prussian army arrived on the field about noon, breaking into the Austrian flank at Chlum, the issue was lost and Benedek ordered retreat. Some of his infantry panicked, but the cavalry kept its spirit and in a number of spoiling charges prevented the Prussian horse from cutting off the Elbe bridges, while the artillery, some batteries firing to the last round, covered the army's withdrawal. The defeated commander, having done all he could, crossed the Elbe towards six in the evening and at ten informed his emperor that a catastrophe had taken place. Losses were very high and some troops panicked, "but," he continued, "I shall endeavor to rally the army and, if possible, lead it back to Olmütz."[109]

Even so, during the next days the retreat on occasion came close to a rout. The troops stumbled along without any clear idea where all the marching was going, their one desire to lie down and sleep. "We are, to tell the truth," one officer wrote to his wife, "no longer able to fight . . . I can hardly go on."[110] The infantry, especially, was losing cohesion and another officer found that orders had to be enforced at the point of the sword.[111] But the bulk of the army escaped and made its way to concentration areas north of Vienna where Archduke Albrecht was forming a new line of resistance.

Appointed commander in chief of all armies on July 10, Albrecht took stern measures to stem the contagion of defeat. Stragglers were to be rounded up, units which had discarded their arms were to be decimated and their officers shot.[112] Belatedly, Vienna decided to evacuate Venetia and switch the bulk of the Southern Army north. Between July 10 and 24, about seventy thousand men were transported to Vienna and with new units formed, some reserves mustered, and some other moves taken, Albrecht was able to mass some two hundred thirty thousand men and eight hundred guns along the Danube from Pressburg to Linz.[113]

Both sides appeared ready for a fight to the finish. Bismarck fostered separatist propaganda in Bohemia and decreed the formation of a Hungarian Legion under the revolutionary veteran, General Georg Klapka, to invade Hungary and arouse the country.[114] At the same time, together with the Italian government, he supported plans for a landing in Dalmatia and for fomenting an insurrection on the Military Border, supplementing incursions from Serbia and Rumania.[115] Although Bismarck had entertained such schemes since 1862, there was not much substance to them. After Admiral Wilhelm von Tegetthoff beat the Italian navy at Lissa on July 20, the prospects of a seaborne invasion dimmed and it was in any case very dubious whether the Croats and Serbs of the Military Border would have been willing to cooperate with Magyar nationalists.[116] In many ways these schemes were threats designed to bring Francis Joseph to the peace table.

The desire to obtain a better bargaining position also appears as one of the main factors behind the Austrian show of determination to continue to war. Albrecht's army was drawn up along the Danube, plans were laid to start a guerrilla war against the Prussian lines of communication in Bohemia, and volunteer units were mustered.[117] Hastily thrown-up field fortifications protected the capital and preparations were made to evacuate the treasury and the archives. Yet, much of this was bluff. The mayor of Vienna assured an anxious city council that the emperor personally had promised him that Vienna would be declared an open city, and this, of course, would have made the Danube front untenable.[118]

In any case, Bismarck had no desire to press Austria too hard. Napoleon's attitude was becoming doubtful and cholera had broken out in the Prussian army. Therefore, on July 21, he concluded an armistice which allowed Austria to return substantial forces to the southern front and to halt an Italian advance beyond the boundaries of Venetia.[119] Meanwhile fighting continued in southern Germany where Prussian forces eliminated the poorly handled armies of Bavaria, Baden, and Württemberg. Having buried the German Confederation, Prussia established her own North German Federation in August, and on the twenty-sixth concluded the Peace of Prague with Austria. After some negotiations, Italy too made peace in October. Austria lost Venetia and was excluded from Germany, but she still remained, at least outwardly, a great power.

In his final order to the army, Archduke Albrecht told the troops that "the Austrian army, though attacked on two fronts by the forces of two powerful states and pursued by bad luck in the decisive theater," had done its very best.[120] But behind these comforting words there was considerable disappointment with the outcome of the war and within weeks the search for a scapegoat began. Given normal expectations, the Austrian rout in Bohemia seemed inexplicable and a stunned Francis Joseph advanced a simplistic theory. Writing to his mother on August 22, he complained bitterly that "all our well-founded hopes have vanished in the course of a few hours." He darkly hinted at treachery and argued that "all this has happened because before the war we had already been sold and betrayed."[121]

Francis Joseph, to be sure, wrote in the anguish of defeat, but attempts to fix the blame and to explain the unexpected defeat have continued. There have been three different schools. The first blames the imperial court and the nepotism and corruption of the military establishment; the second accuses Benedek and his staff of utter incompetence, and finally the third, a predominantly military school, accuses the civilians for starving the army of funds and for thus delaying the vital rearmament of the infantry.[122]

But Benedek, of course, was the obvious and immediate target, and on July 25 Crenneville informed him that there would be an investigation into his conduct.[123] When the commission of inquiry, presided over by Feldzeugmeister Johann Count Nobili, met in Wiener-Neustadt, Benedek stoically accepted all the blame and refused to incriminate his subordinates. The commission promptly indicated that it believed that the general was to blame, but Generalauditor Friedrich von Dratschmiedt, the army's chief judge advocate, courageously argued that the inquiry should not be limited to the period from May 12 to July 25, but that it should also investigate such relevant matters as armament and the lack of coordination with the allied armies. This, however, raised issues which well might have arraigned the entire army hierarchy, implicating the whole system of aristocratic command and privilege which in turn was linked to the dynastic orientation of the military establishment. And finally, the emperor himself had appointed Benedek and there were rumors, in Austria and abroad, that he had personally interfered in the conduct of operations.[124] These issues the government was unwilling to have aired. On November 1, Benedek, Krismanić, and Henikstein were retired, but by imperial fiat, on December 4, further proceedings against Benedek were quashed.[125] Nonetheless, officially inspired newspaper articles intimated that Benedek alone was to be held responsible for the debacle and that only imperial clemency had stopped further judicial action.[126]

Blaming Francis Joseph and Albrecht for these allegations, Benedek returned embittered and resentful. True to a promise given to his former friend Albrecht, he refused to speak out in his own defense and shortly before his death he burned most of his papers relating to the war. His silence, however, did not quiet specualations feeding the continuing controversy over the question of culpability.

In balance, it seems clear that Benedek did indeed make grave mistakes. Even so, the rout in Bohemia was neither, as comforting legend would have it, a sudden and unexpected reversal which could be blamed on the shortcomings of a particular commander, nor a matter of weapon superiority alone. The army which Austria fielded in 1866 was the largest ever; its morale, by and large, was good, and its spirit willing. Despite all organizational and material deficiencies it might yet have made a better showing but for one fundamental defect: the military lived divorced from the life of the people and out of the mainstream of the era. In 1866 the mental climate of the *k.k.* army differed all too little from the days of Archduke Charles. It lacked a broad social and industrial base and it persisted in romantic notions of dash, glory, and individual bravery. It could not prevail against the Prussians who utilized the ideas and techniques of the nineteenth century industrial and social revolution, who employed intellectual commanders, and who drew troops by conscription from the entire national manpower pool. Clearly an era ended at Königgrätz; the question remained as to whether the Habsburg Monarchy could make the fundamental changes required to bring itself and its military establishment into the new age.

6

Dualism and Reorganization: 1867-1874

Although Königgrätz was neither a Cannae nor a Sedan, it forced Emperor Francis Joseph and his generals to made some major changes in the empire and the army. Above all, sweeping concessions had to be made to Hungary, and the new dualistic structure of the realm was reflected in the military establishment. But though the events in Bohemia had convinced some soldiers that the "old-Austrian spirit of death-defying bravery no longer was adequate by itself," the army did not undergo any basic transformation.[1] "The cannon's roar at Königgrätz," one soldier-historian wrote, "was the funeral hymn for the old-Austrian army of German character. In its place there arose the multinational Austro-Hungarian army."[2] But this often-quoted statement needs qualification. Except for the special arrangements with Hungary, the army, though now mass-based and subject to parliamentary approval of its budget, retained its traditional dynastic orientation and character.

Perhaps this was inevitable. Institutions tend to develop a corporate life, purpose, and truth of their own, and Archduke Albrecht and many senior generals were bitterly opposed to change in any form. He believed loyalty to the dynasty, discipline, and *esprit de corps* to be the foundation stones and he regarded reforms as a threat to these fundamentals. "In no other country," he asserted, "is uniformity and the dynastic soldierly spirit as vital . . . because only the dynasty and the army hold this divided monarchy together."[3] But by continuing in this traditional role the army became unable to find a truly popular base among the nations of the empire.[4] During the period from 1867 to 1874, there was much reorganization and some reform, but it was a reluctant accommodation to changes imposed by external circumstances and not a basic revitalization of purpose.

Defeat forced the emperor to strike a bargain with the Magyars. Negotiations had been underway even before the war and the Hungarian Diet was reconvened in December 1865. To conduct the negotiations, the diet named a Committee of Sixty-seven which in turn formed a select Committee of Fifteen with Francis Deák as its guiding spirit. Interrupted by the war, negotiations resumed late in July 1866 and, despite obstruction from conservatives in Vienna and radicals in Budapest, the basic terms of the new relationship between the Habsburgs and Hungary, the *Ausgleich,* were quickly settled. In February 1867 Hungary's government was restored, and Count Julius Andrássy was appointed its first prime minister.

The *Ausgleich* created the Dual Monarchy of Austria-Hungary. Austria, in official parlance "the kingdoms and lands represented in the *Reichsrat*," and Hungary emerged as two distinct constitutional monarchies, joined by one ruler, emperor of Austria and king of Hungary, as well as by an economic union and certain joint instruments of government. The joint (imperial) ministries of war, foreign affairs, and finance were responsible to the emperor, but reported to and were dependent for their appropriations on two bodies, the Delegations, each consisting of sixty members elected by the two legislatures and meeting in alternate years in Vienna and Budapest. Hungary gained considerable leverage in this arrangement because, in contrast to the divided Austrian delegation, the Magyars usually presented a united front. And since the contributions to the joint budget from each half of the monarchy were re-determined every ten years, the very existence of the Dual Monarchy was called into question periodically.

The most critical issue was the military question which almost became a stumbling block during the negotiations and remained the "greatest liability of the *Ausgleich*."[5] Hungary aspired to a national army and in late July 1866 a minority in the Committee of Fifteen, led by Koloman Tisza, asserted that the Pragmatic Sanction only required a common defense and not a unitary army. But Deák and the committee majority, aware that Vienna even now would never accept a complete division of the army, favored the continuation of the unitary army in return for substantial military concessions. And when this division of opinion could not be resolved, the committee decided to shelve the army issue temporarily in order not to block the progress of the political negotiations.[6] Even so, Hungary was determined to assert its claims in military affairs and when in December 1866 an imperial decree introduced conscription throughout the empire, Andrássy, now prime minister designate, protested this "flagrant violation of the nation's rights." Any basic changes in the military system, he declared, could be accomplished only through constitutional processes and not by fiat. In the face of this stand the emperor was forced to retract the order.

Nonetheless, Andrássy realized that a solution to the army issue had to be found unless the *Ausgleich*, then in its final negotiating stage, was to fail. Under his prodding, the Committee of Fifteen agreed in January 1867 that according to the Pragmatic Sanction the army, when actually embodied, was subject to the exclusive command of the sovereign, but that the Hungarian parliament was responsible for recruitment, supply, and quartering within the kingdom. The final version of the *Ausgleich* document reflected this formula, though the language was obscure. Article 11 stipulated that "in accordance with the constitutional prerogatives of the sovereign all matters relating to the command and the internal administration of the entire army, and therefore also of the Hungarian army as an integral part of the entire military establishment, are recognized as being reserved to His Majesty." Terms of service, quartering, and financial support were declared subject to the approval of the Hungarian parliament (Article 12), and all basic changes in the military system affecting Hungary required the consent of the Hungarian ministry (Article 13).

Of course, the reference to the "Hungarian army as an integral part of the entire military establishment" signalled that concessions would be made to Hungary and this was anathema to the conservative military led by Archduke Albrecht. On February 20, 1867, Albrecht, in his capacity as commanding general of the armies, issued an order denouncing military separatism. He acknowledged the establishment of a separate Hungarian ministry of national defense, but asserted, "The army has not changed in the close unity of its components." He fought a separate Hungarian army at court and in ministerial councils and even took his case to the public in several pamphlets assailing "political machinations and the glorification of traitors." In Hungary, meanwhile, the opposition parties exploited Albrecht's activities for their own ends. They introduced motion after motion attacking the government for its failure to achieve a national army, delayed legislation implementing the new recruitment procedures, and generally put the whole *Ausgleich* in danger.

With conscription suspended and the reorganization of the army stalled, Vienna grew more and more impatient during the fall of 1867. If Austria were to recover her position as a great power, army reform was mandatory, and the Hungarian delay raised the specter of a serious confrontation between the two halves of the monarchy. To break the impasse, Emperor Francis Joseph in November 1867 ordered a council of generals to meet in order to work out a comprehensive army reform plan. It was a sign of the changed times that he instructed the council on the one hand to observe the new constitutional framework, but on the other to guard zealously the unity of the army and preserve the old traditions. Moreover, he sent the trusted head of his military chancery, Colonel Friedrich Beck, to negotiate directly with Andrássy.

At the outset of his mission Beck was a determined supporter of a unitary army. In a series of memoranda he tried to convince Andrássy that Hungary could not stand alone and that an independent Hungarian army would become a center of social unrest and provoke similar demands from the Slavic nationalities within the Dual Monarchy. But Andrássy, facing an angry opposition and an aroused country, could not be shaken from his demand for further concessions. However, he now proposed a joint imperial-royal (*k.k.*) army controlled by the emperor and the establishment of separate Austrian and Hungarian national guards (*Landwehr* and *Honvédség*) which were to be under the respective ministries of defense, who also represented the crown in putting the votes for them to the parliaments. Moreover, Andrássy conceded the German language of command for the joint army and promised that he would not press for the dissolution of the Military Borders. On the whole, Beck was well impressed and noted in his report that, considering the temper of the country, Andrássy's position was most courageous. In Vienna, however, Albrecht was not so easily convinced. The existence of national guards, he argued, would provide military training for subversive elements, and at the same time it would induce the two parliaments to reduce their appropriations for the joint army, the only reliable force safeguarding the established order.

Similar fears and objections were voiced by the generals when the council, summoned by Francis Joseph, finally met at the end of February 1868. Some general declared that regardless of the imperial wishes, the unity of the army and its historical legitimacy had to be preserved, and no concessions should be made just to preserve the Andrássy government from its parliamentary opposition. A break with Hungary, asserted Feldmarschall Leutnant Karl Moering, was probably unavoidable in any case, and he compared Andrássy's assurances with those made by the Prussians at Gastein shortly before the outbreak of war in 1866. Feldmarschall Leutnant Ludwig Baron Gablenz replied that this contravened the wishes of the emperor, but Feldmarschall Leutnant Karl Count Bigot de St. Quentin countered that the army was the last and only secure pillar of the monarchy and had to be preserved at all costs. In the end, however, the habit of obedience reasserted itself, and the generals bowed, reluctantly, to the imperial wishes. On March 23, they reported their basic acceptance of Andrássy's proposals.

But this was not yet the end of the controversy. The Hungarians wanted to recreate in organization, uniform, and drill the revolutionary *Honvéd* of 1849, and this was totally unacceptable to Francis Joseph and the military leaders. In April 1868 a series of conferences attended by the ministers of defense; the common war minister, Count Friedrich Ferdinand von Beust; and the emperor's chief adviser and minister for foreign affairs, Andrássy, and chaired by the emperor himself, took place in Buda, but failed to resolve the latest deadlock. In the end the diplomatic Beck once again came to the rescue, and in personal discussion with Andrássy he resolved the deadlock in May. The new *Honvédség* was to be patterned after the joint army in organization and uniform, but its oath of allegiance would be to the Hungarian king as well as to the national constitution. Moreover, it would be authorized distinctive insignia, flags, and the Hungarian language of command. The solution was acceptable to the emperor and pleased Andrássy, who on June 17, 1868, congratulated Francis Joseph on the "resolution of a problem which . . . in the past has bitterly divided the monarchy."

Congratulations, however, were rather premature, because Andrássy, still facing a clamorous opposition, promptly made additional demands. Above all he now demanded that the *Honvédség,* originally restricted to infantry and cavalry only, must receive its full allocation of artillery. But this demand, which would have given the Hungarian units the same combat potential as the joint army, was refused by the emperor, with the strong support of Albrecht and Kuhn. At this point Andrássy, always a political realist, decided that he had reached the full extent of concessions available, and in order not to endanger the political settlement forced the necessary legislation through parliament. However, and this was a portent of things to come, in order to quiet the vehement objections of the opposition, he had to promise that the government would continue to press with all available means for greater military autonomy.

At the same time similar legislation was piloted through the parliament in Vienna, though here too there was opposition. More importantly, outside of parliament the military leadership was still recalcitrant, and in August 1868, during a tour of inspection in Croatia, Albrecht made a symbolic pilgrimage to the grave of Ban Jelačić. Although the meaning of this action was not lost on either Vienna or Buda, this was 1868 and not 1848. The emperor, "who always maintained and protected . . . the compromise law from a strictly Magyar point of view," would tolerate no further obstruction. Once both parliaments had passed the necessary legislation, implementation was rapid. On December 5, 1868, Francis Joseph issued a carefully worded order of the day. "A new element, the *Landwehr* (*Honvédség*)," the order ran, "today joins the army as a valuable augmentation of the common defense." The new organizations, the order continued, "serve the same purpose as the army . . ., and I expect that all officers . . . and in particular the generalcy will do their utmost to further the bonds between all components of My Army and they will strengthen the spirit of order and discipline and combat any potentially divisive and dangerous influences from the very start."

This was plain language indeed, and it settled, for the moment at least, any military opposition to the new order. At the same time, however, the order glossed over the extent of the Hungarian victory. The statement that *Landwehr* and *Honvédség* augmented the army evaded the fact that Budapest regarded the *Honvédség* not just as a second-line home guard, but rather considered it the first step to a fully equipped, completely independent army. Therefore its status, and for that matter that of the Magyar contingents in the joint army, became a source of friction down to the very end of the Dual Monarchy. For all that, the *k.k. Armee* and the *Honvédség* eventually evolved a satisfactory relationship which stood the test of four and a half years of war.

Dualism ushered in constitutional government and the joint army became subject to parliamentary control of its budget. And this created difficulties. In the first ten years following the compromise, the German Liberals, the party of the new bourgeois business element hostile to the "feudal" army, dominated the *Reichsrat*. And though in Budapest the friends of the *Ausgleich* remained in the parliamentary majority, they generally were parsimonious with appropriations for the joint army, though liberal towards the *Honvédség*. In 1867 the military budget was 73 million florins, about one-fourth of the total expenditures. In 1868 it rose to 85 millions.[7] In 1869 the *Reichsrat* cut the military budget request from 80 to 75 millions,[8] though in the following year, due to an insurrection in Dalmatia, actual military expenditures amounted to 99,248,477 florins.[9] The budget for 1870 was the largest for the period up to 1877; army estimates were 78 millions and extraordinary additional requests for fortifications and an ammunition reserve came to another million.[10] But when the war scare passed, military expenditures declined radically and the economic crash of 1873 hit Austria-Hungary hard. By 1875, in fact, some observers doubted that Austria-Hungary could sustain a major war without foreign subsidies.[11]

Military men complained that the army received shabby treatment. To be sure, while the budgets were higher than those of the 1850s and 1860s, the Dual Monarchy spent proportionately less on her armed forces than the other major European powers. But it also must be said that friction in the highest echelons of the army contributed to placing the military in an unfavorable position in their dealings with the parliamentarians.

From 1867 to 1874 there raged an intense and many-sided dispute over the structure of the army's command and control system. On one side stood the traditionalists led by Archduke Albrecht who until the 1890s remained the single most important figure in the military establishment. His immense influence was due to the prestige gained in Italy, to his close relationship with the throne, and finally to his private fortune, estimated to be the largest in the empire. And Albrecht wanted to circumvent all parliamentary interference with the army and therefore advocated a dual command structure. Actual command and control were to be vested in a powerful *Armeeoberkommando,* while the war minister, who represented the army before parliament, was to be restricted to routine administration.[12] Albrecht was opposed by a small group of "liberal-centralist" generals, including Benedek, Hess, Gablenz, John, and Kuhn. Although these officers shared many of Albrecht's ideas, especially his aversion to Hungarian and Slav nationalist aspirations, they believed that a modern army required a broader base than a purely dynastic orientation and favored a strong, centralized, and responsible war ministry on the French pattern. Their leader was Feldmarschall Leutnant Franz Baron Kuhn, a brilliant if volatile German Liberal with excellent political connections.[13] Finally, there existed a third group which in most cases was careful not to offend Albrecht, but which was convinced that modern warfare required a powerful general staff on the Prussian model. Headed by Beck, they supported in practice Albrecht's opposition to a war minister holding any great power. For the moment, however, this group was not strong enough to enter openly into the arena, but from Beck's position close to the emperor he was able to exert influence.

But the major quarrel was between the proponents of a personal and dynastic command structure and those advocating ministerial responsibility. This conflict pitted Albrecht against his former chief of staff, Feldmarschall Leutnant Franz Baron John, and more importantly, against Kuhn. At first Albrecht and John had been close and it was John, appointed acting war minister in the late summer of 1866, who had suggested to the emperor the creation of a new supreme army command, the *Armeeoberkommando*.[14] Francis Joseph took up the suggestion and on September 15, 1866, he established the new agency with Albrecht in charge.[15] But the new agency, controlling not only operations, but also training and military justice, aroused Liberal opposition. The Liberals, not without cause, regarded the *Armeeoberkommando* as a poorly disguised revival of the absolutist *Hofkriegsrat*.[16] Therefore, faced with widespread parliamentary opposition, the new agency was shortlived and had to be dissolved in February 1868.[17] Albrecht, however, retained the title and position of *Armeeoberkommandant* and when this rank became untenable after the introduction of the 1868 army laws, a new position, that of inspector general of the army, was created for him. He assumed his new post on March 24, 1869, and held it until his death in 1895.[18]

Albrecht regarded himself at the first soldier of the monarchy and he was extremely touchy about his prerogatives and position. His conflict with John, who had become the first joint war minister (*Reichskriegsminister*), was largely personal. The two had cooperated well in Italy, but by 1867 the archduke felt that his former chief of staff was claiming an undue share for the victory at Custozza.[19] At the same time, John as war minister had quarrelled with Andrássy by standing firm against Hungarian interference in the joint army,[20] and he also had alienated Beck by refusing greater independence for the general staff.[21] Now these three men combined against John and the general was forced to resign in January 1868. The emperor quickly accepted his request and reassigned him as commanding general to provincial Graz.

But relations between Albrecht and the next war minister, Kuhn, were even worse. Appointed in part because of his excellent connections with the German Liberals dominating the *Reichsrat*, his appointment had aroused some opposition in the army.[22] Moreover, Kuhn was convinced that the decline of Austria's military posture was due to the inefficiency of the "feudal" elements in the army and he was resolved to use the ministry to transform the military establishment. Here, of course, he clashed head on with Albrecht and soon there was open conflict. In his diary Kuhn called Albrecht a Spanish absolutist, a Philip II, and a Torquemada who was scheming to overthrow constitutional overnment.[23] The rift split the army into opposing "court" and "ministerial" factions which lambasted each other in their respective journals, the semi-official *Österreichische Militär-Zeitung* and the liberal-leaning *Österreichisch-ungarische Wehrzeitung*.[24]

Kuhn had the initial advantage in the conflict. Early in 1869 he openly attacked Albrecht's aspirations to the role of generalissimo on the model of his famous father. This division of authority between the war minister and the army commander, the general wrote, not only compromised the emperor's prerogatives as commander in chief, but also had been disastrous in 1859 and 1866. And at the present, Kuhn asserted, "in order to carry out his difficult assignment, the war minister should have the complete and undivided confidence of His Majesty." Kuhn concluded that he had been promised a free hand and threatened to resign unless Albrecht was deprived of command power.[25] This stand, together with parliamentary pressure, had resulted in the abolition of the *Armeeoberkommando*.

Although the events of 1866 had demonstrated the importance of staff work, Kuhn was equally determined not to allow the chief of the general staff to rival the war minister. After Henikstein had been removed late in the summer of 1866, John, who also regarded the general staff merely as an auxiliary of the War Ministry, had combined the offices of chief of staff and war minister.[26] Kuhn went somewhat further. He believed that staff training produced narrow specialists, and because many staff officers adhered to the court party, he, rather unfairly, regarded the staff as a stronghold of aristocratic privilege.[27] Therefore he suppressed the post of *Chef des Generalstabes,* and during Kuhn's tenure as war minister, Generalmajor Joseph Gallina merely ranked as director (*Leiter*) of the staff, itself now a mere section within the War Ministry. In 1871 Kuhn dissolved the separate general staff corps and, in a much disputed promotion regulation, made it possible for line officers who had not attended the war college to sit for special examinations and become eligible for staff appointments.[28]

Kuhn has been attacked for his attitude to the general staff, yet his position was not merely based on hostility to that body, but also reflected his problems as the war minister responsible for changing the army from a long-service professional to a universal-service cadre force. Albrecht's extraordinary power made the position difficult enough and a powerful chief of staff would have further compromised it. Neither Albrecht nor the chief of staff had the responsibility for getting funds from a reluctant parliament, which complicated matters even further.

As it was, the transformation of the army, never before attempted in a state the size of the Dual Monarchy, was difficult. But Kuhn, utilizing his connections with the German Liberals, managed to implement universal service, to rearm the infantry and the cavalry, and to provide the greatly increased number of officers required. When funds ran short in 1869, he utilized moneys accumulated in the *Stellvertreterfond* (money accumulated before 1867 for relief from military service).[29] Although Kuhn did not popularize the army among all the nationalities of the monarchy, he did create the basic framework which lasted until 1918.

Under the provisions of the army legislation of 1868 and further implementing laws passed early the following year, all male subjects of the monarchy were liable for a total of twelve years service. Exemptions were limited to the clergy, theological students, and certain hardship cases. Even so, until World War I, Austria-

Hungary never fully exploited its manpower potential and many eligible men received little or no training. The reason for this was that the annual recruit intake, and therefore the overall strength of the armed forces, was fixed by law at a certain level and not pegged to the increasing population. In 1868 the number was set at ninety-five thousand recruits, of which Austria provided fifty-five thousand and Hungary forty thousand men. The active army numbered two hundred fifty-five thousand, while the war strength, exclusive of the *Grenzer* but including *Landwehr* and *Honvéds*, was projected at eight hundred thousand. Compared with the war establishments of the other great powers, 1,028,946 for the North German Confederation, 1,350,000 for France, and 1,476,000 for Russia, this was by no means an excessive figure.

The annual recruit intake was divided by lot. Those drawing the lowest numbers were inducted for three years into the joint army, then placed for seven years in the army reserve, and finally transferred to the *Landwehr* or *Honvédség* for their last two years. The small number drawing the middle lots spent two years of active service in the national formations. Finally, those drawing the highest numbers received no training at all but were placed in the supplementary reserve, the *Ersatzreserve*, subject to call only in time of war. The law also provided for the establishment of a *Landsturm*, a last levy, but made no provisions for its organization.[30]

Administratively the joint army was divided into sixteen territorial districts, roughly corresponding to army corps areas. These, however, were not tactical formations, and units still drew their replacements from outside the region in which they were normally stationed. In case of mobilization, the emperor appointed a commander in chief, and field armies, usually three corps, were activated. Because brigades had proved too small to carry out their assigned missions in 1866, the division was reintroduced as the basic tactical unit. As for the *Landwehr-Honvédség*, they existed in peace time only as cadres. Men were required to attend one muster a year and a two-week company drill in the autumn, and every two years a battalion exercise was to be held.[31]

The transformation of the army and the demands of the new warfare changed, albeit slowly, the character and the composition of the officer corps. If the noble and well-connected still predominated in the highest ranks, by 1878 commoners constituted 58 percent of the generalcy.[32] This trend was accelerated by the final disappearance of the appointment and promotion powers of the colonel-proprietors. After 1868 these positions became purely honorary and new regulations, pushed through by Kuhn, provided branch-wide criteria for advancement.[33] Nonetheless, promotion prospects differed from branch to branch. The select general staff corps, reestablished after Kuhn left office, advanced the fastest, followed by the cavalry, then the infantry, and finally the artillery, where promotions tended to be slow indeed. For example, in 1870 only 3.13 percent of the majors in the general staff corps were over forty-three years of age, compared with 17 percent in the cavalry, 42 percent in the infantry, and a staggering 94 percent in the artillery.[34]

Perhaps the most important determinant of an officer's career was his method of entry. Disregarding the special cases of the medical, veterinary, judicial, and administrative services, there emerged three basic career patterns: the dynastic, the academic, and the cadet. The dynastic, of course, was reserved for members of the imperial house. If destined for a military career, they usually were commissioned at fourteen, served briefly as subalterns, and in their twenties were given a staff or command position which rarely interfered with their private lives. To be sure, not all members of the dynasty performed only formal service; some, like Archduke Albrecht or Archduke Wilhelm, the long-time director of the artillery, devoted their lives to the career, though their preferment was much more rapid than that of their lesser-born counterparts. Graduates of the two academies, the *Theresianische Militärakademie* and the *Technische Militärakademie,* represented another elite within the army. Normally commissioned at twenty after three years' study, the *Akademiker* had a definite edge in obtaining the best appointments.[35]

The two academies together, graduating only about 230 each year, were inadequate to fill the needs of the enlarged army; therefore, the majority of regular officers came from the cadet schools. These institutions, fifteen for the infantry, and one each for the cavalry, artillery, and engineers, admitted boys between the ages of fourteen and seventeen for four years of study. After graduation, about eight hundred young men entered the service annually as cadet officer deputies. After several years' probation, they would finally be commissioned when a vacancy became available, usually around the age of twenty-four. Although there was no statutory barrier to their advancement, and although some cadets rose to high rank, the great majority lived out their careers as regimental officers.

Materially the condition of the Austro-Hungarian officer corps improved after 1868, though the junior ranks remained hard-pressed. Exclusive of allowances, which varied from station to station according to a schedule keyed to the local cost of living, a second lieutenant received 600 florins a year, a captain 1,200, and a major, 1,680. Colonels jumped to 3,000, major generals received 4,200, and finally, at the very top of the military ladder, a fieldmarschal received 10,500 florins. But whatever their rank, all officers were expected to live in style and for this, as well as other reasons, marriages were strictly regulated. Only one-half of the corps was allowed to be married, and when an officer applied for permission to marry, he and his intended bride not only had to furnish proof of social acceptability, but they also had to provide a marriage bond, the *Kaution,* which assured that the family could maintain a "proper" standard. The *Kaution,* either money, investments, or real estate, was set at varying levels, diminishing with rank, but normally a junior officer without private means wishing to marry a poor girl would have to leave the service.

Little changed in the overall orientation of the corps. The Austrian officer remained intensely loyal to the dynasty, the army, and his regiment. Kuhn, though his dynastic allegiance was never in doubt, had envisaged a more broadly educated officer corps, drawing from a wider range of the wealthy and educated population. He tried to introduce a more humanistic course of studies at the academies, but this proved too difficult and had to be dropped in 1875. Above all, however, it was Albrecht's insistence that the "old Austrian" virtues remained unchanged, thus preserving the character of the corps. The *k.k.* officer continued to find glory in standing above nationality and parties; he was *kaisertreu* and gave his allegiance not to a national flag but to the dynasty. But while the corps remained one of the major factors binding an ever-more divided realm, its apolitical status and education also meant that commanders remained blind to the forces affecting the future of the empire.[36]

Until decimated in the early campaigns of 1914, the regular officer corps shaped the character of the joint army. But the introduction of universal military service required greatly increased numbers of officers, especially for the reserve formations. To provide reserve officers, Austria-Hungary adopted the Prussian institution of "one-year volunteers." Men of education and social standing were allowed to volunteer for one-year training, and after passing an examination received a reserve commission. At first the professionals were not very impressed by the performance of the volunteers, and hopes that they would provide an adequate number of reserve officers were also disappointed. Of 1,355 volunteers in 1869, only half qualified for commissions, and out of 1,752 the following year, only one-third passed the examination.[37] In all, between 1869 and 1885 only 35 percent of the volunteers were commissioned.[38] Gradually, however, the institution took hold and by 1878 there were 12,055 regular and 5,143 reserve officers on the army rolls.[39] Still, even when the officers on the unemployed list and those of the *Landwehr-Honvédség* were added, the Austro-Hungarian army had a shortage. This was a definite handicap because a strong body of non-commissioned officers had never been developed, and many duties which were normally handled by sergeants in other armies had to be handled here by junior officers.

Universal conscription changed the character and the composition of the rank and file. Although recruits were drawn from all parts of the Dual Monarchy, German remained the language of command, though instruction and internal duties were conducted in the national or the so-called "regimental" language. Treatment of the men improved and flogging was abolished in 1867.[40] In 1873 new regulations superseded those in use since the days of Archduke Charles. Whereas in the "old army" officers had, by and large, given little attention to their men, the new regulations ordered them "to pay special attention to the character, abilities, and tendencies of their subordinates; to get to know and understand them, show sympathy for their aspirations and motivate their spirit and attitudes."[41] Still, life in the ranks remained harsh. In 1869 one critical officer complained about the poor food as well as the unsanitary conditions in barracks and hospitals and blamed these for the high mortality rate in the joint army.[42] In part these shortcomings were due to financial stringency. As Kuhn pointed out in 1873, the *k.k. Armee* spent less than the German army, 368 as against 389 florins, on the annual maintenance of a soldier.[43]

The great bulk of the soldiers still served in the infantry, eighty line regiments, the Tyrolean *Jäger* Regiment, and until 1872 the regiments of the Military Border. Uniforms and equipment, however, changed radically. The traditional white coat, dating back to the days of Prince Eugene, was replaced by a dark blue tunic; muzzleloaders were replaced by breechloaders. In August 1866 Albrecht had demanded the immediate rearmament of the infantry.[44] As an emergency measure the Lorenz rifle was converted by a tip-up breechblock, the Wänzel modification.[45] The following year the army adopted the once-rejected Werndl rifle, an 11-mm. single shot breechloader, sturdy and simple to operate. Deliveries of the conversions by the Vienna arsenal were exceedingly slow and by 1870, the Wänzel rifles had not been issued to all troops. Meanwhile the Werndl rifles (M 1867) also were in short supply, but in 1869 Werndl brought American machine tools and by the end of 1872 his company, the Österreichische Waffenfabriksgesellschaft in Steyr, turned out six hundred thirty thousand rifles and carbines.[46]

Despite the new weapons, there was resistance to changes in infantry tactics. Although new field regulations modeled on the Prussian tactics came out in February 1867, were modified in 1868, and were again revised in 1874, officers who had fought in Italy where the bayonet had been victorious still held important commands and continued to favor "cold steel" over fire.[47] Resistance to change was even more pronounced in the cavalry. In 1867 the differences between heavy and light cavalry disappeared and the forty-one mounted regiments—Dragoons, Hussars, and *Uhlans*—received the same horses, arms, and equipment. Individual horsemanship remained at a high level, though little attention was paid to musketry and dismounted fighting. Although recent experience in Europe and America suggested that massed charges were no longer feasible, shock action on the Napoleonic pattern continued to be practiced. During the maneuvers in 1876, in which thirty thousand men and five thousand horses participated, the main event was an old-fashioned frontal charge against emplaced guns. The emperor was present and was well impressed; officers who knew better kept silent.[48]

Because of this continued emphasis on shock tactics, cavalry training neglected reconnaissance and communication duties.[49] Even so, there was slow recognition that the mounted arm would no longer decide battles. Cavalry tacticians now began to advocate the use of mounted troops as a disrupting force which, ranging well ahead of the main army, would interfere with hostile deployment. Since Austria-Hungary was faced with the prospect of numerically superior Russian armies in Galicia, this was an attractive concept; therefore, most of the cavalry, grouped in independent divisions, was concentrated on the eastern frontier.[50]

The war also had revealed that the increased range of infantry weapons required improved artillery performance. But the procurement of new guns was expensive, and therefore no new materiel was introduced until 1875. Trials for a new field gun were started in 1871, and late in 1873 Feldzeugmeister Arthur Count Bylandt-Rheidt recommended that the Krupp steel breechloaders which had proven superior in the tests be adopted.[51] The ordnance experts, however, objected. Austria did not have the capability to produce steel barrels; awarding the contract to a foreign firm might be dangerous. Then too the Vienna arsenal was still smarting from the award of the rifle contract to a private manufacturer. Therefore the army ordnance recommended the adoption of "steel bronze" tubes developed by Generalmajor Uchatius, the head of gun manufacturing at the arsenal. In 1875, field pieces of the Uchatius design both in 8- and 9-cm. caliber were introduced.[52]

Foreign experts rated the heavy 9-cm. piece as good, but considered the light 8-cm. piece to be poor.[53] Austrian experts maintained that the new guns were equal to the new German field artillery and at the same time cheaper and more durable. In fact, however, Uchatius barrels had serious limitations. They were heavy and could not stand up to the pressures developed by heavy calibers so that 17- and 21-cm. siege pieces had to be purchased from Germany. Uchatius, deeply hurt, continued trying to perfect his invention, but he failed and committed suicide.[54] His barrels remained in use, however, and still were part of the Austrian field artillery materiel in 1914.

Most of the changes in organization, training, and materiel were reflected in the *Landwehr* and *Honvédség,* though until the last decade before World War I the war ministry in Vienna regarded these formations as second line and usually did not provide them with the most modern equipment. Moreover, the development of these two forces, administered and financed separately, did not proceed at an equal pace in the two halves of the monarchy. From the outset the *Honvédség* received Liberal support from the Hungarian parliament. Although its nominal commander since 1868 was Archduke Joseph,[55] its real governance was in the hands of the minister of national defense, a portfolio held until 1872 by the prime minister. In 1872 Béla von Szende took over that office with Generalmajor Géza Baron Fejérváry acting as military secretary. Annual expenditures for the *Honvédség* were in excess of 9 million florins, though during the financial crisis of 1873 the allocation was reduced to 7 million for 1874 and to 6 million for the next year. Late in 1877, however, the Hungarian parliament restored most of the cuts and voted additional funds to equip the *Honvéds* with modern arms.

As a result of these efforts the organization grew rapidly, and by 1873 it already numbered 2,868 officers and 158,000 men, organized in eighty-six battalions and fifty-eight squadrons. Many of the original officers either were veterans of 1849 or transfers from the joint army, but in 1872 the Ludovika Academy, formerly a military preparatory school, opened first as a cadet and later as a staff college for the *Honvédség*. In 1870 *Honvéd* brigades participated for the first time in army maneuvers, and in 1873 higher tactical formations and territorial commands, seven divisions and seven military districts, were organized. Of course, these units still lacked artillery, although in August 1870 an attempt to circumvent these restrictions by the formation of twenty Gatling-gun batteries was successful. Kuhn protested, but the emperor ruled that these pieces were infantry weapons, not artillery. But the end of the seventies, then, the *Honvédség* approached, at least in infantry and cavalry if not yet in artillery and auxiliary services, the stature of a national army. By contrast, the *Landwehr,* largely established to maintain the appearance of parity, had made little progress and still consisted only of skeleton infantry units brigaded for administrative purposes with units of the joint army.

Within the *Landwehr* organization, the Tyrol continued to occupy a special position. Conscription, of course, was in force there, but in addition the old obligation of all men to defend the country was retained. In 1864, new regulations established three types of local militia, the *Landesschützen,* which became part of the *Landwehr* after 1868, the *Landsturm,* and the *Standschützen*. The last body, made up of the very young and the very old, was based on government-subsidized civilian rifle clubs which could be found in every village and town. The *Standschützen* elected their own officers and merely received a senior military advisor, usually an officer on the inactive list, when they were called out for active service.[56]

But, as Beck had predicted, the Hungarian example fanned national military aspirations elsewhere in the empire. First reaction came from Bohemia. When recruits were called up under the new conscription laws, there was sullen discontent and in some cases refusal to take the oath of allegiance.[57] The German Liberal cabinet in Vienna, however, refused to make concessions and the commanding general in Bohemia, General der Kavallerie Alexander Baron Koller, was instructed to put down all nationalist manifestations. In October 1868 Prague was placed under martial law which was lifted in April of the following year.[58] For the moment, this harsh measure appeared successful, but it escalated animosity between Czechs and Germans in Bohemia. By the fall of 1869 the situation in Prague once again was tense, and Koller alerted six battalions and one squadron to keep order in the city.[59]

Even more serious events occurred that month in Dalmatia. In the late summer of 1869 it was announced that the new conscription laws would be applied to the Krisvosije, the mountainous hinterland of the Gulf of Kotor. Here traditionally all men carried arms and, though volunteers had served in the small *k.k.* navy, there never had been conscription. The prospect aroused intense antagonism, but the civil and military governor, Feldmarschall Leutnant Johann Ritter von Wagner, assured Vienna that he had the situation well in hand.[60] In late September he ordered disarmament of the population and enforcement of conscription.[61] Fighting promptly broke out, and by October 7 Wagner was forced to call for reinforcements "so that failure would not besmirch the honor of our arms or damage the prestige of the government."[62]

But this was exactly what happened. With some support from neighboring Montenegro and the Hercegovina, the insurgents defeated the detachments sent against them. By November the original five-battalion garrison had been brought up to eighteen battalions, some artillery, and auxiliary troops, with a squadron offshore to provide support. But even this considerable force was unable to pacify some one thousand insurgents. "The blunders committed by FML Wagner," Albrecht commented angrily, "are colossal and he is to blame for this situation."[63] In December 1869 a ministerial council reviewed the problem. Kuhn asserted that the troops should be able to "deal with a few hundred bandits," while Beck and his friend Feldzeugmeister Gabriel Baron Rodich, a Croat who was considered a Balkan specialist, claimed that continued armed dissidence would have serious repercussions in the South Slav areas of the monarchy and argued that appeasement was the only answer. Rodich urged that Wagner be dismissed and that he should be appointed governor with discretionary powers to grant an amnesty.[64] This was done. On January 11, 1870, after giving assurances that conscription would not be enforced, that the inhabitants could retain their weapons, and that all would receive a full pardon, Rodich received the token surrender of the insurgents.[65]

The so-called Peace of Knezlać was a humiliating set-back for the army and the government, but even more threatening was the support which the rebels had received from the South Slavs of the monarchy.[66] For centuries relations between the South Slavs and the army had been close. In 1848 and 1849, the *Grenzer* had been an important reservoir of strength for the dynasty, and volunteers from Serbia had fought under the imperial flag against insurgent Hungary. But in the 1850s the Vienna government had disregarded South Slav national aspirations, and after 1860 it had looked above all to conciliating the Magyars. Finally, the Compromise of 1867 was widely considered as a sell-out of the South Slavs. Even the Military Borders were affected by such sentiments and their military potential became an important consideration in various insurrectionary schemes hatched by Croat and Serb nationalists.[67]

Meanwhile though, Croat politicians did the best they could and in 1868 they concluded a subcompromise, the *nagodba,* with the Magyars. Although this arrangement was condemned by Croat opposition leaders, it provided certain advantages to Croatia. Hungary promised the country limited autonomy, including the right to have special Croatian units, *Hrvatsko Domobranstvo,* within the framework of the *Honvédség*.⁶⁸ In addition, Hungary promised to seek the reversion of the Military Border districts to Croatian control.

The proposed demilitarization of the *Grenzer* aroused opposition both by extreme nationalists and conservative soldiers, now forming a strange, and temporary, alliance. Both Albrecht and Kuhn plotted to make the Military Borders an autonomous *Grenzer* region, but little came of these schemes.⁶⁹ Andrássy charged that the military aimed at subverting the new state of affairs in Hungary and he also warned that the *Grenzer* constituted a potential armed South Slav irredenta threatening the very existence of the monarchy. Perhaps this warning was farfetched, but it was effective. The Dalmatian insurrection, the unrest in Bohemia, and South Slav agitation elsewhere all appeared to be parts of a giant conspiracy. And when Andrássy backed up his demands with threats against the joint army budget, Kuhn and Albrecht hastily backed off from their support for *Grenzer* autonomy. The emperor now agreed to the dissolution of the Military Borders and though there was some delay due to the outbreak of the Franco-Prussian War, in June 1871 a series of decrees spelled out the details ending this ancient military institution.

Demilitarization took time. Until 1873 the *Grenzer* remained in their regiments, and remnants of the military administration functioned until 1881. But the decision had been made and it was not well received on the Military Border. In October 1871 units of the Ogulin Regiment, stirred up by Croat extremists, rose against the "Swabian dogs who have sold us to the Magyars," but the rising was suppressed promptly by loyal *Grenzer* troops. Even so, the rising revived fears of a giant Slav conspiracy in Vienna, and Francis Joseph now decided to break off negotiations for a compromise with the Czechs.

More important even than the end of the Military Border was the decision taken in 1870 not to renew the struggle for supremacy in Germany. Until the summer of 1870 this possibility had been very much alive in the mind of Emperor Francis Joseph and to this end he had appointed Count Friedrich Beust, a former Saxon official, as his foreign minister and chief adviser. On this issue, too, the military closed ranks and accepted Albrecht as the leader of the revanche party.⁷⁰ Some soldiers even entertained more grandiose plans. Kuhn, for one, favored a war against both Russia, which he blamed for fomenting the Dalmatian revolt,⁷¹ and Prussia. But the monarchy needed an ally and France appeared as the most likely prospect. As early as August 1867 Francis Joseph and Napoleon III met in Salzburg to discuss a possible alliance against Prussia. But nothing came out of these talks since Napoleon did not believe that Austrian rearmament had progressed sufficiently.⁷²

Negotiations, however, continued with both France and Italy. In October 1868 Beust indicated willingness to hand over South Tyrol and all territory west of the Isonzo in return for Franco-Italian help to recover Silesia and the establishment of an Austrian protectorate over southern Germany. This time Napoleon was interested, but the Italians above all wanted the French to evacuate Rome and again nothing definite was settled.⁷³ At the same time, unofficial conversations were in progress between the Austrian and French military, and in February 1870 Kuhn informed the French military attaché in Vienna that all preparations were completed and an army of six hundred thousand men could be mobilized within six weeks.⁷⁴ The next month Albrecht went to Paris with concrete strategic proposals. Southern Germany was to be invaded by Austrian, French, and Italian forces and the south German states would be asked to join in a march on Berlin.[75] But the French hesitated and Albrecht concluded, quite correctly, that they were not prepared for a major war. In turn, therefore, when the French changed their mind and early in June dispatched General LeBrun to Vienna to make definite arrangements, Francis Joseph would not commit himself.[76]

The inconsistencies of the sovereigns were shared by some soldiers. By the spring of 1870 the usually belligerent Kuhn worried that Albrecht was dragging the monarchy into a war for which the army was not prepared.[77] But when the outbreak of the Franco-Prussian war appeared imminent, he changed his mind and on July 14 he submitted a lengthy memorandum to the emperor in which he asserted that Austrian intervention could turn the coming conflict into "a struggle involving all of Europe as well as parts of Africa and Asia." And, concluded Kuhn, from this conflagration Austria-Hungary would emerge restored to great power status.[78]

To resolve all these conflicting ideas, on July 18, the day before France declared war on Prussia, a crown council was held in Vienna. Claiming that the army was ready, both Albrecht and Kuhn urged immediate mobilization, while Andrássy and Beck opposed such a move. In the end the emperor, who undoubtedly remembered previous claims of military preparedness, decided to take no chances. Austria-Hungary would observe armed neutrality and only limited military preparations were to be undertaken.[79] At this, the common front of Albrecht and Kuhn dissolved. When the emperor informed Kuhn the following day that in the event of war Albrecht would take overall command, the war minister protested and, claiming that Albrecht would "ruin the work of several years," submitted his resignation.[80] Although the diplomatic Beck persuaded the volatile Kuhn to withdraw his resignation, the minister's temper was not improved when the emperor ordered an investigation into the actual combat readiness of the army.[81] In the event of war, the investigation revealed that six hundred thousand could have been fielded in six to eight weeks, though there would have been severe logistic shortages.[82] Albrecht, always willing to take a swipe at Kuhn, now published an anonymous pamphlet in which he argued that parliamentary parsimony and ministerial maladministration had created a lack of modern weapons and field equipment and that if the reserves had been called out they would have been untrained and unarmed.[83]

To be sure, these statements were in part motivated by Albrecht's dislike of Kuhn, but there also was much truth. The empire was not ready for war and even the limited preparations strained the budget and caused unrest on the Military Border.[84] As early as August 10, Francis Joseph halted most preparations and after Sedan all units were placed on a peace footing.[85] Kuhn, however, undeterred as always, once again dreamed of adventure—a coup to seize Silesia and, after Russia remilitarized the Black Sea in October 1870, a march on Warsaw to raze Poland.[86]

But these were pipedreams. The harsh reality was that unified Germany now dominated the military-diplomatic scene and that Austria-Hungary would have to adjust to this. At home, the situation persuaded the emperor to seek reconciliation with the Czechs, and to this end he appointed a cabinet under the able Count Hohenwart to open negotiations. This encouraged the Slavs and infuriated the Germans and the Magyars. At this point, however, the Ogulin mutiny aborted prospects of settlement. Hohenwart was dismissed and the German Liberals returned to power in Vienna.

Nonetheless, reconciliation with the new Germany had to be accomplished and to carry out this policy Andrássy replaced Beust in November 1871. Like most Magyars, Andrássy regarded Russia as a potential danger, but for the moment he had to accommodate Bismarck who was willing to foster friendship with the Dual Monarchy, though he insisted on preserving his close ties with Russia. A series of monarchical visits to the various capitals provided the machinery. By 1873, on the surface at least, the old amity between the "three northern courts," once the cornerstone of Metternich's system, had been resurrected in the form of the Three Emperors' Alliance.

In appearance the breach between the Habsburg Empire and Russia that had existed since the Crimean War was healed. But the tsar still disliked and distrusted Francis Joseph, and Russia's leaders were leary of Magyar hostility. The Austrian military, however, were delighted. Albrecht wanted an outright alliance with Russia against Germany and was so insistent in pressing his views that Andrássy, regarding this as an interference in his own sphere, complained to the emperor who backed his foreign minister.[87] Forgetting his differences with Albrecht, Kuhn now openly attacked Andrássy and accused him of endangering Russian support because of his own anti-Russian feeling. Kuhn, however, found out that Albrecht would not back him and on this issue Beck joined Albrecht. Faced by opposition from Andrássy, Albrecht, and Beck, Kuhn found himself in an untenable position. He remained in office to present the military budget to an economy-minded *Reichsrat* in 1873, but was obliged to resign in June 1874.[88]

When Kuhn left office the future evolution of the joint army had been determined. Much of his term in office had been spent in conflict with Albrecht and overall Albrecht had won out. And while much of the conflict had been personal, there also had been a fundamental difference about the future character and role of the joint army. Kuhn had pressed for change and modernization on the western European pattern, while Albrecht had stood for tradition and preservation of the army primarily as a guardian of the dynasty. His victory signified that the new Austro-Hungarian army would continue the traditional system and methods of the "old" Austrian army and only change when it became absolutely necessary.

Perhaps this was, in any case, unavoidable. Kuhn's brand of efficiency, combined with his disdain towards Magyars and Slavs, would not have solved the nationality problem and most likely would have aggravated it. The army could not change the basic political structure of the Dual Monarchy, and perhaps Albrecht's insistence on a dynastic army was the only feasible course.

Still, by 1874 the army had only partially recovered from defeat. The *Ausgleich* had solved the most pressing political issue, but it had not really augmented the military posture of the monarchy. Moreover, the special status accorded to Hungary had alienated the Slavic peoples. Within the army the feuds between the leading figures had created much ill feeling and delayed some important reforms, such as the development of an effective general staff. Moreover, it had been shown that the industrial development of the Habsburg Monarchy had fallen behind and that it still was not able to produce first-class heavy weapons. In short, the military posture of the Dual Monarchy remained weak, and if it were to conduct an active foreign policy, it would require an alliance with a first-rate power.

7

The Army and the Balkans: 1874-1881

During the first seven years following the *Ausgleich,* the Austro-Hungarian army was preoccupied with internal reorganization, but between 1874 and 1881 external events and actual operations of war dominated the scene. The army fought two major campaigns in the Balkans, the only fighting it was to see until 1914, while conflicts of interest with Russia brought the monarchy to the brink of war and forced a reassessment of strategy. The weakness revealed by this reevaluation contributed to the country's fateful decision to enter an alliance with Germany.

After 1870, although France was torn by internal dissension and its army was weak, there existed no great unresolved problems in western Europe. On the Balkan peninsula, however, there was dangerous national unrest straining the Alliance of the Three Emperors. By the early 1870s Russia had recovered from her Crimean defeat and embarked once again on a forward policy in the Balkans that appeared to threaten the ramshackle Ottoman Empire. As Metternich before them, Beust and Andrássy believed that the continued existence of the Ottoman Empire was essential for the security of the Habsburg Monarchy. They feared Russian domination of the Balkans and were apprehensive about the rise of any large South Slav state in that region because of the dangerous attraction this would present to the Slavs within the Dual Monarchy. "The creation of such a state," Beust declared, "would produce new centers of attraction which naturally would arouse the inhabitants of our southeastern provinces . . . and thus pose great dangers to the vital interests of the monarchy."[1] Andrássy went further. He disliked a possible Austro-Russian partition of the Balkans because this would add more South Slavs to the population of the empire and prejudice Hungary's favored position. As far as possible Andrássy wanted to strengthen Habsburg influence and prevent Russian expansion on the Balkans by peaceful means, but he would not have shrunk from an appeal to arms.

But there were groups in the Dual Monarchy which opposed war with Russia and strongly favored a partition of the Ottoman Empire. Many of the South Slavs under Habsburg rule wished to include their fellow Slavs in the empire which might then be reconstructed into a triune Austro-Hungarian-Slavic state. Even more important was the attitude of the emperor and the military. Francis Joseph and the soldiers, above all Albrecht and Beck, but also an influential group of slavophile generals, felt that Andrássy was too much influenced by Hungarian dislike of Russia. And while they too were prepared to resist unilateral Russian domination of the Balkans, they favored partition. Such a course would recoup lost prestige, recompense the dynasty for the lands lost in Italy, and, perhaps as an afterthought, by adding to the weight of the Slavic population in the empire, help to roll back Magyar pretensions. Some ambitious soldiers dreamed of an Austrian window to the east, an outlet to the Aegean and control of Salonica.[2]

As their immediate object, these groups wanted to acquire the provinces of Bosnia and Hercegovina, adjacent to Croatia and Dalmatia, where a warlike Christian Slav population simmered with discontent under Turkish rule. In the past, South Slav nationalists, mainly Serbs, had hoped that an insurrection here would produce Serbia's intervention and also, by bringing in volunteers from the Slav *Grenzer* regiments, become the opening episode in the creation of a great South Slav state comprised of Serbia, Bosnia-Hercegovina, and the South Slav parts of the Habsburg realm. Such schemes were current between 1845 and 1870 and they greatly alarmed the military authorities in Vienna.[3] Under these circumstances it was not surprising that Austrian generals repeatedly urged that these provinces should be occupied, both as security for the Austrian possessions on the Adriatic and as a way to forestall disruptive Serb schemes. In 1854 the old Quartermaster-General Staff drew up plans for the seizure of Bosnia,[4] and two years later Radetzky, the monarchy's most influential soldier, strongly urged such a move. "The possession of Istria and Dalmatia," he wrote, "makes it imperative for Austria to obtain both Bosnia and Belgrade."[5] Such feelings were widely shared in the army at that time.[6]

As it was, the Italian and German wars prevented the realization of these ambitions, but after 1867 the military raised the project anew. Beck in particular was convinced that the Italian and German questions were closed and that the future of the monarchy lay in the Balkans. As early as 1869 he sent a memorandum to the emperor recommending that in case of a political change on the Balkans, especially in the event of a Serb-Montenegrin victory over the Turks, Austria would have to seize Bosnia-Hercegovina "unless Dalmatia was to wither away."[7] The uprising in the Krisvosije, which he and others blamed on foreign machinations, strengthened his convictions, and when his close friend and confidant Rodich became governor of Dalmatia, active support was given to pro-Austrian elements in Bosnia-Hercegòvina.

The generals' concern about Bosnia-Hercegovina was complicated by the rise of Pan-Slavism in Russia. Although that movement never was endorsed by the tsarist government and was more effective as a cultural rather than a political force, it nonetheless augmented the apprehensions felt in Vienna. Russian agents were suspected at work among the western South Slavs, though in fact Russia's connections here were of the slenderest. Even so, it was true that certain groups in the Serb Principality and in Austrian Slavonia were eager to exploit any trouble in the two provinces, and Russian promises or not, the rumor was spreading that if large-scale fighting broke out the great Slavic tsar would send money, munitions, and perhaps even soldiers.[8]

And Bosnia-Hercegovina was ripe for revolt. The two provinces were held in a state of semi-feudal serfdom by a Moslem Serb landlord class which mercilessly exploited both Christian and Moslem peasants. In addition, the Christians labored under special legal and social disabilities. At this time, out of a total population of some 1.2 million, 40 percent were Moslem, 42 percent Orthodox, and 18 percent Catholic. The Catholics were especially susceptible to Austrian propaganda and looked to the Habsburgs as their protectors. Several times in the last decades there had been risings in these provinces, and the Turks had promised to make reforms. But nothing was done. Continuing turmoil in the provinces would provide Austria with the opportunity for intervention.

In June 1873 the commanding general in Agram, Feldmarschall Leutnant Anton Baron Mollinary, reported that a number of refugees, fleeing from Turkish mistreatment, had entered Croatia.[9] Andrássy was favorably inclined to the Porte and therefore reluctant to do anything, but when additional refugees arrived, he made representations in Constantinople and urged amelioration of conditions in the two provinces. Meanwhile, however, the expansion-minded military men saw their opportunity. Propaganda among the Catholic clergy was stepped up, and in March 1875 Beck and Rodich persuaded the emperor to tour Dalmatia, a move considered by the well-informed Mollinary as an open invitation to revolt.[10] During the imperial tour, April to May 1875, there were carefully staged demonstrations by the local inhabitants and deputations from Bosnia-Hercegovina appeared to plead for Austrian protection. Prince Nicholas of Montenegro greeted the party at Cattaro and appeared ready to support Austrian aspirations.[11]

In early July 1875 came the expected uprising. It began in southern Hercegovina, but quickly spread north into Bosnia. Although there were allegations that the rising had been engineered by foreign agents, Austrian, Russian, or Serb, depending on the nationality of the commentator, it appears that the initial risings were spontaneous protests by Christian merchants and peasants against heavy taxation and oppressive rule.[12] There were reports that some rebel groups wanted to come under Habsburg rule and carried black and yellow flags. The great majority of the rebels, however, wanted to join either Serbia or Bosnia. There appeared the possibility that the revolt might turn into a national struggle for liberation which would challenge Austria-Hungary's vital interests.

For the moment, both Vienna and St. Petersburg tried to quarantine the fire. Although there was a great amount of popular sympathy for the Christian insurgents both in the Slavic lands of the Dual Monarchy and in Russia, the governments proclaimed their neutrality. Serbia and Montenegro were warned against intervention, while the states of the League of the Three Emperors pressed for reforms, hoping that these would calm the revolt. Such a policy was not popular everywhere. In Russia, Pan-Slav circles argued for a more active line, while in Austria-Hungary, Slavic groups tried to provide assistance to the insurgents. To be sure, the Budapest government sternly put down such attempts within its territorial jurisdiction, but in Dalmatia Rodich took no such action. Dalmatia became both a refuge and a resupply point for the insurgents. Indeed, Rodich was advised from Vienna, probably by Beck, that he was to make preliminary preparations for Austrian intervention in the two provinces. But for the moment, Andrássy, reviving the dread specter of South Slav nationalism, was able to persuade the emperor to halt the "enterprise of the military." He even obtained an order withdrawing units composed of Slav soldiers from the immediate frontier zone.[13] But this did not solve the fundamental question—what was to become of

Bosnia-Hercegovina? Even Andrássy was determined to prevent the establishment of a large national South Slav state on the southeastern borders of the Dual Monarchy and, rather than let these provinces fall to Serbia, he was prepared to take them over. Therefore, military contingency plans were initiated. On July 30, 1875, the emperor informed Mollinary that he had been selected to lead the occupation troops if and when such a move became necessary. The emperor commanded Mollinary to begin staff preparations, because, as he added, "we cannot allow these provinces to fall into other hands than our own."[14]

Although Austria-Hungary's official policy was still non-intervention, the military's determination to find a pretext for intervention in the continuing turmoil soon clashed with Andrássy's desire for neutrality. On instructions from Andrássy, Rodich allowed Ottoman troops to use the Adriatic ports to unload troops and supplies and move them across Austrian territory into the combat zone.[15] At the same time, however, he aided Hercegovinian refugees in Dalmatia, shipped supplies to Montenegro, and aided that principality in the import of arms to the insurgents. Early in June 1875 an astonished Austrian officer witnessed an Austro-Hungarian steamer unload eight thousand Wänzel rifles and 2 million rounds of ammunition at Cattaro which were promptly picked up by native bands and carried into the hinterland.[16] Rodich continued to provide direct assistance to the rebels even after Serbia and Montenegro, driven by popular pressure, drifted towards war with the Porte. Arms and supply dumps for the insurgents were established, apparently with the knowledge and approval of the governor's superiors, in Dalmatia.[17]

Military enthusiasm, popular feeling in Serbia and Montenegro, and Pan-Slav agitation in Russia combined to wreck Andrássy's pacification attempts. In fact, the revolt soon spread further. In April 1876 Bulgaria rose in rebellion, and the hard-pressed Turks reacted with considerable ferocity. For the moment, however, their cruel repression of the insurgents left the Ottoman Empire isolated in Europe. At this moment the Russian general Cherniaev arrived in Belgrade, followed by several hundred Russian volunteers. Their arrival heartened the pro-Russian faction in Serbia and weighted the scales towards war. To counterbalance Russia's growing influence, the Austrian government stepped up its covert efforts in Bosnia. Money was spent liberally, and the Catholic clergy was intensively cultivated, but with small results.[18] Austrian apprehensions became even more acute when Serbia and Montenegro signed a military alliance on June 16 and declared war against Turkey on July 30, 1875.

Cherniaev, in fact, had little official backing, but even so the spectacle of a Russian general leading a Serb army in a national war of liberation was regarded with apprehension in Vienna and open hostility in Budapest where *Honvéd* minister Béla Szende declared that two hundred thousand *Honvéd* were ready down to the last button.[19] Austria-Hungary could not tolerate Russian predominance in the western Balkans, and she moved at once to forestall such a possibility. Although influenced by public opinion in Hungary which clamored for war, the political and military leaders of the Dual Monarchy were not prepared to go this far. At this point Austro-Russian relations were good, while German-Russian relations were temporarily strained. Therefore Andrássy was now willing to talk about a partition of the Balkan peninsula into two spheres of interest while Albrecht once again hoped to obtain Russian support against Germany. During a visit to St. Petersburg in December 1875, the archduke cautiously raised the prospect of an alliance directed against Germany, but the tsar had a healthy respect for Germany's martial prowess and did not respond to the overture.[20] Even so, in the spring of 1876 the Austro-Hungarian general staff prepared the last serious war plan, Case D, against Germany.[21]

More importantly, the tsar was eager to remove a possible Austrian threat against his right flank in case of an involvement in the Balkans and he was willing to come to terms regarding a possible spheres-of-interest agreement. In July 1876 Andrássy met with Prince Alexander Gorchakow, the Russian foreign minister, at Reichstadt. No written agreements were signed and the details of their conversation are disputed. It appears, however, that with a Serb-Montenegrin victory expected, Andrássy accepted a partition of the Ottoman Empire. Constantinople was to become a "free city." Russia was to acquire Bessarabia, Austria was to occupy Bosnia-Hercegovina, while Bulgaria, Rumania, and Albania were to become autonomous states.[22] But despite this agreement, neither side was sure of the other's intentions in the event of a major crisis. Russia made soundings in Berlin as to whether Germany would provide support in case of a showdown with Austria. Bismarck would have liked to have evaded a definite answer, but when pressed, replied that Germany would remain neutral, though he added the warning that a "permanent weakening of Austria is contrary to our interests."[23] At the same time the general staff in Vienna once again studied the problems arising out of a possible conflict with Russia.

War plans against Russia had been formulated by Hess in 1854 and had been updated by John in 1874. At that time John had suggested that Austria-Hungary should take advantage of her interior lines and spoil Russia's superior mobilization capacity by an attack from Galicia. John rejected the concept of concentrating in Transylvania and argued that a decision could only be achieved on the Galician front.[24] In the fall of 1876 Feldmarschall Leutnant Anton Baron Schönfeld, chief of the general staff since June, prepared a war plan which accepted John's basic premises. "It would be advantageous," he wrote, "to have Germany, which flanks Russia, as our ally, but this does not appear likely because of the close relationship between Berlin and St. Petersburg."[25] Also, to offset Russian numerical superiority, British and Turkish aid would be highly desirable. But, he concluded, this at best was uncertain, and the Dual Monarchy had to be prepared to fight alone.

Schönfeld estimated that Russia initially would deploy twenty-nine divisions against Austria-Hungary and could reinforce these up to forty-one divisions within a short time. The Dual Monarchy had thirty-two active divisions, and would have to retain four on guard against Italy, three against Serbia, and two in Transylvania. In addition, there also were nine *Landwehr/Honvéd* divisions, but these would be matched by mobilized Russian reserves. Therefore the problem was how to fight against a numerically stronger enemy. The solution proposed by Schönfeld was to conduct an offensive defense.

In common with most contemporary strategists, Schönfeld was convinced that the course of a future war would consist of rapid mobilization and deployment, followed by a major and decisive encounter. And against Russia, such a battle could only be fought in Galicia. "There," Schönfeld wrote, "lies the decision." He rejected suggestions that the army should stand on the defensive in the Carpathians. That mountain range, he pointed out, could be easily traversed; assuming the defensive there would also mean sacrificing Galicia and jeopardizing Cracow, the monarchy's main concentration point. The best course of action, Schönfeld concluded, was to utilize the advantage of rapid mobilization and interior lines to mount an offensive which would disrupt Russian deployment. Then, having interposed the Austrian army between the various Russian forces, one would be able to deal with the divided enemy armies in turn. The concepts advanced by Schönfeld, the decisive character of the Galician front, the need for rapid mobilization and deployment followed by a spoiling attack to disrupt the Russian dispositions, became a basic part of all Austro-Hungarian war plans up to 1914.

Beck and Albrecht, however, remained daunted by the prospect of war with Russia. They submitted a joint memorandum to the emperor warning that such a conflict would be extended and that the monarchy did not have the resources to sustain it.[26] Nonetheless, Beck had not given up his expansionist objectives. In a second memorandum, dated December 1876, he declared that Austria's major foreign policy goal, roughly described as a drive toward Salonica, should not be abandoned, but that it should be achieved in cooperation with Russia.[27]

In the event, the situation changed when Serbia suffered a crushing defeat in September 1876. Suddenly the Ottoman Empire, the "Sick Man of Europe," seemed fearfully healthy and threatening. This naturally agitated the Pan-Slavs who now pressed for direct intervention, and Tsar Alexander and Gorchakow, who previously had hoped to avoid war, grew more bellicose. At the same time the British, who all along had chosen to believe that the Balkan troubles were the result not of Turkish oppression but of Pan-Slav agitation, showed signs of willingness to stop a Russian move to the south. For the moment, however, the powers continued to negotiate and in December a conference was held at Constantinople to discuss new reform proposals.

Because of British hostility, it became more urgent than ever for Russia to secure her right flank. In January and March 1877, Austria-Hungary and Russia made written agreements, the Budapest Convention and the Additional Act of Vienna. Austria-Hungary promised benevolent neutrality and Russia promised not to create a large Slav state. Meanwhile Serbia and Montenegro, which had been forced to make peace, were to remain neutral. Austria-Hungary was to acquire Bosnia-Hercegovina; the fate of the Sanjak of Novi Bazar, a small strip of territory separating Serbia and Montenegro, was to be decided later. Russia was to acquire Bessarabia, occupy Bulgaria temporarily, and predominate at Constantinople. Thus, Andrássy accepted the partition of Turkey.

With these arrangements completed, the Russian government could now launch its war. After making an agreement on passage with Rumania, the tsar declared war on the Porte on April 24, 1878, proclaiming that his sole object was to improve the sorry conditions of the sultan's Christian subjects. Meanwhile, Austria-Hungary prepared to collect her share of the bargain. On April 20, a military conference in Vienna drew up plans for the occupation of the two provinces. There were to be two columns. The main column, one corps commanded by Mollinary, was to move south from Croatia, while a second column, one division strong, was to enter the Hercegovina from Dalmatia.[28]

It generally was expected that the Turks would not be able to withstand the armies of the tsar and at first such expectations were borne out. The Russian advance reached the Danube in June and continued south to the Balkan mountains. The occupation of Bosnia-Hercegovina appeared to be close at hand and from Vienna orders went out to ready the units earmarked for this operation.[29] But relations between Austria-Hungary and Russia were turning sour. As her armies pushed southward, Russia was beginning to do things with a high hand. And while Andrássy was determined to live up to the Budapest Convention and refused an alliance suggested by England, he did consider ways and means to limit the effects of a probable Russian-imposed peace.[30] During a session of the council of imperial ministers on July 31, he suggested that, if necessary, Russia could be compelled to moderate her designs by an Austrian threat against her lines of communications in Rumania. Such a move, the minister pointed out, had worked in 1855.[31] Both Albrecht and Beck, however, were against the possibility of war with Russia. They agreed that success might be achieved on the Danube, but also warned that a conflict with Russia, once begun, would have to be fought out in Galicia where the chances of success were doubtful at best. Only one thing would be certain: by her perfidious action, Austria would earn Russia's permanent distrust.[32]

The military prevailed and the council merely authorized in principle the mobilization of two corps for use against Serbia, a possible attack by Italy, or the occupation of the two provinces. The time for the actual activation of these two corps was, however, left to the discretion of the foreign minister, and when in August 1877 Beck pressed for mobilization, Andrássy declared that the situation did not warrant it.[33] Russia then was stalled in her advance and the minister did not believe then or later that the occupation of Bosnia-Hercegovina required major military commitments. Moreover, in justice to Andrássy, the minister had not really contemplated war against Russia in July. He was as much aware as the military that "a war between the two empires would not be over in one campaign . . . and would probably end with the destruction or collapse of one of the belligerents." Andrássy was not prepared to take such a risk without "reasons that make such a death struggle inevitable."[34] Russian domination of the Balkans or the creation of a large Slav state would constitute such a reason. Here Andrássy and the military were in accord and it seems likely that the soldiers' feelings that Andrássy wanted a war against Russia were largely motivated by their suspicions that the former rebel would not be adverse to seeking revenge for 1849.

As it was, the need for Austrian preventive measures was delayed for some time. At the end of July 1877, the Russians encountered stiff Turkish resistance at Plevna and were stalled in front of this fortress for over four months. They even were forced to request aid from other Balkan nations. But Russia was able to throw in additional troops and finally the surrender of Plevna on December 10 marked the beginning of the end for Turkish resistance. Russian troops reached Sofia on January 4, 1878, and were close to Constantinople when an armistice was signed on the thirty-first. The terms imposed reflected the expansionist peace program approved by Tsar Alexander II in December. Without a doubt, they clearly contravened the letter and spirit of the Budapest Convention. They envisaged a greater Bulgaria and mentioned nothing about Habsburg claims to Bosnia-Hercegovina. When Andrássy realized that despite her repeated assurances Russia intended to go back on her word, he was incensed, and even the peace-minded emperor was angry. Although Austria-Hungary still refused to enter into definite commitments with Great Britain, Andrássy sounded out Bismarck about his position in case the Dual Monarchy went to war with Russia. At the same time, he once again asked the military to consider the probable course of such a conflict. However, though the British fleet was ordered to Constantinople in mid-February and Bismarck indicated that he was ready to uphold Austria-Hungary's vital interests, the generals still were unwilling to risk war with Russia.

On January 15, 1878, a ministerial council was summoned. The emperor presided and as usual Beck and Albrecht were present. Aware of the soldiers' distaste for a bellicose course, Andrássy tried to limit the discussion to technical questions.[35] He pictured the Russian position before Constantinople as extremely vulnerable and argued that a threat to their line of communications would force them to withdraw from the Balkans. The experience of recent wars, the minister maintained, showed that conflicts between major powers were of short duration, a reversal of his previous assessment, and that there was no danger of intervention from Italy or Germany. The military disagreed. War with Russia was sure to be prolonged, and Italy's intention was not clear. Moreover, the generals were divided on eventual dispositions of the army. Beck advocated an invasion from Transylvania, while Albrecht favored a thrust from the Bukovina. Schönfeld was inclined to support Albrecht, but urged that at least one corps be retained in Transylvania. Because no agreement could be reached, internal military discussion continued for a week. During this time the soldiers became more and more alarmed by the prospect of war, though they now feared that little could be done to arrest developments. "We are moving towards war and disaster," Beck noted in his diary.[36] On February 7 and 12 the ministerial council met again. Andrássy urged immediate and total mobilization, but both the joint finance minister Leopold Baron Hofmann and the Reichskriegsminister Feldzeugmeister Arthur Count Bylandt-Rheidt declared that this would require 310 million florins for the first three months alone. Although the British had mentioned subsidies, Andrássy did not bring this into the discussion, and when the emperor too expressed himself in favor of caution, the meeting reached no final decision.[37]

Even so, Austrian mobilization preparations continued. It was decided to form three armies against Russia and a fourth, an army of observation, against Italy. Albrecht was named commander in chief and appointments, awaiting only signature and date, were drawn up for the army, corps, and divisional commanders.[38] By the end of February the necessary administrative measures were completed and an order of battle drawn up.[39] Still, no actual troop call-ups were made. The general staff pointed out that without deployment, mobilization was useless, and that deployment would carry the state to the brink of war.[40] But England was prepared to provide subsidies only if Austria-Hungary decreed full mobilization, and Beck argued strongly against such a fatal step. "For what purpose," he asked the emperor on February 14, "is this war to be fought? If Your Majesty demands half of Turkey to Salonica then we know what we are fighting for, but merely to expel the Russians is not reason enough." Moreover, asserted Beck, the pressure for war originated from "Hungarian politics" and the desire "to avenge Világos."[41]

Apparently this personal appeal persuaded Francis Joseph. When during the ministerial council of February 24, Andrássy again asked for war credits, he found no support and merely was authorized to request a credit of 60 millions from the

Delegations.⁴² And this credit was, in fact, intended to cover the occupation of Bosnia-Hercegovina. Andrássy was left with the option of either resigning or going to the international conference at Berlin, strongly urged by Bismarck, to secure his claims. Ironically, before the Congress of Berlin actually convened, the military became more bellicose. By this time Turkey had reinforced her troops before Constantinople and had also erected strong fortifications. Meantime the Russian army was beginning to suffer from operating at the end of a long supply line. Therefore, when in May 1878 it looked as if Russia would attempt to bar Austria-Hungary from the strategic Sanjak of Novi Bazar, Beck, just promoted to feldmarschall leutnant, wrote to his friend Rodich that it might be necessary "to use force, regardless of Russia, Serbia, or Montenegro."⁴³ But his was merely talk. The crisis had now definitely moved out of the military into the diplomatic arena.

It now becomes necessary to examine the motives and the reasons why the leading soldiers were so opposed to a confrontation with Russia. The answer lies in two major sets of considerations, one predominantly political and the other military and technical. Political considerations were of a domestic nature as well as of an external one. During this period the army leadership consisted of men who had reached their positions in the wars against Prussia and Italy, and most of them remained antagonistic towards their former enemies. They never were quite convinced of Bismarck's good faith and they respected Russia's military potential. Therefore, while anxious to secure the northeastern frontier and to prevent Russian domination of the Balkans, no leading soldier except Kuhn favored war with Russia during this period. War with Russia was considered an unacceptable military risk and the soldiers still hoped for an alliance against Germany. As late as 1875 Albrecht declared that he would not die happy unless he could once defeat the Prussians in battle, a feeling shared by many senior officers.⁴⁴ Then too, Beck and other generals believed that for Austria-Hungary with her large Slav population, conflict with Russia was particularly risky, while at the same time they continued to distrust the loyalty of the Magyars and suspected devious motives behind the loud Hungarian demands for war.⁴⁵ Finally, the soldiers put little faith in eventual British aid. As Feldmarschall Leutnant Ferdinand Baron Langenau, the monarchy's ambassador in St. Petersburg, put it, in case of war with Russia, England would need an army "which she has not."⁴⁶ At best Great Britain could muster some eighty-five thousand men for a continental campaign, and Austria would have to bear the brunt of the fighting.⁴⁷ To be sure, the British fleet might deter Italy from openly attacking across the Adriatic, but it could do nothing to prevent intrusions by volunteer corps in the mountains.

In fact, relations between Italy and the Dual Monarchy were tense throughout the 1870s and Austrian generals believed that the monarchy was threatened on two fronts. King Victor Emmanuel II of Italy had tried to ease tensions, motivated in part by fear of a French attempt to restore Rome to the pope, but when this danger faded after 1875 there arose again strong pressures to acquire the still "unredeemed" Italian areas of the Dual Monarchy. On the Austro-Hungarian side, however, civilians as well as soldiers were determined to hold the territory salvaged from the defeat of 1866. In April 1868 a commission chaired by Archduke Albrecht met to consider the defense requirements of the new frontier, and as a result new fortifications were built in the Tyrol and in Carinthia.⁴⁸ Because of the financial conditions, however, they were constructed rather cheaply, and in the opinion of one high-ranking engineer officer, were not adequate defenses.[49]

More importantly, Austrian military opinion regarded Italian hostility as an obstacle to Austria's position as a great power. In any major conflict in the East, Austria would have to detach up to one-third of her total strength to watch Italy; she was thus placed, as Schönfeld noted in 1876, in an impossible strategic position.[50] In consequence, the military leaders advocated a preventive war to eliminate Italy once and for all. In December 1876 Albrecht urged war against Italy because of the three potential enemies of the monarchy—Germany, Russia, and Italy—the latter was the most hostile. If Italy were eliminated, Austria would be restored as a great military power because she would be able to deploy all of her forces on one front. War against Italy, the archduke noted, also had "the immense advantage of being inexpensive, because while next to nothing could be obtained in the southeast, contributions and a huge indemnity could be easily procured on the Italian peninsula." Because of all these advantages, Albrecht counseled that nothing should be done to avoid a collision with Italy, and to the contrary, the monarchy should try hard to seize the next opportunity for war.[51] And this was more than talk from an inveterate militarist. Beck also endorsed a preventive war against Italy.[52] Francis Joseph reluctantly agreed, and in the winter of 1877 to 1878, the general staff prepared a plan for an offensive war against Italy. This plan was further elaborated in July 1879. The active divisions were to seize most of northern Italy. Then *Landwehr/Honvéd* troops would be used as an army of occupation, while the regulars would be switched back to the east and southeast.[53]

But despite endorsement by Albrecht and Beck, the emperor would not accept the implementation of these plans. Actual forces on the Italian frontier remained small, and excluding the *Landwehr* and the alpine militia *Landesschützen* in the Tyrol and Vorarlberg, amounted only to twelve battalions of infantry and some fortress artillery companies. When in the summer of 1878 intelligence about irredentist threats was received, the frontier force was increased to eighteen battalions. These proved sufficient to deal with local riots among Austrian Italians, and a plot for the invasion of Tyrol and the region west of the Isonzo organized with the knowledge of some Italian officials failed to materialize.[54]

The second major set of problems making the military cautious of war against Russia was largely an internal military matter. Despite Kuhn's efforts, the Austro-Hungarian military establishment in the later half of the 1870s was not prepared for a major conflict. Both Albrecht and Beck agreed on this and repeatedly warned that the army did not possess the capability to sustain extended hostilities.[55] Knowledgeable foreign observers on the scene shared this opinion. In 1876 Major M. S. Gonne, the British military attaché in Vienna, reported that in the event of war, many of the Slav soldiers in the army would be unreliable, that considerable forces would have to be retained for internal security duties in the South Slav areas, and that Austria would be obliged to stand on the defensive and could provide "little or no help to an ally in want of battalions."[56] But there were other opinions. A noted British military writer, General Hamley, noted in 1878 that the Austrian officer corps was well trained and highly professional, and that the army generally was superior to the Russian. Overall, he concluded, the Austro-Hungarian army would constitute a "very formidable antagonist."[57] But this opinion, especially with regard to the training of the officers, was not shared by Albrecht, who as late as 1884 complained to Beck that he lacked confidence in the competence of the vast majority of corps and divisional commanders.[58]

The archduke's complaint reflected the continued friction and infighting at the highest levels within the army. Although with Kuhn's departure one of the leading contenders for power had disappeared, controversies about the respective competencies of the inspector general, the war minister, and the chief of the general staff continued. Early in 1874 Beck, operating behind the scene, had managed to obtain a temporary reconciliation between Albrecht and John. With Albrecht's reluctant acquiescence, John returned as chief of the general staff and held this post until his death in 1876. John, however, had changed his views. As war minister and chief of the general staff, he had been in favor of giving the general staff very little autonomy; now as chief of the general staff, he expected wider powers and even before he assumed office in February 1874 he asked for greater scope in the new office.[59] At first the emperor refused to give him such powers, but in 1875 John obtained passage of new regulations which allowed the chief of the general staff to submit papers directly to the emperor in matters affecting his office.[60] The war ministers succeeding Kuhn, General der Kavallerie Alexander Baron Koller, 1874 to 1876, and Feldzeugmeister Arthur Graf Bylandt Freiherr zu Rheidt, 1876 to 1878, did not strongly object to the enlarged role of the chief of the general staff, but Albrecht was quick to take offense. And when John presumed to criticize maneuver dispositions made by Albrecht, relations between the two men once again became intolerable.[61]

At that point John's unexpected death resolved a potentially explosive situation. Although there was some speculation that the emperor might choose Beck as John's successor, the choice instead fell on Feldmarschall Leutnant Anton Baron Schönfeld, described by one of his subordinates as a "pleasant and amiable superior who selected his staff solely on the basis of merit without regard to connections."[62] But these very qualifications made Schönfeld the target of criticism by highly placed officers. Albrecht in particular complained that the general was incompetent and Schönfeld, already ill at that time with the disease which killed him in five years, was not strong enough to fight back. Under these circumstances Beck, who carefully maintained good relations with all sides and who also had the ear of the emperor, began to function as a *de facto* chief of the general staff, submitting operational plans and directing policy.[63]

His appellation, "secret chief of the general staff," was indeed appropriate. Beck worked both for his own advancement and for the promotion of the interests of the general staff. In August 1867 he had urged the emperor to institute a general staff on the Prussian pattern and assailed the practice of allowing one officer to hold the two offices of war minister and chief of staff, as Benedek had done and as John was doing.[64] In 1872 and 1873 he made additional proposals. He advocated that the general staff be organized in functional sections, and that greater attention be paid to the critical problems of utilizing the railroads to effect faster mobilization and deployment.[65] Much of this was, of course, beneficial. But at the same time by assuming many of the duties of the chief of the general staff, Beck weakened the position of the incumbent. And because the military chancery lacked the necessary personnel, the additional work was not always done efficiently.

Similar reservations apply to the work of Archduke Albrecht. Despite his undisputed merits as a field commander, his influence on the military establishment was not always beneficial. Born in 1817, Albrecht was no longer young, and his thinking became more and more obsolete. Like his cousin, the emperor, he did not like to hear contrary opinions, and as a result he often was badly informed. This attitude seriously hampered the development of a body of senior officers willing to make decisions on their own. Advancing age made him more and more inflexible and while military apologists have blamed parliamentary obstruction for the retardation and weaknesses of the Austro-Hungarian army, Albrecht, who clung to his post as inspector general until his death in 1895, must also share the blame.[66]

There were yet other factors making the army reluctant to undertake a war against Russia. Overall, the military establishment had nearly reached its projected levels, but many of the reserve units were poorly trained. First-line units generally had been issued the new Werndl rifles, and the field artillery had received its new guns by the end of 1877.[67] But reserve ammunition stocks were low, while the railroad lines and unloading facilities, especially in the strategic northeastern provinces of the monarchy, were still inadequate. The general staff plans counted on speed of mobilization, but in 1878 mobilization and deployment of the field armies was still estimated at over forty-five days.

All these considerations, political and military, explain the lack of bellicosity on the part of the soldiers. In the final analysis, the military were willing to go to war only to prevent the unilateral establishment of Russian hegemony on the Balkans or to prevent Bosnia and Hercegovina from falling to Serbia. But if these provinces could be obtained without conflict with Russia, then the military favored a forward policy.

Such expansionist sentiments, however, were unpopular in Hungary, except for Croatia, and suspect in Austria where the ruling German Liberals were flatly opposed. Only after Andrássy had assured the delegations that the special 60 million florins credit was for general military expenditures, and that no occupation of the provinces was intended, an outright lie, did he receive the requested appropriations.[68] Now, finally, the stage was set. With German and British support, and with Russia willing to abandon Serbia and the western Balkans, the Congress of Berlin on July 13, 1878, authorized the Dual Monarchy to occupy the provinces.

Even before the powers had signed the protocol authorizing this move, Austria-Hungary had begun final preparations and concluded them on July 26. Under the orders of Feldzeugmeister Joseph Baron Philippović (replacing Mollinary who had been removed of command in Croatia after a clash with the Hungarian government), XIII Corps, three divisions strong, had been drawn up on the Save, while Feldmarschall Leutnant Stefan Baron Jovanović, commanding the 18th Infantry Division, stood ready in southern Dalmatia.[69] On July 30 the troops crossed into Bosnia-Hercegovina, advancing in four columns, three from the north and one from the southwest.

The army had expected little or no resistance or perhaps even a welcome, and Andrássy, in an unguarded moment, had claimed that the operation could be carried out by a squadron of hussars and a regimental band.[70] However, instead of welcoming the troops as liberators, Moslems as well as Orthodox took up arms and, aided by some regular Turkish units disobeying instructions from the Porte, defied the invaders. North and northwest Bosnia and parts of the Hercegovina around Livna and near the Montenegrin frontier were defended by organized forces in battalion strength provided with artillery. In all, the Austrians later estimated enemy strength at ninety-three thousand, though not all took the field at any one time.[71] At Maglaj in northern Bosnia, the Austrian advance guard was ambushed and sustained considerable casualties. Even more serious was the setback near Tuszla, where on August 10 the 20th Division had to retire and wait for reinforcements. Logistic arrangements, a weak point in the campaigns of 1859 and 1866, broke down again, and at times ammunition ran short.[72] Even so, the advance was pressed and after artillery prepared the way, Sarajevo was stormed on August 19.

The occupation of the Hercegovina encountered fewer obstacles at first, but continuing resistance in Bosnia led to the resumption of armed opposition in the south. By August 8 Vienna had already decided to mobilize additional forces. The 36th Division was moved from Croatia to Bosnia and the 4th, 13th, 31st, and 33rd divisions, as well as *Jäger* battalions and auxiliary troops, were mobilized. By October 1 the newly formed Second Army under Philippović numbered 159 battalions, 29 squadrons, 26 field and 21 mountain batteries, 37 technical companies and various auxiliary detachments, for a total of 159,380 men and 292 guns. In all, Austria-Hungary mobilized 250,000 men, nearly a third of her entire war strength.[72] On October 19, 1878, the occupation was declared completed. Austrian casualties stood at 5,198 killed, wounded, or missing, including 178 officers.[73]

After the conclusion of the campaign, the planning and execution of operations came in for a great deal of external and internal criticism. Andrássy, eager to explain away his overly optimistic pronouncements, blamed the army for having mismanaged the campaign. By moving too slowly, the army had allowed local resistance to become organized; in particular, Andrássy charged Philippović with deliberately holding back subordinate commanders until he could arrive in person to claim the lion's share in the conquest of Sarajevo.[74] The army countered that Andrássy, for reasons of prestige, had deliberately persuaded the emperor to allow only inadequate forces at the beginning, that the appropriations had been too small, and that Philippović had repeatedly requested additional troops before the occupation but that his requests had been denied.[75] More important, perhaps, was the internal criticism. Even Beck, who significantly had issued the operational orders, admitted that the initial troop requirements had been estimated at too low a figure.[76] Other officers were more sharply critical. Staff and intelligence work were described as poor, tactical groupings had been badly handled, the mountain troops lacked proper equipment, and supply arrangements had broken down.[77] Conrad, who participated in the operations as a junior officer, claimed that the enemy had been treated too leniently and that the troops had not received energetic leadership, while Auffenberg, later a war minister, claimed that the reserve components had shown poor march performance and discipline.[78]

Although much of this criticism was undoubtedly justified, the Second World War experience of partisan warfare in the same region suggests that the Austro-Hungarian forces actually accomplished a difficult task with considerable dispatch. While the army was superior in numbers and weapons to the enemy, its strength differential was far below the ratio considered necessary in the twentieth century to fight a successful guerrilla campaign. As it was, the occupation was a creditable performance and restored some of the confidence lost in 1866 and 1870.

Total pacification, of course, proved more difficult. Sporadic resistance continued in some areas and troops in the occupied zone remained on a war footing. In the first years, the provinces remained under the control of military government. Philippović, the son of an Orthodox *Grenzer* family, was considered too friendly towards the Serbs and too independent towards Vienna, and he was relieved in November 1878. At the same time, the Second Army was dissolved. Feldzeugmeister Wilhelm Herzog von Württemberg was named as the first military governor with Jovanović, of Catholic *Grenzer* origin, as his second in command.[79] Beck visited Bosnia-Hercegovina in November. He concluded that the region should be secured by a network of fortified posts, but that rapid progress was being made towards establishing order, and he assured the emperor that within a short time it would be possible to raise indigenous troops.[80]

On the last score, however, Beck was overly optimistic. Although the Austro-Hungarian administration carried out an extensive modernization program, first handled by the military and later by the Joint Ministry of Finance, it preserved the anachronistic land system which existed under Turkish rule. By 1881, though public security was much improved, there was growing dissatisfaction. The Orthodox were discontent with the character of Habsburg administration which appeared to combine the worst aspects of the Turkish and the Austrian bureaucracy, while Moslems felt that their religion and customs were being violated. Refusing to heed the signs, the military now resolved to introduce conscription. They had never really forgotten the humiliation of 1869; they expected no resistance in Bosnia-Hercegovina, and military garrisons now ringed the recalcitrant Krisvosije. If there were resistance, and some soldiers hoped that there would be, an example could be set to wipe out the memory of the past defeat.[81]

In March 1881 the authorities announced their intention to introduce conscription in the occupied zone as well as in the Krisvosije. The necessary regulations were published on November 4. To appease the Moslems, provisions were made to respect their religious traditions and observances.[82] As expected, and perhaps even intended, this led to a rising in the Krisvosije. To the dismay of the military, however, the revolt spread to the Hercegovina and into southern Bosnia. But this time the army had learned from its earlier mistakes. Outlying small posts were evacuated at once.[83] Feldzeugmeister Hermann Freiherr von Dahlen, commanding in Bosnia-Hercegovina, established an inland cordon isolating the Krisvosije, and reinforcements were ordered in before there was any major fighting.[84] Local volunteers, called *Pandurs,* were enlisted from the friendly Catholic population.[85] Operations against the rebels were pursued with determination, even brutality. In some cases villages suspected of sheltering the insurgents were burned down and the male inhabitants shot.[86] The troops, all regulars this time, adapted to guerrilla war. Uniforms were rough and ready; officers sensibly gave up their distinctive caps, sashes, and sabers in order not to provide targets for marksmen.[87] Special volunteer units, *Streifcorps* locally known and hated as *Strafuni,* were formed for search and destroy missions.[88]

It was an all-out effort. Even diplomacy was used to isolate the guerrillas. Although neither Montenegro nor the Ottoman Empire would openly aid the rebels, they did little to prevent them from slipping across the frontiers for sanctuary and supplies. Serbia, however, cooperated with the Austrians. In June 1881

Prince Milan had signed a secret treaty which made him the virtual vassal of the Habsburgs; now he attempted to seal his frontiers and passed on intelligence about the insurgents.[89]

Even so, the campaign revealed shortcomings in the military establishment. By February 1882 the troops were running short of ammunition, and the War Ministry had to issue a directive ordering its conservation.[90] The number of troops engaged had to be raised repeatedly and by May no fewer than three divisions each were deployed in Dalmatia and Bosnia-Hercegovina. In addition, a naval squadron was employed to police the coastline. All this was expensive, and the government was forced to ask special credits from the delegations. Total costs amounted to over 30 millions. But the effort paid off. By May the troops were able to recapture most rebel-held territory and the revolt, cut off from outside support, was brought under control in May, though some skirmishes were reported as late as August.

Troops remained on the alert in the occupation zone and Dalmatia and the *Streifcorps* continued to be used as a mobile surveillance force.[91] However, except for local incidents, the country was at peace and conscription was introduced without further incidents. Within a few years, Moslem troops from Bosnia-Hercegovina, the famed *Bosniaken,* were considered among the best fighting regiments of the monarchy.

Even before these events had taken place, the Dual Monarchy entered into a new diplomatic and military alignment which dominated the final decades of the Habsburg Empire. Despite the fact that the Congress of Berlin achieved a peaceful settlement of the Balkan crisis, it signified, for all purposes, the end of the Alliance of the Three Emperors. And while this caused Andrássy little concern, Bismarck was alarmed. In August 1879 negotiations for an Austro-German alliance began in earnest, and on October 7 the famous Dual Alliance was signed. In accordance with Andrássy's desires, it was directed against Russia. In case of attack by Russia against one of the two empires, both were obliged to aid the other with all of their resources and to conclude only a joint peace.

The alliance gave Andrássy the powerful support which he had deemed necessary to beef up the military potential of the monarchy. But this did not make Austria-Hungary a great power, and the state was increasingly hard-pressed to keep up its pretensions. From 1871 to 1914 armed peace prevailed in Europe, depending largely on a balance of power. To maintain this balance, the powers increased in an ever-accelerating armament race which, as the ruling circles in Austria-Hungary were well aware, the monarchy could not sustain over a long period. The only remedy would have been, and this too is by no means certain, a radical solution of the internal, predominantly national problems in the state. And this Austria-Hungary could not do.

8

The Era of Beck and Albrecht: 1881-1895

Austria-Hungary had reasserted her great power status during the Balkan crisis, but the real test of a great power is her strength for war, and in the closing decades of the nineteenth century the Dual Monarchy found it increasingly difficult to keep up in the European armament race. Unable to fully exploit her manpower potential, only slowly developing an industrial capacity, divided by national rivalries, and hampered by a cumbersome political structure, the empire gradually was falling behind in relative military strength. Both Albrecht and Beck wrestled with this problem, but were unable to find a solution.

Maintaining a great power posture meant that Austria-Hungary was likely to become involved in every major European crisis. Although Andrássy had steadfastly declined to give Bismarck guarantees in case of a French attack, the possibility of a future Franco-Russian alliance could not be ruled out, and fear of war on several fronts haunted the monarchy's military leaders. In March 1880 Beck gave his assessment of the "military political situation."[1] International tensions, he observed, remained high and all nations, especially Germany, France, Italy, and Russia, were continually augmenting their armaments. Russia remained the most likely opponent for the Dual Monarchy. At the moment, he conceded, this threat was only potential, and despite the large number of Russian troops concentrated on the western frontier, the present tsar did not want war.[2] Pan-Slav pressure, however, Beck wrote, might push him into a warlike course. And while in such an event the German alliance would come into operation, Beck warned that Germany would be hard pressed by simultaneous war against France and Russia, despite the excellence of her military establishment. Russia, moreover, might very well foment troubles with Italy, now rapidly increasing her armed forces, and also create complications on the Balkans. A two- or even a three-front war was possible; therefore, it was imperative that the monarchy continue to increase its active army and its war potential.

But to implement Beck's recommendation the emperor and the army needed the support of the two parliaments, and this proved hard to come by. In Austria the German Liberals were furious about the occupation of Bosnia-Hercegovina and their feelings did not improve when the government was also forced to ask for a retrospective allocation of 15 million florins on top of the 60 million which it had originally obtained to cover expenses of the occupation. Early in 1879 the government found itself hard pressed to obtain a ten-year renewal of the 1868 army law from the *Reichsrat*. Concerned about the continuing imperial deficits, the economy-minded Liberals opposed the ten-year proviso which determined the army's peace and war strength. They favored slashing military expenditures and even attempted to lower the peace-time establishment to two hundred thirty thousand men. In order to deal with the Liberals, the emperor appointed an old friend, Eduard Franz Josef Count Taaffe, as prime minister. By political maneuvering and some chincanery, Taaffe put together a heterogeneous coalition. The Czechs, who for a dozen years had boycotted the *Reichsrat* and received concessions, returned and voted with the government, while the Liberals split and lost power. Passage of the army law was secured.[3] In the long run, however, Taaffe remained in office for fourteen years, and his policies served to escalate the national strife in Austria.

While the *Reichsrat* debated the fate of the army law, the Budapest parliament for once proved acquiescent to the wishes of the imperial military. This action, in curious contrast to previous and later attitudes, was due to the premier, Koloman Tisza, who from 1875 to 1890 dominated Hungarian politics. Although originally an opponent of dualism, he changed his stand and as prime minister was undeviatingly loyal to the settlement of 1867. In 1879, though with some misgivings, he supported the extension of the army law. This, however, did not mean that Tisza did not share the general Magyar desire for a more independent Hungarian role in military affairs and ten years later, when renewal of the army law came up once again, he demanded and received important concessions.[4]

Of course, given the sharply rising costs of armaments in Europe, the army law of 1879 merely held the line, but neither the *Reichsrat* nor the Hungarian parliament were inclined to provide large allocations for the joint military establishment. Although on occasion the Delegations voted extraordinary credits (for instance, almost 7 million in 1884), military spending levelled off at around 100 million florins annually. A memorandum drawn up by the chief of staff in 1892 claimed that in the period 1867 to 1892 Austria-Hungary had spent only about a third as much as Russia, only one-half as much as Germany, and very little more than Italy. Converted into francs, France during this period had spent 23,154,480,000; Russia 22,426,371,000; Germany 14,208,000,000; Austria-Hungary 7,004,511,000, and Italy 6,822,411,000.[5] Austria-Hungary, a British historian concluded, was "slipping òut of the ranks of the great powers."[6]

Actually, the financial position of the Dual Monarchy would have been able to support a larger military expenditure. Although every budget up to 1885 had closed with a deficit, albeit small, in 1889 there was a surplus and in 1892 Austria-Hungary went over to the gold standard. The florin was replaced by the crown at the rate of one gulden for two crowns. By that time, however, the rising nationalist tensions prevented the imperial government from making large military outlays. Irreducible political as well as economic factors then limited the military effort. As Albrecht concluded in 1886, the monarchy could only make very limited moves to improve her military posture. Troops could be shifted, some new cadres created, but not much more was possible.[7]

The necessity to augment the military strength of the monarchy, within the limitations existing, also contributed to the emperor's decision to appoint Beck as chief of the general staff on June 11, 1881. Although Beck's biographer claimed that the general had hoped "that this cup would pass," Beck actually had acted as the real chief of the general staff during Schönfeld's incumbency.[8] Together with Albrecht he was the soldier closest to the emperor and had convinced him that there was "no other servant more loyal, reliable, and honest."[9] Beck knew how to deal with influential men, politicians as well as soldiers. Whenever possible he avoided open conflict and looked for a compromise solution. He had managed to break the deadlock on the military issue during the *Ausgleich* negotiations and had escaped from the bitter fight over the structure of the high command with his relations with Albrecht intact. At the same time he had maintained the friendship of most high-ranking generals. Even so, he never had commanded troops and his appointment caused a certain amount of adverse press comment.[10]

Beck entered his new position under more auspicious circumstances than his predecessors. When his appointment was first broached in March 1881 he asked the emperor for a more precise delineation of the duties and rights of the chief of the general staff.[11] The emperor replied that Beck was "personally under the direct orders of the emperor, but also assistant to the war minister." In fact, the appointment still designated the chief of the general staff as an auxiliary of the War Ministry, but this was largely done to silence parliamentary apprehensions about ministerial responsibility. Beck gained the right of direct access to the emperor and as Albrecht slowly faded out of the picture, Beck gradually gained enormous power. Reichskriegsminister Bylandt-Rheidt acquiesced to Beck's new status and the minister's successors were equally complaisant.[12] In practice, Beck imposed his wishes on the ministers of war and defense. Retaining office for twenty-four years, Beck wielded enormous influence and after Albrecht's death in 1895 he sometimes was considered the "emperor's deputy."[13] Although younger and more flexible than Albrecht, he too grew old in office and towards the end was unable to comprehend the new style of warfare and the new demands it imposed on the army and the state.

But this was yet in the future. For the moment his immediate concern was to strengthen the general staff which he regarded as the "elite of the army." Like almost all military leaders of his time, he believed that future wars would be decided in the first violent collision and therefore he stressed the importance of the active army, of rapid mobilization and deployment. He strengthened the operations and transportation section of the general staff and emphasized hard work and devotion to duty among his officers.[14] Even so, many of the Austro-Hungarian field commanders and line officers continued to regard the general staff with ill-concealed suspicion. Especially at the army and corps level, the Austro-Hungarian staff officer never attained the status of his German counterparts and neither then nor later achieved their decision-making powers.[15]

Continuing resentment against the staff was based in part on the suspicion that it no longer restricted itself to planning but interfered with administration.[16] Even more important, perhaps, were the jealousies aroused by the more rapid promotions gained by officers within the general staff corps. Staff majors and captains usually were six to eight years younger than their comrades in other branches of the service.[17] At the same time, with no more fighting and a restricted budget, promotions once again stagnated in the 1880s. In 1887, for instance, out of 1800 captains in the infantry, only 762 were between the ages of thirty to forty; the rest were older, with 373 between forty-six and sixty. However, of these men, more than 1600 had actual combat experience.[18] Generally speaking, next to the staff, the cavalry promoted the fastest and the artillery the slowest, though it now began to catch up with the infantry.[19]

The army remained short of regular career officers, and since the budgets permitted little expansion of the corps, reserve officers became more and more important. In all, the army had between 17 and 18,000 regular officers, while the number of reserve officers grew rapidly from 5,840 in 1885 to 12,171 in 1892, and remained close to this figure until 1914.[20] Reserve officers were drawn from the ranks of the one-year volunteers, predominantly of German, Magyar, or Czech origins, and Austria furnished more volunteers than Hungary.[21] Not all volunteers worked hard at learning the profession of arms, and substantial numbers failed to pass the required examination. In Austria-Hungary a reserve commission never held the prestige it did in Germany, but for many young intellectuals the year of active duty, during which all problems were temporarily suspended in the service of a remote imperial father figure, was pleasant. Even young Sigmund Freud did his term cheerfully and there were others like Max Vladimir Beck, a future prime minister, who looked back to this year with positive nostalgia.[22]

An increasing complication in the training of the rank and file was the language problem. There were three recognized types of languages, the *Kommandosprache,* the *Dienstsprache,* and the *Regimentssprache.* The first two were German and every recruit was expected to know the eighty words or so necessary for drill movements and also the special military terms necessary for the service. Within each regiment the language spoken by the enlisted men was used for all other purposes, including instruction. Regular officers were expected to learn the language of their regiment. In peacetime this obstacle was not insuperable, though it interfered with postings. In war, however, this might create difficulties. Moreover, instruction, especially in the more complicated tools of modern war, was made more difficult by the continuously low educational level of many soldiers. As late as 1895, 22 percent of the recruits could neither read nor write, compared with 0.2 percent in Germany, 5.5 in France, and slightly over 70 percent in Russia.[23] The army regarded itself, with some justice, as the school of the nation, though this increasingly became an irritant to the more vocal nationalities. Service with the joint army was set at three years, although for reasons of economy soldiers often were placed on permanent leave status after two. Even so, the army opposed legislation reducing the active tour of duty to two years, claiming that the shorter term was inadequate to train effective soldiers and educate responsible citizens.[24]

The military leaders were concerned about the detrimental effects of a shorter term on the allegiance of the rank and file, though perhaps they were reacting to the threat with unwarranted panic. But more important than these considerations was the desire to have the largest number of men available at the shortest notice. Strategic doctrine in the 1880s held that wars would be short and that the decision would be reached in the first great battles. Both Beck and Albrecht had in the past warned that a conflict with Russia would be lengthy, though now they discarded their earlier beliefs. Rapid mobilization and deployment which would ensure local numerical superiority were the keys to victory. And such rapid operations could only be carried out with the troops immediately at hand. Neither the *Landwehr* nor the *Honvéd* were considered combat-ready. Although the Hungarian defense minister, Béla Szende, reported in 1881 that "eventual mobilization could be carried out without any problems,"[25] Albrecht never trusted the *Honvéd* and repeatedly urged its incorporation into the joint army.[26] Moreover, he did not regard the Austrian and the Hungarian second line as prepared for war. "The infantry regiments of the *Landwehr*," he wrote in 1887, "have not reached the state of training and discipline which would permit their employment during the first two weeks of a campaign."[27] Therefore only the active army was really important and even if men were on permanent leave during this last year of duty, they could be recalled on short notice.

Given the attitudes of the two parliaments, any large-scale increase in the joint military establishment, and especially in the size of the peacetime active contingent, was out of the question. Therefore, between 1883 and 1892, the high command was forced to fall back on a number of expedients. It tried to raise the numbers of the joint army slightly and to relieve it of internal duties by improving the war readiness of the reserves and the *Landwehr/Honvéd* formations. Some of these measures were approved by the two parliaments; some could be introduced by administrative orders.

Utilizing existing legislation, the joint war minister decreed in 1883 that in future the *Ersatzreserve*, some ten thousand men annually, was to receive eight weeks' training. The same year the *Reichsrat*, largely motivated by a desire to keep up with Hungary, raised *Landwehr* strength to one hundred thirty-five thousand men, exclusive of the special units in the Tyrol and Vorarlberg.[28] In 1886, after the crisis arising out of the Serbo-Bulgarian war had demonstrated the need for a larger army, the *Reichsrat* and the Hungarian parliament passed legislation creating a third line, the *Landsturm*. Every able-bodied man between the ages of nineteen and forty-two, unless he was a member of the armed forces or the reserves, was obligated to serve in this new organization.[29] The next year, after the Bulgarian crisis had nearly escalated into a collision with Russia, the parliaments passed laws which allowed the army to call up the two youngest classes of reservists without mobilization. This was an important step used by the army in 1908 and 1909 and again in 1912 and 1913 to build up its strength in the face of threatening war.[30]

Utilizing the favorable climate created by the Russian war scare, in April 1889 the joint war minister, ably seconded by Beck, gained a slight increase of 7,500 men in the annual recruit contingent. This allowed an annual intake of 103,100 men for the joint army, 19,970 for the *Landwehr* and 12,500 for the *Honvéd*. The parliamentarians, however, turned down the request that the army be allowed to increase the size of the contingent annually to keep up with the rise in the population of the monarchy, 40 million at this time. Moreover, the proposed army law created stormy scenes in the Hungarian parliament and riots in the streets. In the end, the law was only passed after Prime Minister Tisza obtained concessions which reduced the German language requirements for Magyar one-year volunteers and, more importantly, changed the title of the joint army from *k.k. Armee* to *k. und. k. Armee*.[31] In the Hungarian view, adding the conjunction merely recognized the state of affairs established in 1867, but the Austrians and the military felt that this was one more step on the road toward a total division of the joint army.[32]

Of course, compared with the growth of the Russian and Italian armies, both regarded as the most likely enemies of the monarchy, all these increases were minor indeed. Reluctantly, in view of the political implications, the military had to encourage the *Landwehr* and *Honvéd* to strengthen their cadres, so that they could function as parts of the first line in case of war. By the end of 1892 the chief of the general staff, perhaps somewhat over-optimistically, declared that these bodies could now be considered as part of the first line.[33] Moreover, still driven by the need for immediately available troops, and discounting the needs for later replacements, Beck persuaded the war minister and the inspector general that the army reserves should be formed into provisional tactical bodies, *Marschbrigaden*, and utilized at the very outset of a war.[34]

Whether poorly equipped *Marschbrigaden* really were a good solution to the problem of fielding the largest possible numbers at the very outset of a campaign remained dubious, but Beck's most radical innovation, the abandonment of the traditional principle of stationing troops outside their ethnic areas, must be deemed a success. The core of the new army organization were 102 infantry regiments, increased from 80 by detaching one battalion each from the existing regiments and by converting eight *Jäger* battalions into line infantry. These regiments, together with artillery, cavalry, engineers, and auxiliary troops, formed the divisions for fifteen corps located at strategic points in the empire. Each corps was responsible for administration, training, and supply in its own area, and except for a small number of extra-territorial formations, its component units were stationed in or near their replacement districts so that they could be brought up rapidly to war strength. Moreover, the corps organization also approximated the war time order of battle. Already tried out in Germany, the new system provided for a more orderly and rapid mobilization, a prime consideration in Austrian war plans.

Even before Beck actually became chief of the general staff he had pressed for the adoption of this system of "territorial dislocation," as it was called in the army German.[35] Archduke Albrecht, however, had misgivings and feared that this would undermine troop discipline. "Quick mobilization," he asserted in a personal note to the emperor, "is not the only important factor. Every state has its own characteristics, and even by sacrificing the quality of our army we never can mobilize as fast as the Germans." It was up to the diplomats, Albrecht concluded, to provide the necessary time.[36]

Although he retained his misgivings about the new system for the rest of his life, he dropped his opposition in 1882 and agreed to the appointment of a committee to "study and make suggestions concerning all measures which might improve and hasten mobilization and deployment."[37] On June 30 the committee, headed by Bylandt-Rheidt, reported its support for the territorial army organization.[38] On July 11 and 12 a conference chaired by the emperor took up the matter further, and Generalmajor Leonidas von Popp, Beck's successor in the emperor's military chancery, presented the case for the new system which Francis Joseph also favored. The discussion centered on the problem as to whether the international situation and conditions in Bosnia-Hercegovina permitted such large-scale troop movements.[39] The conference agreed that the time was opportune and on July 30 Francis Joseph informed the war minister that he had obtained the support of the other joint ministers and that the new system should be implemented during the summer.[40]

When all troop movements were completed, the new territorial organization provided for fifteen corps districts and one special territorial command in Dalmatia. Except for XV Corps, Sarajevo, II Corps, Vienna, and Dalmatia, the corps were largely composed of local troops. Out of 102 infantry regiments, 89 were stationed in their home districts, and out of 42 cavalry regiments, only 11 were stationed outside their home areas, mainly in Galicia, where the soldiers expected incursions by the powerful Russian cavalry at the very opening of hostilities. It was feared that the Russian cavalry masses would break through the covering troops, and consequently cavalry regiments in Galicia were grouped into divisional formations and kept at near war strength.[41]

Territorial organization facilitated faster mobilization, but the rapid mobilization and deployment of the mass army required improved rail communications. The railroad had shown its value in 1848 and 1849, and had been essential in the Prussian deployment of 1866 and 1870 to 1871. This mode of transportation had become so much a part of war that the huge armies of the period could not be mobilized, maneuvered, or supplied without it. In 1870 the Dual Monarchy had but ninety-six hundred kilometers of track, much of it in the hands of private foreign-controlled companies. After the 1873 financial crisis, the state took over most of the major lines and on the insistence of the general staff built or expanded a number of strategic communications. Most important were the improvements, mainly double-tracking, of the five lines into northeastern Galicia and the building of two new lines into the northeastern part of this strategic province.[42] To supervise the railroads in war and to provide for better logistics, the general staff railroad section was expanded and a special Railroad and Telegraph Regiment organized in 1883. By the late 1880s deployment time for the Austro-Hungarian army had been cut from six to three weeks, and railroad tracks had expanded by 1896 to 32,180 kilometers.[43]

Weaponry was now in a period of transition. Breech-loading weapons had been generally adopted and the repeating small-bore rifle, the machine gun, and the quick-firing field gun were being tested. By 1885 all major powers had introduced or were in the process of adopting bolt-action repeating rifles. Austria-Hungary, too, tested a number of models.[44] In 1888 the Mannlicher repeater, reduced in caliber from 11 to 8 mm., was introduced as the service weapon and, with various modifications, remained the standard arm until the end of the empire. The artillery also received new heavy and medium field guns, model 1880, in 12-, 15-, and 18-cm. calibers. For their day, these were good pieces, but since Austria-Hungary did not produce adequate heavy steel barrels until after the turn of the century, and also for reasons of economy, these were still equipped with bronze barrels. They rapidly became obsolescent and it was a sign of Austria-Hungary's lag in armaments that the model 1880 pieces formed the mainstay of her heavy and medium field artillery for the first two years of the World War.[45] To provide more flexible fire support, the fifteen field artillery regiments were reorganized in the 1880s. Each corps and each of the forty-two divisions received a field artillery regiment.[46]

In organization and tactics, however, the army responded slowly to the new capabilities and the new demands of modern weaponry. Essentially, the Austro-Hungarian forces remained composed of the three major fighting branches—infantry, cavalry, and artillery. Auxiliary services such as engineers constituted only a very small proportion of the establishment. Technological changes failed to elicit corresponding innovations in tactics. The growing effectiveness of infantry fire was insufficiently recognized and did not lead to an adequate reappraisal of the effectiveness of mass attacks and the alleged value of the offensive. Although a large literature sprang up in which these points were discussed, the verdict in all armies, including the *k.u.k. Armee,* was the same: the new weapons required no basic changes in organization and tactics and even the role of cavalry was unchanged. Austro-Hungarian field regulations recognized the necessity of heavy skirmishing lines and individual fire, but they still maintained that this was preparatory to the decisive bayonet charge. Cavalry, of course, hoped to preserve the traditional shock action. This disregard for changing technological conditions, strengthened by the traditionalist conservatism of Francis Joseph and Albrecht, was to have disastrous results in the years ahead.

The same faith in the offensive dominated strategic thinking. It was the universal assumption of all European general staffs that war, if it should occur, would be brief and decided by massive offensive thrusts delivered at, or soon after, the outbreak of hostilities. Such a doctrine complimented Austria-Hungary's strategic needs. Not only was the Dual Monarchy numerically inferior to her most likely opponent, Russia, but an extended war was also likely to strain the socio-political framework of the monarchy. Therefore, the general staff favored taking the offensive. In the 1870s and 1880s the plans were designed to throw Russia off balance, but later they developed into ambitious schemes for a double envelopment which would destroy the Russian armies near the frontier.[47]

Of course, Austria-Hungary counted heavily on German support, but from the military point of view the Treaty of 1879 had one major weakness—it lacked definite military commitments. For the decade from 1882 to 1892, Beck, Albrecht, and even Crown Prince Rudolf attempted to gain such definite commitments from Germany, and although at times the German military seemed willing, the politicians would not allow such action. The chief obstacle was Bismarck, who felt that binding military arrangements would prevent diplomatic flexibility during a crisis. The chancellor did not wish to have to choose between Austria-Hungary and Russia, and after 1879 he tried to revive the ruptured Alliance of the Three Emperors. Although there were obstacles, especially the new Austro-Hungarian foreign minister, Heinrich Baron Haymerle, who outdid Andrássy in his suspicions of Russia, on June 18, 1881, representatives of the three empires signed a new agreement, pledging their neutrality in case one of their numbers went to war with another major power. But the renewed alliance only gave the impression of stability. Austro-Hungarian and Russian ambitions remained in conflict on the Balkans.[48]

Moreover, German-Russian friendship was strained by the rising intimacy between Berlin and Vienna, and this raised the possibility of a future Russian alignment with France, and thus the specter of a two-front war. With regard to this eventuality, Bismarck believed that a decision should be sought against France.[49] Until late in 1879 the German chief of the general staff, Feldmarschall Moltke, shared this view. By 1879, however, he concluded that the French military revival prevented a quick decision being reached in the west and he now advocated a campaign with limited objectives, designed to knock Russia out of the war. Moltke held that strong blows against the Russian armies in the western provinces and support of national insurrections, above all in Poland, would force the tsar to negotiate. The bulk of the German forces would be used in the east, while holding operations only would be conducted in the west.[50]

The conclusion of the Dual Alliance did not materially alter Moltke's troop dispositions. To be sure, he realized that plans for fomenting an insurrection in Poland had to be modified in deference to the Dual Monarchy's interests in Galicia. Moltke, however, did not believe that the Austro-Hungarian army could carry out a major offensive alone and he feared that unless it was supported by Germany, it would flounder and be forced to assume a defensive posture. This, of course, made coordination of plans desirable and this feeling was shared by Beck. In April 1882 the Austro-Hungarian chief of the general staff concluded that the strategic needs of the monarchy required some definite agreements with Germany regarding "war aims and, at least in outline, coordination of strategic plans."[51] At the same time, Beck warned that in order to concentrate the maximum number of troops against Russia, the monarchy ought to cover her rear by a treaty with Italy.

Negotiations with Italy had in fact been underway since the preceding year, and though Vienna entertained strong reservations about an agreement, the Triple Alliance was signed on May 20, 1882. The treaty was primarily a defensive one against a French attack on Italy and Germany, and it did not measurably improve Habsburg-Italian relations. Even so, it affected Beck's thinking when, in July 1882, he prepared for conversations with the German general staff. In an assessment dated July 12, 1882, he based his concepts on the expectation that Italy would remain benevolently neutral. He expected that Germany would concentrate fifty infantry and nine cavalry divisions in the east, while Austria-Hungary would provide twenty-six joint army infantry divisions, reinforced by nine *Landwehr* (*Honvéd*) divisions as well as all the army's cavalry. Because Germany could mobilize her bulk within twenty-one days, and Austria-Hungary would be only partially ready in thirty days, Beck counted heavily on his allies' assuming the heaviest part of the initial fighting.[52]

Actual conversations between Beck and Moltke's deputy, General Alfred Count Waldersee, took place in August and proved somewhat disappointing. Waldersee explained that the French threat would force Germany to keep some fifteen divisions in the west, but he did promise that in a two-front war Germany would assist Austria with more than half of her forces, twenty active and six reserve divisions, which would take the offensive on the twenty-first day after mobilization. The Germans intended to cooperate with the Austro-Hungarian army in an offensive to envelop the Russian armies in the Polish salient.[53] Beck was pleased by the prospect of a giant envelopment, though the total German support promised fell short of his expectations. Albrecht, who never could quite overcome his resentments against the "Prussians," was even more chagrined. He wrote to Francis Joseph that he put but little faith in the German promises and that in any case he doubted that the Germans could really begin their offensive within three weeks.[54]

Even so, after Beck met with Moltke in September 1882 and received further assurances, the Austro-Hungarian general staff worked out an ambitious war plan aiming to "destroy the Russians during their period of concentration."[55] Beck and Moltke continued to be in touch during the next few years and exchanged private letters on the plans for common operations. But Beck's plans had a fatal flaw.

Under prevailing conditions the bulk of the *k.u.k. Armee* could only be combat-ready and deployed in six weeks and this delay would give the Russians adequate time to complete their concentration. Austria-Hungary, of course, was now moving to speed up her mobilization, but these measures would not become effective for several years.

Beck was extremely concerned that the monarchy should not appear a second-rate power, and he deemed it necessary to begin operations as soon as the German ally. In 1883, therefore, he proposed a thrust northeast from Galicia to be delivered by some sixteen divisions which could be ready by the twentieth mobilization day.[56] The idea that the Dual Monarchy should take the offensive in order to demonstrate her equal status with the more powerful partner in the Dual Alliance was most unfortunate, but it had considerable influence on future war plans.

At the same time, despite the conclusion of the Triple Alliance, Austrian military thinking continued to be apprehensive about the potential danger from Italy. After 1882 there was a marked increase of irredentist agitation among the Italian public and by 1886 Albrecht expressed regrets that this problem had not been solved in 1878 and 1879 by a preventive war.[57] Of course, Austria continued to expand her fortifications along the Austrian-Italian frontier, but there were complaints that the forts were poorly sited and that for reasons of economy they were not up to modern requirements. One high-ranking engineer complained that "works were constructed for very little which in an actual emergency would have been worth very little."[58] A major shortcoming was that the main guns were not placed in armored cupolas, though after 1885 there were attempts to remedy this.[59] The possibility of Italian hostility, however, continued to preoccupy the general staff. During the crisis with Russia in 1886 and 1887, Beck declared that with Italy's benevolent neutrality and Germany's support, Austria-Hungary could deploy her main forces in the east, but if Italy were to be hostile, then the monarchy could not hope to conduct offensive operations against Russia.[60]

Preoccupied with the danger of Russia, Austria-Hungary moved to strengthen her position in the Balkans. In 1883 Rumania signed a secret alliance with the Dual Monarchy aimed at Russia, and in 1885 during the short Serb-Bulgarian war, an Austrian ultimatum halted the advance of a Bulgarian army on Belgrade. In turn, Russia tried to assert her preponderance in Bulgaria where the crown had been given to Prince Alexander of Battenberg who had served in the tsar's army but resented the heavy-handed methods of the Russians. In 1886, with Russian foreknowledge, the prince was first removed by an army coup, then returned, and finally, facing implacable Russian hostility, compelled to abdicate. The removal of Alexander and the search for a successor brought Europe close to war. In late 1886 and the following year, the elevation of Ferdinand of Coburg, a German prince and officer serving in the Austrian army, escalated the crisis. War again seem imminent, and Bismarck wanted to avoid that above all.

The Bulgarian affair had so strained Austro-Russian relations that at its expiration in 1887, the Alliance of the Three Emperors was not again renewed. But since at this point the situation in France once again looked threatening, Bismarck was glad to accept the Russian offer of a mutual Reinsurance Treaty, valid for three years, which promised that either empire would remain neutral if it were to become involved in war with a third power. Although Bismarck made it clear that this provision did not cover an unprovoked Russian attack on Austria-Hungary, the chancellor was aware that the treaty would create an extremely unfavorable reaction in Vienna, and so it was kept highly secret. At the same time, Bismarck created an interlocking system of alliances, the so-called Mediterranean Ports, which engaged both Italy and England to work for the maintenance of the status quo in that region.

Bismarck's complicated and largely secret maneuvers were better understood by the diplomats than by the soldiers in Germany and in Austria-Hungary. In both countries there existed a military party which did not shrink from the thought of preventive war against Russia. In fact, by the end of 1887, most Germany army leaders supported such action.[61] Austrian military opinion, however, was divided. The Dual Monarchy was neither militarily nor politically ready for war. Its army was understrength, the territorial reorganization untried, and the rearmament with the new repeaters not yet completed. In addition, the parliaments were reluctant to vote military appropriations and there was considerable and rising national unrest. A war party, headed by Crown Prince Rudolf and supported by some influential commanders, urged an attack on Russia, but the ever-cautious Beck was worried about the state of military preparedness, and Albrecht vacillated. As always he was suspicious of Germany's good faith, and while he sometimes regarded war as inevitable, he rapidly changed his mind and directed that no reinforcements be sent to Galicia because the Russians might interpret this as a provocation.[62]

It was imperative, however, for the military to ascertain the exact intentions of the German ally, and the general staff tried to gain definite promises about the commitment of German troops in the east. "It is of the utmost importance for the army command," Beck wrote on December 1, 1886, "to know exactly what we can expect because any German deployment against Russia, with half her army or even less, threatens the main Russian line of communications." Every Russian division diverted by the Germans was a help, but unless Germany contained at least thirty-two enemy divisions, Austria-Hungary would find the going difficult. Indeed, considering the prospects of the Dual Monarchy in fighting the Russians alone, Beck concluded that even under the most favorable circumstances her thirty-two to thirty-four divisions could not hope to prevail against an estimated sixty-four Russian divisions.[63] The options available to Austria-Hungary were thus sharply limited and her military dependence on German support all too clear.

In January 1887 Beck began work on the administrative and logistic preparations for an eventual war with Russia,[64] and in February Gustav Count Kálnoky, a former general officer and now joint foreign minister, managed to obtain the necessary special appropriations, 52.5 millions, from the Delegations. Meanwhile the general staff was feverishly improving the mobilization schedules and estimated that thirty infantry divisions could be assembled in Galicia by the twenty-fourth day of mobilization. But even assuming some German aid, this still left forty Russian divisions facing them and Albrecht warned Beck that at least half of the German army would have to be deployed in the east. To obtain some clear indications of German intentions, Crown Prince Rudolf was dispatched to Berlin with instructions to make some definite soundings. Much to Vienna's consternation, Bismarck told the prince that though Germany would stand by her alliance, Austria should refrain from provoking Russia and that if it came to a two-front war, Germany would seek a decision against France first. This announcement, clearly contradicting Moltke's previous assurances, came as a bad shock which seemed to confirm Albrecht's worst apprehensions.[65]

There is no evidence that Moltke actually had switched his priorities at this time, but Bismarck always considered France rather than Russia as the greater danger. Since January, unknown to Moltke, he had been negotiating the Reinsurance Treaty. In any case, Bismarck's maneuver succeeded in sobering the war party in Austria while the Reinsurance Treaty placated the tsar, and so the summer of 1887 passed without incident. By October, however, the situation had worsened. Reports and rumors about Russian troop movements caused grave anxiety in Austria, and Albrecht informed Beck that he now considered war inevitable.[66] Even so, the archduke was not willing to precipitate war at this time; he expected a Russian attack in the spring. Meanwhile he wavered. On the one hand he urged Beck to take all necessary steps to meet a Russian attack; on the other he warned against sending reinforcements to Galicia because this could be interpreted as a provocation.[67] His feelings were shared by the emperor. "We must be careful," Francis Joseph explained to his friend and confidant Albert of Saxony in December, "not to provoke hostilities during a season which we at least consider completely unsuitable for campaigning." He reassured his friend that the monarchy had taken precautions against a Russian coup. The cavalry regiments had been augmented, draft teams provided for the artillery of the two Galician corps, and work was proceeding on the fortifications of Cracow and Przemysl. If necessary, he concluded, "we are prepared to move to a state of increased peacetime preparedness."[68]

Because of a mixture of political, technical, and financial considerations, Vienna moved cautiously, but in Berlin the top soldiers, above all Waldersee who nurtured political ambitions, believed that war was inevitable and that Germany and Austria-Hungary should therefore launch a preventive attack upon Russia at the most opportune moment.[69] Bismarck was opposed to such a move and incensed at military meddling in international policy. He restrained the soldiers by a direct appeal to the emperor and he also informed Vienna that the Dual Alliance was purely defensive and did not oblige Germany to assist Austria in an aggressive undertaking.

The signals from Berlin were truly confusing, but they definitely spelled caution. Albrecht even suspected that the bellicosity of the German generals was deliberately designed "in historic old-Prussian fashion" to lead the monarchy into a trap. Even so, both he and Beck were temporarily affected by the preventive war fever and so towards the end of the year they made proposals to the German general staff which would have enabled Austria-Hungary to change the *casus foederis* in favor of a preventive war.[70] Once again Bismarck stopped the Austrians cold. He revealed the existence of the Reinsurance Treaty to Moltke and in consequence the field marshal told Beck in February 1887 that in case of a two-front war, Germany would engage only one-third of her army, seven corps and four reserve divisions, for an offensive into the Polish salient.[71]

Moltke's announcement was a significant step-down from the promise of more than half of Germany's army made in 1882, and it greatly changed the odds against the Dual Monarchy. This bitter pill was hardly sweetened by Austro-Hungarian staff talks for the use of Italian and Rumanian troops against Russia. In any case, these forces were hardly the equal of the Germans, and Italy declined to engage herself while Rumania gave more definite assurances.[72] Finally, when Waldersee succeeded Moltke in 1888, he too no longer showed any intention of making the main effort in the east and refused to make any binding commitment. The German turnabout was a harsh blow for Beck. In October 1888 he admitted the unpleasant truth to Albrecht. Austria-Hungary, he wrote, had a field army which was weaker than that of Russia, only slightly stronger than that of Italy, and had no margin or strategic reserve to take care of even the minor Balkan powers in the event of a major war. He concluded that Austria-Hungary could only wage war in cooperation with another major power. And Albrecht noted on the margin of the memorandum: "Very unpleasant, but unfortunately true."[73]

But the situation in Berlin was fluid and after the accession of William II, Germany discontinued Bismarck's careful balancing between Vienna and St. Petersburg. In 1889 Waldersee and the German war minister Verdy du Vermois assured Beck that Germany would mobilize on the day of Austria's mobilization, and William confirmed this statement in the same words. Waldersee, however, fell from office soon and although his successor, General Count Alfred Schlieffen, promised that Germany's major effort would be first directed against Russia, he changed his mind in 1892 to favor an all-out attack against France. In 1895 Schlieffen even abandoned the projected joint German-Austro-Hungarian offensive into the Polish salient and instead asked Beck to mount an independent offensive in the general direction of Warsaw, while Germany would limit herself to the defense of East Prussia.[74] Beck, naturally, refused, but Schlieffen, who at this point had a low opinion about Austria-Hungary's war potential, remained unmoved. Military relations had reached a low point in 1896, and Beck noted in his yearly appraisal of the military-political situation that although he did not wish to question German loyalty to the alliance, "one cannot deny that it is not certain under which circumstances we can count on the direct and immediate support of the German armies and if this would be the case in eventualities which first and foremost concern our own interests."[75]

Beck, however, found comfort in the thought that the monarchy's military establishment had made considerable progress since he had taken office. In his annual report of 1892 he noted that the *Landwehr/Honvéd* had improved their combat readiness and could now be considered part of the first line, increasing immediately available forces to forty-two divisions. He reported that the artillery had been strengthened by new batteries, that the changeover to breechloaders was completed, and that fortifications in the Tyrol and in Galicia had been improved. Above all, the speed of mobilization had been greatly accelerated and railroad capabilities increased. At the same time, according to Beck, the international arms race was continuing, and Austria-Hungary was spending proportionately less on her military establishment than other European powers.[76] The same rather optimistic tenor characterized his reports during the next four years. Indeed, in 1896 he claimed that "I can state with confidence that our present army is very good and is improving more rapidly than most foreign armies."[77]

This satisfactory state of affairs, however, would not continue. Even if the international situation had improved, the Dual Monarchy was entering a period of troubles which greatly affected the army because of its domestic affairs. Since the *Ausgleich*, the joint army, the only institution widely present in both parts of the monarchy, had assumed special importance. Its existence and unity was, as a distinguished French historian phrased it, "the last refuge of the old imperial spirit of unquestioning devotion to the supreme warlord."[78] But because of this very spirit, the joint army came increasingly under attack by the forces of a revived nationalism. In the last twenty years of the century, national tensions in the Habsburg empire became transformed into national hatreds. Hungary renewed her demands for military concessions, seeking to convert the Hungarian contingent of the joint army into an instrument of Magyarization. In Austria Taaffe's pragmatic policies, unintentionally, to be sure, alienated a considerable faction of the German speaking population. Since the army, the most visible and vital instrument of an imperial unity in the two halves of the empire, stood "both in principle and in practice on the basis of national equality," it became the object of attacks from all sides.[79]

The army was, in fact, largely free of the national intolerance which flourished elsewhere in the monarchy. Its officer corps, loyal to the emperor alone, steadfastly maintained their allegiance to a dynastic coat of arms and not to any national flag. Many of the officers now held noble predicates and titles, though usually these denoted that the holder had been ennobled after a long period of meritorious service.[80] Despite the growing number of officers from the middle and lower-middle classes, there still remained a few of the international aristocratic soldiers who found their origins not incompatible with loyalty to the warlord. Alexander of Battenberg, ousted in Bulgaria, entered the Austrian service and actually commanded a regiment. The inspector general of engineers in the 1880s, Feldmarschall Leutnant Daniel Baron Salis-Soglio, a native Swiss, was approached by his native government for expert advice on new fortifications. He formulated the classic reply that "as a Swiss I would be delighted to do this, but as an Austrian officer I cannot oblige without His Majesty's permission."[81]

But more important than such isolated remnants of the past was the open entry into the officer corps. Although the regular corps retained an overwhelming German character, neither religion nor ethnic origin was a bar to commissioned rank. The Austro-Hungarian army was almost alone in the pre-war European forces in opening its officer corps to Jews, some of whom, like Feldmarschall Leutnant Eduard Ritter von Schweitzer, reached high rank. Above all, the institution of the one-year volunteers created a rich mixture, though, of course, the educational qualifications tended to sharply reduce the proportion of volunteers from the less developed national groups. In 1896, for example, out of 1000 officers in the *k.u.k. Armee*, there were 791 Catholics, 86 Protestants, 84 Jews, 39 Greek-Orthodox and 1 Uniate.[82]

In fact, the army's liberal attitude aroused violent opposition in Germany where a number of officers wrote pamphlets alleging that this military liberalism had deprived Austrian officers of their proper status and had diluted the corps with freethinkers, Jews, democrats, and even socialists. Such developments, the pamphleteers claimed, had seriously impaired the effectiveness of the Austrian army. Austrian officers took up the pen in defense,[83] and in 1896 Albrecht personally complained to Waldersee about these attacks and was promised that steps would be taken to suppress them.[84]

But the very fact that the army was in fact supranational also involved it in a renewed struggle with the Magyars who now possessed the powerful weapon of parliamentary obstruction. The Hungarian parliament, based on a limited franchise, represented only 6 percent of the population. During most of the period of dualism, the Liberal Party, faithful to the *Ausgleich,* managed to retain itself in office. In opposition were the Independence Party and some radical nationalist splinter groups advocating the principles of 1848. In military affairs the Liberals supported the settlement of 1868, while the Independence Party championed the complete separation of all Hungarian contingents from the joint army. Moreover, both parties were nationalists and shared the desire that the Hungarian components of the joint army should be "magyarized." In addition, the army often incurred the dislike of the unrepresented masses when in his efforts to retain power Premier Tisza frequently called on the military to repress peasant unrest and opposition demonstrations.[85]

Even so, the dispute over the status and the composition of the *Honvéd* had been followed by a period of relative calm, disturbed only on occasion by clashes between regular officers and Magyar radicals. Nationalist commemorations of the war of 1848–1849 and its martyrs incensed the military, while military celebrations honoring Windischgrätz and Jelačić were regarded as deliberate provocations by the radicals. By the 1880s tempers were rising. Independence Party journals opposed military operations in Dalmatia in 1882, and an angered Francis Joseph wrote to Tisza that this undermined the morale of Hungarian troops in the zone of operations and asked the minister to consider suppressing the offending publications.[86] An even more serious incident, at least in Hungarian eyes, occurred in 1886 when the commander of troops in Budapest, Generalmajor Ludwig Janski, decorated the statue of General Hentzi, the defender of Buda against Kossuth in 1849. There were street demonstrations and violent diatribes in the press, and even Tisza protested against this action. In the circumstances the act was perhaps ill-advised, but despite pressure Vienna refused to punish the officers involved, though Janski was transferred to command a division.[87] The incident was symptomatic and in its wake followed a number of verbal exchanges, fist fights, duels, and other collisions between officers and Hungarian nationalists.[88] These incidents, including the celebrated brawl between Gabor Ugron, a radical member of parliament, and Captain Uzelać, often brought an angry reaction from the emperor, but given the constitutional situation, there was little that he could actually do.[89]

By far the most serious and far-reaching developments, however, came out of the debate over the 1889 army law. Indeed, the debate was a turning point in Hungarian politics and in the history of dualism. It marked the introduction of the demand for the Hungarian language of command and service in the joint army as the major grievance of Magyar nationalists. In the 1889 debate both sides of parliament accepted the notions of Count Albert Apponyi that the army was the school of the nation. And with Magyars a minority in the lands of the Crown of St. Stephen, the introduction of Hungarian as the official army language would greatly aid the magyarization of Hungary's non-Magyar subjects.[90] To the army, which recognized ethnic groups (*Volksstämme*) but no nationalities, this clearly was unacceptable, especially since of the infantry regiments recruited in the country only five were purely Magyar, while thirty-seven were linguistically mixed with Magyars predominating only in twelve.[91] Even the conciliatory Beck opposed such a move. It would, he noted, create great difficulties in intra-army communications and greatly complicate the process of mobilization.[92]

The introduction of the Hungarian language, moreover, was widely regarded as a preliminary step to the ultimate division of the joint army, and so the government tried to fight these demands. Baron Fejérváry, the *Honvéd* minister, declared that "one cannot maintain an army subject to notice of dissolution!"[93] The aged Julius Andrássy also entered the fight to defend the arrangements of 1868. Hungary's security, he told parliament, demanded a strong Dual Monarchy. German was a necessary medium of communication in the joint army which should not be regarded as an alien instrument. "The question of a separate Hungarian army," he declared, "was discussed during the *Ausgleich* negotiations, and if we had believed that such an army was necessary for an independent Hungary, then we would have insisted on it." But, continued Andrássy, "we did not deem it desirable; in fact, we considered it dangerous, both for Hungary and for the monarchy."[94]

The parliamentary debate, however, spilled over into the streets; there were riots and demonstrations. To appease the country, Tisza went to Vienna and obtained a number of concessions, above all the change in the title of the joint army. He did not ask for the Hungarian language of command and he refused to support demands for a separate Hungarian army.[95] Even so, parliament, in the end, passed the army law, but the debate had revealed the depth of Magyar national feeling and greatly perturbed the military leadership. Composed of men who personally had experienced the trauma of 1848 and 1849, the generalcy, with few exceptions, was opposed to all Hungarian aspirations. Perhaps a solution might have been possible after all. In retrospect, at least one general believed that "greater flexibility in the externals . . . might have created better internal cohesion in the army." While he did not discuss the language question, he noted that small concessions on the "flag and insignia question" might have yielded large dividends. "Would the gallant Hungarian troops, which since the days of Maria Theresa had worn special uniforms, braids, and tight pants, have really changed if they had displayed the national emblem instead of the double eagle on their belt buckles and helmets?"[96] But these feelings, retrospective in any case, were not widely shared.

The military members of the imperial house were especially set against any concessions to Hungary. Archduke Albrecht never forgave the Magyars for 1848 and his feelings were shared by Crown Prince Rudolf, who during the Hentzi affair in 1886 urged military intervention against Budapest.[97] And when after Rudolf's suicide in 1889, Archduke Francis Ferdinand became the heir apparent, he also manifested the most violent anti-Magyar sentiments. In fact, his feelings were so well known that before he assumed command of the 9th Hussars, a predominantly Hungarian regiment, Francis Joseph cautioned him from making any public announcement on Hungarian affairs.[98] Even so, Francis Ferdinand, convinced that Hungarian nationalism was basically anti-dynastic and revolutionary, and that troops "animated by a Hungarian spirit" could never be trusted, was enraged when officers spoke Magyar in his presence.[99] Of course, Francis Ferdinand was wrong; Magyar was the regimental language of his regiment and if he had not been an archduke he would have been compelled to master it. As it was, his situation became untenable and he soon requested a change of assignment.[100]

National problems also manifested themselves in the Austrian half of the monfiarchy where Beck was angered during his travels by the growing display of national rather than Habsburg black and yellow flags.[101] Here Taaffe, a *Kaiserminister* rather than a representative of any party or nationality, attempted to dampen the conflict by keeping "all nationalities in a balanced state of mild dissatisfaction."[102] In the end, however, this policy backfired. It did not reconcile the Czechs and it alienated the Germans. Before 1878 mistrust between the German Liberals and the army had been based on the memories of 1848 and on the Liberals' dislike of excessive military spending. The Liberal Party was now in decline and, frightened about their status, many Germans, especially the academic youth, turned towards the more radical, greater German doctrines espoused by Georg von Schönerer. To be sure, the conclusion of the Dual Alliance forced even the German nationalists to adopt a more positive attitude towards the military establishment, but this was only temporary.

Universal military service and the one-year volunteer system meant that previously exempt classes of the population, above all university students, found themselves in the army and constituting a large proportion of the reserve officer corps. And as the national struggles in the monarchy assumed an even more violent character, these reserve officers often found that Schönerer's slogan, "Nationalism is more important than dynastic patriotism," was irreconcilable with the military oath of allegiance.[103] Although the German nationalists denied that they were opposed to the state, their creed had a clear anti-dynastic tinge; when in 1888 Kuhn, who had become identified with the nationalist opposition, was retired there was a singular demonstration by some junior officers of the Graz garrison which aroused the wrath of Archduke Albrecht.[104]

In turn, the hardening German attitudes brought about a similar reaction on the part of the Czechs. By the late 1880s Czech groups, above all the militant sports associations like the *Sokol,* were clearly anti-dynastic and anti-military.[105] They were dissatisfied by the concessions granted, and during the spring and summer of 1893 unrest and rioting in Bohemia led to the collapse of Taaffe's finely balanced system. During the disturbances troops had to be called out to quell street fighting, and to the consternation of the high command the Czech rank and file of the 28th Infantry (Prague) proved unreliable and the regiment had to be transferred to Linz in Upper Austria.[106] It appeared then as if the dire prognostications about the territorial system might, after all, not have been without some foundation.

The fears were compounded by the specter of the "red menace" of socialism and anarchism, both active in Austria since the late 1870s. Officers holding socialist views were dismissed; soldiers were closely watched. In 1882 and 1884 workers in Vienna erupted in street riots and troops had to be called out.[107] To deal with potential big city riots, Bosnian-Hercegovinian units were stationed in Vienna, Graz, and Budapest.[108] This action, a significant deviation from the territorial principle, had two advantages. For one, these troops were considered reliable because their language, religion, and customs kept them apart from the populace, and secondly, it also removed these regiments from the continuing pan-Serb agitation in their home stations.

Nonetheless, although in later years it became fashionable to describe the Dual Monarchy as a prison of nations practicing widespread repression, such statements are not correct. The government and the army maintained internal security by means no more ruthless than in other states of their day. To be sure, there were national and social tensions, inhibiting the development of the army and weakening the state, but perhaps more important was the fact that neither the civilian nor the military leadership could free itself from reliance on outmoded concepts and attitudes.

As far as the army was concerned, this was due in large part to the superannuation of its leaders. Although in 1892 a sixty-two-year-old major general complained that "old and combat-experienced generals were being relieved to make way for young men," this was not really the case.[109] By the 1890s the top soldiers were old men indeed. Of the three generals slated to lead armies in case of war, two, Edelsheim and Phillipović, died from old age while on active duty, and Albrecht, the commander in chief designate, clung to his all-important office until his death in 1895. By this time he was "a helpless old man," partially blind, whose horse had to be led by an adjutant.[110] Under these circumstances Beck's boast that the army was improving faster than most other foreign armies was open to doubts.

9

Foreign Equilibrium and Internal Crisis: 1895-1905

The period in the history of the Habsburg army which opened with the death of Archduke Albrecht in 1895 and closed with the dismissal of Beck in 1906 saw a substantial relaxation of tensions in the foreign relations of the monarchy. At the same time, however, and in part because of this reduced outside pressure, internal crises continued and even escalated. In both halves of the monarchy the turbulent opposition by the dominant nationalities almost brought parliamentary government to a halt. In the case of Hungary a confrontation about the character of the army raised the specter of total separation, and by 1905 military leaders seriously considered large-scale intervention against Budapest. Under these circumstances the rapid progress of the army, acclaimed by Beck in 1896, came to a halt and the Austro-Hungarian military establishment entered a period of stagnation.

In the 1890s European power alignments tended to blur and even break down. The main effort of the great powers was directed toward colonial expansion and "global policy." While Austria-Hungary, lacking sufficient naval strength, did not enter the race for colonies, it profited from the preoccupations of Russia and Italy. Although by 1896 Beck was disappointed and somewhat apprehensive about the recent shift in German military priorities and the subsequent weakening of the alliance, the Russian threat to the Dual Monarchy was, temporarily at least, receding. To be sure, the long-feared alliance between Russia and France materialized in the agreements of 1891 and 1894, while the secret Austro-Serb treaty was not renewed after 1895. Even so, the military picture looked rather encouraging. The Chinese-Japanese war of 1894 diverted Russian attention from the Balkans, and Italy's defeat at Adua in 1896 revealed the martial shortcomings of an ally still regarded with grave suspicions. Meanwhile, the Balkan situation remained a source of concern; when Beck visited Rumania in 1896 in order to explore implementation of the Austro-Rumanian alliance, his general impression was that popular opposition in that country might well create serious obstacles to an effective military cooperation.[1] However, the Balkan situation became much less critical when in May 1897 Austria-Hungary and Russia signed an agreement affirming the status quo in that region and pledging consultation and common policy if change became necessary. By the end of 1897 the relaxation in the foreign affairs of the Dual Monarchy was so marked that Beck, now the undisputed first soldier, informed Francis Joseph that a major war was most unlikely in the near future,[2] and he reaffirmed this appraisal in the following year.[3]

In fact, though Beck remained suspicious about Russia's ultimate intentions, her major effort was now made in the Far East. To secure her rear, Russia needed Austria-Hungary's neutrality; the Balkan agreement, reaffirmed in 1903 and 1904, allowed the tsar to enter into the disastrous war with Japan. Although Russian military reverses were welcome news for the *k.u.k.* general staff, the revolution which followed caused some repercussions in the Dual Monarchy. In balance, however, it appeared as though future threats from Russia were much diminished, and Beck noted with satisfaction that Russia "will be crippled for years."[4]

On the other hand, Italy remained a dubious quantity in all diplomatic and military calculations. Friction between Rome and Vienna continued, and Austrian generals still entertained strong reservations about Italy's fidelity to the Triple Alliance. Military misgivings, however, were not shared by the foreign minister, Agenor Count Goluchowski, who opposed military plans for improving the state of defenses in South Tyrol, claiming that it might prejudice allied relations.[5] Therefore, Austro-Hungarian troop strength along the southwestern frontier remained low, and fortifications were not modernized to any extent.[6] Moreover, although Italy had been in a rapprochement with France since 1898, she still remained, at least outwardly, faithful to her treaty obligations. In case of war, Italian divisions were slated for deployment on the extreme left wing of the German front in the Alsace, and consultations continued regarding the best utilization of the Austro-Hungarian railroads to carry these troops.[7] At the same time, reports from the monarchy's military attaché in Rome indicated that Italy would continue to honor her agreements.[8]

The reports from Rome came in response to inquiries raised in 1900 about the probable future Italian course of action when Victor Emmanuel III succeeded King Humbert. In general, Humbert had been sympathetic to the Triple Alliance and suspicious of France, but Victor Emmanuel, married to a Montenegrin princess, favored a more active Balkan policy and closer ties to France. Both moves were sure to be opposed by Vienna as well as by Berlin, but the king and his cabinet continued on their course. And while this was not technically against the letter of the Triple Alliance, it certainly meant that from 1902 on, neither Germany nor Austria-Hungary could be sure of Italy. Although the common foreign minister continued to play down the significance of this development, a difference which in 1911 led to open conflict with the chief of the general staff, the military saw in it confirmation of their worst apprehensions. Old war plans were dusted off and vigilance in the frontier areas was stepped up. With increased tension, fears about irredentist coups returned, and there were several alerts and occasional military intervention against Italian nationalist demonstrations.[9]

And when in addition to Italy's possible defection a revolt in Serbia ousted the Austrophile Obrenović dynasty and brought in the ambitious Peter Karageorgević, military fears increased. An active Serb national program always had been considered a major threat to the monarchy. To be sure, Serbia alone was not dangerous and, as long as Russia remained involved in the Far East and bound by the agreement of 1897, she could offer no assistance to Serbia. Italy, however, was another matter. Since 1859 the possibility of an Italian thrust across the Adriatic had figured prominently in Austrian military speculations, and from 1903 on the general staff once again prepared plans to deal with a possible simultaneous conflict with Italy and Serbia, the so-called "Case I + S."[10] Thus during Beck's last few years in office, the military horizon of the Dual Monarchy began to darken again.

The matter was even more serious because, despite Beck's optimistic prognosis in 1896, the army actually had made little progress during this decade. At the same time Beck's personal position, already powerful, had become dominant. In March 1895, following the death of Albrecht, the emperor discontinued the office of army inspector general and distributed its various functions. Some duties were transferred to the inspector generals of the infantry, cavalry, and artillery, but the most important attributes of the former office were delegated to Beck. In addition to his planning and operational responsibilities, Beck now gained the right to issue army orders in the name of the emperor in minor matters, to coordinate training, and to supervise maneuvers. And when Beck pointed out that this was incompatible with the status of his office as an auxiliary organ of the War Ministry, Francis Joseph changed the army's structure so that the office of the chief of general staff became a direct organ of the supreme command.[11] In 1900, moreover, new instructions extended the competence of the chief of the general staff to the "entire armed forces," including *Landwehr* and *Honvédség*.[12]

As Beck's biographer noted, within the fifty years separating Hess and Beck there had been a tremendous improvement in the position of the chief of the general staff. But this was not all. By 1900 Beck clearly outranked the war minister and as the unofficial "emperor's deputy," he dominated the military establishment. In 1902 he was able to force the resignation of General der Kavallerie Edmund Baron Krieghammer and the appointment of his former deputy chief of staff, Feldmarschall Leutnant Heinrich Ritter von Pitreich, to the position of war minister.[13] Even so, Beck's unique position rested primarily on his special relationship with the emperor and there still was not, and never would be, a clear delineation between the responsibilites of the chief of the general staff and the war minister. Beck attempted to define the relationship. "The general staff," he wrote, "determines what is absolutely necessary for war and what is desirable in peacetime. The war minister determines what can be provided."[14] But since according to the constitution the war minister had to present and defend the military estimates before the deputations, he often was forced to reduce the estimates made by the chief of the general staff and this, of course, created considerable ill-will between the two officials. And while Beck preferred to approach obstacles cautiously and to avoid conflict, the latent controversy came into the open under his successor, the volatile Conrad von Hötzendorf.

Until 1906, and in many respects until 1912, internal political problems within the monarchy, discussed in some detail below, prevented any great expansion of the army. In Vienna and in Budapest the parliamentarians were unwilling to grant new money to the army. By 1898 Beck was forced to report to the emperor that financial limitations and the failure to remove the manpower ceiling of 1889 had limited progress to minor administrative and technical modifications.[15] Actually, the Austro-Hungarian defense budget rose from 262 million crowns in 1895 to 280 million in 1900 and to 306 million in 1906. This increase, however, was not proportionate to the rising military expenditures of the other European powers, and on a per capita basis the Dual Monarchy spent far less than Germany, France, Great

Britain, or Italy, and remained about level with Russia, which had a much larger population.[16] At the same time, the army was not allowed to exploit the growing manpower potential of the state. Although the population had increased to nearly 50 million by 1900, the annual intake of recruits, and therefore the size of the army, remained tied to the ceilings established in the 1889 army law. Austria-Hungary's annual recruit intake remained at 103,100 men, compared to 280,000 in Germany, 250,000 in France, 335,000 in Russia, and 100,000 in Italy. The Dual Monarchy conscripted only 0.29 percent of its population, while Germany trained 0.47; Russia, 0.35, and France 0.75 percent.[17] As a result a considerable number of potential recruits received at best eight weeks of training in the *Ersatzreserve* and the cadres of the regular and reserve formations were understrength. To remedy these serious defects, from 1892 on both the chief of the general staff and the common war ministers pressed for a revision of the 1889 army law, but because of political obstruction, mainly in Hungary, this was not achieved until 1912.[18]

The army remained overwhelmingly an infantry force, as had been the case since the eighteenth century. During the decade from 1896 to 1906, out of one thousand soldiers, about seven hundred served in the infantry, including the *Jäger,* one hundred in the artillery, and eighty-five in the cavalry. About fifty were assigned to the supply services, twenty-eight to the engineer, railroad, and signal units, and eighteen served in the medical branch. There were no significant changes in this mix, except that the ratio of the field artillery declined from seventy-nine in 1896 to seventy-six in 1906, while at the same time the heavy, siege, and fortress artillery contingent rose from twenty-four to thirty-five men per thousand.[19] The rise in fortress artillery personnel reflected the necessity to garrison the new fortifications in Dalmatia built as a result of the political changes in Serbia.

At the same time, however, the Austrian artillery materiel was fast becoming obsolete. The siege pieces introduced in the 1880s had always been rather poor, but they still were better than the fortress guns which in large part were composed of the outdated cast-iron M 1861 pieces. Even more important, however, was the lag in field artillery in the 1880s. The perfection of smokeless powder and the high-explosive artillery shell, together with the development of recoil-absorbing mechanisms, greatly increased the effectiveness of field artillery and rendered the M 1875 pieces obsolete. Although by 1895 the Dual Monarchy had made sufficient technological progress to produce new war materiel, especially in the Skoda Works of Bohemia, the Technical Military Committee was cautious and pending the perfection of the new mechanism merely decided to modify the existing guns. Equipped with a tail spur to reduce recoil and altered to fire heavier charges, the modified guns, designated M 75/96, retained the heavy steel bronze barrels, had inadequate range, and lacked protective shields.[20] Then in 1897 the French introduced the 75-mm. field gun, the first of the modern rapid-firing field pieces with a perfected hydraulic recoil mechanism. And while the new design was immediately adopted in Russia, Austria-Hungary's new field piece, introduced in 1899, was a 10-cm. howitzer with short range, no recoil mechanism, and no protective shield.[21] The lag in Austria-Hungary's armament aroused the concern of her German ally. In 1900 General Count Alfred Schlieffen, the new German chief of the general staff, is reported to have told Beck that the Dual Monarchy would have to move from a "monthly wage to a piece-work system in order to catch up." Otherwise, Schlieffen warned, "we might very well come too late."[22] More directly, in the following year, the German emperor inquired about the state of Austria's field artillery and repeated the query the next year.[23] Even so, the Technical Military Committee accepted designs for rapid-firing field artillery only in 1904 and although production got underway shortly, by 1914 many of the first line *k.u.k.* batteries were still armed with the obsolescent M 99 howitzers.[24]

In general, Francis Joseph and Beck were unwilling to exploit the achievements and talents of the new technology and adapt them to the needs of the army. During the last exercises directed by Beck, the imperial maneuvers of 1906, an armored car invented by Lt. Col. Günther Burstyn was demonstrated. But when this vehicle scared the horses of the imperial suite, Francis Joseph, visibly annoyed, declared that "such a thing would never be of any military value."[25] Beck did, however, press for the expansion and modernization of the Austro-Hungarian railroad network. New rolling stock was acquired, trackage extended, and strategic tunnels, bridges, and loading ramps were constructed. In 1896 the chief of the general staff used his influence to have a former general staff officer, General Emil Ritter von Guttenberg, appointed as head of the newly created common railroad ministry.[26]

Of course, even changes in materiel and armament would not have solved the greatest shortcoming of the Austro-Hungarian military establishment, the nationality problem. The *k.u.k. Armee,* drawn by conscription from a large number of different and often hostile nationalities, was held together by tradition and discipline. But tradition was beginning to suffer when, reflecting the national quarrels which divided the monarchy, the army too became ever more aware of its differences and less conscious of its common heritage. In the past, a great leader like Radetzky had been able to overcome this problem, but after his death there was no one to take his place. Between 1853 and 1918 there were many brave and devoted generals, including some who could claim military genius, but no one else ever inspired the devotion of the rank and file. Benedek had attempted to do this but had failed, and of Albrecht, Kuhn, Beck, or for that matter, Conrad von Hötzendorf, none was ever able to achieve the status of "Father Radetzky." And the Emperor Francis Joseph, though respected, was far too distant and reserved a figure to inspire the personal devotion of his troops.

Under these circumstances, the main burden of maintaining morale and discipline fell on the officer corps which in 1901 was composed of 16,648 regular and 12,265 reserve officers.[27] The German-speaking element continued to prevail both in the regular and in the reserve officer corps. Although the Germans constituted only 24 percent of the population, out of 1000 regular serving officers in 1906, there were 791 Germans. In addition there were 97 Magyars, 47 Czechs, 23 Poles, and 22 Croats and Serbs. The low Magyar contribution was significant and a reflection of the national feeling. Although Magyars constituted some 20 percent of the total population, they provided less than 10 percent of the regular officer corps. In contrast, they provided their full share of reserve officers, serving mainly in the *Honvédség.* Out of 1000 reserve officers, there were 589 Germans, 257 Magyars, 98 Czechs, 29 Poles, and 16 Croat and Serb officers. Here the contribution of the Magyars correlated highly with their percentage within the total population.[28]

At the same time, the widely differing educational standards in the monarchy affected the composition of the officer corps. Because most reserve officers were drawn from the socially and educationally privileged one-year volunteers, only nationalities with a substantial middle class could furnish many officer entrants and the peasant nationalities—Slovaks, Slovenes, Ruthenes—were not represented in the corps.[29] Another striking fact was the number of Jewish officers, especially in the reserves. Although the officer corps was predominantly Catholic, (80 percent of the regulars, 90 percent of the pupils at the military academies, and 68 percent of the reserves), and while the Jewish population of the Dual Monarchy fluctuated around 5 percent, over 18 percent of the reserve officers were Jewish.[30] In fact, religion was given considerable latitude in the Habsburg army and it was not a barrier to promotion.[31]

Of course, the composition of the rank and file was a more accurate representation of the nationality distribution in the empire. In 1906 out of every 1000 enlisted men, there were 267 Germans, 223 Hungarians, 135 Czechs, 85 Poles, 81 Ruthenes, 67 Croats and Serbs, 64 Rumanians, 38 Slovaks, 26 Slovenes, and 14 Italians.[32] Since 1896, reflecting the magyarization efforts of the Hungarian government, the number of Magyars had risen by 40, up from 183.[33] Even so, the common army's impartiality towards special national demands and its retention of the various regimental languages were a constant thorn in the side of Hungarian nationalists. In 1901 out of 256 units of the common army, 94 employed but one language, 133 used two languages, and 28 authorized the use of three or even four languages. And in Hungary, except for the purely Magyar units, there were 26 regiments employing their various national languages: 2 Slovak, 3 Rumanian, 6 German-Magyar, 1 German-Slovak, 3 German-Rumanian, 5 Magyar-Slovak, 6 Magyar-Rumanian, and even 1 Magyar-Rumanian-Ruthene regiments.[34] Clearly, the army's attitude, neutral rather than pro-Hungarian, was an obstacle to extremist goals; in 1903 one delegate complained in the Budapest parliament that all magyarization efforts were futile if the indoctrination begun in the village schools would not be reinforced in the common army.[35]

Although the common army refused to become the tool of any national group, the ever more virulent character of the nationality struggles entered its ranks. At the same time, especially in the German and Czech areas, there was an increase in anti-military agitation by the socialists which usually was mixed with anti-dynastic nationalism.[36] And while the regular officer corps remained loyal to its dynastic orientation and untouched by these currents, the same was not true of the reserve officers who usually retained strong commitments to the national and social ideas of the region and class from which they had come.[37] Many observers believed that the army was drifting towards disintegration and shared the belief of Count Kasimir Badeni, the Austrian prime minister, who declared that "a state of nationalities cannot wage war without danger to itself."[38]

But during this period Austria-Hungary's military leaders were not primarily concerned with the remote prospect of foreign war; they were preoccupied with the possible employment of the army as an instrument of internal security and they feared that nationalism and socialism were eroding the dynastic allegiance of the troops. To counteract this trend they advocated once again stationing units outside their ethnic areas and away from the large cities where seditious agitation was at its most dangerous. Among the strongest advocates of such ideas was

Archduke Francis Ferdinand, the heir presumptive, who in May 1896 sent a lengthy memorandum on this subject to Beck.

"The monarchy," the archduke wrote, "faces a time of crisis. Revolution is threatening in Hungary and there is mounting separatist nationalist disaffection in the other half of the empire."[39] Only the army could protect the throne and the dynasty, and in fact, continued Francis Ferdinand, "the army's main task is not the defense of the fatherland against an external enemy, but the protection and maintenance of the throne and the dynasty against all internal enemies." Hungary, now strengthened by a well-organized *Honvéd,* "more dangerous than that of Kossuth and Görgey," appeared as the most immediate danger, but nationalist, socialist, and anarchist agitation also endangered the spirit of other regiments. Yet, claimed Francis Ferdinand, the solution was simple and had the endorsement of the departed Archduke Albrecht, namely to move the regiments once again out of their ethnic areas. As long as this beneficial institution prevailed, he argued, soldiers had regarded themselves as Austrians and had "recognized nothing else but the emperor and their branch." Beck, however, refused to consider this course of action. There was, he replied, still a very considerable reservoir of dynastic loyalty in the army and, above all, a return to the old "extra-territorial" system would endanger the rapid mobilization schedule. For the moment Francis Ferdinand, lacking a military position of power, let his scheme go, though he always remembered it and made it an important part of his future plans.

In any case, any large-scale troop transfers became impossible because in the following year the full fury of the nationality struggle was unleashed. The crisis began in April 1897 when Count Badeni, in an effort to gain the support of the powerful Young Czech faction in the *Reichsrat,* issued his language ordinances which placed Czech on an equal level with German in the transaction of official business within Bohemia. For some years now, the conflict there between Germans and Czechs had grown more virulent, and the ordinances triggered an explosion of German national resentment not only against the language regulations, but also against the relative decline in their position as the leading nation within Austria. Schönerer's German nationalists, until then a violent and loud minority, found allies among the German moderates, liberals, and even socialists, and for the next three years German obstruction brought the *Reichsrat* to an effective halt. Parliament was crippled by hundreds of motions, resolutions, and interpolations; there were tumults and violence, which soon spilled over into the streets. Throughout the alpine provinces, in Vienna, Graz, and Salzburg, German crowds demonstrated with considerable violence which threatened to disrupt all orderly government. All Austria was shaken and Badeni fell from office in November 1897.

Badeni's fall, however, did not end the crisis in Austria. Though the *Reichsrat* was periodically reconvened, each time noisy obstruction and interruptions forced a suspension of the sessions, and the government had to rule by emergency decrees. Although the language ordinances were eventually repealed in 1899, causing great dissatisfaction among the Czechs, the German nationalists also were not satisfied and riots continued in the large German-Austrian cities. The most serious incidents occurred in Graz, always a hotbed of German nationalist agitation, where a series of confrontations between the garrison and the rioters revealed a potentially serious rift between the army and the national group long considered among the most loyal supporters of the dynasty.

When late in November 1897 the local police in Graz proved unable to deal with student and worker riots, the provincial governor, Marquis Olivier Bacquehem, asked the commander of III Corps, Feldmarschall Leutnant Eduard Succovary Ritter von Vezza, to provide military assistance.[40] On November 27, detachments of the 27th Infantry, the 2nd Bosnian-Hercegovinian Infantry, and the 5th Dragoons were called out to disperse the rioters, but the number of troops employed was insufficient to overawe the crowd, and when a Bosnian patrol was in danger of being overrun by the mob, the officer in charge gave orders to fire. One attacker was killed and several others wounded.[41] The funeral of the victim became the occassion for bitter attacks on the "black-yellow Moslem mercenaries," and on December 1 the Graz city council passed a resolution deploring the presence of Bosnian troops, characterized as "strangers to the country," in the city. Here then was a direct challenge to the basic concepts of a common army and when the resolution was brought before the *Reichsrat* by a German nationalist deputy, the common war minister answered it.

"I can assure you," stated Reichskriegsminister Krieghammer on December 7, "that every regiment of the multinational Austrian army, regardless of its ethnic composition, will always do its duty against all internal and external enemies of the monarchy." And, continued the minister, "it never will make a difference whether the regiment comes from the north or the south of the monarchy, or what language it uses, because in the army every nationality is equal and is equally respected. No officer recognizes any national differences."[42] Even so, the press and the public continued to attack the army, and on December 14 Succovary complained to Krieghammer that the "position of the officer corps and the army would sustain irreparable damage until energetic action was taken against the student ringleaders."[43] In turn, the war minister pressured the civil authorities to take action. A number of students were expelled from the Graz university, while military courts of honor deprived thirty-three students of their reserve officer commissions.[44] And when, in May 1898, this again led to attack against troop units, countered this time with considerable restraint, the emperor demanded to know why assaults on troops had not been repelled by the "use of arms, including firearms."[45]

German nationalist riots created a Czech reaction and by November 1897 there had been Czech riots in Prague which destroyed German and Jewish property. However, the governor, Count Karl Coudenhove, was careful to employ only Czech units to repress the mobs, though other troops from I Corps (Cracow) and II Corps (Vienna) had been alerted.[46] At the same time, Czech nationalists started a campaign asking that recruits called up for muster but not yet in uniform should answer roll call with *Zde* instead of *hier*. Though trivial, at that time it was considered a serious attack on the German language of command. As usual, the military authorities overreacted and the emperor too was adamant. During a state dinner he told a Czech delegate that "on the *Zde* issue I can see no compromise. If necessary I will proclaim martial law to settle this business, because I am very strict in military matters."[47] As it was, the issue contributed to the emperor's decision to terminate once again efforts to conciliate the Czechs.[48] Abandoning attempts to create governments based on parliamentary coalition, he now fell back on governments headed by technicians and after a number of short-lived interim cabinets, he appointed Ernst von Koerber, an experienced civil servant, as prime minister of Austria in January 1900. Relying in large part on the emergency powers of the constitution, Koerber managed to restore a semblance of order, and by 1902 the *Reichsrat* was again functioning. Among its first pieces of business was a request by the War Ministry to increase the strength of the common army. Since 1892 the military had pressed for a revision of the manpower ceilings set in 1889. In fact, in 1899, 1900, and 1901, the government had been forced to call up recruits by the use of its emergency power in Austria and by annual bills in Hungary. But this did not provide more manpower and in 1902 the war minister proposed that while the annual recruit figure remain unaltered, the military be given authority to call up for service men of the supplementary reserves who had not actually done their full term. But when these proposals, introduced in both parliaments in October 1902, met with considerable resistance, Krieghammer withdrew them and in November introduced a new bill asking for a rather modest increase in the annual number of recruits. In all, the war minister proposed that the annual contingent for the common army be raised to 125,000—71,562 from Austria and 53,438 from Hungary—while the annual quota for the *Landwehr* was set at 14,500 and at 15,000 for the *Honvédség*. The increase was modest and justified considering the huge increase in the population of the monarchy. Nonetheless, there was considerable opposition in the *Reichsrat* and the bill was passed after a struggle which lasted nearly a year and even then only on the condition that the Hungarian parliament do the same.[49]

But in Hungary, where Magyar nationalism had become more and more pronounced, introduction of the army bill triggered a crisis which brought the Dual Monarchy to the brink of civil war. Hungarian political affairs were dominated by the quarrel between the Liberal Party which supported the Compromise of 1867 and the parties of "1848," above all the Independence Party, which sought to revive the Hungary established by Louis Kossuth. To be sure, the quarrels of the two groups had little meaning for the great majority of the people. The franchise extended to only 6 percent of the population, more than a third of the adult males were illiterate, and the great mass of the landless proletariat lived in abject squalor. Still, the pressures of the 1848 group led to disagreements within the leadership of the governing Liberal Party. In 1890, Tisza, shaken by the violence displayed over the army bill of 1889, resigned from office and successive Liberal governments, though they purported to support the Compromise of 1867, actually cooperated with the opposition parties in order to strengthen Hungary's political position within the Dual Monarchy and to assert Magyar predominance within the kingdom. A succession of Liberal Party prime ministers, Count Gyula Szapáry (1890–1892), Alexander Wekerle (1892–1895), Baron Dezsö Bánffy (1895–1899), and Kálmán Széll (1899–1903), all tried to make political capital by demanding concessions in return for their support of the common army.

Szapáry tried to gain concessions by refusing to get the Budapest parliament to provide extraordinary funds for the procurement of smokeless powder, and it required the personal intervention of the emperor to budge him from his position.[50] Wekerle as well as Bánffy endorsed the demands of the opposition. As a prominent Liberal politician, Count Kálmán Széchényi wrote to Beck, Hungarian military demands—including the transfer of Magyar officers to Magyar regiments, a Hungarian war academy, and recognition of the Hungarian language for official military transactions—were widely shared in the country. Széchényi advised Beck to give in on these points because, as he put it, an adamant stand would only aid the radical opposition.[51]

But Beck was not prepared to accede to such demands, especially since every concession to Hungary would only be followed by similar demands from the Czechs and Poles. To be sure, there were some minor concessions. For instance, in 1899 the statue of General Hentzi, which had produced the incident in 1886, was quietly removed from its prominent place in the St. George Square and located in the interior court of the Budapest cadet school. But this was not enough to appease the Magyars and when in October 1902 Széll's minister of defense, Géza Féjérváry, presented the army bill before the House of Deputies, there was a wave of national feeling. Liberals joined with the opposition in demanding the introduction of the Hungarian language of command, Hungarian national flags and insignia, and Hungarian officers to command all Hungarian formations, and they interspersed their demands with threats of a complete break-away from Austria.[52]

The reason for this outbreak, the gravest internal challenge facing the monarchy since 1848, was that by 1902 many Hungarians feared that dualism would be abrogated by Austria. Such fears were fed by nationalist radical agitation and found substance in the fact that Emperor Francis Joseph, regarded as a staunch adherent of the compromise, was now over seventy years old and the heir presumptive, Archduke Francis Ferdinand, was known as an open enemy of Hungary. Moreover, the international situation appeared relaxed and to many Hungarian nationalists the common army no longer appeared as a necessity to shield the country against Russia. In the face of the parliamentary uproar, the ruling Liberal Party was thrown into confusion and in May 1903 Széll resigned from office. But, for the moment at least, it appeared as if Francis Joseph would stand firm. He appointed Karl Count Khuen-Hédervary, an energetic Liberal politician and former *Ban* of Croatia, as prime minister. However, the strong man was unable to deal with the obstreperous parliament and he resigned on August 10, though he remained in office pending the appointment of a successor.[53]

The situation in Hungary was considered so serious by the army that Beck counseled the emperor to move two infantry divisions into the country, suspend the constitution and rule *ex lex*. The emperor was unwilling to resort to such extreme measures, but from the maneuver field at Chlopy in Galicia he issued the famous army order of September 18, 1903, asserting that, "My Army shall know above all . . . that I will never abandon the rights and prerogatives entrusted to me as Supreme War Lord. My army shall remain joint and united, a strong force to defend the Austro-Hungarian Monarchy against all enemies." Moreover, in a seeming rebuff to special national claims he proclaimed that, "the armed forces shall continue to honor the various national characteristics . . . and thus utilize the individual qualities of every nationality."[54]

These were determined words and appeared to challenge Hungary. However, the emperor soon wavered in his resolution. A few days later he sent a letter to Khuen-Hédervary which softened the impact of the order and opened the way towards negotiations. Early in October such negotiations opened between the emperor and a Liberal Party Committee of Nine, headed by Count István Tisza. Both sides shrank away from a collision course and in short order agreed to a temporary compromise solution. Magyar officers were allowed transfer to Hungarian units; the Magyar language was accorded greater prominence in Hungarian regiments, military schools, and in the official correspondence between the Hungarian military and the political administration. In addition, Francis Joseph conceded flying of the national colors alongside the imperial flag on military buildings and promised that graduates of the *Honvéd* academy would be eligible for regular commissions. In turn, the committee, though with some reservations, recognized the crown's right to determine the languages of service and command.[55]

Armed with these substantial concessions, Tisza was appointed prime minister of Hungary in November 1903. The emperor evidently believed that the concessions would appease Hungarian nationalism and permit the resumption of recruit inductions, while leaving his power over the common army essentially intact. But he was mistaken. Tisza almost at once was deserted by a number of Liberal leaders who claimed that the government was not doing enough to magyarize the army, and together with the opposition, brought government practically to a standstill for the next two years. There were noisy scenes in parliament and rioting in the streets. Meanwhile taxes were not collected, recruits were not levied, and in order to preserve the active strength of the army, the military authorities were forced to retain men on active duty beyond their due discharge dates.[56]

Francis Joseph had made the concessions, but the task of implementing them was left to General Pitreich, the common war minister. Hoping at least to obtain the recruit contingents laid down in 1889, Pitreich interpreted the provisions of the understanding with the Committee of Nine in a most generous fashion. Above all he conceded that Magyar would be employed as the regimental language in all Hungarian units, even in those where only twenty percent of the troops could speak it. At the same time he appeared favorable towards the demand that the *Honvédség* be permitted to form its own artillery units. Much to the relief of Archduke Francis Ferdinand, however, this was quashed when Koerber protested. The Austrian prime minister pointed out that the principle of parity demanded that similar formations be established for the *Landwehr*, and that Austria did not have the money to do this.[57] Although Pitreich mainly carried out what had been implied in the emperor's understanding with the Committee of Nine, he was sharply attacked by the more intransigent army leaders and dubbed the *Heeresverderber*—the spoiler of the army. Writing in his own defense, Pitreich pointed out that he had always held fast to the two essentials, the sovereign prerogatives of the monarch and the uniform language of service and command.[58]

Pitreich's good intentions, however, neither reassured the army leadership nor placated the Magyars. Hungary continued in turmoil, and Tisza resolved to take a desperate expedient. On the assumption that the electorate would repudiate the state of near anarchy, he dissolved parliament and ordered a national election. But in this election of January 1905, though Tisza challenged the opposition on its own ground by taking over many of the extremist national demands, he was defeated. The anti-government coalition of dissident Liberals and Nationalists won a clear majority and Tisza resigned. The triumphant nationalists now demanded further military concessions as the price of forming a government, but Francis Joseph refused to be intimidated. On June 21, 1905, he appointed General Féjérváry, commander of the Royal Hungarian Bodyguard and chancellor of the Maria Theresa Order, as prime minister and also hinted that he was considering the introduction of a radical suffrage reform in Hungary.

Indeed, a strong stand seemed necessary because the empire was in crisis. In Austria there was increased agitation for a broad electoral reform, the Social Democrats were making gains in the industrial and mining districts, and in Bohemia the army once again was disturbed by Czech nationalist manifestations during the annual reserve musters.[59] Moreover, the foreign horizon was clouding. In March, Emperor William II appeared at Tangiers demonstrating that Germany would not accept a French hegemony in Morocco; Serbia and Bulgaria drew together in a commercial agreement; and finally, in June 1905, Norway unilaterally dissolved its union with Sweden. The last event clearly was not lost on the nationalists in Hungary and seemed to provide a precedent for the dissolution of the Dual Monarchy.

To counter such an eventuality, the *k.u.k.* general staff in Vienna began to prepare plans for an armed intervention in Hungary.[60] The possibility of such a move had passed repeatedly through the minds of Magyar and imperial leaders. During the negotiations of 1868 Andrássy had pressed for the dissolution of the Military Border because he feared that it constituted a potential base for intervention against Hungary.[61] In 1886, during the Hentzi incident, Crown Prince Rudolf had urged such a step, and in 1903 Beck had comtemplated military measures.[62] But now the army leaders were even more disturbed. During the crisis of 1903 many Hungarian reserve officers had openly revealed their dislike of the Austrian connection, and in 1904 there had been other incidents in which Hungarian units rioted and mutilated pictures of the emperor.[63] Foreign developments, parliamentary obstructions, demonstrations, riots, and violence which accompanied the fight against the army bill and for the introduction of the Hungarian language of command hardened the military's conviction that only force could resolve the issue and save the Dual Monarchy.

In February 1904, Feldmarschall Leutnant Moritz von Auffenberg, then commanding the 65th *k.u.k.* Infantry Brigade at Raab, had submitted such a scheme to the emperor's military chancery, to the general staff, and to Archduke Francis Ferdinand. Auffenberg envisaged a concentric attack on Hungary by loyal troops drawn from the non-Magyar units of the common army. He realized that this would provoke a full-fledged national insurrection, but proposed to deal with it by an "offensive *a outrance,* an offensive pushed to the last extremity in every quarter."[64] The chances for success, the general estimated, were excellent because against a potential 400 infantry battalions, 200 cavalry squadrons, and 1,136 guns, the Magyars could only rely on the *Honvéd,* most of the regular Hussar regiments, and 92 regular battalions supported by between 120 to 150 guns.

By April 1905 the operations section of the general staff had produced its own version, designated "*Fall* U." This plan called for a modified general mobilization in all corps areas, except in IV Corps, Budapest, where "one cannot count on the support of the local administration or on the proper functioning of communications and transportation."[65] Between July 19 and August 13, this basic plan was further refined. There now were two variants. The first called for the complete military occupation of Hungary and the appointment of Feldzeugmeister Rudolf Prince Lobkowitz, then commanding IV Corps (Budapest), as military governor. Although the plan did envisage some resistance, it did not consider artillery requirements as important. "Because of its tradition and the composition of its officer corps," the study explained, "the artillery of the Hungarian corps, including that of IV Corps, appears to be reliable."[66] In any case, the fire missions that might be required could be carried out by the monitors of the Danube flotilla.

The second variant was in a much lower key and merely provided for troops to be put at the disposal of the civil authorities in case widespread riots accompanied the reconvening of the Budapest parliament set for September 15, 1905.

On August 24, the chief of the general staff presented a specially prepared outline of the two plans to a joint council of ministers held at the imperial summer retreat at Bad Ischl. The emperor and his ministers approved of the plans, though they showed a marked preference for the second variant—military intervention in support of the civil power.[67] In any case, Francis Joseph reserved final word on giving the signal for beginning actual operations. At heart, he was not prepared to redress the balance of power in the Dual Monarchy by force. He was willing to countenance force as a last resort to save dualism, but not as a means of destroying it.

Throughout September and October 1905, the general staff maintained a close watch over the available transport to throw troops into Budapest. For instance, on September 28, 1905, Danube steamer transportation for three thousand men was reported available, while on October 8, five thousand men could have been lifted.[68] However, Francis Joseph was really looking for a political solution. While disorders continued in Hungary, he called the leaders of the victorious electoral coalition into conference on September 23, and demanded they drop their obstruction to the new army law and accept the continued use of the German language of command, threatening them with the introduction of secret universal manhood suffrage.[69] The threat was not enough; the victorious coalition still insisted on a Magyar army as its condition for taking office.

Meanwhile, however, the political conditions for a military intervention in Hungary were beginning to recede. Although during the night of October 8, general staff officers carried sealed packages of instructions, to be opened only on receipt of orders from the Reichskriegsminister to the various corps commanders, these orders never arrived, and on October 12 the corps commanders were told to return these packages unopened to Vienna.[70] There would be no large-scale military action against Hungary.

The reasons for this change in plans were manifold. Above all there was the emperor's reluctance, reinforced by political developments in the rest of the empire, to unleash a civil war. Even the loyalist Croatians were wavering and on October 14 at Fiume, Croat and Serb representatives agreed on common action and support of the Magyar opposition in return for better treatment. In Russia the revolutionary events following the defeat in Manchuria induced the tsar to grant freedoms which had violent repercussions in Austria. The parties of the left demonstrated for a broader suffrage, and on November 2 and again on November 4, there were bloody clashes in Vienna, Prague, and other cities. In Bohemia VIII Corps had to be mobilized, and there were distinct signs of unreliability among the Czech rank and file.[71] These events contributed to a reconciliation between the crown and the Hungarian opposition. To be sure, when turmoil continued in the Budapest parliament, Francis Joseph finally did employ force, but it was essentially a minor police action. On February 19, 1906, the emperor suspended the

Hungarian constitution, appointed a *Honvéd* officer, Generalmajor Alexander von Nyiri, as royal commissioner plenipotentiary, and used one infantry battalion to disperse the unruly deputies.

Contrary to the expectations and fears of the emperor's military advisors, the country accepted this action without resistance. The myth that the Hungarian parliament represented the people and not just the ruling classes had been called. The Magyars did not spring to arms to defend the privileges of parliament. But at the same time Francis Joseph shrank from pushing his success to its logical conclusions—basic political, social, and national changes. He was too conservative for that. He wanted to save the common army and having achieved an approximation of this goal he was willing to make yet another compromise. The Hungarians too were sobered by the threat of electoral reforms and the specter of the Croat-Serb coalition. Although the opposition swept the country in the elections of 1906, in April the opposition politicians then in office accepted Francis Joseph's proposal for an enlarged recruit contingent and the retention of the German language of command.[72] In return, Hungary received concessions which in all essential aspects made the *Honvédség* a truly national army composed of all branches, including its own artillery.[73]

Thus the crisis ended with substantial Hungarian gains, only a step short of complete victory. Even the promise of an enlarged recruit contingent was not realized until 1912; in the meantime, Budapest continued to exact a high price for its contributions to the common army. "Every strengthening of the army," one general wrote in anger, "every improvement, had to be bought from Hungary."[74] To some officers the outcome actually foreshadowed the end of the monarchy. In a widely read pamphlet, one general staff officer painted the nightmare of a future, but imminent, war in which the monarchy, torn apart internally by Hungarian sedition and socialist riots, was attacked and overwhelmed by a Serb, Montenegrin, Russian, and Bulgarian coalition, with Germany standing by and merely occupying Bohemia to protect its own interests.[75]

Of course, these dire predictions did not come to pass. The Hungarian national army, which is what it had become by 1914, proved loyal during the stress of World War I, and Hungarian troops fought with distinction on all fronts. But soldiers are notably poor prophets, and for the moment they were bitterly disappointed in the failure to redress the dualistic imbalance by force. And since the old emperor stood above criticism, much of the dissatisfaction was vented against his friend and chief of the general staff, Feldmarschall Beck. Beck's paramount influence had already been assailed by many leading officers and was offensive to some members of the imperial house. Now Archduke Francis Ferdinand took the lead in the attack on Beck. Although the archduke held no formal military appointment, in part because Beck was reluctant to surrender power, he had gradually built up influence in the military establishment through his own military chancery, headed since January 1906 by Major Alexander Brosch von Aarenau.[76]

Francis Ferdinand's political notions were crude and he tended towards championing a Habsburg absolutism which portended little good for the future prospects of the Dual Monarchy. Although he too was enamored of the thought of a global policy for Austria-Hungary, and in 1900 had bitterly complained that the monarchy had not sent troops to China "when even dwarf states like Belgium and Portugal have contingents there,"[77] he was not primarily interested in the army as an instrument of foreign policy but above all as a safeguard against internal dangers.[78] Now the archduke blamed Beck as well as Pitreich for the concessions made to Hungary, which he continued to regard as the main internal enemy of the monarchy, and he added his personal influence to the groups persuading the emperor to dismiss his old chief of the general staff.[79]

Although the dismissal, when it came, was abrupt, there can be little doubt that the action was necessary. During the last ten years of Beck's tenure the army had fallen behind. And this was not only due to the inadequate budgets and manpower ceilings, or because of the confusion in government, administration, or parliaments, or because of the nationalist and socialist agitation. These, to be sure, were important. But there also were other reasons which were just as substantial. The army was suffering from an overaged leadership which did not comprehend the requirements brought about by recent technological changes.

When Beck had entered the service, muzzleloaders, bayonets, and smoothbore cannons, unchanged in their principal characteristics since the days of Prince Eugene, had still been the main weapons. By 1905 repeating rifles, machine guns, and quick-firing artillery provided firepower undreamed of in an earlier age, while new weapons—the armored fighting vehicle, chemical weapons, and aircraft—were in their seminal stages. The internal combustion engine was coming into use and electricity, both through the telephone wire and through the airwaves, provided means of instant communication. To be sure, Beck had ceaselessly worked to create bigger battalions and faster mobilization, but he never was able—and this was to be also true of his successor—to look beyond the narrow bounds of dynastic loyalty to the bigger vision of a nation in arms supported by a modern industrial and economic base.

Indeed, by 1905 the limited franchise granted in 1867 and only slightly modified since then caused considerable resentment among the masses who were carrying the burden of universal military service. Moreover, Francis Joseph had threatened to introduce universal male suffrage in Hungary and, as people were saying, the emperor of Austria could not very well refuse what the king of Hungary was willing to grant. Although Baron Gautsch, Koerber's successor as prime minister of Austria in 1905 and 1906, was apprehensive, and the military too were concerned, Francis Joseph himself pressed for the measure and his ministers obeyed. By the end of 1905 the institution of general franchise in both halves of the monarchy was accepted at least in principle, though its introduction in Austria took several years and it was never accomplished in Hungary.

Thus, slowly, the modern age was arriving in Austria-Hungary. Beck, clearly a survivor of the nineteenth century and now seventy-two years old, was expendable. When in the fall of 1906 the emperor was dissatisfied with the conduct of maneuvers, the necessary pretext for dismissing Beck was at hand and he was relieved on September 18, 1906.[80] He was replaced, on Francis Ferdinand's recommendation, by Feldmarschall Leutnant Conrad von Hötzendorf, while Pitreich, whose head the archduke had also demanded, was replaced by General der Infantrie Franz Baron Schönaich.

For the *k.u.k. Armee* these changes in the top command marked the beginning of the twentieth century. It was exactly forty years before that the army had fought its last major war. Therefore Conrad, known as an expert in military tactics and planning, was full of ideas for reorganizing the army, revamping its obsolescent tactics, improving its armament, and reshaping it totally into an instrument for fighting a modern war. He inherited from Beck a position which *de facto* had become the most powerful post in the Habsburg military establishment, but as the new chief of staff also recognized, the portents were not favorable. In domestic and foreign affairs the storm signals were flying, and Conrad suspected that time was running out for the Dual Monarchy.

10

The Conrad Era from His Appointment to the Annexation Crisis: 1906-1909

In the Dual Monarchy the closing decades of the nineteenth century were marked by political and social turbulence arising from the escalation of national conflicts and the stresses of the accelerating industrial revolution. In Austria the conflict between Germans and Czechs had wrecked the constitutional processes of government, while in Hungary a military collision between Vienna and Budapest over the question of the army had only been avoided by the reluctance of the aged monarch to sanction such a radical move. In both halves of the monarchy there was mounting unrest among the industrial and agricultural proletariat, arousing great apprehension among the propertied classes. At the same time, however, since the 1890s the foreign relations of the Dual Monarchy had been in a period of stabilization, reflecting the equilibrium among the major European powers and Russian preoccupation in the Far East. To be sure, Vienna retained deep suspicions of Italian intentions, and relations with Serbia had deteriorated rapidly, but neither of these potential antagonists by themselves represented a major threat to the security of the empire. Therefore Count Goluchowski, Austria-Hungary's foreign minister, with the approval of the emperor, had pursued an essentially passive policy.

The combination of internal conflicts and the absence of a serious menace from abroad combined to hold down the military posture of the Habsburg Empire. Most politicians assumed that no major war was expected in the near future and that therefore military expenditures could be kept down. In the Vienna *Reichsrat*, various national groups brought parliamentary business to a virtual standstill and the government, appointed from senior civil servants, increasingly ruled by decree. Meanwhile in Budapest, parliament dominated by Magyar chauvinist politicians used obstruction in military matters, specifically in that of raising the annual recruit quota, as a means to press for autonomy in military affairs. Actually, as the soldiers pointed out, calculations that there was no need to improve the army were nearsighted. Except for Austria-Hungary, and despite the relaxation in international tensions, European powers continued to increase their armament and neither the new mass armies nor their required equipment could be quickly improvised in the event of war. But to break the deadlock in political affairs would have required strong and perhaps even bloody surgery, and Francis Joseph would not countenance such action. Therefore, in military affairs too, the empire followed a static policy.

By 1906, however, the belief was growing in influential circles that the Dual Monarchy was gradually disintegrating and that desperate efforts should be made to infuse fresh life and vigor into the political structure and to check tendencies towards dissolution arising from internal and foreign pressures. The nationality question and, above all, the position of Hungary within the common framework of the monarchy had to be resolved. In foreign affairs it was evident that Russia, repulsed in the Far East by Japan, would soon revert to her traditional forward policy on the Balkans. Clearly, for both internal and external contingencies, the army would need to be strengthened.

In 1906 important changes took place in the highest political and military positions of the Dual Monarchy. In April a bargain designed to end the deadlocked army issue was struck between the crown and Hungary. The Magyars promised to drop their opposition to the German language of command in the joint army and promised to support the long-stalled bill increasing the size of the annual recruit contingent. In return, the emperor relieved General Fejérváry, his personal appointee, as prime minister of Hungary and appointed Alexander Wekerle, an old-line Liberal, to head a new cabinet of nationalist politicians. And while this obscure transaction (which led to the resignation of the joint war minister, Feldzeugmeister Heinrich Baron Pitreich, who felt that too much had been conceded in return for empty promises) soon became unstuck, and the Budapest parliament did not pass an army bill until 1912 as Pitreich had predicted, the appointment of Wekerle ended, for the time being at least, an acute stage in the confrontation.[1]

Of course, the deal with Hungary in many ways was merely a continuation of previous arrangements, but the other major appointments constituted real changes. On June 3, Max Wladimir Baron Beck, for some years chief civilian advisor to Francis Ferdinand, became prime minister of Austria. On October 24, Count Goluchowski was replaced by Alois Lexa Count Aehrenthal in the Foreign Ministry,[2] and General der Infantrie Franz Baron Schönaich, considered a strong man, replaced Pitreich at the *Reichskriegsministerium*. The series of new appointments concluded with the appointment of Feldmarschall Leutnant Franz Conrad von Hötzendorf replacing Beck as chief of the general staff in November.

In large part these changes reflected the growing influence of Archduke Francis Ferdinand. To be sure, Francis Ferdinand had no influence on the appointment of Wekerle, and he regarded the deal preceeding this appointment with a great deal of alarm. At the same time, however, the archduke enthusiastically supported the appointment of Beck and welcomed the arrival of Aehrenthal.[3] Francis Ferdinand had been disappointed that Goluchowski had not conducted a more active policy while Russia was preoccupied, and Aehrenthal had promised that under his direction Austria-Hungary would act like a great power.[4] Aehrenthal's main objective was to revive the Alliance of the Three Emperors and, in cooperation with Russia, to pursue a program of expansion in the Balkans which would neutralize Serbia, regarded both in Vienna and Budapest as a potential focus of attraction for the South Slavs within the monarchy and as a certain enemy in case of war with either Russia or Italy.[5]

Although Francis Joseph had been slow to grant Francis Ferdinand any real share in the government of the realm, the very fact that the archduke was the heir presumptive gave his views considerable weight. The case that some recent Habsburg apologists have made for Francis Ferdinand as an enlightened spirit who might have solved the nationality problem and transformed the Dual Monarchy into a truly supranational community does not, however, appear very convincing.[6] The archduke was much too self-willed, too autocratic, too reactionary, and too clerical for such developments. To be sure, the little brain trust—in some eyes a shadow cabinet—which he had gradually assembled at the Belvedere Palace included some original thinkers, but, as far as can be determined, Francis Ferdinand's foremost aim was to resurrect the centralized monarchy created by Schwarzenberg and the army after 1848.[7]

The army therefore was a key factor in almost all of Francis Ferdinand's schemes and it was in military affairs that his influence was most apparent, although by 1906 he still did not hold any regular position in the chain of command. Like other members of the imperial house he had entered the service early and had been advanced rapidly regardless of age and experience. Appointed a lieutenant at the age of fourteen, a captain at twenty-two, and a colonel at twenty-seven, he was promoted to major general in 1894 at the age of thirty-one. Although he had received no formal staff training and never attended the *Kriegsschule,* he was considered eligible for senior command. Indeed, after the death of Archduke Albrecht in 1895, Francis Ferdinand was expected to become his successor as commander in chief in case of war, though this appointment was never made official.[8] In 1898, however, he was given a roving commission "at the special disposition of His Majesty" to inquire into all aspects of the military establishment.[9] The three military ministries, the *Reichskriegsministerium* in Vienna as well as the Austrian and Hungarian Ministries of National Defense, were commanded to circulate information copies of all of their major papers to the archduke.

Moreover, in order to carry out his new duties, he also was provided with the rudiments of a military staff. Starting originally with two aides-de-camp, this staff grew into the "little" military chancery with an eventual staff of sixteen rivalling the "great" military chancery of the emperor, headed by Feldmarschall Leutnant Arthur Baron Bolfras, which had only two more staff members.[10] The influence of Francis Ferdinand's military chancery grew rapidly after Captain Alexander Brosch von Aarenau, a brilliant and ambitious young general staff officer, took charge of the office in January 1904.[11] Essentially a political soldier, Brosch had with charm, tact, and discretion not only reinforced the archduke's political convictions, but also created an elaborate network of contacts and unofficial informants which furnished the Belvedere with a great deal of intelligence, superior in many respects to that received through more conventional means by the emperor. Brosch established a working relationship with the conservative and imperial-minded Christian Socialists in Austria, while in Hungary he cultivated relations with minority group politicians who were looking towards Vienna for protection from Magyar oppression.[12]

Hungary, in fact, was a main preoccupation at the Belvedere; like his master, Brosch pursued a hard line on all issues concerning Hungarian aspirations. By 1906 Francis Ferdinand's earlier resentment of the Magyars had grown into a real obsession which colored all his thoughts and actions. And this attitude was revealed in both large and small concerns. Francis Ferdinand regarded the army primarily as an instrument against the "internal enemy" which he once described as "Jews, Freemasons, Socialists, and Hungarians,"[13] and he always considered a revolution as far more likely than a foreign war.[14] Sometimes his resentment of all things Hungarian even interfered with the performance of his duties. Although the archduke probed into all details of the military establishment and the story went that if a rifle toppled from its stand in Kamionka Strumilova, a small Galician garrison, the Belvedere would hear about it the next day, he adamantly refused to inspect any Hungarian units.[15]

Francis Ferdinand's preoccupation with the menace of revolution was reflected in his old-fashioned, arch-conservative approach to military technology. Except for an interest in the navy and in military aviation, he displayed little understanding of the revolution on the battlefield brought about by the repeating rifle, quick-firing field artillery, and entrenchments.[16] The lessons of the Boer and the Russo-Japanese wars he ignored and he retained great faith in the effectiveness of parade ground drill to instill loyalty and confidence in the troops. He even maintained faith in the efficacy of the massed cavalry charge, and after he had been appointed inspector general of the armed forces in 1913, and had been placed in charge of maneuvers, he ordered at the conclusion of the army maneuvers in Bohemia a massed charge by a cavalry corps, eight regiments, against dug-in infantry supported by artillery.[17]

This was a splendid spectacle, but it was not war. However, the archduke did not consider the army primarily as an instrument for war. Because of his association with Conrad, an ardent and persistent advocate of preventive war, he often was regarded both within the Dual Monarchy and outside as the leader of a war party, but Francis Ferdinand was in fact eager to avoid external conflict. Above all he was determined to avoid any conflict with Russia, which he regarded as a stronghold of legitimism, and he was prepared, in order not to offend the tsar, to maintain peace with Serbia. However, he disliked republican France, regarded the House of Savoy as usurpers, and might have gone to war to restore the Papal States. Although he disagreed with Conrad's view on war, he believed that the general was the man to revive the stagnant military establishment and it was largely through his efforts that Conrad was appointed chief of the general staff in November 1906.[18]

The appointment came as a surprise. During the last years of Beck's long tenure as chief of the general staff numerous candidates, most of them senior to Conrad and better placed, had been mentioned for the position which had become the most influential military appointment in the Dual Monarchy. The candidates included Feldmarschall Leutnant Oskar Potiorek, Beck's deputy, Feldzeugmeister Pitreich, the war minister, and Feldmarschall Leutnant Karl Tersztyánszky von Nádas, a general staff officer senior to Conrad by several years.[19] But Conrad, then serving as commander of the 8th Infantry Division in Innsbruck, had attracted the eye of Francis Ferdinand and had served as the archduke's chief of staff during the 1905 maneuvers in the Tyrol. Casting about for a successor to Beck, Francis Ferdinand first suggested the position to Conrad during the late summer of 1906. Though the prospect must have been attractive, Beck was still in office and therefore Conrad declined to take the offer. However, after Beck had actually been forced to resign, Conrad was again summoned to the Belvedere and this time he accepted the archduke's proposal. The following day, November 18, he formally received his appointment during an audience with the emperor.[20]

Although some disappointed candidates were bitter, notably Potiorek, who never forgave the fact that he had been passed over, the appointment of Conrad was widely regarded as a new and welcome departure. The military press was favorable. "The army," one journal noted, "welcomes a man who not only is a highly qualified staff officer, but who also had been a successful troop commander for many years. Both the general staff and the line greet him with equal enthusiasm."[21]

Conrad was then fifty-four years old, the son of a regular cavalry officer, educated at the *Theresianische Militärakademie,* and commissioned a *Jäger* lieutenant in 1871. In 1876 after graduating from the *Kriegsschule,* he transferred to the General Staff Corps, participated in the occupation of Bosnia-Hercegovina, was promoted to major, and served as instructor at the *Kriegsschule* from 1888 to 1892, where he developed a considerable following. Returning to the line at his own request in 1892, he commanded an infantry regiment and then, promoted to major general, the 55th Infantry Brigade in Trieste. After showing considerable energy in quelling a major Italian riot in Trieste in 1902, he was promoted to Feldmarschall Leutnant and commander of the 8th Infantry Division, Innsbruck, the following year. As regimental, brigade, and divisional commander, Conrad did much to further the combat readiness of his troops, demanding great efforts from his officers and men and not sparing himself.[22]

An efficient line officer, an able staff worker, and an inspiring lecturer, Conrad had never been under fire or commanded large bodies in action except for his short tour in Bosnia. Nonetheless, by 1906 he had an army-wide reputation derived mainly from his widely read writings on tactics. While assigned to the *Kriegsschule* he wrote a two-volume work, *Zum Studium der Taktik,* which simplified the soldier's drill and emphasized firing and field training.[23] A strong advocate of psychological factors, Conrad regarded the offensive as the superior element. The work, soon supplemented by a series of teach-it-yourself exercise books, sold well and went through several editions. And though in the following years Conrad wrote a number of other books on tactics, mainly *Die Gefechtsausbildung der Infantrie,* which had five editions, he never changed his basic concepts.[24]

A well-trained, offensive-minded infantry, Conrad argued, was the key to victory. He admitted that the new fire power of the defense had made the approach in closed columns impossible, but advocated that infantry should advance in small columns to reduce shrapnel casualties. And when these parties came into effective rifle range, they should form a firing line and, reinforced by supports, achieve fire superiority over the defenders. After this, with the reserves coming into line, came the ultimate step—the massed bayonet attack.[25] Conrad paid little attention to the question of artillery support and did not take the new trench techniques into account. In his view, infantry could overcome an entrenched enemy relying on its own resources. Neither the Boer nor the Russo-Japanese War changed his thinking and the field regulations of 1911, which largely reflected his ideas, stated that infantry could "without the support of other arms, even in inferior numbers, gain victory as long as it is tough and brave."[26] In his defense, it must be said that his tactical concepts were widely shared by almost all military experts. They contributed much to the very severe casualties suffered by the Austro-Hungarian forces in the first stages of the war.[27]

Conrad also recognized that modern technology and communications had removed the traditional restrictions on the size of armies and he asserted that this was only limited by the willingness and the ability of a state to support its military establishment. But this, of course, was the Achilles' heel of the Dual Monarchy. It was Conrad's fate to serve a multinational empire where there were deep divisions on military policy. To resolve this problem was among the chief tasks facing the man who was chief of the general staff and who in and outside the empire was widely considered the real head of the army.[28] Unless Conrad could obtain broadbased support for the military establishment, Austria-Hungary was doomed to fall further and further behind in the armament race. The real question therefore was whether Conrad was indeed the man to overhaul the armed forces of the Dual Monarchy.

Austrian military historians, almost to a man, have answered this question affirmatively, but an objective historian must have very serious reservations.[29] In political affairs Conrad's approach to the problems of the Habsburg Empire was simplistic. He had formed his convictions long before he became chief of the general staff and he never changed or modified them. He proceeded from the assumption that "all preparations and planning for external war are useless as long as our internal situation is not resolved."[30] And he believed that the resolution of the monarchy's internal situation lay in the centralization of all institutions, "a strong central government, based on a unitary army, and a centralized parliament."[31] Of course, the centralized government and the army were conceived as purely dynastic. Like almost all of the leading soldiers before him, like Charles, Clam-Martinitz, Radetzky, Benedek, Albrecht, and Beck, Conrad regarded the Habsburg Monarchy as a non-organic historic creation, held together only by the army "which can rest only on the dynastic principle."[32] That such views would require an abrogation of the Compromise of 1867 did not bother Conrad, nor did the fact that his views would be equally unacceptable to the other nationalities, especially the Czechs. As the famous historian Josef Redlich, a liberal Habsburg loyalist, once noted in his diary, Conrad was "exclusively a technician. In politics he only recognizes quantifiable and measureable factors, corps, guns, fortresses etc. . . . He lacks the ability and understanding, in short, everything essential for the great concept of a state based on the nationalities."[33]

And this was true. Conrad could never understand the power of nationalism and he regarded all opposition to the dynastic army as inspired by the evil machinations of subversive elements. Soon after he took office he recommended the traditional expedient, repressive measures against the internal enemy, Socialists, Czechs, and above all Magyars.[34] He stressed that it was "intolerable that the very existence of the army is constantly threatened by the refusal of the Hungarian parliament to provide recruits and money,"[35] and soon was dusting off the old plans for a military intervention in Hungary.[36] But Conrad's proposals for a solution by violence were not limited to the internal sphere. "During my peacetime tenure as chief of the general staff," he wrote in his memoirs, "I realized that the very existence of the monarchy was menaced. But my opponents either discounted these dangers, or believed that a policy of patience would diminish them. I, however, was convinced that they could only be removed by preventive action."[37] Therefore Conrad constantly pressured the emperor, the heir presumptive, and the government to wage preventive war against either Serbia or Italy, and on occasion against both, while Austria-Hungary still was strong enough to do so with a good chance of success.[38] And when Aehrenthal heatedly rejected such interference in the conduct of foreign affairs, Conrad boldly asserted that in such matters which were likely to lead to war "the responsibility of the chief of the general staff is far greater than that of the foreign minister."[39]

Some of Conrad's admirers claim that his bellicose statements did not actually represent a program of aggression, and that many of his pronouncements merely were desperate attempts to gain essential allocations to meet the army's most pressing needs. They argue that the powers of the chief of the general staff were limited and that he was still answerable to the war minister who, often without informing Conrad, scaled down military requests before submitting them to the budget-making bodies of the two parliaments.[40] Above all, they assert that Conrad's war schemes must be understood within the political framework of the Dual Monarchy where both the emperor and the heir presumptive were firmly opposed to preventive war. But these apologists miss the point. As chief of the general staff for the entire armed forces, (*Chef des Generalstabes für die gesamte bewaffnete Macht*), Conrad had emancipated himself from any control by the war minister, and with the backing of Francis Ferdinand he held the single most influential military position in the Dual Monarchy. His statements, therefore, had to be taken seriously and, as they were well known in Budapest and not hidden from other powers, they actually contributed to the very situation he tried to avoid by stiffening the resolve of the Magyars to extract further military concessions by any and all means, casting Austria-Hungary into the role of a potential aggressor, and in the end leading the army into multi-front war for which it was not prepared.[41]

Moreover, Conrad's sentiments were shared by the vast majority of senior soldiers and by the regular officer corps. This was especially true with regard to his view of the position of the army in society. Because the emperor valued his army and wore its uniform, and because the army still presented itself with much glitter and panache, the Dual Monarchy was regarded widely as a military state. But actually Austria-Hungary spent less on her military establishment than any other major European power, and despite the emperor's support, and despite forty years of universal military training, the relationship between the army and the population was not close. The absence of an actual foreign menace and the frequent use of the army as an internal security force in domestic tumults had blurred its image in the eyes of the public. And by consciously adopting the pose of a "mute servant of the dynasty," the army on the one hand managed to isolate itself from the disruptive political currents of the times, but on the other had to pay the price of public disinterest in daily life. On both a material and a moral plane, the regular officer corps especially stood increasingly apart from the rest of the people, but, unlike their German counterparts, they realized that they did not play the first role in the state and resented it bitterly indeed.

This difference translated itself into a feeling of superiority, expressed most clearly in a memorandum penned by Feldmarschall Leutnant Blasius von Schemua. The empire, Schemua wrote, was in a period of waning authority and rising discontent. The old values had fallen into disrespect and everywhere in the monarchy "the subjects are rebelling against the government, which no longer stands firm but, swayed by selfish interests, merely tries to appease their demands."[42] Military service is no longer considered as an honorable duty but as an interruption of a civilian career, and everyone merely tries to make as much money as he can. Only the officer has a sense of vocation and commitment to the entire state. But, complained the general, the soldier's profession is not well rewarded. Aristocratic and well-connected civil servants receive more honor and attention from the emperor than his soldiers, the best families no longer send their sons to the military academies, and ill-paid senior officers, unable to keep up with the social pretensions of officialdom, are withdrawing from society.

Of course, feelings of rejection have been common to many armies in peace time and they have survived it. But what was unique and threatening in the Dual Monarchy was the extraordinary position held by Hungary in military affairs. Since the 1890s it had become increasingly clear that many Hungarian politicians no longer recognized the Compromise of 1867 as the final settlement in military affairs, but consciously and by any and all means were aiming to create an autonomous Hungarian army which could be used as a tool of Magyar domination over the various lands of the Crown of St. Stephen. This, clearly, the soldiers could not tolerate, and they bitterly resented the emperor's proclivities toward preserving the compromise by further concessions. They supported the plans of Francis Ferdinand and Conrad to break, if necessary by force, Magyar obstruction to the joint army and its enlargement. But, while their viewpoint was understandable, it did little to bring about a viable solution short of an internal conflict.

At this point the question, only temporarily shelved by the appointment of Wekerle, once again became acute when early in 1906 Vienna and Budapest once again opened negotiations for the decennial renewal of the compromise. This time Prime Minister Beck took the lead. A most able statesman, perhaps the ablest in the decade before the war, Beck had set himself two major objectives. One was to introduce the universal male franchise and to restore parliamentary government in Austria; the other was to keep Magyar extremism in check and to obtain, if possible, a twenty-year compromise with Budapest which would place relations between the two parts of the Dual Monarchy on a stable basis.[43] Beck succeeded in his first objective. In January 1907 Francis Joseph signed a bill introducing universal franchise, and for the next year the *Reichsrat* once again held orderly sessions. But the second objective was much more difficult to obtain. Here Beck realized that his standing as Austrian prime minister gave him but very limited leverage in Budapest; therefore, he decided to approach the negotiations with some concessions in the military sphere. Late in 1906 he asked Emperor Francis Joseph for permission to sound out the military as to what, if any, concessions could be made.[44] On February 25, 1907, Beck met with a military committee chaired by Reichskriegsminister Schönaich. As could be expected, however, with the exception of Schönaich and Feldzeugmeister Anton Galgotzy, the military participants were quite unwilling to make any concessions.[45] Nonetheless Beck, supported by Aehrenthal, continued to explore such possibilities in his preliminary talks with the Hungarians, while Conrad threatened that if any substantive deal were made, he would resign in protest.[46] Conrad need not have feared. The Hungarians were in no mood to offer anything in return and when Francis Ferdinand, who deliberately had been left in the dark about the negotiations, finally got wind of them, he too threw his weight against any concessions and both sides then decided to drop military affairs from the agenda and concentrate on the economic aspects of a renewed compromise.⁴⁷ In October 1907 Vienna and Budapest concluded an agreement which omitted all military issues. Hungary agreed to take over a slightly higher percentage of the common expenses.

Although the renewal of the compromise made it possible for the two halves of the Dual Monarchy to continue under one ruler and with a common army, Francis Ferdinand would never forgive his friend Beck and he now engaged in a ruthless operation to discredit him. Beck was forced to resign in November 1908, and with him went the last attempt to govern Austria with parliamentary means and to find a negotiated solution to the Hungarian problem. Under these circumstances the promises made by Wekerle in 1906 to drive the army bill through parliament became worthless. Conrad now perceived that it might be possible to utilize the various discontent national minorities in Hungary against Budapest. "We can guarantee," he wrote to Francis Ferdinand, "the unity of the army which is the basic prerequisite for the existence of the monarchy only by guaranteeing equal treatment for all nationalities."⁴⁸ The Hungarians want to use the army to magyarize their minorities; we should be able to counterbalance this in the joint army, he added.

Francis Ferdinand, of course, agreed wholeheartedly, but beyond this, he regarded Hungarian intransigence as part of a monstrous conspiracy by Jews, Freemasons, and Socialists "to spoil the army so that it will no longer be reliable when I need it. This is the heart of the matter."⁴⁹ Francis Ferdinand accused Beck and Wekerle of being a conscious part of this conspiracy and even blamed Schönaich for refusing to recognize the danger. But, continued the archduke, "I managed to get rid of Pitreich and if the current war minister continues on his course, I shall get rid of him too." The archduke concluded that if he were emperor, he would get everything necessary for the army—a bigger budget, pay raises, and an enlarged recruit quota.

But for the moment these were pipedreams though, as usual, they did not remain hidden from the Magyars and further aggravated an almost unbearable situation. For their part the Magyars, always ready to profit from the troubles of the monarchy, renewed their demands during the Annexation Crisis of 1908 and 1909. In October 1908 they demanded the immediate implementation of language concessions made during the April 1906 understanding; specifically, they asked for the introduction of the Magyar language of service and command in all units where at least 50 percent of the men could understand it, and the abolition of the title *Reichskriegsminister* with the simple *Kriegsminister* substituted instead. Again, the archduke rose to the challenge. Although, much to his anger, Schönaich appeared inclined to give in, Francis Ferdinand pointed out to Francis Joseph that it was dangerous, as well as useless, to buy Magyar good will with concessions. The Hungarians had not kept their promises to provide more money and recruits, and the war minister's claim that the *Honvéds* were reliable was an untested hypothesis. In any case, he continued, morale was more important than mere numbers and it was the morale of the joint army which these Magyars and their allies wanted to determine. Finally, if such concessions were made to the Magyars, then similar demands would be related by the Czechs and Poles.⁵⁰

And when it appeared as if there would be concessions anyhow, Francis Ferdinand told Conrad that he would resign, and the chief of the general staff promised that he would follow suit.⁵¹ But within a few days, on January 5, 1909, Conrad reneged on his threat and asked the archduke to relieve him of his promise because with war likely he did not wish to appear ready to shirk his duty.[52] Here the matter remained, although the Magyars had gained a point. From 1908 on, both *Landwehr* and *Honvédség* were gradually provided with organic artillery, mainly obsolescent field guns and howitzers, which became available as the first-line batteries were reequipped with more modern armament.[53]

But, as Francis Ferdinand had indicated, the joint army also faced problems in other quarters. These attacks did not come because the army was unduly repressive, but because it functioned as a strong support of the established order. Within the army there was a substantial degree of equality. "All officers must uphold the basic concept that within the army all nations enjoy equal rights," Conrad wrote in 1907.[54] Even critics of the monarchy conceded that this was true.[55] But this did not halt attacks on the army, especially in volatile Bohemia where Czech nationalists and Socialists found common ground in their anti-militarism. To be sure, most Czechs still thought in terms of operating within the framework of the monarchy, and the position of the Czech nationalists on the army issue tended to be opportunistic, but the military authorities were worried indeed. When the events of 1905 revealed that propaganda, both nationalist and socialist, had affected certain units of VIII Corps (Prague) the commander ordered strong countermeasures,[56] and in 1906 a plan to provide military assistance to the civil authorities in case of a general insurrection in Bohemia was elaborated.[57] Even so, during the crisis of 1908 there were some manifestations of discontent when Czech reservists were recalled to active duty.[58]

And while the army could still count on the loyalty of the other nationalities, there too were disturbing signs. From Graz, III Corps reported an increase in anti-military socialist propaganda, while XV Corps (Sarajevo) and XIII Corps (Agram) gave indications that Serb propaganda was not without effect. On one occasion, national and social discontent operated together; in the spring of 1907, a general strike broke out in Bosnia which required the intervention of army, gendarmerie, and police units.[59]

Moreover, and this too was frustrating to Conrad and other senior commanders, the continuing Hungarian obstruction caused the Austro-Hungarian military establishment to fall further and further behind. "When I assumed my present position," Conrad wrote to his friend Feldmarschall Leutnant Auffenberg early in 1907, "I knew that the army was in a poor way, but I had absolutely no conception of how bad it really was."[60] And yet, there was little that Conrad could do about it during his first three years in office. In 1905 the military budget for the Dual Monarchy amounted to 13.2 percent of all expenditures. The next year it sank to 12.2 percent of the total, though in 1907 there was a special appropriation of 13,752,755 crowns for the purchase of new artillery materiel and for work on frontier defenses. Excluding extra credits voted for specific emergencies, the budget for the joint army fluctuated from 308,996,175 crowns in 1905 to 322,000,000 in 1909, an increase but far behind the efforts made by other European powers.[61] At the same time the recruit intake, and thus the size of the army, remained at 126,000 per year, limited by the figure set in 1889. The result was that the active units of the army were far under strength, and that every mobilization would bring in vast numbers of poorly trained reservists and even untrained recruits.

Conrad did what he could to improve the army and to remove the weaknesses which had crept into its system during the last years of Beck's tenure as chief of the general staff. Although hampered by the restrictions on manpower and finances, and on occasion by the prejudices of the emperor and the heir apparent, Conrad introduced changes in the command structure, training, equipment, and organization of the army. Believing in the inevitability of war, he did his best to shake the military establishment out of its lethargy and to implant a sense of urgency.

At the highest command levels, he proposed that each of the four inspector generals of the army, destined to become army commanders upon mobilization, were to be provided with a skeleton staff in peace time, and that a mandatory retirement age of sixty be imposed on all general officers. At that time, however, out of fifteen corps commanders, two were older than sixty-five, eight were between sixty-five and sixty, and only two were younger than sixty. Naturally, Conrad's proposal ran into opposition, especially since the emperor was then seventy-nine years old and regarded sixty-year-old officers as mere youngsters.[62] Conrad also tried to make the staff more flexible and responsive. Under Beck, the general staff had gained influence and status, but it was not necessarily efficient and certainly not Spartan. Conrad demanded that his officers become physically fit and serve for regular periods with troops of their original branch, and he transformed the annual general staff trips into real working exercises. All this created opposition, not only in the War Ministry, but even among the ranks of the General Staff Corps.[63]

In order to make training as realistic as possible, Conrad abolished the set-piece maneuvers which restricted the initiative of commanders and introduced "free" maneuvers in which the offensive was stressed, troops were moved at maximum speed, and left in poor shape for the final grand parade, much to the displeasure of the emperor and the heir apparent. Francis Ferdinand in particular continued to interfere with the conduct of maneuvers, and in 1913 this led to a serious clash with Conrad who claimed that the exercises were "impressive spectacles" but not serious training.[64] In addition, other members of the imperial house, including the later emperor Archduke Charles, also interfered and when acting as referees often showed partiality towards their favorites.[65] Overall, concluded one Austrian critic after the war, maneuvers were not realistic and "neither the troops nor the command were really trained for combat." And even Conrad confessed in 1914 that German troops were much more hardened and inured to privations, "a spirit which is based in their tough peace-time training." But, he continued, "when I tried to introduce similar training methods in our army I was attacked and denounced."[66]

Conrad encountered difficulties too in the procurement of new materiel and in the expansion of the army cadre formations. Although despite many difficulties, the artillery finally received new M 1905 field guns equipped with hydraulic recoil buffers and protective shields, the guns still had steel bronze barrels and were not equal to those of the other powers in range and speed of fire.[67] In addition, Conrad constantly pressed for the procurement of heavier guns, both to rearm the new fortifications necessary in the Tyrol and to smash the Italian forts barring the way into the northern Italian plains.[68] Here he was partially successful.[69] In September 1906 the War Ministry had asked the Skoda firm in Pilsen, which long had produced heavy guns for the navy, to develop designs for a heavy but mobile 30.5-cm. howitzer, and by 1911 they were ready to go into production.[70] Although Conrad's tactical concepts did not give great weight to artillery, his concern here was motivated by his strategic preoccupation of war with Italy. As commander of the 8th Division, he had strongly urged that the southern Tyrol be better fortified and be made into a safe base for an offensive into the Italian plain.[71] Soon after he became chief of the general staff, a commission appointed to check into the state of fortifications in the Tyrol strongly supported Conrad's views,[72] and with the special funds made available in 1907, work was begun to rearm and in some cases rebuild the frontier forts. But since Italy also was strengthening her fortifications, Conrad was eager to procure heavy assault artillery to smash the new Italian armored cupolas and casemates.[73]

The annexation crisis of 1908 and 1909, during which fears of a Greater Serbia scared even the Budapest parliament, provided Conrad with some additional funds which he used to set up a new corps command, XVI Corps (Ragusa) to procure more artillery, to equip a number of infantry battalions with machine gun detachments, and to further strengthen fortifications against Italy. However, there was no overall increase in the personnel ceiling of the army and troops to man the new units, and installations had to be scraped up from administrative personnel, musicians, and by reducing the already weak effectives of the infantry.[74] As a result, the composition of the army changed slightly by 1909. Whereas in 1906 infantry constituted still 70 percent of the army, its share had dropped to 68 percent, and artillery was up from 0.76 percent to almost 1 percent in 1909.[75] Still, the *k.u.k. Armee* remained above all an infantry force with its main punch provided by its 102 infantry regiments, the 4 Tyrolean *Kaiserjäger* regiments, the 26 *Feldjäger* battalions, and the 4 Bosnian-Hercegovinian infantry regiments. And in addition, though both Conrad and Francis Ferdinand disliked this development which they regarded as a further trend towards a divided army, both Vienna and Budapest parliaments often were willing to grant their particular forces, the *Landwehr* and the *Honvédség,* funds which they denied the common army, and as a result these regiments, now regarded as part of the first line, were as well equipped and had higher peace establishments than the line regiments.[76] Moreover, three *Landwehr* regiments based in the Tyrol and Carinthia were specially trained and equipped as mountain troops, and together with the *Kaiserjäger* formed the cadre for Austria's justly famous alpine establishment.

Conrad's preoccupation with the problems of mountain warfare also was expressed in the new pike-grey field uniforms for the infantry, introduced from 1908 on. This color offered good concealment in the Alps, but was hardly suitable for the plains of Galicia. Moreover, Conrad too was unable to make much of an impression on the cavalry which "retained the form it took after 1866 to the outbreak of the World War."[77] Although the cavalry accepted some innovations, such as a pioneer and telegraph troop in each regiment which was equipped for demolition work, and though it also accepted machine gun detachments after 1909, in spirit and training it retained a deliberate emphasis on mounted combat. Marksmanship continued to be neglected and even the machine gunners retained their sabers. Even in externals the cavalry retained its character. While the pike-grey uniform was accepted by the other branches, a special appeal to the emperor gained the cavalry the right to retain their blue blouses and red pants.[78]

Generally, the trends evident in the composition of the officer corps since 1867 continued. While much to the chagrin of Archduke Francis Ferdinand the number of officers from the high aristocratic families continued to decline,[79] a strong hereditary element of sons following in their fathers' footsteps became evident. Sometimes ennobled, these families remained essentially middle class and a military career was substantially enhanced by a pay raise pushed through the parliaments in October 1908 which, in conjunction with their allowances, made officers among the best-paid public servants.[80] During the first three years of Conrad's term in office, the number of regular officers rose from 17,262 in 1906 to 17,570 in 1909. There was, however, a more considerable increase among reserve officers, from 11,621 in 1906 to 12,652 in 1909.[81] This increase reflected the larger number of qualified one-year volunteers who, because of educational and financial requirements, still were largely drawn from the German, Magyar, and Czech populations.

German officers continued to form the backbone of the corps, both among the regulars and the reserves. Although Germans comprised only 24 percent of the total population and 25 percent of all ranks in the armed forces, they provided over 70 percent of all regular and 60 percent of all reserve officers. In the reserves Magyars constituted 24 percent and Czechs 10 percent.[82] The rural nationalities—Galicians, Ukrainians, and Rumanians—contributed only insignificant numbers of officers, though from 1907 on their share rose rapidly, at least statistically.[83] By religion Roman Catholics predominated absolutely, 86.5 percent among the regulars and 70.4 percent in the reserves, though the well-educated and largely middle class Jewish population of the monarchy, constituting only 5 percent, continued to provide over 16 percent of reserve officers.[84]

Even so, the army no longer was as tolerant as it had been under Beck. Francis Ferdinand, a staunch or even bigoted Catholic, was accused by Conrad of discriminating against Protestant officers,[85] though Conrad shared Francis Ferdinand's aversion to Jews.[86] And under the influence of inflamed national feelings, the long-held but largely suppressed anti-semitic attitudes of the military tended to appear. The "best regiments," an estimate often in the eye of the beholder, tended to discriminate against Jewish officers.[87] Nonetheless, measured by the standards of a later age, such discrimination was held in rather narrow limits and certainly Jews were better received in the *k.u.k. Armee* than in other contemporary forces. Neither Francis Ferdinand nor Conrad had any doubts about the loyalty and devotion of the regular officers, but there were increasing, though largely unfounded, fears about the attitudes of reserve officers from the disaffected nationalities.[88]

Regarding the rank and file, there also was little change. In general it was believed that good officers would be able to keep their troops under control, though the continued lack of long-serving non-commissioned officers remained a problem which was never solved satisfactorily.[89]

Despite the many weaknesses of the military establishment, or perhaps because he was aware of them and feared that future developments would weight the scales even more against the Dual Monarchy, Conrad repeatedly and insistently clamored for preventive war. Like many professional soldiers and military writers of his day, he believed that relations between states were based on a permanent state of conflict, that war therefore was unavoidable, and that there was little difference between offensive and defensive wars.[90] In Conrad's view it was the duty of a chief of the general staff to choose the most favorable moment for beginning a war and therefore he unceasingly advocated preventive war at the time and place of the monarchy's choosing. Moreover, he believed that such a well-chosen stroke would restore the waning prestige of the monarchy and solve its internal problems. The actual opponent mattered less than a display of the power of the Dual Monarchy.[91]

In contrast with his predecessor, however, Conrad gave but little attention to Russia and always regarded Italy and Serbia as the most dangerous and immediate enemies, an attitude based perhaps more on emotion than on logic.[92] After barely two months in office, he contended that the future of the monarchy demanded expansion in the Balkans and the extinction of Serbia and Montenegro, because "a sovereign Serbia represents a dangerous enemy and an ever-present attraction for the South Slav lands within the Dual Monarchy."[93] In view of recent Russian set-backs, he argued that there was little danger of interference from that quarter, but that relations with Italy had become so volatile that in case of war with Serbia a partial mobilization against Italy was mandatory. A few months later, however, he changed his mind about the immediacy of the Serb threat and now advocated a preventive war against Italy first. The Serb army, he wrote, was still weak and Serbia's relations with Bulgaria were tense; Montenegro could be bought off, while England and France would remain neutral and Germany was sure to provide support. Therefore, he demanded, "we must strike at Italy the sooner the better." However, on a more cautious note he added that, "in view of the conversion of our artillery, the best possible moment would be the spring of 1909."[94] Indeed, both sides were making active preparations for war, and even when in May 1907 the Italian general staff suggested formulation of more detailed plans for joint operations of the Triple Alliance, Conrad expressed severe doubts about Italy's true intentions and maintained that the Italian suggestion was but a scheme to obtain intelligence about Austrian communications and plans.[95] In any case, mutual suspicions led to an increase in both armaments and intelligence activities along the Italo-Austrian frontier[96] and both Austrian and Italian military journals as well as the general press frequently commented on the possibility of war between the two nominal allies. Discussion centered on the respective state of the armies, fortifications, and navies, and as the influential Vienna *Neue Freie Presse* commented, "On both sides the possibility of war is being seriously considered."[97]

Aehrenthal was much more inclined to accept Italian manifestations of friendship, and he argued that Conrad's war-like preparations actually increased the likelihood of a conflict, but the general rebuffed him, arguing that "treaties can be concluded overnight; but an army needs years of preparations before it can strike and these must never be allowed to be interrupted by diplomatic considerations."[98] By the end of 1907, while still maintaining his belief in the inevitability of a collision with Italy "at a time when we have the advantage," Conrad once again advocated the elimination of Serbia and also the incorporation of the occupied provinces of Bosnia and Hercegovina. Only such a drastic move, he argued, would halt the continued Great Serbian agitation and the eventual secession of the Habsburg South Slav lands which would be a "fatal blow to the great power status of the monarchy."[99]

By 1907 conditions in the South Slav areas of the Dual Monarchy, especially in Croatia and in Bosnia-Hercegovina, had become a source of considerable apprehension in Vienna. Once again the specter of Greater Serbia and the possible loss of these provinces haunted the political and military authorities. Since the Karageorgević dynasty came to power in Serbia in 1903, relations between that state and the Habsburg Monarchy had steadily deteriorated while even the proverbially loyal Croats had shown in the Fiume Resolutions that their support was by no means unconditional. And though cooperation between the Magyars and the Croats was short-lived, a new Croat-Serb coalition party, considered both in Vienna and Budapest to be aligned with Belgrade, was gaining ground in the country. Finally, and regarded as the most immediate danger, there was growing unrest in Bosnia-Hercegovina.

Though much had been done for the material improvements in Bosnia-Hercegovina, the Habsburg government had failed to win the loyalty of the inhabitants. The administration of the provinces was in the hands of a military governor, the *Landeschef,* but his authority was restricted by a civilian assistant representing the authority of the Austro-Hungarian finance minister who was ultimately responsible for the government. In general, the Habsburg authorities had favored the Catholic and Moslem population, and as a result these were well disposed while the majority Orthodox Serbs remained hostile. In November 1907 a Serb convention met in Sarajevo and adopted a series of resolutions demanding franchise reforms, free elections, civil liberties, and far-reaching autonomy for the two provinces "as parts of the Ottoman Empire, which is administered by Austria-Hungary on the basis of a European mandate."[100]

Adoption of these resolutions provoked an immediate and sharp reaction in Vienna. On November 18, Conrad and Aehrenthal had a conversation in which the minister stated that Russia was resuming her forward Balkan policy, but that he thought it possible that an agreement with Russia could be worked out. Austria-Hungary would concede Russia the freedom on the Straits and in return would annex Bosnia-Hercegovina. Conrad replied that under the prevailing circumstances it would be necessary to show a strong hand in the two provinces and squelch any insurrection in the bud, but that for the moment he still considered Italy as the major danger.[101] In a letter sent to Aehrenthal the next day, Conrad repeated his argument that in case of war with Italy only a small covering force should be left in the Balkans—the so-called "brown" mobilization scheme—and that this required a thorough pacification of the provinces. But here, Conrad pointed out, the Treaty of Berlin raised certain legal obstacles which could only be removed if the monarchy gained a free hand by converting occupation into annexation.[102] Conrad was even more outspoken and in his end-of-the-year report on December 31, 1907, he asserted that the security of the monarchy demanded the annexation of Bosnia-Hercegovina, "which should be followed by the incorporation of Serbia."[103] Meanwhile, preparations against Italy should continue.

But Conrad's radical solution was, for the moment at least, not adopted. During the council of common ministers held on December 1, Stefan Count Burian, the finance minister, proposed that the situation in the provinces could be defused by providing the Serbs with a greater voice in the administration. Although Reichskriegsminister Schönaich argued that intelligence from XV Corps (Sarajevo) did not support Burian's assessment of the situation, the council adopted the latter's suggestions.[104] Conrad, who had been excluded from the council, did not agree with the decisions. In February 1908 he sent a letter to Aehrenthal emphasizing that only an energetic resolution of the South Slav problems could guarantee maintenance of order in the two provinces in case of war with Italy,[105] and after inspecting the area in question, he reported in a memorandum dated March 27, 1908, that the situation was serious indeed. Serbia actively encouraged subversive activities in Bosnia-Hercegovina; arms, ammunition, and agents were smuggled across the frontier, and in case the Dual Monarchy became involved in war elsewhere, major complications could be expected in the Balkans.[106]

During April Conrad continued to press for strong action. He urged that troops in Bosnia-Hercegovina and Dalmatia be reinforced and that if this step provoked an insurrection, all of XV Corps should be fully mobilized. Should Serbia, as the chief of the general staff fully expected, give aid to the insurrection, then the country should be invaded and occupied in a rapid campaign.[107] At the same time, Conrad was not unaware that this might lead to complications with both Italy and Russia; therefore, while requesting an opinion from the foreign minister, he also prepared plans for a multi-front war, Case R, I, B (S), to be fought in cooperation with Germany.[108]

Like Conrad, Aehrenthal too wanted to restore the prestige of the Habsburg Empire by some great stroke. He was quite prepared to annex Bosnia-Hercegovina and at times he even thought of partitioning Serbia with Bulgaria. He expected to carry out his plan in cooperation with Russia, and the new and ambitious Russian foreign minister, Alexander Izvolsky, seemed willing. On July 2, Izvolsky sent a note to Aehrenthal offering to support the annexation of Bosnia-Hercegovina in return for Russian designs on the Straits. The question became burning when the next day the Young Turk Revolt erupted, and within three weeks forced the sultan to concede restoration of the 1878 constitution and to call elections throughout the Ottoman Empire. This, of course, would vitally effect the status of Bosnia-Hercegovina and it provided an opportunity to realize plans for annexation.

In August 1908 Aehrenthal proposed this step in the council of common ministers, but was met with opposition by Beck, then still prime minister of Austria. However, Beck changed his mind and in the next meeting, held on September 10 in Budapest, he voted with the rest of the ministers in favor of annexation. Meanwhile, the general staff had begun to press for military measures to counter expected Serb opposition. One report, dated August 25, claimed that Serb and Montenegrin forces numbering between one hundred twenty and one hundred seventy thousand were assembling for an attack north and that units of the XV Corps should be placed on an immediate war footing.[109] Aehrenthal, however, pressed for a diplomatic solution and on September 16 met with Izvolsky at Buchlau. Since no written record was kept, there soon arose disagreement on what took place. It appears that Izvolsky promised to support annexation in return for Habsburg promises to support the Russian position on the Straits. The greatest difficulty arose over the matter of timing. Izvolsky apparently believed that no immediate steps were taken and when on October 6 Aehrenthal announced annexation, preceded by one day by Bulgaria's declaration of independence, there was strong popular and governmental reaction in Russia.

In fact, the annexation caused an immediate European crisis. Aligned since

1907 in the Triple Entente, France, Britain, and Russia called for a European conference; the Ottoman Empire began an economic boycott of the Dual Monarchy. Only Germany, though it had not been informed in advance, decided to support Austria-Hungary, while Italy, which had been informed, was forced to change its initially favorable attitude because of public indignation. As expected, the most violent reaction came from Serbia which traditionally had considered Bosnia-Hercegovina as its rightful heritage. Serbian ministers assumed that war was inevitable; the Serbian parliament hurriedly voted military credits, reservists were called up, and armed irregular bands, *komitadji*, were formed.[110]

It appeared as if Conrad, at last, had his war. He urged the immediate reinforcement of troops on the Balkans and prepared plans for an offensive against Serbia to be mounted in the spring of 1909. At the same time, he once again warned that there was a strong possibility of an Italian attack and recommended contingency plans to deal with it.[111] But Conrad's eagerness for war was not shared either by Francis Ferdinand or Schönaich. The war minister resented Conrad's pressure to place the army on a war footing and on October 18 informed him that in time of peace the war minister alone had the right to make these decisions. And Francis Ferdinand, too, was not happy. Although he told Conrad that in case of war he would take personal command, an assumption never confirmed by the emperor, he also did not want a conflict and on October 20, 1908, instructed Brosch to prevail on the chief of the general staff to "stop all this agitation for war."[112] Therefore only minor reinforcements, fifteen battalions and some reservists, were sent to XV Corps and there was no general mobilization. The reservists were merely called up in accordance with the 1889 law which permitted such action for the two youngest reserve classes.

But despite this opposition, Conrad continued to press for a solution by force. The monarchy, he argued, should seize this favorable moment for the "inevitable" war with Serbia while Russia and Italy were not yet prepared to fight. England and France might disapprove but would remain neutral, and Germany would support the monarchy.[113] To sound Germany out, on January 2, 1909, he sent a letter to Generaloberst Helmuth von Moltke, the newly appointed German chief of the general staff, asking how many divisions Germany would employ in the east in case of a general war.[114] Moltke's reply did not promise as much as Schlieffen had offered to Beck, but still it strengthened Conrad's hand.[115]

But meanwhile Aehrenthal, who once had not been averse at all to war with Serbia, changed his mind; on January 17 he told Conrad that the Dual Monarchy could not digest Serbia, and that preparations should be limited to safeguarding the annexation. Moreover, fearful of Archduke Francis Ferdinand's volatile character, Aehrenthal also opposed making him commander in chief in case war would break out after all. This move, which soon came to the archduke's knowledge, so enraged Francis Ferdinand that he immediately returned to Vienna from his winter resort and, suspecting another grand conspiracy against himself, fulminated to a somewhat discommoded Conrad that he would stand on his prerogatives and that "once I am the commander in chief, everyone will obey me or I shall have them all shot."[116] For the moment, however, Conrad could not do much, though he managed to wrest from a reluctant emperor permission to send a second echelon of fifteen battalions to the Serbian frontier.[117]

Still, agitation and threats from Serbia continued, and finally on March 29 a ministerial council gave its permission to proceed with full mobilization against Serbia—"yellow" mobilization in the general staff language.[118] War was in sight, but in the end German support became decisive. On March 21 a German note was received in St. Petersburg which demanded that Russia allow Austria-Hungary a free hand against Serbia or "matters would have to take their course." And since Russia could not stand against Germany without the support of her allies, and this was not forthcoming, she had to advise Belgrade to submit. On March 31 Serbia issued a formal declaration that the annexation had not infringed on her rights, promised to cease all agitation, and reduced her army to its normal footing. Meanwhile the Turks, almost forgotten in the crisis, had accepted a financial indemnity and the evacuation of the Sanjak of Novi Bazar.

The outcome of the crisis appeared as a great success for the Dual Alliance, but Conrad was by no means satisfied. Serbia and Montenegro were not eliminated and he complained to the emperor that "we have lost an opportunity which probably will never come again."[119] He continued his agitation for preventive war throughout the year. In August he told Aehrenthal that the monarchy should be prepared to wage preventive war,[120] and at the conclusion of the great maneuvers in 1909, he approached the emperor and urged an immediate surprise attack on Serbia.[121]

In a way, Conrad was right, though he refused to see that his own policy had contributed to Serbia's uncompromising hostility. Serbia was rearming feverishly now, and in the end the Dual Monarchy would have to fight her under much more unfavorable circumstances. Russia too began to rebuild her forces and relations with Italy had been strained further. There still remains the question whether Austria-Hungary would have been able to wage a successful war in 1909. Conrad, of course, affirmed this question, though other leading generals later wrote that the army had not been ready for war at that time.[122]

No matter. The crisis brought some prestige to the monarchy but it also aggravated existing external and internal problems. Although on Conrad's insistence an energetic general, Feldmarschall Leutnant Marijan Baron Vareŝanin, was appointed governor in the two provinces, little was done to alleviate the lot of the poor and illiterate peasantry there. Neither did annexation solve the discontent in Croatia, the unrest in Bohemia, or the problem of restoring parliamentary government in Austria. And although Hungary, scared by the Slavic danger, had voted some extraordinary credits for the army during the crisis, the Budapest parliament soon returned to its obstructionist course and continued to block the passage of the bill enlarging the army. Finally, in foreign affairs Russian friendship had been compromised, Italy was uncertain, and the Triple Alliance still faced the Triple Entente. Even the exchange of communications between Conrad and Moltke begun in January 1909 had produced no clear military understanding about cooperation in case of war. The outlook was indeed grim. Aehrenthal returned to the passive policy of his predecessors, while Conrad and Francis Ferdinand continued to promote more aggressive internal and external remedies. Considering the nature of the Habsburg realm, the destructive forces at work, and the limited, traditional outlook of these two men, it remains questionable whether they could have in fact saved the empire. Still, their views represented the nearest approach to a positive policy during the few remaining years.

11

Conrad, Moltke, Aehrenthal, and the Balkan Crises: 1909-1913

Although many circles in the Dual Monarchy hailed the outcome of the Annexation Crisis as proof of the empire's continued vitality, Conrad voiced his bitter indignation in a letter to Francis Joseph. He asserted that the solution was but an illusory triumph and he deplored the failure to crush Serbia and Montenegro. "These two foes," he declared, "have neither been beaten nor crushed by diplomacy, but have been roused and made aware of their weakness."[1] Conrad warned that as a result, Austria one day would find herself involved in a war on several fronts. Moreover, the crisis had made European differences more pronounced. The Triple Entente of France, Russia, and Great Britain drew closer, while Italy drifted further away from the Triple Alliance. Throughout Europe, armaments increased rapidly and only the Dual Monarchy, stalled by the continuing impasse with Hungary, failed to keep up.

As Austro-Hungarian military leaders saw it, the only bright spot was the increased intimacy with Germany, manifested in renewed contacts between the two general staffs. Such contacts had taken place on previous occasions, notably in the decade after 1882 when, in the event of a two-front war against France and Russia, the Germans had planned to make their main effort on the eastern front. But even then, Bismarck had blocked the conclusion of a specific military convention. Moreover, after Schlieffen replaced Waldersee in Berlin, German emphasis had shifted from the eastern to the western front, and contacts between the staffs were allowed to lapse after 1896.[2] In January 1909 Conrad reopened contacts with a letter to Moltke and the correspondence, supplemented by personal meetings, continued intermittently until 1914.[3]

Although the exchange was authorized by the respective foreign ministers, and the German chancellor as well as the two emperors were kept informed, these contacts did not constitute binding military agreements and did not modify the terms of the alliance between Vienna and Berlin. Conrad's main goal was to obtain a German promise of support in case a conflict with Serbia brought Russian intervention. He was tortured by apprehension that Russia would wait until the Austro-Hungarian army was deeply involved and then strike into Galicia. And since France would also become involved, Conrad asked for clarification as to whether Germany intended to make her main effort in the east or the west.

Moltke, who at this point was eager for closer cooperation, assured him that Russian intervention would indeed constitute the *casus foederis,* but also disclosed that Germany intended to stand on the defensive in the east while the decisive blow was struck in the west. He promised, however, that as soon as France had been eliminated, strong forces for an offensive in the east would become available "in a reasonable time," a period which Conrad estimated from subsequent correspondence as four to six weeks. Moltke also told Conrad that Serbia should not be considered a major problem and that no danger was expected from Italy.[4] But Conrad did not share Moltke's confidence in Italy, and in order to persuade him to send as many troops as possible to the eastern front, he now intimated to the German that unless he promised to attack into Poland during the early stages of a war, the Austro-Hungarian forces would have to stand on the defensive along the San and Dniester rivers. Should Germany, however, be willing to undertake such offensive operations, then Austria-Hungary too would press an attack from Galicia, regardless of any involvement in Serbia.[5]

And since Moltke, in order to secure his rear, was eager to have a maximum Austrian engagement in the east, he now gave in to Conrad and in a letter dated March 19, 1909, promised that the Eighth Army in East Prussia would support the projected Austrian offensive from Galicia. "I will not hesitate," Moltke wrote, "to support the Austrian offensive by an attack. Your Excellency can rely on this well-considered undertaking." Moltke, however, hedged his promise by stating that if enemy action made such a move impossible, then both allies should notify each other at once.[6]

Actually, Moltke's promise was of dubious value because if he intended to leave in the east only weak forces, twelve to fourteen divisions, then an attack into Poland with Siedlce, a city east of Warsaw, often mentioned as the target, made neither tactical nor strategic sense. It placed the German divisions in jeopardy and exposed East Prussia to invasion. Moltke gave his promise because he wanted to assure himself of an Austrian offensive and also because he believed that Russian mobilization would be so slow that Austrian fears were unfounded. In any case, he felt Austria-Hungary's fate would be decided on the Seine and not on the Vistula. Moreover, he did not know that Conrad was also less than realistic. Choosing to regard Moltke's letter as a binding commitment, though fully aware that Germany would only employ a dozen or so divisions in the east, Conrad now planned to employ a rather greater portion of his forces than originally intended against Serbia.[7] Thus, despite the continued correspondence, there was no real coordination between the two armies at the highest levels, while little information was exchanged between the lower echelons, and up to the outbreak of the war, officers of these two allied armies remained virtual strangers.[8]

Even so, the exchange gave Conrad his first insight into the shift in German strategy. As late as 1908, in his first war plan against Russia, he still had presumed a main German effort in the east and counted on a Rumanian army covering the right wing of the Austro-Hungarian deployment with Italy remaining neutral.[9] Later that year, however, he worked out a radically different plan which for the first and only time deviated substantially from the traditional *k.u.k.* general staff doctrine that in case of hostilities with Russia all available strength should be concentrated on that front. At that time he reasoned that Russia had not yet recovered from her Asian defeat and therefore, temporarily, represented a lesser danger. If war broke out over the annexation issue, Conrad proposed to deliver a knockout blow against Italy, relying on Germany to neutralize Russia.[10] But Moltke's reaction was totally unfavorable and the plan was dropped after 1909.

From this point on the Habsburg Empire was confronted by potentially hostile powers in three different directions: Russia in the east, Serbia and Montenegro in the southeast, and Italy in the southwest. By 1911 the chief of the general staff realized that this situation was an invitation to disaster, and he informed the emperor that it was up to the diplomats to avoid "getting us into such a position."[11] Nonetheless, from 1909 on Conrad had to make plans for fighting a major war, designated as Case "I" for Italy or Case "R" for Russia, and a minor war against Serbia and Montenegro, Case "B", at the same time. In order to deal with these various contingencies, Conrad formulated alternate mobilization schemes which divided the army into three major groupings.

The main force—designated *A-Staffel*—was composed of nine corps, I (Cracow), II (Vienna), III (Graz), V (Pressburg), VI (Kaschau), X (Przemysl), XI (Lemberg), XII (Hermannstadt), and XIV (Innsbruck), a total of some twenty-eight infantry and ten cavalry divisions, reinforced by twenty-one provisional brigades composed of reservists and *Landsturm*. *A-Staffel* was to be deployed either against Italy or Russia, but because Conrad expected that either contingency would also involve hostilities with Serbia-Montenegro, the second major group, designated as *Minimalgruppe Balkan,* was left in the southeast to protect the territory of the Dual Monarchy. This force consisted of eight infantry divisions from XIII Corps (Agram), XV Corps (Sarajevo), and XVI Corps (Ragusa), again reinforced by *Landsturm* and reserve units.

The third major group—*B-Staffel*—was made up of the remaining four corps: IV (Budapest), VII (Temesvar), VIII (Prague), and IX (Leitmeritz), a total of twelve infantry and one cavalry divisions. These corps, selected because their districts were removed from any endangered frontier, constituted a strategic reserve which could be used either to reinforce *A-Staffel* and make it into a powerful offensive force, or, if there were no danger from either Italy or Russia, to join *Minimalgruppe Balkan* for an offensive against Serbia. This scheme, which also provided for the individual mobilization of each grouping, provided a number of defensive and offensive options and, repeatedly refined in detail, it remained the basic Austro-Hungarian mobilization scheme.[12]

But there existed a flaw in these calculations. Unless in case of a Balkan war Vienna obtained immediate clarification of Russian intentions, *B-Staffel* might well be dispatched to join *Minimalgruppe Balkan;* if Russia then intervened, it would be hard to recall the deployment of *B-Staffel* and almost impossible to extract it if it were already involved in operations. Therefore Conrad continued to ask for a firm German commitment for a major drive in the east which would deflect some of the Russian pressure expected against *A-Staffel*. But Moltke would not make any more specific assurances and on May 12, 1914, when the allies held their last staff talks and Conrad asked him how long it would be after the outbreak of the expected two-front war against France and Russia before Germany would be able to send strong forces against Russia, Moltke replied that it would take approximately six weeks. And with this assurance, contingent on a rapid German victory in the west, Conrad had to content himself.[13]

Meanwhile Conrad again turned to the problem of expanding his army and providing it with more advanced weapons. Additional funds voted during the Annexation Crisis had allowed him to construct some new fortifications, purchase some field artillery, and introduce the Schwarzlose M 1907 machine gun, as well as to organize some new formations. Even so, the manpower ceiling remained static and once the reserves called during the crisis had been released, the peace establishment cadres once again were at a very low level. In his annual estimates of 1909 and 1910, Conrad complained that the defenses of the monarchy were critically inadequate. He decried the lack of manpower, urged further fortifications in the Tyrol, and called for heavy mobile artillery to smash the new Italian forts.[14]

There was, however, no substantial improvement. The size of the military establishment remained fixed by the quotas set in 1889, while Austria-Hungary's overall military expenditures ran well below that of other major European powers. In 1911, for instance, the annual defense budget of the Dual Monarchy was 420 million crowns, compared with 1,786 for Germany, 1,650 for Russia, and 528 for Italy.[15] Both halves of the monarchy, however, were spending large sums amounting to over 20 percent of their total budget on railroads although, especially in Hungary which was trying to promote economic autonomy, the new lines did not always conform with the strategic priorities of the general staff.

The lag in Austro-Hungarian armament was due to the continuing internal crisis, the impasse between Vienna and Budapest over the issue of army expansion which had stalled legislation since 1903. On this issue opinion in Vienna was divided. One party, led by Aehrenthal and supported by Schönaich, was prepared to proceed with the full implementation of the promises made to Hungary in 1906, including a greatly enlarged role for the Hungarian language in the joint army. The second party, headed by Francis Ferdinand and Conrad, bitterly opposed this course. It believed that the inherent weaknesses in the Magyar position, struggling both against the crown and against the national minorities in the kingdom, could be exploited to prevent any further concessions.[16] The old emperor clearly held the decisive vote. Although sincerely dedicated to the principles of the *Ausgleich* and always reluctant to take a firm stand against Hungary, he was at this point equally reluctant to engage in a bitter controversy with the heir presumptive and his supporters.[17] Francis Ferdinand held the upper hand and on April 1909 he informed Wekerle, the Hungarian prime minister, that he would use his influence to block any further implementation of the 1906 promises, and he also hinted that after he acceded to the throne he would attempt to revoke Hungary's special position in military affairs.[18]

Under these circumstances Wekerle, heading a coalition cabinet specifically to implement the 1906 bargain, was forced to resign. But this did not change the mood of the country. In the elections of May 1910, the old Liberal Party, reconstituted by Tisza, secured a substantial majority of 258 seats. The opposition secured 100, while the minority group candidates, despite covert support from the Belvedere, managed to obtain only 41 seats. Tisza, of course, was furious about the threats against the compromise and the delay in the implementation of the 1906 bargain. Still, he regarded the continuation of the Dual Monarchy and a strong joint army as essential to Hungary's future and when parliament opened he once again introduced an army bill designed to revise the recruit quota. The opposition immediately raised demands for greater military autonomy and the situation returned essentially to the conditions of 1903.[19]

Divisions also continued in Vienna. Reichskriegsminister Schönaich was willing to offer further concessions including a reduction of active service from three to two years, but fearing that a shortened service tour would impair troop discipline, especially with the shortage of long-service senior non-commissioned officers, Archduke Francis Ferdinand violently opposed this proposal. He was supported by Conrad who accused Schönaich of making more unnecessary concessions, though both the emperor and Aehrenthal tended to favor the idea.[20]

By this time both Francis Ferdinand and Conrad regarded Schönaich as an arch appeaser of destructive Hungarian nationalist ambitions, and relations between Conrad and the war minister deteriorated even further when Schönaich presented a sharply reduced military budget to the delegations.[21] In late 1910 Conrad had submitted budget requests totaling 1000 million crowns to the minister. The minister, skeptical about his ability to get this approved, promptly reduced the request by more than one-third in his proposal.[22] Conrad had not been consulted about this drastic cut and read about it in the newspapers. He immediately sought an audience with the emperor and on February 13, 1911, he restated his demands for the full amount, threatening resignation if he would not get his way.[23] The emperor told him to be realistic, but through the intervention of Francis Ferdinand, Conrad was permitted to plead his case in person before a special ministerial conference on March 5 in Budapest. He was unable, however, to sway the ministers and the reduced budget remained firm.[24]

The budget issue triggered an explosion in the Belvedere. Francis Ferdinand labelled Schönaich as an enemy of the dynasty and on April 28, 1911, sent him a letter demanding his resignation which the minister ignored.[25] Although legally the archduke had no military authority other than that of inspector general, he felt that Schönaich had violated his dynastic prerogatives and he complained to the emperor. This time, however, Francis Joseph was not overly responsive. The emperor was a stickler for dynastic rights, but he had little affection for his nephew and was becoming concerned about his constant scheming.[23] In particular, Francis Joseph did not like the man Francis Ferdinand advanced as Schönaich's successor—Feldmarschall Leutnant Ritter von Auffenberg, commanding the XVI Corps.

Auffenberg first had come to Francis Ferdinand's attention when he had submitted one of the original proposals for Case "U" and in November 1910 he had submitted a memorandum to the Belvedere, "The Position and Mission of the next War Minister," in which he fully identified himself with Francis Ferdinand's concepts of a dynastic army and with his plans for reducing Hungary's special position.[27] Aehrenthal, who also did not hesitate to move well beyond his own sphere, immediately voiced his opposition to Auffenberg, but indicated that he might accept a trade-off. Aehrenthal wanted Conrad, whose plans for preventive war he opposed, to go; in return, he was willing to accept Auffenberg whom he perceived as a much weaker personality.[28] But Francis Ferdinand was opposed. In July 1911 he told Conrad that "a certain Aehrenthal seems to command the army," and that "as long as such people are in charge, we, my dear Conrad, are cut off." The archduke continued that he hoped to bring about the selection of a new war minister, and Auffenberg, "who is totally devoted to me and will provide an excellent ally against this clique which wishes to push us out of the saddle, is the only possible candidate."[29]

Francis Ferdinand, in fact, entertained even more far-reaching plans. He did not merely wish to remove some recalcitrant ministers; he wanted to restructure the empire on a consolidated, unitary basis. Of course, such plans would have to be carried out at the expense of Hungary, but the heir apparent had never concealed his dislike of the Magyars or his willingness to use force to establish the unity of the monarchy.[30] Since 1906 his military chancery had been working on schemes to be carried out at the time of his accession to the throne, and while the schemes varied from time to time, a more or less definite program had been elaborated during the winter of 1910 and 1911 by Lieutenant Colonel Brosch.[31]

At the heart of the program was the creation of a unified army under the exclusive jurisdiction of the emperor. All concessions made to the Magyars were to be repealed; the army would no longer recognize any Hungarian troops, but only units recruited, trained, or stationed in Hungary. If possible these changes were to be accomplished by negotiations, but if necessary force would be used. The manifesto "To our Peoples," prepared for this eventuality, read, "Every patriotic Austrian must admit that circumstances demanded this action by the crown."[32] At that, the planners did not expect much resistance. "The masses," so Brosch explained, "want bread and will not fight for national flags, insignia, or the Hungarian language of command." But, he continued, only $k.u.k.$ forces should be used, and foreign aid, even German, should be avoided under all circumstances.[33] Even so, Brosch worked out certain precautionary measures, including the strengthening of garrisons and seizure of communications.[34] Moreover, to ensure the reliability of the troops, Francis Ferdinand proposed a large-scale exchange of garrisons, in effect abandoning the "territorial principle."[35]

Despite the faster mobilization provided by the territorial scheme, Francis Ferdinand, like his uncle and mentor Archduke Albrecht, had never wholeheartedly approved of it. The scheme had appeared a necessary measure to both Beck and Conrad, but by 1911 even Conrad was willing to subordinate fast mobilization to safeguarding military loyalty. "Lacking all cohesive basis for a state," he wrote to Francis Ferdinand in January 1911, "the army can only rely on the dynastic principle."[36] In fact, he already had made certain shifts in the direction of counterbalancing national tendencies with troops of a different nationality. When during the crisis of 1909 there was considerable dissension among the Serbs in Slavonia, he had transferred a Magyar infantry regiment to Semlin, and in 1910 he contemplated the transfer of additional Hungarian troops into the Croatian Agram corps district.[37] Detailed elaboration of these proposals was left to Brosch's successor, Colonel Dr. Karl Bardolff, who in late October 1911 took over the military chancery in the Belvedere. "Events have shown," he wrote in a memorandum dated January 1913, "that nationalist propaganda has made certain units unreliable and therefore the distribution of troops should be governed, at least in part, by the principles prevailing before the 1880s."[38] But before this could be done, a conflict between Conrad and Aehrenthal diverted Francis Ferdinand's attention.

By 1911 Aehrenthal had adopted a cautious policy. The foreign minister believed that Austria-Hungary's prestige had been reestablished in the Annexation Crisis and he now wanted to consolidate the gains achieved. Russia, he believed, was willing to accept the new state of affairs in the Balkans and he even expected a detente with Serbia. In contrast, Conrad continued to agitate for an "active" policy against Italy and Serbia. In 1911 he calculated that the time had come to settle accounts with Italy.

Since they first took office, the foreign minister and the chief of the general staff had been in profound disagreement over policy towards Italy. Aehrenthal accepted the Triple Alliance as one of the foundations of his policy and, though not unaware of the tensions between Vienna and Rome, was determined to preserve the relationship. Conrad, on the other hand, was convinced that in any major war Italy would either disregard her obligations or would be openly hostile. Conrad, therefore, favored a preventive war against Italy, a conflict which Aehrenthal described in 1907 as a "violation of Austrian traditions, lacking in popular support. . .[and] an invitation of disaster for the monarchy."[39] Nonetheless, the military continued to regard war with Italy as eventually unavoidable and saw no use in keeping her even as a nominal ally. Intelligence reports of Italian preparations in the Alps and of anti-Austrian sentiment among the population were taken most seriously by the general staff.[40] Therefore, despite Aehrenthal's objections, the military pressed for increased defenses in the southwest. In 1904 Italy had twice the infantry, four times the cavalry, and eight times the field artillery as the Austro-Hungarians in the sectors facing them. In addition, the Italians had built modern fortifications and were procuring heavy siege guns. By 1910 Austria-Hungary had evened out her inferiority in infantry and had created modern fortifications. On Conrad's initiative modern armored forts were built on the high plateau of Lavarone-Folgaria, designed not only to block an Italian offensive but also to provide a secure deployment area for an Austrian offensive into Venetia.[41]

Aehrenthal had objected strenuously to these preparations.[42] As a result, and also because of Aehrenthal's attitudes in matters of the army budget and relations with Hungary, he and Conrad were on extremely bad terms. When in July 1911 an Albanian revolt against Turkey threatened complications in Montenegro and possible Italian or Russian interference, Conrad asserted that Austria-Hungary should make military preparations to exploit all opportunities. Aehrenthal, however, chose to regard these suggestions as a "personal thrust against myself," and demanded that the chief of staff cease interfering in the conduct of foreign affairs.[43] Conrad countered with a lengthy memorandum to the emperor in which he accused the foreign minister of deliberately undermining the military preparedness of the empire.[44]

The final explosion came late in September 1911. At this time Italy was making preparations for a war against the Ottoman Empire and Conrad now suggested to Aehrenthal that Austria should seize this opportunity for an attack against Italy.[45] In October hostilities opened in Tripolitania and Conrad became more pressing in his demands for war. "Austria's opportunity has come," he wrote in an exposition to the emperor, "and it would be suicidal not to use it."[46] Aehrenthal promptly complained to the monarch that the chief of the general staff should not be allowed to determine foreign policy and Francis Joseph sustained him. On October 17 Francis Joseph sent a sharp reply to Conrad telling him that his duty was to prepare the military establishment for war, "while the foreign minister, in accordance with My direction and in agreement with the two prime ministers" was solely responsible for the conduct of external affairs.[47] Although Conrad counted on the backing of Francis Ferdinand, the archduke was no longer committed, having achieved Auffenberg's appointment as war minister in September, (though as a concession to Hungary with the title changed from *Reichskriegsminister* to the more ambivalent *k.u.k. Kriegsminister*).[48] The archduke had become troubled about Conrad's open advocacy of war, was concerned about the new style of army maneuvers, and above all, as an ardent Catholic, objected to Conrad's liaison with Gina von Reininghaus, a married woman.[49] As late as November 15 Conrad still suggested war against Italy, with the most opportune time the spring of 1912, but he found little backing.[50] In fact, that very day the emperor summoned him and told him that "my policy is peace and everyone must conform to this." A fortnight later Francis Joseph again sent for Conrad and told him that he was relieved of his "present duties" and reassigned as inspector general of infantry. "My reasons," the emperor stated, "are well known to you and we need not talk about them."[51] The army regarded Conrad's dismissal as a major turning point, though not necessarily as a catastrophe. "His ideas," an old trooper wrote in a military journal, "have taken root in the army."[52]

Aehrenthal had triumphed, but he did not live to enjoy it and died soon thereafter on February 17, 1912. He was succeeded by Leopold Count Berchtold, a man of no great strength, but charming and well-liked at court. Much the same has been said about Conrad's temporary successor, General der Infanterie Blasius Schemua, a staff officer, described rather unfairly as a "zero" by Ritter.[53] Nonetheless, by 1912 the entire team which in 1906 had come into office with such high hopes had been removed, and its replacement confronted the continuing problems of army reform and a worsening external situation.

Schemua, though he lacked much of Conrad's drive, was in fact a man of some vision and in his first annual assessment of the international situation, submitted in January 1912, he followed many of Conrad's concepts but also showed a much wider concern. After reviewing the dangers to Russia stemming from the rising power of Japan, and asserting that in any Balkan conflict "we must count on Italy leaving the alliance," he recommended a detente with Russia because "a two-front war must absolutely be avoided."[54] The army, Schemua pointed out, was in a weak condition and he listed as his priorities passage of the long-delayed army bill, appropriations for siege and field artillery, fortifications in the Tyrol, radio and aviation equipment, and finally enough funds to provide, if necessary, for a three-month mobilization. At that, Schemua had but little hopes of getting his requirements from the two parliaments. "These," he complained to Francis Ferdinand, "have proved totally incompetent, lacking in sense of duty, and corrupt."[55] His aversion to the civilian politicians were shared by many other generals.[56] In fact, War Minister Auffenberg went even further and in 1911, despairing of getting action to replace the new totally obsolete Austrian siege artillery of Uchatius design with modern pieces, had ordered, on his own authority, twelve mobile 30.5-cm. mortars from the Skoda works in Bohemia. The result, of course, was an uproar in the parliaments, especially in Budapest, but nonetheless a beginning, at long last, had been made to modernize the artillery.[57]

Still, this did nothing to resolve the fundamental deadlock over the new army bill designed to increase the annual recruit contingent and the overall strength of the army. In Vienna, elections held in the summer of 1911 brought defeat for the conservative and pro-army Christian Socialists and stengthened divisive and antimilitary elements in the *Reichsrat*. It was Hungary which finally dissolved the impasse. Here Tisza dominated politics, and while he continued the magyarization policy which further alienated the national minorities, he also realized that strengthening the joint army was a necessity for the future security of his country. In June 1912 he coerced the Budapest parliament to pass the new army law and a reluctant *Reichsrat* followed suit. Francis Joseph was most pleased with Tisza. He never had approved of the ideas promoted by Conrad and Francis Ferdinand of using the minorities against the Magyars, and some months later he told Conrad that after all "the Magyars are the reliable element."[58]

The new army law increased the annual recruit contingent by 42,000, a total of 181,000 annually, which broke down into 136,000 men for the joint army, 20,715 for the *Landwehr* and 17,500 for the *Honvédség*. Also envisaged were further increases in three stages, so that by 1918 the annual contingent for the joint army was to rise to 170,000, and to 35,300 for the *Landwehr* and 31,000 for the *Honvédség*.[59] Of course, there was a price attached. The new law reduced the average service obligation in the joint army from three to two years and it also elevated *Landwehr* and *Honvédség*, in theory at least, to coequal status with the units of the first line by granting them organic artillery.[60]

Finally, supplementing the new army law was the War Services Act, also passed in the autumn of 1912, which incorporated in legal form the theory that in time of war all labor, goods, and services were at the disposal of the state.[61]

In this fashion, after more than a decade of trouble which had brought the Dual Monarchy to the brink of civil war, the army question was resolved. But it was too late to make much difference in 1914. Although the increased recruit contingent helped to flesh out the skeletonized infantry regiments and provided the basis for an increase in artillery as well as a modest beginning for military aviation, the delay had greatly weakened Austria-Hungary's relative military strength, and she took the field in the World War with inadequate materiel and insufficient reserves.[62] "The weakness of the Habsburg army in 1914," one English scholar declared, "stemmed not from the disaffection of its soldiers but from the intransigence of politicians in Hungary."[63] This statement, perhaps, was too harsh. There was disaffection, especially among the Czechs, some generals were notably incompetent, and the handling of the Hungarians had, on occasion, been inept. At least one Austrian general admitted that small concessions in uniforms and insignia might have smoothed over some of the difficulties with the Magyars and compromised nothing.[64]

In any case, Tisza's change of heart in the summer of 1912 was based on the realization of a growing threat in the Balkans. Following the Bosnian crisis of 1909, some Russian diplomats and soldiers decided to redress the balance and bar the southeastern expansion of the Dual Monarchy by promoting a Balkan coalition. Prodded by the Russians, Serbia, Bulgaria, Greece, and Montenegro negotiated offensive and defensive alliances in the spring and summer of 1912, forming the Balkan League. Although the league's primary objective was to push the Turks out of Europe, the allies also agreed to resist any Austro-Hungarian attempt at intervention by force; Poincaré, the French prime minister, characterized the alliance as an agreement for war not only against Turkey but also against Austria. Clearly the arrangement carried the danger of a wider conflict, but the French and Russian general staffs, though not necessarily the diplomats, were willing to accept that risk, calculating that a major Austro-Hungarian involvement in the Balkans would materially improve their own prospects in case hostilities escalated into a general European war.⁶⁵ For Austria-Hungary the situtation presented a grave problem. Since the days of Metternich the Habsburg Empire had been determined to maintain the Balkan status quo and the integrity of the Ottoman Empire, but by 1912 the situation had changed. Austria-Hungary was still opposed to the division of European Turkey and was still capable militarily of keeping the Balkan states in check. But the division of Europe into two hostile camps meant that any intervention would have wider repercussions and it was now necessary for every great power to consult its allies and also take reaction from the opposite camp into consideration.

By the summer of 1912 the impending Balkan crisis aroused attention in Germany and Austria-Hungary, though in both countries the civilian leaders, especially the monarchs and their foreign ministers, tended to underrate the seriousness of the situation. Moreover, through much of the crisis Germany was uncertain of her course and reluctant to risk general war for the sake of Habsburg interests in the Balkans, though resolute Austro-Hungarian action might have been able to limit the damage. Count Berchtold, however, lacked the inclination and the resolution for determined and clear action. Although as early as July 1912 he was willing to permit limited military measures designed to "protect our interests,"⁶⁶ his objective, as stated in the council of joint ministers on September 14, was to "avoid any action which might involve Austria ia a war."⁶⁷ Even after Serbia mobilized on October 1 and the chief of the general staff called for an Austro-Hungarian countermobilization, Berchtold remained adamant. "Our actions during the Annexation Crisis," he told Schemua, "have aroused apprehension in all the foreign offices of the major powers [and] mobilization now would cast Austria-Hungary in an aggressive role."⁶⁸ Berchtold was eager to avoid war and hoped that the Turks would be more than a match for the Balkan allies and that internal dissensions would break up the league. In fact, most western military experts, including Austrian, predicted a Turkish military victory, though Schemua warned the foreign minister against these optimistic forecasts and warned him to assume the worst.⁶⁹

Schemua was no "zero" and his appreciation of the situation was much like Conrad's. He believed, as Taylor put it, that the "victory of Balkan nationalism was a disaster beyond remedy for the Habsburg Monarchy."⁷⁰ To prevent this, he was willing to resort to war and from September 1912 on he began to press for the execution of Plan "B" when fighting broke out.⁷¹ On October 18 he repeated his arguments in a long memorandum to Berchtold and maintained that even if Russia intervened and Germany stood aside, Austria-Hungary's chances were not at all bad as long as the Balkan states still were engaged with Turkey.⁷² But Berchtold could not be moved and neither Francis Joseph nor Francis Ferdinand were willing to risk a general war without a direct danger to the existence of the monarchy.⁷³

Even so, Austria-Hungary took limited military precautions. At the urging of Feldzeugmeister Oskar Potiorek, the influential military governor of Bosnia-Hercegovina, garrisons in these provinces were reinforced, though XV and XVI Corps were not brought up to war strength until December 1912.⁷⁴ The immediate concern in Vienna was with the Russian "trial" mobilizations in certain western districts in October, and with the retention of some four hundred thousand time-expired conscripts with the colors in November. At that Auffenberg, who until then had supported Berchtold, changed his stand and supported Schemua's demand for the mobilization of I, X, and XI Corps in Galicia. But it was not until November 21 that a reluctant Francis Joseph permitted mobilization of these corps as well as partial mobilization of IV, VII, and XIII Corps.[75] Anxiety about a Russian surprise cavalry thrust remained, and in December nine additional regiments of cavalry were sent to Galicia.[76]

By this time public sentiment in Austria-Hungary was becoming more bellicose and on October 29 the Delegations, acting with surprising speed, had voted 250 million crowns in extraordinary military expenditures.[77] Even Germany, until now unconcerned, became worried about the Russian preparations and when in mid-November Francis Ferdinand and Schemua visited Berlin, the Emperor William promised support and Moltke reiterated his previous promises. But, as he repeated, these involved a general war and in that case the main German effort would still be made against France.[78] A general war came closer when the Russian war minister proposed mobilization of the Warsaw and Kiev military districts and partial mobilization in the Odessa district for November 22, 1912. Such large-scale measures most probably would have provoked general mobilization in Austria-Hungary, while Germany, under the circumstances, would have been compelled to follow. And that would have meant war. At the last minute, however, Tsar Nicholas, becoming aware of the dangerous schemes of his soldiers, decided to cancel the proposed mobilization.[79]

Affairs had come to the brink because the course of events in the Balkans had been swift and unexpected. On October 8 Montenegro, brushing aside a last-minute warning from Russia and Austria-Hungary, declared war on Turkey, with Serbia, Bulgaria, and Greece following in a few days. Confounding the experts, the Balkan allies were from the outset victorious on all fronts. One reason for this was the numerical superiority of the combined armies, about seven hundred fifteen thousand men, against some three hundred twenty thousand Ottoman troops. In addition, the allies proved to have better staffs and slightly better equipment. With the Bulgarians bearing the brunt of the fighting, the allies made swift gains, and by November the Turks had lost all their European territories except for the area around Constantinople and the fortresses of Adrianople, Scutari, and Yanina. In the west, meanwhile, Serbian troops drove to the Albanian coast and after Turkey signed an armistice with Bulgaria and Serbia on December 3, Belgrade announced its intent to held on to its outlet on the Adriatic. This Berchtold was not prepared to tolerate, though why he should suddenly have become willing to risk all for the sake of a port is obscure. Perhaps the fact that Italy, for once, was prepared to back the Dual Monarchy and join in its efforts to establish an independent Albania gave Berchtold heart. In any case, though the Russian halt in mobilization had eased tensions in the east, Austro-Hungarian preparations against Serbia were stepped up sharply in December. Although Auffenberg professed misgivings, the emperor acceded to pressure from Schemua and Potiorek and on December 7 ordered mobilization of XV and XVI Corps and the call-up of the *Landwehr* in Dalmatia.[80] Counting the Galician corps, the Dual Monarchy now had over 550,000 men under arms.

At this moment Conrad was brought back to his former post as chief of the general staff. On December 7 Francis Ferdinand called Conrad, who had just returned from Rumania where he had negotiated a reluctant renewal of the alliance, and informed him that he was to resume his old duties, a decision confirmed the same day by the emperor.[81] Apparently Francis Ferdinand now favored a more active policy.[82] This, however, meant that Auffenberg had to go because Francis Joseph would only tolerate one of the archduke's men in a decision-making position in the army. Moreover, Auffenberg had become a liability because part of his 1905 proposals for intervention in Hungary had been published by the press, and his retention jeopardized military appropriations.[83] On December 10 the emperor summoned Auffenberg and rather brusquely told him to submit his resignation.[84] He was replaced by Feldzeugmeister Alexander Baron Krobatin, a friend of Conrad, and it now appeared that the war party was in the ascendancy.

But actually this was not so. Conrad, of course, immediately called for war. On December 30, 1912, he wrote to the archduke that "we have reached the point at which there must be a trial of strength between the monarchy and Serbia. All else, Albania, the seaport question...are but side issues."[85] Conrad saw the issue clearly, but much to his surprise, the ever-volatile Francis Ferdinand now had changed his mind again and would not support him. In fact, for whatever reasons Francis Ferdinand had engineered Conrad's return, it was not for war against Serbia.[86] The archduke now supported Berchtold who put his faith in the diplomatic negotiations between the great powers which were trying to bring an end to the fighting in the Balkans and settle the territorial disputes which had arisen out of it. And these efforts continued even though on January 30, 1913, the Turks reopened the war. Moreover, Germany, though prepared to back Austria-Hungary in an extremity against Russia, would not support her on the question of a seaport. In January 1913 Moltke wrote to Conrad that the solution was now to be found in diplomacy, and that Austria-Hungary should ease tensions by demobilization, a suggestion to which Conrad replied that mobilization remained necessary and that he was most disappointed in the German attitude.[87] But Moltke stood his ground. On February 10 he told Conrad that though in the long run war was unavoidable, a war of nations could only be waged with the support of the people and this would not be forthcoming in a conflict over the frontiers of Serbia and Albania.[88] Moltke hinted that Russia would reciprocate if forces were reduced in Galicia, and despite Conrad's strenuous objections, on March 11 Francis Joseph ordered the stand-down of the Galician Corps.[89]

In part Conrad objected because Balkan peace negotiations were deadlocked. In March Turkey renewed hostilities but did no better in this second round. Adrianople fell and Scutari, besieged by Serbian and Montenegrin troops, became the center of attention. The powers had agreed to establish an independent Albania, but when Scutari surrendered to the Montenegrins on April 23, 1913, the Montenegrins balked at evacuating the port while Serbia continued occupation of some areas earmarked for the new Albania. Berchtold was incensed and Conrad saw an opportunity. On April 18 he told Berchtold that "there are plenty of reasons for war" and Serbia should now be eliminated.[90] Austria-Hungary reinforced XV and XVI Corps and announced that she was ready to use force to expel the Montenegrins from Scutari. But this was not necessary. Nikita of Montenegro bowed to a naval demonstration by the powers and Scutari was occupied by an international force. At the end of May the London Conference negotiated a peace treaty between Turkey and the Balkan allies.

At the same time Conrad once again provided Berchtold with an exposition of his views. Only an appeal to arms could eliminate the danger of a Greater Serbia and the monarchy, together with Bulgaria, should attack that kingdom. "The aim of his operation," the general wrote, "is to be the partition of Serbia."[91] It was Conrad's most total design against Serbia. It has been suggested that, in part at least, Conrad wrote this proposal at a moment when, lacking German support, he really could not take action to divert attention from the treason of Colonel Alfred Redl, one of the army's chief intelligence officers.[92] Answering an inquiry from Berchtold, Conrad hastened to assure the minister that Colonel Redl's treason was indeed serious but that he had not had access to documents determining the outcome of war.[93]

The Redl affair, however, was soon overshadowed by a new flare-up in the Balkans. Bulgaria, feeling betrayed in the distribution of spoils, attacked its former allies, but was in turn attacked by Rumania and even the Turks. Badly defeated in July, Bulgaria had to accept the Treaty of Bucharest in August which resulted in very substantial territorial gains for Serbia, Montenegro, and Greece. Rumania took the Dobrudja, while Bulgaria obtained only a small bit of Macedonia for all her efforts. During the war, Austria-Hungary had attempted to secure intervention by the powers in Bulgaria's favor, but neither Germany nor Italy would go along. As a result, Rumania, already a doubtful ally in 1912, switched to the Russo-French camp. To Austria-Hungary this meant the loss of five army corps in her order of battle against Russia; for Russia this provided direct access to Bulgaria and Serbia, as well as the ability to threaten Hungary through the unfortified Transylvanian passes.[94] Conrad was unable to compensate for this loss. In late August he wrote to Berchtold that he realized that the time for preventive action in the Balkans was over. He now recommended keeping the Triple Alliance in being and hoped that Germany would help to keep Rumania neutral. A war against Serbia, Montenegro, Rumania, and Russia at the same time did not have any chances of success.[95] At the same time Bulgaria began to seek closer relations with Austria-Hungary, but this was tenuous and no definite agreement existed until 1915.

The unsettled state of affairs in Albania where Serb troops continued to occupy some districts revived Conrad's hope for a possible armed intervention. In September an Albanian revolt led to further Serb troop commitments and deeper penetration of the country. Conrad tried to prevail on Francis Joseph to take the opportunity and go to war, but the emperor, now in his eighties, merely wanted to live out his life in peace.[96] Berchtold was also incensed, and after considerable hesitation dispatched an ultimatum to Serbia giving her one week to comply. On October 21 Conrad told Francis Joseph that "a peaceful solution at this time will only cause us to have to go to war under worse conditions later, but in the end the Serbs, not supported in the Albanian question by Russia, complied.[97] The Balkan crisis was over. It had been a great set-back for the Dual Monarchy, which now faced a Greater Serbia with almost boundless national self-confidence and a battle-tested army of two hundred thousand in the first line and another two hundred thousand in the reserves.[98]

Throughout the last year of the Balkan crises Conrad, like Schemua in the months before, constantly and almost frantically called for swift, bold, and violent action. Historians have condemned him as a warmonger, and he certainly was that. But historians also have shown that the victory of Balkan nationalism was fatal for the Dual Monarchy and unless Conrad, who realized this, wanted to let the situation drift by default, the means he advocated were well within the sphere of his competence and sworn duties. Even Albertini argues that Austria-Hungary should have occupied the Sanjak of Novi-Bazar in 1912, and that certainly would have led to hostilities with Serbia.[99] Conrad may be faulted in that he had no real program except for his obsession to destroy Serbia. Would the destruction of Serbia, by occupation, partition, or by bringing her into a relationship to the Habsburg Empire similar to that of Bavaria and Germany, as he proposed in July 1913, have solved the South Slav problem in the monarchy?[100] And finally, did Conrad have the military means to carry out his plans?

Of this, Conrad himself was no longer sure. In October 1913 he told an old friend that in 1908 and 1909 it would have been easy, in 1912 it would have been a "gamble with the odds in our favor, and now it is just a straight gamble."[101] The main problem of the army, as Conrad saw it, was not outdated equipment or numbers, though both worried him, but the reliability of the troops—the old "nationality problem." And because he realized that while the army was still a reliable instrument, its stability might not last much longer, he clamored more and more insistently for preventive war.[102] The long mobilization, causing considerable economic dislocations and hardships, lowered the morale of the troops.[103] Moreover, mobilization revealed that not all units could be considered loyal in case of a war against men of their own ethnic backgrounds. There was a serious mutiny when the 8th Dragoons were sent from Bohemia to Galicia late in 1912, and throughout the crisis there were incidents in Czech, Ruthene, and even South Slav regiments.[104] Foreign observers did not always realize this. In an article on the *k.u.k.* army appearing in an English journal, one author felt that "despite many good qualities. . .[it] lacked spirit and tended towards slackness."[105] But the article said little about the nationality problem, agreeing perhaps with another critic, Seton-Watson, who as late as 1908 had proclaimed that the joint army had overcome all ethnic and language differences and, in that respect at least, was "a splendid institution."[106] Even the Germans were still confident. A staff evaluation of 1913 believed that "the officer corps forms the main and at this time still quite effective counterbalance against the polyglot character of the army," and that the rank and file were "disciplined, willing, patriotic, largely loyal to the emperor, and not yet touched by anti-militaristic agitation."[107] But Conrad did not delude himself. In early 1913 he wrote to Moltke that in the event of a long German-Slav confrontation "we hardly can count on the enthusiastic support of our Slavs, 47 percent of our population."[108] As a result of the events of 1912 and 1913, mobilization plans were changed. Originally VIII Corps (Prague) had been slated for Galicia and the alpine troops of XIV Corps (Innsbruck) for the mountains of Serbia, but now these dispositions were reversed, though this brought tactical disadvantages.[109]

Francis Ferdinand entertained even more far-reaching plans. By 1913 the emperor had finally given him real authority and he had been appointed inspector general of the entire armed forces (*Generalinspektor der gesamten bewaffneten Macht*), a position more powerful than the one Albrecht had held, including the presumptive supreme command in war.[110] Disregarding the undoubted advantages of a faster mobilization, Francis Ferdinand wanted to do away with the territorial system introduced by Beck and to return to the old system of stationing troops outside their ethnic areas. He already had started on this program in 1911 and he returned to it in late 1912. In January 1913 Colonel Bardolff of his military chancery submitted a detailed plan for his approval. "The late events have shown," the memorandum read, "that the existence of national dissension in certain units can no longer be denied and this requires that, at least partially, we return to the system prevailing before the 1880s."[111] The plan, Bardolff continued, intended to assure a maximum of internal security without damaging mobilization requirements. The current stations would be maintained for I, III, VII, XI, XII, and XIV Corps; in IV, V, VI Corps there would be only minor changes, while II, VIII, IX, and XIII Corps would have to make large-scale transfers. Four Czech, five Magyar, one Croat, and two Dalmatian infantry regiments, as well as two Czech and two Hungarian cavalry regiments, would be moved from their home stations and replaced with non-indigenous units. This, Bardolff insisted, would provide a safer ethnic balance. Conrad was reluctant to endanger rapid mobilization, but he agreed, though with certain reservations and modifications, as did Krobatin.[112] All seemed ready for implementation of this scheme. In October 1913, however, news of the plan leaked into the Vienna press.[113] Speculation about Francis Ferdinand's ultimate designs, including his scheme for revising the *Ausgleich,* induced Francis Joseph to cut the proposed station changes. The most he would allow were some of Conrad's proposals which strengthened the order of battle and the transfer of some Hungarian infantry to Croatia.[114]

The emperor's decision hardly endeared Conrad to Francis Ferdinand with whom he had already disagreed over his war policies and his summary disposition of Colonel Redl. Francis Ferdinand would have been a difficult commander for any self-respecting chief of staff, and for a man of Conrad's ambitions the relationship soon became barely tolerable.[115] An open clash between the two men occurred during the autumn maneuvers of 1913 in Bohemia, when the archduke changed certain dispositions without bothering to inform the chief of the general staff. In the argument that followed Francis Ferdinand hinted that Conrad should take care not to become another Wallenstein, a most unfortunate allusion, and the incident was papered over only with difficulty.[116] On this unhappy note ended 1913, the last year of peace for the Habsburg army.

12

Austria-Hungary's Last War: 1914-1915

The outcome of the Balkan Wars shattered many assumptions of Austro-Hungarian military policy. It demonstrated that the potential Balkan enemies had considerable and effective military establishments, and that Russia, with the reorganization and reequipment of her army nearly completed, was willing to embark on an aggressive course. The defection of Rumania jeopardized the right flank of the army's deployment, and Austria-Hungary clearly depended more than ever on the support of her German ally. Above all, the course of the wars revealed that the Dual Monarchy no longer could control events in a vital strategic area. "The Balkan Wars," concluded an English historian, "marked the virtual end of the Habsburg Monarchy as a Great Power." And the reason for this was clear; the monarchy had fallen behind in armaments. In 1914 Austria-Hungary, "though ranking only after Russia and Germany in population . . . spent less than any Great Power—a quarter of Russian or German expenditure, a third of British or French, and even less than Italian."[1] To be sure, there was an effort to catch up. Between 1906 and 1914 armament outlay had risen by 64 percent (actually 123 percent, if the extraordinary allocations made during 1912 and 1913 are taken into account), but even so this represented only 21 percent of the total budget.[2] In any case, the spurt had come too late, and neither trained manpower nor modern equipment could be produced within a few months. Overall, in the words of a German observer more sympathetic than most to the efforts of the monarchy, "the military potential of the Danubian monarchy and its army was adequate for a campaign against Serbia, but she was inadequately prepared for a war against the major European powers."[3]

Few if any historians or military observers would quarrel with this assessment, though the question of who was responsible for the decline remains disputed. Conrad certainly recognized that the balance of power had tilted against the Habsburg Empire. In his "Summation of the Situation at the Beginning of the Year 1914," he conceded that the time for preventive war had passed.[4] Once their forces were mobilized the potential enemies of the Triple Alliance, "a combination of France, Russia, Serbia, and Montenegro," would be clearly superior in manpower and resources. The German alliance, Conrad continued, remained a vital necessity, and, though he really could not have had any illusions about

Italy's future course, he advised that attempts should be made to regain her as well as Rumania for the Triple Alliance. And to redress the balance further, he urged bringing other states into the alliance and suggested that Sweden should be approached.

As in the case of so many of the speculations made by leading Habsburg soldiers, these were but castles in the air. By March 1914 Conrad had reverted to his usual self, and in a memorandum to Francis Joseph he called for "energetic action" against Rumania, "that faithless ally."[5] No, Conrad was right about the need to strengthen the alliance with Germany, but neither he nor Moltke did anything concrete to implement joint planning. Given the strategic constellation, by far the best prospects for success were in exploiting the interior position held by the Austro-Hungarian and German armies in a tightly coordinated common operational plan.[6] In 1914, however, relations between the two general staffs continued much as before and remained based on a set of assumptions not confirmed or worked out in any detail. Germany would seek a rapid victory in the west, while Austria-Hungary, whether engaged with Serbia or not, would undertake an offensive into Russian Poland supported in some fashion by German forces from East Prussia. These understandings were confirmed in May 1914 when Conrad and Moltke had their last conversations, but again no definite plan of joint action was prepared.[7] After hostilities actually had started, Lieutenant Colonel Count Kageneck, the German military attaché in Vienna, sent a despairing telegram on August 1, 1914, to Moltke's chief of staff, Count Waldersee, pleading that "measures to coordinate operations against Russia should be worked out as soon as possible. Everyone had relied on the assumption that the two chiefs of staff had made these most intimate arrangements."[8]

But there were no such arrangements and in fact important changes in operational planning had taken place during the last few months of which the other partner was not informed. In March 1914, partly to replace the earlier plans compromised by Redl's treason, Conrad had elaborated a new offensive scheme against Russia.[9] The new plan, which moved the concentration of *A-Staffel* back behind the San-Dniester line, was designed to reduce the risk of an accidental collision with Russia in case that country held back while Austria-Hungary was settling accounts with Serbia.[10] At the same time the direction and objective of the offensive thrust was changed. The main thrust was to be made by the left flank northward between the Vistula and the Bug towards Lublin and Kholm. The offensive was conceived as a spoiling operation, designed to destroy part of the Russian forces in the process of deployment, and it no longer placed any great weight on cooperation with German forces in a giant pincer movement.[11]

In his 1914 summation, Conrad also had pointed to the numerical weakness of the *k.u.k.* army, only forty-eight divisions compared to ninety-three for Russia, eleven for Serbia, and eighty-eight for France. Although the 1912 army law provided for an increased annual recruit contingent, its effects would not produce substantial augmentations in trained manpower for several years. In the meantime Austria-Hungary would be short of field formations in the vital battles during the initial period of the war which Conrad, like strategists everywhere, expected to be brief. With *Landwehr* and *Honvédség* considered part of the first line, the army did not possess any second line similar to the German reserve divisions. On the other hand, the obligation to serve ten years in the joint army reserve had created a considerable pool of men above the number required to bring the existing formations up to war strength, and late in 1913 Conrad tried to persuade the government to establish a seven-division reserve army on the German pattern.[12] The government refused and Conrad, with the help of Krobatin, now tried to create new formations by resorting to the utilization of the *Landsturm* and the half-trained *Ersatzreserve*. Plans were made to activate on mobilization *Landsturm* and *Marschbrigaden,* provisional field formations not equipped on a combat scale, having small arms and some obsolete artillery, but no machine guns, signal equipment, or transport. This raised immediately disposable forces to about 1.8 million men, forty-eight infantry and eleven cavalry divisions, and thirty-six brigades, organized in seventeen corps and six armies.[13]

But such desperate remedies could not solve the other shortcomings of the military establishment—the insufficient and obsolescent materiel as well as the outdated tactics. Above all, in 1914 the army was short on firepower. Still in the process of reequipment, the Austro-Hungarian field artillery had only forty-two pieces supporting each infantry division, compared to an average of forty-eight pieces for Russia and fifty-four for Germany. And while thirty of these pieces were modern 8-cm. M 5/8 guns, they still were equipped with the outdated heavy steel-bronze barrels and had inadequate range.[14] The remaining pieces were field howitzers, necessary for their high trajectory, but these were 10-cm. M 99 field howitzers, obsolete short-range weapons lacking recoil buffers and protective shields. The same was true of the only heavy field artillery piece, the 15-cm. M 99/04 howitzer, eight of which were assigned to the corps artillery reserve. Ammunition stocks were inadequate, with about 500 rounds for the guns and 330 for the howitzers, and most of this consisted of shrapnel of little use against entrenched troops.[15] Things were better in the mountain artillery whose main weapons still were the obsolete M 99 guns, though new designs, the M 08 and the M 09, were coming into service. Finally, the Technical Military Committee in cooperation with the Skoda Works in Bohemia had designed modern field artillery and, once funds had been received, these were coming into mass production at the outbreak of war.[16] Even so, except for the few batteries of mobile 30.5-cm. mortars, procured by Auffenberg in 1911, the Austro-Hungarian artillery was weak.

The weakness was, in large part, due to financial shortages, but it also reflected faulty tactical thinking by the top command which "with sublime indifference, continued to disregard the lessons of the Manchurian and Balkan wars."[17] None of the senior commanders had any modern war experience, and they expected that infantry would advance without artillerty support against entrenched positions. For that matter, the artillery had no doctrine for indirect targeting and firing against an enemy which had gone to ground, and the cavalry, paying only lip service to dismounted fighting, was still trained for the massed charge. Overall, the spirit of the attack prevailed, though as one post-war commentator observed, "an army lacking adequate artillery cannot fight primarily with offensive tactics."[18] Even the official Austrian war history concluded that "a considerable degree of uncertainty in the choice of tactics was typical of all Austro-Hungarian forces during the initial battles."[19]

It is, of course, easy to single out Austria-Hungary's army for its inability to appreciate the incompatibility of weapons and tactics that had developed in the early twentieth century. But in this the army was by no means alone. The British

Field Service Regulations also overrated the importance of the rifle in the defense and the attack; the French were intoxicated with the cult of the mass offensive, and German infantry advanced in dense waves in the summer of 1914. If the *k.u.k.* cavalry retained its preference for the mounted charge, the Germans shortly before the war reequipped their entire cavalry with lances, a weapon also held in high regard by the British. Only the Russians and the Serbs, having learned from recent experience, habitually dismounted their cavalry to fight, but the practice of entrenching in the field was not always practiced in the tsar's armies. Furthermore, Conrad was not unreceptive to new weapons. He had been instrumental in pushing the development of heavy mobile mortars and artillery, and, anxious to strengthen his infantry, he had ordered troop trials with an automatic rifle, the Revelli, in the spring before the war. Finally, Conrad took a strong interest in the development of the fledgling Austro-Hungarian air arm.

Although military aviation in the Dual Monarchy dated back to balloon detachments established in 1893, Schönaich had regarded aviation as a luxury item for which no funds could be spared.[20] Even so, in 1909 the balloonists, now designated as the *k.u.k. Luftschiffer Abteilung,* had been transferred from the fortress artillery to the more congenial control of the new *Verkehrs Brigade,* which also included motorized transport, railroad, and telegraph troops. At first the new unit experimented with a number of non-rigid dirigibles, but by 1911 the general staff realized that the future of the military depended on the heavier-than-air machines and the dirigibles were gradually phased out, while the balloon detachments were severed from the aviation units and returned to the fortress artillery. But the aviation section was still very small, and Austria-Hungary possessed only four monoplanes and one biplane in 1911.

Schönaich's ouster and the supplementary appropriations of 1912 and 1913 gave Conrad the opportunity to realize his own ideas—an air establishment of 200 planes, projected to be operational by 1915. Still, there were other priorities, and in 1914 the Dual Monarchy spent only a total of eight hundred thousand crowns for military aviation while France in comparison spent twenty million.[21] When war broke out the *k.u.k.* land forces had organized thirteen *Flieger* companies, but with only 48 first-line and 27 training machines, including some German Aviatik and Rumpler machines delivered at the last moment. In contrast Germany had 250, France 136, Russia about 70, and the British Expeditionary Force 48 first-line planes.

Clearly, Austria-Hungary was not prepared for war on the scale of 1914, though perhaps the greatest preoccupation of the leading soldiers remained as it had been for a hundred years—the problems arising out of the multinational composition of the army. Francis Ferdinand and Conrad's scheme for an exchange of garrisons had not yet been accomplished, though in retrospect their fears about nationalist disloyalty seem exaggerated. They must, however, be understood against the growing political tensions which were threatening the conduct of government in both halves of the empire. In Hungary, Tisza, who had become premier in 1913, ruled parliament with an iron hand; he and his party, the reorganized Liberals, were pledged to uphold the compromise and were willing, albeit most reluctantly, to support the military establishment. On the other hand, their magyarization policies drove the minorities, still regarded by Francis Ferdinand and the military as the main elements of loyalty in the kingdom, further and further away from the narrow path of allegiance. As a result of the Balkan Wars, Serbs, Croats, and Rumanians increasingly felt the pull of their compatriots beyond the frontiers, while the Ruthenes were beginning to reveal open Russophile tendencies.[22] Moreover, affairs in Austria were reaching a deadlock. In the *Reichsrat,* Czech obstructionist tactics, frequently seconded by the Socialists, brought business to a standstill and essential legislation had to be passed by emergency decree. Finally in March 1914, Prime Minister Karl Count Stürgkh, prorogued the assembly; it would not meet again during the reign of Francis Joseph.

But despite the fears of the senior soldiers there remained the question of how much all this political turmoil and dissident propaganda really affected the army. The quality of an army, that least democratic of institutions, is largely determined by its officer corps and effective fighting forces have been molded from the most unpromising material when they have had good officers. And despite the problems existing in the highest ranks and the occasional failure of an officer, the corps by and large consisted of able and dedicated men. The large territorial expanse of the Dual Monarchy which included the gentle landscapes of Lower Austria and Bohemia, the mighty ranges of the Alps and the Carpathians, the rich lands of Slovenia and the plains of Galicia, the wild forests of Bosnia and Transylvania, as well as the barren crags of the Dalmatian coast, with garrisons ranging from cities of culture and refinement like Vienna, Budapest, and Prague, provincial towns like Graz, Agram, or Budweis, to small, isolated hamlets, gave service in the joint army a special character. An officer might serve a tour in a big city and find himself during the next in an isolated fort in Bosnia or in the mud of a small Galician hamlet. Described by one English journalist "as hard-working, hard-living men," the average Austro-Hungarian regimental officer was judged the "superior of the average German officer . . . more intelligent, more readily adaptable, in closer touch with his men, less given to dissipation, and remarkably free from arrogance."[23] The writer was equally complimentary about the senior officers and the staff, though he was not impressed by the training and materiel of the artillery and with the supply service. While some may dispute his comparisons with the German officer corps, his overall conclusion that the army was reliable appears correct and has been restated in a more recent study of the decline of the Habsburg Monarchy. "The army which was to fight this war," Professor Zeman wrote, "reflected faithfully the national composition of the empire. It was a reliable instrument at the disposal of the established order."[24]

Even so, the senior officers and the government had misgivings when, in the summer of 1914, Austria-Hungary entered its last war. Certainly the response to the mobilization order against Serbia on July 25, the declaration of war against Serbia on the 28th, and the general mobilization of the *k.u.k.* armed forces on July 31 revealed unsuspected aggressive national solidarity. Much to the relief of the authorities, mobilization, even in the Czech districts where incidents had marred the partial mobilizations of 1908 and 1912, everything proceeded smoothly and everywhere there were scenes of patriotic emotion.[25]

The exuberance and enthusiasm, however, were not shared by the military, only too aware of the monarchy's weaknesses. Emperor Francis Joseph signed the war manifesto against Serbia with tears in his eyes. "It was my profound hope," the manifesto read, "to devote the years which God in His mercy may still grant me working for peace . . . now I put my faith in the Austro-Hungarian army, in its bravery and dedicated loyalty." At heart, though, the aged emperor did not have much confidence. Solferino and Königgrätz had left permanent doubts in his mind about the fortunes of war.[26] For that matter, Conrad was pessimistic. In a letter to Gina written on the evening of the assassination of Francis Ferdinand in Sarajevo, he predicted the conflict's escalation, involving not only Serbia and Rumania, the "coffin nails of our monarchy," but also Russia. "It will be a hopeless struggle," he wrote, "but nevertheless it must be because such an ancient monarchy and such an ancient army cannot perish ingloriously."[27] Even younger men like Colonel Brosch, now commanding the 1st Tyrolean *Kaiserjäger*, had gloomy forebodings. On July 1 Brosch wrote to his old friend Auffenberg that he would witness the final destiny of the empire "not as an uncommitted bystander, but as a resigned combatant who will see the black steamroller, which will obliterate us, approach, but who cannot stop it."[28]

Mobilization activated the war command and control apparatus, the *Armee-Oberkommando* (*A.O.K.*) with the elderly General der Infantrie Archduke Friedrich as titular head. Conrad, however, was in actual command, passing on all questions of major importance and making all major decisions. Effectively, Conrad became the commander-in-chief of all forces. Equipped with far-reaching powers, the *A.O.K.* directed the war essentially independently of the emperor and other authorities.[29] Such an aggregation of power, of course, soon aroused animosity and by the spring of 1915 Arthur Baron Bolfras, the seventy-five-year-old head of the emperor's military chancery, was grumbling that "we are being ruled by the *A.O.K.*"[30] In fact, the war brought a considerable increase in the political power of the army. Military tribunals obtained jurisdiction over a wide variety of offenses connected with national security, and military commanders held unlimited administrative powers in the territories behind the fighting front which, in some cases, extended far into the hinterland. Moreover, with the *Reichsrat* suspended, the usual constitutional checks had disappeared in the Austrian half of the monarchy, though in Hungary, Tisza vigorously, obstinately, and sometimes to the detriment of the war effort maintained parliamentary government and the special status of the kingdom.[31]

For the moment, however, the main responsibility had passed into Conrad's hands. Unfortunately, it soon became evident that he was not equal to the task. Although Austrian military writers have praised his leadership, and even an English military historian estimated that he was the best strategist in the opening phase of the war, a realistic appraisal does not confirm their judgment.[32] In a war that would impose unprecedented strains and stresses on the *k.u.k.* troops, demand bravery, tenacity, and great adaptibility to changing conditions, Conrad isolated himself from the reality of the battlefield. Installed with the *A.O.K.* at Teschen in Austrian Silesia, far from the front, he and his staff were totally out of contact with the troops, living in luxury with uniformed lackeys, candlelit dinners, and frequent female company.[33] Even the official Austrian war history, written by men loyal to his memory, admits that he lacked contact with the troops and during his three years at the head of the *A.O.K.* he visited the front only three times.[34]

Other commanders during World War I have been accused of doing much the same. But Conrad did not compensate for this with victories. A less charitable appraisal was penned shortly after the war by General Josef Count Stürgkh. "Conrad," Stürgkh concluded, "has been overrated. Although by modern standards he lacked tactical expertise and command experience, he erroneously was regarded as the right man for the position of chief of the general staff."[35] Indeed, Conrad, whose capacity for self-deception was to grow under stress, made grave errors. Above all, completely misreading the diplomatic situation, he committed a grave blunder in the disposition of his forces at the outset of war.

On paper Conrad's plans always had an almost Napoleonic sweep, though he often lacked the resolution to carry them out and also forgot that he did not have the instruments to execute them. The day after Sarajevo he urged immediate action against Serbia and perhaps a swift, surgical strike would have provided the Dual Monarchy with the needed prestige, assured Serbian compensations, and avoided international complications. This prospect was unlikely, but when the occasion arose Conrad had to admit that he lacked the necessary forces to carry out such an operation.[36] The cabinet in Vienna also could not make up its mind. Clearly, something had to be done, but Tisza balked at any course likely to add more Slavs to the Habsburg Empire. Still, at this point, Conrad should have pointed out to the responsible ministers that such a course was likely to involve the Dual Monarchy into a two-front war for which the army was not prepared. But he did nothing.[37] In fact Conrad and Krobatin left Vienna for over two weeks in July and went on vacation.[38] In the meanwhile Berchtold had secured promises of German support and reluctant consent from Hungary and the day after mobilization had been ordered against Serbia, on July 26, Berchtold asked Conrad when he could initiate swift action against the enemy. Conrad replied that nothing could be done for several weeks. During this conversation Conrad also touched lightly on the possibility of hostilities with Russia, but did not warn the foreign minister about the likely consequences.[39]

Berchtold showed more perception than the chief of staff. Mobilization and deployment against Serbia had actuated Plan "B" and the question was what to do with *B-Staffel*, now formed as the Second Army of twelve divisions, in case Russia came into the war. In reply, Conrad told him, as he already had done on July 7, that in such an eventuality *B-Staffel* could be rerouted to Galicia, provided that this was done by the fifth day of mobilization—that is within five days after July 28, the actual first mobilization day. After that, the chief of staff admitted, things would be rather more difficult.[40] It is difficult to understand why by July 26 Conrad was still maintaining that the war could be localized. The previous evening intelligence reports had indicated widespread Russian mobilization measures, and during the next few days consular, diplomatic, and military reports confirmed the story.[41] Still, the Second Army continued to muster and entrain for the Danube. After the war Conrad and his apologists explained rather lamely that until July 31, when Russia announced her general mobilization, there still had been hope that she would stand aside and that in any case "technical considerations" made it impossible to switch the Second Army.[42] Conrad, however, never explained why "technical difficulties" appeared suddenly on the 31st of July, a date well within the limits he had indicated to Berchtold. More important remains the question as to why he dispatched the Second Army at all.

Conrad had expected complications with Russia as early as June 28 and said as much to Berchtold some days later.[43] Then, on July 29, before any major formations of the Second Army had been entrained, he had reported to Francis Joseph that "tomorrow or at the latest the day after that we must count on war against the major powers."⁴⁴ And this meant Russia. In that case every man and every gun was needed in the east and Serbia's fate would be decided on the Vistula and not on the Danube. The explanation that Conrad did not switch the Second Army because the "complex war plans prepared did not foresee a Russian involvement in the middle of deployment against Serbia," simply is not true.⁴⁵ The real reason was that Conrad was temporarily blinded to all other considerations by his determination to destroy Serbia. He had, in fact, every intention of using the Second Army for an offensive against Serbia and he was prepared to stand on the defensive in Galicia.⁴⁶ This intention was already noted by one Habsburg general at the time. "One hoped," Feldmarschall Leutnant Alfred Krauss noted in his war diary, "to knock Serbia out quickly and then turn all forces against Russia—only this can explain the peculiar conduct of the *A.O.K.*"⁴⁷

Conrad did indeed have this choice, but he now lacked the resolution to follow it through. On August 3 Moltke informed him that the German forces would remain on the defensive in East Prussia.⁴⁸ Conrad confidently had expected Moltke to carry out his pledge of a German attack into Poland and he was now faced with the prospect that lacking the twelve divisions, his First, Fourth, and Third armies in Galicia faced unsurmountable odds. He therefore belatedly switched the Second Army which already had been partially committed to combat under Potiorek to Galicia. In the words of Churchill it "left Potiorek before it could win him a victory; it returned to Conrad in time to participate in his defeat."⁴⁹ Moreover, when it returned it came with only half of its strength. Four infantry divisions were permanently detached for service on the Balkan front, and two were delayed in transit, so that in the end only six divisions arrived to participate in the great battles fought in Galicia between August 23 and September 12.⁵⁰

After Moltke finally acquainted Conrad with his actual dispositions which effectively cancelled the previously projected attack south from East Prussia, Conrad replied that he still intended to make an offensive with the left wing of his armies north and northeastward on August 20, and, mainly for the record, he repeated his demand for fulfillment of the prewar understandings. Of course, Conrad's current plan, his scheme of March 1914, was no longer based on the premise of complementary German operations; it primarily was designed to prevent the Austro-Hungarian forces from being enveloped by the growing array of Russian armies now assembling in a vast arc around Galicia.

In early August the Austro-Hungarian order of battle in Galicia comprised three armies and two improvised "army groups." From left to right there were the First Army (Dankl), the Fourth (Auffenberg), and the Third (Brudermann). On Dankl's left there was Army Group Kummer while on Brudermann's right there was Army Group Kövess. Conrad had ordered Dankl due north, while Auffenberg was to advance northeastward, and Brudermann due east. The First and Fourth armies were to be the main striking force and for this purpose were to have been reinforced from nine to twelve divisions each by the strategic reserve, the Second Army, but of course, this army was still on the Danube and when it arrived it had to be sent to the badly threatened right wing. And so two armies with only eighteen divisions advanced on divergent axes, each day fanning out more, increasing their frontage and diluting their strength.

To make matters worse, they advanced blindly. Before leaving Vienna for

Przemysl to take personal charge of the offensive, Conrad had ordered his cavalry divisions to make a strategic reconaissance, a wide sweep from the Dniester to the Vistula, some 250 miles wide and some 90 miles deep. It was an ambitious undertaking and it achieved little. When on August 15 the *k.u.k.* cavalry rode across the frontiers, it was, except on the extreme left and right wings, unable to penetrate the Russian screen. Still trained for the mounted charge, it fought but one conventional cavalry battle, on August 21 near Jaroslavice. For the rest, it ran into dismounted Russian cavalry and supporting infantry elements, and suffered heavy losses. "It was the lot of the *k.u.k.* cavalry," one officer commented, "to sacrifice the major part of its combat potential for a phantom."[51] Even more serious were the heavy losses in horses which prevented the cavalry divisions from providing needed tactical reconnaissance when the offensive actually started on August 23.

During the three weeks from August 23 to September 12, the Austro-Hungarian and Russian armies collided in an immense series of combats, the battle of Lemberg. At first, in the battles of Krasnik (August 23 to 26) and Komarow (August 26 to 31), the First and Fourth *k.u.k.* armies were successful, though poor communications and lack of mobility reduced these victories to tactical successes only. Meanwhile the weak right, Brudermann's army, was in trouble, stalled in its advance and with Russian forces threatening its southern flank and penetrating into the gap between the Third and the Fourth armies. Moreover, the Russians also were threatening Auffenberg's right flank and Brudermann as well as Auffenberg were compelled to fall back with Russian cavalry already operating behind their main concentrations. Conrad, even now, refused to accept the situation. Still assuming that the main Russian mass was to the north in the Lublin-Kholm area, he urged Dankl to continue his advance and the two others to stand fast. But Dankl was vastly outnumbered and after two days of murderous fighting, Conrad concluded on September 11 that "there was only one course of action . . . to break off the battle and withdraw all armies behind the San."[52] But even this line could not be held and, leaving behind a strong force to defend Przemysl, the Austro-Hungarians retreated to the Dunajec, a retreat of some 150 miles. Elements of the Second Army, arriving too late for the offensive, also became involved in the rout and suffered badly. With poor strategic direction and outdated tactics and equipment, the troops had shown an aggressive spirit, and the units from the alpine lands in particular had fought exceedingly well.[53] Still, the results of all this were heavy casualties, almost two hundred fifty thousand men, and an additional one hundred thousand lost as prisoners of war. The *k.u.k.* army lost nearly a third of its combat effectives in the first three weeks of war in Galicia, including much of its regular junior officer corps and many noncommissioned officers who could not be replaced easily.[54] Almost all of Austrian Galicia, except for besieged Przemysl with its one hundred fifty thousand-strong garrison, now was in Russian hands, and the strategic situation exposed the entire German flank in southern Poland.

Conrad, of course, has been bitterly criticized for his decision to take the offensive without the Second Army.[55] But his entire orientation favored the offensive and he was convinced that it gave him a greater chance of success than passively awaiting the Russian onslaught.[56] Moreover, he claimed that he had acted in accordance with his pledged word and later chose to blame his disaster on Moltke's failure to honor commitments made before the war.[57] As for the Emperor Francis Joseph, he had learned to suffer setbacks stoically; on September 8 he wrote to the Archduke Friedrich and advised him not to punish defeated generals too harshly, "because today's unlucky commander may well be victorious tomorrow."[58] No such spirit, however, prevailed on the German side. By September, William II and members of his entourage were freely making invidious comparisons of the fighting qualities of the respective armies.[59] And as the war continued, it became common practice to claim the credit for success in all joint German-Austro-Hungarian operations for the Germans and blame all failures on the "slack" Austro-Hungarians.[60]

But while the *k.u.k.* army had been routed in Galicia, the German offensive in the west also had failed to achieve its objectives. With the conflicts becoming a war of attrition, no massive reinforcements would reach the eastern front. By contrast, Russian mobilization now was at full tide and new enemy concentrations in southern Poland threatened both Silesia and Galicia. To prevent their threat, the formidable command team of Generals Paul von Hindenburg and Erich Ludendorff, assisted by Colonel Max Hoffmann, an acerbic but exceedingly able staff officer, suggested a spoiling attack by a newly formed German army, the Ninth, consisting of four corps transferred southward from Eastern Prussia. On September 28 the Ninth Army, followed within days by the four *k.u.k.* armies to the south, attacked against relatively light Russian resistance. By October 10 the Vistula-San line had been reached, and Przemysl was relieved. Russian resistance and superior numbers, however, halted the attack which faltered and then recoiled. The Germans withdrew towards their frontier, while the Austro-Hungarians, leaving Przemysl to its fate, recoiled even beyond their original positions.

During the offensive the four *k.u.k.* armies, their ranks filled with ill-trained replacements, short of artillery and ammunition, suffered heavy casualties.[61] Moreover, the operation was marred by clashes between German and Austro-Hungarian commanders. On September 23 Hoffman noted in his diary that "yesterday we had our first quarrel with the Austrians," and six days later, "everything is fine here except for the Austrians! If the brutes would only move."[62] And Ludendorff felt even more strongly. "If the Dual Monarchy and the *k.u.k.* army," he wrote after the war, "had even halfway done what Germany had every right to expect of them, fewer German troops would have been needed to support the Austro-Hungarian forces."[63] At the same time, however, he admitted that he had no real appreciation of the special difficulties which the political, social, and linguistic conditions of the Habsburg Empire imposed on its army. Of course, the assertions of superiority, which the Germans made little attempt to conceal, angered the Austro-Hungarians. The Germans especially disliked the non-Germans in that multinational army, but even German-Austrians often regarded their northern brothers with "dislike and bitterness."[64]

Altogether it was not an auspicious beginning for a relationship. Although the Austro-Hungarians demonstrated a truly remarkable capacity to absorb terrible casualties and recover from great defeat, more and more German formations had to be used to stiffen the weaker ally. By November 1914 the Austro-Hungarian position once again became critical. The Fourth Army had been compelled to fall back south of Cracow and the Third Army had been pushed deep into the Carpathians. A gap nearly seventy miles wide opened between them, and through this the Russian high command hoped to penetrate into Bohemia and Hungary. Desperate measures were needed. Ludendorff, now chief of staff to *Oberost*, the German high command in the east, reluctantly dispatched the 47th Reserve Division to assist the Austro-Hungarians while Conrad summoned up reserves from the hinterland. In the battle of Limanowa-Lapanow between December 3 and 14, the Russians were defeated though Conrad did not have adequate strength to exploit this success. His forces were now badly in need of rest; most divisions were at half or even a third of their establishment, and new Russian units had forced the Third Army back into the Carpathians. A defensive victory had been gained; Hungary had been saved temporarily from invasion.[64] After that, the bitter winter halted major fighting for several weeks.

In the meantime, however, the Dual Monarchy had suffered another setback which added to the anxieties of the *A.O.K.* Serbia had inflicted a humiliating defeat on the forces deployed against her. In this theater, at least, the Austro-Hungarian army felt confident of victory. Russia with its vast resources had been a dreaded adversary since the time of Napoleon, but Serbia, especially "town and fortress Belgrade," had been a familiar objective for schemes by Habsburg generals since the days of Prince Eugene. Even after the Balkan Wars, Vienna continued to underestimate the prowess of the Serbian army. An intelligence report of 1913 concluded that the "main reasons for recent Serb successes lay in the inferior numbers and general low quality of the Turkish forces in Macedonia. The young Serb army cannot yet be considered the equal of the great power armies."[66] When war came, however, the Serbs were equal in number and superior in training, morale, endurance, and higher direction to the Austro-Hungarians. Ironically, the Serbian chief of staff, the elderly but wily General Radomir Putnik, had been in Budapest when Francis Joseph had signed the war manifesto, but, chivalrous to a fault, the emperor had provided him with safe conduct across the frontier. His adversary was Feldzeugmeister Potiorek, whose excellent connections at court had enabled him to escape blame for the faulty security arrangements at Sarajevo. An ambitious man, and once Conrad's rival for the position as chief of the general staff, he had ruled Bosnia-Hercegovina with almost princely powers, but now his confidence was shaken and throughout the campaign he remained closed off in his heavily guarded headquarters.

Although Russia's entry into the war should have relegated Potiorek's forces, *Minimalgruppe B,* to its purely defensive role, he was determined to restore his good name by winning a decisive victory. Therefore, after the Second Army was removed from his command, he used his connections to obtain virtual independence from *A.O.K.* control and, despite the precarious situation on the Russian front, he retained four divisions of the Second Army to conduct an offensive against Serbia which was primarily political in motivation.[67] His two armies, the Fifth and the Sixth, numbered some four hundred sixty thousand men with 528 mobile guns, but included a high proportion of *Landsturm* brigades, unprepared for modern war. As one officer remembered "men and officers alike were much surprised when new arms and equipment were issued and everything had to be explained."[68] In contrast, the Serbian army on complete mobilization would have four hundred fifty thousand men, though lacking equipment for some units. The army was well trained, war experienced, and equipped with modern artillery. Its officers were excellent, the rank and file tough and highly motivated. Montenegro, of course, had no regular army, but a combat-experienced militia of some forty thousand with poor equipment.

Potiorek deployed the Fifth Army along the Save and Drina rivers and the Sixth further south in order to cover Sarajevo. On August 12 he ordered the Fifth Army across the rivers, followed some days later by the Sixth. Stiff resistance and difficult terrain stalled the advance and Putnik, realizing that the Second Army was being withdrawn, staged a counterattack. By the last week of August not a Habsburg soldier was left on Serb soil. In the first days of September, the Serbs raided across the Save into southern Hungary but were defeated, and on September 8 Potiorek began his second offensive, once again failing to make much headway against an entrenched opponent. Moreover, a Serb thrust against Sarajevo forced him to divert much of the Sixth Army to the defensive and he barely managed to expel the Serbs from Bosnia. The second offensive, too, had failed.

By this time, however, the Serbs were exhausted, while Potiorek, using his influence, had received considerable reinforcements. On November 6 his armies crossed the rivers in a concentric attack and in hard fighting drove into central Serbia, to the Kolubara River. In the north, Belgrade fell and Potiorek issued orders to pursue the beaten enemy. But his forces were exhausted and their supply lines overextended. Marshalling his last reserves, Putnik counterattacked on December 3 and within two weeks pushed the *k.u.k.* armies out of the country, recaptured Belgrade, and threatened Hungary beyond.[69] It was a sharp and unexpected reversal, and Austro-Hungarian troop morale dropped sharply.[70]

Conrad promptly disassociated himself from the debacle. As long as Potiorek had been under the direction of the *A.O.K.*, Conrad pointed out, Potiorek had been ordered to stand on the defensive, but that the "present surprising turn of events is a mystery to the *A.O.K.*"[71] The defeat, Conrad continued, laid Bosnia-Hercegovina, Hungary, and even Austria open to the threat of invasion and he recommended construction of a defense line from Lake Balaton to Budapest. To be sure, Conrad was not entirely truthful about his relations with Potiorek and he exaggerated the Serb threat. In fact, Conrad had urged Potiorek in August to take the offensive "into the heartland of the enemy" in order to prevent him from threatening Budapest.[72] Then too, the Serbs were in no position to exploit their victory. While the *k.u.k.* armies had lost about half of their effectives, with about 28,000 dead, 120,000 wounded, 76,500 taken prisoner, and tens of thousands temporarily disabled with malaria and typhoid fever, the Serbian armies were in not much better condition. The front fell quiet now. After a short period of rehabilitation, the remainder of the Fifth and Sixth armies were transferred to the Carpathians, and the protection of the frontier was taken over by *Landsturm* formations. Potiorek was relieved to join the growing list of compulsorily retired generals; Archduke Eugene took over command of the southeastern front.

Defeat by Serbia was bitter and rankling, "a serious political setback and a grave blow to the prestige and self-confidence of the Dual Monarchy."[73] Even more damaging for the *k.u.k.* army, now fighting its first war with a mass base truly reflecting the multinational composition of the Habsburg Empire, were the openly voiced recriminations against certain troops and certain nationalities. The failure of Potiorek's first offensive was blamed on the conduct of the 21st *Landwehr* Division which had been recruited in Bohemia, and disloyalty was falsely imputed to other Czech units engaged in Serbia.[74] At the same time, there were allegations about large-scale desertions of Czech soldiers from IX Corps on the eastern front, which the *A.O.K.* chose to regard as the result of treasonable propaganda both in Bohemia and among the Russophile Ukrainians of eastern Galicia.[75] Much of this thinking was the result of traditional apprehensions which had long haunted the high command. Although historians of the successor states, each for his own purposes, have made much of the relatively isolated instances of troop disloyalty, it remains open to speculation how many of these desertions were the result of conscious political-national feelings or were instead spontaneous reactions to danger and deprivation. At any rate, as one Czech historian recently noted, "the army remained on the whole an effective instrument until the summer of 1918."[76] But, driven by fears, the Austro-Hungarian military overreacted and tended to generalize isolated instances of treason. As one thoughtful participant concluded after the war, "almost every unit, of whatever nationality, experienced a 'black day'. . . . If this occurred to German or Magyar troops it was considered a 'regrettable disaster' or even a 'heroic sacrifice,' but if Slavic troops, especially Czechs, were involved, it became a 'shameful failure,' . . . and a useful excuse for the shortcomings of the commanders."[77]

In any case, the *A.O.K.* faced a number of more immediate problems at the end of 1914. The heavy losses sustained in the first half-year of war had to be replaced, the shell shortage continued, and by the winter of 1914–1915 even modern rifles were lacking.[78] Most pressing, however, was the situation in the Carpathians where the Russians had reached the crest and threatened descent into the Hungarian plain below. Conrad's apprehensions were not eased by the fear that unless soon relieved, Przemysl would have to capitulate, nor by the growing indications that Italy was getting ready to enter the war against the Dual Monarchy. A victory in the Carpathians, he reasoned, not only would remove the threat to Hungary, but also lead to the relief of Przemysl, and it even might deter Italy. For these reasons he decided to make an attack on this front.

Unfortunately, Conrad's plans always looked better on paper than in reality. This time he planned a frontal assault, supported by a diversion further south. For the frontal attack he planned to use the Third Army (Boroević) and the hastily formed and German-commanded *Südarmee* (Linsingen), constituted around the solid core of three German divisions. To the south, Army Group Pflanzer-Baltin was to create a diversion by attacking in the direction of Czernowitz. The major flaw in the plan was that the terrain was unsuitable for the major attack, the mountains steep and the snow impassable in many locations. Moreover, the Russians were well dug in, and the *k.u.k.* formations short on artillery and winter equipment.[79] Disregarding these obstacles, Conrad ordered the attack on January 23, 1915. Suffering heavy casualties, the attacking troops made but little progress, and by February 8 they recoiled with losses of almost ninety thousand men. Undeterred, Conrad reinforced the assault with the Second Army, which he sandwiched between the Third and the *Südarmee*. On February 27 he launched another attack with much the same results. The fact that within a few short weeks after the disastrous setbacks in Galicia and Serbia, the *k.u.k.* army was able to take the offensive again attests to its astonishing recuperative powers. But the operations in the Carpathian winter used up the last remaining reserves of trained manpower. From now on the Habsburg army became essentially a skeleton, fleshed out with hastily mustered and trained conscripts, "a *Landsturm* and militia army," the official history called it.[80]

Although Pflanzer-Baltin had done much better to the south and had reached Czernowitz, he could not swing north to affect the course of operations there. No relief would reach Przemysl, and the fate of this great belt fortress and its outlying forts was now sealed. On March 22 and 23 the garrison demolished most of the remaining works and some of the artillery, burned what supplies they had left, and then surrendered. Altogether nine generals, ninety-three senior staff officers, twenty-five hundred other officers, and one hundred seventeen thousand enlisted men became Russian prisoners.[81] Having at its disposal the troops released by the end of the siege, the Russian high command decided once again to attempt a breakthrough into Hungary. In a series of battles early in April 1915 the Russians took the important Dukla Pass. The Austro-Hungarian lines seemed in danger of falling apart and Teschen sent out orders to fortify a last-ditch resistance line, from Budapest to Vienna and then on to Innsbruck. But, just as in the Serbian action a few months before, the Russians did not have adequate reserves to exploit their victory, and a hastily assembled German task force, the *Beskiden Korps,* sufficed to plug the breaches in the Austro-Hungarian front.[82]

It was during the Russian April offensive, however, that there occurred a most serious and spectacular incident throwing new and ominous light on the reliability of Czech units. On April 3 the 28th Infantry Regiment, which in its home garrison at Prague had been subject to considerable nationalist and socialist propaganda, surrendered almost without resistance to the Russians during the battle for the Dukla Pass. An outraged Archduke Friedrich asked the emperor to dissolve the unit and this was done on April 17, 1915.[83] It was the first open mass defection, and the incident became and has remained the subject of considerable controversy as to the causes, motivations, and even the actual conduct of the regiment.[84] But most senior officers believed that the affair proved that Czech troops were no longer reliable and from now on special precautions would have to be used when they were committed to action.[85] In turn, this only poured oil on inflamed passions and did nothing to solve the problem of the wayward and uncooperative "Soldier Schwejk," fast becoming the prototype of passive resistance to authority. Finally, the incident encouraged the military to extend their control over the civil administration in Bohemia, which they claimed had been unable to halt subversive activities.[86]

The evident debilitation of its major ally aroused considerable concern in the German Supreme Command, the *Oberste Heeresleitung (O.H.L.),* where General Erich von Falkenhayn had replaced Moltke in September 1914. And although Falkenhayn, because he believed that victory could only be won in the west and also because he was engaged in a bitter rivalry for power and prestige with the Hindenburg-Ludendorff team, was disinclined to send major reinforcements to the eastern front, he could not accept the prospect of an Austro-Hungarian collapse. Therefore, with imperial approval, four German corps newly raised in the late winter of 1914 were transferred to the east, and part of the *O.H.L.,* including the Emperor William and Falkenhayn, established their headquarters at Pless, an hour's drive from the *A.O.K.* at Teschen.[87] Falkenhayn had decided to utilize a plan, originally conceived by Conrad, to stage a major offensive from the north end of the Carpathians to penetrate the Russian front and then, swinging north, envelop and destroy a substantial portion of the enemy's armies.[88] Conrad lacked the necessary instrument for his scheme, and instead Falkenhayn assembled a strong composite force, the German Eleventh Army comprising eight German and four *k.u.k.* divisions with reinforced heavy artillery, in great secrecy. While this force commanded by Generaloberst Mackensen was to smash the Russian front between Tarnów and Gorlice, it was shielded on its northern flank by the *k.u.k.* Fourth Army and by the *k.u.k.* Third Army on the south. Although the Austro-Hungarians played only a subsidiary part, they too were reinforced by German artillery and aviation units, and the power of the massed German batteries came as a revelation to one *k.u.k.* corps commander. "This thundering noise, this volcano of fire," he commented, "was something which for us Austrians, with our weak artillery and our limited ammunition supply, was a totally new experience."[89] On May 2, 1915, the offensive started and within two days, having virtually eliminated the six Russian divisions of the opposing Third Army, it accomplished its breakthrough. Mackensen's army continued to advance at the rate of about ten miles a day, forcing the Russians to evacuate the Carpathians in order to reach the San. Further north, with the offensive becoming general, the Russians pulled back across the Vistula, and despite some ferocious counterattacks, the German-Austro-Hungarian advance continued for several months. By the middle of July the Russians had been thrown back from almost all Austro-Hungarian territory, and when Falkenhayn, eager to return to the west, finally halted the advance, the new line stretched from the outskirts of Riga in the north to the east of Pinsk and south to Tarnopol and Czernowitz.

This great success did little to improve relations between the Austro-Hungarians and the Germans. At the very top, Falkenhayn and Conrad differed not only in personality and style, but also in policy and strategy toward Serbia, Italy, and Rumania, issues on which Conrad felt that the German was far too ready to sacrifice Habsburg interests for the sake of immediate advantage.[90] Even more bitter were the problems of how to direct and control joint operations of the eastern front. From the outset, when nine German divisions were fighting along with thirty-eight *k.u.k.* divisions in southern Poland, and Conrad had asked for authority to issue orders to them, the Germans had refused to accede.[91] Now, with the Germans clearly assuming the role of the senior partner in the alliance, the *O.H.L.* held out for a larger role, in fact a dominant share, in any unified command; this Conrad still was unwilling to accept. Special arrangements had to be adopted for the Tarnów-Gorlice campaign. Although under the nominal command of the *A.O.K.*, Mackensen and his chief of staff, Seeckt, controlled all operations, and Conrad agreed that he would issue no orders to this army without Falkenhayn's approval.[92] At that, the cumbersome system had worked, but there had been friction. Austro-Hungarian staff officers conceded the high level of German performance, but they disliked being patronized and treated as poor relations. The fact that they had become dependent on German help made the situation even less palatable.[93]

Still, in an hour of need, German intervention had saved Austria-Hungary, and even while the advance continued across the dusty Polish plains, trains were transferring major combat elements to the Alps where on May 23, 1915, Italy had entered the war.

13

War on Many Fronts and the Death of Emperor Francis Joseph: 1915-1916

When Italy came into the war the Habsburg army already had fought the greatest, bloodiest, and most exhausting battles in its long history. It had sustained heavy losses in men and materiel which were still only partially replaced, and war weariness had begun to affect its depleted ranks. But against the new enemy, the army showed unexpected strength and determination. Even Ludendorff, who in his memoirs rarely missed an opportunity to complain about the fighting qualities of his Austro-Hungarian ally, admitted that "the $k.u.k.$ troops fought well against Italy; it was the hereditary enemy and no such animosity existed against Russia."[1] And while Ludendorff never really understood the dynamics of a multinational army, for once he was correct. Except for the short campaigns of 1808 and 1812, the Habsburg armies had never fought Russia. That great empire loomed dark and foreboding in the minds of Habsburg soldiers, and the generals repeatedly had warned that here a conflict could have fatal consequences for both opponents. But in Italy the army felt at home. Here it had a traditional emotional and strategic commitment and followed the familiar footsteps of Eugene, Radetzky, and Albrecht. Moreover, the picture of a treacherous Italy, thirsting for German and Slav territories, aroused indignation, and on the Italian front soldiers of almost all nationalities (even Czechs and Slovaks, provided they were well led), fought valiantly up to the late summer of 1918. Above all, of course, the Tyroleans distinguished themselves in defense of their homeland, but South Slavs and "Croats, Slovenes, and Serbs in the armies of Francis Joseph fought Italians with unexampled resolution and passion."[2]

Geography, as always, determined strategy; in this theater, it favored Austria-Hungary which held the high ground almost everywhere. Just east of Switzerland, the South Tyrol, the Trentino, constituted a deep salient into northern Italy, and from this bastion an Austro-Hungarian offensive into the Venetian plain threatened vital railroads and the rear of the Italian army. East of the Trentino the high mountain chains of the Julian and Carnic Alps interdicted major movement. This left the sector between the pre-alpine foothills and the Adriatic, where for some fifty miles the mountains gave way to a high plateau through which the Isonzo River cut a deep gorge. But even here the terrain was difficult. The grim and forbidding limestone plateau of the Carso, a "howling wilderness of stones," made entrenchments difficult, and the splintering stone multiplied the effects of fire.[3] During autumn and winter the plateau was swept by rain and snow, while during the summer months heat and the lack of water inflicted additional hardships on the armies. Even so, geography dictated that this would be the region where most of the major battles took place, though bitter fighting also raged in the high alpine sectors where the adversaries struggled in sub-zero temperatures, attacked and counterattacked, mined and countermined, and where fierce hand-to-hand combats took place on mountain peaks thousands of feet above the valley in the eternal snow and ice. In such conditions, as tough or tougher than any in this war, both sides showed much spirit and proved wrong those military historians and critics who have sneered at their fighting abilities.

For both the Italians and the Austro-Hungarian commands, hostilities began under circumstances not envisaged before 1914. Although for many years both sides had been making extensive and elaborate warplans against each other, the alliance relationship notwithstanding, Austria-Hungary always had assumed that it would take the offensive, while Italy, outclassed both in men and materiel, expected to stand on the defense.[4] By 1915, however, the situation had changed drastically. The great offensive army which Conrad had hoped to assemble on the high plateau of Lavarone-Folgaria in the Trentino no longer existed, and its successor was deeply engaged on the Polish plains, in the Carpathians, and along the Danube and Drina. In consequence General Luigi Cadorna, who had become Italy's chief of the general staff in 1914, changed his plans. Early in 1915 he elaborated an offensive warplan which called for a major effort across the Isonzo in the direction of Trieste, accompanied by a secondary thrust into Carniola-Carinthia along the line Tarvisio-Villach. Meanwhile, facing the Trentino, Cadorna intended to remain defensive, though he did not rule out local advances against Austro-Hungarian forts dominating the high passes. All in all, after mobilization, Italy had at its disposal some eight hundred fifty thousand men, twenty-five first-line and ten reserve infantry divisions, one *Bersaglieri* division, *Alpini* troops amounting to about four brigades, and four cavalry divisions.[5]

As Conrad had pointed out in 1907, Austria-Hungary did not have the resources to fight on the Russian and Serbian fronts and at the same time make adequate provisions against Italy. Therefore from August 1914 to April 1915, the defenses against Italy had consisted of a few skeleton crews in the major forts and some light covering troops. Command of these forces was entrusted in August 1914 to General der Kavallerie Franz Rohr, though because of the delicate political situation the emperor retained the right to call out the *Standschützen* and other local volunteers and to place the frontier fortifications on a war footing.[6] In any case, the usefulness of these fortifications was limited by the developments in siege artillery. The blockhouses built in the 1870s had become obsolete, while the works erected during the next decade could only withstand fire for a limited period. Only the new armored works in the Trentino, constructed at Conrad's insistence, were expected to stand up to the heaviest shelling.[7] There were, however, few fortifications along the Isonzo, now the most likely invasion front, and Rohr did as much as he could with his limited resources to prepare field fortifications, wire obstacles, mine fields, and demolitions, though early in 1915 he was ordered to halt all work so as not to prejudice the increasingly tense relations with Italy.[8]

During the winter of 1914–1915, Italy was negotiating with both sides, and the

German government strongly urged Vienna to make extensive concessions, perhaps even a promise to cede the Trentino. Part of the pressure came from Falkenhayn who feared that Italy's entry into the war might create an unbearable strain for the Central Powers, and repeatedly urged Conrad to use his influence to obtain a settlement, but Conrad was most reluctant. He did not underrate the gravity of the situation, but insisted that success on the Russian front would deter Rome and also suggested that the dispatch of some German troops to the Italian frontier would have a sobering effect. By the end of March 1915, however, Conrad became convinced that Italy intended to enter the war and that any concessions would merely place her in a more advantageous strategic position; he now began to lay plans to defeat the attack which he expected to come in the near future.[9]

On April 6 he informed Falkenhayn that war with Italy, while undesirable at this point, appeared unavoidable. He therefore intended to transfer seven divisions from Galicia to the new front and he asked Falkenhayn to replace these formations with German troops.[10] Falkenhayn, however, refused. The main effort, he maintained, would have to continue on the Russian front and it would be better to let the Italians gain some territory, even sacrificing Trieste.[11] The German general staff was even more perturbed by Conrad's great entrapment scheme which called for allowing the Italians to advance unopposed through the foothills into the Carinthian-Carniolan plain and then destroy them as they debouched from the passes. "If it had been accepted," Falkenhayn contended, it meant that "the continuation of operations against the Russians would have had to be abandoned." On the "peremptory advice of Germany," he continued, "it was therefore decided to carry on a purely defensive war against Italy."[12]

At that, Falkenhayn refused to allow any German troops to become involved on this front and merely prepared to send one division of Bavarian mountain troops, the *Alpenkorps,* to the Dolomites but with orders not to cross the Italian frontier. Pleased that Italy had not declared war on Germany, Falkenhayn did not intend to enter the fighting until it suited him, though this attitude did not make for better relations with the Austro-Hungarians.[13] Conrad was left to make his own preparations as best he could. On April 15 he told István Baron Burián, who earlier that year had replaced Berchtold as foreign minister, that Italy had to be kept out of the war for at least four weeks. "Any and all means appear justified," he declared, "against this perfidious and unfaithful ally."[14] The progress of the offensive in Poland allowed him to plan for the transfer of three divisions from that front, and additional troops were found along the Danube and the Drina where the Serb army was still recuperating. Meanwhile, relations with Italy deteriorated rapidly. On May 11 Emperor Francis Joseph authorized arming of the frontier forts and moving the only available division, the 57th, into the Isonzo line.[15] The following day while troop trains were bringing divisions from Syrmia and Galicia, the emperor called out the *Standschützen* and other volunteer bodies from Tyrol, Carinthia, and Vorarlberg.[16] By May 14 advance elements of three divisions detrained on the Isonzo, and on May 22 Archduke Eugene was appointed commander in chief of the new southwestern front, with Feldmarschall Leutnant Alfred Krauss as his chief of staff.[17] The new front was divided into three major sectors: the Tyrol, commanded by General der Kavallerie Viktor Count Dankl; Carinthia, commanded by Rohr, and the Isonzo region, where the tough and energetic General Svetozar Boroević von Bojna took charge of the hastily forming Fifth *k.u.k.*

Army. However, only the 57th Division was in position by May 23, and even including the local volunteer elements the Italians mustered a very considerable superiority in men and guns. As late as mid-June, when all new formations had arrived, the Italians still were superior by a two-to-one factor, some 460,000 men with 1,810 mobile guns, against 228,000 men with 640 guns.[18]

The *A.O.K.* expected and feared an immediate large-scale Italian offensive, but this failed to materialize. For one month Cadorna restricted himself to probing attacks, allowing the *k.u.k.* soldiers vital time to dig in along the Isonzo.[19] The first clashes, in fact, came in the Trentino and along the Carinthian frontier. Here border forts were heavily shelled and then assaulted by infantry, while fighting patrols from both sides contested strategic peaks. The opening attacks revealed that the Italians, contrary to legend, were by no means reluctant to fight. Their infantry was brave, though their methods inept. On several occasions marching bands advanced together with the assault waves, and generally artillery support, while heavy, was ineffective.[20]

Such small encounters could not, however, yield any decisive results, and the major Italian attack, the First Battle of the Isonzo, was launched on June 23, 1915. The defenders had put the month to good effect, and though the assault was pressed with courage and determination, the battle, lasting until July 7, only resulted in frightful casualties and very minor gains for the attackers. And this remained the pattern for the next four Isonzo battles, July 1915 to March 1916. Each time, the Italians attacked but were unable to break through the Austro-Hungarian defences. Still, a war of attrition as practiced by Cadorna also inflicted heavy losses on the *k.u.k.* forces which, already stretched to the limit, could afford them less than the Italians.

But while the armies bled along the Isonzo, Serbia had finally been eliminated. Although much to Cadorna's disappointment that front remained quiescent during the initial stages of his war, Falkenhayn had become concerned about the Turkish supply situation. On March 21, 1915, he sent a telegram to Conrad proposing a quick strike against Serbia in order to clear the way for supplies to reach Turkey which had joined the Central Powers in October 1914 and now was preparing to meet an Entente attack against the Dardanelles. Conrad, however, replied that he had no forces to spare in view of the situation on the Galician front.[21] But Falkenhayn persisted and hinted that Bulgaria might join in the enterprise, provided the Turks would secure her against Rumanian or Greek intervention. At this Conrad became interested and he told Burian that under these circumstances an offensive against Serbia might have most desirable results, and might even bring Rumania to the side of the Central Powers.[22] At the same time, however, on March 30, he informed Falkenhayn that in such an operation the prestige of the Dual Monarchy would have to be entrusted to a member of the imperial house.[23] Burian did not feel very much inclined to support an extension of the fighting. With Italy turning hostile, he suggested that a settlement with Italy should take precedence over any agreement with Bulgaria, but if action against Serbia was advisable militarily, then he strongly urged Conrad to consider employing only *k.u.k.* troops. It was, considering the military situation, an astonishing proposal and Conrad penned a sardonic comment on the margin of Burian's message: *"Mit was denn?"*[24]

By April the Italian threat had begun to absorb most of Conrad's thinking, though with Falkenhayn continuing to pressure him about a joint operation against

Serbia, he agreed to consider the matter, provided Bulgarian participation could be secured.[25] But Bulgaria continued to sit on the fence, though the breakthrough at Tarnów-Gorlice deterred Rumania from any hostile move and induced her to allow the shipment of war materiel to the hard-pressed Turks. Meanwhile, negotiations with Bulgaria continued all summer, and Falkenhayn finally indicated that he was prepared to allocate substantial German forces for an offensive against Serbia. This, together with an immediate cession of Turkish territory and promises of Serb territorial gains, led the Bulgarians to a decision and on September 6, 1915, they signed a military convention at *O.H.L.* headquarters, now at Pless in Silesia.

The final negotiations were marred by another bitter controversy between Conrad and Falkenhayn. Falkenhayn proposed to give overall command of the operation to August von Mackensen, and the Bulgarians also insisted on German command and control. At this Conrad, chafing at his dependence on German aid and annoyed by Falkenhayn's patronizing attitude, became furious. From the start he had insisted that the operation be headed by a *k.u.k.* general and maintained that anything else would be a slight to the prestige of the Dual Monarchy. For once he remained adamant and in the end the impasse was resolved by a face-saving compromise. Mackensen was appointed to command, but the *A.O.K.* and the *O.H.L.* would jointly decide all major directives and the *A.O.K.* would issue the actual orders.[26]

On October 5, the Third *k.u.k.* Army (Kövess), the German Eleventh Army (Gallwitz), and two strong Bulgarian armies began a concentric offensive. This time the Serbs were outnumbered in men and heavily outweighed in artillery, and an Entente attempt to aid the Serbs with an expeditionary force landed at Salonika failed when its advance was contained by the Bulgarians. Within six weeks the Serb campaign was decided; the Serbian army was beaten, though in an epic fighting retreat its remnants reached the Adriatic to be eventually evacuated to Salonika by French and Italian naval forces. During the campaign, relations between the Austro-Hungarians and their German and Bulgarian allies were strained. Falkenhayn complained that the "Third Austro-Hungarian Army . . . found it difficult to overcome the enemy resistance," though it faced no more difficult task than the neighboring German formation.[27] In turn, Conrad was outraged when, previous agreements notwithstanding, the *O.H.L.* issued orders directly to Mackensen.[28] Considering the command agreement at an end, the Austro-Hungarians now asserted their own particular interests and to Falkenhayn's intense annoyance followed up the conquest of Serbia by quickly overrunning Montenegro. On January 11, 1916, assisted by naval gunfire support, they stormed heavily fortified Mount Lovčen and two days later occupied Cetinje, the country's capital. On January 17 the Montenegrin army capitulated and Austro-Hungarian forces moved into northern Albania.[29]

Although the year ended with strained relations among the allies, it also ended with a much improved position for the Central Powers. With Serbia eliminated, the Central Powers had consolidated their interior position. On the eastern front, where early in the year the situation had been threatening, Russia had suffered enormous casualties and considerable loss of territory. The Ottomans had repulsed the Entente at the Dardanelles and, for a moment at least, Rumania showed no more inclination to abandon her neutrality. To be sure, the German general staff was not completely satisfied. The bloody stalemate continued on the western front, and Russia, while badly hurt, had not been knocked out. There also was disappointment in what Falkenhayn described as the "very moderate achievements of the Allied Army, due far more to the domestic circumstances of the Dual Monarchy than to the enemy." But he also conceded that from the "special Austro-Hungarian view light blotted out the shadows."[30]

The "domestic circumstances" to which Falkenhayn referred also worried the *A.O.K.*, which had become increasingly nervous about the effects of nationalist and anti-military agitation on the troops and on the home front. But the *A.O.K.*, and this meant Conrad, really had no answer to the problem. The immediate response to the growing volume of agitation and discontent was repression, and to this end Conrad tried to expand the powers of the special War Supervisory Office, the *Kriegsüberwachungsamt,* established in August 1914. He felt that the civilian authorities were far too lenient in their attitude towards subversive activities, and he attempted to gain military jurisdiction over a vast variety of offenses, to control the schools and determine the curricula, to purge the state bureaucracy of unreliable elements, and to extend the zones under direct military control. Of course, he had no influence in Hungary where Tisza jealously guarded the special position of that kingdom, but he also failed to gain the wholehearted cooperation of Karl Count Stürgkh, Austria's prime minister. Finally he tried a frontal attack against the civilian authorities. On September 25, 1915, the *A.O.K.* submitted a memorandum to the emperor which recounted the dire consequences caused by the "unreliability and the lack of patriotic feeling of a large part of the population," and suggested the appointment as prime minister of a "personality whose proven ability and unshakeable energy would guarantee a fortunate solution for these problems which determine Austria-Hungary's future fate."[31]

Francis Joseph, however, was far too tired to act, and Stürgkh retained office until assassinated by a socialist in the following year. It was in any case a debatable question as to whether Conrad's hard line would have been more effective than the conciliatory course followed by the civilians. In fact, at this point it probably was too late for any solution to the nationality problem, though victory in the field would, without a doubt, have provided a breathing spell for the Dual Monarchy. Certainly, though their professions may well have been only tactical, the various nationalist politicians with rare exceptions continued to profess their loyalty to the dynasty until in the summer of 1918 the military balance clearly had tilted against the Habsburg Empire.[32]

In the final analysis then, the continued existence of the Dual Monarchy depended on its army and here Conrad felt more optimistic toward the end of 1915. During the spring he had told Burian that Bulgarian and possibly even Rumanian aid would be most desirable because "the war is gradually exhausting the strength of the monarchy."[33] At the end of October, however, he submitted a new evaluation of the situation to the emperor in which he expressed some hope that the defeat of Serbia might induce the Entente to make peace; in that case, he wrote, "we shall not make any great demands, but neither shall we make any territorial concessions."[34]

Conrad's renewed optimism was founded not merely on the improved military situation, but also on the remarkable recovery of the *k.u.k.* army. By the end of 1916, Austria-Hungary had mobilized almost 5 million men, and suffered eight hundred thousand dead and 1 million severely wounded or sick. The losses had been made up, though physical standards for replacements had to be drastically lowered, and twenty new divisions had been formed and equipped.[35] On the other hand, there continued a shortage of officers, only partly replaced by graduates from accelerated courses at the military schools, but still the *A.O.K.* resisted any policy altering the basic social make-up of the officer corps and on June 30, 1915, it sent a memorandum to the War Ministry stressing its desire for quality over quantity.[36] Moreover, in contrast with the armies of the Entente, Austria-Hungary and, for that matter, Germany, did not make wide use of their reserve officers. Few of them reached responsible positions and only as late as 1916 were they allowed to be promoted to captain's rank.[37]

Surprising progress was made in the production of arms and ammunition. During the winter of 1915 to 1916, the field artillery was completely reequipped with new models. The old 8-cm. field guns were withdrawn and each division received a field artillery brigade with modern M-14 field guns and field howitzers, as well as with new 15-cm. M-15 howitzers. With a total of eighty-eight guns, the *k.u.k.* divisions now matched their opponents in the quality and quantity of their artillery. The non-divisional artillery also was refurbished. The heavy artillery was being reequipped with mobile 24-cm. M-16 howitzers, the famed 30.5-cm. mortars were employed in larger numbers, and super-heavy pieces like the 38-cm. *Autohaubitze* and 42-cm. tractor-drawn howitzers were being placed into the firing line. To be sure, the limited industrial capacity of the Dual Monarchy could never furnish the range or quantity of weapons available to the major industrial belligerents. Flamethrowers and trenchmortars were produced in very limited quantities only, there were no tanks, and even light machine guns, the main infantry weapon during the last war years, could only be produced as a modification of the standard heavy piece.[38] The air arm also continued to be weak. By the end of 1915, though several new factories building both German and indigenous designs had been established, Austria-Hungary produced only a total of four hundred aircraft, though the next year production increased to one thousand machines and five hundred spare engines.[39]

But the most difficult and, in the long run, the fatal problem was the provisioning of the army and the population. There was a totally unexpected grain shortage within a few months after the beginning of the war. The Russian invasion of Galicia jeopardized one important source, and there was a decline in both Austria proper and Hungary. The total cereal crop in both halves of the monarchy fell by nearly one-half between 1914 and 1916. By 1915 there were food shortages in the major Austrian cities, and though Hungary prohibited and rigidly controlled exports of grain and the Hungarians were at no time as desperately short of food as the Austrians, there were shortages in Budapest and other major centers. The army did better at first, though rations fell off and became short by the autumn of 1916.[40] Textiles were another problem. Production of military blankets declined from 9.5 million in 1915 to seven million in 1916, and much of the new field grey uniform cloth, which in September 1915 replaced the pike grey introduced by Conrad, had to be imported from Germany.

Still, in 1916 the Habsburg army became in many ways a more formidable instrument than it had been at the outbreak of the war. The old army had perished, but the replacements had become hardened soldiers. In his field grey uniform, but retaining his characteristic puttees and lace-up boots, *Kamerad Schnürschuh*, as the Germans called him, knew how to assault, wire, bomb, and defend. Above all, he was ready to do his duty to endure.

The new face of the war affected even the cavalry, long resistant to all change. In 1915 a number of regiments lost their horses and were employed as infantry. As the war progressed, tactical requirements and shortages of horses and fodder led to the dismounting of additional units, and by 1917, except for one division and some reconnaissance elements, the entire mounted arm fought as *Kavallerieschützendivisionen* on foot.[41] The war also saw a great expansion in the technical and auxiliary branches of the army, and though much of it was improvisation, altogether it was the largest, most complicated, and most comprehensive single organization ever evolved by the Habsburg Empire.

The new organization was to make its first major debut in an offensive from the Trentino. Early in 1916 the consolidated interior position of the Central Powers should have been utilized to deliver a decisive blow against one or the other of the major enemies, but although the open rifts between Falkenhayn and Conrad had been patched up, the two commanders insisted on pursuing their separate plans. Falkenhayn was convinced that a decision could only be achieved in the west. While he considered England the "arch-enemy," he intended to strike at her by forcing France, "England's tool on the Continent," into a battle of attrition in the Verdun sector; the Austro-Hungarians he wanted to assign holding the front in the east. Conrad, on the other hand, wanted to defeat Italy, and since his days as a divisional commander in the Tyrol he had considered a massive attack from the Trentino as the best method of achieving this aim. In December 1915 he asked for German support in this enterprise, but Falkenhayn refused. If this were done, he wrote, it "would benefit Austria-Hungary and her future prospects only and not directly the prospects of the war."[42] Moreover, Falkenhayn, who understood the problems of combat in the high Alps somewhat better than Conrad, pointed out that the proposed forces would be inadequate, hard to assemble, and even harder to supply, and bluntly indicated that he was skeptical both about the immediate as well as the long-range chances of the project.[43]

Rebuffed, Conrad nonetheless decided to carry out his grandiose scheme. His detestation of Italy and his fatal shortcoming, his inability to see the false assumptions on which so many of his grand schemes rested, spoiled his judgment. Although Archduke Eugene, the commander of the southwestern front, was to be in charge, the actual dispositions and plans were made by Conrad who refused to consult with the able Krauss, the archduke's chief of staff.[44] Sweeping out of the high plain of Lavarone-Folgaria, two armies, the Eleventh (Dankl) and the Third (Kövess), were to break through the Italian defenses, penetrate into the northern Italian plain, capture the key rail center of Padua, and envelop the Italian armies in Carnia and along the Isonzo. The Eleventh Army was to assault along the whole front, while the Third was to follow, ready to exploit the breakthrough. Scheduled for the beginning of March, the offensive was delayed by the deep snow still covering the high Alps at this time of the year, something which Conrad, allegedly an expert in mountain warfare, neglected to consider, and it had to be postponed twice more until it actually opened on May 15, 1916.[45]

By this time, of course, the vital element of surprise was totally lost. The concentration of so many troops and guns in a small area could not remain hidden from Cadorna who, taking advantage of his interior lines, reinforced his First Army. When the attack actually started, it gained some initial success. Arsiero and Asiago, the gateways to the northern plains, were captured, but then the momentum of the attack declined due to confusion at the higher command level, difficulty of the terrain, and the stubborn and on many points heroic Italian resistance. On May 20 the Austro-Hungarians regrouped, but valuable time was lost and Cadorna was able to rush in additional reinforcements. Bitter fighting continued around Asiago, but it became clear that no decisive breakthrough could be made and by June 6 the offensive had virtually petered out. Still, operations continued until June 17 when Conrad, shaken by unexpected Russian successes, closed down the offensive.[46]

At best, it had been a limited success. Some territory had been gained; the Italians had suffered casualties and lost some forty thousand prisoners and three hundred guns. Against this, however, were equally heavy Austro-Hungarian losses and a serious morale setback. The operation ended in bitter recrimination among the commanders. Conrad accused Dankl of having mismanaged the attack, and the outraged general asked for immediate relief from command. Archduke Charles, the heir to the throne, who during the offensive had commanded XX Corps, accused the *A.O.K.* of having developed an operational plan without any regard for the realities in the Trentino,[47] and Krauss submitted a long memorandum to the imperial military chancery arguing that attacks in the mountains should be delivered not along the crests but through the valleys.[48] Conrad's defenders have tried to claim that he still might have achieved a major victory if he had not been forced to switch troops back to the Russian front, but terrain, resistance, and exhaustion had already stalled the offensive before the storm broke in the east. Falkenhayn had been right and the Trentino offensive, Conrad's brainchild for which he had denuded his lines in Russia, merely helped Brusilov to make enormous gains.

The Brusilov offensive was mounted in response to a French appeal to draw German troops away from the western front, where Falkenhayn's initial success at Verdun had precipitated a grave crisis. In March, responding to French pleas, General Kuropatkin attacked the German lines in the northwestern sector, but was driven back with heavy losses. In May, after heavy fighting, Fort Vaux, a key position in the Verdun defenses, fell and once again Paris requested Russian aid. Now it was Brusilov's turn, and he decided to attack simultaneously along his entire front, from south of the Pripet Marshes to the Rumanian frontier.

Confronting him was a mixed but preponderantly Austro-Hungarian group of armies under the overall command of the German General Alexander v. Linsingen. From north to south these included the *k.u.k.* Fourth Army (Archduke Joseph Ferdinand); the *k.u.k.* First Army (Puhallo); the *Südarmee,* a composite German-Austro-Hungarian formation, (Bothmer); and the *k.u.k.* Seventh Army (Pflanzer-Baltin). These armies had been in their positions since the end of the great 1915 offensive, and during this time, toiling with intensity, had built strong fortified lines. Yet, the formidable-looking entrenchments concealed rot. Relying on past experience, too many troops had been placed into the first line, and reserves were stationed too close to the front. Then too, the constant entrenching had sapped the spirit of the troops, "they had dug too much and exercised too little."[49] Above all, however, there were serious command problems. Relations between von Linsingen and his Austro-Hungarian subordinates were bad and Archduke Joseph Ferdinand especially resented the German general. At that, Joseph Ferdinand was an extremely poor commander. Paying little attention to his troops, he spent his days hunting with his aristocratic friends and allowed troop morale to decline. Finally nine of the best divisions and much artillery had been withdrawn for the Trentino offensive.[50]

On June 4, 1916, Brusilov attacked, using all his armies simultaneously, along the two-hundred mile front. Although in complete defiance of conventional offensive doctrine, preceeded only by a brief though intense artillery barrage and without the previous massing of reserves, the attack came neither as a strategic nor as a tactical surprise. The withdrawal of nine divisions for the Trentino offensive obviously had weakened the front, and both Archduke Friedrich and Emperor Francis Joseph had expressed their concern. But Conrad personally had assured the emperor only four days before the attack that there was nothing to worry about.[51] Even the exact timing of the offensive had become known because on June 3 Austro-Hungarian intelligence had intercepted Brusilov's attack message to his troops.[52] Yet, despite these forewarnings, the attack succeeded brilliantly. By the evening of the first day, the Russians had overrun the three trench lines of the Fourth Army and punched a hole twenty miles wide and five miles deep into its positions. Considerable gains were also achieved against the Seventh Army in the south and lesser gains were made against the First Army in the north. Almost everywhere along the entire Austro-Hungarian front, control and morale failed. Many formations panicked and there were reports that Slav units, Czechs and Ruthenes, deserted or surrendered without offering any resistance. Even "reliable" formations were washed away in the flood and, unknown before in the annals of the Habsburg army, there were cases where the divisional artillery galloped away and left the infantry to its fate.[53] Only the German and Austro-Hungarian units of the *Südarmee* stood fast and held their positions until forced to retreat because of their exposed flanks. Everywhere else the Russians gained open country by the end of the first week and, stopping only to deal with isolated attempts to delay them, once again tramped their way across the Galician plain towards the Carpathian passes and the very heart of the Habsburg Empire beyond.

During these long June days, dismay and near panic gripped the *A.O.K.* at Teschen. Conrad, recently remarried, advised his wife to prepare for evacuation.[54] More importantly, having gambled and lost, and with no strategic reserve to plug the breakthrough, he had to appeal for German aid. Although at first Falkenhayn was reluctant to provide troops, the dimensions of the catastrophe threatened to bring Rumania into the war, and on June 10 he ordered that the five divisions of *Oberost's* army group reserve be rushed down to help stem the Russian advance. In addition, he withdrew four divisions from the western front and Conrad returned five divisions from Italy. In the end, the speed of the German intervention was effective. By the end of July, Brusilov's supply system was creaking and it broke down in August. Although the Russians continued to press forward against stiffening resistance, they now suffered enormous casualties, and by the end of September the offensive ground to a slow stop. By the time it was over, Brusilov had reached the slopes of the Carpathians and overrun the whole of the Bukovina. The Austro-Hungarian army had been badly shaken, losing seven hundred fifty thousand men, three hundred eighty thousand of whom had been taken prisoner.

To be sure, the *k.u.k.* army was severely hurt, but it was not yet eliminated as a fighting force. In Italy, an Italian offensive, the Sixth Battle of the Isonzo on August 6 to 17, managed to take both Gorizia and Monte San Michele, dominating the northern Carso, but stiff resistance prevented any Italian breakthrough. And the Seventh, Eighth, and Ninth Battles of the Isonzo, September 14 to November 4, 1916, aimed at penetrating along the coast to Trieste, became battles of attrition in which the *k.u.k.* lines held firm.[55] In the east, however, Austro-Hungarian failure led to the insertion of German formations in some twenty places along the front, and this, together with a great many other German interventions and liaison arrangements, placed the *k.u.k.* army into a clearly secondary role. A clear example of this new relationship was provided by the campaign against Rumania which, persuaded by the Brusilov offensive and having received promises of territory, entered the war on August 27, 1916. Although the lower Danube had historically been a primary Austro-Hungarian zone of interest, the main laurels in the quick and decisive campaign, which in three months eliminated a Rumanian army of some five hundred fifty thousand men as a factor in the war, were gained by the Germans.

As expected, the main Rumanian thrust came through the mountain passes into Transylvania where a hastily assembled Austro-Hungarian covering force, skillfully handled by General der Infantrie Arthur Baron Arz von Straussenburg, slowly withdrew to a previously prepared line of resistance. Behind this line Falkenhayn, who had lost Emperor William II's confidence and after Rumania's entry into the war had been deposed as chief of the general staff, was marshalling the Ninth Army, a mixed German-Austro-Hungarian formation, while in the south Mackensen had raised a combined German, Austro-Hungarian, Bulgarian, and Turkish force called the Danube Army, which invaded Rumanian Dobrudja early in September. The Rumanians had relied on Russian support and supplies and on an Entente offensive north from Salonika. The latter stalled after initial advances, while Russian aid did not become available in the required quantity. Forced to fight on two fronts, and lacking capable leadership, the Rumanians were pushed out of Transylvania, recoiled into the interior of their country, lost their capital Bucharest, and finally were compelled to take refuge behind the Sereth River in Moldavia. In the end, Rumania would re-emerge, but meanwhile the armies of the Central Powers, in a campaign which has remained a model of allied cooperation, had taken some 150,000 prisoners, inflicted over 200,000 casualties, and captured 350,000 rifles and 350 guns.

The victory over Rumania, carrying with it visions of access to greatly increased supplies of grain and oil, largely unrealized, brought some cheer to a despondent and gloomy civilian population in the Habsburg Empire, now in the third winter of the war. It also demonstrated the advantages to be reaped from a unified command, while the skill and the decisiveness of the German intervention demonstrated the superior competence of the German general staff. Actually, the Austro-Hungarian forces had done well under exceedingly difficult circumstances. With only a few *Landsturm* units, augmented by a mixed bag of gendarmerie and frontier guards, the energetic Artur Baron Arz von Straussenburg had conducted a model delaying action in Transylvania which had provided the time necessary to assemble the armies.⁵⁶ In the south the *k.u.k.* Danube flotilla and the engineers had played an important role in the crossing of the Danube, and three *k.u.k.* mountain brigades had performed well in the Transylvanian Alps. But still, it had been primarily a German victory and it did little to raise the waning star of Conrad von Hötzendorf.

The repercussions of the Trentino and Brusilov offensives had severely damaged Conrad's reputation within the army and within the Dual Monarchy.⁵⁷ For the first time since the beginning of the war, Conrad was openly attacked in the crown council of June 29 in Vienna, and he could defend himself only by stating that the Central Powers had forces inferior in number to those of their enemies and that reverses had to be expected.⁵⁸ Dissatisfied, the civilian ministers concerned, Burian, Stürgkh, and above all Tisza, demanded more complete information. When the *A.O.K.* stalled in providing it, they approached Francis Joseph, who ordered Conrad to make full disclosure of military plans and operations required by the civilian authorities.⁵⁹ Even more important, the setbacks suffered by the army raised anew the basic problems of relations with Hungary. While Tisza was fully committed to the support of the common war effort, the nationalist opposition in the Budapest parliament gained new strength in 1916, and once again demands for a greater share in the control of the army and even a completely independent army were heard.⁶⁰ The Hungarian nationalists openly compared the efficient conduct of the war by the Germans with the alleged inefficiency of the *A.O.K.*, and claimed that Magyar soldiers were mistreated by Czech and Slav superiors and that the kingdom bore a disproportional burden of casualties.⁶¹

Finally, there was pressure from Germany for a completely unified command in which the *A.O.K.* would be subordinated to German direction and control. Even before the Brusilov offensive, German officers had commanded mixed formations and acted as chiefs of staff to Austro-Hungarian army commanders. Often these relationships were far from happy. For instance, when in June 1916 Generalmajor Hans von Seeckt arrived to take over duties as chief of staff with the *k.u.k.* Seventh Army, the displaced chief of staff wrote that "one cannot avoid the unhappy feeling that the monarchy not only is fighting the external enemy, but also has to resist the Prussian will to dominate, which wants to use the war to subdue Austria-Hungary."⁶² In fact, Seeckt, who after two weeks became chief of staff for the Army Group Archduke Charles, did not have much respect for his new colleagues and told Falkenhayn that only with German aid and under German command could there be any chance to restore the situation on the eastern front.⁶³ Although Conrad protested against being placed "under German guardianship," Falkenhayn prevailed.⁶⁴ At the end of July after a personal intervention by Emperor William with Francis Joseph, Hindenburg was made commander on the whole eastern front, down to Lemberg, while Archduke Charles, the successor to the throne, retained control in the remaining sector but with a German, the much disliked Seeckt, as his chief of staff.⁶⁵ But this was not all. The conduct of the war clearly demanded a more unified control over all military efforts, an arrangement which meant that Austria-Hungary would lose much of her freedom of decision in the conduct of her policy and military operations. Once again Conrad resisted and protested violently. Writing to the emperor, he maintained that he would accept such an arrangement if "this would advance the overall victory in the war and safeguard the military interests of the monarchy. But in my considered opinion neither is the case." He threatened that if the German proposal were accepted, the "*A.O.K.* could no longer be responsible for the conduct of the war," and claimed that "this proposal undermines our future relations with Germany and compromises the future of the monarchy."[66] But neither Bolfras nor the emperor were any more impressed with Conrad's threats of resignation; he had lost much of his credibility. In September 1916 after Hindenburg and Ludendorff replaced Falkenhayn at the *O.H.L.*, an agreement was worked out under which the German emperor became supreme commander of the allied forces on all fronts, with Hindenburg acting in his name. The new *Oberste Kriegsleitung (O.K.L.)* would control major operations and allocation of forces to the various theaters, but the existing relationships between each allied chief of general staff and his field commanders would remain as before. Moreover, Conrad prevailed on Vienna to insist on the inclusion of a secret clause under which Germany undertook to respect the territorial integrity of the Dual Monarchy. On September 13, 1916, the agreement went into effect after being ratified by both monarchs. Later that month Bulgaria and the Ottoman Empire also acceded to this arrangement.[67]

Although in the past Conrad had frequently excoriated Falkenhayn and praised Ludendorff, he soon changed his tune. By October 1916 he complained to Bolfras that whereas Falkenhayn had been willing to conduct a bilateral relationship, "Ludendorff's program appears to aim at the total subjugation of our monarchy to German leadership." He claimed the existence of a German-Hungarian conspiracy directed against the Dual Monarchy and demanded that an explicit political understanding on all questions be reached between the two allied empires.[68] The inconsistent and volatile Conrad would change his tune again, and after the war he claimed that he was dismissed as chief of staff because "he never would have agreed to the conspiracy against Germany."[69]

In any case, the arrangement proved of limited importance and as Ludendorff wrote later, that "we had no clear picture of the internal value of our allied armies and therefore we could not, for example, decree that only so many divisions could remain on the Italian frontier of Austria-Hungary. In practice, reciprocal agreements were necessary."[70] And finally, after Francis Joseph died in November 1916, the new Emperor Charles demanded and achieved a substantial modification of the entire arrangement.

The death of Emperor Francis Joseph on November 21, 1916, was an event of enormous importance for the Austro-Hungarian Monarchy, its peoples, and its army. During the last few months of his life the emperor, never optimistic about the fortunes of war, had lost all hope and had told his intimates "we shall see if we can last out the winter. But next spring I shall make peace under all circumstances."[71] By October 1916 the immediate crisis had passed, but even so, deeply apprehensive about the social and political consequences of a continued war, Francis Joseph together with Emperor William had put out tentative peace feelers which were promptly rejected. The war went on and in the last days of his life the old emperor could find some consolation in the victorious advance of the armies of the Central Powers against Rumania.

Yet, when he died in the eighty-seventh year of his life and the sixty-eighth year of his reign, his life's main endeavor, the consolidation and preservation of the Dual Monarchy, was in growing jeopardy. Two major elements, military victory and the retention of the loyalty of the various nationalities within the empire, were closely related and while defeat was by no means sure at this time, final victory had become equally doubtful. To be sure, as yet the Entente had not decided that the destruction of Austria-Hungary was one of its war aims, but the basically unresolved conflicts between the nationalities, and between the nations and the crown, which had been muted throughout the first two years of the war already had reopened. While the old emperor had lived, he had constituted a strong cohesive force almost by sheer habit. When Francis Joseph passed away, one of the basic foundations of the unity of the realm, affection for the venerable old emperor rather than for the supranational principle he symbolized, also passed and long pent-up forces were released.[72]

The emperor's death also had immense effect on the cohesion of the army. Francis Joseph had been closely associated with his army from the very first day of his reign and during those long years he had seen the army undergo unprecedented technological and organizational transformations. To be sure, the emperor did not always understand nor did he sympathize with these changes, but even so the imprint of his personality and his effectiveness as a symbol had been immense. After 1867 an undeviating adherence to the principles of the compromise with Hungary had been his major policy, and despite repeated provocations, he had always resisted attempts to utilize the army as an active instrument to resolve differences within the dualistic structure.[73] It has recently been suggested by a prominent Austrian military historian that the Compromise of 1868 was only a reluctant accommodation to changes imposed by defeat and that it failed to revitalize the military structure. Continued reliance on tradition and dynastic sentiment, Kurt Peball argued, prevented the Habsburg army from gaining wide popular support, and he suggested that a truly "multinational army" on a federal basis would have in the long run been a better solution for the problems of the Danubian Monarchy.[74]

Despite defeats and defections, the army of Francis Joseph actually did better than many of its critics had predicted. The remarkable thing was that in a war which put extraordinary stress on the capacity to bear and endure on the man in the line, the great bulk of the army did its duty and endured and fought with great tenacity. Panic, desertions, and even mutinies occurred in practically all armies during the war, and afterwards one English critic concluded that "this loosely knit conglomeration of races withstood the shock and strain of war for four years in a way that surprised and dismayed her opponents."[75] In large part, this tenacity was based on tradition and discipline and on the feeling that the government of the old emperor was legitimate. With his death this feeling of legitimacy disappeared; the bonds of discipline and tradition loosened. Even so, the army of Francis Joseph continued to fight even when far behind its lines the empire which it served already had disintegrated.

14

Emperor Charles and the Dissolution of the Habsburg Army: 1916-1918

The old emperor was buried with pomp and circumstance in the family crypt below the Church of the Capuchins. His successor, the Emperor Charles, his grand-nephew, was a well-meaning young man of humanitarian inclinations, but volatile, lacking in balance and experience, and strangely unable to make and stick with decisions. Most of his major civilian advisors, including Ottokar Count Czernin, his new foreign minister and virtual head of all the Austrian governments that succeeded each other from January 1917 to October 1918, and Arthur Count Polzer-Holditz, his private secretary, who detested the Magyar aristocracy, had belonged to the Belvedere circle of Francis Ferdinand. While highly regarded by the civilians, the military members of that group, including Conrad, Krobatin, and Bardolff, were much more skeptical about the new monarch. They were apprehensive about his aspirations for military command, dubious about his firmness, and worried about his announced intention to bring peace at almost any price. They also were perturbed about the influence which his forceful wife, the Empress Zita from the House of Bourbon-Parma, exerted over him.[1]

The new emperor also disturbed the Magyars who feared that Charles might try to appease the Slavs at the expense of the dualistic system and the Kingdom of St. Stephen. To prevent this, Tisza rushed to Vienna, assured the young monarch of Hungary's continued allegiance and support, and in return obtained an early coronation in Budapest which committed Charles to uphold dualism. In the final analysis this act forestalled any immediate change from above in the structure of the Dual Monarchy, though it did little to halt the quarrels among the various national groups for which the death of Francis Joseph had loosened many traditional restraints. "Every class and every nationality," two English historians have observed, "was preparing for a struggle to enforce change, or to resist it."[2]

Even if Hungary had been willing to tolerate some modifications in the imperial and royal structure, the preconditions for any new departure in internal, foreign, and military policies required a substantial reduction in the power of the *A.O.K.* and a redefinition of relations with Germany. And while in military matters Charles was much more self-assured and prepared to assert his sovereign prerogatives, he realized, though he resented it, that he depended on German support and the consent of the Magyars.[3] On November 22, 1916, the day after the death of the old emperor "who has led you, your fathers, and grandfathers," Charles issued his first general order to the armed forces. "Soldiers," the document stated, "I have survived with you the hard and glorious days of the gigantic struggle. In these great times I step from your ranks to the head of my battle-hardened army and navy as supreme war-leader, with unshakable belief in our holy right and in the victory, which, with the aid of God, and in union with our loyal allies, we surely will achieve."[4] Troops everywhere took their oath to their new monarch on November 23, and in the wave of awards and promotions that followed, Archduke Eugene and General Conrad were raised to field marshals, a rank until then reserved to Archduke Friedrich.

But these displays of imperial favor concealed Charles's intention to reduce the power of the military and to assume personal command. His estrangement with the $A.O.K.$ dated back to the autumn of 1914, and the rift had never healed. But Charles always remained strangely incapable of making a firm decision. In September 1916, for instance, when Francis Joseph had asked him to report on Conrad's possible replacement, he had composed a most ambivalent reply. On the one hand, he pointed out that Conrad should be retained because of his high reputation with the Germans and because of the difficulty of finding a worthy successor; on the other hand he wrote that "one cannot clear out the misman-agement of the $A.O.K.$ as long as Excellency Conrad is in control there."[5] He recommended his replacement with Archduke Eugene. Francis Joseph had not acted, but once on the throne, Charles slowly proceeded to strip Conrad of authority. As a first step, on December 2, 1916, he issued an order personnally assuming supreme command of the army as well as operational control of all combat units of the army and navy. Archduke Friedrich was named as the new supreme commander's assistant at the $A.O.K.$[6] This action, of course, reduced Conrad's powers and practically eliminated Friedrich who, on February 11, 1917, was relieved of his post and placed "at the disposition of the supreme command."[7]

Even before that, on January 17, the emperor had transferred the $A.O.K.$ from Teschen to Baden near Vienna. Conrad, who suddenly discovered a desire to remain in close personal touch with the German headquarters at Pless and expressed fears that the move might offend the ally, had opposed violently. Baden, a pleasant resort, offered superior accommodations for the staff and was a more convenient place for the emperor and supreme commander, but its vicinity to Vienna also made for many distractions and did little to bridge the gap between the fighting troops and the high command.[8] Of course, all this was merely a prelude to the greatest change of all, Conrad's dismissal as chief of the general staff. Considering the continual quarrels between the twenty-nine-year-old ruler and the sixty-five-year-old soldier both in small and large matters, the action did not come as a surprise either to Conrad or to informed observers.[9] Although rumor variously ascribed his demotion to Catholic intrigues and the antagonisms of influential court circles (Feldmarschall Leutnant Ferdinand Baron Marterer, the new head of the emperor's military chancery, often was mentioned), the real reasons were Conrad's refusal to play a subordinate role, his failure to achieve victory, and his identification with the party favoring continuation of the war.[10] On being relieved of his post on March 1, 1917, Conrad at first requested retirement, but a personal appeal by Charles asking him to reconsider in view of "important military and political reasons," changed his mind and he accepted appointment as commanding general of the South Tyrolean Army Group.[11]

With Conrad's departure, the importance of the position of the *k.u.k.* chief of the general staff declined sharply. The emperor selected as his successor General Arz von Straussenburg, a relatively junior corps commander, who had gained a good reputation in the field. Arz was known for his unvarying good temper, lack of political ambitions, and reputation for pliability.[12] Lacking his predecessor's standing, he was content to abandon the special standing of his office and reverted to the role of a professional advisor to the imperial supreme commander. Moreover, Arz accompanied the restlessly energetic emperor, who spent much of his time travelling, essentially becoming a travel companion while his deputy in Baden, Generalmajor Alfred Baron Waldstätten, assumed responsibility for much of the operational planning.[13] But Waldstätten, appointed at the express wish of the emperor, was not always up to his difficult position.[14] Altogether, the command arrangement, the emperor acting as the supreme commander taking responsibility for all major operational decisions and the chief of the general staff merely serving in an advisory capacity, resembled the command and control structure prevailing between 1850 and 1859. Needless to say, this broken chain of command did little to promote efficiency or improve the strategic direction of the war.

There were numerous other changes at the highest levels of the military hiearchy, all designed to strengthen the emperor's grip and reduce military power. The most important was the replacement of Krobatin, the war minister and a long-time associate of Conrad's. The search for a new man, acceptable to both the Austrian and the Hungarian governments as well as to the emperor, was prolonged. On April 9, 1917, Marterer noted in his diary, "still no war minister! Today we went to Adelsberg and Marburg where H.M. wanted to interview corps commanders... all blank pages. Arz proposed Schönburg; this was turned down."[15] In the end, the emperor agreed to one of the corps commanders, General der Infantrie Rudolf Stöger-Steiner, "more the courtier than the hard-fisted soldier," while Krobatin, too, went to assume command on the Italian front.[16] Rounding out the new men at what became known as the "second *A.O.K.*" was the former Hungarian minister of defense, Generaloberst Samuel Baron Hazai, who became chief of the replacement branch, reporting directly to the emperor.[17]

Headed by a sovereign who combined the functions of ruler, supreme warlord, and commander of the army in one person, the second *A.O.K.* became an even more unwieldy organization, little suited to the energetic pursuit of war. But then Charles was no longer expecting victory or even determined to continue the war. In fact, most of his interventions in military affairs were regarded by the soldiers, including even Arz and Stöger-Steiner, as misplaced humanitarian gestures which eroded discipline and encouraged defeatism and even treason. Among his first orders, allegedly issued because of pressure from the Empress Zita, was an order to the air arm to halt all strategic bombing, including that of railroad targets, if it could endanger civilians. At the same time the order prohibited the use of incendiary projectiles in air-to-air combat and forbade the employment of gas without previous imperial sanction. Arousing much anger among the troops, the order had to be altered within a few months.[18] Other imperial orders, in March and June 1917, modified the articles of war and ended, against the opposition by Arz who claimed that this would endanger discipline, all physical punishments in the field.[19] At the same time, Charles prohibited summary executions of military and civilians even in the actual combat zone,[20] and in the fall of 1917, much to the consternation of traditionalists, Charles, an ardent and devout Catholic, outlawed the time-honored practice of duelling in the army.[21]

By far his most controversial step, however, was the relaxation of military rule, combined with the granting of amnesty for political crimes. In contrast to Germany, the *A.O.K.* at its most powerful never had achieved a military dictatorship and assumed control of political affairs.[22] In certain areas, to be sure, the *Kriegsüberwachungsamt* had interpreted its competence rather liberally and in a number of designated areas, military rule prevailed. Soon after his accession, Charles granted amnesty for a number of political offenses,[23] and also restricted the scope of military jurisdiction to areas immediately behind the fighting fronts.[24] In the spring of 1917, hoping to coopt opposition leaders in Hungary, Charles met with such radical leaders as Count Mihaly Károlyi, a move which eventually toppled Tisza, and tried to appease national discontents in Austria by recalling the *Reichsrat*. Finally, in spite of strong opposition from the military and the German nationalists, in July 1917 the emperor granted amnesty to a number of major political prisoners, including the Czech radical politicians Karel Kramář, Alois Rašin, and Václav Klofač, who promptly returned to Prague where they resumed their previous activities. These conciliatory gestures, however, had little influence on the loyalty of Czech units,[25] and some observers considered them counterproductive. The emperor was seeking wider support for his policies, but he lacked the strength to take a really decisive step.

Moreover, any decisive move to end the war required a redefinition of relations with Germany which actually might have occupied the country.[26] Although Charles realized his dependence on the powerful and dominant ally, he resented it and immediately after his accession revoked the unified command agreement of September 1916. For more than a year relations between the two allies proceeded again on the basis of nominal equality, though Arz still had to repeatedly request German assistance.[27] In another effort to assert his independence, as well as a demonstration of his humanitarian principles, the emperor protested against the German decision to resume unrestricted submarine warfare in early 1917.[28] Finally, between February and April 1917 he attempted to negotiate behind the back of his ally with the French government, using Prince Sixtus of Parma, his brother-in-law, then serving with the Belgian army, as his channel of communication. In the end, the negotiations failed; nothing that Charles could offer was acceptable to Italy, and at this point large territorial concessions, a peace that would have been a confession of military defeat, still would have been opposed both by the Germans in the *Reichsrat* and by the majority in the Hungarian parliament. The emperor may have been justified in his attempt to extricate his empire from the war, but his methods were clumsy, and little remained hidden from the Germans.[29] When a year later the French published certain correspondence regarding the negotiations, the emperor was accused of duplicity, regarded as treacherous by many, and forced to accept an even higher degree of subservience to Berlin.

The fact remained that no matter how much the emperor desired peace, the preservation of his dynasty and empire depended, as it had done so often in the past, on the strength of his army. Early in 1917, German plans contemplated retreat to shorter prepared positions in the west, holding actions in east, and unrestricted submarine warfare to bring England down. The Entente, in contrast, was planning simultaneous attacks in France, Russia, and Italy. In the spring of 1917 the *k.u.k.* armed forces numbered 3.5 million men, of whom, however, only seven hundred eighty thousand were at the front, though two hundred fifty thousand additional combat troops could be found in training and replacement units. Infantry continued to predominate, six hundred eighty thousand strong; cavalry had shrunk to fifty-one thousand, of whom over one-half were dismounted. Technical troops had increased to thirty-seven thousand. The operating armies were organized in sixty-seven infantry and eleven cavalry divisions, eight independent brigades and other local defense units, equipped with 7,000 machine guns, 3,200 light and heavy mortars, 5,700 field and mountain guns, and 1,530 pieces of heavy artillery.[30] For the moment, production of weapons and ammunition was adequate, though in the air, with Italy having become the main center of operations, Austria-Hungary continued to be weaker. In 1917, 1,740 planes and 1,230 spare engines were built, and in 1918, despite material and personnel shortages, 2,378 aircraft were produced. Even so, this was not enough to gain air superiority against the Italian, now actively joined by British and French, opponents.[31]

In 1917, the replacement situation began to tighten up again. Up to February of that year the armed forces had suffered 14,520 officers and 562,738 men killed, while 18,762 officers and 1,342,697 men were reported captured or missing in action. There were about 1.5 million wounded and 1.8 million sick, and of these two groups a million died or were permanently disabled.[32] The number of those succumbing to wounds and illness rose, in part because of the increasingly desperate food situation, from 26 percent in 1914, to 48 percent in the following year, and to 60 percent in 1917.[33] Hazai was told to comb the rear area services for combat-fit men, employ naval personnel ashore, and investigate the utilization of female auxiliaries.[34]

On the all-important question of fighting morale, the answer was not clear. Although at home the emperor and his foreign minister were extremely pessimistic, especially after the United States had entered the war in April 1917, troops at the fronts continued to fight stubbornly. Along the Isonzo, the army, more than half of which was composed of Slav units, stoutly resisted Italian attacks, though on the Russian front, Slav units, especially Czechs, defected in considerable numbers during the last Russian offensive in June 1917.[35] In part these defections were undoubtedly caused by nationalist propaganda, but they were also due to the growing war-weariness appearing in all armies, and to the totally inadequate rations. Front troops now received only one ounce of meat daily, as compared to nine ounces in Germany, and the quartermaster announced that while the worms found in the rations might not be appetizing, they were not dangerous to health.[36] And though an imperial decree of February 27, 1917, had established a joint food administration, the Hungarians, also short of supplies, cooperated only very reluctantly, while the exploitation of the occupied territories also fell much below expectations.

The various changes in the Austro-Hungarian military establishment induced the *O.H.L.* to seek a clearer picture, and in June 1917 Seeckt, still serving with the *k.u.k.* armies in Galicia, submitted his assessment. On the whole, he believed that the common Austro-Hungarian soldier still was willing to fight, though he perceived great differences in their combat willingness and rated the German and Hungarian soldiers as the best. At the same time, however, he pointed out that the Magyars were not reconciled to a unitary army. Seeckt was less favorable in his judgment of the *k.u.k.* officer corps and the high command. The officers showed too little initiative and willingness to accept responsibility, the staff lacked prestige and education, and the *A.O.K.* was too isolated and had too little understanding of the needs of the combat troops.[37] Of course, what he said about the supreme command applied with equal force to all armies during this conflict.

At the beginning of 1917 more than half of the Austro-Hungarian army, forty-one infantry and eleven cavalry divisions, were committed on the eastern front; sixteen divisions were on the Italian front, and the remainder served on the Balkans. In accordance with Entente decisions, the Italians, reinforced by British and French heavy artillery, attacked in the Tenth (May 12 to June 6) and the Eleventh (August 18 to September 15) Isonzo battles. In the Tenth Battle the Italians, suffering enormous casualties, gained some ground, about two miles on both flanks, and in the Eleventh Battle they drove the Austro-Hungarians off the Bainsizza plateau, but failed to exploit their success. Again, Italian losses were huge, almost double that of the defenders, but the *k.u.k.* armies were shaken. Meanwhile on the eastern front, Kerensky, who after the March revolution had first become minister of war and then prime minister, with Brusilov as his commander-in-chief, launched an offensive in Galicia in July. After initial successes, during which the appearance in the Russian ranks of a brigade of Czech legionaries mainly composed of former *k.u.k.* soldiers was a dangerous portent of things to come, the offensive faltered.[38] A counteroffensive regained all ground and more, and for the rest of the summer the eastern front remained in an uneasy state of calm. But the Russian army had been broken as a major fighting force, and Arz could congratulate himself on his decision to leave the majority of his troops in the east.[39]

Reductions of the Russian menace and apprehension about a possible Italian breakthrough in a Twelfth Battle at the Isonzo made Emperor Charles send a personal appeal to William II. "My commanders and troops feel," he wrote on August 26, "that an offensive would be the best way to master the difficult situation." But he asked for no more than the loan of some heavy German artillery and the relief of Austro-Hungarian troops on the eastern front. "You will certainly understand," the letter continued, "that I particularly wish to conduct the offensive against Italy only with my own troops. My entire army considers the war against Italy as 'our war'. Since childhood, every officer has inherited from his forefathers the desire to fight against the hereditary enemy."[40] But the Germans were reluctant to underwrite a purely Austro-Hungarian enterprise; they had, by this time, little confidence in the efficiency of their ally and also feared that a victory against Italy might permit Charles to leave the alliance. To be sure, Ludendorff recognized the precarious position along the lower Isonzo and he now offered a joint operation, but with a strictly limited aim. Rejecting more ambitious proposals made by *k.u.k.* officers, Ludendorff indicated that he would provide seven divisions for a quick push from the Isonzo west to the Tagliamento, a distance of some thirty miles. In no position to argue, the *A.O.K.* accepted.[41]

The assault force, designated as the German Fourteenth Army, consisting of two Austro-Hungarian and two German corps with some special formations, was commanded by General Otto von Below, with Krafft von Dellmensingen, Ludendorff's Bavarian mountain warfare expert, as chief of staff. Though Archduke Eugene as the commander of the front was supposedly in charge, as usual in joint operations the Germans reserved for themselves all tactical decisions and his influence was only nominal. Based on the latest German assault methods, which substituted surprise and a sudden unregistered saturation bombardment for the lengthy fire-plans and rigid attack schemes, the Fourteenth Army was assembled by circuitous routes, marched by night into its carefully camouflaged jump-off positions, and the entire movement was covered by a strong German air umbrella and wireless deception. However, the Italians were warned of the impending attack by deserters, two Rumanian officers, and the attack, scheduled for October 22, had to be postponed for two days due to adverse weather.[42]

The area chosen for the attack was the upper Isonzo in the high Julian Alps, a twenty-mile wide sector from Flitsch (Plezzo) in the north to Tolmein (Tolmino) in the south. Approximately in the center of the area was the village of Karfreit (Caporetto) from which the battle was to take its name. Below had formed his army into four assault groups: the Krauss Group, three *k.u.k.* and one German divisions in the north; the Stein and Berrer groups, predominantly German with German commanders in the center; the Scotti Group, about evenly divided, in the south, and the Austro-Hungarian Tenth Army in the Carniolan Alps. The Tenth Army and the First and Second Isonzo armies were to support the attack by limited demonstrations, and Conrad was to tie down the Italians on his front. Even so, the attackers were inferior in number, thirty-three against forty-one divisions, to the defense which Cadorna had reinforced during the first part of October.

But the attack, preceded by a short saturation bombardment delivered by nearly two thousand guns including some five hundred heavy pieces, and firing gas against which the primitive Italian gasmasks were useless, achieved a breakthrough. Infiltrating through the valleys while other units took the commanding heights, the Germans and Austro-Hungarians moved swiftly forward in wretched autumn weather. In the two northern sectors Italian resistance collapsed, and some thirty thousand men were taken prisoner the first day marching into captivity in formed units.[43] The Second Italian Army was routed, and on the flanks of the breakthrough the other Italian armies fell back to escape entrapment. An attempt to stand on the Tagliamento on November 2 was foiled when Krauss managed to gain a bridgehead, and even Ludendorff wavered for a moment and permitted the offensive to continue rolling on its own momentum. By November 7, Austro-Hungarian and German spearheads reached the broad obstacle of the Piave, seventy miles behind the original Isonzo front. Here the Italians held, rushing new forces to the line, and French and British divisions were hurriedly brought up from France. The limited Austro-Hungarian and German strength was inadequate to break through here, and even Conrad's attack from the Trentino with an army which had been weakened by withdrawals for the main attack failed to change the situation.[44]

Caporetto was a great disaster for the Italians who suffered more than three hundred thousand casualties, including two hundred sixty-five thousand prisoners, evidence of demoralization in their ranks. The attackers captured some three thousand guns and tremendous quantities of supplies. Still, there were recriminations among the commanders. Krauss later accused Boroević of the Second Isonzo Army of having failed to close the trap from the south and there also were rumblings that Ludendorff, who never considered the Italian theater decisive, had prematurely closed down the offensive.[45] During the operations, coordination between the two allies had been good, but lacking cordiality. Before Caporetto an imperial order had demanded that all personnel, on or off-duty, observe cordiality and cooperation with the German ally.[46] After the offensive, Austrian officers, especially Major General Heinrich Wieden, commander of the elite Edelweiss Division, accused some of the German units of looting and showing a lack of respect for Austro-German troops.[47] Even so, as winter closed in over the Italian front, and another revolution rocked Russia, the Austro-Hungarian position had improved immeasurably.

The Emperor Charles gained new heart and during the winter of 1917 to 1918 a number of schemes for the reorganization of the army, both for during and after the war, were drawn up, while Hungary, clinging single-mindedly to its dream, once again made demands for an independent national army. Though diametrically opposed in their ultimate purposes, the plans had their common conceptual basis in the experience of the war. The rulers of Hungary felt that their country's contribution to the war effort entitled it to a separate national army; the *A.O.K.* believed that the war clearly had demonstrated the need for a larger, more modern, and more unified military establishment in the future.

As early as March 1915, the Operations Division of the *A.O.K.* elaborated a scheme for the reorganization and modernization of the army after the end of the war.[48] Repeatedly modified during the following years, this scheme, the so-called "Conrad Plan," had to be radically changed in 1917. As Arz, the new chief of the general staff, put it, "however the war would end, it was evident that one could not count on obtaining in peacetime the necessary means for the creation of a modern army."[49] Given this realization, and taking into account the attitude of the new monarch, the *A.O.K.* proceeded to scale down its planned peacetime army expansion and to proceed at once with the implementation of its minimal objectives.[50] The new program, approved by Charles in March 1917, called for a future peace establishment of 594,000 men, with a permanent supreme command, sixty infantry and ten cavalry divisions, a greatly strengthened artillery complement, a combined sapper-engineer corps, and an eighty-two-squadron air arm. Based on the lessons of combat, the new infantry divisions were to be triangular rather than square; comprised of three regiments of three battalions each, instead of four regiments with four battalions each. There was to be a special assault battalion, a mortar battalion, and a strong divisional artillery brigade with seventy-two light and twenty-four heavy guns as well as an anti-aircraft battery and sapper, signals, and communications detachments.[51]

Losing no time, the *A.O.K.* proceeded with the reshuffling of troops as soon as the Caporetto operations had ended. Reorganization produced a total of sixty-six triangular infantry divisions with at least part of their projected artillery and with a greatly augmented number of machine guns.[52] The decision to proceed with the reorganization of the army in the middle of war, attended by a great number of troop exchanges and marches and much dislocation, caused a highly adverse reaction. Krauss excoriated it as an example of the bureaucratic mentality which took no account of the hardships it inflicted on the troops;[53] a more moderate writer commented that it "caused a considerable amount of headshaking in the army,"[54] and even the official war history, written by staff officers, spoke of "not always quite understandable troop movements."[55] In defense, Arz claimed that a great number of provisional formations had been formed which were not of equal combat value and could not be interchanged. Moreover, he wrote, the reorganization of the army at that time would provide the basis for the future peace establishment.[56]

In any case, the reorganization, the ultimate implications of which were constantly protested by the Hungarians, was only carried out at the divisional level.[57] It coincided with a determined Hungarian push to obtain their own national army. Friction between Austria and Hungary over this issue had not been laid to rest and had reemerged in 1915 and 1916 when, during negotiations concerning the decennial renewal of the *Ausgleich*, the Austrian delegation proposed that it wanted to conclude an agreement for twenty years instead of ten. The Hungarians countered with stiff demands both economic and military, and even Tisza, a life-long champion of the *Ausgleich*, asserted the kingdom's claim to an independent army. This Francis Joseph had rejected, but, in spite of Conrad's vehement objections, he conceded the introduction of new dualistic emblems for the armed forces.[58] Such measures hardly solved the basic issue, the differences over the control of the army, which for hundreds of years had disturbed the relations between Hungary and the crown. And as the war continued, and with the possibility that the Habsburg Empire might break up or become subordinated to Germany, there was a growing resolve among Magyar politicians of all shades not to be pulled down with Austria and to safeguard the interests of the kingdom by a separate military establishment.

The issue had become enmeshed in the negotiations for the renewal of the compromise and in internal Hungarian political problems, especially the question of extending the franchise. Tisza had promised not to bring up the army issue during the war in an acute form, but in May 1917 the leaders of the national opposition coalition persuaded Charles to dismiss the premier.[59] After considerable hesitation, the emperor-king appointed Prince Moritz Esterházy, a well-intentioned but weak young man, who resigned after an uneasy two months in office during which nothing was resolved. At this point Charles fell back on Alexander Wekerle, a veteran politician, to whom he promised in principle a separate Hungarian army after the war.[60] In November 1917 Wekerle pushed through a limited electoral reform, but facing opposition from many sides, he decided to bolster his position by reopening the army issue. In November 1917 General der Infantrie Alexander Baron Szurmay, the *Honvéd* minister, also compiled a lengthy memorandum which demanded nothing less than a division of the common army into separate Austrian and Hungarian armies.[61]

In response to these demands a special crown council convened on December 4, 1917, in Vienna. Besides the emperor, who personally chaired the session, Archduke Friedrich, and Generals Arz, Böhm-Ermolli, Czapp, Dankl, Hazai, Sarkotić, Stöger-Steiner, Szurmay, and Tersztyanszky were present.[62] Sarkotić opened the discussion by stating that the Hungarian demands were quite inadmissible, and what was required was a "small unitary army. . . prepared and ready to repress revolutionary subversions and coups." Böhm-Ermolli protested against the suggestion that the army was not reliable, while Szurmay repeated his demands, asserting that "all groups in Hungary are united on the issue of a Hungarian army." The conciliatory Stöger-Steiner then submitted that it would be tactically unsound to concede under pressure something that would be conceded sooner or later anyway, and suggested that it should be done in such a way as to constitute a "genuine coronation of dualism." In any case, he concluded, it would have to wait for the end of the war. Dankl then remarked, "later, much later," and the emperor concluded the session by stating that it appeared to him that all were agreed that the issue could not be resolved during the war.

In January 1918, in order to strengthen this position and at the same time reassure the Magyars that the question was under active consideration, all army commanders assembled in Baden for a council of marshals. No protocol was kept, but only Archduke Joseph voted for division of the army, while the eleven remaining officers were opposed.[63] Even before this, however, the emperor had ordered Stöger-Steiner that negotiations on this question should continue, but that these "negotiations and their results have to remain strictly secret."[64] On the other hand, he also informed Wekerle after the council of marshals that the lop-sided vote confirmed that nothing could be implemented until after the war.[65] The negotiations, as could be expected, leaked out and there were repercussions in Hungary, though these merged into the bigger anti-war and hunger strikes of January 1918. Negotiations did continue and with a spectacular disregard for the real situation and the real intentions of the Entente and the nationalities, the Hungarian representatives during these discussions insisted on their separate army, including air squadrons.[66] In fact, as late as September 12, 1918, the Hungarian representative indicated that unless these demands were granted Hungary would proceed on its own to implement them.[67]

In retrospect, the schemes for the reorganization of the army, its peacetime establishment, and Hungary's demand for an independent army assume a rather anachronistic character. All presumed that the war would end with the Dual Monarchy substantially intact, and though at the close of 1917 the situation of the Central Powers looked better than before, the entry of the United States had altered the real balance of power beyond repair. Politically, President Wilson's Fourteen Points, published on January 8, 1918, though they did not necessarily call for an end to the Habsburg Empire, encouraged the nationalities to seek independence instead of the federal solution which they might have accepted earlier. Militarily, Caporetto had merely been a shot in the arm, but no more than that. Even the reluctant Austro-Hungarian advance in the Ukraine, in accordance with a rather contrived treaty with its government (the "bread peace," as it was called), did little to improve the desperate food and supply situation of the empire and its army.

The stark reality of the situation already had been exposed by Stöger-Steiner in an August 1917 memorandum to the emperor. Discussing the "Possibilities of our lasting through the Winter of 1917/18," the minister concluded that it would, in all probability, just be possible. Replacements could be provided up to May 1918 and arms and ammunition supply were adequate, though the production of machine guns had to be cut from three thousand to fifteen hundred per month and due to material shortages no ground sheets would be available after December 1917. Above all, there were serious shortages of coal and food, and it would be absolutely essential to increase rations for the industrial workers.[68]

But this could not be done. On the contrary, in January 1918 it became necessary to reduce the already meager bread ration to 200 and then to 165 grams a day. This was the last straw. Since 1917, scattered strikes, work stoppages, and sabotage had plagued the war industry; now, despite pleas for moderation from the Austrian Social-Democratic leadership, a strike broke out in Wiener-Neustadt, rapidly spreading to other Austrian industrial areas and to Hungary. Only in Bohemia, where the Czech workers were firmly in the hands of their political leadership which feared a German intervention, the strike was limited to a one-day demonstration demanding national freedom. Elsewhere the strike assumed an almost revolutionary character, taking the government by surprise. The Vienna garrison seemed not totally reliable; the police powerless.[69] In this emergency Emperor Charles appealed to the army which responded with operations "Mogul" and "Revolver," rushing seven reliable divisions from the front to Austria and Bohemia. In addition, the emperor appointed General der Kavallerie Prince Alois Schönburg-Hartenstein as commander of troops at home and discussed plans for a military government with the prince at its head and Bardolff as his deputy.[70]

In the end the government ended the strike by a mixture of military coercion and political concessions, including promises to revise the electoral laws and reopen the Russian peace negotiations that had broken down. An increase in bread rations was promised to the factory workers, but this increase had to be made at the expense of the army. And the food situation of the army, especially in Italy, already was desperate. By the end of 1917, the military had used up their reserve stocks and merely were existing hand to mouth.[71] Weekly rations were down to two hundred grams of bread, sometimes replaced by three ounces of corn meal, and six ounces of meat for troops in the front and half of that for troops behind the line. Dried vegetables were the main staple of diet and horse meat a delicacy seldom seen. It was no wonder that many batteries were down to three or five horses, and some had but one.[72]

Meanwhile the armed forces themselves became infected with revolutionary sentiments. The first major incident was the mutiny of the Fifth *k.u.k.* Fleet in the Gulf of Cattaro on February 1, 1918, which was fairly easily suppressed.[73] Still, the sailors' demands for better rations and an immediate peace found a responsive cord in the hearts of many soldiers. War weariness, hunger, want, national and social agitation had entered the ranks and the situation became more volatile when in March Austro-Hungarian prisoners in large number, six hundred thirty thousand in all, began to come back from Russia.[74] These men had seen and lived through the Bolshevik revolution and the military authorities were worried about their possible indoctrination with Bolshevik ideas. Of course, the majority were glad to come home; a minority had revolutionary ideas, and others resented all authority. Attempts to screen them were counterproductive and rather than rejoin the army, many deserted, roaming the countryside in armed bands.[75]

This large number of deserters, estimated early in 1918 at almost a quarter of a million, as well as the mutinies which occurred in April and May of that year in several replacement units, did not yet mean the end of the army's ability to fight. Desertions and mutinies were in large part due to the reluctance of returned prisoners to return to active duty, and not a conscious effort to end the war or overthrow established authority.[76] In February 1918, albeit reluctantly, the

Austro-Hungarians participated in the offensive operations against Soviet Russia designed to force conclusion of the peace treaty and take possession of the supposedly rich granaries of the Ukraine.[77] On the Italian front, Monte Pasubio was blown up after months of intensive mining and countermining efforts, and in March the German *O.H.L.* requested one hundred heavy Austro-Hungarian guns for its great spring offensive.[78] And in far-off Palestine, *k.u.k.* gunners detached to assist the Turks managed to impress the enemy by their calm courage amidst chaos and retreat.[79]

At the same time, however, the various nationalities were becoming more vocal in their determination to destroy the Dual Monarchy, and no solution to the national issue could be found in Vienna or Budapest. The Entente was changing its policy towards open recognition of independence for the "oppressed" nations. In 1915 Russia had formed a Czech Legion, and an independent Czecho-Slovak army, partially recruited in the United States and partially from prisoners of war in Italy, was set up in the spring of 1918.[80]

Entente feelings against Austria-Hungary were hardened by the sequel to the Sixtus affair. In April 1918, Count Czernin, speaking in Vienna, declared that the French had opened peace negotiations, but that these had failed because of their aspirations for Alsace-Lorraine, which he had rejected in loyalty to the German ally. Infuriated, the French now published a letter written by Charles during the previous year's negotiations in which the emperor had promised support for "France's just claims to Alsace-Lorraine." Revelation of the "Sixtus Letter" not only embarrassed Charles, it also forced Germany to secure its relations with the Dual Monarchy. Although as late as 1917 Ludendorff had opposed any permanent military agreement, it now seemed vital to assure Austria-Hungary's continued participation in the war. On May 13, 1918, Charles signed agreements at Spa, the *O.H.L.'s* location, providing for the closest military, political, and economic cooperation between the two empires.[81] Although it has been claimed that these agreements foreclosed any possibility for his future independent action, they were not altogether disadvantageous. They provided for economic cooperation in exploiting the Ukraine, a hope not realized, and for uniform training, organization, armament, and joint planning between the armed forces. And especially in the military sphere, the agreements remained largely on paper and there were no negotiations to implement them.[82]

Still, Austria-Hungary was dependent on Germany and the emperor was unhappy about this development. As a token of his good intentions, he had agreed at Spa to undertake a major offensive in Italy.[83] Although pressured by the Germans into this fatal undertaking, both Arz and Conrad also favored such a move. The collapse of Russia and the success of the German offensive in the west, partial though it was, made another attempt to knock Italy out of the war, or at least forestall her expected offensive, a great temptation.[84] It was a grave mistake. Austria-Hungary would have been better off remaining on the defensive, husbanding her resources. No decision affecting the overall war situation could be reached in Italy; even the repetition of Caporetto, unlikely under prevailing conditions, would not have done much. On the other hand, with the army intact, the secessionist nationalities might have been overawed and perhaps Austria-Hungary might have gained better terms from the Entente. As it was, the monarchy's last resources were wasted in an unnecessary gamble.

Although Austria-Hungary, relieved by the capitulations of Russia and Rumania, was free to deploy the bulk of its army's fifty-three divisions with ten in reserve against Italy, these units were in most cases only hollow shells without much fighting spirit. Infantry divisions were reduced to between five thousand and eight thousand men, with cavalry divisions at about half that level. In the artillery about a third of the batteries lacked draft horses, tractors were without fuel, and the railroads no longer able to carry additional traffic. Rations were at starvation level, clothing was of the poorest quality, and even arms, ammunition, and equipment had become worn out for lack of spare parts. The army hoped to feed and supply itself from stocks to be captured during the offensive and special units were formed to collect and distribute supplies.[85]

Moreover, the Austrian commanders, Conrad in the Tyrol, Boroević along the Piave, and Arz and Waldstätten at Baden, could not agree on a common strategic plan. Conrad stuck to his favorite concept: a thrust from the South Tyrolean Alps into the Venetian plain, taking the main Italian body in the flank. Though this scheme had failed in 1916, his starting positions now were improved and with adequate forces (about thirty-four divisions were estimated as the requirement), it might have been possible. Waldstätten and the *A.O.K.* proposed strong attacks on both extreme flanks, but with the main effort in the center. Boroević favored the defensive, but when pressed he made the most foolish suggestion—a frontal attack across the Piave. When the commanders failed to reach agreement, the final decision was left to the Emperor Charles who believed that the had strategic gifts and was capable of directing his armies in the field. Always indecisive, however, he could not make up his mind between the competing plans and personalities and in the end he struck a compromise which satisfied no one. Both Conrad and Boroević were allotted roughly equal forces, so that neither had sufficient strength.[86]

The offensive was, in any case, doomed before it started. Opposing forces were about equal and the Italians, reinforced by British and French divisions, had the advantage of interior lines and good communications. When the attack started, delayed from May 28 to June 6, it even lacked the element of surprise. Wireless intercepts and deserters had revealed the coming attack and the night before Italian guns put down heavy fire on the Austro-Hungarian assembly areas. In spite of all these handicaps, the *k.u.k.* troops attacked with considerable spirit and persistence. Conrad made some gains in the mountains but was stopped by the French and British defense; on the Piave a bridgehead fifteen miles wide and five deep was gained. But the river rose and the combined Entente airpower, against which the 170 Austro-Hungarian planes were unable to prevail, destroyed the pontoon bridges. With their supplies running low and facing an armor-supported counterattack, the *k.u.k.* positions west of the Piave became almost hopeless. On June 20, Emperor Charles, who had arrived in person to direct operations, ordered a withdrawal across the river.[87]

Although the Austro-Hungarians took fifty thousand prisoners, losing twenty-four thousand of their own, other casualties were very heavy. The June offensive was a clear military defeat with enormous repercussions on the morale and cohesion of the army and an already shaky empire. To be sure, even now the army remained capable of stubborn defense and in July and August 1918, Generaloberst Pflanzer-Baltin managed to mount a limited counteroffensive against French-Italian forces in Albania. But this was of minor importance. Deprived of hope, the army on the whole lost morale and its leaders the last shreds of public confidence. In an effort to divert criticism, Conrad, described as "a broken man," was dismissed on July 15, 1918.[88] In the *Reichsrat* the military leadership came under open attack. Deputy Leuthner, a Social Democrat, declared that too many units had been diverted to internal security duties and "one cannot simultaneously conduct war on the foreign and the domestic front. At least the army leaders should spare us irresponsible offensives for which the army is neither morally nor physically prepared. Tens of thousands were sacrificed for nothing at the Piave."[89] These sentiments were echoed in the Budapest parliament where speakers contended that Hungarian troops had been deliberately sacrificed.[90] More and more Hungarians began to follow Károlyi who rather naively believed that if Hungary broke ties with Austria, introduced democratic reforms, made concessions to the nationalities, and concluded a separate peace, then the Entente would respect her territorial integrity and treat the country leniently.

Although the army still managed to hold its lines against Italy, behind the front the breakdown of the military establishment accelerated at an increasing rate. After the Piave mutinies, refusals to go into action, and mass desertions became frequent and were no longer confined to Czechs. Slovene, Ruthene, Polish, Serb, and even Croat units were also affected. Whenever possible, mutinous units were surrounded and captured, but many escaped to join the deserters in the "green cadres" roaming in the hills.[91] Although orders were issued to attack and suppress armed deserters, they managed to maintain themselves and especially in the south of the monarchy became a veritable plague. By the summer of 1918, the "green cadres" had machine guns or even field artillery, and when Emperor Charles visited Sofia and Constantinople in May, heavy precautions had to be taken to safeguard the imperial train.[92]

The dissolution of the military infrastructure and the escalating domestic turbulence placed a heavy stress on the troops still in the trenches. In July 1918 the *A.O.K.* informed the War Ministry and General Hazai that the fifty-seven divisions in Italy actually had a combat effectiveness equal to only thirty-seven divisions and that it was most unlikely that they could withstand an attack by the seventy or so enemy divisions facing them.[93] But it became harder and harder to scrape up replacement units. The problem was further complicated by the fact that the seven divisions used to break the January strikes were never returned to the front, though the *A.O.K.* frequently requested them and the situation occasioned a sharp and prolonged exchange between the *A.O.K.* and Stöger-Steiner.[94] But in the end, domestic considerations prevailed and after the matter had been appealed to the emperor, Arz was forced to agree to maintain a minimum of sixty-six battalions in the interior of the monarchy, though he obtained assurances that as soon as enough internal security units, *Assistenz Bataillone* as they were termed, had been formed, the combat troops would be sent to the front.[95] At that time, in September 1918, *k.u.k.* forces in Italy numbered fifty-seven divisions, four divisions were in the Ukraine and on the Sea of Azov, six divisions were in or enroute to the Balkans, and three divisions were fighting in Albania. In addition Ludendorff, who previously had turned down Austro-Hungarian troops for the western front, had changed his mind and had asked for the maximum number to shore up the German defenses. Two divisions had been dispatched and two more were being prepared for service there.[96]

Considerations about troop distribution were, however, becoming academic. In August 1918 during his last visit to the *O.H.L.*, Arz had already informed Hindenburg and Ludendorff that the monarchy could continue the war only up to the end of the year; thereafter, "the army would be needed to maintain order and bring about the solution of certain internal political questions."[97] Evidently, Arz still believed that the army could be used to repress social and national revolutions now brewing in both Austria and Hungary, but by September even combat troops were not that reliable anymore. They still clung to their positions against an enemy who refused to test their resolution and preferred for the process of internal disintegration to complete its work. Even so, reports from the front indicated that many officers had lost confidence in a successful outcome and that troop morale, already low, was ebbing fast.[98] The major cause of this was hunger and deprivation, many men now were in rags, and in at least one unit there were only enough uniforms for men directly in line; the remainder had to await their turn in their ragged underwear. Hopes of getting additional supplies from the Ukraine had faded as only seventy thousand tons of food reached Austria-Hungary from that source, and even the belated creation of a special Army Food Council (*Armee Ernährungsrat*) could not change this situation.[99]

The initiative had gone over to the Entente. In September, British and Dominion forces cracked the Turkish defenses in northern Palestine and Syria and eliminated the Ottoman Empire from the war, and on September 15, the Entente Armies around Salonika attacked and quickly smashed the Bulgarian lines. Within ten days Bulgarian resistance collapsed and Entente forces, with reconstituted Serbian divisions in their van, rapidly approached the Hungarian plains.[100] During a hastily summoned crown council on September 27, Arz stated that he might be able to bring some troops from Venetia and the Ukraine to help Feldmarschall Hermann Baron Kövess stabilize a new defense line along the Danube-Save line, but that this would take time, and that in any case peace would have to be made by the end of the year.[101]

Austria-Hungary clearly was at the end of her rope, and her powerful German ally was in very little better condition. Her last offensive in the west had failed and on August 8, the "black day of the German army," British and French forces, accompanied by 450 tanks, tore a great hole into the German front. After over four years of war, discipline even in the German army eroded and on that day there was straggling and disorder as units fell back. Before a week was over, the German *O.H.L.* decided that the war had to be brought to a speedy end. By September 29, Hindenburg called on the German imperial government to initiate immediate negotiations for an armistice. In the end, the much-maligned and belittled Habsburg army had managed to hang on just as long as its powerful ally who so frequently had patronized it.

In Vienna, meanwhile, Emperor Charles tried desperate expedients to save the Habsburg inheritance. An appeal for peace made on September 14 had gone unanswered. A second appeal was made on October 4, when Austria-Hungary joined Germany in asking for an armistice on the bais of Wilson's Fourteen Points. Meanwhile, national councils resembling quasi-governments were forming in Prague and Agram, and without even waiting for a reply the emperor, in a last-ditch effort to preserve some future role for the dynasty, issued a manifesto on October 16 reorganizing Austria into a federal state with complete self-government for its nationalities. But the formula came much too late to satisfy the Czechs or for that matter the Poles or the South Slavs. And, threatened by an adamant Hungarian government with an interruption of food shipments, the manifesto specifically promised that it would not "disturb the integrity of the lands of the Crown of St. Stephen."[102]

The manifesto left the Habsburg civil service and military thoroughly confused and instead of shoring up the tottering monarchy, it became the instrument of its dissolution, the death-warrant of the empire signed by its last emperor. There was much which was confusing in this episode, and it revealed the inconsistencies which so often before characterized many of Charles's actions. Arz had feared it would lead to the disintegration of the army and he had managed to delay publication for several days.[103] Emperor Charles disseminated a special order-of-the-day to the armed forces stressing the special relationship between them and the crown and expressing confidence that this would continue unimpaired.[104] But this was a pipe dream. The manifesto essentially dissolved the empire into various national groups, and it was quixotic to expect that soldiers would continue to fight and die for an empire which no longer existed. In fact, even Charles recognized the new circumstances and on October 31 issued a follow-up order which permitted officers to take service with the new national governments established by the end of the month.[105] Moreover, a week later on November 8, the joint war minister, "at the specific order of HM," told all commanders that in case of conflict, the new oath should have precedence over the old oath to the monarch.[106] Even so, when two years later Charles was eager to resume the Hungarian throne, he claimed that he never had released his soldiers from their oath of allegiance. "Officers and men," he wrote, "merely were permitted to give their allegiance to the new national governments, but without infringing on their personal oath to me."[107] He did not, however, explain how these two contradictory positions could be reconciled.

Although it is of course true that the manifesto was issued in anticipation of certain military defeat, and this was the real cause of the monarchy's collapse, the manifesto destroyed the remaining legitimacy of Habsburg rule. At the same time, on October 21, Wilson replied to the emperor's plea and announced that he no longer could accept mere autonomy for the Czecho-Slovak and South Slav peoples. By the end of October, in city after city, in Prague, Agram, Laibach, Budapest, Cracow, and finally even in Vienna, the imperial and royal authorities were repudiated as every ethnic group within the empire abandoned the Habsburg and established its own national state. Although in some cases energetic local commanders contemplated offering armed resistance, Charles refused to sanction the use of force.[108]

This state of affairs did not prevent the army, sustained by tradition and the last remnants of discipline, from continuing to hold its lines and in fact, though only for a few days, to continue fighting even after the monarchy already had dissolved into its various components. As late as mid-October 1918, some commanders still were optimistic about containing an Italian offensive.[109] Others who were more realistic began to think about the duties ahead, though in the end this too would provide an ugly controversy. "My remaining duty," Schönburg-Hartenstein wrote to his family, "is to preserve discipline and to protect the new Austria."[110]

On October 24, the long-awaited enemy attack came. The Entente armies in Italy launched an offensive along the entire front, with the main weight along the Piave in the vicinity of Vittorio Veneto. Fifty-one Italian, one Czecho-Slovak, and three French divisions were hurled against the Austro-Hungarian lines. For two days the *k.u.k.* front units fought back with astounding tenacity, but then the army began to melt away. Hungarian, Croatian, Czech, and finally even German-Austrian formations demanded to be transported home, refused to go into action, mutinied, and on occasion fought officers and still-loyal units.[111] Some Tyrolean regiments resisted until November 2, but by then the "*k.u.k.* army had ceased to be a military instrument."[112]

By October 25, Krobatin, speaking for Archduke Joseph, had called for the immediate conclusion of an armistice and on October 29, the Tyrolean Army Group command informed the *A.O.K.* that "only an unconditional cessation of hostilities, guarding the honor of our arms, can avoid a catastrophe."[113] That day Arz cabled Hindenburg that more than half of the Austro-Hungarian divisions in Italy refused to fight any longer and that the army was finished.[114] Allegations by some historians that an order to the Hungarian soldiers in Italy to return home at once "left gaps in the front which could no longer be plugged" are false.[115] To be sure, Béla Linder, war minister of the Hungarian National Council headed by Károlyi, which took over in Budapest on October 31, had in fact issued such an order on November 1, 1918.[116] But to be effective it had to be disseminated through command channels, and Arz refused to transmit it until Linder prevailed on the emperor by telephone to give his consent. Then the order went out, and on November 2 Linder and Waldstätten talked on the telephone and confirmed the arrangement.[117] While it may be possible that Charles was trying to separate Austrian from Hungarian affairs at this point, perhaps hoping to continue playing a political role in the kingdom, the message at this point had no effect on the tactical developments in Italy.

On November 2 the emperor, his advisors, and the *A.O.K.* were debating whether to accept the armistice negotiations offered by the Entente. Since early October a delegation of *k.u.k.* officials had been standing by for such negotiations and on October 31 the delegation, headed by General Viktor v. Weber, arrived at Italian headquarters in the Villa Giusti near Padua.[118] On the morning of November 2 they were given the terms which had to be accepted or rejected in their entirety. Austro-Hungarian troops were to cease fighting at once; the army was to be demobilized to a skeleton force of twenty divisions; half of its artillery was to be surrendered; all occupied territories were to be evacuated; all Entente prisoners of war were to be released at once, and the Entente was to have free access to all transportation facilities of the Dual Monarchy. The last point, obviously related to operations against Germany, was particularly disconcerting to the emperor and the military, who regarded it as incompatible with their honor.[119]

Charles discussed the problem with Arz, with the new German-Austrian Council of State, and with the former joint Austro-Hungarian ministers. Arz told him that he had no choice but to accept. The emperor tried to shift the odium of the armistice, especially that incurred by permitting Austria to become a possible base of operations against Germany, to the new Council of State, which refused. "We," Viktor Adler, the Social-Democratic leader pointed out, "did not make this war."[120] Still Charles dithered. There was talk about shifting the court to

Innsbruck and a telegram was drafted to William II assuring the "faithful friend" that if the Entente tried to invade Germany through the Tyrol, the emperor would place himself at the head of his German-Austrians and die sword in hand.[121] But all these dramatics could not change matters. Even as the discussions went on in Schönbrunn, the tense capital remained uneasily poised on the edge of revolution and anarchy, while in Italy men were dying in hopeless efforts to stem the enemy advance. Finally, still hoping to avoid responsibility, the emperor stepped down as supreme commander at about 2 a.m. on November 3, and pending the arrival of Feldmarschall Kövess, the senior general, handed over the army to Arz.[122] About an hour later orders went out to the troops to cease fighting at once.[123]

But then Charles reversed himself again. A last attempt to have the armistice ratified by the Council of State delayed transmission of the decision to Weber at Padua until 10 a.m. on November 3, and when the Italians finally signed at noon, they insisted, not unreasonably in view of the vast front, that it could only take effect in twenty-four hours. But the *A.O.K.* had not revoked its first order, and as a result the now-uncontested Italian advance netted some three hundred fifty thousand additional prisoners.[124] Allegations persisted that the *A.O.K.*, fearful of having the masses of armed and undisciplined soldiers flooding the country, preferred to have them taken prisoner.[125] The question cannot be resolved definitively. At best, as one writer maintains, there was a gross malfunction at the *A.O.K.*[126] On the other hand, there is evidence, particularly the signals from the Army Group Tyrol command, which pointed to the danger of having "masses of undisciplined and armed men" erupt into the country, and which claimed that "even captivity is a better fate than starvation or the ruin of all of the northern Tyrol."[127] But whether by command malfunction or deliberate design, the *k.u.k.* army deserved a better end. When the final tally was made, of the 8 million men mobilized in Austria-Hungary, 1,016,200 had died. In all, 518,000 were killed in action, 1,943,000 were wounded, and 1,691,000 were taken prisoners, of which some 480,000 died. The small regular officer corps lost 13.5 percent in action, while non-commissioned officers and enlisted men had 9.8 percent killed in action. Among the population groups, Southern Moravia lamented 44 killed for every thousand population, followed by Carinthia with 37 and the German Sudeten areas with 34 per thousand. Vorarlberg, Tyrol, Styria, and Salzburg had losses ranging between 30 and 34 per thousand. Upper and Lower Austria, including Vienna, suffered between 22 and 27 dead per thousand. Of the non-German peoples of the Dual Monarchy, the Magyars suffered the most, with 28 killed out of each thousand inhabitants.[128]

The remarkable thing was that the Habsburg army, shackled by a complicated and unsteady political and social structure, with an inefficient mechanism of coordination and control, had held out for so long. "It was," one Austrian historian wrote many years later, "a good army...and while there never was much faith in victory, it had good regimental spirit and comradeship. It fought for the honor of the flag, for its officers, perhaps even to earn a decoration."[129] These qualities, essentially those of a professional army, had sustained it throughout the eighteenth and the nineteenth centuries, and they had been adequate to support it for over four a half years of a conflict in which it fought on all fronts. Yet in the end all this was not quite enough.

15

Epilogue

Great wars usually do not end neatly with a cease-fire. The dissolution of government and armies and the attendant disruption of authority create a confused period before the new order takes firm hold. And so it was in November 1918. From Russia and the Balkans and above all from the southwestern front, hundreds of thousands of soldiers had only one thought—to get back to their homes. Magazines, supply dumps, depots, installations, guns, and equipment, all were abandoned in a mad scramble as a hungry, ragged, and largely undisciplined mass of troops poured into the rear areas. Every train was crammed with troops; thousands unable to push their way into the packed carriages travelled on the roofs, where hundreds were swept off and fell to their deaths in the alpine tunnels.[1] But some made their way back in formed units, bringing back their arms and equipment, and withstanding on occasion confrontation by local resistance groups acting in the name of the new national authorities.[2] The most sizable armed body still flying the ancient imperial-royal standard was Pflanzer-Baltin's army group in Albania, which, out of touch with events, was retreating towards the supposed safety of Cattaro. On November 1 its commander queried the A.O.K. about his future objective, but he received no reply; on the following day he recorded in his diary that "I have the uneasy feeling that everything is collapsing and for what purpose my army group remains in existence I do not know."[3] But, a soldier of many years, he carried on and when he finally was informed on November 5 that an armistice had been signed he refused to believe it. Only when he finally arrived in Cattaro and found it in the hands of the Yugoslav National Committee did he realize that it was all over. Even then, he held out for repatriation and, finally unable to keep his troops under discipline any longer, was evacuated by a French warship on November 18, 1918.

Austria-Hungary's imminent collapse also elicited a German reaction. In mid-October there were discussions about possible political and military interventions, either by imperial or state forces. General Cramon, the O.H.L. delegate at the A.O.K., suggested action in Bohemia by Prussian or Saxon forces, but the state officials were not prepared to do much.[4] By the end of the month the O.H.L. became concerned about the strategic alpine passes and made plans for their defense in case of an Austro-Hungarian collapse.[5] On November 8 some Bavarian battalions under General Krafft v. Dellmensingen actually appeared on the Brenner Pass, and the *A.O.K.* issued orders not to resist them, but to provide no aid and to inform then that "they were not welcome."[6] Two days later, with revolution at home, the Bavarians stuck red cockades in their caps and went home.

The imperial family still continued to live at Schönbrunn, but its security was becoming precarious. Thousands of soldiers, many of them armed, moved around Vienna and its vicinity; many tore the imperial emblem from their caps and there were some assaults on officers. The police worried about looting and a proletarian uprising.[7] At the same time, there were rumors about a possible monarchist countercoup. From Klagenfurt in Carinthia, where he had established his headquarters after a well-executed retreat from Italy, Feldmarschall Boroević put out feelers for possible action, but he did not receive any encouragement from the emperor.[8] In any case, it was dubious that troops for such an enterprise could be formed. "It was clear," Prince Schönburg-Hartenstein wrote, "that the country opposed the emperor and the field army and only formed units could have made any impression, and even this was doubtful. I saw no such units and neither Waldstätten nor Arz could tell me about them."[9] In fact, there were not enough soldiers to guard the imperial family. The always largely decorative noble guards, the *Arcièren Leibgarde,* had decamped in the first days of November.[10] Regular troops called for duty had disappeared and Schönbrunn palace was guarded by some two hundred men of the *Leibgarde Infantrie Kompanie,* inadequate for such a large object.[11] Therefore, though the military academies had been closed on November 2, two platoons of volunteers were formed from the cadets to help guard their former supreme commander.[12] On November 10, when news of Emperor William's flight reached Vienna, the leaders of the provisional Austrian government warned the emperor that they might no longer be able to provide for his security unless he announced his abdication. But Charles refused to do so even now. In the early morning hours of November 11, he signed a proclamation renouncing his share in the conduct of state affairs of German-Austria, and later that evening left the palace for the more remote castle of Eckartsau.

Just as the emperor did not formally abdicate his throne, neither did his army come to a formal end. At first the *A.O.K.* had remained in Baden, but the enlisted personnel refused to obey orders any longer, and on November 5 the last remaining officers removed themselves on the interurban train to Vienna.[13] After a number of moves, the *A.O.K.* found refuge at the War Archives. Here, surrounded by dusty records dating back to Maximilian I, in a building originally erected by Prince Eugene, obscurely hidden in one small room was the "supreme command of an army whose outposts, but a few weeks ago, had stood on the Italian plain, on the Sea of Azov, in Albania, and in France."[14]

Meanwhile the War Ministry continued to work out a demobilization scheme which never went into effect. On November 5, Stöger-Steiner, the last *k.u.k.* war minister, requested the emperor to sign a demobilization decree, placing the army on the twenty-division peace footing permitted by the armistice.[15] Of course, the army no longer existed and there is no documentary evidence that the emperor ever signed such an order. The Habsburg army, in fact, was not demobilized. It fragmented first along ethnic lines, and the fragments sought their native lands. Once home, the soldiers either dispersed or found themselves incorporated into new armies. The emperor also never said a formal farewell to his soldiers. A proclamation dated November 8 was drafted but never published. "A whole world of enemies has finally beaten us down," the draft read. "Though our sword is broken, our shield of honor remains untarnished. I always have looked for peace—peace both at home and abroad. As you return home to rebuild, may you rebuild together as you have fought together. My best wishes accompany you on your journey. May God be with you."[16]

But the unity of which Charles spoke failed to come. On November 7 Hungary, which had hoped to secure its own safety by cutting loose from the Dual Monarchy, was forced to sign a military convention at Belgrade which left her with only eight divisions and boundaries yet to be determined. Before the year was over, Carinthian volunteer units clashed with Slovene troops, and Czechs and Germans exchanged fire in the Sudeten area. The break up of the Habsburg Empire did not bring an era of national cooperation and amity to the Danubian region, and in later years there were many who regretted the passing of Habsburg rule. Political fragmentation was, of course, accompanied by military fragmentation, though the armies of the successor states had numerous personal, doctrinal, and material links in differing degrees with the former *k.u.k.* army.[17] Above all, as time passed and the memory of the bitter controversies of the past was replaced by the apprehensions of new controversies, many who had not been its supporters began to think better of it. Julius Deutsch, a leading Austrian Social Democrat, could write fondly of the tolerance accorded to dissidents in its ranks, and Professor Oskar Jászi, a prominent critic, conceded that the joint army handled national antagonisms in a "delicate and tactful way."[18]

Like all other national institutions, the Habsburg army was to a large degree the product of its historical experience. The evolution of the Habsburg Empire, its pluralistic composition, and its unique state concept were all mirrored in its army. To be sure, since the early eighteenth century the Habsburgs were moving toward greater centralization, but this goal, intermittently and sometimes half-heartedly pursued, was never wholly realized, and particularist national elements survived in considerable strength and gained renewed vigor in the latter part of the nineteenth century. The army, which in the Habsburg Empire never achieved separate or superior standing from the political authorities, served as an important factor in the unifying process and indeed after 1867 remained as one of the few institutions functioning in both halves of the monarchy. It never managed to fully accomplish the transition from a dynastic to a people's army, let alone a multinational force, but its very real achievements are reflected in the fact that this army went to war in 1914 lacking national cohesion and motivations and still "managed for over four years to maintain itself not only against a superior enemy, but also against internal nationality and social revolutionary currents."[19] It may have been concerned too much with tradition and too little with the future, but if it is true that armies always reflect the body politic of which they are a part, then to the extent that the predominating problems of the Habsburg Monarchy, and above all the problems of nationalism, could not be solved outside the army, they also could not be solved within.

While it existed, the army carried out its mission, did its duty, and remained faithful, and in the bitter end the army outlived the empire and the dynasty it had been meant to defend.

Notes

Sources

A listing of the collections, published or unpublished, as well as the numerous books I have read, most with profit though some without, would be entirely too cumbersome and I have provided complete citations in the notes. It seems, however, desirable to list a number of bibliographical tools which may be used as a starting point for further research.

The most important depository of materials on the Habsburg army is the Kriegsarchiv in Vienna. No serious work on the army can be done without this well-organized and highly cooperative institution whose holdings are summarized in Rainer Egger, "Das Kriegsarchiv Wien," *Militärgeschichtliche Mitteilungen,* 7(1970), 113–20; 8(1970), 167–75, and 9(1971), 173–81. For many years, official military history was written there, and the works published are listed in the *Inventar des Kriegsarchivs,* 2 vols. in 1 (Vienna, 1953), 2: 106–24. Most of these works are campaign histories, but some writing was done on institutional changes, reorganization, and other such matters. Apart from the multivolume campaign histories dealing with the seventeenth, eighteenth, and nineteenth centuries, the most outstanding work here is *Österreich-Ungarns Letzter Krieg 1914–1918,* 7 vols. and 10 suppls. (Vienna, 1930–1938). Both the merits and limitations of this set have been ably discussed by Kurt Peball, "Österreichische militärhistorische Forschung zum Ersten Weltkrieg zwischen 1918 und 1968," pp. 308–17 in Richard G. Plaschka and Karlheinz Mack, eds. *Die Auflösung des Habsburgerreiches* (Vienna, 1970).

A second important institution devoted to research in military history is the Kriegsgeschichtliche Museum in Vienna which has started to issue a most complete and up-to-date bibliography of all writing, Austrian as well as foreign, on the history of the Habsburg armies. The first list, Johann C. Allmayer-Beck and F. Fritz, "Verzeichnis der zwischen 1945 and 1966 erschienenen Arbeiten zur österreichischen Heeres-und Kriegsgeschichte von deren Anfängen bis 1938," *Schriften des Heeresgeschichtlichen Museum in Wien,* 3 (1967): 190–265, has been supplemented by several additions in subsequent volumes, including a complete bibliography on the Military Border, Kurt Wessely and Georg Zivković, "Bibliographie zur Geschichte der k.k. Militärgrenze," ibid., 6 (1973): 291–324. A recent American bibliography by Laszlo M. Alfodi, "The Armies of Austria-Hungary and Germany 1740–1914," U.S. Army Military History Research Collection, *Special Bibliographic Series,* no. 12 (April 1975), 1:94.

Standard bibliographies of the Habsburg monarchy include A. and M. Uhlirz, *Handbuch der Geschichte Österreichs und seiner Nebenländer Böhmen and Ungarn,* 3 vols. (Graz, 1937, with supplement 1941), and with a new 1968 edition, F. R. Bridge, *The Habsburg Monarchy 1804–1918* (London, 1968), and the continuing listing of recent works in the *Austrian History Yearbook,* published by Rice University.

Abbreviations

Archival material:
- AOK — Armee-Oberkommando
- CA — Conrad Archiv
- CK — Central Kanzlei
- FA — Feldakten
- Gstb. Op. B. — Generalsstab Operations Bureau
- HKR — Hofkriegsrat
- HKR Präs. — Hofkriegsrat Präsidialreihe
- HHStA — Haus, Hof-und Staatsarchiv
- KA — Kriegsarchiv
- Kdo — Kommando
- KM — Kriegsministerium, Kriegsminister
- Mem. — Memoires
- MK — Militärkanzlei
- MKFF — Militärkanzlei Franz Ferdinand
- MKSM — Militärkanzlei seiner Majestät
- RKM — Reichskriegsministerium, Reichskriegsminister

Printed materials:
- *JMH* — *Journal of Modern History*
- *MÖStA* — *Mitteilungen des österreichischen Staatsarchivs*
- *ÖIGL* — *Österreich in Geschichte und Literatur*
- *ÖMZ* — *Österreichische Militärische Zeitschrift*
- *ÖULK* — *Österreich-Ungarns Letzter Krieg 1914–1918*

Military ranks:
- FM — Feldmarschall
- GO — Generaloberst
- FZM — Feldzeugmeister
- GdK — General der Kavallerie
- GdI — General der Infantrie
- FML — Feldmarschall Leutnant
- GM — Generalmajor

Introduction

1. B. H. Liddell Hart, *The Real War: 1914–1918* (Boston, 1930), p. 39.
2. A. J. P. Taylor, *The Habsburg Monarchy: 1815–1918* (New York, 1965), p. 229.

1 The Evolution of an Army: Origins to Archduke Charles

1. Edmund Glaise-Horstenau, "Österreichs Wehrmacht im deutschen Schicksal," in *Österreich: Erbe und Sendung im Deutschen Raum*, eds. Josef Nadler and Heinrich v. Srbik (Salzburg-Leipzig, 1937) p. 207; Hans Meier-Welcker, *Deutsches Heerwesen im Wandel der Zeiten* (Frankfurt a.M., 1956), p. 18, and Walter Hummelberger, "Der Dreissigjährige Krieg und die Entstehung des kaiserlichen Heeres," in *Unser Heer*, eds. Herbert St. Fürlinger and Ludwig Jedlicka (Vienna, 1963), p. 3.

2. Alphons v. Wrede, *Geschichte der k.u.k. Wehrmacht,* 5 vols. (Vienna, 1893–1900), 5: 173–82. Documents in Karl Oberleitner, "Österreichs Finanzen und Kriegswesen unter Ferdinand I vom Jahre 1522–1564," *Archiv für Kunde Österreichischer Geschichtsquellen,* 22 (1860): 1–231. Discussion in Jürgen Zimmermann, *Militärverwaltung und Heeresaufbringung in Österreich bis 1806,* vol. 3 of *Handbuch zur deutschen Militärgeschichte 1648–1939* (Freiburg i. Br., 1965), pp. 9–27.

3. Gunther E. Rothenberg, *The Austrian Military Border in Croatia: 1522–1747* (Urbana, Ill., 1969), pp. 5–23.

4. Ibid., passim.

5. Oskar Regele, *Der österreichische Hofkriegsrat: 1556–1848* (Vienna, 1949), passim. Cf. Rothenberg, pp. 35–36 and the older literature cited there.

6. Ibid., pp. 47–49.

7. Bohdan Chudoba, *Spain and the Empire: 1519–1613* (Chicago, 1952).

8. Gordon A. Craig, "Command and Staff Problems in the Austrian Army, 1740–1866," in *War, Politics, and Diplomacy: Selected Essays* (New York, 1966), pp. 4–5.

9. Hugo Toman, *Das böhmische Staatsrecht und die Entwicklung der österreichischen Reichsidee vom Jahre 1527–1848* (Prague, 1872), pp. 32–36.

10. Wrede, 1: 13–14; Hermann Meynert, *Geschichte der k.k. österreichischen Armee,* 4 vols. (Vienna, 1854), 3: 37.

11. Regele, p. 12.

12. For Montecuccoli, see the forthcoming study by Thomas M. Barker, *Raimondo Montecuccoli and the Thirty Year's War,* which the author kindly allowed me to use.

13. Max Braubach, *Prinz Eugen von Savoyen,* 5 vols. (Munich, 1963–65), 5: 217, 230, and passim.

14. Thomas M. Barker, *Double Eagle and Crescent: Vienna's Second Turkish Siege in Its Historical Setting* (Albany, 1967), pp. 160, 207–208.

15. Alfred Arneth, *Prinz Eugen von Savoyen,* 3 vols. (Vienna, 1858), 1: 309–10; Selma Stern, *The Court Jew: A Contribution to the History of Absolutism in Central Europe* (Philadelphia, 1950), pp. 23–29.

16. KA Nachlass Montecuccoli (B/492). I am indebted to Professor Barker for this reference.

17. Béla K. Király, *Hungary in the Late Eighteenth Century* (New York, 1969), pp. 104–105.

18. Karl A. Roider, *The Reluctant Ally* (Baton Rouge, 1972), pp. 17–25.

19. From the collection of memoranda known as "Maria Theresa's Political Testament," published in *The Habsburg and Hohenzollern Dynasties in the Seventeenth and Eighteenth Centuries,* ed. C.A. Macartney (New York, 1970), pp. 130–31.

20. For a convenient summary of the Theresan reforms, see Johann C. Allmayer-Beck, "Wandlungen im Heerwesen zur Zeit Maria Theresia's, *Schriften des Heeresgeschichtlichen Museums in Wien,* 3 (1967): 7–24. For the Josephinian reforms see Edith Kotasek, *Feldmarschall Graf Lacy* (Horn, 1956), pp. 78–135. A summary of both periods can be found in Gustav A. Auffenberg-Komarow, "Das Zeitalter Maria Theresia's," pp. 108–68 in Fürlinger and Jedlicka.

21. KA Mem. IX–29.

22. Macartney, pp. 125–26.

23. Gunther E. Rothenberg, *The Military Border in Croatia: 1740–1881* (Chicago, 1966), pp. 18–29.

24. Király, pp. 173–87.

25. In general the following discussion is based on Gunther E. Rothenberg, "The Habsburg Army in the Napoleonic Wars," *Military Affairs,* 37 (1973): 1–5. Cf. Manfried Rauchensteiner, *Kaiser Franz und Erzherzog Carl* (Munich, 1972), pp. 17–111 passim for a discussion of the conflict between the monarch and his brother.

26. Peter Paret, *York and the Era of Prussian Reform* (Princeton, 1966), p. 199.
27. Cited in ibid., p. 201.
28. Király, pp. 187–90.

2 The Austrian Army in the Age of Metternich

A shorter version of this chapter appeared previously in *The Journal of Modern History* and is published here with the kind permission of the editors.

1. Cited by Kurt Peball, "Zum Kriegsbild der österreichischen Armee und seiner geschichtlichen Bedeutung in den Kriegen gegen die französische Revolution und Napoleon I," in Wolfgang v. Groote and Klaus-Jürgen Müller, *Napoleon I und das Militärwesen seiner Zeit* (Freiburg i. Br., 1968), p. 162.
2. Carl H. Hermann, *Deutsche Militärgeschichte* (Frankfurt a.M., 1966), p. 174.
3. Karl Fürst Schwarzenberg, *Feldmarschall Fürst Schwarzenberg* (Vienna, 1964), pp. 357–58.
4. Oskar Regele, *Feldmarschall Radetzky* (Vienna, 1957), pp. 217–18; Adolf Beer, *Die Finanzen Österreichs im 19. Jahrhundert* (Prague, 1877), pp. 134–36.
5. Gordon A. Craig, "Command and Staff Problems in the Austrian Army 1740–1866," in *The Theory and Practice of War*, ed. Michael Howard (New York, 1965), pp. 40–52; and Oskar Regele, *Der österreichische Hofkriegsrat 1556–1848* (Vienna, 1949), pp. 31–32.
6. FM Radetzky to FML Latour, Sep. 30, 1848, KA HKR Präs. 1848–216.
7. KA Mem. XI-96; Oskar Regele, *Generalstabschefs aus 4. Jahrhunderten* (Vienna-Munich, 1966), p. 27.
8. *Militär-Schematismus des österreichischen Kaiserthums* (Vienna, 1816), pp. 485–87.
9. KA Mem. XI-232 of 10 August 1835.
10. Ibid., XI-331 of 2 July 1835.
11. Ferdinand to Charles, 21 October 1835, cited in Regele, *Hofkriegsrat*, pp. 51–52.
12. Regele, *Radetzky*, p. 118.
13. Friedrich Fenner v. Fenneberg, *Österreich und seine Armee* (Leipzig, 1847), pp. 96–97. Overall see Nikolaus v. Preradovich, *Die Führungsschichten in Österreich und Preussen 1804–1918* (Wiesbaden, 1955), pp. 43–44, and Oscar Jaszi, *The Dissolution of the Habsburg Monarchy* (Chicago, 1929), p. 141.
14. See the accounts of Fenner, pp. 28–32; Wilhelm Ritter Gründorf v. Zebegény, *Memoiren eines österreichischen Generalstäblers 1832–1866* (Stuttgart, 1913), pp. 18–33; Anton Freiherr v. Mollinary, *46 Jahre im öesterreichungarischen Heere 1833–1879*, 2 vols. (Zurich, 1905), 1:5–31, and Moriz Edler v. Angeli, *Wien nach 1848* (Vienna, 1905), pp. 94–118. The title of the last work is misleading, as the book deals only in small part with Vienna after 1848. The major portion is devoted to a critical consideration of the Austrian army in the years 1840 to 1859. The author served in the Pioneer Corps, was later on staff duty, and finally became a well-known military historian.
15. Mollinary, 1:40–41; Angeli, pp. 121–27.
16. Fenner, pp. 170–76.
17. Schwarzenberg, p. 358; Angeli, pp. 140–49.
18. Ibid. pp. 133–34 estimates that a subaltern had to spend at least one-third of his pay on uniforms and equipment. Cf. Gründorf, pp. 36–37.
19. Schwarzenberg, pp. 358–59.
20. Compiled from the *Militär-Schematismus des österreichischen Kaiserthumes* (Vienna, 1847), passim.
21. Fenner, pp. 50–54.

22. Angeli, pp. 168–69, 181–83.
23. KA Mem. IX–211 of 12 May 1829.
24. Memo., 26 February 1810, KA HKR 1810 G 1-156/15.
25. Fenner, p. 53.
26. KA Mem. XI–281 of 22 February 1837.
27. Alphons Freiherr v. Wrede, *Geschichte der k.u.k. Wehrmacht*, 5 vols. (Vienna, 1893–1900), 1:48.
28. The article "Gedanken über Militärverfassung und stehende Heere," appeared in *Miszellen aus dem Gebiete der militärischen Wissenschaften* (Vienna, 1820), pp. 86–118; Radetzky's view in "Militärische Betrachtungen über die Lage Österreichs," KA Nachlass Radetzky (A/1) Lit. F–19. Cf. his memo of 1828 in Ernst Molden ed., *Radetzky-Sein Leben und Wirken* (Leipzig, 1916), p. 40.
29. Paul Müller, *F. M. Fürst Windischgrätz. Revolution und Gegenrevolution* (Vienna, 1934), p. 63.
30. KA Nachlass Radetzky (A/1) Lit. F–64.
31. Wrede, 1:105–108.
32. Mollinary, 1:33; Regele, *Radetzky*, p. 218, and KA (Kriegsgeschichtl. Abt. d. k.u.k. KA) *Sechzig Jahre Wehrmacht 1848–1908* (Vienna, 1908), pp. 18–19.
33. Fenner, pp. 297–305; Gründorf, pp. 51–52; Angeli, pp. 183–87, and Mollinary, 1:40–41.
34. KA Mem. XI–331.
35. Angeli, pp. 183–85.
36. KA, *Wehrmacht*, pp. 18–19.
37. Otto Stolz, *Wehrverfassung und Schützenwesen in Tirol* (Vienna-Munich, 1960).
38. Gunther E. Rothenberg, *The Military Border in Croatia: 1740–1881* (Chicago, 1966), pp. 122–42 and the literature cited there.
39. Maja Ludin, "Die Leibgarden am Wiener Hof," (Diss., University of Vienna, 1965), pp. 20–22.
40. Estimate by Rudolf Kiszling, *Die Revolution im Kaisertum Österreich 1848–1849*, 2 vols. (Vienna, 1948), 1:25.
41. M. v. Xylander, *Das Heer-Wesen der Staaten des deutschen Bundes* (Augsburg, 1842), pp. 4–25; Hermann, pp. 188–89, and Wrede, 1:48.
42. Angeli, p. 134.
43. Wrede, 1:18–19; Fenner, pp. 210–13.
44. Anton Dolleczek, *Geschichte der österreichischen Artillerie* (Vienna, 1887), pp. 324–26, and G. A. Jacobi, *Beschreibung des Materials und der Ausrüstung der k.k. österreichischen Feld-Artillerie* (Mainz, 1843).
45. Erich Gabriel, *Von der Luntenmuskete zum Sturmgewehr* (Vienna, 1967), pp. 16–18. The pill lock was invented in 1835 by Joseph Console of Milan and involved only minor modifications of the flintlock. The Augustin system introduced a cone to carry the explosion from the percussion pill to the main charge, making ignition more certain.
46. Regele, *Radetzky*, p. 246; Mollinary, 1:52–53. The system described by Karl v. Birago, *Untersuchungen über die europäischen Militärbrückentrains und Versuch einer verbesserten allen Forderungen entsprechenden Militärbrückeneinrichtung* (Vienna, 1839).
47. KA, *Wehrmacht*, p. 18.
48. Regele, *Radetzky*, p. 42, and Angeli, pp. 206–24.
49. *Exercir-Reglement für die k.k. Linien Infanterie 1844* (Vienna, 1844), pp. 217–18.
50. Fenner, pp. 14–16.
51. Archduke Charles to Archduke Albrecht, 18 June 1841, in Carl v. Duncker, *Feldmarschall Erzherzog Albrecht* (Vienna, 1897), p. 205.
52. Rothenberg, pp. 128–31.

53. Müller, p. 52.
54. Conventions of 3 December 1832 and 28 November 1840, KA MKSM Sonderreihe F 82 2/3.
55. Cited in Johann C. Allmayer-Beck, *Der Konservatismus in Österreich* (Munich, 1959), p. 17.
56. Regele, *Radetzky*, p. 217.
57. Eduard Ritter v. Steinitz, "Denkschrift über die Reichsbefestigung," KA MS Rb. pp. 27–53.
58. Regele, *Radetzky*, pp. 199–209.
59. "Maneuver-Instruction," 1831, KA Nachlass Radetzky (A/1) Lit. E–17, the first of many pieces on this subject.
60. Fenner, pp. 17–20.
61. Archduke Charles to Archduke Albrecht, 21 October 1840 in Duncker, p. 107.
62. Julius Miskolczy, *Ungarn in der Habsburger Monarchie* (Vienna, 1959), pp. 48–49, 81–83.
63. Fenner, pp. 84–96.
64. Circular HKR to all commands, Vienna, 5 and 18 November 1833, KA HKR Präs. 1833–1835.
65. Report GdK Ignaz Count Hardegg, Vienna, 13 February 1843, in Gyula Miskolczy, *A Horvát Kérdés*, 2 vols. (Budapest, 1928), 2:38–41. Cf. Rothenberg, pp. 140–42.
66. Gustav Amon v. Treuenfest, *Geschichte des k.k. Infantrieregimentes Hoch-und Deutschmeister Nr. 4* (Vienna, 1879), passim. Cf. KA, *Wehrmacht*, p. 20.
67. Compiled from the *Militärschematismus. . . 1847*.
68. Except for one gendarmerie regiment in Lombardy-Venetia and several small military police guard detachments (Militär-Polizeiwachen) in Vienna and other major cities, there existed no organized police units in the empire at this time. Franz Neubauer, *Die Gendarmerie in Österreich 1849–1924* (Vienna, 1924), pp. 28–31. Cf. Wrede, 1:48. On the general topic of the use of arms during military assistance to the civil power see August Wilfling, *Der administrative Waffengebrauch der öffentliche Wachorgane und des Heeres* (Vienna-Leipzig, 1909), pp. 196–97, 226–27, 245–47.
69. Anton Springer, *Geschichte Österreichs seit dem Wiener Frieden 1809*, 2 vols. (Leipzig, 1865–67), 2:114.
70. Report by Ban Haller in Miskolczy, *A Horvát Kérdés*, 2:304–305. The regiment, IR 43, from Padua, left thirteen dead and sixty-nine wounded and had to be transferred to Buda.
71. Oskar Regele, *Feldzeugmeister Benedek* (Vienna-Munich, 1960), pp. 32–39.
72. Regele, *Radetzky*, pp. 215–16.
73. KA FA 1834–1847, Armee in Italien 1847, F1/4. Cf. Josef A. Freiherr v. Helfert, *Geschichte der österreichischen Revolution*, 2 vols. (Freiburg-Vienna, 1907), 1:102–103, 113–14.
74. KA FA 1834–1837, Armee in Italien 1847, F 7/2 3, 11, and 12.
75. Ibid., F 7/4, 5, 6, and 7.
76. Radetzky to GdK Hardegg, HKR, 17 September 1847, Ibid., F 9/11.
77. Richard Prince Metternich-Winneburg ed., *Aus Metternich's nachgelassenen Papieren*, 8 vols. (Vienna, 1880–1884), 7:473.
78. Metternich to Fiquelmont, 15 October 1847, in Karl Obermann, "Unveröffentliche Materialien zur Diplomatie Metternichs 1821–1848," *MÖSTA*, 19 (1966), 250.
79. Metternich-Winneburg, 7:344.
80. Radetzky to HKR, 15 and 25 December 1847, KA FA 1834–1847, Armee in Italien 1847, F 12/8, 20.
81. Cited in *Carl F. v. Kübeck v. Kübau. Tagebücher*, ed. M. v. Kübau, 2 vols. (Vienna, 1909), 1:777.
82. Helfert, 1:135, 195.

3 Guardians of the Empire: The Army 1848–1849

1. KA (HKR) Präs. 1848–750. Cf. Heinrich Ritter v. Srbik, *Metternich: der Staatsmann und der Mensch*, 3 vols. (Munich, 1925–54), 2:247–50.
2. Carl v. Duncker, *Feldmarschall Erzherzog Albrecht* (Vienna, 1897), pp. 100–104. For the outbreak of fighting see Wilhelm Brinner, *Geschichte des k.k. Pionier-Regimentes*, 2 vols. (Vienna, 1878–81), 2:45–46. A short, if biased, account of military operations by Hugo Kerchnawe, *Die Überwindung der ersten Weltrevolution* (Innsbruck, 1932), pp. 12–17. R. John Rath, *The Viennese Revolution of 1848* (Austin, 1957), remains the standard political account.
3. Zanini, a self-made man who had risen from private to general, was one of the four non-aristocratic generals on active duty as of 1 January 1848. On that date a total of 253 generals were carried on the army list. KA (Kriegsgeschichtl. Abt. d. k.k. Kriegsarchivs), *Sechzig Jahre Wehrmacht 1848–1908* (Vienna, 1908), p. 4. Zanini's appointment in KA KM (MK) Präs. 1848–795.
4. Latour's appointment, ibid., 841. Discussion in Walter Wagner, *Geschichte des k.k. Kriegsministeriums I* (Graz-Cologne, 1966), pp. 11–16.
5. For an account of conditions in the HKR during this period of transition and for Latour's feelings see Wilhelm Weckbecker, *Von Maria Theresia zu Franz Joseph* (Berlin, 1929), pp. 61, 64–65, 156–57, and 167.
6. Heinrich Friedjung, *Österreich von 1848 bis 1860*, 2 vols. (Stuttgart-Berlin, 1912), 1:51.
7. Julius Miskolczy, *Ungarn in der Habsburger-Monarchie* (Vienna, 1959), pp. 94–96; Wagner, pp. 16–17.
8. KA KM (MK) Präs. 1848–918.
9. Ibid., 948 and 1444.
10. Rudolf Kiszling et al., *Die Revolution im Kaisertum Österreich 1848–1849*, 2 vols. (Vienna, 1948), 1:75–76.
11. See the discussion and citations in Gunther E. Rothenberg, *The Military Border in Croatia: 1740–1881* (Chicago, 1966), pp. 143–45.
12. Ibid., pp. 145–46.
13. Kiszling, 1:75. Cf. Lazar Mészáros, *Emlekiratai*, 2 vols. (Pest, 1866), 1:691.
14. Radetzky reports on the developments in Milan, 5 January 1848, KA FA 1848, Krieg in Italien-Hauptarmee, F 1/3. Cf. reports by GM Karl Graf Buol-Schauenstein, ambassador at Turin, 10 and 21 January 1848, ibid., 77. Cf. the letter by Lt. Col. Johann Count Wratislaw, Milan, 28 February 1848, printed in Joseph A. Freiherr v. Helfert, *Geschichte der österreichischen Revolution*, 2 vols. (Freiburg-Vienna, 1907), 1:490–91.
15. Proclamation printed in Duncker, p. 98.
16. Oskar Regele, *Feldmarschall Radetzky* (Vienna, 1957), pp. 251–52. On efforts to suborn Italian units see Helfert, 1:153, 195, and 321–22.
17. KA FA 1848, Krieg in Italien-Hauptarmee, F 1/90.
18. KA, *Der Feldzug der österreichischen Armee in Italien im Jahre 1848* (Vienna-Milan), part 1, 6–7. An official but slanted account. Cf. Hermann Kriebel, *Über die Bezwingung innerer Unruhen nach den Erfahrungen der Geschichte in der ersten Hälfte des XIX. Jahrhundertes* (Innsbruck, 1929), pp. 12–15.
19. Radetzky to GdK Fiquelmont, Pres. HKR, 19 and 22 March 1848, KA FA 1848, Krieg in Italien-Hauptarmee F 3/5 and 24 a, b, c. Report by FML Anton Ritter v. Martini, Venice, 22 March 1848, to Ficquelmont, ibid., 10 1–2. A detailed eye-witness account of the events in Venice in Daniel Freiherr v. Salis-Soglio, *Mein Leben und was ich davon erzählen will, kann, und darf*, 2 vols. (Stuttgart, 1908), 1:33–43. Cf. Kiszling, 1:94–101.
20. KA, *Feldzug . . . 1848*, part 1, 38–49.
21. For the desertions see among others Carl v. Prybila, *Geschichte des 27. Linien Infantrie Regimentes* (Vienna, 1853), pp. 133–37; C. J. Torreseni, *Erinnerungen eines*

Ordonnanzoffiziers Radetzky's (Vienna, 1904), pp. 15-17, and the report, Innsbruck, 5 April 1848, KA HKR (MK) 1848-538.

22. Gorzkowski to Radetzky, Mantua, 1 and 4 April 1848, KA FA, 1848, Krieg in Italien-Hauptarmee, F 4/19 and 27. There also is the anecdote, well-founded if not true, that when a nationalist citizen committee demanded that the general remove the cannon menacing the city, Gorzkowski replied in his broken Italian: "Mantovani buoni, Gorzkowski buono! Mantovani cattivi; Gorzkowski boom, boom, boom!" Cf. Eduard Stäger v. Waldburg, *Ereignisse in der Festung Mantua 1848* (Vienna, 1853), pp. 2-21.

23. Kiszling, 1:111.

24. KA, *Feldzug . . . 1848*, part 4, 1-32; Weckbecker, part 2, 156-57.

25. Kiszling, 1:121-22. Official battle reports in KA FA 1848, Krieg in Italien-Hauptarmee, F 5/122a, b, and c.

26. Helfert, 1:448-49; Paul Müller, *Feldmarschall Fürst Windischgrätz: Revolution und Gegenrevolution in Österreich* (Vienna, 1934), p. 110.

27. FML Graf Leopold Kolowrat-Krakowsky, *Meine Erinnerungen aus den Jahren 1848 und 1849*, 2 vols. (Vienna, 1905), 1:15-10, 62-63.

28. Müller, p. 110; Rothenberg, pp. 146-48; Wagner, pp. 21-23.

29. Ibid., p. 21.

30. Characterization by Joseph Redlich, *Emperor Francis Joseph of Austria* (New York, 1929), p. 25.

31. Ibid., p. 26; Müller, p. 128.

32. In general see Stanley Z. Pech, "The June Uprising in Prague in 1848," *East European Quarterly*, 1 (1968), 341-70, which also provides an excellent survey of the literature. By the same author, and with much additional material, *The Czech Revolution of 1848* (Durham, 1969). For Windischgrätz's military dispositions, see his orders of 3 to 5 June KA FA 1834-48, Juniereignisse in Prag, F 6/1.

33. Windischgrätz to Latour, Prague, 20 June 1848, ibid., 6/8.

34. Pech, *Czech Revolution*, p. 152.

35. A. J. P. Taylor, *The Habsburg Monarchy: 1809-1918* (New York, 1965), p. 69.

36. Ferdinand to Mészáros, Innsbruck, 8 June 1848 [Information copy] KA FA 1848, Krieg in Italien-Hauptarmee, F 6/33a. Cf. Rothenberg, pp. 147-49; Kiszling, 1:163-65, and Kolowrat-Krakowsky, 1:48-49.

37. Radetzky to Latour, 27 June 1848, KA FA 1848, Krieg in Italien-Hauptarmee, F 7/450.

38. Strength figures for the Hungarian forces vary considerably. Miskolczy, pp. 103-104, Kiszling, 1:173-74, and Kerchnawe, pp. 106-107, give numbers of up to seventy thousand trained men. On the other hand, Hungarian writers give a much lower figure. See George de Poor Handlery, "General Arthur Görgey and the Hungarian Revolution of 1848-49," (Ph.D. diss., University of Oregon, 1968), pp. 78-79.

39. KA, *Wehrmacht*, p. 6.

40. Kiszling, 1:263-68; Anton Springer, *Geschichte Oesterreichs seit dem Wiener Frieden 1809*, 2 vols. (Leipzig, 1863-65), 2:493-95.

41. Ferdinand to Jelačić, KA FA 1848, Jellachich, F 9/7-1/2.

42. Rothenberg, p. 152.

43. Handlery, pp. 68-70. Cf. Alfons Danzer, *Dembinszki* (Budapest, 1874), pp. 64-65.

44. Cited by Springer, 2:553.

45. Rothenberg, p. 154.

46. Springer, 2:548-59.

47. Ibid., pp. 516-17.

48. Radetzky to Latour, Milan, 30 September 1848, KA KM (MK) Pras. 1848-5299.

49. Cited in Müller, p. 126.

50. Windischgrätz, movement orders, KA FA 1834-1848, Cernierung Wien's 1848, F

10/60-14. On attempts by railroad workers to delay the movement see Kolowrat-Krakowsky, 2:30-31.

51. FML Karl Count Auersperg, commanding officer Vienna, reports evacuation, KA FA 1834, Cernierung Wien's 1848, F 10/60—15, and the arrival of Jelačić, ibid., 18.
52. Rath, pp. 335-55; Kiszling, 1:293.
53. Assault described in Rath, pp. 355-58. On the encounter at Schwechat see J. G. Horn, *Arthur Görgey, Oberkommandant der Ungarischen Armee* (Leipzig, 1850), pp. 31-35.
54. Handlery, pp. 77-79.
55. Moriz Edler v. Angeli, *Wien nach 1848* (Vienna, 1905), pp. 3-28. Though forty-six hundred suspects were arrested and held for investigation, there were only twenty-six executions. Cf. Josef K. Mayr ed., *Das Tagebuch des Polizeiministers Kempen von 1848 bis 1859* (Vienna, 1931), p. 15, and Müller, p. 160. Even the liberal American chargé d'affaires in Vienna, William H. Stiles, conceded that reprisals had been few. See his *Austria in 1848-49*, 2 vols. (New York, 1852), 1:138-39. The figure does, however, exclude the considerable number of civilians killed during the fighting.
56. KA FA 1848, Gouvernment Wien unter Welden, F 11/1.
57. Kiszling, 1:297-302; Müller, p. 165, and Friedjung, 1:92-93.
58. E. Andics, *Das Bündnis Habsburg-Romanow* (Budapest, 1963), p. 92, and Springer, 2:591-92.
59. Schwarzenberg to Radetzky, 22 October 1848, HHStA, Korrespondenz Schwarzenberg mit verschiedenen Generalen, F 9/12.
60. Redlich, pp. 22-24.
61. Walter Rogge, *Oesterreich von Világos bis zur Gegenwart*, 3 vols. (Leipzig-Vienna, 1872-73), 1:54-55.
62. Redlich, pp. 22-23.
63. Kiszling, 2:6-7; Müller, pp. 179-83.
64. Handlery, pp. 81-84.
65. Anon. *Der Winter-Feldzug 1848-1849 in Ungarn. Unter dem Oberkommando des Feldmarschalls Fürsten zu Windischgrätz* (Vienna, 1851), pp. 21-28.
66. Dispositions for the attack, 4 January 1849, KA FA 1849, Krieg in Ungarn-Hauptarmee, F 1/26a-d. Report on the occupation of the city, 5 January 1849, ibid., 36.
67. Ibid., 177 1/3. Cf. Friedjung, 1:131-32.
68. Windischgrätz to Francis Joseph, 27 February 1849, KA FA 1849, Krieg in Ungarn-Hauptarmee, F 2/26. Cf. Kiszling, 2:53-55.
69. Springer, 2:700.
70. Ludwig v. Welden, *Episoden aus meinem Leben. Beiträge zur Geschichte der Feldzüge der österreichischen Armee in den Jahren 1848 u. 1849*, 2nd ed. (Graz, 1853), p. 72-3.
71. Windischgrätz to FZM Nugent, 15 March 1849, KA FA 1849, Krieg in Ungarn-Hauptarmee, F 3/166 a-c; the Hungarian offensive discussed in Handlery, pp. 142-55.
72. Görgey's proclamation, 8 April 1849, enclosed in KA FA 1849. Krieg in Ungarn-Hauptarmee, F 4/89-1/2.
73. Windischgrätz to Francis Joseph, 10 April 1849, ibid., F 4/147.
74. See the "Anträge welche Welden stellt im Fall das ihm das Oberkommando der in Ungarn und Siebenbürgen stehenden Truppen anvertraut werden sollte," 11 April 1849, ibid., F 4/136. Cf. Welden to War Minister Cordon, 21 April 1849, HHStA Kriegsakten, F 512. Also Müller, 227-28, and Friedjung, 1:204.
75. Redlich, p. 53; Adolph Schwarzenberg, *Prince Felix zu Schwarzenberg, Prime Minister of Austria, 1848-1852* (New York, 1946), pp. 51-52.
76. Hübner's report to the council of ministers and excerpts from the council protocol in Hugo Kerchnawe, *Radetzky* (Prague, 1944), pp. 368-75.

77. KA FA 1849, Krieg in Ungarn-Hauptarmee, F 4/199.
78. Circular, 30 April 1849, KA MKSM 1849-1371.
79. KA FA 1849, Krieg in Ungarn-Hauptarmee, F 4/211, 212.
80. Horn, pp. 82, 88, and W. Rüstow, *Geschichte des Ungarischen Insurrektionskrieges in den Jahren 1848 und 1849*, 2 vols. (Zurich, 1860), 2:47.
81. Appointment of Haynau, KA FA 1849, Krieg in Ungarn-Hauptarmee, F 5/706.
82. KA FA 1849, Krieg in Italien-Hauptarmee, F 3/121, 175, and 278.
83. Regele, pp. 296-99.
84. Report on capitulation, KA FA 1849, Krieg in Italien-Hauptarmee, F 8/108.
85. Pech, *Czech Revolution,* pp. 252-53.
86. Andics, p. 154.
87. HHStA, Kriegsakten F 512, Feldzug in Ungarn, Windischgrätz's letter of 13 January 1849; for Welden's appeal see Friedrich Walter, ed., *Aus dem Nachlass des Freiherrn Carl Friedrich Kübeck von Kübau* (Graz-Cologne, 1960), pp. 23-24.
88. Schwarzenberg, p. 53.
89. Helfert, 1:383-84; Handlery, pp. 199-201.
90. Andics, pp. 186-91.
91. Schwarzenberg (copy), KA FA 1849, Krieg in Ungarn-Hauptarmee unter Haynau, F 5/723.
92. Kiszling, 2:161-64, and John S. Curtiss, *The Russian Army under Nicholas I: 1825-1855* (Durham, N.C., 1965), pp. 306-309.
93. FML Haynau to Francis Joseph, 21 June 1849, KA FA 1849, Krieg in Ungarn-Hauptarmee unter Haynau, F 6/346.
94. Arthur v. Görgey, *Mein Leben und Wirken in Ungarn in den Jahren 1848 und 1849*, 2 vols. (Leipzig, 1852), 2:437, and Haynau to Schwarzenberg, 24 November 1849, HHStA, Nachlass Schwarzenberg, Cart. 10, F 3/156.
95. Haynau to Radetzky, 2 September 1849, KA FA 1849, Krieg in Ungarn-Hauptarmee unter Haynau, F 8/510-1/2.
96. Weckbecker, pp. 177-78.
97. KM to Haynau, KA KM (MK) Pras. 1849-6794.
98. Included among the thirteen were Count Karl v. Leiningen, a cousin of Queen Victoria, two Serbs, Damjanich and Knezics, and one Austrian, Polterling. On the reprisals and reactions see Rogge, 1:154-58; Freidjung, *Österreich,* 1:220-27, and Miskolczy, pp. 116-19.
99. Schwarzenberg, pp. 55-56.
100. A. Schütte, *Ungarn und der Ungarische Unabhängigkeitskrieg,* 2 vols. (Leipzig, 1850), 1:170.
101. Rothenberg, pp. 158-59.
102. Kiszling, 2:293-94.
103. Angeli, pp. 14-16.
104. Regele, p. 351; KA, *Sechzig Jahre Wehrmacht,* pp. 37-38.

4 The Emperor's Personal Command: 1849-1859

1. Friedrich Walter, ed., *Aus dem Nachlass des Freiherrn Carl Friedrich Kübeck von Kübau* (Graz-Cologne, 1960), p. 34.
2. Cited in Egon C. Conte Corti, *Mensch und Herrscher* (Graz-Vienna, 1952), p. 27. Even after many years as a ruler, Francis Joseph could still fly into a towering rage about a misplaced button on a uniform or when a tired detachment did not pass the saluting base as smartly as he required. Lt. Gen. Baron Margutti, *The Emperor Francis Joseph and His Times* (New York, 1921), pp. 38-39. Cf. Johann C. Allmayer-Beck, "Das Heerwesen," in

Friedrich Engel-Janosi and Helmut Rumpler, eds., *Probleme der Franzisko-Josephinischen Zeit 1848-1916* (Vienna, 1967), pp. 67-69.
 3. Joseph Redlich, *Emperor Francis Joseph of Austria* (New York, 1929), pp. 88-89, and Heinrich Friedjung, *Österreich von 1848 bis 1860*, 2 vols. (Stuttgart-Berlin, 1908), 2:263-68.
 4. Redlich, pp. 43-45, 91-92; Corti, pp. 6-7, and the discussion in Walter Wagner, *Geschichte des k.k. Kriegsministeriums 1848-1866 I* (Graz-Cologne, 1966), pp. 32-33.
 5. KA MKSM 1849-37c.
 6. Francis Joseph to GM Cordon, 4 March 1849, KA MKSM 1849-171.
 7. Franz Schnürer, ed., *Briefe Kaiser Franz Joseph I und seine Mutter* (Munich, 1930), p. 131.
 8. Wagner, p. 39; KA MKSM 1849-915-1/2.
 9. Wagner, pp. 127-28.
 10. For the relief of Haynau see Friedrich Walter, "Von Windischgrätz über Welden zu Haynau," in *Die Nationalitätenfrage im alten Ungarn und die Südostpolitik Wiens*, eds. F. Walter and Harold Steinacker, (Munich, 1959), pp. 126-57; for the complaints about Radetzky's "senile regime," see Schnürer, pp. 258-59. Cf. Friedjung, 2:263.
 11. Wagner, p. 36; Josef K. Mayr, ed., *Das Tagebuch des Polizeiministers Kempen von 1848 bis 1859* (Vienna-Leipzig, 1931), p. 44. Gyulai's appointment, 2 June 1849, KA KM Präs. (MK) 1849-4052.
 12. Friedjung, 2:263-65; Wagner, pp. 57-60.
 13. Ibid., pp. 79-80.
 14. KA MKSM (MZK) 1853-2008.
 15. Redlich, p. 91, and Friedjung, 2:268.
 16. Gordon A. Craig, "Command and Staff Problems in the Austrian Army, 1740-1866," in *War, Politics, and Diplomacy* (New York, 1966), p. 12.
 17. Proposals, curriculum, and other materials, KA Mem. XI-181,2,3.
 18. Edmund v. Glaise-Horstenau, *Franz Josephs Weggefährte* (Zurich-Vienna, 1930), pp. 31-32.
 19. Order establishing the new corps, 14 February 1856, KA MKSM 1856-119.
 20. Anton Freiherr v. Mollinary, *46 Jahre im österreich-ungarischen Heere*, 2 vols. (Zurich, 1905), 1:250-51; 2:60-61. Cf. John Presland, *Vae Victis: The Life of Ludwig von Benedek* (New York, 1934), pp. 165-66.
 21. K.K. Direktion der Administrativen Statistik, *Statistisches Handbüchlein für die Oesterreichische Monarchie* (Vienna, 1854), p. 311. Cf. Friedjung, 1:244. See Mayr, pp. 147, 448-49, on the conflicts between the soldiers and the finance ministers.
 22. C. A. Macartney, *The Habsburg Empire: 1790-1918* (London, 1968), pp. 468-70, 485-86.
 23. Related by Col. Moriz Edler v. Angeli, *Wien nach 1848* (Vienna, 1905), pp. 142-43.
 24. Overall see Nikolaus v. Preradovich, *Die Führungsschichten in Österreich und Preussen, 1804-1918* (Wiesbaden, 1955), pp. 44-45. The Prussian observer, Prince Kraft zu Hohenlohe-Ingelfingen, *Aus meinem Leben*, 4 vols. (Berlin, 1897-1907), 1:259.
 25. Schnürer, p. 232.
 26. Order, 31 May 1852, KA MKSM Sonderfasz. 30.
 27. KA (Kriegsgeschichtl. Abt. d. k.k. KA) *Sechzig Jahre Wehrmacht 1848-1908* (Vienna, 1908), pp. 42-44.
 28. Ibid., p. 40.
 29. Details of army organization see order of 16 October 1849, KA KM Präs. (MK) 1849-25, and modifications of 3 August 1852 KA MKSM Sonderfasz. 30.
 30. Gunther E. Rothenberg, *The Military Border in Croatia: 1740-1881* (Chicago, 1966), pp. 155-59.
 31. KA, *Wehrmacht*, pp. 80-81. The combat effectiveness of this army had declined since 1849. See Oskar Regele, *Feldzeugmeister Benedek* (Vienna, 1960), pp. 109-11.

32. KA, *Wehrmacht,* p. 42.
33. F. Schmitt, *Statistik des österreichischen Kaiserstaates* (Vienna, 1854), pp. 303–304.
34. Rothenberg, p. 181.
35. KA, *Wehrmacht,* pp. 51–53. Cf. the report by Maj. R. Delafield, U.S. Army, "The Art of War in Europe," U. S. Senate, 1st Sess., 36th Congress, Senate Documents (Washington, D.C., 1860), pp. 6–7. The Lorenz rifle is described in A.B.M. *Das kaiserlich-königliche österr. Infanterie-Feuergewehr* (Vienna, 1856).
36. Schmitt, pp. 303–304.
37. KA, *Wehrmacht,* pp. 59–61.
38. See order of 3 August 1852, KA MKSM Sonderfasz. 30, and Radetzky's complaints about lack of battle cavalry with the other corps, KA Radetzky Nachlass (A/1) Lit. F-31 of 1853.
39. Anton Dolleczek, *Geschichte der österreichischen Artillerie* (Vienna, 1887), pp. 403–12.
40. Wilhelm Ritter Gründorf v. Zebégeny, *Memoiren eines österreichischen Generalstäblers 1832–1866* (Stuttgart, 1913), pp. 39–43 and Hugo Kerchnawe, *225 Jahre Technische Militärakademie 1717 bis 1942* (Vienna, 1942), p. 11.
41. KA, *Wehrmacht,* pp. 67–69.
42. KA AOK Präs. 1857-1066.
43. Friedrich Engels, *Ausgewählte militärische Schriften,* 2 vols. (Berlin-East, 1958–64), 1:425.
44. Hohenlohe-Ingelfingen, 1:280–84; Mollinary, 2:5,11.
45. Hans Delbrück et al., *Geschichte der Kriegskunst im Rahmen der politischen Geschichte,* 7 vols. (Berlin, 1900–1937), 5:229–30.
46. Rudolf Kiszling et al., *Die Revolution im Kaisertum Österreich,* 2 vols. (Vienna, 1948), 2:311; Mayr, p. 300.
47. Angeli, pp. 4–21; Walter Rogge, *Oesterreich von Világos bis zur Gegenwart,* 3 vols. (Leipzig-Vienna, 1872–73), 1:90–92.
48. Letter cited in Jean de Bourgoing ed., *Briefe Kaiser Franz Josephs an Frau Katherina Schratt* (Vienna, 1949), p. 15. Cf. Rogge, 1:105–106.
49. Ilsa Barea, *Vienna: Legend and Reality* (London, 1966), pp. 235–37, and Walter Wagner, "Die Stellungnahme der Militär-Behörden zur Wiener Stadterweiterung in den Jahren 1848–1857," *Jahrbuch des Vereins für Geschichte der Stadt Wien,* 17–18 (1961/62): 216–85.
50. Delafield, p. 261.
51. Instructions of 28 February 1857, updating instructions of 1853. KA KM Präs. 1857–460.
52. Archduke Wilhelm to all commanding generals, 7 November 1859, KA KM Präs. 1859–7615.
53. Mayr, p. 24.
54. Angeli, pp. 9–11.
55. Mayr, p. 27.
56. Ibid., pp. 27–29, and Rogge, 1:98–99. For a more favorable view see Franz Neubauer, *Die Gendarmerie in Österreich 1849–1924* (Vienna, 1924), pp. 35–41.
57. Engels, 1:426.
58. Eduard Bartels Ritter v. Bartberg, *Der Krieg im Jahre 1859* (Bamberg, 1894), pp. 6–8.
59. Julius Miskolczy, *Ungarn in der Habsburger-Monarchie* (Vienna-Munich, 1959), pp. 120–23.
60. Angeli, pp. 59–61. KM Gyulai issued instructions "that all officers always must remember that the amnesty can only become effective ... if special care is exercised to avoid all insults and defamations ... and every effort is made to achieve complete reconcil-

iation and reintegration of these troops." Order of September 1849, cited in Friedjung, 1:253–54.

61. Rothenberg, pp. 158–62.
62. FML Leopold Graf Kolowrat-Krakowsky, *Meine Erinnerungen aus den Jahren 1848 und 1849*, 2 vols. (Vienna, 1905), 2:52–54.
63. Walter, p. 52.
64. Rogge, 1:298–99; Regele, p. 343.
65. KA Radetzky Nachlass (A/1) Lit. B-10.
66. Hess to Schwarzenberg, 20 December 1849, "Memoire über einen eventuellen Krieg mit Preussen," KA Nachlass Hess.
67. KA FA Böhmen und Mähren 1850, F 12/162 and F 16/2–3.
68. Schwarzenberg to Hess, 9 and 18 April 1850, ibid., F 4/5 a, b, c.
69. Adolph Schwarzenberg, *Prince Felix zu Schwarzenberg* (New York, 1946), p. 160.
70. Erich-Günter Blau, *Die Wiener Militärkonferenzen im Oktober 1850* (Munich, 1933), pp. 9–21.
71. Regele, p. 371; KA, *Wehrmacht*, p. 87; Friedjung, 2:106–12.
72. Alfred Vagts, *Defense and Diplomacy* (New York, 1956), p. 24, and Gordon A. Craig, *The Politics of the Prussian Army 1640–1945* (New York, 1964), pp. 131–32.
73. KA Mem. XI-303, December 1850, "Operative Aussichten bei einem Krieg gegen Preussen." Cf. Blau, pp. 36–40.
74. Documents in KA MKSM Sonderfasz. 82/107–11. The Prussian point of view and documents are in Heinrich v. Poschinger, *Preussens auswärtige Politik 1850–1858*, 3 vols. (Berlin, 1902), 2:155–56. Hess's appraisal is in his letter to Schwarzenberg, 18 November 1851, KA MKSM Sonderfasz. 82/7.
75. Oskar Regele, *Feldmarschall Radetzky* (Vienna, 1957), pp. 90, 201–202.
76. Wilhelm Weckbecker, *Von Maria Theresia zu Franz Joseph* (Berlin, 1929), pp. 196–97.
77. Rothenberg, p. 66, and Franz Zwitter et al., *Les problèmes nationaux dans la monarchie des Habsbourgs* (Belgrade, 1960), pp. 48–49.
78. Paul W. Schroeder, *Austria, Great Britain and the Crimean War* (Ithaca, N.Y., 1972), pp. 14–15.
79. Cited in Eduard Heller, *Mitteleuropas Vorkämpfer: Fürst Schwarzenberg* (Vienna, 1933), p. 171.
80. A.J.P. Taylor, *The Struggle for Mastery in Europe* (Oxford, 1954), pp. 51–52.
81. KA Schriftgut Militärgrenze, "Serbisch-Banater Armee Korps," pp. 87–90, 131–37.
82. Schroeder, pp. 143–68, provides the most recent and persuasive discussion. Cf. Franz Eckhardt, *Die Deutsche Frage und der Krimkrieg* (Berlin-Königsberg, 1931), pp. 48–54. For Buol's alleged support by press and stock-exchange, see Walter, *Nachlass*, p. 137.
83. Hess to Francis Joseph, memorandum of 25 March 1854, KA FA 1854 13/181. Extensive discussion is in Paul W. Schroeder, "A Turning Point in Austrian Policy in the Crimean War: The Conferences of March 1854," *Austrian History Yearbook*, 4–5 (1970): 159–203.
84. Schroeder, *Austria*, pp. 155–56.
85. Ibid., pp. 162–68. The convention and other documents are in KA MKSM Sonderfasz. 82-11/12.
86. Proposed order of battle, 28 March 1854, KA KM Präs (CK) 1854–1012, copy in MKSM Sonderfasz. 30.
87. KA FA 1854–55, Oberkommando der III and IV Armee unter Hess, F 5/3. Cf. Heinrich Friedjung, *Der Krimkrieg und die österreichische Politik* (Stuttgart-Berlin, 1907), pp. 60–69.
88. Redlich, p. 181; Corti, pp. 153–52; Mayr, 330–39.

89. Radetzky to Francis Joseph, 5 August 1854, KA Nachlass Radetzky (A/2) B-15.
90. "Operationsverhältnisse Österrichs und Russland," (prepared by GM Nagy), KA FA 1854–55, Oberkommando der III und IV Armee unter Hess, F 13/133. Cf. Friedjung, *Krimkrieg*, pp. 77–78.
91. Ibid., pp. 97–99; Francis Joseph to Archduchess Sophia, Schnürer, pp. 232–33.
92. "Vortrag des treugehorsamsten Oberkommandanten der III und IV Armee," KA MKSM Sonderreihe F 73/18.
93. Walter, Nachlass, p. 162, Mayr, p. 346, and Schroeder, *Austria*, pp. 221–22.
94. Friedjung, *Krimkrieg*, pp. 116–17.
95. See the vivid account by Moriz Edler v. Angeli, *Altes Eisen* (Stuttgart, 1900), pp. 96–107.
96. Redlich, pp. 151–52.
97. Regele, *Benedek*, pp. 346–52.
98. KA, *Wehrmacht*, p. 88.
99. Craig, p. 16.
100. Compare Regele, *Benedek*, pp. 124–27 with Vagts, p. 497, and Charles W. Hallberg, *Franz Joseph and Napoleon III: 1852–1864* (New York, 1955), pp. 190–92.
101. For an account of the ministerial conferences, see the protocols 5 January to 27 April 1859, KA MKSM Sonderreihe F 7.
102. Ibid., protocol of 27 April 1859. Cf. Corti, pp. 220–21.
103. Thus told by Friedrich Ferdinand Graf v. Beust, *Aus drei Vierteljahrhunderten*, 2 vols. (Stuttgart, 1887), 2:343.
104. See the observations of FML Anton Freiherr von Bils, KA Mem. III–126, and above all Gyulai's apologetic "Denkschrift über mein Armee Kommando in Italien von Ende April bis Mitte June 1859," KA MKSM Sonderreihe F 7/10.
105. Daniel Freiherr v. Salis-Soglio, *Mein Leben und was ich davon erzählen will, kann, und darf*, 2 vols. (Stuttgart, 1908), 1:117.
106. Gyulai to AOK, 3 May 1859, KA MKSM Sonderreihe F 7/362.
107. Bartels, pp. 58–61.
108. Gyulai to AOK, 27 May 1859, KA MKSM Sonderreihe F 7/431.
109. Craig, p. 18, but compare Regele, *Benedek*, p. 143.
110. Mollinary, 2:45–47, 60–64, and Bartels, p. 161.
111. Paul Schmitthenner, *Politik und Kriegsführung in der neueren Geschichte* (Hamburg, 1937), pp. 249–50, and Heinrich Friedjung, *Der Kampf um die Vorherrschaft in Deutschland 1859 bis 1866*, 2 vols., 9th ed. (Stuttgart-Berlin, 1916), 1:31–32.
112. Rothenberg, pp. 162–64.
113. Angelo Tamborra, *Cavour e i Balcani* (Turin, 1958), pp. 212–20; Attilio Vigevano, *La Legione Ungherese in Italia, 1859–1867* (Rome, 1924), pp. 47–50; and Albert de Berzeviczy, "L'émigration hongroise et la campagne d'Italie en 1859," *Revue des Études Hongroises et Finno-Ougriennes*, 4 (1926): 129–47.
114. Cited in H. Helmert, *Militärsystem und Streitkräfte im deutschen Bund am Vorabend des preussisch-österreichischen Krieges von 1866* (Berlin-Potsdam, 1964), p. 168 n.1.
115. Macartney, p. 493.
116. Friedjung, *Kampf*, 1:31–32; Rogge, 1:300–301, and Mayr, 516, 521.
117. Bartels, p. 261.

5 The End of an Age: 1860–1866

1. Carl Freiherr v. Bardolff, *Soldat im alten Österreich* (Jena, 1938) pp. 73–74.
2. Joseph Redlich, *Emperor Francis Joseph of Austria* (New York, 1929), p. 105.
3. Wilhelm Rüstow, *Der italienische Krieg 1859 politisch-militärisch beschrieben* (Zurich, 1859), pp. 81–82.

4. Kurt Peball, "Sendung und Erbe. Die österreichische Armee und das Schicksalsjahr der Donaumonarchie 1866," special issue *ÖMZ*, November 1966, pp. 57–58.
5. Archduke Albrecht to Crenneville, 5 November 1862, in Heinrich v. Srbik, *Aus Österreichs Vergangenheit* (Salzburg, 1949), pp. 138–40.
6. Ibid., pp. 112–21. For the citation see Benedek's circular of 24 March 1861, in *Benedeks nachgelassene Papiere*, ed. Heinrich Friedjung (Leipzig, 1901), pp. 279–82.
7. Oskar Regele, *Feldzeugmeister Benedek* (Vienna-Munich, 1960), pp. 212–15. Cf. Anton Freiherr v. Mollinary, *46 Jahre im österreich-ungarischen Heere 1833–1879*, 2 vols. (Zurich, 1905), 2:93–94.
8. Peball, p. 64.
9. Heinz Helmert, *Militärsystem und Streitkräfte im deutschen Bund am Vorabend des preussisch-österreichischen Krieges von 1866* (Berlin-Potsdam, 1964), pp. 173–74.
10. Regele, pp. 222–26.
11. K. K. Statistische Central-Commission, *Statistisches Jahrbuch der oesterreichischen Monarchie für das Jahr 1866* (Vienna, 1868), pp. 403–404. Cf. Regele, pp. 311–26.
12. Hugo Kerchnawe, *Die Vorgeschichte von 1866 und 19??* (Vienna, 1909), passim. A. Regele, pp. 358–63.
13. Helmert, p. 147, and Walter Rogge, *Oesterreich von Világos bis zur Gegenwart*, 2 vols. (Leipzig-Vienna, 1873), 2:165.
14. Ibid., 36–37. Records of the Eynatten case, KA AOK Präs., 1860–3027.
15. Friedrich Engels, unsigned article, *Manchester Guardian*, 20 June 1866.
16. KA KM (CK) 1862–2335 cited by Helmert, p. 157.
17. Benedek's memo on situation in Hungary, August 1860, in Friedjung, *Papiere*, pp. 271–75: Francis Joseph to Benedek, 23 July 1860, KA MKSM 1860–2881.
18. Gunther E. Rothenberg, *The Military Border in Croatia: 1740*–1881 (Chicago, 1966), pp. 164–65.
19. I. Pavlović, "Vojna granica i srpska vojska," *Glasnik Istorijskog društva*, 9 (1936): 335–46.
20. See the articles by Richard Blaas, "Österreich und die Einigung Italiens zwischen den Konferenzen von Teplitz und Warschau," *MÖStA*, 21 (1968): 251–330, and "Vom Friauler Putsch im Herbst 1864 bis zur Abtretung Venetiens 1866," ibid., 19 (1966): 264–338.
21. On Crenneville see Srbik, pp. 116–17. A critical view in Anon. (Bartels v. Bartberg), *Oesterreich und sein Heer* (Leipzig, 1866), pp. 6–7.
22. Mollinary, 2:78.
23. Walter Wagner, *Geschichte des K.K. Kriegsministeriums I* (Graz-Cologne, 1966), pp. 174–76.
24. Regele, pp. 162–70.
25. Mollinary, 2:80–81.
26. Friedjung, *Papiere*, p. 76.
27. Ibid., pp. 301–303, and John Presland, *Vae Victis: The Life of Ludwig von Benedek* (New York, 1934), pp. 179–81.
28. Wagner, pp. 192–93; Regele, pp. 167–68.
29. L. v. M., "Über den Einfluss der Eisenbahnen und Telegraphen auf die Kriegsoperationen." *ÖMZ*, 2 (1860): 148–54.
30. Edmund v. Glaise-Horstenau, *Franz Josephs Weggefährte* (Zurich-Vienna, 1930), pp. 70–71.
31. Benedek to Crenneville, 3 April 1863, in Preland, p. 209.
32. Eugen Frauenholz, "Feldmarschall Leutnant Alfred Freiherr von Henikstein im Jahre 1866," *Münchener Historische Abhandlungen*, 2nd ser., 3 (1933): 34–36.
33. Ibid., Cf. Johann C. Allmayer-Beck, "Der Feldzug der österreichischen Nordarmee nach Königgrätz," in Wolfgang v. Groote and Ursula v. Gersdorff eds., *Entscheidung 1866* (Stuttgart, 1966), p. 124.

34. Gordon A. Craig, *The Battle of Königgrätz* (Philadelphia-New York, 1964), p. 12.
35. Ferdinand Petrossi, *Das Heerwesen des österreichischen Kaiserstaates*, 2 vols. (Vienna, 1865), 1:283–85. For the Military Borders see Rothenberg, pp. 162–65.
36. K.K. Statistische Central-Commission, *Statistisches Handbüchlein des Kaiserthumes Österreich für das Jahr 1865* (Vienna, 1867), p. 23.
37. Petrossi, 1:277–83 gives the peace strength at two hundred sixty-nine thousand and the war strength at five hundred ninety thousand. For the actual figure mobilized in 1866 see Craig, p. 7.
38. Helmert, p. 41.
39. Ibid., p. 67.
40. KA (Kriegsgeschichtl. Abt. d. k.k. KA) *Sechzig Jahre Wehrmacht 1848–1908* (Vienna, 1908), pp. 102–103.
41. Wilhelm Ritter Gründorf v. Zebegény, *Memoiren eines österreichischen Generalstäblers 1832–1866* (Stuttgart, 1913), pp. 278–79.
42. J. Schweinitz, *Entwurf einer Reorganisation der österreichischen Armee* (Vienna, 1861), pp. 8–9, 76–77. The author admits, however, that his proposals depend on a solution of the nationality problem in the empire.
43. Maj. J. N. Nosinich, *Österreich und seine Wehrkraft* (Vienna, 1862), pp. 13–21.
44. Regele, p. 401.
45. Compiled from the *Militärschematismus des österreichischen Kaiserthumes für 1865* (Vienna, 1865) passim.
46. Mollinary, 2:105–107.
47. KA KM Präs. 1860–4031.
48. Helmert, p. 136.
49. *Mitteilungen über Gegenstände der Ingenieur-und Kriegswissenschaften* (1865) and *Mitteilungen über Gegenstände der Artillerie-und Kriegswissenschaften* (1866).
50. KA KM (CK) 1862–715.
51. Srbik, p. 132.
52. KA, *Wehrmacht*, pp. 101–103, and Nikolaus v. Preradovich, *Die Führungsschichten in Österreich und Preussen* (Wiesbaden, 1955), pp. 43–45.
53. Egon Caesar Conte Corti, *Maximilian and Charlotte of Mexico*, 2 vols. (London, 1928), 1:152–55.
54. Ibid., 2:555.
55. Andreas Cornaro, "Österreich und das Mexikanische Freikorps," *MÖStA*, 14 (1961): 64–79.
56. Petrossi, 1:23–27, 121–129.
57. Mollinary, 2:206.
58. Petrossi, 1:261–64, 277–80.
59. KA, *Wehrmacht*, pp. 115–17, 135.
60. Ibid., pp. 116–17. Cf. *Provisorisches Reglement für die kaiserl. königl. leichte Cavallerie* (Vienna, 1862) and the *Abrichtungs-Reglement für die kaiserl. königl. Kavallerie* (Vienna, 1863).
61. Helmert, pp. 171–72.
62. Petrossi, 1:146–98, gives descriptions, tables, and illustrations. Cf. Friedrich Müller, *Das österreichische Feld-und Gebirgs-Artillerie Material vom Jahre 1863* (Vienna, 1864). Rocket batteries continued to exist within the framework of the mountain artillery. See Walter Nemetz, "Die Kriegsraketen im österreichischen Heer," *MÖStA*, 20 (1957): 257–74.
63. Heinrich Friedjung, *Der Kampf um die Vorherrschaft in Deutschland*, 10th ed., 2 vols. (Stuttgart-Berlin, 1916), 1:384.
64. Anton v. Mollinary, *Studien über die Operationen und die Tactique der Franzosen im Jahre 1859* (Vienna, 1864), pp. 12, 27.

65. Petrossi, 2:283–84. Cf. *Abrichtungs-Reglement für die kaiserl. königl. Fusstruppen* (Vienna, 1862) and the *Manövrir-Reglement für die kaiserlich-königliche Infanterie* (Vienna, 1863).
66. Hans Delbrück and Emil Daniels, *Geschichte der Kriegskunst im Rahmen der politischen Geschichte*, 7 vols. (Berlin, 1900–36), 5:229–30, 425–28. This idea is indignantly rejected by Srbik, pp. 130–31, but accepted by a modern Austrian writer, Anton Wagner, "Österreichische Stosstaktik gegen preussische Feuertaktik im Kriege von 1866," *Truppendienst*, 5 (1966): 211–15.
67. Appointment, 22 December 1863, KA FA 1864, Krieg gegen Dänemark, F 1/35.
68. The official Austrian work, Friedrich v. Fischer, *Der Krieg in Schleswig und Jütland im Jahre 1864* (Vienna, 1870), is highly critical of the Prussian command. A more balanced treatment is in Heinz Helmert and Hans-Jürgen Usczeck, *Preussischdeutsche Kriege von 1864 bis 1871* (East Berlin, 1970), pp. 51–89.
69. Ibid., pp. 60–61.
70. FML Gablenz to Crenneville, 3 February 1864, KA FA, Krieg gegen Dänemark, F 2/106.
71. Battle report, 8 February 1864, ibid., 172.
72. Helmert and Usczeck, pp. 81–83.
73. Gründorf, pp. 257–66. Gründorf served as Gablenz's chief intelligence officer during the campaign.
74. FML Gablenz to Crenneville, 3 May 1864, informing him that he has told the Prussians that an amphibious landing is a "risky operation." KA FA 1864, Krieg gegen Dänemark, F 4/40.
75. Cited in Gründorf, p. 264.
76. Emil Franzel, *1866 Il Mondo Casca: Das Ende des alten Europas*, 2 vols. (Vienna-Munich, 1968), 2:376–77.
77. KA, *Wehrmacht*, p. 129.
78. See his "Instruktion für die Generalität und höhere Offiziere einer k.k. Armee in Deutschland," and the later "Einige Ideen als Beiträge für den Krieg Österreichs mit Preussen," KA Mem. XI 337, 338.
79. Glaise-Horstenau, pp. 88, 96.
80. Regele, p. 363, makes this assertion.
81. FZM Augustin to Francis Joseph, Vienna, 15 November 1851, KA MKSM Sonderreihe F/3.
82. KA Gstb. Präs. 1864-242. The often-cited story about the emperor brusquely terminating an audience with Lt. Col. Gründorf, Chief Intelligence Officer VI Corps, when the officer recommended adoption of a breechloader, cannot, however, be substantiated from the records.
83. KA KM Präs. 1865-155/1. Helmert and Usczek, pp. 44–46, and Peball, p. 68.
84. KA MKSM 1866-64-2/1.
85. Friedjung, *Kampf*, 1:379–80; Mollinary, 2:117.
86. KA MKSM 1866-51-1/1.
87. Memo, Albrecht to Francis Joseph, 27 August 1866, ibid., Sonderreihe F 74/5.
88. Even Heinrich v. Sybel conceded that the Austrian military did not press for war. *Die Begründung des Deutschen Reiches durch Wilhelm I*, 7 vols. (Munich-Leipzig, 1889), 5:3–4. Cf. Franzel, 2:503.
89. KA KM Präs. 1866-46/7; 47/4–8.
90. Unsigned article *Manchester Guardian*, 20 June 1866. Cf. John W. Bush, *Venetia Redeemed* (Syracuse, 1967), p. 60.
91. Franzel, 2:424–25; Helmert and Usczek, p. 99.
92. Allmayer-Beck, pp. 117–21; Regele, pp. 396–405; Craig, pp. 12–13, and Franzel, 2:524–30.

93. Presland, pp. 220–21.
94. Originally written in English and cited in Adam Wandruszka, *Schicksalsjahr 1866* (Graz-Vienna-Cologne, 1966), p. 259; Franzel 2:530, Craig, p. 15.
95. Appointment of Henikstein, KA KM Präs. 1866–122; discussed in Allmayer-Beck, p. 126. Cf. Frauenholz, p. 37.
96. For the strength of the Northern Army see Austria, Generalstab *Österreichs Kämpfe im Jahre 1866*, 5 vols. (Vienna, 1867–69), 3:13, and for the Southern Army, ibid., 2:7. For allied contingents as well as for another, slightly higher, tabulation of Austrian strength see Helmert and Usczek, pp. 11–13.
97. Generalstab, 1:73–74. Cf. Allmayer-Beck, pp. 115–22.
98. C. v. Cammerer, *Die Entwicklung der strategischen Wissenschaften im 19. Jahrhundert* (Berlin, 1904), p. 55.
99. See Beck's report, "Zu den Sendungen des Oberstsleutnants Beck in das Hauptquartier der Nord-Armee," KA MKSM Sonderreihe F 75/2. This report, written sometime in August or September 1866, must, however, be used with caution since it has the tendency to blame Benedek exclusively.
100. *Sammlung der Armeebefehle und speziellen Anordnungen des k.k. Feldzeugmeisters Benedek, Kommandanten der k.k. Nordarmee vom Jahre 1866* (Vienna, 1866), passim.
101. "Taktische-und Dienst Instruction für die k.k. Nord Armee," *ÖMZ*, 7 (1866): 234–36.
102. Helmuth v. Moltke, "Bemerkungen über den Einfluss der verbesserten Schusswaffen auf das Gefecht," ibid., 6 (1865): 403–409.
103. Franzel, 2:484–85. The best short account of the Italian campaign is Anton Wagner, "Der Feldzug gegen Italien," pp. 27–37, in *1866-Wendepunkt in der Geschichte Österreichs*.
104. Friedjung, *Kampf*, 1:452–53; Franzel, 2:488–89.
105. Friedjung, *Kampf*, 2:76–77.
106. Army Order No. 41, Josefstadt, 28 June 1866, KA MKSM Sonderreihe F 15. The Lorenz rifle was sighted to one thousand paces, the needlegun only to six hundred. In artillery the Austrians were not so much superior in numbers, 736 Austrian and 58 Saxon guns against 798 Prussian pieces, as in experience, training, and quality. All Austrian guns were muzzleloading rifles, while the Prussian guns were mainly breechloaders but with only 492 rifled. In all, one informed historian gives the Austrian artillery a 30 to 35 percent higher fire capability. Franzel, 2:499–500, and also Regele, p. 372.
107. Message in KA MKSM Sonderreihe F 75/2. Discussion in Eduard Ritter Bartels v. Bartberg, *Kritische Betrachtungen zur Geschichte des Krieges vom Jahre 1866* (Zurich, 1906), pp. 245–46; Craig, pp. 79–80, and Regele, pp. 443–46.
108. Benedek's tactical dispositions criticized in H. Bonnal, *Sadowa-A Study* (London, 1907), p. 166. The battle is eloquently and critically described by Craig, pp. 92 ff.
109. Friedjung, *Papiere*, pp. 382–83.
110. GM Carl Count Coudenhove, 6 July 1866, in Franz Coudenhove, "Erinnerungen an unsern Vater, Mai 1866 bis August, 1866," Typescript, KA Library, pp. 37–38.
111. Report of Maj. Fejérváry, "Zu der Sendung des Majors Baron Fejérváry in das Hauptquartier der Nordarmee," KA MKSM Sonderreihe F 75/2.
112. Army Order No. 4, 17 July 1866, Ibid., F 15.
113. Generalstab, 4:108–14, 151–57.
114. For details of Bismarck's schemes see Harodd L. Kirkpatrick, "Bismarck's insurrectionary projects during the Austro-Prussian War 1866," (Ph.D. diss. University of California at Berkeley, 1966).
115. Among others see Hermann Wendel, *Bismarck und Serbien im Jahre 1866* (Berlin, 1927); Johann A. Reiswitz, *Belgrad-Berlin, Berlin-Belgrad 1866–71* (Munich, 1936), and the classic by Andreas A. Kienast, *Die Legion Klapka* (Vienna, 1900).
116. Franzel, 2:647–49.

117. Heinrich Mast, "Die Ereignisse im Rücken der preussischen Armee im Juli 1866," pp. 21–26 in *1866-Wendepunkt der Geschichte Europas,* and Friedjung, *Kampf,* 2:392–97.
118. KA FA 1866, Operierende Armee unter Erzherzog Albrecht, F 7/427. This report of Dr. Andreas Zelinka, Mayor of Vienna to the city council, is also printed as *Administrazions-Berichte des Bürgermeisters der k.k. Reichshaupt-und Residenz Stadt Wien Dr. Andreas Zelinka für die Jahre 1865 und 1866* (Vienna, 1867), p. 208. Cf. Franzel, 2:693.
119. Wagner, "Feldzug gegen Italien," p. 36.
120. Army Order No. 40, Vienna, 17 August 1866, KA MKSM Sonderreihe F 15.
121. Franz Schnürer, ed., *Briefe Kaiser Franz Josephs an seine Mutter* (Munich, 1938), p. 52.
122. Allmayer-Beck, pp. 106–110, has an excellent survey of the controversy.
123. Friedjung, *Kampf,* 2:604.
124. Corti, p. 382; Presland, p. 321.
125. Friedjung, *Kampf,* 2:604.
126. Ibid., pp. 605–608, reprints the article appearing in the *Wiener-Zeitung,* 8 December 1866.
127. Franzel, 2:704–708.

6 Dualism and Reorganization: 1867–1874

1. FML John to Francis Joseph, 9 September 1866. Note on future role of the army, KA KM Präs. (CK) 1866 16–18/2.
2. Edmund v. Glaise-Horstenau, "Altösterreichs Heer in der deutschen Heeresgeschichte," in R. Linnebach ed., *Deutsche Heeresgeschichte* (Hamburg, 1935), p. 145.
3. Cited in Heinrich v. Srbik, *Aus Österreichs Vergangenheit* (Salzburg, 1949), p. 145.
4. Kurt Peball, "Sendung und Erbe," in *1866-Wendepunkt in der Geschichte Europas,* special issue *ÖMZ* (1966), pp. 59–61.
5. Julius Miskolczy, *Ungarn in der Habsburger Monarchie* (Vienna-Munich, 1959), p. 163. For a similar formulation from a Marxist point of view see Peter Hanák, "Hungary in the Austro-Hungarian Monarchy," *Austrian History Yearbook,* 3 (1967): pt. 1, 298.
6. Ivan Zolger, *Der staatsrechtliche Ausgleich zwischen Österreich und Ungarn* (Leipzig, 1911), pp. 5–12. For details of the negotiations and conclusion of the military compromise see Gunther E. Rothenberg, "Toward a National Hungarian Army: The Military Compromise of 1868 and its Consequences," *Slavic Review,* 31 (1972): 807–11, which also contains the required documentation.
7. K. K. Statistische Central Kommission, *Statistisches Jahrbuch für das Jahr 1869* (Vienna, 1871), pp. 79–80.
8. Walter Rogge, *Oesterreich von Világos bis zur Gegenwart,* 3 vols. (Leipzig-Vienna, 1873), 3:201, 244.
9. K. K. Statistische Centralcommission, *Statistisches Jahrbuch für das Jahr 1871* (Vienna, 1872), p. 60.
10. Rogge, 3:387–89.
11. Estimate of the British military attaché in Vienna, cited in George H. Rupp, *A Wavering Friendship: Russia and Austria 1876–1878* (Cambridge, Mass., 1941), pp. 234–35. Cf. Edmund v. Glaise-Horstenau, *Franz Joseph's Weggefährte* (Zurich-Vienna, 1930), pp. 144–45.
12. Albrecht to Francis Joseph, 2 January 1868, Note on the necessity for an AOK, KA KM Präs. (CK) 1868 16–5/1.
13. Srbik, pp. 174–77; Georg Franz, *Liberalismus* (Munich, 1955), pp. 140–41.
14. FML John to Francis Joseph, 9 September 1866, KA KM Präs. (CK) 1866 16–18/2.

15. Carl v. Duncker, *Feldmarschall Erzherzog Albrecht* (Vienna, 1897), p. 267. There does not exist a modern critical biography of Albrecht.
16. Rogge, 3:91–93.
17. KA KM Präs. (CK) 1868 16–3/1.
18. Glaise-Horstenau, *Beck,* p. 148.
19. Srbik, p. 114.
20. Eduard v. Wertheimer, *Graf Julius Andrássy,* 3 vols. (Stuttgart, 1910–13), 1:276–78.
21. Glaise-Horstenau, Beck, p. 148.
22. Srbik, p. 114.
23. For the rift see also Arthur Skedl, *Der politische Nachlass des Grafen Eduard Taaffe* (Vienna, 1926), p. 106.
24. For an example of the bitterness of the dispute see the editorial "Die Freiheit in der Armee" *Österreichisch-ungarische Wehrzeitung,* 22 December 1869.
25. KA MKSM 1869 9–1/1.
26. "Organisationstatut für den Generalstab," 15 November 1866. KA Mem. XI–228. Cf. Oskar Regele, *Generalstabschefs aus vier Jahrhunderten* (Vienna-Munich, 1966), pp. 33–34.
27. Srbik, pp. 186–88, 190–91. Also Moritz Ritter von Auffenberg, *Aus Österreichs Höhe und Niedergang* (Munich 1921), p. 41.
28. Karl Went v. Römo, *Ein Soldatenleben* (Vienna-Leipzig, 1904) pp. 138–39; KA *Wehrmacht,* p. 144. See also Beck's protests, KA MKSM Sonderreihe 7 76/20.
29. Bundesministerium f. Landesverteidigung, *100 Jahre allgemeine Wehrpflicht in Österreich* (Vienna, 1968), pp. 36–38.
30. Heinrich v. Nauendorff, *Die Kriegsmacht Oesterreichs,* 2nd ed., 3 vols. (Vienna, 1875–76), 1:16–39.
31. Ibid., pp. 30–32, 400–404.
32. Nikolaus v. Preradovich, *Die Führungsschichten in Österreich und Preussen* (Wiesbaden, 1955), pp. 43–45.
33. KA, *Wehrmacht,* p. 144.
34. *Militär-statistisches Jahrbuch für das Jahr 1870* (Vienna, 1871), p. 211.
35. Auffenberg, pp. 14–15. In the army, officers of equal rank employed the familiar "Du" when off-duty. The differences in status, real or imagined, between the academicians and the cadets led to the bitter joke, "Bist Du ein Akademiker oder sind Sie ein Kadett Herr Leutnant?"
36. Oscar Jászi, *The Dissolution of the Habsburg Monarchy* (Chicago, 1929), p. 141. Cf. Johann C. Allmayer-Beck, "Der Ausgleich von 1867 und die k.u.k. bewaffnete Macht," in Forschungsinstitut f. d. Donauraum, *Der österreichisch-ungarische Ausgleich vom Jahre 1867* (Vienna-Munich, 1967), p. 122.
37. *Militärstatistisches Jahrbuch für das Jahr 1870,* p. 70.
38. Compiled from the above publication for the years 1870 to 1888.
39. Ibid., 1878, p. 121.
40. KA MKSM 1867 57–1/2. Cf. Glaise-Horstenau, *Beck,* pp. 142–43, and Srbik, pp. 185–86.
41. *Dienstreglement für das kaiserlich-königliche Heer* (Vienna, 1873), p. 41.
42. Anon. "Einige Bemerkungen über die hohe Sterblichkeit in der Armee," *Österreichisch-ungarische Wehrzeitung,* 25 June 1869.
43. Rede seiner Excellenz des Herrn Reichskriegsministers Franz Freiherrn von Kuhn (Vienna, 1873), p. 4.
44. Albrecht to Francis Joseph, 27 August 1866, KA MKSM Sonderreihe F 74/5.
45. Order to modify the Lorenz rifles, ibid. 64–3/6.
46. Glaise-Horstenau, *Beck,* p. 161. For the Werndl enterprises and the rifle contract,

see Heinrich Benedikt, *Die wirtschaftliche Entwicklung in der Franz Joseph Zeit* (Vienna-Munich, 1958), pp. 74–76.

47. Anton Freiherr v. Mollinary, *46 Jahre im österreich-ungarischen Heere*, 2 vols. (Zurich, 1905), 2:182–83. Foreign observers, too, noted the close resemblance of the Austrian and Prussian tactics. See Maj. Gen. Emory Upton, *The Armies of Asia and Europe* (New York, 1878), p. 303.

48. Alfred Jurnitschek, *Die Wehrmacht der österreichisch-ungarischen Monarchie im Jahre 1875* (Vienna, 1876), pp. 538–39.

49. Mollinary, 2:324–25.

50. Anon. "Die strategische und taktische Verwendung der Reiterei," *ÖMZ*, 40 (1899): 195–259.

51. Report to Francis Joseph, 22 November 1873, KA MKSM Sonderreihe F 69/5.

52. Anton Dolleczek, *Geschichte der österreichischen Artillerie* (Vienna, 1887), pp. 554–55. On the steel versus bronze controversy, see Daniel Freiherr v. Salis-Soglio, *Mein Leben und was ich davon erzählen will, kann, und darf*, 2 vols., (Stuttgart, 1908), 2:69–70.

53. Gen. Sir Edward B. Hamley, "The Armies of Russia and Austria," *The Nineteenth Century*, 3 (1878): 856–57.

54. Ottomar Volkmer, "Vergleichende Gegenüberstellung des neuen österreichischen und deutschen Feld-Artillerie Materiales," *ÖMZ*, 18 (1877): 151–60.

55. For development of *Honvédség* see Rothenberg, pp. 811–12.

56. Alphons v. Wrede, *Geschichte der k.u.k. Wehrmacht*, 5 vols. (Vienna, 1898–1905), 5:165; Otto Stolz, *Wehrverfassung und Schützenwesen in Tirol* (Innsbruck-Vienna, 1960), pp. 181–82.

57. Arthur J. May, *The Hapsburg Monarchy 1867–1914* (Cambridge, Mass., 1951), p. 52; Hermann Münch, *Böhmische Tragödie* (Berlin-Hamburg, 1949), p. 346.

58. Kuhn to GdK Koller, 10 October 1868, IA MKSM 1868 28–1/2.

59. Münch, p. 341.

60. FML Wagner to Count Taaffe, Austrian defense minister, Zara, 12 September 1869, cited in Skedl, pp. 108–110.

61. GM Dormus, Cattaro, to military command, Zara, 25 September 1869, and military command, Zara, to Dormus, 29 September 1869, KA FA 1869, Aufstand in Dalmatien, F 9/5 and 9/7.

62. Wagner to Kuhn, 7 October 1869, ibid., 10/29.

63. Albrecht to Taaffe, 24 November 1869, in Skedl, p. 110.

64. Protocol ministerial council, 8 December 1869, KA MKSM Sonderreihe 74/15.

65. Ceremony described in Karl Vrbanić, *Geschichte der Bocche di Cattaro* (Zagreb, 1887), pp. 100–101.

66. Glaise-Horstenau, *Beck*, p. 158.

67. Gunther E. Rothenberg, *The Military Border in Croatia 1740–1881* (Chicago, 1966), pp. 165–72.

68. Ivan Babić, "Military History," in Francis H. Eterovich and Christopher Spalatin, *Croatia* (Toronto, 1964), pp. 146–48.

69. For details and notes on the following paragraphs see Gunther E. Rothenberg, "The Struggle over the Dissolution of the Croatian Military Border, 1850–1871," *Slavic Review*, 23 (1964): 63–78.

70. Wertheimer, 3:477. The most recent and revisionistic interpretation of this period is István Diószegi, *Österreich-Ungarn und der französisch-preussische Krieg 1870–1871* (Budapest, 1974), pp. 27–79, 138–53.

71. Srbik, pp. 194–95.

72. Hermann Oncken, *Die Rheinpolitik Kaiser Napoleons III von 1863 bis 1870*, 3 vols. (Stuttgart, 1926), 3:23–26.

73. F. Engel-Janosi, *Geschichte aus dem Ballhausplatz* (Vienna, 1963), p. 199.
74. Archives historiques de l'Armée, Rec. Autriche-Hongrie 1869–1872, carton 1608, report of Colonel Vassart for 21 February 1870.
75. Barthélemi L. J. LeBrun, *Souvenirs Militaires*, 1866–1870 (Paris, 1895), pp. 69–79.
76. Ibid., pp. 95–103; Rudolf Kiszling, "Die militärischen Vereinbarungen Österreich-Ungarns, 1867–1914," *Österreich in Geschichte und Literatur*, 10 (1966): 428–29.
77. "Aus den unveröffentlichen Tagebüchern des Kriegsministers Freiherrn von Kuhn," *Neue Freie Presse*, (Vienna), 24 August 1930, entries for 29 April and 11 July 1870.
78. Excerpts from Kuhn's memorial printed in Glaise-Horstenau, *Beck*, pp.456–60.
79. Srbik, pp. 69–71, 199–200. A recent book by a Hungarian historian challenges this interpretation. Andrássy, he asserts, favored mobilization, though not against Prussia but for war against Russia. Diószegi, pp. 51–59.
80. Kuhn to Francis Joseph, KA MKSM Sonderreihe 71/70.
81. Srbik, pp. 201–203.
82. KA KM Präs. 1870 16–13/3.
83. Anon. (Albrecht), *Das Jahr 1870 und die Wehrkraft der Monarchie* (Vienna, 1870), especially pp. 71–72. Cf. Glaise-Horstenau, *Beck*, pp. 170–71.
84. Rothenberg, *Military Border*, p. 176.
85. Archives historiques de l'Armée, Recon. Autriche-Hongrie, 1869–1872, carton 1608, report of Lt. Col. Bouille, 10 August 1870.
86. Srbik, pp. 211–13.
87. Rupp, pp. 72–73; Glaise-Horstenau, *Beck*, p. 176.
88. Srbik, pp. 212–14.

7 The Army and the Balkans: 1874–1881

1. Cited in David MacKenzie, *The Serbs and Russian Pan-Slavism 1875–1878* (Ithaca, N.Y., 1967), p. 12.
2. Edmund v. Glaise-Horstenau, *Franz Josephs Weggefährte* (Zurich-Vienna, 1930), pp. 184–85; Anton Freiherr v. Mollinary, *46 Jahre im österreichungarischen Heere 1833–1879*, 2 vols. (Zurich, 1905), 2:281–82; George H. Rupp, *A Wavering Friendship: Russia and Austria 1876–1878* (Cambridge, Mass., 1941), pp. 29–31.
3. Gunther E. Rothenberg, *The Austrian Military Border in Croatia, 1740–1881* (Chicago, 1966), pp. 166–67.
4. KA MKSM 1854–1874.
5. Memo 30 August 1866, printed in Theodor v. Sosnosky, *Die Balkanpolitik Österreich-Ungarns seit 1866*, 2 vols. (Stuttgart, Berlin, 1913), 2:289–90.
6. Mollinary, 2:288–89.
7. Beck, pp. 179, 184–85.
8. B. H. Sumner, *Russia and the Balkans* (Oxford, 1937), pp. 126–32; MacKenzie, pp. 13–26.
9. Mollinary to Andrássy, 16 June 1873, No. 1 in *Aktenstücke aus den Korrespondenzen des k.u.k. gemeinsamen Ministerium des Äusseren vom 6 Mai 1873 bis 31 Mai 1877* (Vienna, 1877).
10. Mollinary, 2:281–82.
11. Ibid., 283–84; Glaise-Horstenau, pp. 182–83.
12. Mackenzie, p. 31.
13. Eduard v. Wertheimer, *Graf Julius Andrássy*, 3 vols. (Stuttgart, 1910–13), 2:254, 260–61.
14. Mollinary, 2:288–89.
15. See the exchange of telegrams between Andrássy and FML Rodich, 5, 6, and 7

October, 29 and 30 November 1875, and 6 and 8 February 1876, KA MKSM Sonderreihe F 73/20.
16. Karl Went v. Römo, *Ein Soldatenleben* (Vienna, 1904), pp. 158–59. For other, earlier, arms shipments see V. Djordjević, *Crna Gora i Austrija, 1814–1894* (Belgrade, 1924), pp. 414–15.
17. Rodich to Beck, Zara, 10 February 1878, KA Nachlass Beck A/2 F V I/179. Cf. MKSM Sonderreihe F 73/20.
18. Mollinary, 2:300–301.
19. Anon. *Géza Baron Fejérváry* (Pressburg, 1901), p. 87.
20. Rupp, p. 176.
21. KA Gstb Op. B. F 173. It should be noted, however, that such plans were in part routine exercises and that other Case D studies were worked out in 1879 and 1907 at which time they no longer represented serious intent.
22. Barbara Jelavich, *The Habsburg Empire in European Affairs 1814–1918* (Chicago, 1969), p. 117.
23. Rupp, pp. 202–204.
24. Chef d. Gstb. "Zur Lage," Vienna, 14 February 1874, in KA Gstb. Op. B. F 1.
25. "Betrachtungen zum Kriegsfall gegen Russland," Vienna, 20 November 1876, ibid.
26. Glaise-Horstenau, p. 191.
27. Ibid., pp. 191–92.
28. Mollinary, 2:305–306.
29. Glaise-Horstenau, p. 193.
30. M. Stojanović, *The Great Powers and the Balkans 1875–1878* (Cambridge, 1939), p. 165.
31. Wertheimer, 3:41–46.
32. Glaise-Horstenau, pp. 188–89, 193–95.
33. Ibid.
34. Andrássy to Beust, 22 June 1877, cited in Rupp, p. 402.
35. Glaise-Horstenau, pp. 196–98.
36. Ibid., p. 199.
37. Rupp, pp. 451–53.
38. KA MKSM Sonderreihe F 82/1, and instructions for "Kriegsfall Russland," of 5 June 1878, KA KM Präs. 76-27/1.
39. Report by Schönfeld, 20 February 1878, KA MKSM Sonderreihe F 75/8.
40. Draft, 16 February 1878, KA Gstb. Op. B. F 1.
41. Glaise-Horstenau, p. 200.
42. Ibid., p. 201; Wertheimer, 3:76–79.
43. Glaise-Horstenau, pp. 205–206.
44. Wertheimer, 2:290.
45. Glaise-Horstenau, pp. 189–90. Cf. C. Conte Corti and Hans Sokol, *Der alte Kaiser* (Graz, 1955), pp. 58, 74, 79.
46. Langenau to Andrássy, 22 November 1876, cited in Rupp, p. 280.
47. Sosnosky, 1:168.
48. Reichsbefestigungskommission, Protocol, Sessions April 1868, KA Gstb. Op. B. F 162.
49. On the defects of the new fortifications see the account by the chief of engineers, FZM Daniel Freiherr v. Salis-Soglio, *Aus meinem Leben*, 2 vols. (Stuttgart, 1908), 2:7–38.
50. Memo of 20 November 1876, KA Gstb. Op. B. F 1.
51. "Zur militärischen Lage der Monarchie," December 1876, KA MKSM 1876 78–4/1.
52. Glaise-Horstenau, pp. 86, 186, 200.
53. Study prepared by Col. Anton Galgotzy, drafts and summary of previous work, 4 August 1878, KA Gstb. Op. B. F 162; KA MKSM 1879 29-½-2.

54. Arthur J. May, *The Hapsburg Monarchy 1867–1914* (Cambridge, Mass., 1951), pp. 139–40. Cf. Editorial "Die 'Italia irredenta' und deren Bedeutung für unser Vaterland," *Österreichisch-ungarische Wehrzeitung*, 8 February 1879.
55. Glaise-Horstenau, p. 191.
56. Gonne's reports, 11, 14, and 18 October 1876, cited in Rupp, pp. 233–34.
57. Gen. Sir Edward B. Hamley, "The Armies of Russia and Austria," *The Nineteenth Century*, 3 (1878): 857–59.
58. Glaise-Horstenau, p. 241.
59. Memo, John to Francis Joseph, February 1874, KA MKSM 50-20/1.
60. Glaise-Horstenau, p. 242. Organisatorische Bestimmungen f. d. Generalstab, 24 December 1875, KA KM Präs. 1875 54/3–168.
61. For a brilliant discussion of the organizational disputes within the highest echelons, see Walter Wagner, *Geschichte des k.k. Kriegsministeriums II* (Vienna-Cologne-Graz, 1971), pp. 31–35, 128–30, 165–68, and passim.
62. Franz Graf Conrad v. Hötzendorf, *Mein Anfang* (Berlin, 1925), pp. 149–50.
63. Glaise-Horstenau, pp. 246–47.
64. KA MKSM Sep. Fasz. 75–3. KA Nachlass Beck A/2 F VII/161, 162.
65. Wagner, pp. 228–29.
66. Heinrich v. Srbik, *Aus Österreichs Vergangenheit* (Salzburg, 1948), p. 112. GdI Moritz v. Auffenberg, *Aus Österreich-Ungarns Teilnahme am Weltkriege* (Berlin, 1920), pp. 32–33, concluded that Albrecht could not be considered a great field commander.
67. KA MKSM Sonderreihe F 75/8.
68. Sosnosky, 1:177–78.
69. Order of battle, ibid., pp. 291–94.
70. KA (Abt. f. Kriegsgesch. d. k.k. KA) *Die Okkupation Bosniens und der Herzegovina durch die k.k. Truppen im Jahre 1878* (Vienna, 1879), p. 874; Wertheimer, 3:153.
71. KA, *Okkupation*, p. 206.
72. Ibid., pp. 809–11.
73. Sosnosky, 1:241–42.
74. Wertheimer, 3:144–46, 150–53. The attack also was taken up by the German Liberal press; see *Tagespost*, Graz, 15 January 1879.
75. Ludwig Ritter v. Przibran, *Erinnerungen eines alten Österreichers*, 2 vols. (Stuttgart-Leipzig, 1910–12), 2:78–79.
76. Glaise-Horstenau, p. 206. Evidently, he too had counted on a peaceful occupation.
77. Georg Freiherr v. Holtz, *Von Brod nach Sarajevo* (Vienna, 1907), pp. 184–91. On the other hand, the report of an official commission of inquiry headed by Archduke Albrecht declared itself satisfied with the overall performance. KA MKSM 1879 20-2/1.
78. Conrad, pp. 31–35; Moritz Ritter v. Auffenberg, *Aus Österreichs Höhe und Niedergang* (Munich, 1921), p. 45.
79. Glaise-Horstenau, p. 211; Przibran, 2:78–79.
80. "Militärische Verhältnisse in Bosnien und der Herzegovina," Buda, November 1878, KA MKSM Sonderreihe F 70/58.
81. Josef Graf Stürgkh, *Politische und militärische Erinnerungen*, (Leipzig, 1922), pp. 11–12, 80; Charles Jelavich, "The Revolt in Bosnia-Hercegovina 1881–82," *Slavonic and East European Review* 31 (1953): 421–23.
82. KA KM Präs. 1881 60–14/59.
83. KA, FA 1881–82, Insurrection in Süd-Dalmatien und der Hercegovina, F 1/2.
84. RKM to Dahlen, 3 December 1881, ibid., F 1/4–8.
85. Enlistment of *Pandurs*, 19 January 1882, ibid.
86. Conrad, p. 218.
87. Stürgkh, pp. 35, 46–51.
88. Ibid. Orders to establish *Streifcorps*, KA FA 1881–82, Insurrection, F 5/22–25.

89. Jelavich, "Revolt," pp. 425-38.
90. RKM to FML Jovanović, 2 February 1882, KA FA 1881-82, Insurrection, F 2/8-1.
91. Stürgkh, pp. 72-73.

8 The Era of Beck and Albrecht: 1881-1895

1. "Die militärisch-politische Situation im Jahre 1880," KA Nachlass Beck F VI/185.
2. It is not clear whether Beck here refers to Alexander II, assassinated March 13, or to his successor, Alexander III. The memorandum is dated 31 March 1881, but may have been composed earlier.
3. William A. Jenks, *Austria under the Iron Ring 1879-1893* (Charlottesville, Va., 1965), pp. 33-50.
4. Ibid., pp. 25-26, 42.
5. Beck, "Denkschrift über die allgemeinen militärischen Verhältnisse im Jahre 1892," KA MKSM Sonderreihe F 90/3, p. 54.
6. Statistics from A. J. P. Taylor, *The Struggle for Mastery in Europe 1848-1918* (Oxford, 1954), p. xxviii.
7. Albrecht, Memo December 1886, "Die Vermehrung der Wehrkraft der Monarchie," KA MKSM Sonderreihe F 70/38.
8. Edmund v. Glaise-Horstenau, *Franz Josephs Weggefährte* (Zurich-Vienna, 1930), pp. 243-44.
9. Josef Graf Stürgkh, *Politische und militärische Erinnerungen* (Leipzig, 1922), pp. 261-62.
10. Glaise-Horstenau, pp. 255-56.
11. Memo, 15 March 1881, KA MKSM 1881 50-30/1. The emperor ordered Beck to report in person at least once a week, KA KM Präs. 1881 1-33/2. Cf. Glaise-Horstenau, p. 254.
12. Ibid., p. 364.
13. Ibid., pp. 374-77; Stürgkh, p. 269.
14. Glaise-Horstenau, pp. 262-70.
15. Hans v. Seekt, *Gedanken eines Soldaten* (Berlin, 1929), p. 160.
16. *Stürgh*, pp. 278-81.
17. *Militär-Statistisches Jahrbuch für die Jahre 1883 und 1884* (Vienna, 1885), pp. 171-72.
18. Alfons Danzer, *Unter den Fahnen* (Vienna-Leipzig-Prague, 1889), pp. 185-95.
19. *Militär-Statistisches Jahrbuch ... 1883 und 1884*, pp. 171-72.
20. Ibid., 1906, p. 145.
21. Ibid., 1896, p. 7.
22. Ernest Jones, *Sigmund Freud: His Life and his Work*, 2 vols. (London, 1953), 1:211, and Johann C. Allmayer-Beck, *Ministerpräsident Baron Beck* (Vienna, 1956), p. 20.
23. Tabulation from Georg Schreiber, *Des Kaisers Reiterei* (Vienna, 1967), p. 269.
24. See the editorial "Zweijährige Präsenzpflicht," in *ÖMZ* 34 (1893): No. 2, 25-27.
25. 28 April 1881, KA MKSM 1881 64-4/1.
26. Glaise-Horstenau, p. 357.
27. KA MKSM Sonderreihe F 70/38.
28. KA (Kriegsgeschichtl. Abt. d. k.u.k. KA), *Sechzig Jahre Wehrmacht 1848-1908* (Vienna, 1908), pp. 197-97.
29. Alphons v. Wrede, *Geschichte der k.u.k. Wehrmacht*, 5 vols. (Vienna, 1898-1905), 5:583-85, 591-93.
30. Glaise-Horstenau, p. 322.
31. Jenks, pp. 245-46.

32. Julius Miskolczy, *Ungarn in der Habsburger Monarchie* (Vienna-Munich, 1959), pp. 163–64.
33. Beck, "Denkschrift über die allgemeine militärische Lage Ende 1892," KA MKSM Sonderreihe F 90/3.
34. Conference protocol, 10 October 1892, ibid., 90/2.
35. "Anträge zur Vorbereitung der Mobilisierung und des strategischen Aufmarsches der Armee," KA GStb Op. B. F 1. Cf. Glaise-Horstenau, pp. 273–74.
36. KA MKSM 1881 70–1/41. Cf. the discussion in Walter Wagner, *Geschichte des k.k. Kriegsministeriums II* (Vienna-Cologne, 1971), pp. 209–22.
37. "Studien über die Armee Reorganisierungs Frage," KA MKSM Sonderreihe F 30.
38. Report, 3 June 1882, KA MKSM 1882 38–3/2.
39. Protocol, ibid.
40. Ibid.
41. "Kavallerie in Galizien," Memo, 22 July 1886, Albrecht to RKM and CGStb., KA MKSM Sonderreihe 70/40.
42. Emil Ratzenhofer, "Militärische Verkehrsprobleme Österreich-Ungarns, in Carnegie Institution, Austro-Hungarian Series, *Verkehrswesen im Kriege* (Vienna, 1931), pp. 164–67.
43. Glaise-Horstenau, pp. 302–304.
44. RKM, "Memoire über die Nothwendigkeit der Beschaffung von Repetiergewehren," June 1866, KA MKSM Sonderreihe F 69/6.
45. GM Otto Kerchnawe et al., *Ehrenbuch unserer Artillerie*, 2 vols. (Vienna, 1935), 1:131–32.
46. Glaise-Horstenau, pp. 272–73.
47. See the preparatory work for Case "R" in KA Gstb. Op. B. 676 of 1883.
48. Taylor, pp. 259–71.
49. Eberhard Kessel, *Moltke* (Stuttgart, 1957), pp. 703–705.
50. Gordon A. Craig, *The Politics of the Prussian Army 1640–1945* (New York, 1964), pp. 274–77; Gerhard Ritter, *The Sword and the Scepter* (Miami, 1969), I: 230–31.
51. Memo, Beck to Albrecht and Francis Joseph, KA MKSM Sonderreihe F 74/16.
52. "Expose über die militärische Situation in einem Kriege Österreich Ungarns und Deutschland mit Russland als Grundlage für eventuelle Verhandlungen mit dem königl preussischen Generalstabe," KA Nachlass Beck F VII/205.
53. Report of conversations with Waldersee, Strobl, 3 August 1882, ibid., 207.
54. Albrecht to Francis Joseph, 19 August 1882, ibid., 208/1.
55. Max Freiherr v. Pitreich, *1914. Die militärischen Probleme unseres Kriegsbeginnes* (Vienna, 1934), pp. 19–21; Kessel, pp. 706–707.
56. Pitreich, pp. 19–21.
57. Glaise-Horstenau, p. 282.
58. FZM Daniel Freiherr v. Salis-Soglio, *Aus meinem Leben*, 2 vols. (Stuttgart, 1908), 2:126–27.
59. "Denkschrift über die Reichsbefestigung der ehem. öst.-ung. Monarchie," KA MS Rb. pp. 60–78.
60. Memo, 1 December 1886, KA MKSM Sonderreihe F 69/29.
61. Craig, p. 268.
62. Glaise-Horstenau, pp. 308–14.
63. KA MKSM Sonderreihe F 69/29.
64. "Vorbereitungsmassnahmen für einen Krieg mit Russland," 12 January 1887, ibid., 111.
65. Glaise-Horstenau, pp. 301–306. Cf. the letter and memo from Albrecht to Beck, 8 March 1887, cited in Stephan Verosta, *Theorie und Realität von Bündnissen* (Vienna, 1971), pp. 143–44.
66. Albrecht to Beck, 30 October 1887, Glaise-Horstenau, pp. 460–61.

67. Albrecht to Beck, 13 and 21 November 1887, ibid., pp. 308-309.
68. Francis Joseph to Albert, 14 December 1887, in Otto Ernst ed., *Franz Joseph I in seinen Briefen* (Vienna-Leipzig-Munich, 1924), pp. 184-85.
69. Ritter, 1:232-33.
70. Glaise-Horstenau, pp. 311-12. Instructions to Lt. Col. Steininger, Austr.-Hung. plenipotentiary, 22 December 1887, ibid., pp. 461-63.
71. Gerhard Ritter, "Die Zusammenarbeit der Generalstäbe Deutschlands und Österreich-Ungarns vor dem ersten Weltkrieg," in *Zur Geschichte und Problematik der Demokratie* (Berlin, 1958), pp. 528-29.
72. Rudolf Kiszling, "Die militärischen Vereinbarungen Österreich-Ungarns 1867-1914," *ÖIGL*, 10 (1966): 431-32. Austro-Hungarian-Italian staff agreements in KA GStb. Op. B. F 105.
73. KA Chef d. GStb. Res. 236 EB.
74. Glaise-Horstenau, pp. 337-38.
75. "Denkschrift über die allgemeinen militärischen Verhältnisse Ende 1896," KA Gstb Op. B. F 93. Verosta, pp. 181-82.
76. "Denkschrift ... Ende 1892," KA MKSM Sonderreihe F 90/3.
77. "Denkschrift ... Ende 1896," KA GStb. Op. B. F 93.
78. L. Eisenmann, *Le Compromis Austro-Hongrois de 1867* (Paris, 1905), p. 505.
79. Oscar Jaszi, *The Dissolution of the Habsburg Monarchy* (Chicago, 1929), p. 143.
80. Karl Kandelshofer, "Der Adel im k.u.k. Officierskorps," *ÖMZ* 38 (1897): 248-50.
81. Salis Soglio, 2:208.
82. Friedrich F. Kleinwächter, *Der Untergang der österreichisch-ungarischen Monarchie* (Leipzig, 1920), pp. 107-110. Cf. *Militär-statistisches Jahrbuch für das Jahr 1896* (Vienna, 1897), p. 146.
83. A. E. *Offene Worte über die österreichisch-ungarische Armee im Verhältnisse zum deutschen Reichsheer* (Leipzig, 1891) and the reply by Oscar Teuber, *Offene Worte über die österreichisch-ungarische Armee* (Vienna, 1891).
84. "Gespräche mit Waldersee," 22 June 1896, KA MKSM Sonderreihe F 70/40.
85. Peter Hanák, "Hungary in the Austro-Hungarian Monarchy," *Austrian History Yearbook* 3 (1967), pt. 1, 295-98.
86. Francis Joseph to Tisza, 22 February 1882, in Ernst, p. 297.
87. Egon C. Conte Corti and Hans Sokol, *Der alte Kaiser Franz Joseph I* (Vienna-Graz-Cologne, 1955), pp. 71-73.
88. Miskolczy, pp. 162-63.
89. Ernst, p. 306.
90. Miskolczy, pp. 167-69.
91. Jaszi, p. 144.
92. "Die Ungarische Dienstsprache," KA Nachlass Beck A/2 F VIII/301.
93. Speech of 26 January 1889 in Anon. *Géza Baron Fejérváry* (Pressburg, 1901), pp. 184-54.
94. Speech of 5 April 1889, printed as *Die Einheit der österreichisch-ungarischen Armee* (Vienna, 1889), pp. 17-19.
95. Theodor v. Sosnosky, *Die Politik im Habsburgerreiche*, 2 vols. (Berlin, 1912), 2:170-71. Cf. Jenks, pp. 245-46.
96. Anton Pitreich, *Der österreichische-ungarische Bundesgenosse im Sperrfeuer* (Klagenfurth, 1930), p. 67.
97. Corti-Sokol, pp. 172-73.
98. Rudolf Kiszling, *Erzherzog Franz Ferdinand von Österreich-Este* (Graz-Cologne, 1953), p. 19.
99. Glaise-Horstenau, pp. 404-406.
100. Ibid., p. 476.
101. Ibid., pp. 397-98.

102. A. J. P. Taylor, *The Habsburg Monarchy: 1809-1918* (New York, 1965), p. 157.
103. Carl Freiherr v. Bardolff, *Soldat im alten Österreich* (Jena, 1938), p. 39; Paul Molisch, *Geschichte der deutschnationalen Bewegung in Österreich* (Jena, 1926), pp. 104-105.
104. Albrecht to Beck, 28 July 1888, Glaise-Horstenau, pp. 465-66.
105. Konrad Leppa, *General der Infanterie Alfred Krauss*, (Munich, 1932), pp. 34-35; Jenks, pp. 291-93.
106. Jenks, pp. 291-93.
107. Arthur J. May, *Vienna in the Age of Franz Josef* (Norman, Okla., 1966), p. 93.
108. Wrede, 1:623-36. The change of garrisons took place in 1894.
109. Karl Went v. Römö, *Ein Soldatenleben* (Vienna-Leipzig, 1904), pp. 178-79.
110. Stürgkh, pp. 86-87; and Erich Graf Kielmansegg, *Kaiserhaus, Staatsmänner und Politiker* (Vienna, 1966) pp. 181-82.

9 Foreign Equilibrium and Internal Crisis: 1895-1905

1. Edmund v. Glaise-Horstenau, *Franz Josephs Weggefährte. Das Leben des Generalstabschef Grafen Beck* (Zurich-Vienna, 1930), pp. 390-91.
2. "Denkschrift über die allgemeinen militärischen Verhältnisse zum Ende 1897," KA MKSM 1898 25-1/1.
3. "Denkschrift ... 1898," KA GStb. Op. B. F 93.
4. Ibid., F 94.
5. Glaise-Horstenau, pp. 395-96.
6. Theodor v. Sosnosky, *Die Politik im Habsburgerreiche*, 2 vols. (Berlin, 1912-13), 1:108-109.
7. KA GStb. Op. B. F 105, "Italien im Dreibund."
8. Ibid., F 89a, 3,4,5,6,7,9, and 11.
9. Josef Graf Stürgkh, *Politische und militärische Erinnerungen* (Leipzig, 1922), pp. 250, 258-60.
10. Glaise-Horstenau, p. 393. "Denkschrift ... 1904," GStb. Op. B. F 94.
11. Glaise-Horstenau, pp. 374-75.
12. Oskar Regele, *Generalstabschefs aus Vier Jahrhunderten* (Vienna-Munich, 1966), pp. 36-37.
13. Glaise-Horstenau, pp. 401-402.
14. Cited in August v. Urbanski, *Conrad von Hötzendorf* (Graz-Leipzig-Vienna, 1938), pp. 114-15.
15. "Denkschrift ... 1898," GStb. Op. B. F 93.
16. Oskar Regele, *Feldmarschall Conrad* (Vienna-Munich, 1955), pp. 160-63.
17. Ibid., p. 163.
18. "Denkschrift ... 1904," KA GStb. Op. B. F 94.
19. Figures compiled from the *Militärstatistisches Jahrbuch* for 1896, 1900, and 1906.
20. "Die Feldgeschützfrage," *ÖMZ* 45 (1904): 131-41.
21. "Denkschrift" ... 1900," KA GStb. Op. B. F 93.
22. Alfred Freiherr v. Margutti, *Vom Alten Kaiser* (Leipzig-Vienna, 1921), p. 283.
23. Reports of Lt. Col. Stürgkh, Austro-Hungarian military attaché, Berlin, 29 November 1901 and 13 January 1902, KA Nachlass Beck F VII/297.
24. Erich Gabriel, "Die wichtigsten Waffen der österreichischungarischen Armee 1918," *ÖMZ* 6 (1968): 436-37.
25. Ludwig v. Tlaskal, *Die Entwicklung des Militär-Kraftfahrwesens in Österreich vom März 1896 bis März 1938* (Vienna, 1960), pp. 5-6.
26. Glaise-Horstenau, pp. 394-95.
27. *Militärstatistisches Jahrbuch*, 1906, p. 143.

28. Ibid., 1901, pp. 144–45.
29. Norman Stone, "Army and Society in the Habsburg Monarchy, 1900–1914," *Past & Present*, no. 33 (1966): 99.
30. *Militärstatistisches Jahrbuch*, 1906, p. 145. By 1910 there were 500 Jewish officers in the Italian army, 720 in the French, and 2,179 in the Austro-Hungarian army. By contrast there were no Jewish officers in the Prussian army after 1885. See Martin Kitchen, *The German Officer Corps 1890–1914* (Oxford, 1968), p. 40, and Walter T. Angress, "Prussia's Army and the Jewish Reserve Officer Controversy before World War I," *Leo Baeck Institute Year Book*, 17 (1972): 19–42.
31. Regele, *Conrad*, pp. 92–94.
32. *Militärstatistisches Jahrbuch*, 1906, p. 146.
33. Ibid., 1896.
34. Ibid., 1906, p. 147.
35. Gábor G. Kemény, *Iratok a nemzetiségi kérdés történetéhez Magyarországon a dualizmus korában*, 4 vols. (Budapest, 1952–66), 4:91–92. For this reference, as well as other information on Hungarian nationalist aspirations and the common army, I am deeply obliged to Professor George Barany of the University of Denver.
36. Lt. Col. Dr. Emil Dangelmeier, "Abwehr gegen für den Geist des Heeres schädliche Ideen," *ÖMZ* 40 (1899): 37–45.
37. Franz Conrad v. Hötzendorf, *Aus meiner Dienstzeit*, 5 vols. (Vienna, 1921–25), 1:329; Paul Molisch, *Geschichte der deutschnationalen Bewegung in Österreich* (Jena, 1926), pp. 102–105.
38. Cited in Arthur J. May, *The Habsburg Monarchy, 1867–1914* (Cambridge, Mass., 1951), p. 491.
39. 6 May 1896, KA Nachlass Beck A/2 VII/272. Printed in Glaise-Horstenau, pp. 474–81.
40. Berthold Sutter, *Die Badenischen Sprachenverordnungen von 1897*, 2 vols. (Graz-Cologne, 1960–65), 2:185–86.
41. Succovary to Krieghammer, Graz, 28 November 1897, KA KM Präs. 52–26/26. Actually, the troops in Graz delayed beyond the point where fire was permissible by regulations. See the *Dienst-Reglement für das kaiserlich-königliche Heer* (Vienna, 1886), pt. I, para. 516–18.
42. Sutter, 2:213.
43. KA KM Präs. 1897 52–26, memorandum by Succovary.
44. Ibid. 26–11/2.
45. Marginal note by Francis Joseph to KA KM Präs. 1898 52–5/9.
46. Sutter, 2:231–36.
47. Gustav Kolmer, *Parlament und Verfassung in Österreich 1848–1904*, 8 vols. (Vienna, 1902–14), 4:489. Cf. Dangelmeier, pp. 39–40.
48. C. A. Macartney, *The Habsburg Empire 1790–1918* (London, 1968), pp. 666–67.
49. Kolmer, 8:515–17, and Rudolf Kiszling, *Erzherzog Franz Ferdinand von Österreich Este* (Graz-Cologne, 1953), p. 73.
50. Egon C. Conte Corti and Hans Sokol, *Der alte Kaiser Franz Joseph I* (Vienna-Graz-Cologne, 1955), pp. 151–52.
51. "Betrachtungen über die Lage in Ungarn," KA Nachlass Beck A/2 F VIII/282.
52. For the political developments see Norman Stone, "Constitutional Crises in Hungary, 1903–1906," *Slavonic and East European Review*, 46 (1967): 163–82.
53. Kiszling, p. 81.
54. Glaise-Horstenau, pp. 403–06.
55. Sosnosky, 2:181–83; Kiszling, pp. 74–78, and Stone, "Crises," pp. 170–72.
56. Sosnosky, 2:188.
57. Rudolf Sieghart, *Die letzten Jahrzehnte einer Grossmacht* (Berlin, 1932), p. 65.

58. Heinrich Freiherr v. Pitreich, *Meine Beziehungen zu den Armeeforderungen Ungarns* (Vienna, 1911), pp. 9–13.
59. Jan Beranek, *Rakouský militarismus a boj proti nemu v Čechách* (Prague, 1955), pp. 156–58.
60. For a detailed analysis of the plans and copies of the relevant documents see Kurt Peball and Gunther E. Rothenberg, "Der Fall U. Die geplante Besetzung Ungarns durch die k.u.k. Armee im Herbst 1905," *Schriften des Heeresgeschichtlichen Museums in Wien,* 4 (1969), pp. 85–126.
61. Eduard v. Wertheimer, *Graf Julius Andrássy,* 3 vols. (Stuttgart, 1910–13), 1:393.
62. Conti-Sokol, p. 72.
63. Sosnosky, 2:175; Glaise-Horstenau, p. 405.
64. Moritz v. Auffenberg-Komarov, *Aus Österreichs Höhe und Niedergang* (Munich, 1921), pp. 85–91. Actual copy of proposal, KA GStb. Op. B. F 182/6.
65. "Weisungen für eine allgemeine Mobilisierung des k.u.k. Heeres-Kriegsfall U," Reservat to KA RKM Präs. 1904–7100.
66. Ibid.
67. "Ergebniss der Ischler Beschlüsse und der kommissionellen Beratungen im Kriegsministerium," 24 August 1905, KA GStb. Op. B. F 182/10.
68. Ibid., 182/5.
69. Kiszling, p. 79.
70. Peball and Rothenberg, p. 126.
71. Report from VIII Corps, 7 November 1905, KA MKSM 1905 28–1/4.
72. A copy of the April 1906 agreement in KA MKFF Carton 187 16/4.
73. *ÖULK,* 1:27–29. Cf. Wilhelm Schüssler, *Das Verfassungsproblem im Habsburgerreich* (Berlin, 1918), p. 87.
74. Alfred Krauss, *Die Ursachen unserer Niederlage* (Munich, 1920), p. 64.
75. Anon. (Hugo Kerchnawe), *Unser Letzter Kampf* (Vienna-Leipzig, 1909) passim. Even the more sober evaluation by Beck concluded that "the struggle for the army law and the Hungarian language of command reveals that the final aspirations of the opposition are directed against the unity of the common army, the strongest pillar of the unity and the great power status of the monarchy." "Denkschrift ... 1905," KA GStb. Op. B. F 94.
76. On the rising political-military influence of Francis Ferdinand see Friedrich Funder, *From Empire to Republic* (New York, 1963), pp. 98–100, and Johann C. Allmayer-Beck, *Minister-Präsident Baron Beck* (Munich, 1956), pp. 165–71.
77. Ibid., p. 101.
78. Theodor v. Sosnosky, *Franz Ferdinand, der Erzherzog Thronfolger* (Leipzig, 1929), p. 106.
79. On Francis Ferdinand's opposition to Beck see Leopold v. Chlumecky, *Erzherzog Franz Ferdinands Wirken und Wollen* (Berlin, 1929), pp. 359–60.
80. Glaise-Horstenau, pp. 422–24, 431–35, Margutti pp. 282–91.

10 The Conrad Era from His Appointment to the Annexation Crisis: 1906–1909

1. C. A. Macartney, *The Habsburg Empire: 1790–1918* (London, 1968), pp. 762–63, provides an account of what the author describes as "this obscure transaction." Pitreich's resignation, KA KM Präs. 1906 16–1/6.
2. Johann C. Allmayer-Beck, *Ministerpräsident Baron Beck* (Munich, 1956), pp. 94–100.
3. Rudolf Kiszling, *Erzherzog Franz Ferdinand von Österreich-Este* (Graz-Cologne, 1953), p. 94.

4. On Aehrenthal's program see, among others, G. P. Gooch, *Before the War: Studies in Diplomacy*, 2 vols. (London, 1936), 1:373–415.
5. See the "Denkschrift ... Ende 1904," in KA Gstb. Op. B. F 94.
6. For this view see Leopold v. Chlumecky, *Erzherzog Ferdinands Wirken und Wollen* (Berlin, 1929); Georg Franz, *Erzherzog Franz Ferdinand und die Pläne zur Reform der Habsburger Monarchie* (Brno-Munich-Vienna, 1943); Theodor v. Sosnosky, *Franz Ferdinand, der Erzherzog-Thronfolger* (Leipzig, 1929), and Emil Franzel, *Franz Ferdinand d'Este: Leitbild einer konservativen Revolution* (Vienna, 1964).
7. Kiszling, pp. 248–52.
8. Ibid., p. 37.
9. Ibid., pp. 63–65.
10. Franzel, pp. 46–48; Carl v. Bardolff, *Soldat im alten Österreich* (Jena, 1938), pp. 118–19.
11. Kiszling, pp. 94-96. Allmayer—Beck, pp. 100–101, makes the rather spurious point that Brosch was a politically conscious, but not a "political," soldier.
12. A first-hand account of these activities is provided by Friedrich Funder, former editor of the Christian-Socialist *Reichspost*, in his memoirs, *From Empire to Republic*, pp. 98–101, 111–21.
13. Letter to Conrad, Celerina, 18 February 1908, printed in Conrad v. Hötzendorf, *Aus meiner Dienstzeit 1906–1918*, 5 vols., (Vienna, 1921–1925), 1:564.
14. Sosnosky, p. 106; Allmayer-Beck, p. 101.
15. Franzel, p. 47; Kiszling, p. 65: Conrad, 3:81–82.
16. Ibid., pp. 63–65. The archduke's attitude was seconded by Brosch who also regarded the old-fashioned virtues of a soldier and unquestioning obedience above all as far more important than the "technical means which of late have been grossly overvalued." See Brosch's annotations to the memo by FML Auffenberg, November 1910, in KA MKFF 201/16.
17. Kiszling, pp. 263–64.
18. Vladimir Dedijer, *The Road to Sarajevo* (New York, 1966), pp. 146–47.
19. August Urbanski, *Conrad von Hötzendorf* (Graz-Leipzig-Vienna, 1938), pp. 99–100.
20. Ibid., 100–102.
21. *Die Militärische Welt*, 2 (1906): 199–200. Cf. *Wiener Armee-Blatt*, no. 46, 1906, and *Der Armeefreund*, no. 34, 1906.
22. Conrad's career is outlined in Urbanski, pp. 21–98.
23. *Zum Studium der Taktik* (Vienna, 1891).
24. *Taktikaufgaben*, issued in three parts, (Vienna, 1892–96), *Vorgang beim Studium taktischer Reglements* (Vienna, 1895), and *Die Gefechtsausbildung der Infantrie*, 1st ed. (Vienna, 1900).
25. *Gefechtsausbildung*, 5th ed. (Vienna, 1913), pp. 212–38.
26. See his *Infanteristische Fragen und die Erscheinungen des Burenkrieges* (Vienna, 1903) and the later editions of the *Gefechtsausbildung*. As Kiszling, p. 158, conceded, "Conrad surprisingly paid little attention to the lessons of the Russo-Japanese War." Cf. *Exercierreglements für die k. u. k. Fusstruppen* (Vienna, 1911).
27. After the war many generals blamed Conrad for his insistence on offensive tactics and his neglect of artillery support. See Artur Baron Arz v. Straussenburg, *Kampf und Sturz der Kaiserreiche* (Vienna-Leipzig, 1935), p. 122; Moritz Freiherr v. Auffenberg-Komarov, *Aus Österreichs Höhe und Niedergang* (Vienna, 1925), pp. 79–80; Ernst Kabisch, *Streitfragen des Weltkrieges 1914–1918* (Stuttgart, 1924), pp. 103–104; Alfred Krauss, *Die Ursachen unserer Niederlage* (Munich, 1920), p. 97.
28. In many circles the army was referred to as "Conrad's army," Oskar Regele, *Feldmarschall Conrad* (Vienna, 1955), pp. 515–16.
29. See the adulatory summation in ibid., pp. 442–50, which summarizes the attitude of

Austrian military writers. Civilian historians are slowly becoming more critical. See the introductory remarks by Kurt Peball, "Briefe an eine Freundin," *MÖStA*, 25 (1972): 493.
30. Conrad cited in Regele, p. 81.
31. KA Conrad Archiv, Aphorismen, 1:20.
32. Conrad to Francis Ferdinand, 24 January 1911, KA Gstb. Op. B. F 90.
33. Fritz Fellner ed., *Das politische Tagebuch Josef Redlichs 1908–1919*, 2 vols., (Graz-Cologne, 1953–54), 1:272.
34. Conrad, 1:333. Cf. Rudolf Sieghart, *Die letzten Jahrzehnte einer Grossmacht* (Berlin, 1932), pp. 462–63.
35. Memorandum of 8 April 1907, Conrad 1:503–505.
36. Ibid., pp. 504–505, and Allmayer-Beck, p. 169.
37. Conrad, 1:13.
38. See the summation in Gerhard Ritter, *Staatskunst und Kriegshandwerk*, 4 vols., (Munich, 1954–68), 2:284–86.
39. Notation on Aehrenthal's memorandum rejecting Conrad's demand for preventive war against Serbia, 15 August 1909, KA Gstb. Op. B. F 89 (a).
40. See Regele, pp. 108–23, for a discussion of Conrad's views on preventive war.
41. Solomon Wank, "Some Reflections on Conrad von Hötzendorf and his Memoirs based on Old and New Sources," *Austrian History Yearbook*, 1 (1965): 75–88, presents an excellent and dispassionate summary.
42. FML Schemua, "Militärpolitische Denkschrift Angangs 1912," KA Gstb. Op. B. F 95. Cf. the sentiments expressed by Krauss, pp. 74–76.
43. Allmayer-Beck, pp. 164–73.
44. Ibid, pp. 173–74.
45. Minutes, 25 February 1907, KA KM Präs. 1907 52/61. Cf. Walter Hetzer, "Franz von Schönaich: Reichskriegsminister von 1906–1911," (Diss., University of Vienna, 1960), pp. 55–59, 107.
46. Allmayer-Beck, pp. 175–76; Regele, p. 91; Kiszling, pp. 103–104, and documents in KA Nachlass Putz, "Ausgleich 1907."
47. Allmayer-Beck, pp. 175–76.
48. Conrad to Francis Ferdinand, "Most Secret," Vienna, 7 February 1908, KA Gstb. Op. B. F 95. Also printed in Conrad, 1:552–54.
49. Reply, Francis Ferdinand to Conrad, Celerina, 18 February 1908, ibid., pp. 565–66. Cf. Chlumecky, pp. 260–61.
50. Francis Ferdinand to Francis Joseph, 11 November and 24 December 1908, cited in Kiszling, pp. 131–33.
51. Notes on audience, 30 December 1908; Conrad, 1:133.
52. Conrad to Francis Ferdinand, Vienna, 5 January 1909; ibid., pp. 635–36.
53. "Denkschrift zu Ende 1907," KA Gstb. Op. B. F 95 already mentions plans to transfer the obsolete M 75/96 pieces to the second-line units.
54. Ibid.
55. R. W. Seton-Watson, *Racial Problems in Hungary* (London, 1908), p. 256.
56. Memorandum, 17 November 1905, RKM to FML Czibulka, VIII Corps, KA RKM Präs. 1905–7003.
57. Jan Beránek, *Rakouský militarismus a boj proti němu v Čechách* (Prague, 1955), pp. 202–204.
58. Norman Stone, "Army and Society in the Habsburg Monarchy, 1900–1914," *Past & Present*, no. 33 (1966): 101–102.
59. K. Ivović, *Generalno strajk u Bosni i Hercegovini* (Sarajevo, 1963), passim. A collection from the official archives, including records of XV Corps.
60. KA Conrad Archiv F B/1, letter of 27 February 1907.
61. Regele, pp. 150–57.
62. Conrad, 1:335–37.

63. Ibid., pp. 45–46.
64. Kiszling, pp. 64–65, 69–70.
65. During the same maneuvers, September 1913 in Bohemia, Archduke Charles clearly favored General Brudermann over former War Minister Auffenberg, who had fallen from favor. Reinhold Lorenz, *Kaiser Karl* (Graz-Vienna-Cologne, 1959) pp. 122–23.
66. Krauss, pp. 96–98.
67. Conrad to Arthur Frhr. v. Bolfras, Chef MKSM, 10 October 1914, KA Conrad Archiv F B/12.
68. *ÖULK*, 1:31.
69. Conrad, "Denkschrift zu Ende 1907," Beilage, KA Gstb. Op. B. F 95.
70. Regele, pp. 210–15.
71. Memo. "Über Südtirol," Appendix I, in Conrad, 1:457–71.
72. Report of local inspections commission, 12 January 1907, KA KM Präs. 1906-33/22.
73. For the new Italian fortifications, see reports in ibid., 1907-35-5/12. On Austrian fortifications see ibid. 33-22/7. Cf. Conrad, 1:430–33.
74. Ibid., 1:295–96, and "Denkschrift ... 1909," KA Gstb. Op. B. F 95.
75. *Militärstatistisches Jahrbuch für das Jahr 1907* and the same for 1910, (Vienna, 1907-10), p. 146.
76. Alois Veltzé, *Internationaler Armee-Almanach 1909/10* (Vienna-Leipzig, 1910), pp. 375–77.
77. Alphons Bernhard, "Die österr.-ung. Kavallerie," Reprint from *Militärwissenschaftliche Mitteilungen*, nos. 7–8 (1931): 8–9.
78. Georg Schreiber, *Des Kaisers Reiterei* (Vienna, 1967), pp. 273–75.
79. Kiszling, p. 259. Cf. Schemua to Auffenberg, 17 February 1912, KA Gstb. Op. B. F 95.
80. The new pay scale, exclusive of allowances, started a second lieutenant with 1,680 crowns annual base pay, rising to 1,880 in three years and to 2,000 after six years' service. Captains went from a previous scale of 2,400 to 3,600 crowns to a new scale of 3,000 to 4,400, colonels from 7,200 up to 8,000 crowns, and major generals from 11,400 to 13,000 crowns annually. *Gebührenvorschrift für das k.u.k. Heer* (Vienna, 1909) passim.
81. *Militärstatistisches Jahrbuch*, 1907 and 1910, pp. 143–45.
82. Ibid.
83. Wilhelm Winkler, *Der Anteil der nicht-deutschen Volksstämme an der österr.-ung. Wehrmacht* (Vienna, 1919), p. 2.
84. *Militärstatistisches Jahrbuch*, 1910, pp. 145–46.
85. Conrad, 1:328.
86. Urbanski, pp. 99, but Regele, p. 94, strongly denies these allegations.
87. Michael Károlyi, *Faith without Illusion* (New York, 1957), p. 68.
88. *ÖULK*, 1:55; Conrad, 1:331–34; Krauss, p. 71.
89. Although the army paid premiums for reenlistment and after twelve years' service secured minor civil service positions for discharged non-commissioned officers, the number of men electing to stay on was inadequate, and by 1907 the army was short some six hundred senior non-commissioned officers.
90. Conrad, 1:125–30; Regele, pp. 108–23.
91. Ritter, 2:284–86.
92. Rudolf Krieger, *Die Entwicklung des Conradschen Offensivgedankens* (Stuttgart, 1934), p. 10.
93. Conrad, "Denkschrift Ende 1906," KA Gstb. Op. B. F 95.
94. Memo of 6 April 1907, with postscript of 8 April 1907, Appendix 5 in Conrad, 1:506–10.
95. Ibid., 1:66–68; Cf. documents in KA Gstb. Op. B. F 105, "Freibundsvertrag."
96. For a discussion, see Theodor v. Sosnosky, *Die Politik im Habsburgerreiche*, 2

vols., (Berlin, 1912), 2:107-110. For Italian fortifications see KA Gstb. Op. B. F 62, "Italienische Befestigungen," and ibid., F 38, "Aufmarschpläne-Italien 1907/08".
97. Issue of 28 August 1908.
98. Conrad, 1:40.
99. "Denkschrift Ende 1907," KA Gstb. Op. B. F 95.
100. Report on the Serb assembly, Conrad, 1:511-12.
101. Notes on conversation with Aehrenthal, ibid., p. 514.
102. Conrad to Aehrenthal, 19 November 1907, ibid., pp. 516-17.
103. "Denkschrift Ende 1907," KA Gstb. Op. B. F 95.
104. Kiszling, pp. 125-26; Conrad, 1:518-20.
105. Conrad to Aehrenthal, 16 February 1908, ibid., p. 557.
106. Conrad to RKM, "Situation im Okkupationsgebiet," 27 March 1908, ibid., pp. 567-71.
107. Conrad to Aehrenthal, 2 April 1908, ibid., pp. 572-75, and the memorandum, 17 April 1908, concerning complications to be expected from action in Bosnia and Serbia, ibid., pp. 578-81.
108 Memo, "Kriegsfall Ö.-U. mit D. Reich Kontra R., I., B. (S).," ibid., pp. 582-87.
109. Report, CGstb., 25 August 1908, KA Gstb. 63/1908.
110. Kiszling, pp. 128-29.
111. "Grundlagen für die konkreten Kriegsvorbereitungen für das Jahr 1909," Conrad, 1:604-13.
112. Chlumecky, p. 99; Regele, p. 104, and Sieghart, p. 147.
113. Conrad, 1:142-44.
114. Conrad to Moltke, 2 January 1909, ibid., pp. 631-34. Cf. KA Gsbt. Op. 90 a-l.
115. Moltke to Conrad, 21 January 1909, ibid., p. 2. On the continuing exchange of letters see Norman Stone, "Moltke-Conrad: Relations between the Austro-Hungarian and German General Staffs, 1909-14," *The Historical Journal*, 9 (1966): 204-11.
116. Conrad, 1:149-58.
117. Ibid., p. 157.
118. "Kriegsfall gegen Serbien und Montenegro," memo, 8 March 1909, ibid., 640-55. On the mobilization for Case Yellow—which meant partial execution of Case B—see ibid., pp. 162-63.
119. Report (audience) with Francis Joseph, 2 April 1908 in ibid., pp. 166-68.
120. Conrad to Aehrenthal, August 1909, KA Gstb. Op. B. 89a-10.
121. Thus the story in the idealized but revealing account by Gina Conrad v. Hötzendorf, *Mein Leben mit Conrad von Hötzendorf* (Leipzig, 1935), p. 67.
122. Arz, p. 119; Auffenberg, p. 125. Also the reservations about the combat readiness of the army expressed by Col. Repington, London *Times* military correspondent, reported to Vienna by Capt. Friedrich Prince Liechtenstein, military attaché, 24 January 1909, KA Gstb. 1909 25-2/8. Schönaich also felt that the army was ill-prepared. Memorial of 29 December 1908, in KA KM Präs. 1908 49-39/1.

11 Conrad, Moltke, Aehrenthal, and the Balkan Crises: 1909-1913

1. L. C. F. Turner, *Origins of the First World War* (New York, 1970), pp. 8-9.
2. Gerhard Ritter, *The Schlieffen Plan* (London, 1958), pp. 31-32.
3. Hans Meier-Welcker, "Strategische Planungen und Vereinbarungen der Mittelmächte für den Mehrfrontenkrieg," *ÖMZ* special issue 2 (1964): 18-20. The correspondence discussed in detail by Norman Stone, "Moltke-Conrad: Relations between the Austro-Hungarian and German General Staffs, 1900-14," *The Historical Journal*, 9 (1966): 201-228. The letters exist in draft and original in KA Gsbt. Op. B. 89a and are also printed

in part in Conrad v. Hötzendorf, *Aus meiner Dienstzeit, 1906–1918,* 5 vols., (Vienna, 1921–25), 1:379 and passim.
  4. Ibid., pp. 379–84. It should be noted, however, that some historians regard this exchange as fundamentally modifying the defensive character of the Dual Alliance. For an exposition of this point of view see Stephan Verosta, *Theorie und Realität von Bündnissen* (Vienna, 1971), 341–48.
  5. Conrad, 1:384–93, 396–99, and Stone, p. 209.
  6. Ibid., p. 210; KA Gstb. Op. B. 89a 7.
  7. Conrad's presentation to Francis Joseph, memo, 1 February 1910, ibid., 4. Cf. Gerhard Ritter, *Staatskunst und Kriegshandwerk,* 4 vols. (Munich, 1954–68), 2:305–307, and Stone, 224–26.
  8. Carl Freiherr v. Bardolff, *Soldat im alten Österreich* (Jena, 1938), pp. 90–91; Gordon A. Craig, "The World War I Alliance of the Central Powers in Retrospect: The Military Cohesion of the Alliance," *JMH,* 37 (1965): 48.
  9. "Grundzüge für den Kriegsfall gegen Russland," KA Gstb. Op. B. 89a.
  10. "Kriegsplan ÖU mit D. Reich kontra R, I, B (S)," 17 April 1908, Conrad, 1:582–87. See the observations of Max Freiherr v. Pitreich, *Die militärischen Probleme unseres Kriegsbeginnes* (Vienna, 1934), pp. 32–33. Pitreich was one of the few military writers critical of Conrad.
  11. Memorandum, 15 December 1911, Conrad, 2:445.
  12. Summarized by Rudolf Kiszling, "Kriegspläne und Aufmärsche der k.u.k. Armeen und der Feindheere im Sommer 1914," *ÖMZ* special issue 1 (1965): 2–4. Cf. Conrad passim and Pitreich, pp. 52–85.
  13. *ÖULK,* 1:10–15; Conrad, 3:674.
  14. "Denkschrift Ende 1910," and same memorandum for 1911, KA Gstb. Op. B 95. The 1910 memo also in Conrad, 1:255–74.
  15. Oskar Regele, *Feldmarschall Conrad* (Vienna-Munich, 1955), p. 160; C. A. Macartney, *The Habsburg Empire 1790–1918* (London, 1968), p. 791.
  16. R. W. Seton-Watson, *Corruption and Reform in Hungary* (London, 1911), pp. 184–86. On Schönaich's position, see Walther Hetzer, "Franz von Schönaich: Reichskriegsminister von 1906–1911" (Diss., University of Vienna, 1960), pp. 55–59, Cf. Regele, p. 91.
  17. Rudolf Sieghart, *Die letzten Jahrzehnte einer Grossmacht* (Berlin, 1932), p. 152.
  18. Rudolf Kiszling, *Erzherzog Franz Ferdinand von Österreich-Este* (Graz-Cologne, 1953), pp. 141–45.
  19. Ibid., p. 153. For the political activities of the Belvedere and its attempts to influence the national minorities in Hungary, see Friedrich Funder, *From Empire to Republic* (New York, 1963), pp. 113–21.
  20. Kiszling, *Franz Ferdinand,* p. 157. By 1908 there was a shortage of 600 hundred senior non-commissioned officers in the army establishment. Cf. Schönaich's defense, KA Nachlass Bolfras, B 75–17, 15–5.
  21. Regele, p. 165. Relations had become so bad that the two men never spoke to each other except on official matters. Alfred Krauss, *Die Ursachen unserer Niederlage* (Munich, 1920), p. 107.
  22. Moritz Ritter v. Auffenberg, *Aus Österreichs Höhe und Niedergang* (Munich, 1921), p. 141; Regele, p. 165.
  23. "Vortrag," 13 February 1911, KA Gstb. Op. B. 95. Account of audience, Conrad, 2:113–16; discussion in Regele, pp. 167–68.
  24. Protocol of the session, Budapest, 5 March 1911, Conrad, 2:134–39.
  25. KA MKFF 1911–281/1.
  26. Bardolff, p. 147.
  27. Sarajevo, 10 November 1910, KA MKFF 201/16.
  28. Kiszling, *Franz Ferdinand,* pp. 160–61.

29. Conrad, 2:146–47, and again 232.
30. Macartney, p. 805.
Georg Franz, *Erzherzog Franz Ferdinand und die Pläne zur Reform der Habsburger Monarchie* (Brno-Munich-Vienna, 1943), pp. 47–67.
31. Ibid., p. 86.
32. Text printed in ibid., pp. 146–47.
33. Ibid., p. 145.
34. Heinrich Lammasch, *Seine Aufzeichnungen, sein Wirken, und seine Politik* (Vienna, 1922), p. 91. Lammasch, a university professor and later Austrian prime minister, participated in the formulation of the plans.
35. Although Kiszling, *Franz Ferdinand*, pp. 258–59, doubts that this was a firm program, he confirms the change of garrisons proposal.
36. "Denkschrift über die militärischen Verhältnisse in Ungarn," KA Gstb. Op. B. 90, of 24 January 1911.
37. Rudolf Kiszling, *Die Kroaten*, (Graz-Cologne, 1956), pp. 89–90.
38. Bardolff to Francis Ferdinand, 5 January 1913, KA MKFF 33–12.
39. Aehrenthal to Francis Joseph, 1 April 1907, in Alfred F. Pribram, *Die politischen Geheimverträge Osterreich-Ungarns 1879–1914*, 2 vols. (Vienna, 1920), 2:144.
40. Intelligence reports, KA Gstb. Op. B. 25–2/75.
41. Theodor v. Sosnosky, *Die Politik im Habsburgerreiche*, 2 vols. (Berlin, 1912), 1:107–110 provides the statistics.
42. Conrad, 2:218–33; Regele, p. 170.
43. Conrad to Aehrenthal and Aehrenthal to Conrad, 18 and 21 July 1911, KA Gstb. Op. B. 90, "Korrespondenz in Angelegenheiten Aehrenthal."
44. Memorandum, "Behinderungen des Ausbaues der Wehrmacht durch das Ministerium d. Äusseren," ibid.
45. Letter of 24 September 1911, ibid. Cf. Conrad, 2:172–74.
46. Conrad, 2:275–76.
47. KA MKFF 1911 170/11.
48. Auffenberg, pp. 153; Franz, p. 31, and Kiszling, *Franz Ferdinand*, p. 133.
49. Bardolff, pp. 147–50.
50. Memorandum of 15 November 1911, KA MKFF 1911 Mo/81.
51. Conrad, 2:282–84.
52. *Vedette*, 6 December 1911.
53. Ritter, *Staatskunst und Kriegshandwerk*, 2:287.
54. "Militärpolitische Denkschrift Anfang 1912," KA Gstb. Op. B. 95.
55. Schemua, "Denkschrift für 1912," KA MKFF 34/128.
56. Krauss, pp. 72–73.
57. Auffenberg, pp. 71, 156–57, 177, and 200. Cf. Regele, p. 213. The demand for better artillery originated with Conrad who in early 1911 had asked for the mortars to smash the Italian fortifications. KA Gstb. Op. B. 58, has numerous letters, drafts, proposals, etc., regarding artillery material.
58. Conrad, 3:84–86.
59. Text of the law in Bundesministerium f. Landesverteidigung, *100 Jahre Allgemeine Wehrpflicht in Österreich 1868–1968* (Vienna, 1968), pp. 60–62. Cf. Sosnosky, 2:200–202, Kiszling, *Franz Ferdinand*, pp. 170–71.
60. *ÖULK*, 1:30, and documents in KA Gstb. Op. B. 57.
61. Joseph Redlich, *Austrian War Government* (New Haven, 1929), pp. 57–58.
62. Regele, pp. 161–64, 184; Auffenberg, p. 212.
63. Norman Stone, "Army and Society in the Habsburg Monarchy, 1900–1914," *Past and Present*, no. 33 (1966): 103.
64. Gen. Anton Pitreich, *Der österreichisch-ungarische Bundesgenosse im Sperrfeuer* (Klagenfurt, 1930), p. 67.

65. Turner, pp. 26–47 provides the latest and best balanced account of the Balkan crisis.
66. L. Bittner and H. Uebersberger, eds., *Österreich-Ungarns Aussenpolitik von der Bosnischen Krise 1908 bis zum Kriegsausbruch 1914*, 8 vols. (Vienna, 1930), 4:3633.
67. Hugo Hantsch, *Graf Leopold Berchtold*, 2 vols. (Graz-Vienna-Cologne, 1963), 2:306–308.
68. Berchtold to Schemua, 2 October 1912, KA Gstb. Op. B. 161.
69. Schemua to Berchtold, ibid., 165–3946.
70. A. J. P. Taylor, *The Struggle for Mastery in Europe 1848–1918* (Oxford, 1954), p. 491. See idem; *The Habsburg Monarchy: 1809–1918* (New York, 1965), pp. 228–29.
71. Schemua to Potiorek, 23 September 1912, KA Gstb. Op. B. 61 and to Francis Ferdinand, 29 September 1912, KA MKFF 1912 Mb/11–74.
72. Turner, p. 40.
73. Bardolff, p. 177.
74. Potiorek to Francis Ferdinand, 12 July 1912, asking for additional troops, KA MKFF 1912 Mb/7; troop movement orders, 31 October 1912, KA KM 10 Abt. nr. 944, and KA MKFF 1912 Mb 11/4.
75. KA Gstb. Op. B. 1912–3980. Cf. Auffenberg's memo in KA KM 10 Abt. nr. 720.
76. Ibid., 2026, 3566, 3988.
77. Hantsch, 2:322; Auffenberg, p. 209.
78. KA Gstb. Op. B. 89a 1912/7.
79. Turner, pp. 43–47.
80. KA MKSM 1912 69–2913; Auffenberg, pp. 210–15.
81. August v. Urbanski, *Conrad von Hötzendorf: Soldat und Mensch* (Vienna, 1938), p. 130.
82. Hantsch, 2:359; Kiszling, *Franz Ferdinand*, pp.180–82.
83. Auffenberg, pp. 223–25; Conrad, 2:374.
84. Resignation, KA MKSM 1912 70–1/121.
85. Conrad to Francis Ferdinand, KA MKFF Mb/11–234. Cf. Conrad, 2:410–12.
86. "The exact circumstances of Conrad's return remain uncertain and lacking documentation; one must rely on guessing." Horst Brettner-Messler, "Die Balkanpolitik Conrad v. Hötzendorfs von seiner Wiederernennung zum Chef des Generalstabes bis zum Oktober-Ultimatum 1913," *MÖStA*, 20 (1967): 181. Cf. Kiszling, *Franz Ferdinand*, p. 204.
87. Conrad, 3:151, 154, 167.
88. Fritz Fischer, *Germany's Aims in the First World War* (New York, 1967), p. 33.
89. Conrad to Potiorek, asking for support against demobilization plans, 3 March 1913, KA Gstb. Op. B. F 61; decision for demobilization in Galicia, Conrad, 3:161–63.
90. 18 April 1913, KA Gstb. Op. B. 61.
91. Ibid.; Conrad, 3:333–34.
92. Brettner-Messler, pp. 227–28.
93. KA CA B 3, Conrad to Berchtold, 31 May 1913. However, Col. M. Ronge, *Kriegs- und Industriespionage: Zwölf Jahre Kundschaftsdienst* (Zurich-Leipzig-Vienna, 1930), pp. 77–79, claims that Redl compromised the Austro-Hungarian war plans. After being found, Redl was given the opportunity to commit suicide in order to save face for the army, but the case could not be hushed up. See KA MKFF 1913 14–2/3, 4, 5, and 6 regarding the affair. The report of his suicide in KA MKSM 1913 28–2/24. An excellent book, obviously resting on documents in the KA, is Robert Asprey, *The Panthers Feast* (London, 1959). The author, however, seems to overestimate the effects of Redl's treason.
94. Conrad, 2:363–64.
95. KA Chef d. Gstbs. 1913 Res. 3512; Regele, p. 177. For Conrad's appeal to Moltke to keep Rumania neutral, see KA Gstb. Op. B. 89a, letter of 14 February 1914.
96. Notes for a report to Francis Joseph, 15 October 1913, KA Gstb. Op. B. 91.

97. Ibid., notes for report of 21 October 1913. In slightly changed form in Conrad, 3:447.
98. Maj. Otto Jellinek, *Resüme über d. serb. Armee im Feldzug* 1912/13. Printed in three copies for the Chef d. Gstb. Ev. B. Nr. 1274.
99. L. Albertini, *The Origins of the War of 1914*, 3 vols. (London, 1952–57), 1:388–90.
100. Conrad to Berchtold, 2 July 1913, cited in Brettner-Messler, pp. 238–39.
101. L. v. Chlumecky, *Erzherzog Franz Ferdinands Wirken und Wollen* (Berlin, 1929), p. 106.
102. *ÖULK*, 1:41.
103. In the notes for a report of Conrad to Francis Joseph, 15 April 1913, KA Gstb. Op. B. 91.
104. On the mutiny in the 8th Dragoons see KA MKFF 1913 14–1/6–5; KA MKSM 1914–57–3/1. For dissidence in the 6th Infantry, KA MKSM 1912 69–2962. For the desertion of one lieutenant and twenty-three local civilians to Montenegro in October 1912, KA MKFF 1912 Mb 11/27. Cf. *ÖULK*, 1:41, which also mentions incident in the 16th and 18th Infantry and the 36th Dragoons.
105. OTC, "The Austrian Army," *Westminster Review*, 179 (1913): 142–44.
106. R. W. Seton-Watson, *Racial Problems in Hungary* (London, 1908), p. 256.
107. Cited in Alfred Vagts, *A History of Militarism* (New York, 1937), p. 273.
108. Letter to Moltke, 15 February 1913, Conrad, 3:149–50.
109. Rudolf Kiszling, "Die letzten Dezennien ...," *ÖMZ* special issue 2 (1964):33.
110. Franz, p. 33; Kiszling, *Franz Ferdinand*, pp. 252–53.
111. Bardolff to Francis Ferdinand, 5 January 1913, KA MKFF 1913 33–12.
112. Conrad to Francis Ferdinand, (strictly secret), ibid., 12/6; Krobatin to Francis Ferdinand, (confidential), 24 August 1913, ibid., 12/21.
113. MKFF to Krobatin, subject leakage of information to press, 14 October 1914, ibid., 12/22.
114. KM Krobatin to MKFF reports emperor refuses assent, 16 October 1913, ibid., 12/23.
115. Chlumecky, p. 357.
116. Karl F. Nowak, *Der Weg zur Katastrophe* (Berlin, 1919), p. 153.

12 Austria-Hungary's Last War: 1914–1915

1. A. J. P. Taylor, *The Habsburg Monarchy 1809–1918* (New York, 1965), p. 229.
2. Oskar Regele, *Feldmarschall Conrad* (Vienna, 1955), pp. 180–84.
3. August v. Cramon, *Unser Österreich-Ungarischer Bundesgenosse im Weltkrieg*, 2nd rev. ed., (Berlin, 1922), p. 200. Cramon was German liaison officer with the *A.O.K.*
4. KA Gstb. Op. B. 95.
5. Franz Conrad v. Hötzendorf, *Aus meiner Dienstzeit*, 5 vols. (Vienna, 1921–25), 3:561–63.
6. Ludwig Beck, *Studien*, ed. Hans Speidel (Stuttgart, 1955), p. 158.
7. Conrad, 3:673–74.
8. Beck, p. 102. Cf. Gordon A. Craig, "The World War I Alliance of the Central Powers in Retrospect: The Military Cohesion of the Alliance," *JMH*, 37 (1965):339.
9. Conrad, 3:606–609.
10. Max Freiherr v. Pitreich, *1914 Die militärischen Probleme unseres Kriegsbeginnes* (Vienna, 1934), pp. 124–25.
11. Ibid., pp. 40–42.
12. Memo, 24 December 1913, KA MKSM 1914 38–1/4.
13. Exact figures vary between forty-eight and fifty infantry divisions. In August 1914

four *Landsturm* brigades were formed into two divisions and together with one cavalry division formed provisional Army Group Kummer. The latest figures are in Anton Wagner, *Der Erste Weltkrieg* (Vienna, 1968), pp. 13–17.

14. Ludwig Ellmannsberger, "The Austro-Hungarian Artillery in the World War," *Coast Artillery Journal*, 62 (1925):199. Cf. Erich Gabriel, "Die wichtigsten Waffen der Österreichisch-ungarischen Armee 1918," *ÖMZ*, no. 6 (1968):436–38.

15. Ammunition stock report, 25 July 1914, KA Nachlass Krobatin B 162. Cf. Anton Pitreich, *Der Österreichisch-ungarische Bundesgenosse im Sperrfeuer* (Klagenfurt, 1930), pp. 78–79; Alfred Krauss, *Die Ursachen unserer Niederlage* (Munich, 1920), pp. 94–95.

16. Gabriel, pp. 437–39; KA Gstb. Op. B. 57, "Stand der Projektgeschütze mit Jänner 1914."

17. Pitreich, *Bundesgenosse*, p. 82. Cf. Hans Meisl, "Der russisch-japanische Krieg 1904/05 und die Balkankriege 1912/13 in den Berichten der österreichisch-ungarischen Kriegs, Militär, und Marineattaches," (Diss., University of Innsbruck, 1964), pp. 424–39; August Urbanski, *Conrad von Hötzendorf* (Graz-Leipzig-Vienna, 1938), p. 81; Lothar Rendulic, *Soldat in stürzenden Reichen* (Munich, 1965), pp. 24–25, and Regele, pp. 201–202.

18. Ernst Kabisch, *Streitfragen des Weltkrieges 1914–1918* (Stuttgart, 1923), pp. 103–104.

19. *ÖULK*, 1:449.

20. Gunther E. Rothenberg, "Military Aviation in Austria-Hungary 1893–1918," *Aerospace Historian*, 29 (1972): 77–80. In addition the author is indebted to Douglas Pardee of Melbourne, Australia, for his extensive communications on the Austro-Hungarian airforces.

21. Regele, pp. 214–15.

22. Z. A. B. Zeman, *The Break-Up of the Habsburg Empire* (London, 1961), pp. 1–35.

23. Henry Wickham Steed, *The Hapsburg Monarchy* (London, 1914), p. 61.

24. Zeman, p. 39. Adverse reflections on the loyalty of officers and men, especially those by Krauss, p. 71, appear to be largely self-serving. For a more balanced judgment see *ÖULK*, 1:42–47, and Pitreich, *Bundesgenosse*, pp. 390–91.

25. Arthur J. May, *The Passing of the Hapsburg Monarchy 1914–1918*, 2 vols., (Philadelphia, 1966), 1:86–89, and *ÖULK*, 1:26, Zeman, p. 46. Even Conrad was surprised and relieved by the response. See Fritz Fellner, ed., *Schicksahljahre Österreichs, 1908–1919: Das Politische Tagebuch Josef Redlichs*, 2 vols. (Graz, 1953–54), 1:252. The anti-war socialists, too, were swept up in the wave of emotions; see Friedrich W. Adler, *Vor dem Ausnahmsgericht* (Jena, 1923), pp. 44–46. Nonetheless, the high command was nervous and ordered partial disarmament of certain Bosnian-Hercegovinian formations. KA, AOK 1914 Op. Nr. 133, 602.

26. A. v. Krobatin, "Aus meinen Erinnerungen an den Kaiser," in *Erinnerungen an Franz Josef*, ed. E. v. Steinitz (Berlin, 1931), p. 325.

27. Letter, Karlstadt, 28 June 1914, in Gina Gräfin Conrad von Hötzendorf, *Mein Leben mit Conrad von Hötzendorf* (Leipzig-Vienna, 1935), p. 114.

28. Brosch to Auffenberg, 1 July 1914, in Ludwig Jedlicka, "Alexander Brosch von Aarenau und Moritz von Auffenberg-Komarov," in Emil Franzel, ed., *Virtute Fiduque: Festschrift für Otto von Habsburg zum fünfzigsten Geburtstag* (Vienna, 1965), p. 100.

29. Order appointing Archduke Friedrich, KA MKSM 1914 69–6/9 1–2. On his relations with Conrad see among others Artur Arz v. Straussenburg, *Kampf und Sturz der Mittelmächte* (Vienna, 1935), p. 208; Moritz v. Auffenberg-Komarow, *Aus Österreichs Höhe und Niedergang* (Munich, 1921), pp. 79–80; August v. Cramon and P. Fleck, *Deutschland's Schicksalsbund mit Österreich-Ungarn* (Berlin, 1932), pp. 70–72. For the status of the *A.O.K.*, see *ÖULK* 1:58–61. On the whole question, see also Karl F. Nowak, *Der Weg zur Katastrophe* (Berlin, 1919), pp. 143–47, which gives a much too favorable appraisal of Conrad's abilities.

30. Edmund Glaise v. Horstenau, *Die Katastrophe: die Zertrümmerung Österreich-Ungarns* (Vienna, 1929), p. 66.
31. On this problem see Josef Redlich, *Austrian War Government* (New Haven, 1929), esp. pp. 55–62. On the Austrian part see Christoph Führ, *Das K. u. K. Armeeoberkommando und die Innenpolitik in Österreich 1914–1917* (Graz-Vienna-Cologne, 1968), passim.; Zeman, pp. 40–41.
32. Cyril Falls, *The First World War* (London, 1960), pp. 17–19. Cf. the adulatory appraisals by Oskar Regele, *Gericht über Habsburgs Wehrmacht* (Vienna, 1968), p. 53, and Urbanski, p. 346.
33. KA, Nachlass Oberst Theodor v. Zeyneck (B 151), "Das Leben eines öst.-ung. Generalstabsoffiziers," p. 119.
34. *ÖULK*, 1:58.
35. Josef M. Baron Stürgkh, *Politische und militärische Erinnerungen aus meinem Leben* (Leipzig, 1923), pp. 288–89. General Stürgkh was the brother of Premier Stürgkh and Austro-Hungarian plenipotenitary with the German Supreme Command.
36. Regele, *Conrad*, p. 239.
37. Stürgkh, p. 287; Auffenberg-Komarow, p. 174.
38. Conrad, 4:61–62.
39. Ibid., pp. 131–32.
40. Ibid., pp. 52–54.
41. KA, Nachlass Ronge, Tagebuch d. Landesgendarmeriekommando Galizien, entries for 25 July to 28 December 1914. Cf. Conrad, 4:132, 142, 150–51.
42. Ibid., 110–13, 156–57, and Regele, pp. 245–46.
43. Discussion of 26 July 1914, Conrad, 4:131–32, and Gina v. Hötzendorf, p. 114.
44. KA AOK 1914 Op. Nr. 33.
45. *ÖULK*, 1:5, 322.
46. This is the conclusion reached by Norman Stone, "Moltke-Conrad: Relations between the Austro-Hungarian and German General Staffs, 1900–14," *The Historical Journal*, 9 (1966): 22–25.
47. KA, Nachlass Krauss, Kriegstagebuch, entry for 24 August 1914. Cf. Krauss, pp. 129–30.
48. Conrad, 4:318–21.
49. Winston S. Churchill, *The World Crisis: The Eastern Front* (London, 1931), p. 133.
50. Johann C. Allmayer-Beck, "Der Sommerfeldzug von 1914 gegen Russland," *ÖMZ*, special issue 1 (1965): 32–34.
51. Conrad was so disappointed with the poor showing of the cavalry that he wrote to Bolfras that the branch would have to lose its special position in the future. Cited in Regele, *Conrad*, p. 204. Cf. Pitreich, *Bundesgenosse*, pp. 82–83. For a more favorable evaluation see Heinrich Mast, "Die Aufklärungstätigkeit der österr.-ung. Kavallerie bei Kriegsbeginn 1914," *ÖMZ*, special issue 1 (1965): 12–17.
52. Conrad, 4:701–702.
53. Pitreich, *Bundesgenosse*, pp.130–31; Churchill, p. 159.
54. *ÖULK*, 1:344–45; but see Regele, *Conrad*, pp. 339–40, who points out that all armies experienced heavy losses among their regulars in 1914.
55. Among others see Erich Ludendorff, *Meine Kriegserinnerungen* (Berlin, 1919), p. 46; Krauss, pp. 135–37; Churchill, pp. 121–22, 230–31, and Kabisch, pp. 59–60.
56. Urbanski, p. 279; *ÖULK*, 1:155, and Conrad, 4:324–26, 712–14. Cramon and Fleck, p. 26, support Conrad's contentions.
57. Conrad, 3:637, 4:536–37, and 467. Cf. his statement to Josef Redlich in Fellner, 1:270.
58. KA MKSM 1914-53.
59. Josef Count Stürgkh, *Im deutschen grossen Hauptquartier* (Leipzig, 1921), p. 40.
60. Regele, *Conrad*, pp. 299–300, 482–87, and Nowak, pp. 128–29.

61. Pitreich, *Bundesgenosse*, pp. 138–39; *ÖULK*, 1:391–449.
62. Major General Hoffman, *War Diaries and Other Papers*, 2 vols. (London, 1929), 1:45.
63. Ludendorff, p. 91.
64. Krauss, pp. 60–61.
65. *ÖULK*, 1:812.
66. Maj. Otto Jellinek, "Resume über die serbische Armee in Feldzug 1912/13," KA, k.u.k. Chef. d. Gstb. Ev. Bureau N 1274.
67. The best account by far of the campaign in Serbia in 1914 is Kurt Peball, "Der Feldzug gegen Serbien und Montenegro im Jahre 1914," *ÖMZ*, special issue 1 (1965): 18–30. For an unfavorable evaluation of Potiorek, see Nowak, pp. 99–102.
68. Josef Neumair, *Im Serbischen Feldzug 1914: Erlebnisse und Stimmungen eines Landsturm Offiziers* (Innsbruck, 1917), pp. 34–35. Cf. Pitreich, *Bundesgenosse*, p. 108.
69. *ÖULK*, 1:707–59.
70. Krauss, p. 167.
71. "Denkschrift des Chef d. Generalstabes," 14 December 1914, KA MKSM 1914 69–8/15.
72. Pitreich, *1914*, pp. 97–98.
73. *ÖULK*, 1:762.
74. Ibid., p. 151. Cf. Regele, *Conrad*, p. 517.
75. Reinhold Lorenz, *Kaiser Karl und der Untergang der Donaumonarchie* (Graz-Vienna, 1959), pp. 175, 178–79. Not only Czechs, but also Ruthenes and Poles were beginning to show signs of disaffection. Cf. Rudolf Hecht, "Fragen zur Heeresergänzung der gesamten bewaffneten Macht Österreich-Ungarns während des Weltkrieges," (Diss., University of Vienna, 1969), pp. 195–98.
76. Zeman, p. 39.
77. Pitreich, *Bundesgenosse*, p. 151.
78. Regele, *Conrad*, pp. 214–15; for the shortage of rifles see KA MKSM 1914 69–12/5.
79. Pitreich, *Bundesgenosse*, pp. 191, 198–99, is bitterly critical of the conduct of the winter offensive which "practically ruined the *k.u.k.* infantry."
80. *ÖULK*, 2:271.
81. Wagner, p. 82.
82. Pitreich, *Bundesgenosse*, pp. 198–99.
83. Official version and documents in KA MKSM 1915 52–4/16.
84. See the excellent discussion in Zeman, pp. 52, 54–57.
85. Edmund Glaise v. Horstenau, *Die Katastrophe: Die Zertrümmerung Österreich-Ungarns* (Zurich, 1929), p. 65.
86. May, 1:363; Zeman, p. 56.
87. Cramon, pp. 22–23.
88. Ibid., pp. 12–13, holds that Conrad conceived Tarnow-Gorlice as a limited tactical operation only.
89. Artur Arz. v. Straussenburg, *Zur Geschichte des grossen Krieges 1914–1918* (Vienna-Leipzig-Munich, 1924), pp. 58–60, clearly relates the German support and influence on the new tactics. Most of the artillery support was provided by German batteries.
90. Regele, *Conrad*, pp. 183–86. Falkenhayn complained that Conrad was the "typical writer of exposé and memorandum. As soon as one dispute appeared settled, there appeared at once a sarcastic counter-memorandum from the *A.O.K.*" Gisbert Begerhaus, *Einheitlicher Oberbefehl. Ein Problem des Weltkrieges* (Munich, 1938), p. 27.
91. Conrad, 5:178.
92. Cramon, pp. 13–14.
93. Krauss, pp. 58–61. For a German view see KA Ms. WK, "Die Deutsche Südarmee von Anfang Januar bis Anfang Juli 1915," pp. 15–16, and passim.

13 War on Many Fronts and the Death of Emperor Francis Joseph: 1915–1916

1. Erich Ludendorff, *Meine Kriegserinnerungen 1914–1918* (Berlin, 1919), p. 132.
2. Arthur J. May, *The Passing of the Hapsburg Monarchy 1914–1918*, 2 vols. (Philadelphia, 1966), 1:200. Cf. Oskar Regele, *Feldmarschall Conrad* (Vienna, 1955), p. 525.
3. James E. Edmonds, *Military Operations, Italy 1915–1919* (London, 1949), p. 11.
4. Hugo Schäfer, "Die Kriegspläne Italiens gegen Österreich-Ungarn," *ÖULK*, supp. 2 (1931):1–7.
5. Anton Wagner, *Der Erste Weltkrieg* (Vienna, 1968), pp. 96–100.
6. Appointment of Rohr, 27 August 1914, KA MKSM 1914 69–10/1.
7. KA MS. Rb., "Denkschrift über die Reichsbefestigung der ehem. öst.-ung. Monarchie."
8. KA MKSM 1915 69–10/14.
9. Gerard E. Silberstein, "The High Command and Diplomacy in Austria-Hungary, 1914–1916," *JMH*, 42 (1970): 592–96.
10. Conrad to Falkenhayn, 6 April 1915, KA AOK Op. B. 8822.
11. Erich v. Falkenhayn, *The German General Staff and its Decisions 1914–1916* (New York, 1920), p. 102; Karl F. Nowak, *Der Weg zur Katastrophe* (Berlin, 1919), pp. 157–59.
12. Falkenhayn, pp. 104–105.
13. Regele, p. 377.
14. KA AOK Op. B. 9645.
15. KA MKSM 1915 69–2/11.
16. Ibid., 69–10/17–5.
17. Ibid., 69–3/32–3. Cf. Alfred Krauss, *Die Ursachen unserer Niederlage* (Munich, 1920), pp. 175–76.
18. Wagner, pp. 99–100.
19. For the initial confusion along the Isonzo see KA Nachlass Kuttig v. Domberg, Diary, 2:8–10, 25–26; Krauss, pp. 176–77.
20. Fritz Weber, *Das Ende der alten Armee* (Salzburg-Stuttgart, 1959), pp. 11–51, gives a graphic account of the first weeks of fighting in the Trentino. Cf. Anton Pitreich, *Der österreichisch-ungarische Bundesgenosse im Sperrfeuer* (Klagenfurt, 1930), pp. 220–21.
21. KA AOK Op. B. 8273.
22. Ibid., 8533 of 29 March 1915.
23. Ibid., Conrad to Falkenhayn, 8585 of 30 March 1915.
24. Ibid., Burian to Conrad, 8656 of 30 March 1915.
25. Gerard E. Silberstein, *The Troubled Alliance: German-Austrian Relations 1914–1917* (Lexington, Ky., 1970), 281–82.
26. Ibid., pp. 291–93; August v. Cramon, *Unser österreichisch-ungarischer Bundesgenosse im Weltkriege* (Berlin, 1922), pp. 31–35. Compare Falkenhayn's draft of military convention, September 1915, KA AOK Op. B. 14810 with Conrad's counter proposal, 5 September 1915, ibid., 14890.
28. A. v. Cramon and P. Fleck, *Deutschlands Schicksalsbund mit Österreich-Ungarn* (Berlin, 1932), pp. 112–13.
29. Final reports, KA MKSM 1916 69–13/1–22.
30. Falkenhayn, pp. 220–22.
31. Discussion and full text of memorandum in Kurt Peball, "Um das Erbe. Zur Nationalitätenpolitik des k.u.k. Armeeoberkommandos während der Jahre 1914 bis 1917," *ÖMZ*, special issue (1967): 30–36.
32. Ibid., p. 36, and Leo Valiani, *The End of Austria-Hungary* (New York, 1973), pp. 173–76.

33. Conrad to Burian, 30 March 1915, KA AOK Op. B. 8577.
34. Conrad to Francis Joseph, 22 October 1915, ibid., 17238.
35. May, 1:126. Edmund v. Glaise-Horstenau, *Die Katastrophe: Die Zertrümmerung Österreich-Ungarns* (Vienna, 1929), pp. 62–63.
36. KA KM Abt. 6, 1–2/168.
37. *ÖULK*, 1:56.
38. Erich Gabriel, "Die wichtigsten Waffen der österreich-ungarischen Armee 1918," *ÖMZ*, no. 6 (1968): 437–40; Pitreich, pp. 312–15.
39. Gunther E. Rothenberg, "Military Aviation in Austria-Hungary, 1893–1918," *Aerospace Historian*, 19 (1972): 80–81.
40. Valiani, p. 177; May 1:329–34. On the military supply situation, see Ottokar v. Landwehr Pragenau, *Hunger* (Zurich-Leipzig-Vienna, 1931), p. 9.
41. Alphons Bernhard, "Die österr.-ung. Kavallerie," *Militärwissenschaftliche Mitteilunger*, nos. 7–8 (1931): 15–16.
42. Falkenhayn, pp. 246–47.
43. The exchange in full in Cramon and Fleck, pp. 121–27. Original KA AOK Op. B. 19974.
44. Krauss, pp. 189–90.
45. Ibid., Cf. August v. Urbanski, *Conrad von Hötzendorf* (Graf-Leipzig-Vienna, 1938), pp. 332–35.
46. *ÖULK*, 4:251–59.
47. Draft of letter to chief of MKSM, KA Brougier Nachlass (B-133). Lt. Col. Brougier was Charles' adjutant.
48. Krauss to Bolfras, KA MKSM Sep. Fasz. 79/42.
49. *ÖULK*, 4:374. Cf. FML Székelely de Doba, "Study concerning experiences gained during Russian June offensive," 16 August 1916, KA AOK Op. B. 28136.
50. FML Otto Berndt, chief of staff Fourth Army, "Betrachtungen über die Schlacht von Olyka-Luck 1916," KA AOK Op. B. Fasz. 524, sep. enclosure. Cf. Nowak, pp. 173–76.
51. Fritz Fellner ed., *Schicksalsjahre Österreichs, 1908–1919: Das politische Tagebuch Josef Redlichs*, 2 vols. (Graz-Cologne, 1953–54), 2:123.
52. Regele, pp. 365–66.
53. Cyril Falls, *The Great War 1914–1918* (New York, 1959), p. 227. Cf. Nowak, pp. 174–76.
54. Gina Gräfin Conrad v. Hötzendorf, *Mein Leben mit Conrad von Hötzendorf* (Leipzig-Vienna, 1935), pp. 151–52.
55. Pitreich, pp. 280–300.
56. Arthur Baron Arz von Straussenburg, *Zur Geschichte des Grossen Krieges 1914–1918* (Vienna-Leipzig-Munich, 1924), pp. 102–20. Cf. KA MKSM 1915 69–4/47.
57. Cramon and Fleck, pp. 138–39.
58. Regele, p. 369.
59. Cramon, pp. 65–66; Silberstein, *Troubled Alliance*, pp. 315–16.
60. May, 1:396–97; Valiani, pp. 165–66.
61. Zoltán Szende, *Die Ungarn im Zusammenbruch 1918* (Oldenburg, 1931), pp. 37–39; Michael Károlyi, *Memoirs* (London, 1956), p. 69.
62. Col. Theodor Ritter v. Zeyneck, "Das Leben eines österreichisch-ungarischen Generalstabsoffiziers," KA Zeyneck Nachlass (B-151), diary p. 167.
63. Hans Meier-Welcker, *Seeckt* (Frankfurt a.M., 1967), pp. 79–80. Cf. also the allegations in Karl Freiherr v. Werkmann, *Deutschland als Verbündeter* (Berlin, 1931), pp. 38–39, 57–63.
64. Conrad's protest, 19 July 1916, KA MKSM 1916 69–2/6–1. Falkenhayn, pp. 310–11.

65. KA MKSM 1916 2/6–2,3,4,5. Reinhold Lorenz, *Kaiser Karl und der Untergang der Donaumonarchie (Graz-Vienna-Cologne, 1959), p. 210.*
66. KA MKSM 1916 69 2/10–1.
67. Correspondence, stipulations, and agreements, ibid., 2/10–12. Regele, pp. 272–300.
68. KA MKSM 69 1 3/200.
69. Rudolf Kiszling, "Feldmarschall Franz Graf Conrad v. Hötzendorf," *Gestalter der Geschicke Österreichs*, ed. Hugo Hantsch (Innsbruck-Vienna-Munich, 1962), p. 563.
70. Ludendorff, pp. 202–203.
71. A. Freiherr v. Margutti, *Kaiser Franz Joseph* (Vienna, 1924), p. 459.
72. On the impact of the emperor's death see Z. A. B. Zeman, *The Break-up of the Habsburg Monarchy 1914–1918* (London, 1961), pp. 98–99; May 1:430–33.
73. An overall appreciation of the relationship between Francis Joseph and his army by Johann C. Allmayer-Beck, "Das Heerwesen," in Friedrich Engel-Janosi and Helmut Rumpler, *Probleme der Franzisko-Josephinischen Zeit 1848–1916* (Vienna, 1967), pp. 67–78.
74. Kurt Peball, "Sendung und Erbe," *ÖMZ*, special issue (1966): 59–65.
75. Basil H. Liddell-Hart, *The Real War 1914–1918* (Boston, 1930), p. 39.

14 Emperor Charles and the Dissolution of the Hapsburg Army: 1916–1918

1. For an overall assessment, see Arthur J. May, *The Passing of the Hapsburg Monarchy 1914–1918*, 2 vols. (Philadelphia, 1966), 1:436–42. For the negative military evaluations, see Carl Freiherr v. Bardolff, *Soldat im alten Österreich* (Jena, 1938), pp. 267–68; Karl F. Nowak, *Der Weg zur Katastrophe* (Berlin, 1919), pp. 207–10; August v. Cramon, *Unser österreichisch-ungarischer Bundesgenosse im Weltkriege* (Berlin, 1922), pp. 88–95; and Alfred Krauss, *Die Ursachen unserer Niederlage* (Munich, 1920), pp. 199–205.
2. C. A. Macartney and A. W. Palmer, *Independent Eastern Europe* (London, 1966), p. 66.
3. Reinhold Lorenz, *Kaiser Karl und der Untergang der Donaumonarchie* (Graz-Vienna-Cologne, 1959), pp. 240–41.
4. Ibid.
5. In Karl Freiherr v. Werkmann, *Deutschland als Verbündeter* (Berlin, 1931), pp. 87–88.
6. KA MKSM 1916 69–6/33.
7. Ibid., 1917 69–2/7.
8. Ibid., 65–2/4–2. The memoirs of Gina Gräfin Conrad v. Hötzendorf, *Mein Leben mit Conrad v. Hötzendorf* (Leipzig-Vienna, 1935), pp. 156–58, provide an intimate glimpse into this affair. Cf. A. v. Cramon and P. Fleck, *Deutschlands Schicksalsbund mit Österreich-Ungarn* (Berlin, 1932), pp. 112–13.
9. Fritz Fellner, ed., *Schicksalsjahre Österreichs, 1908–1919: Das politische Tagebuch Josef Redlichs*, 2 vols. (Graz-Cologne, 1953–54), 2:181.
10. Among others see E. Zeno v. Schonta, *Aus den Erinnerungen eines Flügeladjutanten* (Vienna, 1928), pp. 93–95; August v. Urbanski, *Conrad von Hötzendorf* (Graz-Leipzig-Vienna, 1938), p. 714; Cramon, p. 100; Nowak, pp. 225–26, and *ÖULK*, 4:72.
11. Charles to Conrad, 1 March 1917, in Nowak, pp. 223–44. Cf. Hötzendorf, pp. 163–70, and KA MKSM 1917 69 2/9.
12. A discussion of Arz and some assessments in Oskar Regele, *Gericht über Habsburgs Wehrmacht* (Vienna-Munich, 1968), pp. 54–58. Notably lacking in this collection are the harsh judgments by Krauss, p. 249, and Cramon, pp. 134–35.
13. Regele, pp. 60–61; Krauss, pp. 249–50.

14. Werkmann, pp. 90–91; Cramon, p. 135.
15. Reinhold Lorenz, "Aus dem Kriegstagebuch des Generaladjutanten Freiherrn von Marterer," Institut für österr. Geschichtsforschung u. Wiener Katholische Akademie, *Festgabe für Hugo Hantsch* (Graz-Vienna-Cologne, 1965), p. 495.
16. KA MKSM 1917 70–1/26; May, 1:440.
17. KA MKSM 1917 70–1/7. Cf. KA Marterer Nachlass (B-16), diary for 9 February 1917.
18. KA MKSM 1916 11–2/16–2; Regele, 124–25; Cramon, pp. 95–97.
19. Artur Arz v. Straussenburg, *Zur Geschichte des grossen Krieges 1914–1918* (Vienna, 1924), pp. 134–35.
20. Ibid., p. 136.
21. KA MKSM 1917 57–2/5–2,3. Bardolff, p. 275; Regele, pp. 123–24.
22. Christoph Führ, *Das k.u.k. Armeeoberkommando und die Innenpolitik in Österreich 1914–1917* (Graz-Vienna-Cologne, 1968), p. 182.
23. KA MKSM 1916 85–3/2,3,4.
24. Führ, pp. 175–77.
25. Z. A. B. Zeman, *The Break-up of the Habsburg Empire 1914–1918* (London, 1961), p. 189; Cramon, pp. 113–15; Krauss, pp. 279–80.
26. Leo Valiani, *The End of Austria-Hungary* (New York, 1973), p. 184.
27. ÖULK, 5:732.
28. Cramon, pp. 96–97; May, 1:474–80.
29. Discussed in detail by Robert A. Kann, *Die Sixtus-Affäre und die geheimen Friedensverhandlungen Österreich-Ungarns im Ersten Weltkrieg* (Vienna, 1966). Cf. Werkmann, pp. 220–21.
30. Arz, pp. 141–42; Anton Pitreich, *Der österreichisch-ungarische Bundesgenosse im Sperrfeuer* (Klagenfurt, 1930), pp. 312–15.
31. Gunther E. Rothenberg, "Military Aviation in Austria-Hungary, 1893–1918," *Aerospace Historian*, 19 (1972): 80–81.
32. KA MKSM 1917 93–2/60. Cf. Edmund v. Glaise-Horstenau, *Die Katastrophe: die Zertrümmerung Österreich-Ungarns* (Vienna, 1929), pp. 62–63.
33. ÖULK, 6:46–47.
34. KA MKSM 1917 82–2/15 and 12/14.
35. Lorenz, *Kaiser Karl*, p. 410.
36. Ottokar v. Landwehr-Pragenau, *Hunger* (Zurich-Leipzig-Vienna, 1931), pp. 167–68 and passim.
37. Hans Maier-Welcker, *Seeckt* (Frankfurt a.M., 1967), pp. 129–33.
38. Gerburg Thunig-Nittner, *Die tschechoslowakische Legion in Russland* (Wiesbaden, 1969), pp. 24–26.
39. Arz, p. 162.
40. Printed ibid., p. 171.
41. See Cramon, pp. 126–27 for the attempt by Charles to prevent participation of German troops; on the limited aim see Erich Ludendorff, *Meine Kriegserinnerungen* (Berlin, 1919), pp. 386–88.
42. Arz, p. 175.
43. Alfred Krauss, *Das Wunder von Karfreit* (Munich, 1926), p. 65. Other works on the battle include Krafft v. Dellmensingen, *Der Durchbruch am Isonzo* (Berlin, 1926), and Cyril Falls, *Caporetto 1917* (London, 1966). A brief and objective account by Anton Wagner, "Die 12. Isonzoschlacht- Vom Isonzo zur Piave," *Der Donauraum*, 12 (1967), 193–204.
44. Ibid., pp. 202–203; Nowak, pp. 262–66.
45. Krauss, *Ursachen*, pp. 232–33; Werkmann, pp. 132–36. But compare Ludendorff, pp. 400–401, and Regele, pp. 86–88.

46. KA MKSM 1917 69–23/4.
47. KA Nachlass Wieden (B-30), F 1/4.
48. Johann C. Allmayer-Beck, "Heeresreorganisation vor 50 Jahren," *ÖMZ* special issue (1967): p. 18.
49. Arz, pp. 257–58.
50. Allmayer-Beck, p. 19.
51. KA MKSM 1918 38–2/2.
52. Arz, pp. 259–60.
53. Krauss, p. 247.
54. Glaise-Horstenau, p. 248.
55. *ÖULK*, 7:55.
56. Arz, pp. 257–58.
57. Allmayer-Beck, p. 21.
58. Conrad Regele, *Feldmarschall Conrad* (Vienna, 1955), pp. 90–91. Cf. KA MKSM 1915 37 1/10–2, and 1916 25–1/2.
59. Johann C. Allmayer-Beck, "AOK und 'Armeefrage' im Jahre 1918," *ÖMZ*, 6 (1968): 431–32.
60. Glaise-Horstenau, *Katastrophe*, pp. 112–13.
61. Allmayer-Beck, "Armeefrage," p. 432.
62. Protocol, KA MKSM 1918 38–2/1.
63. Regele, *Conrad*, 439–41; a slightly erroneous version in Bardolff, pp. 292–94.
64. Arz, pp. 213.
65. KA KM Präs. 1918 49–5/1.
66. Allmayer-Beck, "Heeresreorganisation," pp. 25–26.
67. KA MKSM 1918 38–2/1, report of the sessions of 12 September 1918.
68. Stöger-Steiner, "Memoire über die Möglichkeit des Durchhalten im Winter 1917/18," KA MKSM 1917 69–2/7.
69. Valiani, pp. 212–13. The most comprehensive treatment of the disruptions, subversions, revolts, and mutinies during the last year of the war is Richard G. Plaschka, Horst Haselsteiner, and Arnold Suppan, *Innere Front: Militärassistenzen, Widerstand, und Umsturz in der Donaumonarchie 1918*, 2 vols. (Vienna, 1974).
70. Documents in Rudolf Neck ed. *Österreich im Jahre 1918* (Vienna, 1968), pp. 30–34. Cf. KA MKSM 1918 69–3/17–22; Arz, 223–24; Bardolff, p. 295, and Glaise-Horstenau, pp. 141–42.
71. Report of AOK 119 083, appendix 3, in KA MKSM 1918 25–1/9.
72. Glaise-Horstenau, p. 247.
73. Richard G. Plaschka, *Cattaro-Prag. Revolte und Revolution* (Graz, 1963), the best study on the Cattaro mutiny.
74. See Inge Przybilovszki, "Die Rückführung der österreich-ungarischen Kriegsgefangenen aus dem Osten in den letzten Monaten der k.u.k. Monarchie," (Diss., University of Vienna, 1965).
75. Karel Pichlik, "Der militärische Zusammenbruch der Mittelmächte im Jahre 1918," in *Die Auflösung des Habsburgerreiches,* ed. R. G. Plaschka and K. Mack (Vienna, 1970), p. 252. Cf. by the same author and in greater detail "Das Ende der österreichisch-ungarischen Armee," *Österreichische Osthefte* 2 (1963): 353–54.
76. Ibid., pp. 355–56. For May mutinies see *ÖULK*, 7:98.
77. Arz, pp. 238–44; Cramon, p. 145.
78. Arz, p. 280; *ÖULK*, 7:183.
79. John Laffin, *Anzacs at War* (London, 1965), p. 83.
80. Richard G. Plaschka, "Die revolutionäre Herausforderung im Endkampf der Donaumonarchie," in Plaschka and Mack, pp. 19–23.
81. KA MKSM 1818 69–23/5. A version more favorable to Charles is in Werkmann, pp. 168–69. Cf. Arz, pp. 248–52.

82. Gerhard Ritter, *Staatskunst und Kriegshandwerk*, 4 vols. (Munich, 1954–68), 4:293–94.
83. Peter Fiala, *Die letzte Offensive Altösterreichs* (Boppard, 1967), pp. 21, 25–31; Neck, p. 19.
84. Arz, pp. 262–64, defends the decision, as does Regele Gericht, pp. 93–99. For Conrad's part in this decision, see Konrad Leppa, "Heeresgruppe Conrad. Die Tragödie eines Feldherrn," *Allgemeine Schweizerische Militärzeitschrift*, 125 (1959): 442–45.
85. Amedo Tosti, *La guerra Italo-Austriace 1915–1918*, 2nd ed. (Rome, 1938), p. 333. For a participant's account of the army's condition, see Fritz Weber, *Das Ende der alten Armee* (Salzburg-Stuttgart, 1959), pp. 211–23. Even Archduke Joseph, the front commander, had little faith in the enterprise. See his letter to Seeckt, 4 August 1918, in Ludwig Jedlicka, *Ende und Anfang: Österreich 1918/19* (Salzburg, 1969), pp. 18–23.
86. Peter Fiala, "Die letzte Offensive gegen Italien," *ÖMZ* 6 (1968): 397–402. Werkmann, p. 272, blames Arz for the misallocation of forces.
87. Fiala, pp. 403–404. Cf. *ÖULK*, 7:228–359; Cramon, pp. 164–73.
88. KA MKSM 1918 69–3/71. Cf. Werkmann, p. 274.
89. Report of secret session, 24 July 1918, in Neck, pp. 53–54.
90. Zoltán Szende, *Die Ungarn im Zusammenbruch 1918* (Oldenburg, 1931), p. 18.
91. Pichlik, "Das Ende," pp. 357–61; Plaschka, "Die revolutionäre Herausforderung," pp. 22–23. Cf. Sarkotić to *A.O.K.*, 5 July 1918, KA AOK Op. B. 108961; *ÖULK* 7:98, 361, and passim.
92. KA MKSM 1918 3/3–26, and 69 15/2–2 orders action against deserters; on the precautions during Charles' journey, see Glaise-Horstenau, p. 244.
93. KA MKSM 1918 69–4/33.
94. KA KM Präs. 1918 34/327–5, MKSM 1918 69–4/21.
95. KA MKSM 1918 69–20/19 of 27 September 1918.
96. Arz, pp. 279–80, 297–99; figures provided to the crown council of 27 September 1818, KA MKSM 1918 69–2/10–2.
97. Arz, pp. 283–84.
98. Hugo Kerchnawe, *Der Zusammenbruch der österreichisch-ungarischen Wehrmacht im Herbst 1918* (Munich, 1921), p. 25.
99. Alfred Krauss and Franz Klingenbrunner, "Die Besetzung der Ukraine 1918," in *Die k.u.k. Militärverwaltung in den besetzten Gebieten*, ed. H. Kerchnawe (Vienna, 1928), pp. 388–90.
100. KA MKSM 1918 69–20/19.
101. Minutes of the crown council, ibid., 69–2/10–2.
102. Police report on repercussions of manifesto, ibid., 69–20/17.
103. David F. Strong, *Austria: Transition from Empire to Republic* (New York, 1939), p. 99. Arz, pp. 323–26.
104. KA MKSM 1918 64–20/17–1.
105. KA MKSM 1918 69–27/10. Text printed in Werkmann, pp. 327–28.
106. KA KM Präs. 1918 10–24/2.
107. Letter to Kövess, 29 June 1920, printed in Heeresgeschichtliches Museum, *1918–1968: Die Streitkräfte der Republik Österreich* (Vienna, 1968), p. 142. The oath issue had given rise to polemics between various officer groups in the postwar period. Cf. KA Nachlass Krauss, nos. 6–8; Bardolff, pp. 342–43, and Ludwig Jedlicka, *Ein Heer im Schatten der Parteien* (Graz-Cologne, 1955), pp. 27–29.
108. Among others, Plaschka, *Cattaro-Prag*, pp. 267–71; Lorenz, *Kaiser Karl*, p. 535; Szende, p. 88. KA MKSM 1918 69–27/4–1,2.
109. Kerchnawe, pp. 65–67.
110. Letter to his family, 21 October in Neck, pp. 61–62.
111. Documented account in Kerchnawe, pp. 95–122.
112. Glaise-Horstenau, pp. 406–12; *ÖULK*, 7:632–36; Kerchnawe, p. 174.

113. KA AOK Geh: Fasz. 493, Op. Nr. 2074.
114. Ibid., Nr. 2058. Y. Tedlicka, p. 52.
115. Hugo Hantsch, *Geschichte Österreichs,* 2 vols., (Graz-Vienna-Cologne, 1962), p. 539; Rolf Bauer, *Österreich-Ein Jahrtausend Geschichte im Herzen Europas* (Berlin, 1970), p. 371, are typical for this version. A slightly modified account in Lorenz, *Kaiser Karl,* p. 537.
116. Linder to *A.O.K.,* telegram, KA Chef d. Gstb. Op. geh. 2090.
117. Neck, pp. 108–109. The version of events in Arz, pp. 364–65, is false.
118. Emil Ratzenhofer, "Der Waffenstillstand von Villa Giusti," *ÖULK* suppl. 2 (1931): 37–41.
119. Terms of the armistice, KA MKSM 1918 69–2/16–2.
120. Werkmann, pp. 340–41; KA Nachlass Arz (B 63) 2; Arz, p. 364.
121. KA MKSM 1918 69–20/20; Cramon, p. 197.
122. Kövess' appointment, KA MKSM 1918 69 27/9–3; Arz, p. 368.
123. Neck, pp. 111–13.
124. Ratzenhofer, pp. 40–42; Glaise-Horstenau, pp. 418–22.
125. Jedlicka, pp. 54–55.
126. Neck, pp. 111–13.
127. Lt. Col. Alfred v. Wittich, chief of staff Army Group Tyrol, KA Umsturzakten; signal from Army Group Tryol, 5 November 1918, Kerchnawe, p. 156; dated 4 November in Arz, p. 379; Glaise-Horstenau, pp. 410–17.
128. Figures taken from Anton Wagner, *Der erste Weltkrieg* (Vienna, 1968), pp. 316–17.
129. Heinrich Benedikt, *Monarchie der Gegensätze* (Vienna, 1949), p. 195.

15 Epilogue

1. Arthur J. May, *The Passing of the Hapsburg Monarchy,* 2 vols. (Philadelphia, 1966), p. 800. Cf. the description by Prince Schönburg-Hartenstein, in Rudolf Neck ed., *Österreich im Jahre 1918* (Vienna, 1968), p. 101.
2. Among others, Zoltán Szende, *Die Ungarn im Zusammenbruch 1918* (Oldenburg, 1931), pp. 108–79 passim; Rudolf Kiszling, *Die Kroaten* (Graz-Cologne, 1956), pp. 124–25.
3. KA Nachlass Pflanzer-Baltin (B-50), Tagebuch July-November 1918.
4. Jiri Koralka, "Germany's attitude towards the national disintegration of Cisleithania (April-October 1918)," *Journal of Contemporary History,* 6 (1969): 92–93.
5. Wilhelm Gröner, *Lebenserinnerungen* (Göttingen, 1957), p. 447.
6. KA Chef. d. Gstb. Op. geh. 2138 of 8 November 1918.
7. Julius Deutsch, *Ein Weiter Weg* (Zurich-Leipzig-Vienna, 1960), pp. 115–20.
8. Friedrich Funder, *From Empire to Republic* (New York, 1959), 183–84.
9. In Neck, pp. 100–101.
10. Karl Freiherr v. Werkmann, *Deutschland als Verbündeter* (Berlin, 1931), pp. 326–27.
11. Carl Wolff, "Erinnerungen des letzten Kommandanten der k.u.k. Leibgarde-Infanterie," KA Gardeakten 308-3/8.
12. Egon Pechnczek, *Die Letzten Tage der Theresianischen Militärakademie* (Vienna, n.d.), pp. 13–14, 18–19.
13. August v. Cramon, *Unser österreichisch-ungarischer Bundesgenosse im Weltkriege* (Berlin, 1922), pp. 197–98.
14. Edmund Glaise-Horstenau, *Die Katastrophe: die Zertrümmerung Österreich-Ungarns* (Vienna, 1929), pp. 429–30.
15. KA MKSM 1918 69–24/6.
16. Ibid.

17. Ludwig Jedlicka, "Die Tradition der Wehrmacht Österreich-Ungarns und die Nachfolgestaaten," *ÖMZ*, 6 (1968): 441–47.
18. Oskar Jászi, *The Dissolution of the Habsburg Monarchy* (Chicago, 1929), pp. 142–43.
19. Johann C. Allmayer-Beck, *Der Konservatismus in Österreich* (Munich, 1959), pp. 18–19. Cf. the characterizations by Heinrich Benedikt, *Monarchie der Gegensätze. Österreichs Weg durch die Neuzeit* (Vienna, 1947), p. 195, and Otto Bauer, *Die Österreichische Revolution* (Vienna, 1923), pp. 89–91. For a different view, see Kurt Peball, "Sendung und Erbe," in *ÖMZ*, special issue (1966): 59–61.

Index

Unless otherwise indicated, all entries for individuals, military personnel and organizations, weapons, and materiel refer to the Habsburg, Austrian, or Austro-Hungarian armed forces.

Academic Legion (Vienna), 23
Adelsberg, 203
Adjutant general, first. *See* Crenneville-Poutet, Grünne
Adjutanten Corps: establishment of and duties, 41; merger with General Staff Corps, 60
Adler, Dr. Viktor, Austrian socialist leader, 217
Adrianople, Turkish fortress, 167
Adriatic: Italy opposes Serb outlet on, 167; mentioned, 91, 98, 124, 187
Adua, battle of (1896), 123
Aehrenthal, Alois Lexa Count, Austro-Hungarian foreign minister: appointment of, 140; policy goals, 140, 154; conflict with Conrad, 142, 152, 156, 162–63; his appraisal of Italian intentions, 152; on Russian aims in Balkans, 153–154, 162; and the annexation of Bosnia-Hercegovina, 154; his opposition to war, 155, 163; opposes Francis Ferdinand's appointment as commander-in-chief, 155; denounced by Francis Ferdinand, 155, 161; favors shortening active duty tours for conscripts and military concessions to Hungary, 161; supported by Francis Joseph against Conrad, 163–164; death of, 164
Aegean, 91
Africa, 88
Agram (Zagreb), 15, 20, 93, 176, 216
Airplanes: in Austro-Hungarian service, 175, 193, 205, 213; British, French, and Russian, 175
Air service, 142, 164, 165, 175, 193, 205, 213
Air superiority, 205
Air support: German during Caporetto operations, 207; at the Piave, 213
Albania: military advocate occupation of, 50; Austro-Hungarian policy towards, 94, 168–169; revolts against Turkish rule, 163, diplomatic and military crisis over, 167–169; Austro-Hungarian troops in, 191, 213–214, 220
Albert, King of Saxony, informed by Francis Joseph of military precautions, 116
Albertini, Luigi, Italian historian, quoted on Austro-Hungarian policy during Balkan Wars, 170
Albrecht, Archduke FML, FM: in Vienna 1848, 22–23; as commander Third Army, 51; mission to Berlin 1859, 52; proponent of dynastic army, 57, 74, 79–80, 144; distrusts military intellectuals, 62; commands Southern Army, 67, 69; appointed commander-in-chief, 71–72; his final army order quoted, 72; denounces military concessions to Hungary, 76–77; favors continued dynastic control of army, 78–79; opposes ministerial control of army, 79–80; appointed inspector general, 79; quarrels with Kuhn, 79–80, 88–89; accused of absolutist leanings, 79–80; on Dalmatian insurrection, 86; schemes for *Grenzer* autonomy, 87; and alliance with France, 87–88; views on mobilization in 1870, 88–89; advocates Russian alliance, 93–94; on war with Russia, 96, 97, 115; distrusts Germany, 98, 113, 115; proponent of war against Italy, 99, 114; views on powers of general staff, 100; limited outlook retards reconstruction of army, 101, 112; on improving Austria-Hungary's military position, 106; critical of combat readiness of *Landwehr-Honvéd*, 108–109; opposes Beck's new corps dispositions, 110; concedes monarchy dependence on German support, 117; defends officer corps against

273

Albrecht (*continued*)
German criticism, 118; distrusts Hungary, 120; opposes German nationalists in Austria, 121; in old age, 122; mentioned, 127, 187
Alexander of Battenberg: as prince of Bulgaria, 114; as Austro-Hungarian officer, 118
Alexander II, Tsar of Russia, and war with Turkey, 95, 96
Algeria, 17
Allerhöchstes Armee Oberkommmando (1849), 40. *See Armee Oberkommando*
Alliances and military conventions: against Napoleon, 7; with Prussia, 17, 22, 49, 50; with Russia, 17, 35; with Bavaria, Saxony, and Württemberg, 48; Dual Alliance, 104–105 and *passim;* with Rumania, 114, 123; with Ottoman Empire, 190; with Bulgaria, 191
Alpenkorps, German mountain division, 184
Alpini, Italian mountain troops, 188
Alps: Carnic, 187; Julian, 187, 207; Carniolan, 207 and *passim*
Alsace-Lorraine, 212
Alsen, Danish island invaded by Prussians, 65
America, sale of surplus arms to, 58
Ammunition supply: inadequate in 1870s, 101, 102; in 1882, 104; in World War, 174, 181, 184, 210, 213
Amnesty, 204
Andrássy v. Csik-Szent Király u. Kraszna-Horka, Julius Count, Hungarian prime minister, Austro-Hungarian foreign minister: opposes universal conscription, 75; and *Ausgleich*, 75–76; suggests creation of *Honvéd*, 76; and military compromise of 1868, 77; quarrel with John, 79; at the crown council of July 18, 1870, 88; and the Three Emperor's Alliance, 89; policy in Balkan crisis 1877–1878, 90–97 *passim;* and occupation of Bosnia-Hercegovina, 101–102; and conclusion of Dual Alliance, 104; quoted in defense of joint army arrangements, 120
Annexation Crisis: and Hungarian demands, 147; Austro-Hungarian policy during, 154–156; military measures during, 155; unrest in Slav units during, 148; results of, 156–157
Apponyi, Count Albert, on the army as the school of the nation, 119
Appropriations, military: before 1815, 3, 4, 5; in Metternich era, 9–10; after 1849, 41–42; effects of Crimean mobilization on, 51–52; in 1859 to 1866 period, 57–58; extraordinary, 1866, 60; 1867–1879 period, 78; 1867–1892 period, 106; compared to other European powers, 106, 125–126, 145, 148, 160, 172; Conrad and Schönaich dispute over, 161; Schemua complaint about, 164; supplementary 1912–1913, 167; inadequate to close armament gap, 172
Arad, executions at (1849), 36
Arcièren Leibgarde, 15, 220
Armament increases, European: Beck comments on 105; mentioned, 104, 117, 139, 157, 172
Armee Ernährungsrat (Army Food Council), 215
Armeeoberkommandant, Archduke Albrecht appointed as, 79
Armee Oberkommando, 1850–1860: formation of, 40–41; functions of, 41–42; discontinued, 59
Armee Oberkommando, 1866–1868, 78–80 *passim*
Armee Oberkommando (*AOK*), 1914–1918: activation of, 177; powers of, 177, 192, 201; isolation from combat troops, 177, 202, 206; and Potiorek, 182–183; concerned about nationalist agitation, 184–185, 192; relations with *OHL*, 186, 191, 198–199, and *passim;* resists changes in officer procurement, 193; Charles I reduces its powers, 201–203; move to Baden and the "second" *AOK*, 202–203; weaknesses of new high command structure, 203; accepts German conditions for Italian offensive, 206; and the army reorganization of 1917, 208–209; and Piave offensive, 213–214; on fighting capabilities of army, 214; requests return of troops from interior of monarchy, 214; role in armistice negotiations, 217–218; and German intervention in Tyrol, 219–220; end of, 220
Armistice of Villa Giusti (1918): confusion regarding timing, 217–218; allegations concerning, 218
Armored vehicles: Francis Joseph fails to appreciate, 127; introduction in warfare, 137. *See also* Tanks
Army inspector general: Albrecht appointed as, 79; office discontinued after his death, 125
Arsenal (Vienna): description, 45; rifle production of, 66; artillery production of, 84
Arsiero, 195
Artillery: original establishment of, 3; in post-Napoleonic period, 15–16; reorganization of, 43–44, 59, 63, 111; evaluation of, 44, 111, 126–127, 174; in war against France and Sardinia, 53–54; in war against Prussia (1866), 65, 70; slow promotion of, 81; technical lag of in late nineteenth century, 84, 111, 126; German concern about Austro-Hungarian field artillery, 126–127; weakness at outbreak of World War, 126, 174; heavy artillery, requirement for, 149, 160, 164; divisional artillery, 149, 174; expansion in World War, 193, 205; performance during

Brusilov offensive, 196; at Caporetto, 207; on western front, 212; in Palestine, 212, 215, and *passim*
Artillery Academy, Olmütz, 44
Artillery Committee: reviews lessons of Crimean War, 44. See also Technical Military Committee
Artillery, French: in 1859, 53–54; introduces rapid-firing field gun, 126; on Italian front, 206
Artillery, German, 174, 186, 207
Artillery, Italian, 163, 190, 207
Artillery pieces: muzzle-loading, 16, 44; muzzle-loading rifled, 63; breech-loading M 1875, 84; M 1880, 111, 126; M 1899, 126; M 99/04, 174; 30.5-cm. Skoda, 149–50, 164, 174; M 1905, 149; M 1908, 174; M 1909, 174; M 1914, 193; M 1915, 193; M 1916 24-cm. howitzer, 193; 38-cm. *Autohaubitze*, 193; 42-cm. howitzer, 193
Artillery, Russian: new field gun, 126; divisional, 174
Artillery, Serbian, 182
Artillery support: concentration of fire, 44; in support of bayonet charge, 65, 70; Conrad's neglect of, 143; absence of proper doctrine, 174
Arz v. Straussenburg, Artur Baron, GdI, chief of general staff: defends Transylvania, 197; appointed chief of general staff, 203; requests German aid, 204; favors Piave offensive, 212; and the question of troops for internal security duties, 214; on army continuing to fight, 214; delays publication of October 1918 manifesto, 216; informs Hindenburg army is finished, 217; temporary commander-in-chief, 218
Asia, 88
Asiago, 195
Aspern, battle of (1809), 7
Assault troops: at Caporetto, 206–207; as divisional troops, 208
Assistenz Bataillone, 214
A-Staffel: composition and proposed deployment, 159; deployment moved back, 172
Auersperg, Karl Baron FML, 23
Auffenberg v. Komarow, Moritz Baron, FML, KM: critical of reserve units in occupation of Bosnia-Hercegovina, 102; plan for military intervention in Hungary, 134, 168; Francis Ferdinand's choice as war minister, 161; orders heavy Skoda mortars, 164, 168; relieved, 168; commands Fourth *k.u.k.* Army, 178–180
Augustin, Vincenz Baron FML, FZM, director of artillery: improves percussion lock, 16; reorganizes artillery, 43–44; disapproves of needle gun, 65–66

Ausgleich: conclusion of, 74–75; military stipulations of, 75; additional military compromise, 76–78; decennial renegotiations and army question, 109, 119–120, 130–131, 146–147, 209–210. See also Dualism, Hungarian National Army, Hungarian Parliament
Austria, Ministry of National Defense, 141
Austria and Austria-Hungary, finances, 4, 10, 12, 41, 51–52, 106, 172, and *passim*
Austro-Hungarian-German command problems: pre-World War contacts, 112; Beck's contacts with Moltke and Waldersee, 113–114; Austria-Hungary desires equal status, 114; contacts between Conrad and Moltke, 157–158, 179, 180; lack of concrete arrangements, 173, 180; Conrad feels that Moltke has not kept his promises, 180; Germany refuses to accept Austro-Hungarian command, 186; special arrangements for Tarnow-Gorlice, 186; Falkenhayn vetoes Conrad's plan in Italy, 189; strained relations during Serbian campaign, 190–191; Germany refuses to support offensive in Italy, 194; Archduke Joseph Ferdinand and Linsingen, 196; Germany assumes senior role, 197; takes charge of campaign against Rumania, 197–198; *OKL* agreement signed, 198–199; and Charles I, 199, 204; before and during Caporetto operations, 206–208; Spa agreements concerning, 212. See also *Armee Oberkommando*, Conrad
Austro-Italian war of 1866: operations on land, 69, 71; naval operations, 71
Austro-Prussian war of 1866: foreign and domestic expectations, 66–67; mobilization, 67–68; command controversy, 67; staff problems, 67–68; war plans, 68–69; operations in Bohemia, 69–71; final phase of, 71; responsibility for defeat, 72–73. See also Albrecht, Benedek, Königgrätz
Austro-Prussian War against Denmark, 1864: fought as a limited war, 64; operations, 64–65; tactical lessons of, 65
Austro-Sardinian war in 1848–1849, 24–26, 28, 34. See also Radetzky, Revolution of 1848
Austro-Sardinian French war of 1859: diplomatic shortcomings, 52–53; lack of strategic direction, 53–54; operations, 53–54; appraisal of, 54–55. See also Buol, Francis Joseph, Grünne, Gyulai, Hess
Azov, Sea of, 214, 220

Bach, Alexander, Austrian minister: advocates cooperation with England and France, 50; mentioned, 33
Bacquehem, Marquis Olivier, governor of Styria, 130

Baden, Grand Duchy, 71
Baden near Vienna, 71: location of "second" *AOK*, 202, 212
Badeni, Kasimir Count, Austrian prime minister: quoted on Austro-Hungarian war potential, 128; and language conflict in Bohemia, 129
Bad Ischl, council of joint ministers discusses intervention in Hungary, 135
Bainsizza plateau, 206
Balaton Lake, 183
Balkan League: formation, 165; regarded as challenge to Austria-Hungary, 165–166; its victory over Ottoman army, 167–168; internal dissension, 169
Balkans: and Austro-Russian relations, 49, 91–97 *passim*, 114–116, 123–124, 165–170 *passim*; military advocate expansionist policy on, 49–50, 90–91, 92–93, 96, 115, 168–169. *See also* Bosnia-Hercegovina, Dalmatia, Serbia
Balkan wars: mistaken assessments of military capabilities, 165–167; effect of wars on Austro-Hungarian position, 166, 169–170, 172; operations during first Balkan war, 167–168; Austro-Hungarian military measures during, 167–168, 169–170; second Balkan war, 169
Balloon detachments, 175
Banat: Military Border in, 14, 40
Banderial (portal) militia in Hungary, 1
Banditry: in Hungary, 46; deserter bands, 214
Bánffy, Deszö Baron, Hungarian prime minister, 131
Bardolff, Carl Baron, Colonel, FML, director MKFF: on Francis Joseph as a soldier, 56; recommends return to "extraterritorial" troop dispositions, 162, 171; scepticism about Charles I, 201; and role in projected military government, 211
Batthiany, Louis Count, Hungarian prime minister: forms government, 24; resigns, 29; executed, 36
Battalion: amphibious *Grenzer (Tschaikisten)*, 16; Richter Grenadiers, 30
Bavaria, Kingdom: as Austrian ally, 48, 71; occupies Holstein, 64
Bavarian troops: *Alpenkorps*, 184; on Brenner, 220
Beck, Max Wladimir, Baron, Austrian prime minister: appointed, 140; attempts to renegotiate *Ausgleich*, 146; willing to make military concessions to Hungary, 146; mentioned, 108
Beck-Rzikowsky, Friedrich, Baron (later Count), Lt. Colonel, Colonel, FML, FM, director MKSM, chief of general staff: on *Stosstaktik*, 65; missions to Benedek, 69, 70; assists in negotiating military compromise with Hungary, 76–77; views on functions and powers of general staff, 79, 100; growing influence of, 79, 89, 106, 107; urges seizure of Bosnia-Hercegovina, 91–92; advises against war with Russia, 95, 96, 97; willing to use force to protect vital interests, 98; agrees to preventive war against Italy, 99; visits zone of operations in Bosnia-Hercegovina, 102–103; views on military situation in 1880, 105; 1892, 117; 1896, 117; appointed chief of general staff, 107; efforts to speed up mobilization, 110–111, 114, 117; seeks coordination of plans with German general staff, 113–114, 117; uncertain of German support, 114–117 *passim;* on chances of fighting Russia alone, 115; reports improvement of army, 118; opposes Hungarian language demands, 119, 132; concerned with rising national agitation in monarchy, 120–121; visits Rumania, 123; asserts war unlikely in near future, 123–124; concerned over possible Italian-Serb alliance, 124–125; becomes chief of general staff of the entire armed forces, 125; redefines the powers of his office, 125; improves railroad system, 127; defends his new corps dispositions, 129; recommends military intervention in Hungary, 132, 134; comes under attack, 136; responsibility for stagnation of army, 137; forced resignation and legacy, 137–138; mentioned, 88, 142, 144
Belgium, 66, 136
Belgrade: as symbol of Habsburg ambitions in Balkans, 182, 183; mentioned, 50, 91, 93, 114, 153, 167
Belgrade, Military Convention of (1918), 221
Below, Otto v., Prussian (German) GdI: commands Fourteenth German Army at Caporetto, 207
Belvedere Palace: residence and center of political and military activities of Francis Ferdinand, 141, 160, 161, 171; mentioned, 201
Benedek, Ludwig Ritter v., FZM: on dynastic mission of army, 57; denounces liberals, 57; his qualities and limitations, 57; as governor of Hungary, 58; views on staff work, 60; dislike of military intellectuals, 62; accepts command of North Army, 67; staff problems, 67–68; hesitant to advance, 68–69; orders change in tactics, 70; at Königgrätz, 70–71; commands retreat, 71; faces court of inquiry, 72; evaluation of his performance, 72–73; mentioned, 78, 144
Berchtold von u. zu Ungarschitz, Fratting u. Pulitz, Leopold Count, Austro-Hungarian foreign minister: character, 164; opposes mobilization during Balkan crisis, 166; agrees to military measures against Serbia,

167; sends ultimatum to Serbia, 169; in July 1914, 178
Bergamo, 19
Berlin, 48, 52, 68, 88, 167, and *passim*
Berlin, Congress of (1878), 98, 104
Berlin, Treaty of (1878), 153
Berrer, Albert v., Württemberg (German) General, commands assault group at Caporetto, 207
Bersaglieri, Italian elite troops, 188
Beskiden Corps, German task force, 185
Bessarabia, 94
Beust, Friedrich Ferdinand Count, Austrian chancellor, Austro-Hungarian foreign minister: and negotiations on military compromise, 77; views on possible revenge on Prussia, 87–88; replaced, 89; views on Ottoman Empire, 90
Bigot de St. Quentin, Karl Count, FML, 77
Birago, Karl v. Major, 16
Bismarck-Schönhausen Otto v., Count, Prince, Prussian prime minister, German chancellor: prepares for war with Austria, 66; promotes insurrectionary schemes, 71; favors a strong Austria-Hungary, 94, 97; promotes Berlin Congress, 98; is distrusted by senior Habsburg officers, 98; and the Dual Alliance, 104; is opposed to military commitments to Austria-Hungary, 112, 157; and Triple Alliance, 112; favors main German military effort against France, 112; and the Bulgarian Crisis, 114; negotiates Reinsurance Treaty, 114–115; opposes preventive war, 115, 116
Black Sea, 88
Boer War, and neglect of its tactical lessons, 143
Bohemia: and military prerogatives of the crown, 3, 5; in revolution of 1848, 27–28; as base of operations against Prussia, 48, 69, 71; reactions to military compromise in, 85–86; anti-military agitation in, 121, 148, 185, 204, and *passim*; Czech-German conflict in, 121, 130; uprising feared, 148; dissension during war, 184, 185, 204; mentioned 18, 35, 170, 211, 219, and *passim*
Böhm-Ermolli, Eduard Baron, FM, on division of the joint army, 209–210
Bolfras, Arthur Baron, FML, director MKSM: on excessive *AOK* powers, 177; and Conrad, 199; mentioned, 141
Bolshevik revolution, 211
Bombardeur Corps, 16, 44
Boroević v. Bojna, Svetozar, GdI, FM: commander on Isonzo front, 189–190; and Piave offensive, 213; and alleged schemes for counterrevolution, 220
Bosnia: and frontier skirmishing, 17; military urge acquisition of, 49–50, 90–91, 101; conditions in, 91–92; Austro-Hungarian covert activities in, 93; resistance to occupation, 101–102; general strike in, 148; in 1914, 183
Bosnia-Hercegovina: events leading to occupation of, 91–101 *passim;* operations in, 101–102; criticism of, 102; pacification, 103; and Dalmation insurrection of 1881, 103–104; unrest under Austro-Hungarian rule, 103, 121, 153; Conrad opposes concessions in, 154; annexation of, 154; Potiorek as governor of, 182; mentioned, 110.
Bosniaken (Bosnian Infantry): units established, 104; used for riot control, 121, 130, 150
Bothmer, Felix Count, Bavarian (German) GdI: commander of *Südarmee* during Brusilov offensive, 195
Bourbon Dynasty in Spain, 6
Breechloaders: investigation of practicability as artillery pieces, 44; controversy over adoption as rifle, 65–68; adopted as rifle and as artillery, 83–84. *See also* Artillery pieces, Firearms, Wänzel, Werndl, Mannlicher
Brenner Pass, 220
Brescia, 34
Brigades: composition and tactical employment, 42–43, 63; 55th, 143
British army: strength of, 98; Field Service Regulations, 174–175; British Expeditionary Force, 175; on Italian front, 206, 207; in Palestine offensive, 215; ruptures German lines, 215; mentioned, 15, 16
British navy, 97, 98
Brosch v. Aarenau, Alexander, Captain, Major, Colonel commanding 1st *Kaiserjäger* Regiment, director MKFF: as Francis Ferdinand's advisor, 136; characterization of, 141; directs Francis Ferdinand's planning staff, 162; pessimistic about outcome of war, 177
Bruck, Karl Ludwig Baron, Austrian finance minister: favors cooperation with England and France, 50
Brudermann, Rudolf Ritter v., GdK, commander Third *k.u.k.* Army, 179, 180
Brünn, 15
Brusilov, Alexexej Alexandrovich, Russian general: ruptures Austro-Hungarian front, 195–196; as commander-in-chief under Kerensky, 206
B-Staffel: composition and proposed deployment, 159; controversy over actual deployment, 178
Bucharest, fall of (1916), 197
Bucharest, Treaty of (1913), 169
Buchlau agreement (1908), 154
Buda, 15, 34

Budapest: conquered by Windischgrätz, 32; retaken by Hungarians, 34; revolution in, 216; mentioned, 24, 25, 27, 29, 31, 32, 33, 74, 78, 120, 134, 161, 183, 193, and *passim*
Budapest, Convention of (1877), 95, 96
Budweis, 16, 176
Bug River, 173
Bukovina, 196
Bulgaria, principality and kingdom: rises against Turks, 93, 95; crisis over, 114; joins Balkan League, 165; fights Turkey, 167; turns against allies and is defeated, 169; enters World War, 190–191; mentioned, 134, 152
Bulgarian army: participates in conquest of Serbia, 191; in Rumanian campaign, 197; collapse of, 215
Buol-Schauenstein, Karl Count, FML, Austrian foreign minister: policy during Crimean War, 49–51; his Italian policy and the war of 1859, 52–53; mentioned, 61
Bürgerwehr, k.k. privilegierte (Vienna), 23
Burian v. Rajecz, István Count, Austro-Hungarian finance minister, foreign minister: suggests concessions in Bosnia-Hercegovina, 153; becomes foreign minister, 189; proposes to eliminate Serbia with Austro-Hungarian forces alone, 190; and *AOK*, 198
Burstyn, Günther, Lieutenant Colonel; invents armored car, 127
Bylandt zu Rheidt, Arthur Baron, FZM, KM: recommends purchase of Krupp artillery, 84; on expenses of mobilization, 97; as war minister, 100, 107; favors new corps disposition, 110

Cadet officer deputies, 82
Cadet schools, 11, 82
Cadorna, Luigi Count, Italian Lieutenant General: war plans, 188: practices war of attrition, 190; during Trentino offensive, 195; at Caporetto, 207
Cannae, battle of (216 B.C.), 74
Cannon: muzzle-loading, 16, 44; rifled, 63; breechloaders, 85, 111, 126, 174, 193. *See also* Artillery, Artillery pieces
Caporetto (Karfreit), battle of (1917), 207, 212
Capua, 19
Career patterns, military, 11–12, 42, 81–82
Carinthia: fortifications in, 98–99; *Landwehr* of, 150; volunteers of called out, 189; mentioned, 14, 36, 59, 221
Carniola, 14, 59
Carpathians: Russians cross into Hungary, 35; winter battles in, 182, 184, 185, 186; Russian breakthrough, 185; Brusilov almost reaches range, 196; mentioned, 94–95

Carso (Karst), 187–188, 197
Casualties. *See* Losses
Catholics: in Bosnia-Hercegovina, 92, 93, 103; predominance in officer corps, 118, 128, 151
Cattaro: as supply base for Hercegovinian insurgents, 93; naval mutiny at, 211; mentioned, 82, 219. *See also* Kotor
Cavalry: organization, 16, 43, 63, 84, 150, and *passim;* arms, 16, 43, 150; tactics and doctrine, 16, 43, 63, 84, 112, 150, 174; reforms of, 59, 63, 84, 150; concentrated in Galicia, 84, 111, 167; long-range reconaissance mission, 84, 180; dismounted in World War, 194, 205; mentioned, 61. *See also Chevauxlegers,* Cuirasseers, Dragoons, Hussars, *Kavallerieschützendivision, Uhlans*
Cavalry, British, 175
Cavalry, German, 175
Cavalry, Hungarian (1848–1849), strength and quality of, 29, 32
Cavalry, Russian: capabilities, 84, 111, 167; dismounted tactics of, 175, 180
Cavalry, Serbian, 175
Cavour, Count Camillo, Sardinian prime minister: seeks foreign support, 47; traps Austria into war, 52; mentioned, 59
Central Military Investigating Commission (1848–1850), 46
Central Powers: joined by Ottoman Empire, 190; desire to eliminate Serbia, 190; joined by Bulgaria, 191; in Rumanian campaign, 197; form *OKL*, 199; strategic position at end of 1917, 210
Cetinje, Montenegrin capital, 50, 191
Charles V, Holy Roman Emperor, 1–2
Charles of Styria, Archduke, 3
Charles VI, Holy Roman Emperor: decline of army during his reign, 4–5; and Pragmatic Sanction, 4–5
Charles, Archduke: and military reforms, 6; dubious about *Landwehr*, 6–7; at Aspern, 7; retirement, 7; suggests revival of generalissimo position, 11; quoted on army, 17; on army in Italy, 18; warns about Russian danger, 49; mentioned, 144
Charles, Archduke, FML, heir apparent: interferes in maneuvers, 149; commands XX Corps, 195; on eastern front, 198; report on Conrad, 202
Charles I, Emperor-King: relations with Germany, 199, 201, 204, 206, 212, 218; qualities and defects, 201–202; his chief civilian and military advisors, 201–202; moves to reduce *AOK* prerogatives, 201–202; and Hungary, 201, 216; assumes personal command, 202; removes Conrad as chief of general staff, 202–203; appoints Arz as his successor, 203; humanitarian gestures, 203–204; and unre-

stricted submarine warfare, 204; peace initiatives and Sixtus affair, 204, 212, 215–216; asks William II for support of Italian offensive, 206; October manifesto, 216; permits officers to serve national authorities, 216; refuses to countenance use of force against revolutions, 216; and armistice negotiations, 217–218; renounces role in Austria, 220; final proclamation to army, 221

Charles Albert, King of Sardinia: declares war, 26; concludes armistice, 28; reopens hostilities, 34; defeat and abdication, 34

Cherniaev, Mihail Gregorevich, Pan-Slav Russian general, 93

Chevauxlegers regiments: number of, 16; converted to *Uhlans*, 43

China, 136

Chinese-Japanese War (1894), 123

Chlopy, army order of (1903), 132

Chlum, fighting at (1866), 70

Christian Socialists: and Francis Ferdinand, 141; in elections of 1911, 164

Churchill, Winston S., British statesman and historian, quoted on Austro-Hungarian deployment in 1914, 179

Civil-military relations: Wallenstein's legacy, 3, 171; conflict between Emperor Francis and Archduke Charles, 6–7; Metternich's views on, 7, 9, 11; Radetzky's comments on, 10, 30; Schwarzenberg's conflict with Windischgrätz, 33–34; rise of military power in post-1848 period, 38, 40; Schwarzenberg removes Haynau, 40; conflict over conduct of foreign affairs, 47, 48, 49–51, 52–53, 90–93 *passim*, 124, 145, 152, 161, 163–164; Benedek on civilians, 57; *Reichsrat* and army, 58, 78, 89; German Liberals and Bosnia-Hercegovina, 101, 105; Conrad and Prime Minister Beck, 146; Schemua on the army and society, 164; in World War, 177, 192, 198; and *passim*

Civil servants, 10, 38, 146, 216

Clam-Gallas, Eduard Count, GdK: as corps commander in Italy, 55; at Gitschin, 70

Clam-Martinitz, Karl Josef Nepomuk Count, FML: advocates army reforms, 10–11; on treatment of common soldier, 14; on role of army, 21; mentioned, 144

Clergy, 92, 93

Clothing and equipment, supply of, 53, 68, 184, 193, 210, 215. *See also* Uniforms

Committee of Fifteen: and *Ausgleich* negotiations, 74; and military compromise, 76–77

Committee of Nine, and attempts to solve the Hungarian crisis, 132–133

Compromise of 1867. *See Ausgleich*

Congreve rocket, 16

Conrad v. Hötzendorf, Franz Baron, (Count), FML, GO, FM, chief of general staff of the entire armed forces: criticism of operations in Bosnia-Hercegovina, 102; not a charismatic leader, 127, 177; appointment as chief of general staff, 137, 142; tactical concepts of, 137, 144; early career, 143; limited views on politics, 144, 148; demands greater role for chief of staff in foreign policy decisions, 144; 152; advocates use of army as instrument for internal policy, 144, 162; and the Magyars, 145, 160, and *passim*; discussion of his views on preventive war, 144–145, 169–170; advocacy of preventive war, 144, 151–152, 155–156, 163–164, 168–169; makes maneuvers more realistic, 149; his concern for effective weapons, 149, 175; favors annexation of Bosnia-Hercegovina, 152–154 *passim*; elaborates war plans, 154, 158–159, 172–173; contacts with Moltke, 155, 156–157, 179, 180; decides to employ larger forces against Serbia, 158, 173, 178–179; relations with Schönaich, 161; willing to modify corps dispositions, 162; relations with Aehrenthal, 163–164; relieved temporarily, 163–164; returns to his post, 167–168; becomes pessimistic about future of Habsburg monarchy, 170; on balance of power shift, 172–173; lacks confidence about outcome of war, 177; assumes actual command of army, 177; evaluation as a commander, 177–178; controversy about mobilization and deployment in 1914, 178–179; his Galician offensives, 179–180; and Potiorek, 183; and the Carpathian offensive, 184; and Tarnow-Gorlice operations, 185–186; changes his war plans against Italy, 189; and operations against Serbia, 191–192; becomes more confident by end of 1915, 192; conducts Trentino offensive, 194–195; and Brusilov offensive, 196; his standing damaged, 198–199; opposes subordination to Germany, 199; claims Germany endangers future of monarchy, 199; relations with Charles I, 199, 202; relieved as chief of staff and transferred to Tyrolean front, 202–203; army reorganization scheme, 208; and Piave offensive, 212–213; dismissed by Charles I, 214; mentioned, 125, 137, 207

Conscription, in Prussia, 73

Conscription, selective: Josephinian, 6, 42; in era of Metternich, 13–14; law of 1852, 42. *See also* Recruitment

Conscription, universal: on Military Borders, 14–15; objections to, 61, 75; introduced, 75–77 *passim*; annual quota for, 81, 109, 126, 131, 164–165; opposition to, 85, 86, 103; annual levy compared with other European powers, 126

Constantinople, 94, 95, 98, 214
Cordon, Franz Baron, FML, KM, 34, 39, 40
Corps, Austrian army: I, II, 25; permanent organization of, 43; Serb-Banat, 50; II, IV, IX, X, XI, XIII during 1854, 50; composition of after 1859, 63; VI, 64–65; I at Gitschin, 70
Corps, Austro-Hungarian army: XIII in Bosnian campaign, 101; new territorial organization of, 110–111; opposition to new system, 110, 129, 162, 170–171; II (Vienna), 111, 130, 171; XV (Sarajevo), 111, 148, 153, 154, 155, 166, 167; III (Graz), 130, 148, 171; I (Cracow), 130, 171; VIII (Prague), 135, 148, 170, 171; IV (Budapest), 134–135, 167; XIII (Agram), 148, 167; XVI (Ragusa), 150, 166, 167; corps dispositions for mobilization and deployment, I–XVI, 159; VII (Temesvar), 167; X (Przemysl), 167; XI (Lemberg), 167; XX in World War, 195; and *passim*
Coudenhove, Karl Count, governor in Bohemia, 130
Council of common ministers, 88, 96, 97, 151, 153, 154, and *passim*
Councils, general officers and marshals, 76–77, 209–210
Cracow: occupied by Austria, 20; fortifications improved, 116; mentioned, 46, 50, 181, 216
Craig, Gordon A., historian, quoted on Austrian staff problems, 61
Cramon, August v., Prussian (German) GM, liaison officer at *AOK*, suggests intervention in Bohemia, 219
Crenneville-Poutet, Franz Count Folliot de, FML, Adjutant General: succeeds Grünne, 57, 59; conservative views, 62; telegram to Benedek, 70
Crimea, 51
Crimean War (1853–1856): military lessons of, 44; and Austrian policy, 49–51; mobilization and war plans, 50–51; consequences of, 51–52
Croatia: nationalist tendencies in, 24–25, 36, 47, 54, 59, 148 and *passim;* and Military Border, 36, 47, 87; sub-compromise with Hungary, 86–87; mentioned, 2, 95, and *passim*
Croat-Serb Coalition, 135–136, 153
Croats, in Habsburg army: under Jelačić, 25, 28–29; percentage in ranks, 61, 128; as officers, 217; reliability of in 1918, 214, 217; mentioned, 18. *See also* Military Border
Crown Councils, 89, 209–210, 215, and *passim*
Csorich v. Monte Creto, Anto Baron, FMK, KM, 40
Cuirasseers, 16, 43, 63
Custozza, battle of (1848), 28
Custozza, battle of (1866), 69, 79
Czapp v. Birkenstätten, Karl Baron, FML,

Austrian defense minister, 209
Czech Legion, 206, 212
Czech National Council, 215
Czecho-Slovak army: formation of, 212; at Vittorio Veneto, 217
Czechs: political unrest among, 19, 27–28, 85–86, 88–89, 121, 129, 134, 148, 204, and *passim;* Czech-German conflicts in Bohemia, 85, 121, 130; mentioned, 106, 144, 147, and *passim*
Czechs and Slovaks, in Habsburg army: dissension among, 18–19, 85, 130, 148, 165, 170; percentage in ranks, 61, 128; *Zde* incidents, 130; conduct during World War, 176, 184, 185, 187, 196, 198, 204, 205, 214
Czernowitz, 183–184, 186
Czernin v. u. zu Chudenitz, Ottokar, Count, Austro-Hungarian foreign minister, 201, 212

Dahlen v. Orlaburg, Hermann Baron, FZM, 103
Dalmatia: Italian landings feared, 59, 78; uprisings, 86, 91; as support base for Hercegovinian revolt, 92; mentioned, 91, 95, 104
Danewerk, Danish fortified position, 64
Dankl v. Krasnik, Viktor Count, GdI, GO: commander First *k.u.k.* Army, 179, 180; on Tyrolean front, 189, 194, 195; on division of army, 209–210
Danish army, 64–65
Danish navy, 64–65
Danube Army, combined, under German command, 197
Danube flotilla, 135, 198
Danube River, 50, 59, 71, 95, 178, 179, 180, 188, 198
Dardanelles, 190, 191
D'Aspre v. Hoobreuk, Constantin Baron, FML, 25, 26
Deak, Francis, Hungarian politician, 74, 75
Debreczen, 33
Defections, 26, 29, 53, 54, 69, 184, 185, 205. *See also* Desertions, Mutinies
Degenfeld-Schonburg, August Count, FML, KM, 57, 59, 60
Delafield, Richard, Major, U.S. Army, report on Vienna arsenal, 45
Delegations, Austro-Hungarian: role of, 75; vote credits for occupation of Bosnia-Hercegovina, 98, 101; and military expenditures, 106, 115, 167
Dembinszki, Henry Count, Polish general in Hungarian revolutionary army, 32
Demobilization, 221
Dempscher, Franz, regimental agent, 12
Deployment of Austrian and Austro-Hungarian field armies, 15, 50, 51, 53, 64, 68, 101, 159, 166–167, 178–179, 206, 214
Denmark, 64–65

Deputation, Habsburg fiscal agency, 4
Desertion: in early nineteenth century, 14; in revolution of 1848–1849, 29; in 1859, 54–55; of *Grenzer* to Serbia, 59; in World War, 184, 185, 196, 207, 211
Deutsch, Julius, Austrian socialist politician, 221
Dienstsprache, 108. *See also* Language problem
Discipline: Archduke Charles's regard for dignity of common soldier, 6; strictness of, 14; regulations of 1873, 83; compared to German army, 149; and death of Francis Joseph, 200; modified by Charles I, 203–204
Divisions: as tactical units, 42; discontinued, 63; reestablished, 81; 4th, 13th, 31st, 33rd, 36th, in Bosnia-Hercegovina occupation, 101–102; 8th under Conrad, 143; numbers available compared to other European powers, 173–174; 21st *Landwehr*, 183; 57th, 189; Edelweiss, 208; combat effectiveness of in 1918, 214
Dniestr River, 158, 180
Doblhoff, Anton Baron, Austrian minister, 29
Dobrudja, 169, 197
Dolomites, 184
Dragoons: regiments, 16, 43, 63; mutiny of 8th Dragoons, 170
Dratschmiedt, Edler v. Mährentheim, Auditor General, 72
Drina River, 183, 188
Dukla Pass, 35, 185
Dual Alliance, (1879), 104, 112, and *passim. See also* Austro-Hungarian-German command problems, Beck, Bismarck, Charles I, Francis Joseph, Moltke, William II
Dual Monarchy: structure of, 75, 76–78; and nationality conflicts, 85–86, 87, 120–122, 121–138, and *passim;* challenged by Hungary, 106, 109, 146–147, 131–137 *passim;* 164–165, 209–210; plans to change character of dualism, 134–136, 162, 215–216; pessimistic views regarding the future of, 136, 170, 177; and the death of Francis Joseph, 200–201; and *passim*
Düppel, Danish fortifications, 64, 65
Dunajec River, 180

East Prussia, and German operational plans, 117, 158, 173, 179
Eckertsau castle, 220
Edelsheim-Gyulai, Leopold Baron, GM, GdK: and reform of cavalry, 63; death, 122
Edelweiss Division, 208
Elbe River, 70
Engels, Friedrich: quoted on Austrian army in Italy, 54; compares Austrian and Prussian armies, 66

Engineers-Pioneers-Sappers, 10, 16, 61, 150. *See also* Technical troops
Entente: offensive plans for 1917, 205; changes its policy regarding preservation of Dual Monarchy, 212; final offensives, 215–217; mentioned, 191, 192, 200. *See also* Triple Entente
Erfurt, 48
Ersatzreserve, 81, 126, 131, 174
Estates, of Habsburg lands, 1, 2, 3, 5
Esterhazy v. Galantha, Moritz Prince, Hungarian prime minister, 209
Eugene, Archduke, GdK, FM: appointed commander southwestern front, 189; at Caporetto, 194; promoted to FM, 202; on Piave operation, 202
Eugene of Savoy, Prince, president HKR, FM: reforms of, 4; his advice disregarded, 5; mentioned, 49, 83, 182, 187, 220
Eynatten, August Baron, FML, 58
Exemptions, military service, 61–62, 80

Falkenhayn, Erich v., Prussian (German) GdI, chief of general staff: succeeds Moltke as chief of staff, 185; and Conrad, 186; urges Austria-Hungary to appease Italy, 189; opposes Conrad's plans against Italy, 189; favors joint attack on Serbia, 190–191; critical of Austro-Hungarian troops, 191–192; insists on Verdun operation, 194, 195; dismissed as chief of staff, 197; conquers Rumania, 198; favors unified command, 198–199
Fall U, military intervention in Hungary: Andrássy's apprehensions, 134; proposals for, 134; general staff operational plans, 134–135; Francis Joseph refuses to authorize action, 135; cancellation of, 135; as contributory cause for Auffenberg's dismissal, 168; mentioned, 161
February Patent (1861), 57
Fejérvary de Komlos-Keresztes, Géza Baron, FZM, *Honvéd* minister, Hungarian prime minister, 88, 133, 140
Feldjäger, 14, 17, 43, 62
Feldzeugamt, 16
Ferdinand I, Archduke, Holy Roman Emperor, 1–2
Ferdinand III, Holy Roman Emperor, 3
Ferdinand I, Emperor of Austria: rebuffs Archduke Charles, 11; concessions to Hungary, 24; flees Vienna, 26, 29; deposes Jelačić, 28; abdication of projected, 27; mentioned, 32
Ferdinand of Coburg, King of Bulgaria, 114
Ferrara, 20
Feuerwerker Corps, 16, 44
Ficquelmont, Karl Ludwig Count, Prince, GdK, president HKR, 20, 23

Firearms: cavalry carbines, 16, 43, 63; change from flintlock to percussion, 16; percussion, 43; breechloader debate, 65–68; introduction of breechloaders, 83; introductions of repeaters, 111. *See also* Artillery pieces, Muskets and rifles
Fiume, resolution of (1905), 135, 153
Flags: Habsburg, 92; Hungarian, 77, 120, 132; national, 120–121
Flamethrowers, 193
Fleet, Fifth *k.u.k.*, mutiny of, 211
Flitsch (Plezzo), 207
Food shortages, 193, 205, 210. *See also* Rations
Fortifications: of monarchy in early nineteenth century, 18; in Bohemia, 48, 68; on Italian frontier, 98–99, 114, 117, 124, 149–150, 163, 188, 189; in Bosnia-Hercegovina, 103; improvement of, 116, 117, 124, 149–150, 160; in Dalmatia, 126; mentioned, 68
Fort Vaux, French key position at Verdun, 195
Fourteen Points, 215
France: as danger to the monarchy, 9, 13, 15, 22, 49; intervenes in Italy, 1859, 51, 54 *passim;* seeks an alliance with Austria, 87–88; military expenditures of, 106; and Austro-Hungarian peace moves, 204, 212; mentioned, 152, 165, 194, 195, and *passim*
Franchise, in Austria-Hungary: limitations of, in Hungary, 117–118, 131; Francis Joseph threatens reforms of, 133, 135, 137; demands for universal manhood franchise in Austria, 134, 135, 137; introduction of in Austria, 146; Wekerle and the franchise reform issue in Hungary, 209
Francis I, Holy Roman Emperor, Emperor of Austria, 6, 10
Francis Ferdinand d'Este, Archduke: opposes all military concessions to Hungary, 120, 132, 142, 147, 160; considers the army primarily as an internal instrument, 129, 137, 142, 146, 162; opposes Beck's system of corps dispositions, 129, 162, 171; regards the *Honved* as a threat, 129, 133, 147; political ideas of, 136, 141, 147, 162, and *passim;* military career and talents, 136, 141, 142; dislikes Pitreich; 137; and the appointment of Conrad, 137, 142–143; military chancery of, 141, 162; asserts army threatened by subversion, 142, 147; differs with Conrad, 145, 161, 164, 171; turns against Beck and Wekerle, 147, 160; and Schönaich, 147, 161; has ambitions to be commander-in-chief, 155; relations with Aehrenthal, 155, 161; favors Auffenberg as RKM, 161; his succession program, 162; appointed inspector general, 170; assassination of, 177; mentioned, 165

Francis Joseph, Emperor-King: mentioned as potential ruler, 27; his accession, 31; assumes personal control of army, 31, 34, 39–40, 41; asks for Russian aid, 35; military talents and qualities, 38–40, 56, 127; dislike for learning, science, and technology, 38–39, 127; observations on recruitment, 42; views army as internal instrument, 45; policy in Crimean War, 51; supports Buol, 52; personal command in 1859, 54, 56; instructions to Gablenz, 65; on breechloaders and bayonets, 66; his telegram to Benedek, 70; quoted on cause of defeat in 1866, 72; during negotiations for military compromise, 77–78; fears great Slav conspiracy, 87; cautious on French alliance, 87–88; decides to give up the fight against Prussia, 87–89 *passim;* tours Dalmatia, 92; and Bosnia-Hercegovina, 93; unwilling to wage preventive war against Italy, 99, 163–164; his special relationship with Beck, 110; supports new corps dispositions, 110; and danger of war with Russia, 116; in crisis with Hungary, 131–137 *passim;* and suffrage reform, 133, 135, 137, 146; backs Aehrenthal against Conrad, 163–164; considers Magyars reliable, 165; assents to partial mobilization, 167; orders demobilization, 168; desires peace, 169; vetoes Francis Ferdinand's scheme to relocate garrisons, 171; declares war against Serbia, 176–177; fatalism about the chances of war, 177; advice to Archduke Friedrich, 181; and Putnik, 182; orders precautions on Italian front, 188–189; and Brusilov offensive, 196; orders *AOK* to furnish more information, 198; determined to make peace soon, 199; death of, 199; his role in army and state assessed, 200; mentioned, 62, 71, 119, 130, 142, 201, 209, and *passim*
Franck, Karl Ritter v., FML, KM, 59
Franco-Prussian War and Austro-Hungarian policy, 88
Frankfurt a. M., 48
Franzensfeste, fort, 18
Frederica, Danish fortress, 65
Frederick IV, King of Prussia, 48–49
French army: in Italy 1859, 52–54 *passim;* in Mexico, 63; annual recruit intake of, 126; on Italian front 1917–1918, 206, 207, 217; mentioned, 6, 15
French revolutionary and Napoleonic wars, 6–8
Freud, Sigmund, 108
Friaul, 59
Friedrich, Archduke, GdI, FM, head *AOK*: appointment largely titular, 177; and dissolution of 28th Infantry, 185; and Brusilov offensive, 196; removed by Charles I, 202; mentioned, 181, 209

Frimont, Johann Prince, GdK, president HKR, 10, 18
Freemasons, 142

Gablenz, Ludwig Baron, FML: commands IV Corps, 64–65; on Hungarian military demands, 77; mentioned 78
Galgotzy, Anton, FZM, 146
Galicia: and Polish nationalism in, 7; in operational plans against Russia, 50–51, 84, 94–95, 111, 114, 167; fighting in, 179–180, 185, 186; mentioned, 27, 38, 142, 170, and *passim*
Gallwitz, Max Karl Wilhelm v., German general, 191
Garibaldi, Giuseppe, Italian revolutionary leader, 14, 59
Gallina, Joseph, GM, 80
Garrisons, 19, 43, 110–111, 128–129, 162, 171, 176
Gas warfare: restricted by Charles I, 203; at Caporetto, 207
Gastein, 77
Gatling guns, 85
Gautsch v. Frankenthurn, Paul Baron, Austrian prime minister, 137
Gefechtsausbildung der Infantrie, 143
Gendarmerie, 43, 46
Generalate, 61
Generalinspektor der gesamten bewaffneten Macht, 170
Generalkommanden (General Militärkommanden), 14–15
General officers: social origins of, 11, 62; oppose war with Prussia, 48; and Balkan policy, 48–49, 51, 91, 97–98; performance in 1859, 53; purge of, 59; show lack of confidence, 57, 101, 170, and *passim;* debate concessions to Hungary, 76–77, 209–210, and *passim;* liberal-centralist grouping among, 78–79; superannuation of, 121, 138, 149; not charismatic leaders, 127; alienation from society, 145–146; and *passim*
General Quartiermeister bei meiner Person, 39. See also Quartermaster-General Staff
General Staff: low status in Habsburg army, 10, 39, 41, 60–61; Kuhn's dislike of, 80; Beck's views on and his tenure as chief of, 100, 107, 125, 126, and *passim;* improvements in position of, 107, 125, 145
General Staff Corps: status of, 10, 60, 80; assessments of, 60, 107, 176, 206; Beck's efforts to improve morale, 107; Conrad and personal fitness of, 149
General Staff, Prusso-German: compared to Austro-Hungarian, 107, 181
German-Austrian Council of State (1918), 217
German armies: Eighth, 158; Ninth, 181, 197; Eleventh, 186, 191; *Südarmee,* 184, 195–196; Danube Army (composite), 197; Fourteenth, 206–207
German army: deployment of, 113, 115–116, 117, 179; and preventive war, 115; assessment of Austro-Hungarian ally, 118, 170, 172, 181, 187, 191–192, 205–206; annual recruit intake, 126; supports Austro-Hungarian armies, 184, 185, 186, 191, 195–196, 197, 198, 199; requests Austro-Hungarian help on western front, 214–215
German confederation: and Austrian military commitments, 15, 17; and confrontation with Prussia, 48–49, 68–70 *passim;* troops of, in Schleswig, 64
German Liberals in Austria: in *Reichsrat,* 57, 78; and army, 58, 106; support Kuhn, 79; and Bosnia-Hercegovina, 101, 105; decline of, 106, 121; mentioned, 89
German nationalists in Austria: opposition to dynasty, 12; clash with army, 129–130
Germans in Habsburg army: officers, 11, 42, 127, 151, 181, 208; enlisted men, 18, 19, 61, 128, 187, 206, 218, and *passim*
Gitschin, battle of (1866), 70
Goluchowsky, Agenor Maria Adam Count, Austro-Hungarian foreign minister, 124, 139
Gonne, M.S., Major, British military attaché Vienna, 99
Gorchakov, Alexander Mihailovich Prince, Russian foreign minister, 94, 95
Görgey de Görgo et Toporcz, Arthur, Hungarian revolutionary general, 32, 33, 35–36; mentioned, 129
Görz (Goricia), 197
Gorzkowski v. Gorzkow, Karl Ritter v., GdK: in Mantua, 26; besieges Vienna, 34
Graz, 3, 15, 45, 79, 121, 130
Great Britain: aid from desired in possible war against Russia, 94; suggests action to halt Russia, 96, 97; lacks army, 98; and assessment of Austro-Hungarian army, 99, 170; mentioned, 50, 101, 152
Greece, kingdom; and Balkan League, 165; declares war on Turkey, 167
"Green cadres," 214
Grenzer: duties and privileges, 2, 6; military actions of, 2, 6, 15, 17, 29, 30, 50, 55, 67; regiments, 14, 16, 43, 63, 67; disaffection, 19, 25, 29, 30, 36, 47, 50, 55, 59, 86, 87; in Kossuth's schemes, 71; in South Slav schemes, 91; mentioned, 61. *See also* Military Border, Ogulin Regiment, *Székler*
Grünne, Karl Ludwig Count, FML, GdK, First Adjutant General: views on role of army, 39; centralization of command, 40; conflict with Radetzky, 40; eliminates KM, 40; reduces powers of staff, 41; achieves dominant posi-

Grünne (*continued*)
tion, 41; favoritism of, 42; on availability of junior officers, 42; and war of 1859, 52–53; removed, 59; mentioned, 62

Guerrilla war: army concerned about, 34, 53, 65; attempts to foment, 71; in Dalmatia, 86, 103–104; in Bosnia-Hercegovina, 102–103

Guttenberg, Emil Ritter v., FML, Austro-Hungarian railroad minister, 127

Gyulai v. Maros-Németh u. Nádaska, Franz Count, FML, FZM, KM: and Grünne, 40; in Italian campaign, 53; limitations, 53, 57

Habsburg armies, *k.k.* Austrian to 1867: in Italy, 15, 17–18, 25–26, 34; in Hungary, 24–25, 34, 35; before Vienna, 30; dispositions of in 1849, 40; Third, 51; Fourth, 51; Second, 53, 59; Northern, 67–70; Southern, 67, 71

Habsburg armies, *k.k.* and *k.u.k.* Austro-Hungarian, 1868–1918: Second, 102, 178–179, 182–183, 184; Third, 179–180, 182, 184, 185, 194; Fourth, 179–180, 181, 185, 195–196; First, 179–180, 195–196; Fifth, 182–183; 189–190; Sixth, 182–183; Eleventh, 194; Seventh, 195–196; First and Second Isonzo, 207; Tenth, 207 and *passim*

Habsburg Army, *k.k.* Austrian to 1867: origins, 1; surviving medieval institutions, 1–3, 14; command and control apparatus, 2, 4–5, 6, 9, 10, 24, 40, 41, 59–61; strategy and tactics, 2–3, 5, 7, 16–17, 25–26, 31–33, 34, 35, 42, 48, 53–54, 63, 64–65, 68–69, 70; first standing regiments, 3–5 *passim*; organization, 3, 5–6, 15–16, 42–44, 63; strength of, 3, 5, 7, 15, 17–18, 22, 35, 38, 42, 43, 51, 53–54, 61, 68, 71; composition of, by branches, 3, 16–17, 43, 63; finances of, 3, 4, 5, 9–10, 41–42, 51–52, 57–58, 66; reforms 4–7 *passim*, 18, 44, 59, 63, and *passim*; officer corps, 5, 11–13, 26–27, 36, 44, 62; nationality problem in, 6, 7, 13, 18–19, 26, 36–37, 46–47, 54–55, 58, 64, 69; enlisted men, 6, 13–14, 18, 26, 42, 61, and *passim*; resistance to change, 9, 10–11, 13, 17, 39, 44, 56–57, 59, 63–66, and *passim*; dynastic orientation of, 9, 21, 26–27, 29–31 *passim*, 57; armament, 16, 43–44, 63–64, 65–66; employed as internal security force, 19–20, 21, 27, 38, 45–46, 47, 54, 59; evaluations of, 36–37, 54–55, 66; and *passim*. *See also* all entries to specific branches, officers, units, political bodies, etc.

Habsburg army, *k.k.* and *k.u.k.* Austro-Hungarian, 1867–1918: changed character, 74; and *Ausgleich*, 74–75; formation of dualistic army, 76–78, 81, 120; internal conflicts over command and control, 78–80, 81, 88–89, 177, 202–203, and *passim*; recruit quotas, strength, and war potential of, 80–81, 88–89, 94, 99–100, 106, 109, 115, 117, 126, 131, 165, 170, 172, 173–174; officer corps, 81–83, 100, 118, 127, and *passim*; composition by branches, 83, 84, 126, 150, 205; attitude towards nationalities within, 108, 118, 119, 130, 147, 184, 221, and *passim*; new corps dispositions, 110–111; national composition of, 127, 128, 151; conflict with Hungary, 119, 131–165 *passim*; and society, 145–146; on eve of war, 173–175; changed nature of, 184–185, 193–194; war expansion and re-equipment of, 193, 205; effects of death of Francis Joseph on, 199–200; deployment in 1917, 206; reorganization and proposed post-war establishment, 208–209; Hungary demands the division of the dualistic army, 208–209; disintegration of, 211, 214–221 *passim*; final evaluation of, 218, 221. *See also* all entries to specific branches, officers, units, political bodies, etc.

Habsburg dynasty and army: view of, as a dynastic instrument, 6, 39, 57, 74, 129, 137, 142, 146, 162; military talents and careers of members of the dynasty, 6–7, 38–40, 56, 67–69, 82, 112, 141, 177, 196, 200, 203, 213; distrust of outstanding military leaders, 3, 7, 11, 39–40, 171. *See also* Albrecht, Archduke Charles, Charles I, Francis Ferdinand, Francis Joseph

Habsburg navy, Austrian and Austro-Hungarian, 71, 86, 104, 191, 205, 211

Hamley, Sir Edward B., British general, quoted on Austro-Hungarian war potential, 99

Hammerstein, Wilhelm Baron, GdK, 27

Hannover, kingdom, 48, 68

Haymerle, Heinrich Baron, Austro-Hungarian foreign minister, 112

Haynau, Julius Jakob Baron, FML: reputation of, 34; in Hungary 34–36; relations with Russians, 35–36; dismissal of, 40

Hazai, Samuel Baron, GdI, GO, chief replacement branch, 203, 205, 209, 214

Henikstein, Alfred Baron, FML, chief of general staff: character and limitations, 57, 68; as chief of staff, 59–60; in Bohemia 1866, 67–70 *passim*; retired, 72; mentioned, 80

Hentzi, Heinrich Edler v. Arthurm, GM, 34, 119, 132, 134

Hercegovina, 86, 92, 103–104

Hermannstadt, 15

Hess, Heinrich Baron, FML, FZM, chief of Quartermaster-General Staff: characterization, 39–40; and Francis Joseph, 39–40; loss of power to Grünne, 40–41; war plan of 1850, 48–49; and war with Russia, 50–51; on condition of army in 1859, 52–53; frustra-

tions of, 53–54; retired, 59; mentioned, 78, 94
Hesse, Grand Duchy, 48, 68
Hindenburg, Paul v. Beneckendorff, Prussian (German) GO, GFM: on eastern front, 198; conduct of war by, 199; calls for armistice, 215
Hoch-und Deutschmeister Regiment, 19, 45
Hofburgwache, 15
Hofkriegsrat (Inner-Austrian), 3
Hofkriegsrat (HKR): formation and scope of activities, 1, 3–4; relations with field commanders, 6; internal conflicts, 6; relations with civilian authorities, 10; fears about troop loyalty, 19; reinforces Italian garrisons, 20, 25; replaced by KM, 23–24; mentioned, 10, 11, 12, 79
Hoffmann, Max, Prussian (German) Colonel, GM, 181
Hofmann, Leopold Baron, Austro-Hungarian finance minister, 97
Hohenwart, Karl Siegmund Count, Austrian prime minister, 88–89
Holstein, 64
Holy Alliance, 59
Holy Roman Empire, 2
Holy See, 17
Honvéd, Hungarian defense force 1848–1849: formation of, 28–29; fights Jelacić, 29; conflict among its officers, 30, 32; in campaigns of 1848–1849, 32–35; reprisals against, 35–36, 47; mentioned, 77, 129. *See also* Hungarian national army
Honvéd, Hungarian defense force, 1868–1918: negotiations for its formation, 76–78; arms and equipment of, 77, 84–85, 133, 136, 148, 165; expansion of, 85, 93–94, 110; combat readiness of, 93, 109; operational plans for, 94, 113, 165, 173; considered dangerous by Francis Ferdinand, 129, 147; considered possible opponent by general staff, 134; assumes status of national army, 136; considered equal to first line, 165, 173
Horses: in cavalry service, 43, 48, 180, 194; as draft animals, 48, 53, 116, 211, 212
Howitzers: muzzle-loading, 16; breech-loading, 126; Skoda, 149–150. *See also* Artillery, Artillery pieces
Hrabowsky v. Hrabova, Johann Baron, FML, 36
Hrvastko Domobranstvo, Croatian defense force, 1868–1918, 86–87
Hübner, Joseph Alexander Baron, 33
Humbert, King of Italy, 124
Hungarian Committee of National Defense (1848–1849), 32
Hungarian Diet: accepts standing army, 4–5; and *insurrectio,* 4–5, 7; and demands for national army, 18; of 1847–1848, 22; mentioned, 74
Hungarian Legion (1866), 71
Hungarian Ministry of National Defense (1867–1918), 76, 141
Hungarian national army: early aspirations for, 6–7, 18, 24–25, 28; in 1848–1849 revolution, 30, 32, and *passim;* demands for during *Ausgleich* negotiations, 76–77; *Honvéd* as step towards, 78, 85, 136; revival of demands, 109; as an issue in Hungarian crisis, 131–135 *passim;* continued desire for, 146; demands renewed during World War, 198, 208, 209–210
Hungarian national council, 215, 217
Hungarian Noble Guard, 15
Hungarian parliament (1848–1849), 28, 29, 34–35
Hungarian parliament (1867–1918): military demands of radical opposition in, 76; accepts dualistic army, 77; liberal in appropriations for *Honvéd,* 85; demands additional military concessions, 106–109; non-representative character of, 117–118, 131; and national minorities, 119, 128, 175–176; demands Magyarization of common army, 119, 128; obstructs expansion of common army, 131–136, 139, 140, 146, 156, 160; dissolution of, 135–136; during Annexation Crisis, 150, 156; ends its obstruction, 164–165; called responsible for weakness of Austro-Hungarian army in 1914, 165; remains in session during war, 177; and military leadership, 198
Hungarians, ethnic. *See* Magyars
Hungary, kingdom of: special position in military affairs, 1, 4–5, 13, 24, 75–78, 126, 131–137 *passim,* 164–165, 209–210, and *passim;* and renewal of *Ausgleich,* 75, 146–147, 208–210; political crisis in, 118–119, 131–137 *passim;* solution of, 140, 164–165; renews demands for control of national army, 198; reluctant in cooperation for food supply, 205; attacks on army leadership and demands for break with Austria, 209, 211, 214; and October Manifesto, 216; responsibility for collapse of front, 217; mentioned, 13, 14, 18, 22, 35, 38, 45, 48, 50, 54, 55, 58, 177, 182, 183, 185, and *passim*
Hussars, 11, 16, 19, 29, 43, 63, 120, 134

Imperial Military Chancery. *See Militärkanzlei seiner Majestät*
Incendiary projectiles, use in air combat prohibited, 203
Independence Party, Hungarian, 119, 131
Industrial capacity, Austro-Hungarian, 84, 89, 111, 193, 205
Infantry: organization of, 6, 16, 42, 63; weapons

Infantry (*continued*)
   and tactics, 16, 17, 43, 64–66, 70, 83–84, 143, 174; numerical preponderance in army, 15, 16, 43, 63, 110, 126, 150, 205
Inner-Austria, 2–4, 17, 32
Inner City (Vienna), 22–23, 45
Innsbruck, 3, 26, 27, 185, 218
Insignia: demand for separate Hungarian, 18, 77, 120, 132, 165; concessions regarding, 77, 120, 209
Inspector general, branch, 125, 150
Insurrectio, 1, 5, 7, 18
Irredentist activities: in Austrian Italy, 20, 47, 59, 98, 99, 114, 124; on Military Border and in South Slav areas, 59, 86, 91
Isonzo, battles (1915–1917): First through Fifth, 190; Sixth, 197; Seventh, Eighth, Ninth, 197; Tenth, Eleventh, Twelfth, 206
Isonzo River, 98, 187, 188–189, 194, 205, 206
Istria, 59, 91
Italian army: in 1866, 69; operational plans for, in Triple Alliance, 116, 124; annual recruit intake of, 126; strengthened, 163, 188; bravery in combat, 190; at Caporetto, 207–208; at Piave, 213; at Vittorio Veneto, 217; mentioned, 158 and *passim*
Italian navy, 71
Italian-Turkish War (1911), 163
Italians in Habsburg army: disaffection, 18, 26, 69; percentage of, in army, 61.
Italians in Habsburg Empire, 25, 47, 57, 59, 98, 114, 124, 143
Italy, Austrian interests in: strategic importance of, 15, 17, 43, 54; military interventions in, 17–18, 20, 47. *See also* Lombardy-Venetia, Milan, Radetzky
Italy, kingdom: considered as a potential adversary, 61, 97–99 *passim;* 114, 144, 152, 163, 188–189; war with Austria, 69–71; military expenditures of, 106; in Triple Alliance, 113, 114, 115, 124, 152, 167; wavers in 1914–1915, 184, 188–189; mentioned, 14, 35, 38, 48, 59, 94, 113, 117, 204, 212, 220, and *passim*
Izvolki, Alexander Petrovich, Russian foreign minister, 154

Jacobins, Hungarian, 18
Janski, Ludwig, GM, 119
Japan, 140, 164
Jaroslavice, cavalry battle of (1914), 180
Jászi, Oskar, Hungarian historian, quoted on national tolerance in Habsburg army, 221
Jelačić de Buzim, Joseph Baron (later Count), FML, Ban of Croatia: appointment and defiance of Hungary, 25; deposition and reinstatement, 28–29; invades Hungary, 29–30; apprehensive about unity of army, 29–30; before Vienna, 30–31; in Hungary, 1849, 35; mentioned, 77, 119
Jews, in Habsburg army: as regular officers, 118; as reserve officers, 128, 151; disliked by Francis Ferdinand and Conrad, 142, 151
Johann, Archduke, FM, 39
John, Franz Baron, FZM, RKM, and chief of general staff: as chief of staff to Albrecht, 69; as KM, 79; and general staff, 80; updates war plans against Russia, 94, 100
Josephstadt, fortress in Bohemia, 48, 68
Joseph II, Holy Roman Emperor: military reforms, 5–7; Turkish War, 6; mentioned, 13, 39, 49
Joseph, Archduke, FML, GdK, commander of *Honvéd*, 85
Joseph, Archduke, GO: favors national Hungarian army, 210; demands immediate armistice, 217
Joseph Ferdinand, Archduke, GO, shortcomings as a commander, 195–196
Jovanović, Stefan Baron, FML, commander 18th Division, governor of Dalmatia, 101, 103
Jutland, 65

Kageneck, Karl Count, Prussian (German) Major, Lieutenant Colonel, 173
Kaiserjäger (until 1815 Tyrolean *Jäger* Regiment), 14, 43, 83, 150, 177
Kaisers-Ebersdorf, 19
Kalnócky, Gustav Siegmund Count, FML, Austro-Hungarian foreign minister, 15
"*Kamerad Schnürschuh,*" German term for Austro-Hungarian soldiers, 194
Kamionka-Strumilova, garrison in Galicia, 142
Kapolna, battle of (1849), 32
Karageorgević, Peter, King of Serbia, 124
Karageorgević dynasty, 153
Karfreit. See Caporetto
Károlyi v. Nagykároly, Michael Count, Hungarian prime minister, 204, 214, 217
Kavallerieschützendivision, 194
Kaunitz-Rietberg, Wenzl Anton Eusebius Prince, 17
Kaution, 82
Kempen v. Fichtenstamm, Johann Baron, FML, chief of gendarmerie and minister of police, 45
Kerensky, Alexander F., Russian prime minister, 206
Kholm, 173
Khuen-Héderváry, Karl Count, Ban of Croatia, Hungarian prime minister, 132
Kiew, Russian military district, 167
Klagenfurt, 220
Klapka, Georg, Hungarian revolutionary general, 71

Klofáč, Václav Jaroslav, 204
Knezlać, Peace of (1870), 86
Koerber, Dr. Ernst, Austrian prime minister, 130–131, 133
Koller, Alexander Baron, GdK, KM, 85–86, 100
Kolowrat, Franz Anton Count, 10, 23
Kolubara River, 183
Komarow, battle of (1914), 180
Kommandosprache, 108. *See also* Language problems
Komitadji, 155
Komorn, battle of (1849), 35
Komorn, fortress, 18, 33, 34
Königgrätz, battle of (1866): account, 70; results of, 71, 74; mentioned, 59, 61, 63, 177
Königgrätz, fortress, 48, 68
Kossuth, Louis, Hungarian revolutionary leader: calls for national freedom, 22; in Hungarian government, 24; presses for national army, 25; forms government of national defense, 29; reorganizes army, 32–33; assumes full powers, 35; schemes in Croatia and on Military Border, 54; mentioned, 129
Kotor (Cattaro), Gulf of, 86
Kövess v. Kövessháza, Hermann Baron, FM: commands provisional army group, 179; commands Fifth *k.u.k.* Army, 191; and Third *k.u.k.* Army, 194; on Danube in 1918, 215; last commander-in-chief of army, 218
Krafft v. Dellmensingen, Konrad, Bavarian (German), Lieutenant General, 207, 220
Kramárč, Dr. Karel, Czech radical politician, 204
Krasnik, battle of (1914), 180
Kremsier, 33
Krauss, Alfred, FML: quoted on deployment controversy, 179; as chief of staff to Archduke Eugene, 184; on Conrad's conduct of Trentino offensive, 194; on mountain fighting tactics, 197; criticism of 1917 army reorganization, 208; mentioned, 207
Krieghammer, Edmund Baron, GdK, RKM: resignation forced by Beck, 125; replies to German nationalist attacks on army, 130; attempts to raise recruit quota, 131
Kriegsarchiv, 12–13, 220
Kriegsfaktor, 4
Kriegsminister: substituted for *Reichskriegsminister*, 147
Kriegsschule: Radetzky urges establishment of, 12; first course, 41; and Conrad, 143
Kriegsüberwachungsamt (War Supervisory Office), 192, 204
Krismanić, Gideon Ritter v., GM: as assistant chief of staff, North Army, 67–68, 69; characterization by Moering, 68; faces court of inquiry, 72

Krisvosije: first uprising in, 86; alleged Russian inspiration of, 87, 91; second uprising, 103–104
Krobatin, Alexander Baron, FZM, FM, KM: appointed KM, 168; supports garrison shift, 171; and reserve army, 174; in July 1914, 178; sceptical of Emperor Charles, 200; removed to front command, 203; counsels armistice, 217
Krupp artillery, 84
Kübeck v. Kübau, Carl Friedrich Baron, quoted on dominant position of army, 38
Kuhn v. Kuhnenfeld, Franz Baron, Colonel, FML, RKM: as Gyulai's chief of staff, 53; opposes *Honvéd* artillery, 77; desire to transform character of army, 79; quarrels with Albrecht, 79–80, 88; opposes greater power for general staff, 80; on troop expenditures, 83; protests *Honvéd* Gatling guns, 85; schemes for *Grenzer* autonomy, 87; his schemes in summer 1870, 88; attacks Andrássy, 89; resignation of, 89; evaluation of his work, 89; funeral of, 121; mentioned, 78, 81, 98, 127
Kummer v. Falkenfeld, Heinrich, GdK: commands provisional army group, 179
Kuropatkin, Alexey Nikolayevich, Russian general, 195

Laibach, (Ljubljana), 46, 216
Laibach, Congress of (1820), 15
Landesaufgebot: in alpine lands, 1; on Military Border, 14
Landeschef, military governor in Bosnia-Hercegovina, 153
Landesschützen (designated *Kaiserschützen* in 1917), 14, 85, 99
Landsturm: legislation for enacted, 81; in Tyrol, 85; actual formation of, 109; utilization in combat, 174, 182, 197; deficiencies in equipment and training, 182
Landwehr (1809–1830): establishment, 6–7; record, 13; Radetzky's opinion of, 13
Landwehr (1868–1918): proposed by Andrássy, 76; recruit intake, 81; arms and equipment of, 85, 150, 148; retarded development of, 85; in army order of battle, 94; as occupation force in Italy, 99; combat readiness, 109; strength increases, 109, 150, 165; provides mountain troops, 150; regarded as first line, 165, 173; mobilized in Dalmatia, 167
Langenau, Ferdinand Baron, FML, 98
Langenau, Karl Friedrich Baron, FML: quoted on mission of army, 9
Language of command controversy: Hungarian demands for Magyar language in army, 18, 28, 29; German as language of command, 76, 108; Magyar conceded to *Honvéd*, 77; Hun-

Language (*continued*)
  gary concedes Croatian, 86–87; as a major issue in Hungarian politics, 119, 131–137 *passim;* Francis Joseph on, 132; Hungary renews her demands, 147, 160; and *passim*
Latour, Theodor Count Baillet de, FZM, KM: as minister, 23–24; tries to preserve army intact, 24; supports counterrevolution, 24–27 *passim;* murdered, 30; mentioned, 34
Lavarone-Folgaria plateau: fortifications on, 163; as assembly area, 163, 184, 194
LeBrun, Barthélemi Louis Josephe, French general of division, 88
Legeditsch, Ignaz v., FML, 48
Legnano, fortress, 18
Lehensaufgebot, 1
Leibgarde Infantrie Kompanie, 15, 220
Leitha River, 32
Lemberg, 15, 19, 50
Lemberg, battle of (1914), 180
Leopold I, Holy Roman Emperor, 4, 19
Leuthner, Dr. Karl, Socialist *Reichsrat* deputy, 214
Libell (1511), 14
Liberal Party, Hungarian: Joins with opposition to demand military concessions, 119, 131–132, 133; gains majority, 160; rules, 175
Light infantry, 17
Limanowa-Lapanow, battle of (1914), 182
Linder, Béla, Colonel, Hungarian minister of national defense, 217
Linsingen, Alexander v., Prussian (German) GdI: commands *Südarmee,* 184; and Brusilov offensive, 195–196; relations with Austro-Hungarian subordinate commanders, 196
Linz, fortified camp, 18, 71
Lissa, naval battle of (1866), 71
Literacy: in army, 61, 66; compared to other European armies, 108
Lobkowitz, Joseph Prince, Duke of Raudnitz, FML, 27
Lobkowitz, Rudolf Prince, FZM: projected as military governor of Hungary, 134
Lombardy, 20, 25, 26, 34, 42, 54
Lombardy-Venetia, kingdom of: military service in, 13, 42; Austrian army in, 17–18; dissension in, 25; state of siege, 45; terrorist activities, 47; mentioned, 52
London, Conference of (1913), 168
Losses, Habsburg armies: from disease in Moldavia-Wallachia, 52; in Italy, 1859, 54; in Danish war, 59; due to faulty tactics, 59, 69–70, 143; in occupation of Bosnia-Hercegovina, 102; in Galicia, 1914, 180, 182; in Serbia, 1914, 183; in Carpathians, 184; overall, 1914–1915, 184, 192–193; during Brusilov offensive, 196–197; overall up to February 1917, 205; during Piave offensive, 213; grand total during World War by nationalities, 218
Losses: Serbian, 183; Italian, 190, 207, 213; Rumanian, 197
Lovčen, Mount, 191
Lower Austria, 218
Lublin, 173
Ludendorff, Erich, Prussian (German) General, First Quartermaster General: and Hindenburg, 181; criticism of Austro-Hungarian army, 181; at *Oberost,* 182; on Habsburg army in Italy, 187; criticized by Conrad, 199; agrees to provide troops for Italy, 206; blamed for breaking off Caporetto offensive, 208; desires better coordination with Austria-Hungary, 212; asks for Austro-Hungarian divisions on western front, 214
Ludovika Academy, Budapest, 85
Ludwig, Archduke, FZM, 39
Luftschiffer Abteilung, 175
Lutheranism, 2

Machine guns, Schwarzlose M 1907 and M 1907/12: introduction of, 150, 160; modified as light weapon, 193; production numbers, 205, 208; production cut, 210
Macedonia, 169
Mackensen, August v., Prussian (German) GdK: at Tanow-Gorlice, 186; in Serbia, 191; commands Danube Army, 197
Magenta, battle of (1850), 53
Maglaj, encounter at (1878), 102
Magyars: Montecuccoli, opinion of, 4; Maria Theresa on, 5; in Habsburg army, 18, 61, 69, 119, 128, 151, and *passim;* oppose Habsburg dynasty, 32–33, 35; boycott *Reichsrat,* 57; at Custozza, 1866, 69; Beck doubts their loyalty, 98; attempt to use the army to magyarize minorities in Hungary, 119, 131–132; Francis Ferdinand on, 120, 132, 144, and *passim;* Conrad desires action against, 144; Francis Joseph regards them as basically loyal, 165; German opinion of their combat effectiveness, 206, and *passim*
Main River, 68
Maneuvers: under Radetzky, 15, 18, 44; Francis Ferdinand and, 142, 149, 171; Conrad's attempt to make more realistic, 149
Manifesto, October 16, 1918, 215–216
Mantua, fortress, 18, 26
Marburg a. Drau, 203
Maria Theresa Order, 133
Maria Theresa, Queen: describes army at time of her accession, 5; reforms, 5–6; mentioned, 3, 120
Marie Ann, Empress of Austria, 27
Marksmanship, neglect of, 16, 43, 150

Marschbrigaden, 110, 174
Marterer, Ferdinand Baron, FML, GdI, 202, 203
Maximilian I, Holy Roman Emperor, 220
Maximilian, Archduke, Emperor of Mexico, 62
Mazzini, Giuseppe, Italian revolutionary, 19, 47
Mediterranean pacts (1887), 115
Mensdorff-Pouilly, Alexander Count, Prince of Dietrichstein zu Nikolsburg, GdK, Austrian foreign minister, 61
Mészáros, Lázár, Colonel, Hungarian war minister, 24, 28
Metternich, Klemens Lothar Prince, Austrian chancellor: views on civil-military relations, 7–8, 11; on military power, 9, 12; fears renewed French aggression, 17; intervenes in Italy, 17, 20; reinforces army in Italy, 20; calls on Prussian aid against revolution, 22; driven from office, 22–23; views on maintenance of Ottoman Empire, 50
Meyer, Heinrich, regimental agent, 12
Mexico, 62, 63
Milan: Radetzky warns citizens of, 21; evacuation of, 25–26; reoccupation of, 28; coup attempted in, 47; Gyulai evacuates, 53
Milan I, Prince and King of Serbia, 103–104
Militarism and Austria-Hungary, 145
Militärkanzlei seiner Majestät (*MKSM*), 79, 100, 141, and *passim*
Militär Schematismus, 10
Military academies, 42, 82. See also *Technische Militärakademie*, *Theresianische Militärakademie*
Military assistance to the civil power: before 1848, 19–20; in Hungary, 119; in Graz and Vienna, 130; in Prague, 130; and *passim*
Military Border *(Militärgrenze)*: origins, 2; Hungarian desire to control, 5, 24–25, 28, 76; reorganizations of, 5–6, 14–15, 40, 61; under French control, 7; operations of, 17, 24, 28–29, 30, 50, 67; disaffection on, 19, 25, 29–30, 36, 43, 47, 50, 59; dissolution of Transylvanian regiments, 43; insurrectionary schemes on, 54, 71, 86, 87; demilitarization of Croat and Banat Military Borders, 87; mentioned, 58, 61, 63, 81. See also Banat, Croatia, *Grenzer*, Jelačić, *Székler*
Military Compromise of 1868, 76–78 and *passim*
Military conventions, 17, 22, 48, 199, 212
Military intellectualism: low status of, 12–13, 41, 42, 44; opposition to, 38–39, 41, 42, 44, 61, 62, and *passim*
Military intelligence, 66, 99, 152, 153, 154, 169, 178, 196
Military journals, 13, 62, 80, 143, 152, 164
Military professionalism, 5, 12–13, 38–39, 44, 60, 61, 62, 82, 100, 149, 176, 206

Military service: duration of active duty, 13, 42, 61, 81; shortened for fiscal reasons, 42, 61; political pressure for two years' tour, 108; approved by Schönaich, 161
Militärzentralkanzlei (also *Militärkanzlei*), 39–40
Mincio River, 54
Minimalgruppe Balkan: composition and deployment, 159; offensive and defeat against Serbia, 181–182
Mobilization: in 1850, 48; in 1853–1854, 50–52; in 1859, 52–53; in 1866, 67–68; slowness of, 67–69 *passim*, 101, 104; partial, 88, 156, 166–168; preparations in 1878, 97; efforts to speed up process, 101, 110–111, 114, 117; Albrecht dubious about German mobilization schedule, 113; preparations for multifront scheme, 125, 159; scheme for *Fall U*, 134; shift in mobilization dispositions after Balkan wars, 170; in 1914, 174, 176–179 *passim*
Moering (also Möhring), Karl, GM, FML: quoted on Krismanić and Henikstein, 67–68; denounces Hungarian military demands, 76–77
Modena, 17, 20
Moga, Johann v., FML, later *Honvéd* general, 29
Mogul, operation, 211
Moldavia, 197
Moldavia-Wallachia, principalities: Russian intervention in 1848, 35; Russian occupation and evacuation, 50–51; Austrian occupation, 51; losses during occupation, 52
Mollinary, Anton Baron, FML: reports on conditions in Bosnia-Hercegovina, 92; designated to lead occupation troops, 93, 95; removed from command, 101
Moltke, Count Helmuth C.B., Prussian (German) General FM, chief of staff: on infantry fire tactics, 69; western front in plans of, 112, 115–116; shifts major deployment to eastern front, 112–113; meets with Beck, 113–114; shift back to western deployment, 115–116; so informs Beck, 116
Moltke, Count Helmuth J.L., Prussian (German) GO, chief of staff: and Annexation crisis, 155; contacts with Conrad, 155, 157–158, 159, 168, 179; intends to make main effort on western front, 158; promises early redeployment east, 158; warns Conrad against preventive war, 168; informs Conrad that he will stand on defensive in east, 179; blamed by Conrad for failure of his offensive, 180; replaced, 185; mentioned, 170
Montecuccoli, Raimondo Count, FM, 4
Montenegro: conflict with Turkey, 1853, 50; support for Dalmatian rising, 86; supports

Montenegro (*continued*)
  insurrection in Hercegovina, 93; declares war on Turkey, 93, 167; in Balkan Wars, 165; in World War, 191; mentioned, 198
Montenegro, army of: before Scutari, 168; in 1914, 182–183; capitulates, 191
Monte Pasubio, operation (1918), 212
Monte San Michele, operation (1916), 197
Morale, 18, 44, 48, 53, 54, 65, 127, 180, 183, 192, 196, 211, 213–214
Moravia: as troop assembly area against Prussia, 48, 68; casualties of in World War, 218; mentioned, 27
Morocco, 134
Mortality rate: in peacetime army, 42, 83
Mortara, battle of (1849), 34
Mortars, 193, 205
Moslems: in Bosnia-Hercegovina, 91–92, 101, 103; formation of Moslem regiments, 104; their use denounced by German nationalists, 130
Mountain troops, 102, 150, 188, 190, 198
Münchengrätz, Agreement of (1833), 35
Muskets and rifles: flintlock converted to percussion, 16; introduction of rifled musket (M 54), 43, 64; the breechloader controversy, 65–66; Prussian needle gun, 66, 69, 70; Wänzel modification of M 54 rifles, 83; Werndl (M 67) introduced, 88, 101; Wänzel rifles delivered to insurgents in Hercegovina, 93; Mannlicher rifles (M 1886/88) and modifications (M 1895) introduced, 111; Revelli automatic rifle, troop tests of, 175
Mutinies: Richter grenadiers, 30; Ogulin *Grenzer*, 87, 170; 8th Dragoons, 170; naval, 211; military, 214

Nagodba, (1868), 86
Nagy-Sarló, battle of (1849), 34
Nagy de Alsó-Szopor, Ladislaus Baron, FML, deputy chief Quartermaster-General Staff, 60
Naples, 17, 19
Napoleon I, 6, 7, 9, 182
Napoleon III: rise of, 47, 49; supports Sardinia, 52, 54; policy of, in 1866, 71; negotiates for Austrian alliance, 87–88
National Guard (Hungary), 29
National Guard (Vienna), 23, 29
National guards: in Compromise negotiations, 76–78 *passim*
National composition, Habsburg armies of: officers, 11, 42, 118, 127–128, 151; all ranks, 13–14, 18–19, 61, 119, 128
Nationality problem, within the army: as a fundamental problem, 6–7, 18, 20, 54, 56, 74–78 *passim;* 120, 129, 170, 200, 221; and *passim;* military attempts to deal with, 19,
58, 110, 118, 119, 147, 162, 170, 171; during 1848 revolution, 26–27, 29–30; Hungarians and, 29, 30, 52, 55, 58, 129, 196, 206; South Slavs and, 36, 47, 54, 55, 86–87, 91–92; detrimental effects on military potential, 46, 55–56, 64, 73, 128, 170, 206; Francis Joseph and, 58, 132, 200; and Czechs, 85, 121, 130, 148, 165, 184, 187, 204, 206; army provides fair treatment for nationalities, 118, 119, 147, 170, 221; Germans and, 121, 129–130, 187, 196, 206; Francis Ferdinand's proposals for dealing with, 120, 129, 141–142, 162, 171; Conrad's views on, 144, 147, 170; problem forces changes in mobilization deployment, 170; general discussion of problem during World War, 170, 184, 200, 221; and *passim. See also* entries to specific nationalities, controversies, and incidents.
National problems, in Habsburg Empire: 7, 18, 24, 37, 46–47, 74–75, 119, 120–121, 129–130, 139, 145–146, 162, 165, 176, 192, 201, 204, 212, 215–216, and *passim. See also* entries to specific nationalities, issues, and personalities.
Needle gun: introduced in Prussia, 65; evaluated by Augustin, 65–66; effectiveness in war, 70
Neue Freie Presse (Vienna), quoted on war with Italy, 152
Nicholas, Prince of Montenegro, 92
Nicholas I, Tsar of Russia: military support of Austria, 17; congratulates Windischgrätz, 31; decides to intervene in Hungary, 35; pardons Görgey, 36; joins alignment against Napoleon III, 49
Nicholas II, Tsar of Russia: prevents partial mobilization, 167
Nobili, Johann Count, FZM, 72
Nobility and military careers, 11–12, 42, 62, 81–82, 118, 146, 151
Non-commissioned officers: quality of, 61; shortage of senior, 61, 83, 151, 161; casualties, 180, 218; mentioned, 11
North German Confederation, 71, 81
Norway, 134
Novara, battle and armistice of (1849), 34
Novi Bazar, Sanjak of, 95, 98, 156, 170
Nyiri v. Székely, Alexander, GM, royal commissioner in Hungary, 136

Oath, military: conflict over in 1848–1849, 26–27, 29–30, 32; refusal to take in Bohemia, 85; and German nationalism, 121; controversy over release from, 216
Oberost (German High Command East), 182, 196
Oberste Heeresleitung (OHL), German Supreme Command: concern over Austro-

Hungarian situation, 185, 205; demands senior role in combined operations, 186, 191; demands German control on eastern front, 198; requests Austro-Hungarian aid on western front, 212, 214–215; decides to end war, 215; and intervention in Austria, 219–220; and *passim*. See also Falkenhayn, Ludendorff, William II
Oberste Kriegsleitung (OKL), Supreme Command Central Powers, 199, 204
Obrenović dynasty, 124
Obrenović, Milan, Prince of Serbia, 103
October Diploma (1860), 57
Odessa district, 167
Oeversee, battle of (1864), 65
Officers, Habsburg army, regular: procurement of, 5, 11–12, 42, 62, 108, 118, 127; qualities and limitations, 11–13, 42, 44, 57, 62, 82, 100, 127, 149, 170, 176, 206; origins and national derivations, 11, 12, 42, 118, 127–128, 151; promotion and pay, 11–12, 42, 62, 81–82, 107–108, 146, 151; loyalties during 1848–1849 revolution, 26–27, 29–30, 32; court-martials of, 36; Francis Joseph's dislike of learned officers, 38–39; Grünne's views on, 40, 42; career patterns of, 42, 81–82; purge of incompetents, 59; resignations, 62; Prussian-German views of, 42, 44, 118, 170, 181, 206; alienation from society, 57, 145–146, 164; religious distribution of, 118, 127, 161; numbers of, 127, 151; Francis Ferdinand and Conrad sure of their loyalty, 151; losses of, 180, 218, and *passim*
Officers, Habsburg army, reserve: need for, 83; one-year volunteers, 83, 108, 127, 151; national composition and reliability of, 121, 127, 128, 130, 134, 151; predominance of Germans among, 128, 151; promotions of, during World War, 193
Officers, *Honvéd* (1868–1918), 83, 127
Officers, *Landwehr* (1868–1918), 83
Ogulin Regiment, 15, 87
Olmütz, fortress, 16, 27, 68, 69, 70
Olmütz, Punctation of (1850), 49
Oppenheimer, Samuel, 4
Österreichische Militärische Zeitschrift, 13, 62
Österreichische Militär-Zeitung, 80
Österreichisch-ungarische Wehrzeitung, 80
Österreichische Waffenfabriksgesellschaft, 83
Ottinger, Franz, GM, provisional Hungarian war minister, 24
Ottoman Empire: as threat to Austria, 4; decline of, 49; Austrian interest in its preservation, 50, 90, 92, 166; partition negotiations, 94, 97; considered as ally against Russia, 94; defeated in Balkan Wars, 167; reorganization of, 168–169; joins Central Powers, 190; collapse of, 215; mentioned 153, 156
Ottoman troops, 166, 182, 197

Padua, 194
Pakozd-Velenze, engagement of (1848), 29
Palestine, 212, 215
Pandurs, 103
Pan-Slav Congress (1848), 27–28
Pan-Slavism: fears of, 36, 87, 91, 93; support of, for Serbia, 93, 95; British opinion of, 95
Papal states, 142
Paris, 13, 22, 195
Parma, 17
Paskievich, Ivan Fedorovich, Prince of Warsaw, Russian FM, 35–36
Pavia, 25
Peball, Kurt, Austrian military historian, quoted on character of Habsburg army, 200
Pesciera, fortress, 18
Pest, 16, 34
Peterwardein, fortress, 15
Pflanzer-Baltin, Karl Baron, GdK: commands provisional army group, 184; commands Seventh *k.u.k.* Army, 195; counterattacks in Albania, 213–214; last active force commander, 219
Philip II, King of Spain, 79
Philippović v. Philippsberg, Joseph Baron, FZM: during occupation of Bosnia-Hercegovina, 101–102; relieved, 103; death of, 122
Piedmont. See Sardinia
Piave River, 207
Piave offensive (1918), 212–214
Pillersdorf, Franz Baron, Austrian prime minister, 23
Pitreich, Heinrich Ritter v., FML, RKM: appointment of, 125; attacked for making concessions to Hungary, 132, 137; leaves office, 140
Pius IX, Pope, 20
Pless, Silesia, *OHL* location, 185
Pless, Convention of (1915), 191
Plevna, Turkish fortress, 96
Poincaré, Raymond, French prime minister, 165
Poland, 112–113, 180
Polish troops in Austrian army, 7, 18, 19, 61
Polish troops in Austro-Hungarian army, 128
Polzer-Holditz, Arthur Count, 201
Ponsonby, John Viscount, British minister in Vienna, quoted on military counterrevolution, 30
Popp, Leonidas Baron, GM, FML, director *MKSM*, 110
Porte, 50, 95. See also Ottoman Empire, Turkey
Portugal, 136

Potiorek, Oskar, FML: as candidate for chief of general staff, 142; urges reinforcements for Bosnia-Hercegovina, 166; gains independence from *AOK*, 182; defeated, 182–183; mentioned, 179.
Pragmatic Sanction: and military affairs, 4–5; interpretation of, challenged, 75
Prague: state of siege in, 45, 85–86; riots in, 130; mentioned, 15, 16, 185, 204, 216
Prague, Revolution of 1848 in: uprising, 27–28; repression of, 28; importance of, 28
Prague, Treaty of (1866), 71
Pressburg, 22, 32, 71
Preventive war: Beck and Albrecht suggest against Italy, 99; considered against Russia, 115–116; Conrad's advocacy of, 144–145, 151–152, 155–156, 163–164, 168–170; evaluation of his advocacy, 145, 169–170; opposition to, 152, 164, 169
Pripet marshes, 195
Prisoners of war: Austro-Hungarian, 180, 185, 197, 211, 212; Italian, 195, 207; Rumanian, 197
Proprietors, regimental, 11–12, 15
Prussia: wars with Austria, 5, 67–71; military relations with Austria, 17, 22, 49, 50–52; in conflict with Austria over policy in Germany, 48–49, 67; policy of in 1859, 52, 54; joins Austria against Denmark, 64–65; and war with France, 88; mentioned, 57, 87, and *passim*
Prussian army: as model for Austria and Austria-Hungary, 5, 10, 83; compared with Austrian and Austro-Hungarian institutions, 10, 39, 41, 60–61; reforms after 1850, 49; armament, 65; as intervention force in Bohemia, 219; mentioned, 10, 15, 54
Przemysl, fortress: strengthened, 116; siege of, 180, 181; relief of, attempted, 184; capitulation of, 185
Puhallo v. Brlog, Paul, GO, commander First *k.u.k.* Army, 195
Putnik, Radomir, General, Serbian commander-in-chief: allowed to proceed to Serbia, 182; defeats Potiorek, 183

Quadrilateral: fortresses of, 18; Radetzky retreats into, 25–26; Gyulai retreats into, 53–54; mentioned, 28
Quartermaster-General Staff: creation of, 6; low status of, 10, 39, 41; conflict with *Adjutanten Corps*, 41; in 1850, 48; in 1859, 53–54; Benedek and, 59–60; evaluation of, 60–61; plan to seize Bosnia, 91. *See also* General Staff, General Staff Corps

Radetzky v. Radetz, Josef Wenzl Count, FML, FM: as chief of staff to Schwarzenberg, 7–9; on army finances, 9, 12; on staff needs, 10, 41; and civil-military relations, 10, 20, 25, 30, 40; views on *Landwehr*, 13; advanced ideas on discipline and morale, 18; defends Austrian position in Italy, 20–21, 25–26, 34; conflict with Grünne, 40; puts down terrorism, 47; appointed to command army in case of war with Prussia, 48; his ideas on danger from Russia, 49; mentioned 36, 37, 39, 54, 59, 91, 127, 187
Railroads: delays in construction, 42, 101, 160; military use of, 48, 111, 213; in staff planning, 60, 109, 111, 160; expansion of capabilities, 111, 117, 127
Railroad and Telegraph Regiment, 111
Rainer, Archduke, viceroy in Lombardy-Venetia, 20, 25
Ramming v. Riedkirchen, Wilhelm Baron, FML, 54
Rašin, Alois, Czech radical politician, 204
Rations: military, 14, 16, 193, 205, 211, 213; for industrial workers, 210–211
Rechberg-Rothenlöwen, Johann Bernhard Count, Austrian foreign minister, 40, 61
Recruitment: up to 1852, 6, 13, 14; Francis Joseph's comments on, 42; Law of 1852, 61–62; universal conscription debated, 61–62; attempted, 75; Law of 1868, 77; quotas, annual, 81; increase of annual quota, 109; increase resisted, 131, 148; Law of 1912, 165. *See also* Conscription
Redl, Alfred, Colonel, 169, 171, 173
Redlich, Josef, Austrian historian, quoted on Conrad, 144
Regimental agents, 12
Regiments: Tyrolean *Jäger (Kaiserjäger)*, 14, 43, 150; Ogulin, 15, 87; Hoch-und Deutschmeister, 19, 45; 26th Infantry, 26; 5th Artillery, 29; 19th Infantry, 54–55; 34th Infantry, 54–55; infantry, in Hungary, national composition of, 119; 28th Infantry, 121, 185
Regimentssprache, 83, 108. *See also* Language of command
Reichskriegsminister, Hungary obtains title modification, 147, 164. *See also* War minister
Reichsrat (1861–1918): and military appropriations, 57–58, 78, 89, 105–106, 164; and new weapons, 65–66; boycotts and obstruction in, 57, 59, 129, 139, 164; and recruit quota, 109, 196; attacks on military leadership in, 130, 214; suspension of, 176; reconvened, 204
Reichstadt, conversations at (1876), 94
Reichstag, Vienna and Kremsier, 30, 33
Reininghaus, Gina v., later Countess Conrad v. Hötzendorf: her liaison with Conrad, 164; his letter on war chances to, 177; at *AOK*, 196

Reinsurance Treaty (1887), 114–115, 116
Religion: military distrust of Orthodox, 36, 37; tolerance toward, 118, 151; distribution in officer corps, 118, 128, 151; Catholic preponderance in officer corps, 128; Jewish reserve officers, 128; Conrad accuses Francis Ferdinand of discrimination against Protestants, 151
Remington rifles, 66
Remount service, 16
Replacements in World War: lowered quality of, 193; shortage of, 205; no longer available, 210, 213
Reserve components: *Ersatzreserve*, 81, 131, 174; combat readiness, 101, 109, 110, 148, 174, 182; attempts to increase strength, 109, 131, 174; dissension among Czech reservists, 130, 148. *See also Honvéd, Landwehr,* Officers, reserve
Revelli automatic rifle, 175
Revised Land Ordinance (1627), 3
"Revolver" operation, 211
Revolution, in France, 6, 13, 22
Revolution of 1848, Vienna: spring and summer, 22–23, 29; radicalization of, 30; siege and conquest of city, 30–31
Revolution of 1848, Hungary: demand for national autonomy, 22; national ministry formed, 24; conflict over military powers, 24–25, 28; national army formed, 28–29; revolutionary government formed, 33; national armies defeated, 34–35; reprisals, 36
Revolution of 1848, in Italy: spring and summer of 1848, 25–26; Radetzky defeats Sardinia, 26, 34; Milan reoccupied, 34; Venice capitulates, 34
Rhineland, 48
Riga, 186
Riots: military regulations concerning, 19; Agram, 20; Galicia, 20; Vienna, 23, 121, 130; Milan, 25; Prague, 85–86, 130; Graz and Salzburg, 130; Hungary, 133 and *passim*
Ritter, Gerhard, German historian, cited on Schemua, 164
Rocket Regiment, 16, 44
Rodich, Gabriel Baron, FZM: advises appeasement of Dalmatian insurgents, 86; and Balkan schemes, 91, 92, 93; mentioned, 98
Rohr, Franz, GdK, 188–189
Rome, 98, 163, and *passim*
Rothkirch und Panthen, Leonhard Count, FML, 11
Royal Military Chancery, Prussian, 39
Rudolf, Archduke, crown prince: negotiates for military agreement with Germany, 112; and war party, 115; urges military intervention in Hungary, 120, 134
Rumania, kingdom of: allies with Austria-Hungary, 114, 123; in Balkan Wars, 165–169 *passim;* becomes unreliable ally, 169; denounced by Conrad, 173; wavers, 190–191; enters war, 197; conquered, 197–198; mentioned, 71, 94, 95
Rumanian army, 116, 197
Rumanians in Habsburg armies, 47, 61, 128, 176
Russia: military cooperation with Austria, 17, 35, 49; friction over Russian actions in Hungary, 35, 36; over Balkan policy, 49–52, 97–98, 114, 123, 140, 153, 165; military consider her a potential enemy, 49, 88, 91, 105, 112, 113, 114, 115, 187; and Andrássy, 89, 90–91; agreements for division of Balkans, 94, 95, 154; declares war on Porte, 95–96; Francis Ferdinand and, 142; reaction to annexation of Bosnia-Hercegovina, 154; backs down before German threat, 156; Schemua recommends detente with, 164; and Balkan League, 165; and trial mobilizations of, 166–167; makes gains as result of Balkan wars, 169
Russian army: in Hungary, 1849, 35–36; annual recruit intake of, 126; success and defeat in Galicia and Carpathians, 180–182, 185, 186; in Brusilov offensive, 195–196; mentioned, 9, 15, 17, and *passim*
Russian Revolution (1905), 135
Russian Revolution (1917), 210
Russo-French alliance, 123
Russo-Japanese War (1904–1905): neglect of its tactical lessons, 143; mentioned, 124
Russo-Turkish War (1877–1878), 95–96
Rüstow, Wilhelm, Swiss Colonel and military writer, quoted on nationality problem in Austrian army, 56
Ruthenes in Habsburg army, 18, 61, 128, 170, 184, 196, 214

St. Gotthard, battle of (1664), 4
St. Petersburg, 50, 92, 94, 98, 156
St. Stephen, Crown of. *See* Hungary
Salis-Soglio, Daniel Baron, FML: quoted on obligations of an Austrian officer, 118
Salonica, 91, 95, 97, 191, 197
Salzburg: meeting of Francis Joseph and Napoleon III, 87
Salzburg, province: casualties of, 218
San River, 158, 180, 186
Sanitary cordon, 43
Santa Lucia, battle of (1848), 26, 28
Sarajevo: captured, 102; Serb concentration in, 153; assassination of Francis Ferdinand in, 177; mentioned, 178, 182
Sardinia: prepares to invade Lombardy, 25; defeated, 28; war with Austria, 52–54; mentioned, 47
Sardinian army: in campaign of 1848, 26, 28; in

Sardinian army (*continued*)
1849, 34; in Crimea, 51; in war of 1859, 52–54
Sarkotić v. Lovčen, Stefan Baron, GO, 209
Save River, 183
Savoy, dynasty of: Radetzky and, 34; Albrecht, dislike of, 142. *See also* Charles Albert, Humbert, Victor Emmanuel
Saxony, army of: as Austrian ally, 48, 68, 69; occupies Holstein, 64; proposed as intervention force in Bohemia, 219
Saxony, kingdom, 48
Schemua, Blasius, GdI, chief of general staff: quoted on army and society, 145–146; his qualities, 164; and Balkan crisis, 166; in Berlin, 167; mentioned, 169
Schlieffen, Count Alfred, Prussian (German) Lieutenant General, chief of general staff: deployment plans, 117; concern over obsolete Austro-Hungarian artillery, 127; mentioned, 155, 157
Schlick zu Bassano u. Weisskirchen, Franz Count, GdK, 51
Schleswig-Holstein, 64–65
Schlitter v. Niedernberg, Karl Baron, GM, FML, 40
Schönaich, Franz, Baron, GdI, RKM: appointed, 137, 140; and concessions to Hungary, 146, 160; denounced by Francis Ferdinand, 147, 161; and military aviation, 175
Schönbrunn Palace, 221
Schönbrunn, Treaty of (1809), 7
Schönburg-Hartenstein, Alois Prince, GO: proposed as war minister, 203; as proposed head of a military government, 211; considers the war lost, 216; on military counterrevolution, 220
Schönerer, Georg Ritter v., German nationalist leader in Austria, 121
Schönfeld, Anton Baron, FML, chief of general staff: and war plans against Russia, 94–95; on danger from Italy, 99; assessment of, 100; mentioned, 107
Schwarzenberg, Felix Prince zu, FML, prime minister of Austria: appointment, 31; program, 31, 38; and Windischgrätz, 35; accepts Russian aid, 35; asserts civilian supremacy over generals, 40; policy towards Prussia, 48–49; towards Russia, 49; mentioned, 47, 141
Schwarzenberg, Karl Prince zu, FM, president *HKR:* as allied commander, 7; on the financial state of the army, 9–10
Schwechat, encounter at (1848), 30
Schweitzer, Eduard Ritter v., FML, 118
Scotti, Karl, FML, commands assault group at Caporetto, 207
Scutari, Turkish fortress, 167–168

Sebastopol, 51
Sedan, battle of (1870), 88
Seine River, 158
Seeckt, Hans v., Prussian (German), GM: as chief of staff to Mackensen, 186; and Archduke Charles, 198; on Austro-Hungarian army, 198, 205–206
Semlin, 162
Serb-Banat Army Corps, 50
Serbia, principality and kingdom: military misgivings about, 49–50, 59, 86–87, 90–91, 124–125, 146, 152–153; as center of operations against Habsburg territory, 66, 71, 91–92; supports revolt in Bosnia-Hercegovina, 93; declares war on Turkey, 93, 167; defeated, 95; ties with Austria-Hungary, 103–104; Francis Ferdinand willing to maintain peace with, 144; Conrad wishes to wage preventive war against, 152–153; and the annexation of Bosnia-Hercegovina, 155; crisis with Austria-Hungary, 155–156; joins Balkan League, 165; gains power, 169; remains primary target for Conrad, 178–179; mentioned, 101, 134, 162
Serbian army: formation of, 59; victorious in Balkan Wars, 169; underestimated by Austro-Hungarian intelligence, 182; defeats invasion, 183; defeat and evacuation of, 191; reconstituted, 215
Serbo-Bulgarian War (1885), 109, 114
Serbs in Habsburg armies, 21, 29, 32, 36, 47, 61, 128, 170
Serbs in Southern Hungary: defy Budapest government, 21; declare autonomy, 28; fight Magyars, 29, 32; military suspicious of, 36, 47; favor insurgents in Bosnia-Hercegovina, 92; become less loyal after Balkan Wars, 176
Sereth River, 197
Seressaner, 14
Seton-Watson, Robert W., British journalist, quoted on Austro-Hungarian army, 170
Siedlce, 158
Silesia, 87, 181
Sixtus of Parma, Prince, go-between in peace move, 204, 212
Skoda arms factory, 126, 164, 174, 149–150
Slavonia: Military Border in, 14; support in for Bosnian-Hercegovinian revolt, 92; dissension in, 162; mentioned, 50
Slovakia, 32
Slovaks in Habsburg armies, 61, 128
Slovenes in Habsburg armies, 61, 128, 214
Slovenes, as hostile troops in Carinthia, 221
Socialists: and workers' riots, 121; anti-military agitation of, 128, 148, 185; denounced by Francis Ferdinand, 142, 147; and strike of January 1918, 211; mentioned, 176
Sofia, 96, 214

Sokol, Czech nationalist sports association, 121
"Soldier Schwejk," 185
Solferino, battle of (1859), 54, 56, 57, 61, 177
Sophie, Archduchess: and the ouster of Metternich, 23; relations with Windischgrätz, 27; and Grünne, 39
South Slav National Council (Agram), 215
South Slavs: national movement of, 19, 36–37, 49–50, 86–87, 90–91, 135–136, 153; a great South Slav state considered a mortal danger for the Habsburg monarchy, 36, 49–50, 86–87, 90–93 *passim,* 152–153; Conrad's solution for, 170. *See also* Bosnia-Hercegovina, Croats, Dalmatia, *Grenzer,* Serbs
Soviet Union, 210
Spa, agreements of (1918), 212
Spanish military establishment, 1, 3
Spitzer, Alois, regimental agent, 12
Staatsrat, 10
Stadion, Johann Philip Count, 6
Standschützen, 85, 188, 189
Steel-bronze, 84
Stein, Hermann Baron, Bavarian (German) Lieutenant General, commands assault group at Caporetto, 207
Stellvertreterfond, 62, 80
Steyr, 83
Stöger-Steiner, Edler v. Steinstätten, Rudolf, FML, GdI, KM: appointment of, 203; on division of army, 209–210; his report on continuing the war, 210; wishes to retain troops for internal security, 214; and demobilization, 220
Stosstaktik: description of, 64; defects of, 65; Benedek's insistence on, 69; modifications of, 70; defended, 84
Strategic bombing, restricted by Charles I, 203
Strategy: against Turks, 2; against Napoleon, 7; Radetzky, 25–26, 34; in Hungary, 31–33, 35; plans in 1850, 48; lack of, in Italy in 1859, 53–54; in 1866, 67–69 *passim;* planning against Russia, 94–95, 158–159, 173, 179; at Tarnow-Gorlice, 186; in Italy, 187–189 *passim,* 194, 207, 213; and *passim. See also* War plans
Strategy, general: eighteenth century precepts, 68; short war doctrine, 108, 112; incompatibility of weapons, strategy, and tactics, 112, 174–175. *See also* War plans, weaponry
Streifcorps (Strafuni), anti-insurgency units, 103–104
Strength, Habsburg army: in period to 1848, 3, 7, 15, 17; in Italy in 1848, 25; before Vienna, 30; against Hungary in 1849, 32, 35; in 1850, 38; in 1854, 43, 51; against France-Sardinia, 53–54; in 1860s, 61; in 1866 war, 61, 68, 71; peace establishment after compromise, 81; claimed by Kuhn, 87, 88; against Russia, 94; on Italian frontier, 99, 190; in Bosnia-Hercegovina, 102; in Dalmatia, 104; Beck's estimates, 113, 115; revised by 1889 law, 109, 126, 148, 160; increase blocked by Hungarian parliament, 131, 136, 139, 140, 146; raised by 1912 law, 165; mobilized in Balkan crisis, 167; compared to other European powers, 173–174; on mobilization, 174; against Serbia, 182; end of 1916, 192–193; in 1917, 205; projected peace establishment, 208; in summer of 1918, 313

Strength, other European armies: Hungarian revolutionary forces, 29, 32; Russian, 35, 51, 81, 94, 115; Sardinian, 53; Danish, 64; Prussian, 68; Saxon, 68; French, 81; North German Confederation, 81; British, 98; Serbian, 154, 169, 182; Italian, 163, 188, 190; Ottoman, 167
Strikes: Prague 1844, 20; Bosnia 1907, 148; general strike of 1918, 210–211
Students, university; radicals, 23, 28, 44; German nationalist, 130
Stürgkh, Joseph Count, FML, *AOK* delegate to the *OHL,* quoted on Conrad, 177–178
Stürgkh, Karl Count, Prime minister of Austria: appointed, 176; denounced by *AOK,* 192; demands more military information, 192; mentioned, 192
Styria, losses in war, 218
Submarine warfare, unrestricted, 203–204
Subversive activities: denounced by military, 57, 121, 145, 184, 204, and *passim;* attacked by Francis Ferdinand, 142, 147; pardoned by Charles I, 204
Succovary, Eduard Ritter v. Vezza, FML, 130
Südarmee, 184, 195–196
Südbahnhof, 45
Sudetenland, 221
Sweden, 134, 173
Supply, transportation, and quartermaster services, 41, 52, 53, 58, 68, 102, 176, 213
Switzerland, 20, 47, 118
Sylvester Patent (1851), 41
Syria, 215
Syrmia, 189
Szapáry, Gyula Count, Hungarian prime minister, 131
Széchenyi, Kálmán Count, on Hungarian military demands, 131–132
Székler regiments, 29
Széll, Kálmán, Hungarian prime minister, 131–132
Szende, Béla, Hungarian minister of national defense: appointed, 85; declares *Honvéd* prepared for combat, 93, 109
Szurmay, Alexander Baron, GdI, Hungarian minister of national defense, 209–210

Taaffe, Eduard Franz Josef Count, Austrian prime minister, 106, 121
Tactics: close order and bayonet, 16–17, 43, 63, 64, 65, 69; retained to control troops, 64; modified, 70, 84; cavalry shock, 16, 43, 63, 84, 112, 150, 174; artillery, 44, 63, 65, 70, 174; combined, 44, 65, 70, 174; infantry fire and shock, 84, 112, 143, 174; antiinsurgency, 102–104; mountain fighting, 195; infiltration, 207. *See also Stosstaktik,* Weaponry
Tactics, general: French light infantry, 17; French assault, 64, 175; Prussian fire, infantry, 69, 84; incompatibility of weapons and tactics, 112, 143, 175; Russian and Serb dismounted cavalry, 175; German assault, 175, 207; British infantry, 175
Tagliamento River, 206
Tangiers, 134
Tanks, 193, 215
Tarnopol, 186
Tarnów-Gorlice, battle of (1915), 186
Tarvisio, 188
Taylor, A. J. P., English historian: quoted on results of repression of Prague insurrection, 28; and on effects of Balkan Wars, 166
Technical Military Committee, 126, 174
Technical troops, 16, 43, 60, 63, 112–113, 175, 194, 205
Technische Militärakademie, 11, 82
Tegetthoff, Wilhelm v., Vice-Admiral, 71
Telegraph, military utility discounted, 60
Teleky, Adam, revolutionary *Honvéd* general, 29
Temesvár, 15
Tersztyánszky v. Nádas, Karl, FML, GO, candidate for chief of staff, 142; mentioned, 202
Teschen: location of *AOK,* 177, 185; panic during Brusilov offensive, 196; mentioned, 202
Textiles, 193
Theiss River, 35
Theresianische Militärakademie: foundation, 5; status of graduates, 82; mentioned, 11
Theresienstadt, fortress, 48, 68
Three Emperors' Alliance (1873), 80, 104
Three Emperors' Alliance (1881), 112, 114
Ticino River, 53
Tisza de Boros-Jenö, Istvan, Hungarian prime minister: and Committee of Nine, 131–132; tries to form government, 133; attempts to break deadlock on recruit quota, 160; forces new army law through parliament, 165; rules Hungary, 175; maintains civil government, 177, 192; demands more military information, 198; commits Charles I to dualism, 201; and national Hungarian army, 209; mentioned, 175, 178

Tisza de Boros-Jëno, Hungarian prime minister: and Compromise of 1867, 75; and his concept of the common army, 75, 106, 120; obtains change in title of, 109, 119; resigns, 131
Tolmein (Tolmino), 207
Torquemada, 79
Trabanten Leibgarde, 15
Tradition and change, 9, 11, 12, 38–39, 44–45, 56–57, 73, 74, 78–79, 89, 112, 127, 137, 199–200, 221
Training: emphasis on drill, 16–17, 44, 142; Conrad tries to make tougher and more realistic, 149. *See also* individual branches and Tactics.
Transylvania: *Grenzer* regiments of, 14, 29, 43; in 1848 revolution, 33, 35; state of siege in, 45; Rumanian invasion of, 197; mentioned, 50, 51
Trautenau, battle of (1866), 70
Trentino, 187–188, 190, 194–195, 207
Treviso (Tarvis), 51
Trieste, 143, 188, 189
Triple Alliance (1882): Austro-Hungarian misgivings about, 113, 114, 124, 152; and Aehrenthal, 163; Schemua expects Italy's defection; 164; Conrad favors it after Balkan War, 169; Conrad believes balance of power shifted against, 172–173; mentioned, 155
Triple Entente (1907), 155, 156
Tripolitania, 163
Turin, 34, 52, 54
Turkey. *See* Ottoman Empire
Tuszla, engagement at (1878), 10
Tyrol: special military institutions of, 13, 14, 85, 100, 109; troops in, alerted, 27, 189; conscription extended to, 42; fortifications in, 98–99, 149–150, 188–189; *Landwehr* of as mountain troops, 150. *See also Kaiserjäger, Landesschützen, Standschützen*
Tyrolean *Jäger* Regiment. *See Kaiserjäger*
Tyrolean Army Group, and controversy regarding armistice, 217–218
Tyrolean troops, 189, 217

Uchatius, Franz Baron, GM, artillery designs of, 84, 164
Ugron zu Abránfalva, Gabor, Hungarian nationalist politician, 119
Uhlans, 16, 43, 63, 84
Ukrain, 210, 212, 214, 215
Uniforms: elaborate and costly, 42; changes after 1866, 83; pike grey introduced, 140; cavalry retains old style, 150; shortage of, 193, 215; field grey adopted, 193; mentioned, 53, 68, 77, 120, 165
United States, 205, 212

Upper Austria, province, losses in World War, 218
Uzelać, Michael, Captain, 119

Varešanin, Marijan Baron, FML, 156
Venetia, 25, 26, 53, 59, 69, 71, 163, 215
Venice: war against (1615–1617), 3
Venice, republic of: established, 25; blockaded, 26; besieged, 28; capitulated, 34
Verdun, French fortress and battle of (1916), 105
Verdy du Vernois, Julius v., Prussian (German) GdI, war minister, 117
Verkehrsbrigade, 175
Verona: location of *Generalkommando*, 15, 40; fortress, 18, 19, 26; headquarters Second Austrian Army, 60
Victor Emmanuel II, King of Sardinia and then Italy, 34, 98
Victor Emmanuel III, King of Italy, 124
Vienna: revolution of 1848 in, 22–23, 26, 30–31; under state of siege, 38, 51; military considerations in urban development of, 45; fears of renewed uprising in, 45–46; preparations for defense of, 71, 185; riots in, 121; strike in, 210; revolution in, 216, 220; mentioned, 1, 3, 11, 15, 19, 22, 25, 35, 67, 74, 88, 102, 124, 152, 160, 161, 163, 176, 178, and *passim*
Vienna, Additional Act of, 95
Vienna, Congress of (1814–1815), 49
Vienna, Peace of (1864), 65
Világos, Hungarian surrender at (1849), 35
Villach, 188
Villafranca, Peace of (1859), 54
Villa Giusti, Armistice of (1918): conditions, 217; controversy over, 218
Vistula River, 158, 173, 179
Vittorio Veneto, battle of (1918), 217
Vojvodina, 21, 28, 36
Vorarlberg, province: militia of, 99, 100, 129, 189; losses in World War, 218

Wagner, Johann Ritter v., FML, and Dalmatian uprising, 86
Wagram, battle of (1809), 7, 11
Waldersee, Count Alfred, Prussian (German) Lieutenant General, deputy chief and chief of general staff: meets with Beck, 113; refuses to make commitment, 117; promises all-out support, 117; mentioned, 118, 157, 173
Waldstätten, Alfred Baron, GM, deputy chief of general staff: gains influence, 203; on Piave operations, 213; and Hungary's decision to recall troops, 217
Wallenstein, Albrecht Eusebius Count: organizes army, 3; legacy of, 11, 171; mentioned, 1
Wänzel modification, 83
Wars, Austrian and Austro-Hungarian army to 1914: against Turkey, 1564–1566, 2; against Turkey 1593–1606, 3; against Venice, 1615–1617, 3; Thirty Years' War, 1618–1748, 3; War of the Spanish Succession, 1701–1715, 4; war against Turkey, 1716–1718, 4; War of the Polish Succession, 1733–1735, 5; war against Turkey, 1737–1739, 5; War of the Austrian Succession, 1740–1748, 5; Seven Years' War, 1756–1763, 5; war against Turkey, 1788–1791, 6; French Revolutionary and Napoleonic wars, 6–8; wars against the Revolution of 1848–1849, 22–36; war against France and Sardinia, 1859, 52–55; war against Denmark, 1864, 64–65; war against Prussia and Italy, 1866, 67–71; Occupation of Bosnia-Hercegovina, 101–103; Dalmatian uprising, 1869, 86; Dalmatian uprising, 1881, 103–104
War government (1914–1918): in Austria, 177; in Hungary, 177, 191; *AOK* attempts to expand powers, 192; restricted by Charles I, 204
War Ministry (*Kriegsministerium, KM*), 1848–1853: formation of, 23–24; difficulties of, 24; support of Radetzky and Jelačić, 27, 30; eclipse and elimination of, 39–40
War Ministry (*Kriegsministerium, KM*), 1860–1867, 59, 61
War Ministry, common (*Reichskriegsministerium, RKM*, later *Kriegsministerium, KM*), 1868–1918: dispute over powers of, 79–80, 107, 125, 145, 161; seeks increase in recruit quota, 109, 126, 131, and *passim;* change of title, 147; wishes to retain troops for internal security duties, 214; and demobilization, 220; mentioned, 149, 193
War plans: Austrian and Austro-Hungarian, against Prussia, 48, 68–69; against Russia, 51, 94–95, 97, 112–114, 158, 173; against Germany, 94; against Italy, 99, 158–159, 188–189; plan for multi-front war, 125; Conrad's plans, 154, 158–159, 173, 178–179, 188–189
War plans, German, 112–113, 115, 116, 117, 157–159, 173
War production, 174, 193, 205, 210
Warsaw, 35, 117, 158, 167
War Services Act (1912), 165
War Supervisory Office. See *Kriegsüberwachungsamt*
Weaponry, influence on strategy and tactics, 17–18, 44, 64–65, 69–70, 84, 111–112, 137, 143, 174–175
Weber, Edler v. Webenau, Viktor, GdI, 217

Wekerle, Alexander, Hungarian prime minister: appointed, 140; clashes with Francis Ferdinand, 160; reopens army issue, 209–210
Welden, Ludwig Baron, FZM: appointed military governor of Vienna, 31; intrigues against Windischgrätz, 33; command in Italy, 33–34; recommends appeal to Russia, 35; mentioned, 45
Werndl Arms Factory (*Österreichische Waffenfabriksgesellschaft*), 66, 83, 101
Wieden, Heinrich, GM, 208
Wiener-Neustadt, 72, 210
Wilhelm, Archduke, FML, 46, 59
Wilhelm, Duke of Württemberg, FZM, military governor of Bosnia-Hercegovina, 103
William II, German Emperor, King of Prussia: promises support for Austria-Hungary, 67, 117; critical of Austro-Hungarian army performance, 180; induces Francis Joseph to accept German predominance on eastern front, 198–199; is assured by Charles I that Austria will not become base for operations against Germany, 218; abdicates, 220; mentioned, 206
Wilson, Woodrow, president of the United States, 215, 216
Windischgrätz, Alfred Prince, FM: characterized, 27, 31; plans military counter-revolution, 27; represses Prague insurrection, 27–28; conquers Vienna, 30–31; appointed commander-in-chief, 31; invades Hungary, 31–33; fails to break resistance, 33; opposes Schwarzenberg, 33; relieved, 33–34; political goals, 33; recommends appeal for Russian aid, 35; mentioned, 36
WJR, acronym for Windischgrätz, Jelačić, Radetzky, 31
Wolhynia, 17
World War I (1914–1918): confusion of initial deployment, 178–179; first battles in Galicia, 179–180; collapse of offensive, 180–181; Austro-German friction emerges, 180–181, 186, 191, 196, 208; Russian breakthrough threatened in Carpathians, 181–182; defeat in Serbia, 183–184; Carpathian winter offensive, 184; changes in character of Austro-Hungarian army, 184–185; German aid stabilizes front, 185–186; defense preparations against Italy, 188–189; initial battles against Italy, 190; Serbia defeated, 191; Montenegro overrun, 191; expansion and reequipment of Austro-Hungarian forces, 193; Trentino offensive, 194–195; Brusilov offensive, 195–196; joint Central Power conquest of Rumania, 197–198; Isonzo battles continue, 206; Caporetto operations, 206–207; occupation of the Ukraine, 212; Piave offensive, 213; disintegration of army commences, 214; Vittorio Veneto, 217; and armistice, 217–218; last fighting in Albania, 219
World War II (1939–1945), 102
Wrangel, Friedrich v., Prussian FM, 64
Wratislaw v. Mittrowitz, Johann Wenzel Count, FML, 25
Württemberg, Grand Duchy, 48, 71

Yanina, Turkish fortress, 167
"Young Italy" movement, 19
"Young Turk" revolution (1908), 154
Yugoslav National Committee (Cattaro), 219

Zanini, Peter, FML, KM, 23–24
Zde incidents, 130
Zeman, Zbynek A. B., Czech historian, quoted on the reliability of the Austro-Hungarian army, 176
Zeughaus, 45
Zita of Bourbon Parma, Empress-Queen, 201
Zsigard, battle of (1849), 35
Zum Studium der Taktik, 143

www.ingramcontent.com/pod-product-compliance
Lightning Source LLC
Chambersburg PA
CBHW022105150426
43195CB00008B/270